D1395487

The Benn Diaries

The Regeneration of Britain
Speeches
Arguments for Socialism
Arguments for Democracy
Parliament, People and Power
The Sizewell Syndrome
Fighting Back: Speaking Out for Socialism in the Eighties
A Future for Socialism
Common Sense (*with Andrew Hood*)

Years of Hope: Diaries, Papers and Letters 1940–1962
Out of the Wilderness: Diaries 1963–1967
Office Without Power: Diaries 1968–1972
Against the Tide: Diaries 1973–1976
Conflicts of Interest: Diaries 1977–1980
The End of an Era: Diaries 1980–1990

TONY BENN

THE BENN DIARIES

Selected, Abridged and
Introduced by
Ruth Winstone

HUTCHINSON
London

© in this edition Tony Benn 1995

The right of Tony Benn to be identified as Author
of this work has been asserted by Tony Benn in accordance
with the Copyright, Designs and Patents Act, 1988

This edition first published in 1995 by
Hutchinson

10 9 8 7 6 5 4 3 2 1

Random House (UK) Limited
20 Vauxhall Bridge Road, London SW1V 2SA

Random House Australia (Pty) Limited
20 Alfred Street, Milsons Point, Sydney,
New South Wales 2061, Australia

Random House New Zealand Limited
18 Poland Road, Glenfield,
Auckland 10, New Zealand

Random House South Africa (Pty) Ltd
PO Box 337, Bergvlei, 2012 South Africa

A CIP record for this book is available
from the British Library

Papers used by Random House UK Limited are natural,
recyclable products made from wood grown in sustainable
forests. The manufacturing processes conform to the
environmental regulations of the country of origin

ISBN 0 09 1792231

Typeset by Deltatype Ltd, Ellesmere Port, Cheshire
Printed and bound in Great Britain by
Mackays of Chatham PLC

CONTENTS

Illustrations

Neil Kinnock	*Srdja Djukanovic / Camera Press London*
Billy Bragg with Tony Benn	*Paul Slattery*
Mikhail Gorbachev with John Major	*The Hulton Deutsch Collection / Sportsphoto*
With Claire Rayner & Bill Owen	*Grimsby Evening Telegraph*

Brief Chronology

April 1940	Anthony Wedgwood Benn 15 years old.
Dec 1941	William Wedgwood Benn MP is created a Labour peer, Lord Stansgate
July 1943	Tony Benn joins RAF
June 1944	Brother Michael killed in RAF
July 1945	General Election. Clement Attlee PM
Aug 1945	Atomic bomb dropped on Hiroshima
Jan 1946	Tony Benn to New College, Oxford
June 1949	Marriage to Caroline De Camp
Nov 1949	Tony Benn becomes producer with BBC
Feb 1950	General Election. Clement Attlee PM
June 1950	Korean War
30 Nov 1950	Tony Benn elected for Bristol South East in by-election
Oct 1951	General Election. Winston Churchill PM
Apr 1955	Churchill resigns. Anthony Eden PM
Dec 1955	Gaitskell elected Leader of Labour Party
June 1956	Nasser nationalises Suez Canal
June–Nov 1956	Suez crisis
Jan 1957	Eden resigns. Macmillan PM
Oct 1959	General Election. Macmillan PM
Nov 1959	Tony Benn elected to NEC
Nov 1960	Father dies. Benn disqualified from Commons
May 1961	By-election Bristol South East. Tony Benn re-elected but is refused admission to the Commons
July 1961	Election Court unseats Tony Benn
Jan 1963	Gaitskell dies. Harold Wilson Leader of Labour Party
Jan 1963	Joint Select Committee recommends reform of peerage law
July 1963	Peerage Act passed. Tony Benn renounces Stansgate peerage
20 Aug 1963	By-election, Bristol South East. Tony Benn re-elected
Oct 1964	General Election. Wilson PM. Tony Benn Postmaster General
Jan 1965	Winston Churchill dies
March 1966	General Election. Harold Wilson PM
June 1966	Tony Benn Minister of Technology
June 1970	General Election. Edward Heath PM

1971/1972	Tony Benn Chairman of Labour Party
Nov 1971	Tony Benn contests deputy leadership of Labour Party
Feb 1974	General Election. Harold Wilson PM. Tony Benn appointed Secretary of State for Industry
Oct 1974	General Election. Harold Wilson PM
Feb 1975	Margaret Thatcher becomes Leader of Conservative Party
June 1975	Common Market Referendum. Tony Benn moved from Department of Industry to Energy
March 1976	Harold Wilson resigns. Tony Benn contests leadership. James Callaghan PM
Feb 1977	Anthony Crosland dies
May 1979	General Election. Margaret Thatcher PM
Nov 1980	Michael Foot elected Leader of Labour Party
June 1981	Tony Benn in hospital with Guillain-Barre syndrome
Sept 1981	Tony Benn contests deputy leadership of Labour Party
Apr–June 1982	Falklands War
June 1983	General Election. Margaret Thatcher PM
	Tony Benn loses in Bristol following Boundary Commission changes to constituencies
Oct 1983	Neil Kinnock elected Leader of Labour Party
March 1984	Tony Benn elected MP for Chesterfield
June 1987	General Election. Margaret Thatcher PM
Oct 1988	Tony Benn contests leadership of Labour Party
Nov 1990	Tony Benn visits President Saddam Hussain in Iraq
	Margaret Thatcher resigns. John Major PM

Foreword

My family have not only had to endure the burden of a politician as husband and father, but also a compulsive diarist. Over the years they have sustained, advised and encouraged me during the ups and downs of political life, and have borne the many real hardships that my life has imposed upon them. To Caroline, Stephen, Hilary, Melissa and Joshua I am eternally thankful.

The main, huge task of transcription fell to Sheila Hubacher, my private secretary, who took it on with good humour and occasional frustration. Tony Whittome of Hutchinson has gently seen this and other volumes through from the start to finish. To both I am extremely grateful.

The main credit for the Diaries must go to Ruth Winstone, the editor of the series over a decade, whose judgement, tenacity and skill have made their publication possible and who has selected and edited this volume with little or no help from me.

Tony Benn
July 1995

Introduction

One of the intriguing aspects of a diary is that it is impossible to predict what posterity will make of it. The fascination of Samuel Pepys's diary, now over 300 years old, lies not in the political events, nor in the drama of the Great Fire rolling through London, but in the incidental insights that it gives. It is the labour trouble down at the docks, the types of river transport used, the difficulties Mrs Pepys is having with her servants, and the character of Pepys himself that make an impression in a diary that was written as a very matter-of-fact record of his daily activity.

It is much too soon to know what the enduring interest and value of Tony Benn's diary will be to future generations, though I am sure that the names of the great and the good sitting round the cabinet table will be forgotten long before the sit-in at UCS. But the process of selecting extracts for this abridgement, from diaries spanning fifty years, has forced me to think afresh about the outstanding features of the diaries and the diarist.

There is no doubt that keeping a diary has been part of an obsession by Tony Benn with Time. Time is a currency to be spent not wasted, and as a youth he kept a time chart on which were marked the hours per day devoted to work, conversation, exercise, leisure and sleep, all of which had to equal 24. As a 35-year-old he drew up a forward diary-plan to the year 2025 (his 100th birthday); and as a Minister he recorded, usually at midnight, the day's unfolding events. To waste time is unendurable, as the war-time diaries, written during periods of enforced idleness in the barracks, reflect.

It is the compulsion to note down the minutiae of working life, in a daily audit of Time spent, that has often exasperated those who have typed and edited the diaries; but that process in the long-run has also established the authority and the credibility of the diaries. To have kept such a record for so long is a phenomenal achievement drawing on extraordinary energy and tenacity.

Yet this self-imposed apparently puritanical regime is contrasted by a good temper, great sense of humour and quick wit which, according to Barbara Castle's diaries, endeared 'Wedgie' to his colleagues, however infuriating he might otherwise have been.

And how he did drive his colleagues to fury! The later diaries candidly reveal the battles, particularly with Labour leaders Wilson, Callaghan and

Foot, who found themselves continually frustrated or irritated by Tony Benn's dogged refusal as a Cabinet Minister and member of the National Executive to let rest uncomfortable issues about which he and others in the party felt strongly. Tony Benn's courage in the face of adversity, if at times misplaced, is undeniable.

Having worked on the diaries for many years, my impression of the political life that they chronicle is that the Labour Party (in power for only 17 of the past 50 years despite its great talents, commitment and organisation) contains inherent conflicts that prevent it from ever wielding power effectively or for long. These contradictions (sometimes known as 'checks and balances') have in practice meant that every Labour leader, from Attlee to Kinnock, has been caught between the interests of the parliamentary party (of ideologically diverse MPs), the National Executive representing the Conference, and a Cabinet or Shadow Cabinet appointed by the leader. Most of the rows (quickly forgotten) between Callaghan and Benn revolved around these irreconcilable differences. But 'splits' have riven the Labour Party in every decade since the war as this volume demonstrates.

Attempts to change the party both by the left-wing in the 70s and 80s and the 'modernisers' in the 1950s and the Kinnock-Blair era have recognised this conundrum but have failed to resolve it, while supporters have got bored with the arguments and the language, and the original issues have got lost.

Tony Blair, the eighth Labour leader since the war, has made the most dramatic leaps yet in repudiating the Party's democratic infrastructure, and its ideology; it remains to be seen how successful his strategy will be in personal and political consequences.

Alongside Tony Benn's life-long fascination with the political process, he has maintained a vigorous scepticism of the current wisdom of the day, scepticism that continually pokes through the diary. It is well known that in December 1978, the 'Winter of Discontent', as it was popularly dubbed, was 'caused' by uncontrollable workers, and trade unions who refused to collect rubbish, bury the dead and were generally obnoxious. Yet since 1990, Denis Healey, the Chancellor from 1974–9, has publicly declared that the policies adopted by the Labour Government after the IMF 'crisis' of 1976 (strict wage control, penalties against employers flouting it, and huge public expenditure cuts) were mistaken. They were, he said, based upon wrong Treasury figures, were unnecessary and were bound to lead to the crisis of 1978–79 as members of the workforce tried to maintain their living standards. A few lone voices, including Tony Benn's, stood out against the measures and questioned the assumptions. Books and PhDs have been written about the crisis; it remains to be seen whether the history books put the record straight.

Unlike the six volumes from which this abridgement is drawn, this book has dispensed with footnotes and chapter notes, and bridging passages have been kept to a minimum. It is not an academic text, or a history, and many characters appear fleetingly: to have attempted explanations would have spoiled the impressionistic nature of the work, in contrast to the detail of the earlier volumes.

It has been a great privilege to edit *The Benn Diaries*. The frustration and exhaustion have been well rewarded. I'm sorry I shan't be around in 2295 to re-assess them.

Ruth Winstone
Editor
July 1995

1

1940–49

In May 1940 Tony Benn was still at school, his older brother Michael had joined the RAF and his younger brother David (nicknamed 'The Proff') was being taught at home, due to a childhood illness. Winston Churchill had by now, with the help of Lloyd George, replaced Neville Chamberlain as war-time Prime Minister; Clem Attlee was leader of the Labour Party in a coalition Government. At this stage also, William Wedgwood Benn, Tony Benn's father, was Labour MP for Gorton, having until 1926 sat as a Liberal MP. He was shortly to be made a Labour peer, with the title Lord Stansgate, and thus his eldest son Michael would become heir to the title.

In this first chapter, letters and other papers are included as well as early, episodic extracts from the diaries and journals of Tony Benn which only become continuous in 1963. From 1940 until 1950 Benn was continuously on the move, first as a wartime evacuee, then as a trainee pilot whose training took him to Southern Africa, and the Middle

East, and after the war as a student at Oxford and in America. In family letters at this time Tony Benn is often called James.

During the war also, his father, at the age of 63, joined the RAF for the second time in his life, and his mother, Margaret, taught at a girls' boarding school – Blunt House – much to the delight of her young sons.

Westminster School Report 1940
Wedgwood-Benn A Age: 15.8

Greek: Place 18   No. in set 22

Does not work hard enough in school or out. He prefers to think Greek is too difficult and therefore not worth attempting to master.

French: Place 24   No. in set 25

His learning French is really a quite unsatisfactory performance. He could do very much better but it would now cost him a great effort.

History: Place 14

Lively and intelligent, as always. He is keen to get on and works hard and I think he ought to do well in the Certificate. His knowledge is patchy, e.g. he will sometimes take a political allusion which no one else in the form sees, and at other times he is ignorant of commonplace matters. He still has a rhetorical style of writing which is unsuitable for history essays.

> Buckenhill
> Bromyard
> Hereford
>
> [Autumn 1941]

Dear Mike

How are you? The ATC uniforms arrived the day I arrived back here. I was promoted that afternoon to one stripe. I hope to get my corporal's stripe before the end of term. Tonight I go on a Home Guard patrol. From 10 to 6 in the morning there are patrols of two in two-hour shifts in the church tower and the streets.

Your affectionate brother
L/Corporal Benn ATC

> Buckenhill
> Bromyard
> Hereford
>
> 12 March 1942

My dear Mike

What a good weekend we did have. My first exploit on the motorbike was entirely your fault! When I join the RAF proper I shall probably see even less of you than I do now.

I am so glad that I found that you have the same view about females that I have. It is the only major omission that the parents have made in our upbringing. I suppose if we had a sister we should have met her friends. I don't know anything about them. I don't know what they are interested in, what they think about, and when I do meet them I feel most embarrassed.

We are having lessons in unarmed combat and I have bought an instructional book on the subject.

New College
Oxford

29 January 1943

My dear Proff

Just a line to let you know how I'm getting on.

Last night we had another debate about helping the Jews in Europe. The motion was 'that this House urges that a more energetic and practical policy be pursued by the Government towards the rescue of Jews in Europe'. At the beginning of the debate there were an equal number of people for and against the proposal. But after Victor Gollancz had spoken, everyone supported the motion, including those who had *spoken against* it. The motion for helping the Jews was carried by 188 votes to 21.

Much love
James (Tony)

Extract from the Oxford Magazine *on the visit to the Oxford Union of Richard Acland*:

'The speech of Sir Richard Acland, who was making his first visit to the Union since founding Common Wealth, enlivened the proceedings which culminated in an equal division of 82 votes for each side. The President gave his casting vote for the motion.

The Hon A.N. Wedgwood Benn proposed the motion, and began by maintaining that the prevailing popular distinction of domestic from international problems largely rested on false assumptions. The economic system at home was dependent upon the conditions of our foreign trade and both involved the fundamental issue of capital versus socialism. The natural outcome of industrialisation had been amalgamation and combination among capitalists, the essence of whose system was to restrict output and so increase prices . . . which had helped to force Germany into Nazism. He concluded by referring to the Malvern Conference, which emphasised the ethical and religious arguments against capitalism . . .

'In reply, Sir Richard Acland Bt MP contrasted the political crisis at home, where the Government was being conducted by an eighteenth-century aristocrat in uneasy partnership with a sorrowful ruling class, and the outside world, where the war was being won by the forces of common ownership . . . Our need was to combine political with economic democracy, since the country that first did this would lead the world . . .

'Capitalism could not meet the crying needs of Europe for food and fuel after the war. In England it would be nonsense to raise again the objection that it 'doesn't pay' when we had men, machines and materials enough to meet all our needs . . .

'Mr C.A.R. Crosland (Trinity), ex-Treasurer, ably endeavoured to refute the argument that work is less well done by the State's employees than the capitalist's, though admitting that he found himself in uneasy partnership with Sir Richard Acland.'

Blunt House
Oxted
Surrey

31 March 1943

My dear old Mike

On Monday night I bought eight bottles of fizzy drinks, some chocolate, cigarettes, rock cakes and buns, costing 6/6, in all and got two half tins of salmon. I woke Lesley, Linnet, Barbara and Fiona at midnight and they all came into my room in their pyjamas. After eating we tried a game. I suggested that we should play a game where we gambled our clothes. I couldn't find any cards, so we decided on a spelling game. Barbara is very bad at spelling . . . I think I can say that a good time was had by all.

Mike, what do you feel about Fiona?

Now to politics and the Beveridge Report. You wrote to the effect that you didn't think that the Beveridge Report solved anything. I don't agree with you there. Remember that Beveridge was asked to make a report on 'The social insurance and allied services', and an idea sprang up that it was a complete plan for post-war reconstruction. I absolutely agree with you that socialist planning is necessary. Capitalism is obsolete. It has ceased to perform the function for which it originated. It is not possible for a man to set up a business in competition with say HMV or Imperial Chemicals or the Nuffield combine. They can afford to push him out of business because of their superior capital.

Out of 32,000,000 men and women who are employed in this country – 14,000,000 work in factories, docks, railways and other big privately owned concerns. They must be enlisted on our side and as is quite evident from their membership of the trade unions, they want national control. It ought to be quite evident by now that a changeover to nationalised industries and services is necessary. What part does the Beveridge Report play in this changeover? I am myself against a sudden breakaway from things as they are today. The new must evolve from the old and the evolution must be accomplished with as little fuss or disruption as is possible with the needs of the moment.

Well, Mike, I feel that this letter is some sort of compensation for a week's neglect.

Your most devoted and affectionate bro.

James

Wednesday 9 June 1943

I regard my death in the RAF as very possible. I am aware in vague bursts that entering the RAF is a great and dangerous venture. When I think of the technical knowledge necessary before I can fly and the number of things I will have to think of and do it fills me with foreboding, but I suppose that all can be done if I work hard at my training. That is only the learning side; it is the problem of judging the exact moment for flattening out and worse still the problem of whether I can keep my nerve in a spin or when the flak is at me. I am filled with depression and then I cheer up and say, 'Well, what if I do get killed? I shall be a hero and I won't have to plan my life which I realise will be an almost impossible task.' I think my new and most earnest wish is that Mike should survive the war unhurt.

Why am I fighting? In short it is because I think there is something worth fighting for. If I think that it is worth fighting for – it is presumably worth making any sacrifices possible?

I shall be terrified most of the time but the conquest of cowardice is a personal struggle and I can say that it will never be my policy to be a coward. I can't guarantee that in a panic I shan't give way – God preserve me from doing so – but I can't do anything now about it except prepare myself and train myself.

RAF Elmdon
Birmingham

September 1943

My very dear brother

In case you haven't had my last two air letters let me congratulate you on (1) your DFC and (2) your 22nd birthday. A junior brother and friend is very proud of you.

At last I am at an aerodrome and I am happier than ever before in my life. We are only here for three weeks but in that time we are really taught to fly Tigers – and go solo – I simply can't believe it. We wear blue battledress and with my pipe I really look quite operational. We are called 'pupil pilots'. On Sunday I shall have my first lesson. Details of the 'drome I can't give you by letter but I know you will understand how every little aspect of this sort of life appeals to me.

> 1850035 AC2C BENN ANW
> Hut 41
> F Flight
> No 1 Squadron
> RAF Station
> Heaton Park, Manchester
>
> [December 1943]

Dear Family,

Here is my address. I am almost certain that I have been selected for pilot training. This will be overseas though I cannot say where. On the nominal roll prepared by the RAF we are divided into two groups – potential officers and NCOs. I am in the first group. The prospects of leave are uncertain.

Conditions here are dreadful. Rains all the time. No baths, and no hot water. There are twenty of us in a Nissen hut which is unheated. But I mustn't go on. I came into Manchester today to have a bath and write some letters. The latter is almost impossible in a crowded canteen and there isn't a bath in the city.

Love James

Friday 14 January 1944 – SS Cameronia

I woke up occasionally but it was not until about 6.15 that I began getting up. A quarter of an hour later we stopped at Glasgow.

We moved off again at about 1430 and about half an hour later came aboard the SS *Cameronia*. I went down to our mess and attempted to settle in. We were situated on D4 Mess Deck where in an area not more than eighty feet square and not higher than six foot five, 296 of us were accommodated. There we ate, sat and wrote. At night the space above the floor and tables was crowded with the hammocks slung from bars on the ceiling. Our kit was stored on wooden racks above these bars and the crush was incredible. Many had to sleep on mattresses on the tables. The first few hours were desperate – you could not be certain what was yours and where were your possessions. However, after the evening meal it was more tolerable and I went on deck. Four enormous cranes were at work loading the ship, two powerful lights shining on each crane, illuminating the decks like the streets of London before the war.

I slung my hammock at 8.30 and slept soundly.

Friday 21 January

I didn't get out of bed till ten to seven. I felt weak with the stink of 300 bodies in so confined a space. We have nothing but artificial light twenty-four hours each day on our mess deck and the fresh air comes through air conditioning vents.

Tuesday 25 January

I went along to a lecture on aircraft recognition which later turned into a discussion of the colour bar, and instructions on how to behave towards negroes and half-whites. We had a few phrases of kaffir language. I went downstairs and started an argument with Stan, Ken and Johnny on the colour bar and whether the Christian church could sanctify marriage based on the love of a black woman by a white man.

Wednesday 2 February

A tanker came alongside of us and while it was filling us up the mechanics on board the tanker sold us handbags, wallets and bracelets, which they sent by rope to the ship on previous receipt of money sent down in a tin.

We are more cramped now. There are twenty-eight on a table designed for eighteen as two tables have been given over to the army and there are a number of stories about women coming on board – WRNS, WACS, ATS and so on. I must say that I hope that they are true.

The Tannoy played music by Victor Sylvester and I lay watching the moon and stars and the lights of Suez.

Wednesday 16 February

A ground staff RAF fellow died this morning in sick quarters of heat stroke. He was evidently working in the bakery where there is a constant temperature of 115 degrees. The flag is at half mast and he is being given a military burial tonight. We were also told that a sailor has gone blind from the sun.

After pay I got dinner and read, showered and talked. Then I attended the funeral of the airman. It was quite impressive though, despite the fact that it was the first funeral, I didn't feel at all spiritually or emotionally moved. It was rather cheap and everyday in a way. In the first place I think his life could have been saved and then the funeral arrangements weren't quite perfect and it went off rather like a parade not quite up to scratch, with all the shabbiness that that involved.

I slept on deck again.

[No date]

My Dearest Dad

Just a very short note to tell you that I have arrived at my port of disembarkation. I don't know where you are or how you are so I am sending this to your ME address.

I was addressing a meeting on Saturday on board ship. The subject was

'War Aims'. It is very different from the Union and my first experience of an ordinary public political speech with heckling and cat calls.

You've no idea how much I've thought of my Pa these last weeks on board and missed him.

Ever your loving son James

Thursday 24 February
Johannesburg 10.50 – great mines and piles of slag. We passed on today through more of the bush country. The gradient was sometimes as steep as 1:4 and the train went on so slowly that some people jumped off it and ran beside, stopping to pick wild peaches and jumping on again. At one station some kind ladies distributed tea and grapes etc. free. At Mafeking (where I relieved myself!) there were a lot of natives though no town to speak of. Periodically we would pass through native settlements or villages and very rough they were. Mud huts made of lumps of clay hewn in brick form, with hay rather than properly thatched roofs, and very often no windows but a wide space for a door. The natives were sitting around quite lazily outside watching, although I fancy their men were railway workers, leaving only their old, infirm, children and womenfolk at home in the daytime.

Friday 25 February
In the afternoon we passed from Bechuanaland to Southern Rhodesia and by 7 o'clock we were at Bulawayo where we disentrained and were marched to Hillside Camp. There we were issued with bedding, given huts and a meal, and left. The camp had been a dairy farm and the buildings were originally cattle sheds.

Saturday 4 March
It is very amusing to hear the natives in the compound in the morning. A native comes in about 0615 and shouts in Bantu, interspersed with the emphatic imperative 'WAKEY, WAKEY'. There is more shouting and laughing followed by silence when the 'waker' departs as sleep regains its prey. This continues until the man returns and reawakens us, which he may have to do two or three times.

Monday 10 April
Today I was very depressed indeed. I think that the boil on my face, the sore on my behind, and the blister on my toe tended – if anything – to worsen things. This depression squashes life itself and any interest in it. Anyway this evening I saw Rita Hayworth in *Strawberry Blonde* and this cheered me quite a lot.

Wednesday 26 April
We were woken this morning at 03.30 hrs but as I had gone to bed early I

didn't feel too bad. We were issued spats, maps and compasses and we boarded the lorry just as the dawn was lifting. The lorry moved off and the flight began to sing as we drove through Bulawayo, the old sentimental soldier songs which in these surroundings were very pleasant. The sky in the east was yellow and orange and above a bank of black cloud shone Venus, the morning star. We were dropped at a gate with a course of 168 degrees and fifteen miles of rough bundu ahead. I pushed on and gradually as the heat increased and the country grew more difficult I stumbled more often, and began to swear under my breath.

We had lunch at a hotel and the lorry came back at 2.30. I had a deadly headache and I felt pretty ghastly but some Anadin soon put that right and despite my sore feet, I went into town to see Gloria. She was there and I noticed a definite difference. She was dressed very much more attractively and when she came over to the table she was much sweeter and her earlier chilliness had completely vanished. I went to bed tired but happy with feet that hurt like the devil.

Thursday 4 May
In the evening Noël Coward came to the camp to give his one-man show. John, Les, Ken and I queued up between 6 and 6.30. The doors opened at 7.30 and from then until 8 the 'Hillside Scamps' played. Then the great moment arrived and Coward came on with his pianist Norman Hackforth. He was very smartly dressed in a khaki shirt and tie, light brown soled suede shoes. His programme which lasted a little over an hour long was absolutely first rate. I admire Noël Coward for being so low despite the ladies present. He used the words 'bloody, bitch, Christ, bastard, short arm inspection, sexy' and so on despite them.

Sunday 21 May
In the evening I went to the Services Club and Gloria was there. She was very sweet and charming to begin with – in fact extremely so. All the signs were OK and Les Boughey came over to my table and said that she had been miserable until I came in and then she had cheered up like billyo. This optimistic statement I should have taken with a pinch of salt, but anyway she did appear to be favouring me so I determined to say something tonight. Unfortunately I found that my heart was throbbing so fast and I felt so hot I was blushing a deep red.

Stubborn in my determination to get somewhere I asked her to 'come and sit at my table and make the last evening of my leave gay', but she turned scornfully away and said, with a sting in her voice, 'I think I'll get you a glass of water to recover.' That finished me. I got up and left at once, muttering to myself and fuming with rage and almost self-pity at this sudden humiliation which had fallen so swiftly after my seeming victory.

Tuesday 6 June 1944 – Liberation Day for Europe and the World
I went up for over an hour and a half during which time I finished spins and
started on my final and crucial task – finding out whether I will ever be able
to land an aircraft. It was not until breakfast time that I heard the great news.
The story was consistent and persistent, then during the airmanship period
F/O Freeman told me the real 'gen'. He had heard General Eisenhower's
broadcast announcement to the world of an Allied invasion of the French
coast and containing the gist of issued orders to the underground
movement. The strain of having old Mike in the front at a time like this must
be very great for Ma, for the burden is probably more heavy on those near
and dear to the fighting men who are left behind than on the men
themselves. I am still depressed.

Thursday 8 June
The WingCo's inspection was strict and searching. We were all in best blue
and the sun came down blazingly on the ranks. One man halfway down our
rank suddenly fell forward limp on to his face with a soft thud; he was carried
off.

The WingCo began by saying that he was sure that we all agreed that the
occasion of the King's birthday was significant at this time and that our
minds were probably not only turned to the King personally or to all that the
Crown stood for but also to the men engaged in the second front. I for one
certainly failed to see why the King's birthday mattered at such a time since
everyone was solely preoccupied with the European onslaught.

Then swinging to the right after an order to remove headgear and give
three cheers for the King which was certainly not rousing, the WingCo
walked over to the native Rhodesian Air Askari Corps and addressed them
through an interpreter in this manner. 'Everything here, the land, the
hangars, the aircraft are all the King's and it is all your duty to guard them.
Do your duty well.' I felt sick at the failure to thank them or refer to
Matabeleland as their country, used by us. It was a dictatorial speech that
Goering might make to the conscripts of an occupied country about Hitler.

Wednesday 14 June
At six this morning Crownshaw told me to get into 322 straightaway, a PT-
26A Cornell trainer. I apologised to him for boobing the check yesterday
and he remarked that they were really only nominal things and that they
didn't really matter. However we took off, did a circuit or maybe two, and
then as we taxied up to the take-off point, he said to me: 'Well, how do you
feel about your landings?' I replied: 'Well, that's really for you to say, sir.' He
chuckled. 'I think you can manage one solo,' he said. 'I'm going to get out
now and I'll wait here for you,' he went on.

So this was it, I thought. The moment I had been waiting for came all of a
sudden just like that. 'OK, sir,' I replied. 'And don't forget that you've got a

throttle,' he said. 'Don't be frightened to go round again – OK? And by the way,' he added – he finished locking the rear harness and closing the hood then came up to me, leant over and shouted, in my ear – 'you do know the new trimming for taking off?' 'Yes, sir,' I replied, and he jumped off the wing and walked over to the boundary with his 'chute.

I was not all that excited. I certainly wasn't frightened and I hope I wasn't over-confident but I just had to adjust my mirror so that I could really see that there was no one behind me.

I remembered my brother Mike's words: 'Whatever you do don't get over-confident: it is that that kills most people and I only survived the initial stages through being excessively cautious.' So I brought my mind back to the job, checked the instruments, looked all around and when we had reached 500 feet began a gentle climbing turn. It was very bumpy and the wind got under my starboard wing and tried to keel me over, but I checked it with my stick and straightened out when my gyro compass read 270 degrees. Then I climbed to 900, looked all round and turned again on to the downwind leg. By the time I'd finished that turn we were at 1,000 feet, so I throttled back, retrimmed, got dead on 180 and I felt pretty good about things. I thought I was a little high as I crossed the boundary so I eased back to 800 rpm, and as I passed over, I distinctly saw Crownshaw standing watching where I had left him. Now we were coming in beautifully and I eased the stick and throttle back. A quick glance at the ground below showed me to be a little high, so I left the stick as it was, gave a tiny burst of engine and as we floated down I brought both back fully. We settled, juddered and settled again for a fair threepointer.

I was as happy as could be. I taxied up, stopped and braked. Try as I did, I couldn't restrain the broad grin which gripped me from ear to ear and Crownshaw, seeing it, leant over before he got in and said ironically with a smile. 'Happy now?' I was more than happy, I was deliriously carefree, and as he taxied her back I thought about it all and I realised that the success of my first solo flight was entirely due to the fine instruction I had received; it was a tribute to that instruction that I never felt nervous once, and all the time had imagined what my instructor would be saying, so used had I got to doing everything with him behind me. We climbed out, and attempting to restrain my happiness I listened while he told me where and what to sign. Then I wandered back to my billet and one of the greatest experiences of my life was behind me. The lectures were pretty ordinary, and it being my free afternoon I had a bit of lemonade in the canteen and then wrote this.

Tuesday 20 June
The whole afternoon Ken Brown, Phil James and Johnnie Walker were in my hut and the time was wasted absolutely in worthless nattering. I tried to keep my temper and in fact never showed any annoyance at all and pretended that I was in a listening competition or that this was practice for

political work. The evening went in the same manner though the room became more crowded still.

Sunday 25 June

In a 5,000-word letter to Mike I wrote out a full description of my flying and the lessons I learned. It gave me a chance to clear my mind. After tea I went along to listen to the Padre on the text, taken from the Christ-child's visit to the temple where he amazed the professors. After which, according to the story, he 'waxed strong in body and in wisdom and gained favour among men and with God.' He constructed his talk round the belief that everyone should make their life like the life of Christ and should develop in those four ways – bodily, mentally, be a tower of strength among men, and be close to God. On physical fitness, which the Padre started with, the three main reasons for developing and maintaining it were: first because our bodies are the temple of God, secondly because if we are really fit we are less likely to fall into temptation, especially the temptations of drink and sex. And lastly because we must keep as fit as possible so as to do our own work the better for the glory of God. Very sound arguments, I thought. He bitterly attacked those who despised an intelligent interest in religion. Gaining favour with men did not mean that we should be so ordinary and popular that we didn't strike a line of our own.

After the service I went along to the last of F/Lt Goulton's gramophone recitals. He played Chopin's first pianoforte concerto which was absolutely wizard and the *Dance of the Hours* which I must get when I'm home again.

Tuesday 27 June

We did PT this morning and the first lecture was meteorology. Gannicliffe brought the mail in and there was a telegram for me. I don't like telegrams as a rule so I didn't open it immediately, and when I did it was quite unhurried.

R5 OXTED 41 24 1440
1850035 BENN

DARLING JAMES OUR PRECIOUS MICHAEL GAVE HIS LIFE JUNE 23RD AFTER OPERATIONAL ACCIDENT DAVE AND I REACHED HIM DONT GRIEVE DEAREST HE SUFFERED NO PAIN IS SAVED COMPLETE PARALYSIS FAMILY HOLDS TOGETHER FOR ALWAYS DEAREST LOVE.

YERMA-STANSGATE

When I saw the words at first, I was stunned and felt as if something inside me had stopped.

For a few minutes I didn't think about it really, and I just went on writing meteorology notes. The realisation of the desolation came to me in waves. For the rest of the period I was either on the verge of tears or quite calm.

When at last the lesson ended I went into the post office, picked up some telegraph forms and walked to my hut. There I let go and sat sobbing for ten or fifteen minutes. It was good to give vent to my feelings – it eased things a lot. I was sick at heart. I never knew how much Mike's example, his interest and advice, were responsible for maintaining my desire to be a pilot.

The outburst over, I sent a telegram to mother:

MIKE'S GREAT SACRIFICE AN INSPIRATION TO US ALL. FAMILY MORE UNITED THAN EVER. GOD BLESS YOU ALL. JAMES

Then I went back into the lessons and stayed until lunchtime. I wanted to share my sorrow but it was difficult to speak about it. I was eating my dinner with Jim Boulton, Ken Brown, Tony Evans, Budgett and Peter Smith and Bob Morgan when a fresh wave of realisation caught me. I was asked whether I had bad news. They were very kind and after just expressing their sorrow they went on as usual and I was glad for the diverted attention, as my lower lip was quivering.

When I got back to my room I made my bed and lay on it once more in the grip of the instincts of affection and friendship which tie me doubly to old Mike who is a brother and my best friend.

I went and sat in the station chapel where before and beside God and with Mikie very near me I began the task of pulling together the shattered fabric of love and companionship which had protected me. I began to realise that the greatest blow fell not on me but on Mother and Father and little Dave. They gave him life and nourished him to healthy boyhood and courageous manhood.

I went across this afternoon to fly with Crownshaw. We did steep turns and forced landings, spinning and compass courses and all the time I thought of Mike. It wasn't until this evening, when I faced the problem squarely, that I reached a new peace and harmony. I did realise when I was flying that a new determination had entered me and that his courage was to become mine. I felt a special sense of mission and of duty that while a Benn still flies with the Air Force, my standard would be as high as his. I asked Crownshaw when I came down how I could get on twin-engined bombers.

After tea I dressed myself up in my battledress and great coat, I pushed my cap on my head, took my pipe and tobacco and went out to have a walk round the aerodrome. I thought of Mike as a pilot flying in North Africa or over France and Germany, I felt proud I was following in his footsteps. I thought of him as a companion through life and as a partner and a colleague in times of struggle for a better world which we can and will create out of this war. I thought of him as a friend with whom so many plans had been made.

When I had finished thinking of the past a great calmness came over me.

Friday 30 June
Prepared for the weekend in Salisbury. Changed my clothes and packed the stuff in my blue pack.

Monday 10 July
I had a letter from Mike today written on the day before he was killed – bless him. It was full of his activities – how sweet and natural it was. It finished 'Oh James, how I miss you – but we must see this through. Ever your old, M'.

Wednesday 19 July
I had many letters today about Mike. They were so sweet and sympathetic that I had a new outburst of emotion which I could not control. I wept bitterly when I read the inspiring words with which the RAF Padre concluded his sermon at Golders Green. The hymn was 'I vow to thee my country all earthly things above'. This made me sob as I haven't since I heard the news.

Wednesday 2 August
Crownshaw and I took off just after 1300 hours for low-level cross-country. Most of the flight was carried out over the native reserve. Of the natives I saw the majority were women. Stark naked, jolly little piccaninnies waved and jumped about. If we were passing fifty yards or more to the side of a village they would stand up and wave. But if we passed closer or over them, they ran in all directions, or crouched on the ground. At the eastern side of Longwe in the foothills, I saw one poor mother kneeling with her two children, attempting to shield them, as we roared across. I felt quite ashamed and I was preparing to climb Longwe when Crownshaw took her off me and began to beat up this village mercilessly. I was really sorry to see him do that because I felt so warmed in my heart at the spontaneous welcome they all gave when they first saw us, that to frighten them, as our dives undoubtedly did, seemed needlessly unkind.

As soon as we had gone over, out they all came to watch and the whole process was repeated.

Previously to our shoot-up at Longwe we had been up and down the Lundi river looking for crocodiles. We saw three hippos in the centre of the river and as we flew over them they submerged like U-boats.

I went back to the billet to gloat over the tobacco and cigarettes that my dearest Ma had sent me. I had reached the stage where my pipe was laid aside because I couldn't find any smokeable tobacco for it.

Saturday 5 August
I saw and heard things tonight which have strengthened my determination to remain teetotal all my life. There was a cabaret show which I left after a few minutes. There were only two sorts of turn, those that were dirty and in thoroughly bad taste, and those that were clean and not funny at all. The

dance was rather a flop. You couldn't hear the band and most people were tipsy. I paid a visit to the Corporals' Club and saw Crownshaw obviously having had too much to drink but quite steady as a policeman invariably is, the only visible sign being that he was enamoured of some deadly popsy well in her thirties. I was caught in a conversation with a drunk Rhodesian sergeant with whom I nattered for five or ten minutes and was then shaken warmly by his hand and bidden good-night and lifelong good luck.

As I wandered by the dining hall I saw in a corner two men fighting. One was lying on the ground and the other was standing over him, picking him up only to knock him down again. Then he hurried back into the dance and as he passed me. I saw that it was Taffy Hinds – quite a pleasant fellow when he's sober. Jim Martin and I hurried over to where the other fellow lay, his face a mass of blood and his clothes crumpled and bloodstained. He was unconscious – in fact he looked half dead.

With the help of a couple of ground staff wallahs we started to carry him across to the sick quarters. However, he woke up halfway, started to mutter and swear and began to kick. I wasn't prepared to help someone who for two pins would have attacked us so we all dropped him and he ran, or rather staggered, to his billet and sat up in a stupor on the steps there.

It all arose because Hinds called De Sylva a bastard and De Sylva called Hinds a Welsh shithouse.

Friday 15 September
We arrived in Bulawayo about six and after a cup of tea at the canteen we walked to the Services Club for breakfast. Our luggage had all been left in error in Gwelo station.

We embussed and arrived at RAF Heany in due course where I was billeted in the old church – an extremely grim building with no box, locker or wardrobe.

Tuesday 17 October
There were three letters for me in the sergeants' mess. One from Dad was on the subject of standing for Parliament. Apparently he had opened a letter for me, from John Parker, in error, in which Parker requested me to consider contesting a seat at the next General Election as a Labour Party candidate. My first sensation was amazement, then of intense pleasure, in the first place at having been remembered by my Party friends and in the second at having been considered as a suitable candidate by Parker, the MP for Dagenham, whom I hardly know. Pa wrote a few words of sound advice. I know that it is his heartfelt wish that I should finish at Oxford. Bless him for promising to use his influence with the Party to get me a good seat if I decided so, and also for his generous offer of the necessary financial support.

Wednesday 25 October
The flick was not very good except for Veronica Lake, who is lusho. Anna

was pretty unresponsive tonight and I almost had a crick in the neck. I wonder why she is like this, because she is always very eager when speaking to me.

Monday 30 October
We had the first fatal accident on the station since I have been here this morning. An instructor and a pupil hit the high-tension cables while on low-level cross-country. The kite caught fire and they were burnt. As a matter of fact, of course, they were killed by the kite striking the deck probably at 140 mph, so they were already dead. It is just another example of what unauthorised low flying does for you. I feel strangely calm about it, and everybody jokes about it. I can't make up my mind if this is wrong or not. If I thought of it too seriously and pondered each implication it might worry me to the extent of affecting my morale and my flying.

   Frankenstein's Monster meets the Wolfman was on tonight and I took Anna. The question of popsies arose and she asked me if I had one in England. I made a joke of it and said, 'I have six – one in England, two at Heany, two at Bulawayo and one at Salisbury.' This solved the problem.

Saturday 25 November
At a quarter to ten Bob, Ken and I were summoned to the Chief Instructor's office. We had to wait an hour and three-quarters while he interviewed five scrubs.

   He saw us individually and the conversation went something like this:

   CI: 'Benn, you have been recommended to me as an under-officer. Do you want to do this and live in the officers' mess?'

   'Yes, sir.'

   CI: 'You are young and may find it difficult at first – a lot of men older than yourself will be under you and you will have to use tact. Don't be put off by the "old chum" racket. If an old chum disregards an order he will expect you to report him and you must do so.'

   Then we went across to the Chief Ground Instructor's office. He gave us a long talk referring especially to home troubles. When he had given Willshire two buttons and Ken and me one each as cadet leaders he told me that I was to be moved to the other group so that Willshire could keep an eye on me and give me a hand with discipline. Then he dismissed us and told us to meet him at the officers' mess for lunch.

   We went into lunch and it was the best scoff I have seen in Rhodesia. I suppose I shall get used to it but at the moment it is strange. I find that I have forgotten some of my table manners. It is an ideal place for spare time and I enjoy the easy chairs and the music from the radiogram. I was going to go to the flicks tonight but I can only sit with the officers and that cuts out Tommy Stout and Anna, so what's the use?

Monday 27 November

I found Johnny Harris to pay him the 15/- I owe and there were some of the boys, so I stayed and nattered. When I looked back. I felt a despair and was unhappy about it while it went on, though the company was friendly enough. I wasted two or more hours; I sunk into the lowest and cheapest form of humour, partly because I hadn't sufficient determination and strength to clear off and partly I suppose because I wanted them to know that even though I have a blue band on my sleeve I am still one of the lads. As it was I stayed and talked and laughed over the lowest filth and lost complete control of myself. I writhed when I thought of it afterwards and lay awake for half an hour conscious of self-disgust.

Tuesday 13 March 1945

I collected a package from the post office and closed my savings account. The package contained Mike's Wings – the actual pair that he wore on his battledress. They were taken off that tunic and sent me, so I at once removed the Wings that I had won ten days ago, and that I had put on my own battledress, and sewed on his pair. I prayed that I should be found worthy of the Wings I wore.

Wednesday 28 March

I finished my packing and after saying cheerio to one or two people we left Heany for the last time at 0945. The train journey wasn't particularly exciting but I stood on the end of the railway carriage and saw the sun set for the last time in Rhodesia. It was most impressive and I felt the magic of Africa.

Friday 13 April – Alexandria

We heard on the news today that President Roosevelt was dead. We were all gathered round the sergeants' mess when the eight o'clock news was read and the first, long item concerned his sudden collapse and death. Everyone was absolutely hushed for some minutes, a more marked silence than is ever accorded to great items of war news.

Without a doubt, everyone was as shocked and as sad as if Churchill himself had died.

Service life – particularly in air crew – gets you accustomed to death of friends and colleagues. It was rather strange and impressive to be there.

Sunday 14 April

I reminisced with Mike aloud and compared notes of my growing fear of operations. The implications of fighting in the air – responsibility for the crew – the possibility of ditching, crashing, being taken prisoner, torture by Japs, these things are working on my imagination and frightening me.

Tuesday 17 April

Today a Warwick, doing fighter exercises with a Corsair at 2,000 on the 'drome, was violently thrown about, it spun in and hit the ground just across the canal, about 300 yards from where I was in the cinema. The petrol tanks blew up and all the crew of eight (six officers and two sergeants) were either killed by the impact or burned to death – a grim business. We heard the thud, rushed out, and a great column of smoke was rising in the air.

As I watched I saw two or three bits of plywood and fabric floating down. They landed very gently a few yards away.

The fire burnt for some time. Two dead and half-burnt men were brought out.

Thursday 26 April

After lunch we went across to the orderly room and learnt that we had got our leave, plus a railway warrant to Jerusalem. This is joyous news.

Sometimes I get quite worried about my inability to get on with people. I really cannot get on with Eddy and I feel that it is not his fault. I get nagging, short-tempered and rude. He is patient most of the time and I wonder if I shall ever be able to get on with my crew later, and later on with my wife, if I am so intolerable to live with.

Tuesday 1 May – Palestine

I woke up early – it was cold. The train was steaming through the Sinai desert and by the light of the full moon I could discern an expanse of silver sand.

We got up and washed before the train pulled into Gaza. Here we had breakfast at the NAAFI and afterwards we wandered up and down the platform and were attracted by the quantity of lavatories. There was one for British officers, one for nursing sisters, one for women officers and one for Indian officers, and separate ones again for women other ranks, British other ranks and South African other ranks – class distinction *par excellence*. Beyond Gaza were green fields well cultivated – I was quite reminded of Blighty – the hedges were well tended, the farm houses fine stone buildings, that pink granite that in England we associate with churches and buildings like the New Bodleian. None of the tumbledown plaster and mud house-huts that mark the Egyptian agricultural land. I saw straight away that this was the land of promise.

At Lydda we changed and there were crowds of peasants waiting for the Jerusalem train, whom we took to be pilgrims to the city for the Easter Holy Week. The journey from Lydda to Jerusalem was full of surprises. The train twisted and turned through the valleys and climbed painfully between the rough bare mountains. Finally, on the dominating summit we reached the Holy City.

After seeing the service police we started hunting for accommodation and we went to the Church Army hostel. This was very cheap and very comfortable.

27 May 1945

My dearest family

I left you in my last letter on the top of the Mount of Olives at dawn.

At lunch we revisited the old city of Jerusalem and found our way to the church of the Holy Sepulchre. I had been expecting to be disappointed. And it was frightful – orange peel and paper on the floor, shouting guides, jabbering masses, police and beggars. I lost the whole atmosphere of Christianity in the building which of all others in the world is – or should be – the focal point of Christian devotions. In the sepulchre itself, of all places, they collected money for the candles! I came away full of rage at this desecration and disappointment.

To the old city to watch the Abyssinian ceremony of 'searching for the body of Christ'. The Abyssinian monks (who are incredibly poor) live in hovels on the roof of the Holy Sepulchre and their church is a 'lean-to' tent. They broke away from the early Church in about the fifth century and have remained almost unchanged liturgically and doctrinally since then. For a while we could neither see nor hear what was going on. Then the crowd parted and from the church came one black brother, the Abyssinian patriarch, richly clad and followed by other Abyssinian dignitaries and monks. The music was provided by tom-toms, of all instruments, and the procession began.

On the morning of Monday 7 May we got up at about 7 and went in for breakfast, which consisted of laban, bread and tea. Laban is a large dish of thick sour milk and lumps of cream cheese which I found hard to stomach but gallantly ate. After breakfast we set off through the fields, joined a dusty and rough road and walked across into Syria. We joined the road to Tiberias and got a lift in.

We hired a rowing boat and rowed out into the Sea of Galilee, trying to pick out Capernaum on the side of the lake further up. Coming in, we entered a little Arab restaurant for refreshment and as we walked towards the place, a Jew hurried up with a smile and said 'The war – finished!'

We didn't know whether to believe it or not so we smiled back. It seemed to be confirmed by a special edition of the paper. So we solemnly celebrated with an orange squash and ice cream each – hardly believing it could be true, hardly thinking of it, it seemed so remote. Returning later to Shaar Hagolan, via another settlement, we found them preparing for a festival to celebrate peace.

It was nearly 10 o'clock and we understood that the King was to speak so we asked to listen to the wireless. As you know, he didn't, but in consequence we missed the gathering on the lawn when the leader of the settlement gave an address of welcome in Hebrew to 'the three English officers'. Think of the wonderful opportunity for replying with a speech – what we missed! I was disappointed.

Outside on the grass an effigy of the swastika was burned and the settlement crowded into the eating hall, where a little wine and lots of biscuits and nuts were laid along tables.

I asked for an orange squash and was given one, however one old boy emptied half a cupful of wine into it, and I drank it up – it was practically communion wine – rather an appropriate beverage to celebrate peace.

Then the national dances began – Germans, Czechs, Poles, Turks, Yugoslavs, all did their national dances. Then there was a pause and an announcement in Hebrew. Everyone looked at us and it was explained that the RAF officers would do an English national dance. Hurriedly deciding to do the boomps-a-daisy, two of us took the floor – it was an instantaneous success and everybody joined in.

That is how I celebrated the peace.

Your devoted

James

March 1946 – Oxford

Last night I heard that Group Captain Cheshire was going to give a talk on the atomic bomb and I decided to go along.

I stepped into the University Air Squadron building and there were the pictures of past members of the Air Squadron around the walls and amongst them a picture of me. There were hardly more than one in six still alive.

The CO came in and asked us not to drop our cigarette ends on the floor, then he introduced Cheshire.

Cheshire is a young man of perhaps 26. He came up as an undergraduate in 1937 and joined the Air Force. He was described as the greatest air bomber pilot ever and he is probably the most highly decorated officer of the war. He started off his talk by describing more or less factually the events leading up to 'Operation Manhattan'.

In 1944 the Superfort bomber made a direct raid on Japan possible and the Pacific stragegy was organised to procure bases for this. Guam was selected a year later as the base for the atomic raids. The utmost secrecy was required and no one, however senior, outside the project, was informed. They got the mechanism for the bomb transported out there, but the problem was moving the atomic cores. One went by cruiser, the other by C54 US Air Transport – carried by a colonel and a sergeant – in a little yellow box.

Cheshire did not go on the Hiroshima raid. He described the Nagasaki one. The aircraft (two for observations, one for the bomb) rendezvoused over South Japan at 9 o'clock and went in to the target at 10. They were flying at 34,000 feet. The kite was pressurised, heat and soundproofed so they were wearing khaki slacks and shirts, with no oxygen or intercom. They put dark glasses on, so dark that the sun was just a blur in the centre and when the bomb went off it lit up the whole scene as if a light had been turned on in a darkened room. The heat generated is ten million degrees C, very nearly as hot as the internal heat of the sun. After three minutes they were able to take off their glasses.

At the moment the bomb dropped there was a flash of fire and a column of smoke rose at about 20,000 feet a minute, to 60,000 feet, where it flattened out into a mushroom shape. They dropped radio sets with instruments attached to record pressure waves, etc.

Cheshire said quite plainly he did not want to discuss the ethics of the thing but he sobered everyone up by putting to us quite plainly the facts. If we have another war it will mean the end of our physical civilisation, for man might survive but buildings can't. He spoke quietly and slowly. 'Realise this, that if these bombs are ever going to be used there is not much point in anything that you are doing now.'

He was quite remote and above us and no doubt the whole world seemed as unreal to him as he to it.

Sunday 25 August
Last Saturday I went out with B. I didn't realise till I came to pay the bill (£3/10/-) what a waste of time and money it had been. The truth of the matter is that she is a shallow, selfish, dull and expensive little girl. She is very physically attractive, but she has no sort of personality, sparkle or life and absolutely no character. She has got nothing original to say about anything. I found conversation extremely difficult. It petered out almost entirely after a time. What is more she was utterly frigid and didn't respond at all to the pressure of my arm while we were dancing.

In June 1947 an 'unsigned' article appeared in the Isis *magazine of Oxford University*
'The facts about Anthony Benn's early life are simple and unexciting. Born in London just over twenty-two years ago he was educated at Westminster, a period unmarked by any distinction in the fields of school activity in which he participated. He left utterly convinced of the desirability of co-education.

'Along with most of the war-time generations, he spent his three terms in a leisurely way before joining the RAF in summer 1943. He spent a year in Southern Rhodesia, learning to fly which he thought was great fun, though his feelings were not shared by his new instructors.

'His extremely youthful appearance had at least one amusing repercussion. After his first round of the cook-house, as a very new Pilot Officer, the sergeant-cook offered him an orange to take away. Benn accepted this gratefully and fled, blushing furiously. From there he went to the Middle East. His stay in the Middle East was brief and pleasant. It included a leave in Palestine, where he and two others stayed over VE Day as guests in a

Jewish communal settlement. At the victory festivities there, the Jews of all nations did their traditional folk dances and the three English officers were asked to do an English national dance. Boompsa-daisy is said to be still popular in the Sea of Galilee area.

'Posted home in time for the General Election he drove a loudspeaker van round his local constituency in Westminster and soon afterward, full of boyish enthusiasm, transferred to the Fleet Air Arm for service in the Far East. However, armed with the atom bomb, the UN Supreme Command decided that Benn's services could be dispensed with and he was sent on indefinite leave . . .

'What can be said of him as a person? He dresses scruffily, talks too much and is rather boisterous. His interests are mainly political (being a rather idealistic socialist) but he also enjoys discussing a great many other subjects of which he is even more ignorant. He collects pipes, believes in complete social and political equality as between the sexes, gets rather too easily embarrassed for comfort and laughs at his own jokes. Being by nature somewhat unmethodical he attempts to organise his life with three mechanical devices. A petty cash account (to keep him economical), a job list (as a substitute for imperfect memory) and a time chart (to give him an incentive to work).

'Of the future he does not like to think overmuch. He is on the list of Labour Party parliamentary candidates (potential) and hopes to make something of this when he has had time to supplement his rather inadequate PPE education, by gaining a little first-hand knowledge and experience of some aspect of political activity.'

Thursday 1 April 1948
All is not well with the Abbey Division of Westminster Labour Party. The growth of the organisation has produced cliques and endless bickering. Wilf Messer is a wonderfully reliable and steady chap. Jack Jones, the chairman, is the best type of trade unionist. But there is an ambitious, bitter and intriguing group. The measure of the tragedy is that it has reached the point where Mrs Hammond, a splendid woman, is resigning and if we can't keep a woman like her in the Party, what hope is there of increasing our membership? Abbey is, I hope, an exception.

Saturday 3 April
My twenty-third birthday. Today the world is heading straight for war. I wonder whether these words will ever be read by anyone who survives.

I know that everyone tends to believe that every war is bound to be the last but this time with atom bombs and bacteria I can't see how life can go on in a form worth living, when it is over.

On this 23rd birthday of mine I am faced with the problem of what to do with my life. In a year's time I shall have left Oxford behind and shall be working for a living.

Is politics really my place? Should I earn my living in business? (Benn Brothers for example). Or should I go down a mine for a year? Just where do I stand politically? *Am* I a socialist? Am I prepared for the personal sacrifices that must necessarily involve?

I must sort out my own position and see if I can't resolve the present confusions and make out of all this a coherent whole on which to base everything.

While I am on my own weaknesses and faults, another shortcoming is that I want the limelight too much. Another thing that has always worried me is my self-consciousness. I have always worried terribly what people thought of me and made all sorts of efforts to please. This has probably done me more harm than good.

If I am really hated by someone even now it still worries me a lot, but generally speaking I am much more at ease with people and with women. A reputation for insincerity is rather a damaging thing, let alone the fundamental badness of insincerity itself. Am I insincere?

Letters from Anthony Crosland to Tony Benn on the eve of Benn's marriage to Caroline De Camp; Crosland always called Benn 'Jimmy'.

Trinity College
Oxford

11 March 1949

My dear Jimmy

How are you? All I've ever heard from you was a note saying 1. Carol was perfect, 2. the prospect of marriage was perfect, 3. life in general is perfect and 4. you were perfect.

From all of which I deduced that you were happy and things were going well. I imagine you are now engaged in ceaseless entrepreneurial activity on behalf of this rather shady publishing firm. I hope the job hasn't turned out to be as disagreeable as you expected.

Nothing much happens or changes in Oxford. Of the Labour Club I now see little, being very much persona non grata as a result of certain goings-on at the Club dinner where I provided, during the speeches, a background of shrewd comment which was not highly appreciated by the more humourless members present (the majority).

The main things that have happened to me are that I nearly got South Hammersmith and that I have turned down Oxford. The South Hammersmith thing was disappointing. I was rung up by Gordon Walker to know if I would let my name go forward. I said yes: there was than a fight at the NEC level between me and Douglas Houghton (for the candidature). Houghton won and went down to the selection conference with full Transport House backing and was then quite unexpectedly beaten by Tom Williams, who was a Co-op nominee. Then Oxford fell vacant since they finally got tough and pushed Stewart Cook out. I was nominated by four wards, and had a terrible time making up my mind. But I finally said No, I think wisely. Lady Pakenham in the end was the only candidate and she has now been accepted.

The only person who is still optimistic about my chances is dear old Hugh [Dalton] whose reputation you will be glad to hear I have now entirely rehabilitated by a sensational article in *Tribune* saying he was the greatest Chancellor since Gladstone.

My love to Carol, God help her. And drop me a line with your news.

Yrs

Tony

Trinity College
Oxford

4 June 1949

My dear Jimmy

I gather, both from your letter, and your elegantly-printed invitation which is (if I may say so) quite dominated by your lengthy nomenclature, that you propose to carry this thing through to the bitter end. So be it. You do so with my prayers and good wishes, and I shall think of you on 17 June 1949 at 6 o'clock.

It is a great relief to me that you are being married in evening dress, though I should hope that you will have a more elegant one than that which you used to wear here. Try not to make a fool of yourself at the wedding: I suggest that you keep off the ginger-beer: you know how it goes to your head.

I won't give you all my news now as I shall see you in a few weeks.

So my very best wishes for the 17th and afterwards: and give Carol an avuncular kiss on the forehead from me and tell her how much I look forward to seeing her.

Yrs

Tony

2

1950–60

During the last years of the 1940s and the first years of the 1950s Tony Benn's political diary is very sporadic. At this time he spent a miserable time as a salesman of Benn trade books in America, relieved only by the prospect of his impending marriage to Caroline De Camp of Cincinnati, in 1949. By November 1950 he had been nominated and elected for Bristol South East in a by-election. Earlier that year a General Election had considerably reduced the Labour Government's majority, and Clem Attlee, now Prime Minister, faced with the dilemma of whether to hold another Election to improve Labour's parliamentary position, did so and lost. Thus Churchill became Prime Minister for a second time in 1951.

Between 1951 and 1958, the Benns' four children – Stephen, Hilary, Melissa and Joshua – were born and Tony Benn and his father started to plan a constitutional and legal campaign that would relieve Tony Benn of an unwanted hereditary title to which he became heir following the death of his brother Michael in the war.

January 1951

I am going to try out a political diary. What I want to do is to highlight the most significant events of which I am a witness and set down contemporary opinions and accounts which my memory would probably distort to suit current purposes were I to try and recall them later on. This is surely the politician's greatest weakness, if published memoirs are anything to go by.

I am a very new Member of Parliament and it is still exciting to bump into Winston Churchill in the Member's Lavatory, as I did the other day. It is still pleasant to be called by my Christian name by Aneurin Bevan and to call him Nye.

Monday 29 January

Returned to the Commons, still feeling like a very new boy. After Questions the Prime Minister made a long-awaited statement on the new Defence plans, involving rearmament costing £4,700,000,000 over the next three years and the call-up of 235,000 reservists this summer. It was received in glum silence on our side of the House. Some Labour MPs asked hostile questions and this was used by the Tories as fresh evidence of a Labour split. I went away wanting to discuss it with my colleagues, but I don't really know them well enough and this frustrated me.

Wednesday 31 January

This morning the Parliamentary Labour Party met to discuss foreign policy and the defence plans.

Clem's statements were moderate and I think he made a strong case for what he has done. But of course a call for party unity means that everyone must make concessions to different viewpoints. I am unhappy and undecided about German rearmament. And 100 per cent against Japanese rearmament. The defence programme I would be inclined to support as I do think that there is a threat of aggression in Europe, though I am not satisfied that enough has been done to negotiate with Russia about Germany or that we have made every possible effort to allay Polish and Czech fears. I think we might do well to guarantee the Oder-Neisse line and perhaps try direct negotiations with the Eastern European countries.

In Korea I am very fearful of MacArthur, but quite what we could have done about the American resolution at the UN I don't know. They would have carried it (without the modification we achieved) in any case as the Latin American countries are satellites of the USA. It is the same problem we Labour MPs have to face: whether we stay in as loyal members accepting what is done and try to shape policy or whether to rebel and become lone voices in the wilderness. What terrific pressure there is on us. A spell in

Opposition would do us a world of good, if not for the grim prospect of Tory rule and the sad depletion of ranks that a General Election would cause.

Wednesday 7 February
I made my maiden speech today on the advice of various people that it should be 'about the middle of February'.

Roy Jenkins suggested steel nationalisation. I know nothing about steel except what anyone can mug up and it was almost impossible to speak non-controversially about it.

Father had said, 'A maiden speech is like a canter at a horse show. You are just expected to show your paces in a graceful way.'

A message came from the Whips' office asking me to move to the benches above the gangway and shortly afterwards my name was called.

I would certainly have abandoned the whole attempt after the opening speeches had not the family all been present – Mother and Caroline, Father and Dave.

The benches falling away from below me made me feel very tall and rather conspicuous.

I stumbled a bit over 'right honourable friend' and 'right honourable and gallant gentleman'. At one point, speaking of the bad psychological effect of a profitable steel industry while rearmament threatened our living standards, I sensed a change of feeling – and a wave of hostility. But towards the end of my speech I was aware of growing friendliness and laughter. I could see our Front Bench – Strauss, Bevan, Dalton and Strachey – all looking up at me.

I sat down after about fifteen minutes. Sir Ralph Glyn, Conservative Member for Abingdon, followed and paid a very warm tribute which Father enjoyed as much as I did. It had been a success. Conceit compels me to record that I had letters of congratulation from the PM, Strauss, Bevan, Steven Hardie (Chairman of the new Iron and Steel Corporation), and others. I do feel much more at home in the place.

Crosland and I went in to the Smoking Room to join Nye, Hugh Dalton and Dick Crossman. Crossman was under attack by Dalton for the defeatist *New Statesman* policy. Nye's personality was electric. His vigour and grasp and good humour and power of arguement paralysed me with excitement. Seeing him beside Dalton one could not but notice the difference. Dalton – saturnine, wicked, amusing, intellectual, roguish: Bevan open, honest, good-humoured, and devastating.

Thursday 22 February
I went to Number 10 for tea today. The Prime Minister and Mrs Attlee make a point of entertaining Labour MPs in one way or another. Welsh MPs Llywelyn Williams and Dorothy Rees, and Coventry MP Elaine Burton were the other guests. We went over at 4.30 by car and up to the flat.

Mrs Attlee received us and Clem came in later and stayed for half an hour.
There had been a row at Questions, over the appointment of an American
admiral over NATO sea forces and Clem had come out of it rather badly.
We had been warned by Clem's PPS not to talk shop and so we were slightly
taken aback when Vi went for Clem and asked him why he had knuckled
under to the Americans yet again. Clem said nothing, but I got the
impression that he really hadn't cared a bit one way or another and hadn't
even known about the decision before Churchill put down his question.

Tea was not exciting and Clem's conversation never rose above the
ordinary except in his digs at Churchill. I think he has an inferiority
complex.

Vi was very la-di-da in her latest creation, with long red fingernails. She
might have been a leader of society and her comments were very 'upper
class', especially her reference to the proposal to open Chequers to Festival
of Britain visitors, which was 'How awful'!

Wednesday 11 April
I must describe the events which have led up to the present crisis in the
fortunes of the Party.

When Gaitskell came to consider his budget he was faced with the need
for a considerable increase in revenue to meet the rearmament programme
and the inflationary dangers that accompanied the rise in world prices.

He also had to demand, even more firmly than is usual for a Chancellor,
that government expenditure be held down tightly. The Cabinet Committee which considered the various ways in which these objectives could be
achieved reached the provisional conclusion two weeks ago that no charge
should be made for dentures and glasses on the Health Service. At about
that time Nye Bevan made a speech in public at Bermondsey in which he
said that no Government of which he was a member would introduce such a
charge.

This was taken to be a statement of fact. It now appears it was nothing of
the kind – rather an ultimatum to Gaitskell designed to intimidate him.

Perhaps I should say at this point that Nye's Celtic pride has been deeply
hurt during the last six months. When Cripps resigned as Chancellor he was
bitterly disappointed that he, Nye, did not replace him. Harold Wilson felt a
similar resentment – of which more later. Then a few weeks ago, when Ernie
Bevin resigned the Foreign Office, Nye felt that he should have had first
refusal. Instead Herbert Morrison got it. These rebuffs and the emergence
of Hugh Gaitskell, which shifted the old balance of forces in the Cabinet,
produced all sorts of results. Nye, who had accepted the defence programme
reluctantly, believed a socialist budget could make the sacrifices more
palatable. When he learned, as late as Monday last, that Gaitskell intended
to impose the health service charges, he decided to act.

The Cabinet met at 10.30 last Monday morning. The charge was disclosed as a definite feature and Nye announced his decision to resign if it were not withdrawn. Gaitskell, backed by the whole Cabinet (except Harold Wilson), stood firm. The Prime Minister, of course, was in hospital with a duodenal ulcer and he was kept in touch. By lunchtime no decision had been reached and so the Cabinet met again on Monday evening at 6.30 and sat for three hours. Nye and Harold Wilson decided that they would resign the following day and letters between them and the PM were actually exchanged with the understanding that they would be published the following evening at 7pm.

After the Cabinet had adjourned, Hugh Dalton (according to his own account) stayed late, with Nye, to dissuade him. Nobody seemed to care very much whether Harold Wilson resigned or not and from this one could learn that indispensability should not be assumed, nor tested too often.

At about 3.40 on Tuesday, after Questions, Hugh Gaitskell, looking pale and nervous and complete with buttonhole, came along the Front Bench to open his Budget.

I looked along the Treasury Bench. Dalton and Chuter Ede, Herbert Morrison and Douglas Jay – they were all there, even the dying Ernie Bevin. But Nye was not.

The Chancellor began. His speech lasted for more than two hours, a brilliant exposition: there is no doubt that speech made his reputation secure. When he came on to the detailed proposals we heard definitely of the decision to charge for glasses and false teeth under the Health Service. I looked at once to the group standing beside the Speaker's chair. Nye and Jennie Lee and Michael Foot had just entered and they stood there to hear the announcement. As soon as it had been made Nye peered anxiously at the Labour benches, eyes going back and forth up and down. The announcement was greeted without a sound. We all took it absolutely quietly. Nye looked crestfallen and disappeared through the glass doors.

The Tea Room and Smoking Room received the Budget well. We had all expected far worse things and the most noticeable reaction was sheer relief.

Monday 23 April

The resignation of Nye was announced this morning. Harold Wilson's position was uncertain though it was announced later today that he too intended to go. I arrived at the Commons at 2 and went up into the Members' Gallery. With the sunlight pouring through the windows opposite, the Chamber was suffused in a warm glow of light. Jennie Lee came in at about ten past three and sat, flushed and nervous, on the very back bench, below the gangway. At 3.20 Nye walked in briskly and jauntily and went straight to his seat three rows back. He looked pale and kept shifting his position and rubbing his hands. The Front Benches on both sides were very full – Churchill, Eden and the Tories sat quietly.

Morrison, Chuter Ede, Noel-Baker, Dalton, Gaitskell and the others sat unhappily together. Then the Speaker called Nye Bevan to make his resignation statement.

His rising was greeted by a few 'hear, hears'. Not many. The Government Front Bench looked sicker and sicker as the speech went on and the violence of the attack intensified. Jennie Lee behind him sat forward and became more and more flushed. Every now and again he pushed back the lock of his iron-grey hair. He swung on his feet, facing this way and that and his outstretched arm sawed the air. He abused the Government, he threw in a few anti-American remarks for good measure. He attacked the Treasury, economists, and the unhappy combination of an economist at the Treasury. Gaitskell showed clearly the contempt he felt. Dalton looked like death once warmed up and now cooled down.

The fact is that though there was substance in what he said Nye overplayed his hand. His jokes were in bad taste. I felt slightly sick.

He sat down, the hum of conversation started and the exodus began. Nye stayed put for a few moments. He rose to go, and Emrys Hughes shook his hand as he passed the Front Bench.

It has to be said that he was written the Tory Party's best pamphlet yet. I predict it will be on the streets in a week.

Tuesday 24 April
Nearly twenty-four hours have elapsed since I wrote the account of the dramatic scene in the House. Nye's attack was bitter and personal. His style was that of a ranting demagogue. But there was substance in what he said and his speech reads better than it sounded. Nye will never be in another government until and if he forms his own.

Wednesday 10 October
The large Gallup poll majority against us (still 7 per cent) seems too big to beat in two weeks.

Monday 15 October – General Election Campaign
Harry Hennessy took me to my first dinner-hour meeting, outside the Co-op furnishing factory. Not a single soul came out of the factory to listen and I began to wonder what was wrong. We had a lot of kids from the school which made some sort of an audience, but either through a mistake in timing, or through hostility, we got no one out.

I disappeared after lunch to help Tony Crosland in Gloucestershire South. He did very well in his personal canvassing but I didn't think much of his speech.

Tuesday 16 October
At 7 Caroline and I went over to the Central Hall, Bristol for the great rally which the Prime Minister was to address. There were nearly 3,000 people

there. Harry Hennessy was a wonderful master of ceremonies. His introductory speech was blunt and honest.

Every Labour candidate in Bristol spoke and as I stood up to speak I felt sick with emotion. Mastery of an audience of that size is a strong task, but what an intoxicating experience it is.

We all did a second speech in an overflow meeting upstairs and Harry started a collection off. We collected £138.

Then Clem and Vi could be seen on the way to the platform. Everyone stood up and cheered lustily, shouting themselves hoarse. 'Hello Tony,' he said as if we were old friends! I shook Vi's hand as she passed. Harry took control again and we all sang 'For he's a jolly good fellow'. Then Harry introduced 'Comrade Clem Attlee', and pushed him forward. But the bouquet had been forgotten and Alderman Mrs Keel gave Vi the flowers with a moving little speech.

Clem quietly and sensibly reviewed the work of the Government abroad and at home, linking each to the work of two famous West Countrymen, Ernest Bevin and Stafford Cripps. 'They have both left us now,' he said, 'but other younger ones have come to take their place. Christopher Mayhew, one of the most brilliant young men, to replace Ernie Bevin, and Tony Wedgwood Benn, another brilliant man, to replace Stafford Cripps.'

When he sat down Tony Crosland moved his vote of thanks, and paid his tribute somewhat back-handedly by saying there has never been an anti-Attlee faction in the Party (which was both patently untrue and damning with faint praise).

We ended with the first verse of 'The Red Flag'.

Thursday 25 October
The first thing to notice on polling day is the weather and today dawned clear and blue, with a good winter nip in the air. Everyone was cheerful and there was a crowd of small boys helping by running as messengers and checking numbers at the polling stations.

The first indications were of a moderate swing – Labour majorities reduced by about 1,500 and Tory votes similarly up. It looked as if this would give a working majority to the Tories but only two Conservative gains were reported in the first hours.

We reached Wick Road School at about 11.45 pm after having left Stephen at Winifred Bishop's house. My agent, Eric Rowe, standing behind the returning officer, had a huge smile on his face. The growing piles of votes in 250s showed us to have about a two to one lead. We almost doubled the by-election majority, although it was down 2,000 compared with Cripps.

I spoke briefly in the count, about the efficiency of the official staff, the clean way the campaign had been fought, and the miracle of British democratic decision making. I was carried on the shoulders of supporters to Ruskin Hall where I thanked them more personally.

A very tired MP and his wife got back to their hotel at 3 am. We listened to the results as they came in until about 3.45.

After the inflation caused by the Korean War, the arguments within the Party, and the drive towards rearmament in Britain and Europe, the defeat of the post-war Labour Government was perhaps inevitable. But the Labour vote remained high and was actually greater than the popular vote that carried Winston Churchill back to power.

Although Clem Attlee carried on as Leader of the Labour Party until after the General Election of 1955, it was obvious that the Party was moving to the right, with the rise of new leaders, of whom Hugh Gaitskell was the most significant; while the left under Aneurin Bevan's leadership was on the defensive. After the Election Tony Benn only kept an intermittent record of those years in opposition, as a humble backbencher.

Wednesday 31 October
This evening David Butler came to dinner. He had been summoned before the 1950 Election to Chartwell and had spent the evening with Churchill discussing electoral possibilities, and he remained overnight as a guest.

Another summons came and David presented himself at Hyde Park Gate at about 10.30 in the morning, where he found Winston in bed drinking a whisky and soda. The first thing that struck him was how he had aged in the last eight months.

He asked several questions about his chances of success in the Election. David was cautious and indicated that an overall majority of forty or so was likely. Putting it into betting odds, he got a more lively response and they had a little backchat.

Churchill remembered almost exactly David's remarks about eighteen months earlier.

Before he left, Churchill asked him quietly and soberly, 'Mr Butler, do you think I am a handicap to the Conservative Party?' It was said without dramatic intent – indeed with a rather pathetic desire for reassurance. David did not answer for a while. 'Come Mr Butler, you need not be afraid to tell me.'

'Well,' replied David, 'I do not think that you are the asset to them that you once were . . . the public memory is short, you know.'

'But the people love me, Mr Butler. Everywhere I go they wave and workmen take off their caps to cheer me . . .'

A Note on Hugh Gaitskell
Just before the Election was announced I wrote (as radio adviser to the Party) to Hugh Gaitskell asking him whether I could give him any help with the Party political broadcast he had been asked to give on 29 September. He sent a message asking me to come to his room at the Treasury and I asked Michael Young, Secretary of the Party's Research Department, to come with me.

Gaitskell walked across from his desk to greet us, and as we were ushered in his smile was welcoming. We sat round his desk and he outlined to us the script that he proposed to deliver.

He was immaculately dressed in a brown suit, with the very slightest aura of aftershave lotion and talcum powder about him. His curly hair and receding chin gave him a boyish but also slightly ineffectual appearance. His smiles are slightly distant and complacent – his mind appeared to be working on its own and only part of it was devoted to the people who were with him.

After he had finished I asked him to what audience he would be directing his remarks – floating, middle-class, trade unionist, unhappy Bevanite? He looked a little pained and bored when I pressed the point and countered by a reminder that honest politics meant speaking the truth, and what fine service Cripps had done to establish this tradition.

Under the mildest form of criticism, he always reverted to this slightly detached and hurt off-handedness so reminiscent of Tony Crosland. The similarity between the two was too noticeable to be missed and no wonder that Crosland thinks so highly of him.

I could see very clearly how the character of Gaitskell and his mannerisms would have driven Nye Bevan to fury. I won't say he is slippery because he is too straightforward to be that, but he could easily by a gesture or smile or frown or word-choice make it clear he wished to avert a head-on collision in argument with those who disagreed with him.

In a way it was his attractive, public-school character that made him both pleasant and detestable.

I thoroughly enjoyed it even though it made me more sympathetic to Nye Bevan than I had been at the start.

Tuesday 20 November
Should I join the Bevanites?

I am not in sympathy with the methods used by the Bevanites since the resignations in April. *Tribune* has been scurrilous and the personal bitterness engendered has been far greater than was necessary. Particularly obnoxious do I find the complacent assumptions by the Bevanites that the ark of the socialist covenant resides with them.

From a personal point of view I am anxious to settle down independently. This last year has been very frustrating and I am only just starting to venture forth on my own.

Thursday 28 February 1952 – PLP Foreign Affairs Group
Today there was another Foreign Affairs Group meeting to discuss German rearmament. It was interesting because for the first time decisions were taken. The characteristic of Party discussions all this time has been talk and

no vote. The Foreign Affairs Group was the first to do anything but of course its decisions were not binding on the Party.

The following motions were moved:

Eric Fletcher: 'That this group is opposed to any proposals for a German contribution to Western Defence which would violate all four conditions laid down by the present Leader of the Opposition on 12 February 1951; and is of the opinion that the whole question of German rearmament should be postponed for the time being; and protests against Her Majesty's Government's support for the creation of what the Prime Minister has openly described as a German army.' [Carried by 30 votes to 24.]

John Strachey: 'That this party shall reaffirm the view that we shall not agree to German rearmament until the conditions laid down by Mr Attlee have been fulfilled. These conditions include in particular the condition that the building up of the forces in the democratic states must precede the creation of German forces and that the agreement of the Germans themselves must be obtained. That this party shall urge that the British Government shall indicate its willingness to become a member of the European Defence Community if a treaty containing suitable safeguards can be negotiated.' [Defeated]

Denis Healey: 'That this party believing that the defence of Western Europe can best be achieved within a closely integrated European Defence Community, but that a European Defence Community limited to the nations of continental Europe is inadequate for this purpose, maintains that the British Government should approach the Administration of the USA to propose that both countries offer to place a proportion of their armed forces inside the European Defence Community.' [Defeated]

Emrys Hughes: 'That this party declares its opposition to any form of German rearmament, welcomes the opposition to German rearmament recently expressed by the socialist parties of Germany and France and calls for joint consultation with our continental comrades with a view to halting armament in Europe, formulating a policy for disarmament and the reconstruction of Europe as a planned socialist economy.' [Defeated]

Freda Corbet: 'That this group accepts the necessity for a German contribution to Western defences with safeguards against a resurgence of German militarism as laid down by Mr Attlee in his four points on 12 February 1951.' [Defeated]

Thursday 24 September 1953

I am satisfied that my personal position in Bristol South East is secure. This is a great relief as I must admit that over the last three years I have worried about it a great deal. I am much more relaxed at meetings – for the very first time ever in Bristol I have made jokes. I am gradually escaping from the personality created for me by circumstances as a young Cripps, earnest, sincere, humourless and churchgoing.

I spent the evening working on Gaitskell's script for the TV broadcast on 15 October. Gaitskell realises its importance and is prepared to work hard, but he is intellectually arrogant, obstinate and patronising. I respect – but cannot quite admire – him.

Thursday 1 October – General Impressions of Conference
This year's Conference did not want to fight. Most delegates are sick of abuse and threats and splits. Herbert Morrison's withdrawal from the treasurership was a fine start.

The right wing of the Party won almost every vote of importance. Land nationalisation and other more extreme proposals were all defeated by big votes.

A great deal of the friction between the trade unions and the constituencies arises from differences in the feelings between 'unpractical' people and the unions, with their huge roles.

It was a good Conference and one senses the great labour movement as a real living organisation, warm and generous, and dedicated. We can look forward to a good year in Parliament now and victory in a General Election.

Monday 2 November
A complete session has gone by between 1952-53 virtually unrecorded.

Ever since 1950 when I was elected, the peerage has been a constant problem. Various proposals for reform have been discussed in these last three years. Lord Simon's Bill a year ago reopened the controversy and led to a government proposal for an all-party conference. But this was rejected by a small Party meeting in the spring.

I was approached by a group of Tories due to inherit peerages who asked whether I would care to talk it over with them. It came to nothing.

The story has been the same since 1711 when the first resolution on reform was moved in the Lords.

I decided I must make an attempt and so, although he was ill and away from work, I wrote a personal letter to Churchill on 27 August in which I set out my problem simply and asked for his guidance.

On 2 September he replied in a very sympathetic way. I thanked him and dared to hope the Queen's Speech might deal with it.

Today the Queen's Speech was read from the throne and did contain a reference to 'Further consideration of the question of the Reform of the House of Lords'.

Thursday 11 February 1954
At 8pm a very important meeting took place – to establish one body for colonial activity – the Movement for Colonial Freedom. It is what is badly needed at the moment for we are frittering away our energies in little tinpot groups with chronic money troubles and too great a diffusion of energy and

skill. The four groups emerging to make up the nucleus are: Congress of Peoples against Imperialism, Seretse Khama Council, British Guiana Association, the Central African Committee. We want an income of £2,000 per year, a paid secretary and typist.

Tuesday 6 April
This evening I was the guest of the Mirror Pictorial Group at the Savoy for dinner. Among those present on the Mirror side were Hugh Cudlipp, Sidney Jacobson, Philip Zec and Labour MPs Woodrow Wyatt, Ernest Davies, Jim Callaghan, Tony Greenwood, Kenneth Younger and self.

The journalists asked us what the Labour Party stood for and what we were doing and how they could help us. During the fascinating evening Jim Callaghan and Tony Greenwood emerged rather as traditionalists – 'nationalise and be damned'. Woodrow was an excellent and strong chairman. Hugh Cudlipp was dynamic, stimulating and unbalanced. Ernest Davies was leading us towards a new foreign policy in the H-bomb age. I talked too much but hit upon a theme that I must develop: 'Socialism is a creed that must be based on the doctrine of liberation or the release of energy.'

We discussed foreign affairs. The age of the H-bomb means a complete reassessment of East–West relations, and survival. The Cold War is dead, we must start afresh.

We agreed to meet again and see if we couldn't hammer out a real working policy, a theme and a basis for co-operation.

Thursday 8 April
Earlier this afternoon I put a question to Churchill about whether the 1943 Quebec A-bomb agreement covered the use of the H-bomb. He said it did, and I quoted Eisenhower and Truman to say it didn't and asked for him to withdraw the charge that Attlee had 'gambled with the national interest'. I thought it a good point but Attlee called me over at the Party meeting and said, 'Wouldn't it have been wiser to have consulted me before putting your question – after all *only* I know the whole truth.' This was stumbling into big things, so I apologised simply. I guess the truth cannot be told yet.

Saturday 23 October
To Bristol for a recording of a programme for the younger generation (15-25-year-olds). What emerged was:

1. Great ignorance about Parliament and its work.
2. Cynicism about politicians and their sincerity.
3. Great gap between politicians and young people.
4. No inspiration of young people by politicians.
5. Healthy disregard of politicians' conceit.

6. Dislike of party or intra-party squabbles except as entertainment.

All very revealing and disquieting.

June 1955 – General Election Post-mortem
Why did we lose the Election? What do we do next?

For a while I have felt very miserable. I took the defeat personally and got too deeply involved. In the last two years I have remained a little more detached. But the rot spread to the constituency Parties very rapidly. I could not help but feel that a party unable to co-exist with itself was really unfit to govern and conduct international negotiations.

Now we are defeated again. The Right will blame Bevan. The Bevanites will interpret it as the price paid for the right-wing policies and leaders.

But since 1951 the Tories have had good luck with the economic climate, people are generally better off and the end of most shortages has enabled rationing to be ended on everything but coal. There has been no unemployment. A family in a council house with a TV set and a car or motorcycle-combination on hire purchase had few reasons for a change of government. The Tories on a turnout 7 per cent lower than 1951 won a greater majority.

Bristol is still a very safe seat indeed and I needn't get panicky but I am frightened that the thing is disintegrating through the absence of a real livewire at its head. The old days of petitions, indoor meetings, 100 per cent canvasses and the rest, are probably dead and gone for ever.

Wednesday 8 June
Invited to Dick Crossman's cocktail party with Nye and the Bevanites plus the left of centre 'Keep Calmers'. Harold Wilson briefed us on the current position on the leadership.

Should Nye oppose Herbert for Deputy Leader? Should Jim Griffiths be put up instead? Do we really want Herbert *or* Hugh Gaitskell? What should Nye do about the Shadow Cabinet?

I found the atmosphere very depressing. The hatred for Morrison and Gaitskell is if anything stronger than their hatred for Nye. In the end it was agreed (almost) that Nye would not oppose Herbert but would stand for the Shadow Cabinet and that we should all plead with Clem to remain indefinitely. Pa advised me to steer clear of intrigues. They all sicken me.

Roy Jenkins cares desperately about getting rid of Morrison for the deputy leadership – to pave the way for Gaitskell.

Sunday 28 October 1956
To Newport last night for a conference. Harold Finch, the Member for Bedwelty, met me and took me to his home, then into the miners' welfare institute where there was a crowded room of serious-minded people. I spoke

for an hour about the challenge of coexistence. It was a wonderful audience to address and the questions were good and pointed. One old boy in a quavering voice asked, 'Can Mr Wedgwood Benn tell us what value he thinks the hydrogen bomb has as a detergent?' I sat listening to the miners talking of the bad old days – the soup kitchens, the struggles with the police, the terrible hunt for work and the agony and humiliation of destitution. It was very moving and more than history – for in the crowded smokey club room were many men gasping for breath from silicosis or limping about from some industrial injury.

Today's news is mainly of the Hungarian crisis reaching its climax. The spontaneous rebellion against the Communist Government has virtually succeeded. The Iron Curtain has risen and people are moving freely in and out of Hungary with supplies and relief. Mr Nagy, the Prime Minister, broadcasts further concessions every hour and the red, white and green have reappeared to replace the hated scarlet banner of the Communist Government. Everyone in the world is breathless with hope that this may lead to a rebirth of freedom throughout the whole of Eastern Europe.

Monday 29 October
The news came through this morning that Britain has raised the matter of Hungary at the UN. I decided to try to raise this as a matter of urgent public importance and get a debate on the adjournment of the House. I worked all morning (and most of last night) on this and phoned Gaitskell to ask him to take it up officially on behalf of the Front Bench. He asked me to come and see him immediately after lunch and I found that he had summoned a meeting of those members of the Party most concerned with foreign affairs. They all feared that a debate might lead to the expression of damaging opinions from left and right extremists which again might harm our capacity to help. I greatly resented all this but on reflection they may well have been right. The Foreign Secretary made a statement and I had acquired for Gaitskell the full text of the Ambassador to the UN, Sir Pierson Dixon's speech which he used most effectively from the Front Bench. I asked whether the Foreign Secretary would make provision for the British people to send blood, relief and money to show their solidarity, without provoking the Soviet Union into a new policy of repression. This last phrase was almost drowned by Conservative boos.

Tuesday 30 October
I heard on the news bulletin this morning of the Israeli attack on Egypt. The weekend news had been grave from the Middle East but I don't think anybody except those in the know had expected it to explode so rapidly and so seriously. I went to the House of Commons after lunch and heard the Prime Minister's statement announcing the ultimatum to Egypt and the decision to demand the right to occupy the Suez Canal. Rumours of this had

been reaching us for a few hours and for a moment the Party was in a state of some uncertainty. Here was aggression and it had to be stopped. Yet we knew the real motives of government policy – how could we say what we felt in a clear way?

In the event Gaitskell made a brilliant comeback following the Prime Minister's statement. The lead he gave us will certainly set the tone of the Party's attitude to this whole crisis. The House was in complete uproar. There was a Party meeting in the evening at which I did speak. I said that this ultimatum was an act of aggression because it denied Egypt's right to self-defence under Article 51 of the Charter and it violated the Tripartite Declaration, the 1888 Convention, the Suez Canal Base Agreement of 1954 and the Baghdad Pact. This was a bold assertion of the law from a layman but on further study it turned out to be absolutely correct.

It is impossible to see how this can now end without far graver disasters. But the impending aggression by Britain has touched a very deep chord in the hearts of every member of the Labour Party bar one or two. This is the same old struggle of collective security versus naked power politics. It has united Phil Noel-Baker and Konni Zilliacus who for twenty years have diverged so enormously since their joint struggles against Hitler.

Wednesday 31 October
I rang the Movement for Colonial Freedom and asked them to book Trafalgar Square for a rally on Sunday afternoon. This they did at once and the meeting was handed over to the Labour Party the same day.

The character and volume of the public protest now developing is most interesting. It has rallied round informed people of every political allegiance. The *Manchester Guardian* provides the intellectual leadership in the country and the Churches, leading figures in science, universities and among professional people are coming out solidly on this. For example, David Butler – normally most conservative – rang me urgently from Oxford to describe the horror with which the news had been received, to confess his feeling of helplessness and to give support.

Thursday 1 November
This morning's news of the bombings added additional tragedy to the situation. The news contained an item that Egypt was contemplating withdrawal from the UN because of the failure of the UN to help her. I decided to ring the Egyptian Embassy at once to urge them not to do this. I spoke to the Ambassador's Private Secretary and explained that the veto cast yesterday by Britain and France was not the end of the matter. Today the General Assembly meets and its decision is a foregone conclusion. I asked the Secretary to ask the Ambassador to send an urgent message to Cairo to get this decision reversed. I also added these words: 'Please convey this message to the Ambassador and add to them an expression on behalf of

the vast majority of the British people of the feelings that he must know we all have.' The Secretary took this down verbatim. No doubt the telephone was tapped, which is why the exact words should be recorded. At any rate, very late tonight the Egyptian Government announced that the reports of its intended withdrawal from the UN were quite without foundation.

This afternoon, after Questions, the Prime Minister made a statement. Gaitskell asked him whether we were at war with Egypt. Eden would not reply. The House burst into uproar. I have never seen Members so angry. I appealed to the Speaker to act for us in ascertaining the legal position. It touched the Royal Prerogative and he was the spokesman of the Commons against the Executive. Silverman asked about the status of our troops if captured. Eden would not reply. The rage and passion reached such a climax that the sitting was suspended.

Friday 2 November
Kenneth Younger drove me to Cambridge for a meeting on Suez and we went at once to the Union where the Committee was waiting. By now sixteen different clubs had united to sponsor the meeting. I sat with the Arab Society officials – two of them Egyptians. One of them, a graduate student of my own age, was crying through the whole of the dinner. He did not know what had happened to his family as all news had been cut off. It was a most awful occasion and I could not convey the shame and disgust that I felt.

The Union debating hall was absolutely packed tight with crowds round it trying to get in through the windows and jamming the entrance thirty deep. We struggled to reach our places. The UN flag had been stolen and there were wildly noisy scenes and shouts. Great posters hung from the gallery reading, 'Support Eden, not Nasser' and 'We are now committed and must support our troops'. The crowd of students laughing and screaming for war gave me an icy hatred of them. The uproar and noise and silly funny remarks when the world was on the brink of disaster were completely revolting, disgusting and shameful.

Sunday 4 November
Bought all Sunday papers. Nutting, a Minister in the Foreign Office, has resigned on principle. Russia is crushing Hungary and has issued an ultimatum. A tragic, heartbreaking day with news flashes every moment that brought us all near to weeping. The last day of freedom in Budapest and the agonising goodbye to Mr Nagy in his dramatic appeal to the world. Then the Hungarian national anthem and total, total silence.

To Gaitskell's house at eleven where he was sitting at his desk beginning to think of his broadcast. Woodrow Wyatt joins us. For an hour we talk to straighten our ideas and work out a plan for the speech. The news is coming in so fast that it is necessary to have someone watching it for us. At my suggestion Gaitskell agrees gratefully that my brother Dave should be asked to go to the *Daily Herald* office and sit by the tape machine. This he does, phoning with news whenever it comes in. A wonderful service and greatly helpful.

By 12 we had sorted out the order for the broadcast. While we made arrangements to get a secretary to him, Gaitskell began dictating on to his tape machine. Woodrow and I talked and read the papers and I answered the phone calls that were flooding in. I really felt that at that house at that moment one was in the centre of the world. By 2.30 Gaitskell had completed his dictation and Woodrow and I lunched with him in the kitchen. Mrs Gaitskell cooked and fed us and washed up. It was a friendly and amusing meal: for 15 minutes we could forget the job.

After lunch we altered the script and recast it until there was a veritable pile of flimsy carbons with unrecognisable scribblings and scratchings upon them. At six we had finished. Woodrow went off and while Gaitskell changed I went on ahead by car to the studio.

Gaitskell arrived at 6.30 and we went straight on to the set. Gaitskell said a word to the assembled engineers, thanking them and apologising for their long frustrating stand-by.

We began together re-dictating the whole script with two secretaries and two reporters from the *Daily Herald* to take it down. Finally, at 8.27 we had a script and were ready to go to the studio for a run-through.

It was a most impressive rehearsal. Absolutely solemn and obviously moved, Hugh went through the whole thing. What he had to say was so compelling that all the technicians stood completely silently and listened to every word. What a contrast to their usual lolling and whispering and hurried glances at the sports news from the evening paper.

At 9 o'clock that was over and we had to cut five minutes from the broadcast. This was done by striking out a single passage completely and it was most certainly the right thing to have done. At 9.50 I took the completed script and sat beside Hugh while he was powdered and brushed, in the long chair. The whole thing had an eerie unreality about it. At 9.55 he began reading it through to check for mistakes. At two minutes to 10 he sat down at the desk in the studio before the camera with the pages in front of him and just time to draw a breath before the red light flashed on.

I watched from downstairs in any easy chair. It was a very good broadcast, I thought, though I knew that I was far too involved in it by then to be able to judge. Certainly it set a precedent in every sort of way. It was the first ministerial broadcast which ever had a reply. It was the first time the Leader of the Opposition had demanded the resignation of the Prime Minister on the air and it was the first time that we had been able to test our capacity to put out a message to the nation with about 11 hours' notice. Afterwards we sat and talked for a little while and then dispersed. Hugh autographed his script for me inscribing it, 'A thousand thanks'.

Monday 5 November
This evening I did three meetings in Gravesend. They were not very big and rather confirmed what I had suspected: that ordinary people are not yet moved on this issue. Part of the explanation too may lie in the fact that every British soldier who has ever served in Egypt hates the Egyptian people.

Tuesday 6 November
A really useful day – made possible by the fact that my secretary, the incomparable Mrs Small, was here all the time. She is going to be here all week, which is an enormous comfort.

This morning's news of a Russian near-ultimatum has made the situation far more grave and we could be within a few hours of a third world war complete with the hydrogen bomb. Very, very, very depressed as a result.

To the House of Commons at 7 pm where the Lobby was full of excited chattering members, talking about a cease-fire. I do not believe it – it is too incredible. Two other members confirm it. It must be true. It is true. Feel like jumping in the air and cheering. Am engaged in a mild caper when spot Bessie Braddock. 'Bessie, I want to kiss you,' I said. Bessie, with a huge smile, replied, 'Not now, dearie, with all these people about.'

Home at 8. Happy and very exhausted. But couldn't go to bed till 2 for trying to think out what all this means and what the lessons are. Will try to set down some first reactions tomorrow.

Thursday 8 November
Today the Tory Party is breaking up, as I suspected it would. Jacob Astor, Alec Spearman and other Tory MPs spoke against the Government. The biggest news of all is of Edward Boyle's resignation from the Treasury. Reggie Paget saw him this afternoon and said a friendly word, at which Edward actually burst into tears in the corridor and Reggie had to stand very close so that three Tories going by wouldn't notice.

Therefore when I saw him after the vote it was with some trepidation that I clasped his arm and said, 'I don't want to embarrass you with my support, but I felt I must say one word.' He was terribly friendly and suggested we have a drink. In fact he came to talk to David, Caroline and me for almost an hour. He said he was sure history would prove him right and he felt a great sense of relief that it was all over. He decided to do it a week ago and was glad the announcement came after the cease-fire to prove that success or failure of the operation could not affect his judgement on it.

He confirmed – very tentatively – what I suspect may happen. Eden, feeling betrayed by his colleagues, may resign and carry the Parliament with him to an Election. It was a most charming talk with Edward who is an old, old friend, but who in the last year or two I have not liked to worry because he has been so busy.

Thursday 15 November

David Butler who came to our party last night asked to see me urgently alone and so we came to the office for a talk. He has seen William Clark who was, until his resignation a few days ago, the Prime Minister's adviser on public relations. He's an exceptionally able man but an appalling name-dropper and snob. His story, as told to David Butler, was this.

Eden's personality underwent a complete change towards the beginning of the Suez crisis. Clark dates this at about the time that he collapsed with a fever when he visited Lady Eden in hospital. He is, said Clark, and I quote, 'a criminal lunatic'. Knowing what a middle-of-the-road, moderate, wishy-washy man Clark is, I was very surprised to hear such strong language used. However, he had more to say in confirmation. Evidently the Government themselves were not kept informed by Eden and various people were taken off the secret list for documents as the plan progressed. Clark himself was sent on leave (which he did not want) the day after he had explained to the PM what the likely public reaction would be to the use of force against Egypt. Clark thought that only an inner group of Cabinet Ministers had been told the plans Eden had made. Clark thought that there was no doubt about the charge of collusion with the French PM, Guy Mollet, and Ben-Gurion. He said that the final proof would come from the State Department in Washington. Apparently when the Israelis were building up for their attack a news blackout descended on London and Paris and consultation with the US came to an abrupt and sinister halt. However, the State Department intercepted and decoded messages passing between Paris and Jerusalem and discovered what was afoot. These messages are likely to leak out from the State Department and destroy the whole basis of Eden's case. Far from claiming the credit for putting out a small fire, he will be charged with having incited the Israelis to start it. This should surely produce more resignations from the Government and alter the whole position once more.

As Hugh Massingham said in Sunday's *Observer*, 'Meanwhile the little time bomb – the charge that there was collusion between Britain, France and Israel – ticks quietly on. If it goes off one day, a lot of beliefs and favourite figures will disappear in the ruins.'

Other items from Clark's story are these:

First, Mountbatten opposed the attack as did Sir Norman Brook, the Secretary of the Cabinet. Sir Roger Makins, Permanent Secretary to the Treasury, first read of it in the newspapers. Finally, the dirtiest thing of all was when Eden told Clark to tell the newspapers privately that Nutting's resignation was not on principle but because of personal difficulties he was in. Clark says he replied, 'If you want that put out, you must put it out yourself.'

One final titbit from today which might be worth following up. Shirley Catlin of the *Financial Times* said that *The Times* itself had been secretly briefed of the Israeli attack and the British intervention four days before it took place. I wonder.

Thursday 29 November
Our Party meeting at 6.30 ended with a most touching little scene. Gaitskell announced the new Shadow Cabinet appointments under which Nye Bevan takes over Foreign Affairs from Alf Robens who is looking after Transport, Fuel and Power. Alf got up to say that he wished Nye all good luck and felt no bitterness at what had happened. Nye responded with a graceful little speech, contrasting our present happy unity with the acrimonious discussions of the past. The Party cheered itself silly in delighted relief at the formal recognition of the final end of all our splits.

Sunday 2 December
Today was the third conference of the Movement for Colonial Freedom. It was held in the Bonnington Hotel in Southampton Row and was a much smaller conference than before. This, however, was itself a good sign. Only the representatives from area councils and nationally affiliated trade unions had been invited. So that everyone who came carried weight. The Fire Brigades' Union, Electrical Trades Union, National Union of Railwaymen and the Miners from South Wales and Derbyshire of course represent hundreds of thousands of members. Our total strength is over five million and there are 109 Labour MPs amongst them. Jim Callaghan, who has just been appointed Shadow Colonial Secretary, sent a message of good wishes and this was very much appreciated. In short we felt that we were a going concern, as indeed we are. It is a fantastic achievement that less than three years after our foundation we should be so well established and so influential.

The greatest change in our policy statement this year has been the decision to urge the summoning of a conference from all the colonial territories as soon as a Labour government is returned to office. With these representatives we should work out a specific timetable for our withdrawal and the transfer of power. This will achieve a psychological revolution and set the people free to work towards its realisation.

After some discussion we passed a resolution demanding the withdrawal of Soviet troops from Hungary. We, above all people, were entitled to do this, and it was supported by John Horner, the General Secretary of the Fire Brigades' Union, and other ex-Communists.

Saturday 8 December
This afternoon I went to the Hanham Labour Party children's party and then looked in at the old people's Christmas sale at Memory Hall. Neither of these was really planned, but being in Bristol it was very nice to be able to get to them.

Saturday 15 December

Travelling to Bristol by train I found myself in the dining car with Sir Walter Monckton. After I had eaten he beckoned me over and we had an hour's talk. He was extremely cordial and most indiscreet about Eden.

Monckton had not seen him since Eden got back from his holiday in Jamaica but has heard he was still rather jumpy, 'which is bad news'. Monckton made it perfectly clear that Eden would have to go although the problem of the succession was a tricky one. Macmillan speaks of his retirement and Rab has behaved so oddly in the last two months that no one trusts him. He agreed that an Election was a remote possibility early in the New Year, though he said he would urge very strongly against it. 'If I were your boys I should prefer next summer as a large number of chickens will have come home to roost by then, and I don't just mean the Suez ones.'

He made his opposition to the Suez policy very plain. Evidently from the start Eden knew what his view was and when he wrote in September and said he wanted to resign the Ministry of Defence, Eden asked to see him and arranged for Head to come half an hour later so that a successor was planned from the outset. Monckton said he told Eden, 'I don't want to dodge this enterprise (presumably the Egyptian attack) but I thought it better to go now rather than later.' He resigned as Defence Minister and was made Paymaster-General.

He quoted one incident in the Cabinet during a Suez discussion. 'Paymaster-General, you are very silent,' said the PM. 'I am, Prime Minister, but I have heard that lawyers should only speak when they know that what they have to say will get a fair hearing and is likely to help their case. I am not sure of either of these things now.'

He spoke a little bit about Clarissa Eden, who is apparently a powerful force in politics and has a great influence on Eden. Monckton says that now she knows he opposed Eden she won't have anything to do with him.

I asked about Winston and whether Monckton saw him. He said he saw him quite often but the old boy has had another stroke and said rather pathetically, 'I still have the ideas, Walter, but you know I can't find the words to clothe them.' He never will speak in the Commons again, partly because he just couldn't stand up to make a speech. I asked what Churchill would have said of Suez. Monckton replied, ' "I wouldn't have had Anthony's courage – or his recklessness." '

Monckton said he had been happiest at the Ministry of Labour under Winston. 'Winston wanted industrial peace at all costs and even thought on occasions that I was too tough. He once sent for me at 10.30 in the morning during a strike. He was in bed and he asked me what I proposed to say in the Commons that afternoon. When I had finished he said "Walter, you're handling this all wrong. You should give them the money. I can't have strikes." He then developed this and finished up by saying "Are you going to take my advice or follow your own reckless course?" ' Monckton said he would obey an order but would still prefer to keep the offer in reserve, at any rate for the present. 'All right, my boy,' said Winston, 'you pursue your foolish course and I shall have the satisfaction of being able to say I told you so.' Eden apparently was much tougher than Monckton and on the famous occasion in May 1955 when he said in his broadcast that the railwaymen must go back before negotiations could start, he did it on the insistence of Clarissa and against the strong and urgent advice of Monckton himself and all the civil servants.

Finally, the train drew into Bristol and he went off to his meeting and I to mine. I was naturally most flattered that he should have been willing to talk so freely and I was delighted to get an inside glimpse of what is going on at his level in the Government. However, it's a great mistake to think of Monckton as a fighter. He has hawked his conscience round quite a number of people the last three months but I very strongly doubt whether under any circumstances he would have resigned from Cabinet altogether.

Wednesday 19 December

At lunchtime a group of us (Fenner, Barbara Castle and others) went to South Africa House to present a letter of protest to the High Commissioner about the Treason Trials. He refused to see us but we left our message and there was a certain amount of publicity which is good for the MCF and helps to focus attention on what is going on. Our great scoop was to interest the Labour lawyers including Gerald Gardiner in the trials and through them the Conservative and Liberal lawyers. Finally all three associations approached the Bar Council who decided to send Gerald as an observer to the preliminary hearings. He is on the point of leaving and his influence should be considerable.

Monday 21 January 1957

The first working day at home after my visit to Germany. It certainly was extremely interesting though an exhausting visit. I am glad I went. There was a little cyst or boil of anti-German feeling in me which was lanced as a result of seeing the country. The bomb damage was phenomenal. The scale of the reconstruction was also interesting. The shops, hotels and petrol stations were so modern and impressive that the visitor might think the country better off than we are. Yet no doubt millions still live in very poor conditions. Berlin was particularly tragic. The total destruction was enormous and the division of the city pathetically obvious.

Now Parliament meets again tomorrow and we enter a new political phase. The resignation of Eden has thrown everything into the melting pot. In a few months one will know whether it really was health or not. The leading articles certainly regarded it as a minor factor compared with his monumental failure over Suez. Macmillan has shown just the right quality of drama in his opening days at Number 10. His government is bold and his television performance was evidently a very dramatic one. His call for an 'opportunity state' has created interest and discussion just when things looked so soggy in his own party. If he succeeds in making an impact it will call for great skill by the Labour Party to make a successful challenge to him.

Sunday 10 February
For some time Geoffrey de Freitas has been bothering me to take an interest in defence and particularly the Air Force. It's not at all my line but as an ex-RAF pilot I suppose I must be one of the very few in the PLP who knows anything about the Air. My reluctance to take the Air job on is heightened by the fact that Geoffrey recommends it as a sure way to get office in the next Government. That he should think that this argument would convince me is intensely irritating and much as I would like office, the thought of the Air Ministry depresses me beyond belief. However, I promised I would watch it for the next few months and I have been attending the various committees.

My dreams of being efficient have been brought a little closer by the purchase of a beautiful four steel drawer cabinet and a suspension filing system to go in it. With all the lovely coloured plastic tabs I think it is the most beautiful thing I have ever seen. Everything now has a place and I find that there is no more enjoyable relaxation than standing looking at it with its drawers proudly pulled out and all the things I ought to do neatly filed away out of sight.

Monday 18 February
Caroline went to the hospital today. The baby is now two weeks late on the most cautious estimate. They have decided to bring it on on Wednesday.

Wednesday 20 February
Slept fitfully and called the hospital at 5.20 fully expecting to hear the good news. Alas, the contractions had stopped and Caroline was sleeping and would be pushed along the road as planned at 12 o'clock. The same story at 7.50 and 10.15. However, they let me go there from 11-12 and I sat beside her for an hour in a white coat and mask. The contractions began again – and it looked as if she still had a sporting chance of doing it unaided. As dawn had broken she saw the lights go on in the cells in the Scrubs opposite and the prisoners looking out through the bars at another cold, clear morning. However, when I left at 12 things were well on their way and I expected news by tea time. As it was, I rang at 1.50 for an interim report and heard that Melissa Anne had been born at 1.35. Caroline was delivered by Sister Tweddle, the Sister in charge of the Labour and Delivery ward. After sending off all the appropriate telegrams and messages, I was allowed to see them both at 3 o'clock and Caroline was looking wonderful.

March
I was forced to miss the annual meeting of the Party in Bristol by the arrival

of Melissa and I gather there has been some criticism there of the rarity of my visits. This is partly my fault and partly theirs. However, I shall have to devote more time to the constituency than I have been doing.

18 April – 8 May
Dick Crossman's party was on 1 May and we went along. No one quite knows what his political position is at the moment. Ever since he parted with Nye he has been a Gaitskell fan. He denounced the ending of the H-bomb tests and has now come out against the H-bomb itself. I'm afraid it has ruptured his personal relationships with other members of the Party but we seem to be on his 'new friends' list. He had a different crowd of guests than before but we enjoyed it very much. He told me afterwards that the little group who had stayed for a talk had voted Caroline 'the best wife for a leader of the Labour Party'.

Tuesday 21 May
A Party meeting this morning on the new National Superannuation Pensions Plan. Dick Crossman introduced it with all the lucidity that he commands. It is such a complicated new idea that it will take weeks for the Party to understand it and years for the local Parties and the general public. It is certainly the most exciting thing that has happened since the Beveridge Report. Dick Crossman will undoubtedly be the first Minister of Pensions after the Election and will find a haven for his talents after the storm since 1945.

This evening Nye Bevan spoke to the Commonwealth and Colonies group of the Party. It was a joint meeting with the Foreign Affairs group and he kept us enthralled for fifty minutes. He described his talks with Nehru and the significance of the Communist victory in Kerala. The brilliance of the word-spinner captivated the audience, who listened with rapt attention. But on reflection I was more than disappointed with what Nye had said and the way he had said it. As in his speech in the House last Thursday night, he took a much more anti-Egyptian line than is reasonable and became an advocate of *realpolitik* with a certain zest. The doctrine that backward countries could not nationalise their industries for fear of losing foreign credits was, I thought, a very dangerous one. Nye will have to be watched for fear that he become not only the darling of the Tory Party – which he is already – but that by his speeches and actions he deserve that title.

Saturday 25 May
This evening to Tony Crosland's party. His divorce came through two days ago and this must have been some sort of celebration. I only knew two people there – Hugh Dalton and Roy Jenkins. The rest were a sort of rootless crowd of nondescript men and rather sulky women between twenty-

five and thirty-five. Tony is, of course, a very unhappy person. I've known him for eleven years and at one time we were very close friends indeed.

The main trouble is his strict Nonconformist background. His parents were Plymouth Brethren and against them he has been in constant revolt. His years in the war gave him the excuse for thinking that his youth had gone and he has been trying to catch up since 1945. At thirty-nine it is rather silly. But he is in fact a very kind man. He taught me economics as a favour in the evenings and we went to the cinema together. Without his recommendation I should never have got Bristol SE and without the redistribution in my favour he would never have lost South Gloucestershire. He is unusually gifted as an economist and has a very clear mind with a very great faith in the power of reason. But the proof of his unhappiness is his curious death wish, which he showed when in the Commons, and which now takes the form of affecting to be bored with current politics. If he gets back into Parliament he will get high office. If he does not, then his life could be a very tragic one.

Friday 31 May
This evening Caroline and I went to Hampstead to a party given by the Gaitskells. Adlai Stevenson was the guest of honour and he had been there for dinner. It was very crowded and we stayed from 9.30 until about 1.45. It was amusing to see who had been invited. Nye was not there but most other members of the Parliamentary Committee were. The only trade union leader was Frank Cousins with his wife.

There was dancing in one room and people got slightly tight. In many ways it was a little depressing to see the Leader of the Party halfway to being sozzled. But it might have been a great deal worse and certainly Winston always looked that way from lunchtime onwards so it can't be a complete bar to a successful premiership.

Monday 15 July
Although I have forgotten to mention it in the last few days Lords' Reform is coming back into the news.

Father and I agreed that it would be worth asking for an interview with Macmillan. Accordingly I rang his Private Secretary, and asked whether the PM could spare a few mintues of his time. He said that I would hear in due course. Today I had a message to go and see Ted Heath, the government Chief Whip. He is a most amiable and friendly soul whom I have known casually since very early 1951. I had then been in Parliament about two months and he about eight months. He has done brilliantly well to have risen to his present position of eminence within such a very short period.

Anyway that is all by the way. He told me that the PM was too busy to see me before the recess and was in any case doubtful about forming a precedent in agreeing to see an Opposition backbencher on a point of policy. He would, however, be glad to receive a letter from me 'which would then be sent to the right people'.

Thursday 18 July

To the Buckingham Palace Garden Party this afternoon. What an occasion it is. The spacious royal park with its ornamental lake and bridges and the splendid front of the Palace dominating it. There in the private enclosure are the royal family surrounded by the Diplomatic Corps and the 'distinguished' guests. Outside promenading on the lawns are 9,000 more guests. The occasional bishop, the invariable sultan with his umbrella, the sprinkling of turbans, saris and white duck jodhpurs, the grey toppers and the flowery dresses with the wide-brimmed hats. The two Guards bands under their tents blowing for all they are worth in their scarlet tunics. The whole pattern is like a gigantic ballet – a Cecil B. de Mille crowd scene.

There is a secret way of eating two teas. One at the beginning when the royal family are arriving and everyone is crowding for a peep, leaving the tea tent deserted, and the other at the end when they're leaving and the same thing happens. In the middle when everyone else is jostling, pushing and shoving, you promendade yourself looking disapprovingly at those who seem 'only to have come for the food'. Actually Joe Lyons and Co. do quite a good job with the catering, though the bridge rolls were soggy.

But like the story of Cinderella the romance evaporates. At the end hundreds of people were waiting for their cars to be called over the loudspeaker. You could see the guests still immaculate, if a little tatty. And you would hear: 'The Town Clerk of Little Chippings' – that tall figure whom you thought was a central European Ambassador (at least) scuttles away to get into his Austin 7 driven by his son. 'The Chairman of the S.W. Area Gas Board' the flunkey announces . . . and so it goes on. Now we know the secret and slip out the back door and catch a bus.

30 September – 4 October – Labour Party Conference, Brighton

This week at Brighton was a very exciting one. Everyone thought it was going to be the dullest Conference ever, but they turned out to be wrong.

The elections offered no surprises and Jim Callaghan displaced Sydney Silverman from the National Executive. I stood for the first time. I missed election by two places and 48,000 votes. But to get 517,000 on first standing was wonderful.

The first day we spent in condemning the Government's economic policy and bringing forward our own emergency resolutions on rents. Of course all this can only work if there is co-operation between the trade union movement and the Labour Government. What has to be got across discreetly to the public is that this co-operation will be forthcoming without any binding undertaking on either side.

We then reached two very important decisions on pensions and public ownership. After excellent debate the national superannuation scheme was adopted. The new policy of share-purchasing in place of nationalisation was also overwhelmingly adopted after an important speech by Hugh Gaitskell. Finally, in a day full of drama the Party decided to continue with the manufacture of the H-bomb, although it expressed its readiness to suspend tests unilaterally.

The Party thus can claim to have reached firm decisions about important matters and to have done so in an atmosphere of unity. The decay of this Cabinet and the prospects of a Labour government within a short period has helped to bring us to our senses again in our personal relations. The triumphs of individuals are worth recording. Harold Wilson delivered two speeches: one on the economic situation which was well received, and one on public ownership which was less well received. I admit I never find him very convincing although he has great ability. Nye Bevan cut away his left-wing support by his cruel wording during the speech on the H-bomb. Though I think he was right in the line he took, it was a very unhappy speech. It earned praise from the *Daily Telegraph* and the *Daily Worker*. Neither of those is a good indication of his talent and I still distrust him profoundly.

Dick Crossman was probably the greatest personal success. After his difficult change of front over the years and the rage he had stirred from the Bevanites he had then annoyed the trade unionists with his unwise article in the *Mirror* saying that only a handful were fit for high office. Therefore when he rose it was to a polite handclap. But so brilliant was his speech and so lucid his exposition that he sat down to a thunderous ovation that carried him to the inner councils of the Party.

Tuesday 5 November
The trouble about a personal diary is that it is entirely subjective. It is not a history, nor has it any value except such as it gets from the personal slant it shows on events. But of course these events are the framework on which the thin personal story is woven. Every now and again one has to step back a little and assess the changes that are taking place outside.

This is particularly true this autumn. The staggering news in October of the launching of the Russian satellites, Sputnik I and II, has really changed the course of world history. It shows the brilliance of Soviet technology, alters the balance of military power, and more important than either of these two, it marks the beginning of the space age. As long as recorded history exists, 4 October will be remembered and remarked upon. It is far more momentous than the invention of the wheel, the discovery of the sail, the circumnavigation of the globe, or the wonders of the industrial revolution.

Looking at the political situation there are not so many momentous events to report.

The Government is losing popularity steadily. Despite this, Macmillan remains confident and Lord Hailsham wanders about the country making ebullient speeches. What drift there is against the Government is not coming to Labour but is going to the Liberals.

The Labour Party on the other hand is in really good shape. Hugh Gaitskell has emerged as a popular Leader in Parliament, although he lacks certain dramatic qualities and loses effectiveness thereby. Nye Bevan is determined to be Foreign Secretary and is touring the world making speeches and influencing people. Whether he is winning friends is another question. His Russian talks were evidently cordial and he is at this moment engaged in lecturing the Americans about their own affairs and policies in a way that is causing a lot of excitement, but not a little interest. Americans like people who 'talk turkey'. There is none of the diplomatic hypocrisy about Nye Bevan. I do not altogether trust him, for I think he lacks the qualities of self-confidence, serenity, generosity and personal loyalty, which are desperately necessary for high office. On the other hand he has energy, imagination, the gift for good human relations, directness, courage, vividness of expression, a wide view, a good political sense, a colourful personality, most lovable faults and a lot of other things which are missing in those who possess the qualities he lacks.

Thursday 5 December
To Robin Day's party. He was voted TV personality of the year yesterday. It is a tremendous honour that he richly deserves. He was celebrating by producing a girlfriend who was Miss Great Britain – a not very glamorous blonde. All our Oxford contemporaries were there.

Saturday 7 December
Drove to Oxford for the Nuffield College dance. Caroline came down by train from London and we had dinner with David Butler beforehand in his rooms. Nuffield is vigorous and forward-looking. It has absolute equality between men and women and close camaraderie between teacher and student. It draws its Fellows from a wide social background. There is no snobbery about it at all.

Tuesday 7 January 1958
Today's sensational news of Thorneycroft's resignation has reawakened everyone to politics again with a bang.

The political implications of this resignation are not hard to see. The question at stake was whether the Government's economic policy should be carried to the point where the structure of the welfare state was to be partially dismantled. The Prime Minister and most of the Cabinet shrank from a course of action which would have such grave political consequences. Thorneycroft was willing to wield the axe even against the Social Services.

Inside the Conservative Party therefore, this is a left versus right struggle.

The Butler wing have won a tactical victory over the wild men of the City. We should all be grateful for small mercies but the consequences for the Conservative Party need to be assessed.

There is already a nucleus of disgruntled right-wingers inside the ranks of the Tory MPs. They first appeared in 1954 as the Suez Group. During the war against Egypt in November 1956 they thought they had captured the Prime Minister. Then came the sell-out and the humiliation of the evacuation. Eight of them resigned the Whip and decided to sit as Independents. They are still there in open opposition.

Now Thorneycroft, Birch and Powell are thrown up as real leaders of this dissident group. The financial issues on which they have resigned will attract the support of the Independent Conservatives. And the Cyprus problem looms up right ahead.

Tuesday 10 February
To Lime Grove for Nye Bevan's TV party political programme. Nye arrived a bit late and was just impossible for the first three-quarters of an hour. He launched into an attack on the BBC for bias, distortion and discrimination against himself and all the rest. It was an ignorant attack, so easily refuted by the facts. The atmosphere was extremely tense and I was unhappy since I could not support him. The programme was going to be terrible if this went on. To make it worse, Nye wouldn't drink anything before the broadcast so he was on edge even more.

Then between the steak and the cheese we got on to farming. Nye, the farmer, mellowed before our eyes. On grazing and pigs and subsidies he found common ground with Gerald Beadle. He began to laugh and do imitations of Tom Williams, who was our Minister of Agriculture, and by the time he came up for the first run-through the tears were running down his cheeks with good humour and giggly laughter. *NOTE*: Nye must never do another broadcast without having some of his intimate friends there beforehand to keep him sweet.

The show itself was very good, I thought. Reckoning the limitations we had to face, a talk with a lot of young people was undoubtedly the best projection of his personality. The *Daily Telegraph* next morning said it was the best Labour Party political yet.

Thursday 20 February
Had a talk to Frank Barlow at the Commons. He told me that some sections of the Party (Jim Callaghan, Tony Greenwood, Alf Robens and Nye) were sick to death of my campaign on the peerage and were being very rude about it. This plunged me into depression.

Nye Bevan opened the debate today. Apparently he made a most appalling speech – his worst flop yet. He tried to explain what he had said at the Conference at Brighton about the H-bomb. All he succeeded in doing was alienating his new friends as well as his old ones.

Friday 21 February
To dinner with Cecil King at the Dorchester, with a lot of commerical TV tycoons. I must say they thoroughly irritated me. Here were these extremely powerful men who were not interested in programmes as such but only in making money. The whole conversation was the financial carve-up of the world. I came away feeling that the public-accountability issue is a really important, live one. Couldn't all public companies be put in the same position as nationalised industries and made subject to directions from a Minister in the public interest? I shall do some work on this.

Monday 3 March
At 7 o'clock in the Division Lobby I saw Geoffrey de Freitas and asked for a word with him privately. He knew what it was about before we had sat down in the Members' Lobby. I asked to be relieved of the responsibility of being No. 2 on Air matters. I explained that I had had many anxious hours of thought about it (as indeed I have) and that I had come to one definite conclusion: under no circumstances would it be right or sensible for Britain to use the hydrogen bomb. I said I did not know yet in my own mind what the right course of action was, but I could not conscientiously be the spokesman of a policy with which I was in disagreement.

Geoffrey was very sweet. He said he absolutely understood my view and the motives that had prompted it. He said he wished he could be relieved of the burden of the Air Force but there was nobody willing to do it. I pointed out that it wasn't reluctance to do the donkey work that influenced me, and he understood that. We left it that he would tell the Chief Whip that I was from that moment discharged.

Without making too much of this it was, of course, a tiny resignation and may not be popular in high quarters. But I really can't help that. If one allowed oneself to be dragged along doing something one thinks is wrong, it would be hopeless.

Friday 7 March
To Bristol this evening for a meeting in support of the South African Treason Trial Defence Fund organised by the MCF. About a hundred people turned up in the Grand Hotel to watch the film *African Conflict* made by Howard Smith for CBS. We raised £25 for the fund. More important even than the money was the feeling that a little group of Bristolians who had never been to South Africa were expressing solidarity with these people on trial for their beliefs.

Saturday 8 March
This evening we went to dinner with Enoch Powell, who resigned with

Thorneycraft over public expenditure. He and I had a long post-mortem on
Suez. As he was a member of the 'Suez Group' at the time of the Canal Zone
Base Agreement in 1954, I naturally took him to have been a violent
supporter of Eden in 1956. But as it turned out I was quite wrong, and for a
most interesting reason. His argument ran like this. 'To be a great empire,
sustained by military strength, requires military bases at strategic points. In
1954 Eden tried to pretend to us that we could still be a great military power
without maintaining by force a base in Egypt. I said then that that was
hypocrisy and humbug. When Nasser nationalised the Canal I was proved
right. But by then it was too late to get it back. World opinion would not have
it, and militarily we could not do it. I therefore watched with amused
detachment the outbreak of hysteria from July to October which had come
two years too late to be effective. I didn't think it was right or could be
successful to attempt to invade and get back what we had lost. As far as the
position now is concerned, we have given up the means by which we can
maintain our empire by force.'

This is not an exact quote, of course, but a précis of his argument.

Wednesday 12 March
To Torrington for the by-election this evening. The first meeting drew in six
people. The Chairman said it was because of a Methodist film show in the
village hall. It was a more original excuse than the weather, which is always
too bad for people to come out or so good that they're gardening. I just sat
and got them to put questions to me.

Back to Exeter by car dog-tired, and to bed at once without a meal.

Friday 14 March
Still extremely depressed. No particular reason, but on the trade cycle
theory of ups and downs, a down has been due for some time.

Tuesday 1 April
Messaoud came in a great state of excitement to finalise the resolution for
tonight's meeting in the Caxton Hall, which was a tremendous success. The
Tunisian, Moroccan and Libyan Ambassadors were there in person and
also various other Ministers from Afghanistan and the Lebanon and so on.
About 600 people crowded the hall and there was a small overflow meeting
of about 50. The speakers were not really all that good and the meeting
flagged a bit until Barbara Castle gave it a fillip at the end. But we collected
£305 for Algerian relief and this in itself justified the meeting. I did the
appeal and felt rather pleased.

Tuesday 15 April
Parliament met today and it was Budget Day. I didn't go in at all as our new

baby showed signs of arriving last night and really seems imminent. I missed the vote on the budget as a result and am in trouble with the Chief Whip!

Tuesday 29 April
Caroline went into hospital this morning with labour pains. It's quite a relief to have her under close medical attention though I shall miss her daily judgement on affairs very much. Our half-hour survey of the day each evening is always the stabilising and comforting part of the day.

To Lime Grove for the party political broadcast. After the show Hugh Cudlipp invited us back to his house in Cheyne Walk. It is the most charming place, overlooking the river. His wife, Eileen Ascroft, is the fashion editor of one of the evening papers. She's a rather catlike creature – an impression strengthened by tight black slacks and a leopardskin blouse. We stood around and talked and listened to gramophone records. Hugh Cudlipp conducted his favourite pieces from opera and kept insisting that we should hear just one more side. It bored me stiff after a time, but although everyone else felt the same no one had the courage to go first. So I decided to leave at about 12.30. But no bed till 2.15, for Dave was here for the night and there was lots to talk about.

Friday 9 May
Working at home this morning with the usual round of chores: reading *The Times*, answering letters, sorting my papers and the rest. The phone rang: 'This is Hammersmith Hospital. Your wife has had a beautiful baby boy.' And so after ten days of waiting, all is well. Caroline wouldn't let them tell me that they were inducing it today. She didn't want me to worry. But, of course, not having paced the room for three hours meant I didn't earn my relief.

I rushed over to the hospital in time to see her wheeled in on a trolley from the labour ward to her room. She was very well and happy. Later that evening I met Joshua. He looks just like the others, with straggling, waving, crinkly fingers which are always exercising in front of his face. Once he opened his eyes and closed them again with an expression which reminded me irresistibly of Gilbert Harding.

In between two visits to hospital I went to see the Sultan of Lahej. He is a very well-groomed man of thirty-six who speaks perfect English and has an aristocractic bearing; he is the direct descendant of a line of Sultans of Lahej going back 250 years.

Not knowing exactly how to begin, I simply asked if he would explain the situation that has arisen. He began talking and we weren't able to get away for two and a half hours. We frequently interrupted him with questions, to which he gave a frank answer.

Tuesday 27 May
The French situation is now critical. Civil war seems quite likely. On top of

this de Gaulle issued a statement today saying he was forming a government but a lot is going on under the surface. One does not know whether de Gaulle is coming in by a coup or whether by abject surrender of the politicians. It looks as if the lights are going out in France.

Wednesday 4 June

To Television House for a run-through of a new programme I've been asked to take over on an experimental basis. The idea stems from *My Fair Lady* and *Pygmalion*. Does accent really betray background? ATV have got together two members of the Faculty of University College, London: Dr Fry, the Head of the Phonetics Department and Mr Trim, a lecturer. They have added a woman called Dr Eisler, a psychologist doing research at UCL. I am the chairman. The idea is to play over a one-minute recording of a voice and then for seven or eight minutes the Panel discuss it and say all they can think of about it: what region, what origin, what occupation, what age, what build, what height, what features, what sort of clothes, everything. A cartoonist draws as the team decide and finally the person appears. Then follows a post-mortem.

We had a run-through with about five recordings and then met the people. Two were absolutely spot on. It was almost uncanny. Two were pretty wrong and one was half and half. But it was tremendous fun to do and what pleased me was that I was almost as good as they were. They are a very nice crowd.

Monday 23 June

To dinner with Mr and Mrs Edward Sieff and the Tynans. He is 'Mr Marks and Spencer'. Ken Tynan is a contemporary of mine from Oxford. After dinner when the women had gone, we sat for an hour talking politics. Ken was a real 'eighteen-year-old Red'. Of course I don't keep up with these things but I gather that he is a leading Angry Young Man. He pressed on me afterwards the view that young people were looking for a new lead. He thought they were sick of both parties and really wanted something that took them outside themselves and made them feel there was something worth worrying and thinking about.

This conversation set my mind on to the general political problem that faces this country. The population of the world will be 7,000 million in the next forty years – far and away the greatest part being in Asia. That fact and the tremendous industrialisation in China and India will turn Britain into a little Denmark. How are we to adjust ourselves to this new world without becoming wildly frustrated and defeatist and bitter and apathetic? This problem of power contraction does threaten our political system. Someone said the Angry Young Men were a symptom of the shrinking pains of the British Empire. The answer probably lies in two things – a widening of

Britain's horizons so that we can get satisfaction from the achievements of others, and a domestic revolution to modernise ourselves. It presents a serious psychological problem for politicians.

Wednesday 9 July
Today Stephen and Hilary came to the Houses of Parliament. The trip had been long planned and as luck would have it the weather was simply super. Their hair had been specially cut and they looked very tidy. They behaved simply beautifully. We saw the Speaker's Procession and then went to the Lords to await Tappa (Father). Black Rod put us in the Diplomatic Gallery and then waved to the boys. We met him later in the Lobby and he was so friendly. The boys had seen him on television and were very interested in his buckle shoes and nylon stockings. Then we went to the Commons where they were put in the special gallery behind the peers. Father sat in the row in front and I took my place. Those tiny heads with the hair so short just poked above the back of the seat and looked like two little eggs all ready to fall like Humpty-Dumpty. We met a lot of people and went over to the Jewel Tower before we had strawberries and cream on the terrace. They were so excited. I was so proud. We also went to the Control Room and watched the Commons through the periscope. I almost forgot. Wherever they went Father said, 'These boys' father, grandfather, and both great-grandfathers have sat in the Commons.' It's quite something.

Tuesday 15 July
Father had Paul Robeson and his wife to tea at Lords. I didn't know what to expect. I wondered if he would be an embittered Red, but my doubts were dispelled in five seconds. I have never been more quickly attracted to a personality than I was to his. He is a giant of a man, towering above us all, and has a most mobile face and greying hair. He was immensely easy to talk to. You only had to mention a song of his (or of anyone else's) for him to begin singing very softly. It was just too tempting for us to go through the ones we liked best, and it was irresistible for him to sing them. I thought it might be embarrassing to have him singing in the Lords' Tea Room but he did it so naturally and so softly that it was only properly audible a few feet away. Beyond that it must have reverberated like some tube train passing deep beneath the building.

Afterwards I took him to the Commons Gallery for a moment and through the lobbies down to the Terrace. It was a journey of triumph. Everybody gathered round – MPs, police, visitors, waitresses from the Tea Room – for unlike most celebrities who make you want to stare, Paul Robeson made you want to shake him by the hand. Two negro women from Florida were almost ready to embrace him. A jet-black Nigerian was touched as if by a magic wand, and nearly split his face with a smile. You just couldn't help feeling that he was a friend of everyone there. He greeted people as if he knew them and those he really knew he remembered. There was no hint of embarrassment, whoever it was who came up. Herbert Morrison shook him by the hand on the way out and as we marched down St Stephen's Hall the crowds queueing for the Strangers' Gallery stood and lined the route as if it were a triumphal march.

Thursday 17 July
I did a very rare thing for me nowadays and went into the Smoking Room for a drink and a gossip for an hour and a half. Nye was there and Dick Crossman, Dingle Foot, Curly Mallalieu and Sir Tom O'Brien.

In the other corner was the Prime Minister sitting and gossiping with his cronies. At the table next to him was Winston, looking much as ever but a bit more shaky. It really is exciting to feel that one is in the middle of events and the Smoking Room after a great debate has an atmosphere that is very thrilling.

Tuesday 2 September
The Notting Hill race riots trouble continued last night. I toured the area before breakfast and saw the debris and the corrugated iron up behind the windows of the prefabs where the coloured families live. The use of petrol bombs and iron bars and razors is appalling. There is a large area where it is not safe for people to be out. I saw Chief Inspector Simmonds at Notting Hill police station for a short talk. He is confident that the police can handle it.

This afternoon I toured the area again by car and even at 5 o'clock there was an ugly atmosphere and people hurried along the streets. The Labour Party really must say something about this.

Tuesday 30 September
By train to Scarborough this morning for the Labour Party Conference. Everyone in the related fields of politics, journalism, television and diplomacy are all in one place at one time. That's what makes Conference such fun.

Wednesday 1 October
Harold Wilson made an excellent speech today in the economics debate. He is certainly Number 3 in the party now.

I missed Donald Soper at the *Tribune* rally, who apparently made a wonderful speech. Michael Foot was a pleasure to listen to as a craftsman. He is a real master of the open-air technique. But the audience didn't take to him all that well. Nye, speaking last, made one of the very worst speeches I have ever heard him make. It rambled. It was self-contradictory. It was repetitive. It had neither information, thought nor uplift. In fact it was like someone sitting down at an organ and trying all the most stirring chords in turn, with no one pumping to give them voice and no one in the choir to accompany them with responses. I came away completely dejected and feeling he had nothing to offer.

Thursday 2 October

Nye Bevan opened the Foreign Affairs debate today with a speech as good as last night's had been bad. He struck just the right note. It was serious, helpful and with as much uplift as was reasonable in the circumstances. The foreign-policy statement is very good and Conference received it well despite the renewed H-bomb debate. I wasn't called, which rather disappointed me. But that is the luck of the game.

Saturday 18 October

Went to Barton House – the new fourteen-storey skyscraper of modern flats – this morning. A man from the Housing Department and Mr Solomon, the caretaker, took me round. It was a perfect autumn day with the sky blue and a shimmer of sunshine, on the whole of Bristol. We went right to the roof and visited various flats. To see the bright airy rooms with the superb view and to contrast them with the poky slum dwellings of Barton Hill below was to get all the reward one wants from politics. For this grand conception of planning is what it is all about. The people were happy, despite the grumbles about detail.

Dora Gaitskell arrived to open the Hanham Sale of Work in Bristol. She was very nervous but did a good job and was very well and warmly received. But for me the best part of the day was driving her home from Bristol to Hampstead. It took three and a half hours and we talked the whole time.

She is a most intelligent woman. She is Jewish and was actually born in Russia, coming to England when she was four. She is as sharp as a needle and altogether an extremely good influence on Hugh. She is 100 per cent loyal to him against all comers, which is as it should be. But she is also very critical of him in private and I know that's a good thing too. There are only a few people who can speak absolutely frankly to him. She is also an extremely perceptive woman and her comments about people are very much to the point. This is probably her greatest asset. You can't take her in and she forms very strong impressions, which I would think are usually correct.

We talked about people most of the time. About Clem and Vi, about Morgan Phillips and other Party figures. She detests Morgan but thinks he is very able and competent. She loves Sam Watson. She is very anti-Hartley Shawcross, who she felt had betrayed Hugh. About him and others she was very critical of what she termed their being 'too fond of money'. She said this about Frank Soskice with his work at the Bar and about Dick Crossman with his column on the *Mirror*. I think her motives were that she thought that any sincere socialist should devote himself 100 per cent to the work of the Party and should not combine it with other occupations, and that a simplicity of living conditions was an essential element of the leadership of the Labour

Party. She took real pride in the fact that she has no help at home other than someone to do part of the cleaning. She cooks and washes up and does the housework herself. And whether it's the American Ambassador or Clem or anyone else who is coming to dinner, there is nothing fancy laid on. 'I'm a very good cook,' she said 'and they must all see us as we are.' I admired her greatly for this.

But when it came to the royal family and social distinctions I found her curiously insecure. She said how she had admired Hugh for his easy way with people (!) and how difficult she had found it to overcome her nerves. This was very human but it was coupled with a sort of feeling for the aristocracy as if it still had some meaning and as if she felt on the outside. It wasn't envy so much as quite inappropriate respect. This did really surprise me.

But the time passed most delightfully and rapidly and her anecdotes were amusing. She talked very frankly about her first husband who was a Communist psychiatrist. She said she thought my current 'I Hear, I See' series was probably explained by telepathy, in which she took a great interest. And she touched my heart by saying how devoted she was to Caroline and admiring her for the way she ran the house and brought up four children without any fuss.

Wednesday 19 November
At 10.30 to the House for the morning committee of the Election campaign.

The most important item that came up was the Gallup poll figures showing that of all British institutions the trade unions were the most unpopular; 26 per cent take an unfavourable view of them and 11 per cent a very unfavourable view. This I raised as a major problem for the Labour Party. To my surprise everyone agreed, including the trade unionists. Apparently the Trade Union Group are very concerned and are engaged in some sort of study of the question. In the end it was agreed that I should prepare a memorandum on the subject setting out very briefly how the public relations of the unions might be improved.

Took a party of schoolchildren round the House of Commons, which took nearly an hour and a half.

Tuesday 2 December
Charlie Pannell told me today his delightful story of his visit to Anglesey to speak for Cledwyn Hughes. Throughout his speech he was much struck by an old man who sat there impassively with his head on his stick. Charlie said he couldn't keep his eyes off him, and after the meeting asked Cledwyn who he was. Cledwyn said he was an old, old man well over ninety who had been a friend of Lloyd George.

'Go and talk to him,' said Cledwyn. 'He'd be delighted.'

Charlie moved to the back of the hall and sat down beside the old man.

'Sir,' he said, for he couldn't address him in any other way, 'I understand you knew Lloyd George.' The old man raised his head slowly and spoke. 'Lloyd George,' he said, 'had a prick like a donkey.'

Charlie was taken aback. 'Ah, well.' he said. 'He was a man of many parts.'

'I know he was.' said the old man. 'And he'll be remembered more for that part than any other.' He gave a deep chuckle.

Tuesday 9 December

Collected Dick Crossman at his home this morning. He was sunk in deep despair about the future of the Labour Party and even the future of democracy. I have days like that too and his tummy trouble probably hadn't improved things. He said he wondered whether we were not just spectators at the funeral of democracy. But he then cheered up and said he thought Mr Khrushchev probably had the same problem in the Supreme Soviet. Most people in politics were, he thought, essentially third rate under any system of government.

Tuesday 30 December

At 8 o'clock this evening there was a dinner at the Charing Cross Hotel in a private suite for us to meet with Donald Baverstock and Cliff Michelmore of the BBC, who had expressed readiness to give us their advice on the series of TV party politicals. On our side it was a very high-level affair: Gaitskell and Barbara Castle, Herbert Bowden and Morgan Phillips. Woodrow, Ken Peay, Chris Mayhew and I completed the party.

After coffee we talked for a couple of hours around the programme. My main job next year will be the television and radio. It is a gigantic responsibility that could decide hundreds of thousands of voters. It is clear I shall hardly get to Bristol at all in the Election and must make it up as much as I can. I am sure they will understand. This means cutting down still further on MCF, other committees and all speaking outside my own division. It also means fewer articles and broadcasts even if they are offered.

This policy will have to be reviewed again immediately after the Election. And that should come in March or May.

Wednesday 7 January 1959

Felt very sick this evening but had to go to dinner with Jim and Audrey Callaghan in her new house in Blackheath. It really is modern and is very effective. Also there were Margaret, her daughter, now at Oxford, Peter Cox, son of Geoffrey of ITN, and Julia Gaitskell, who is the spit image of her mother.

Monday 19 January

We had a very pleasant dinner party tonight with the Crossmans, the Enoch

Powells, David Butler and Dave. Dick was in a very mellow mood and everyone got on very well. Enoch is really very depressed. His resignation now looks to have been fatally ill-advised. He was urging an even tougher policy than the policy which has now led to unemployment, so he is in the wilderness of wildernesses as far as the Tories are concerned. And there is the added bitterness of the resignation on the eve of Macmillan's Commonwealth tour. He wonders how the future will shape for him. But I told him that I thought his sheer ability and lucidity would carry him upwards. As a working-class Tory he has the social barrier to overcome. He has not been offered any directorships since his resignation and he has taken a heavy fall in his standard of living. But he was as nice and friendly as ever.

Wednesday 21 January
Day largely devoted to christening Joshua. Pouring with rain and very chilly, but the service went off all right and we had a riotous tea party. Hilary said thank you very loudly after Canon McLeod Campbell had pronounced the benediction; Melissa pointed and said 'You' and 'Baby' several times during the service. Hilary also asked the battery of photographers, 'Can't you click your cameras together? I can't smile for each of you separately.'

Thursday 5 February
Long and bitter discussion in the Smoking Room with Dick Crossman, George Wigg and Ungoed-Thomas about Wilfred Fienburgh's novel *No Love for Johnny*. Kenneth Robinson had told me earlier in the afternoon that Wilfred told him, at the Brighton Conference in 1957, that Johnny Byrne (the hero) was an amalgam of the worst characteristics of himself (Fienburgh), Desmond Donnelly and Jim Callaghan.

The novel gives a totally cynical view of Labour politics and has stirred colossal controversy in the Party. Dick Crossman regarded it as a piece of pure betrayal, and George Wigg – as one would expect – described it as an epitaph not only on social democracy but on the parliamentary system.

Wednesday 11 March
At home all day and must have made 25 to 30 phone calls in quick succession, on lining up people for our Election testimonial films. I rang Bertrand Russell in North Wales, but he wouldn't do it. 'I'm rather dissatisfied with the Party over this nuclear business,' he said. 'I don't think I can do anything to support it.' I reminded him of the developing African crisis and the Party's role. 'Yes, yes, well, well, I know,' he said rather more sympathetically. 'Even so, I think I won't.' Compton Mackenzie, on the other hand, was far more jovial. 'Well, dear boy,' he said. 'The Tories are simply terrible and they have been the same all my life. But you know I'm mixed up with the Nationalists up here and there'd be an awful stink if I came out for the Labour Party – though, of course, I admire your line on

these things.' He paused. 'No – damn it – I will do it. After Cyprus and now
Malta and Central Africa, I must do it. But I don't guarantee what I'll say.' I
jumped in and arranged to fly to Edinburgh the week after next with a film
unit to get him to do it before he changed his mind.

Thursday 12 March
To Transport House this morning for two more testimonial filmlets from
writers. C.R. Hewitt (C.H. Rolph of the *New Statesman*) was the first, and
Ritchie Calder. It is a lot easier doing it in the studio but what a slow
business. Two hours' hard work for one minute of material. And the cost,
probably £60.

Wednesday 25 March
Flew up to Edinburgh today to make the film with Sir Compton Mackenzie
at his house. We only wanted twenty-five seconds of him saying why he
supports the Labour Party.
      I arrived at 31 Drummond Place at 2.15. Sir Compton was still dressing,
and he appeared in a few minutes in a bright blue tweed suit looking twice as
large as life. He remembered having met me before, and beckoned me into
his room where he kept me talking until 4 o'clock when the film unit was
ready.
      His testimonial was delivered so amusingly that the film crew began
laughing and ruined the take. So we did it again. Afterwards we all shook
hands again, and they took photographs, got autographs, and hurried away.
      Sir Compton took me round his house and showed me a huge empty
room being redecorated in the basement. 'I am opening a ladies'
hairdressing salon,' he said. I thought he was joking. But he wasn't. His
secretary has a sister who is a hairdresser, and he said he thought it would be
a nice idea if she could practise.
      I knew he was a busy man, and kept trying to get away, but he insisted on
my staying, and regaled me with stories and anecdotes until 7.30, when I
had to catch my plane home.
      It was a most amusing day. For him it was the beginning. He gets up after
lunch, dresses, and starts work after tea at 4 o'clock. He works from then till
7, when he has dinner. He watches TV from 8 to 10, and works again from
10 to 2 am. He then goes to bed, reads and does crossword puzzles until 4
am, when he goes to sleep.
      He was full of anecdotes.
      Finally I left him and flew home to London in an hour and a half.

Monday 30 March
Took the boys to watch the Aldermaston marchers as they came in. They
were 1,500-strong at Trafalgar Square, and had Frank Cousins amongst
them. This movement is a force to be reckoned with.

A representative of the White Defence League was there with some Fascist propaganda. Mosley is standing in North Kensington constituency at the next Election.

Saturday 27 June
To Bristol for the most dejected, depressing, inadequate, badly run, deadbeat sale of work that I have ever attended. If that is the Labour Party's image, then something is wrong.

Monday 7 September
Filming all morning, this evening to Lime Grove to see 'Tonight' go out. It was interesting.
   Prime Minister has left for Balmoral. Announcement expected any day.

Tuesday 8 September
Polling Day – 8 October – is announced. Tea with Peter Shore; both very pessimistic about outcome. His chances in Halifax are slightly better than average.
   Rush of work begins in earnest.

Wednesday 9 September
John Osborne the playwright came in to do a 'testimonial' film. The production unit (Mayhew, Woodrow Wyatt, Alasdair Milne and myself) is now meeting regularly to review progress. Our current headache is: who will be in charge at Transport House during the Election? Will it be Dick Crossman? And, if so, will he interfere with us? We feel we must write orders for ourselves to safeguard ourselves.

Sunday 13 September
Russian rocket hits the moon. Socialist economies are certainly overtaking capitalist ones now.

Sunday 20 September
To Lime Grove from 2 to 8 for the first rehearsal of 'Britain Belongs to You'. The set is superb and Alasdair was able to knock us into shape. Tom Driberg is our resident political commissar and fairly easy to deal with. I was rather wooden and stilted. Just could not go to sleep for worrying.

Tuesday 22 September
Left by car for Bristol before breakfast and drove like a madman to be there for a lunchtime factory-gate meeting at Strachan and Henshaw.
   Canvassing all afternoon in the car, and it works like a dream. I have recorded a ten-minute speech on the issues of the Election (the Summit, pensions, housing, education, and Africa) and this lasts just long enough for

me to go round to the houses with window bills. I got lots of them up completely single-handedly.

To the Colston Hall where Hugh Gaitskell is addressing a big meeting. 600 were turned away. The size of the crowd and the tremendous reception given to Gaitskell surprised us all. He was on top of his form and made a really grand, clear, forceful speech. It included a most friendly reference to me among the other Bristol MPs. Afterwards police with linked arms had to hold back the crowd to let his car go back to the Grand Hotel.

I had dinner with Hugh and Dora, John Harris (Hugh's political adviser), and the regional organiser, Ted Rees. We are now frankly much more optimistic about the outcome of the Election. The trememdous meetings, the successful TV, and the Gallup poll showing a shrinking margin, have got us to the point where we think that the Liberals holding the balance with us only just behind the Tories is now a distinct possibility. Walked round Bristol talking to John Harris until very late. His appointment is the best thing that has happened to Hugh for years.

Thursday 24 September

Herbert Rogers had brought a black woolly cat and arranged for some kid to give it to me to make a good publicity picture. But the kid screamed so hard that its mother had to give it to me instead.

Lunch with the six Bristol candidates and immediately drove back to London. To Israeli Embassy for goodbye party to the Ambassador Eliahu Elath and his wife, who are returning to Israel.

Thursday 1 October

Transport House this morning. The pledge that there would be no income tax increases that Hugh gave in his speech, coupled with the purchase tax pledge released by Morgan, has upset us all. We feel the Tories have now got us on the defensive. This is partly true but partly a question of counter-attack. They are now attacking and we are bound to feel the effect of this. Of course the purchase tax thing is just a muddle by Morgan and stems from old material that was hanging about the office. The income tax pledge was done to forestall an anticipated scare that there would be 2s. 6d. on the income tax to pay for Labour's programme. Neither of these was discussed with Crossman before release.

Saturday 3 October

Liverpool. To the Adelphi Hotel and breakfast with Hugh, Dora and Harold Wilson in Hugh's room. Dora in her nightie is quite a sight. Hugh was a bit frowsy and looked like the man who used to be on the Bovril bottle in his pyjamas. We were all cautiously optimistic about the outcome of the Election. Hugh has had a gigantic reception everywhere (20,000 people at

Trafford Park yesterday) and the Gallup poll still suggests that we are on the up-grade.

Spend the morning writing Hugh's broadcast, which he then rewrites and I rewrite, etc. We then walk to the BBC studio and record it.

Thursday 8 October

Up early and a perfect day. The Gallup poll suggests that the enormous 'don't know' group may be inclining to the right.

The usual senseless and exhausting visits to 36 polling stations and 30 committee rooms. Shaking hands with the policemen, asking the returning officer how many people have voted, nodding at the clerks, and heading off for the next.

Finally the usual loudspeaker 'knocking up' and a rather quiet end to the day. People were voting earlier. Then to Unity House when the polls closed to remove all the Election equipment from the car, and to the Grand Hotel for a bath and tea and sandwiches.

Just about 10 the first results begin coming out and it is clear within a short while that the Tories have won and increased their majority. We have gained a bit in Lancashire and Scotland, but otherwise are out. The count is thus very depressing with the Tories crowing and our people very dejected. Indeed my result looked like being in the balance at one stage, and I thought I might have been beaten. But my vote is up 1,000 even though my majority is down 2,000 with a 3 per cent swing.

The arrangements for the count were appalling, inefficient, long-drawn-out. Back to the Grand Hotel too depressed to watch TV.

Sunday 11 October

To the Gaitskells'. Hugh was tired but mellow and said he wanted a holiday, which he deserved. He says it would be a good idea to have a meeting next weekend to review the work of the Election and this will presumably take place under Dick's auspices. I then proposed that a number of changes should be made, including a political permanent vice-chairman, a new Secretary, a Shadow Leader of the House, new Whips and John Harris on a permanent basis.

I said that I thought Harold Wilson would be the obvious Shadow Leader of the House if that wasn't an insuperable difficulty – taking him away from finance. 'Oh no, not at all – in a way it would suit me nicely,' said Hugh. He said he intended to appoint younger men to the Front Bench but thought I would get elected to the Shadow Cabinet anyway.

He also said several times, 'I'm not prepared to lose another Election for the sake of nationalisation.' He laid great stress on the disadvantages of the name Labour, particularly on new housing estates, and said, 'Of course Douglas Jay is going to urge us to adopt a new one.' I reminded him that the prune had been resuscitated without a change of name by clever selling.

Hugh also thought we must review our relations with the trade unions, especially the need for greater freedom and in local authorities.

Dora was bubbling with hate of left and right. She is game!

Monday 12 October

To Manchester for a Granada 'Searchlight' programme on the next five years with Keith Kyle (who was Liberal, was on the Tory candidates' list until Suez, campaigned for Liberals in this Election, and joined the Labour Party last week), and journalists Bernard Levin and Paul Johnson, a very defeatist, rootless young man who was saying that we must drop nationalisation, end links with the trade unions and join up with the Liberals. I said that morale was high and that what we wanted was to revitalise the Labour movement by modernising its constitution, driving its policy thinking forward, creating a new Youth Movement, and making the Opposition more effective.

Flew home to London and saw Roy Jenkins on 'Panorama' advocating very modestly that you should drop nationalisation, watch out for the dangers of the union links and not rule out an association with the Liberals.

He dropped in here with Jennifer on his way back home and we had a flaming row. As a matter of fact I was very calm and collected and he got into a semi-hysterical state. Usually it's the other way round. 'We must use this Election shock to drop nationalisation entirely at this forthcoming Conference,' he said, and I concentrated on the dangers to our integrity if we were to be so reckless. In the end he half apologised for his temper and went off.

Wednesday 21 October

Tea with Harold Wilson, who is extremely bitter. Hugh certainly has failed to keep us together.

Tuesday 10 November

Peter and Liz Shore, Gerald Kaufman and Ivan Yates came to dinner tonight and we discussed the idea of a 1964 Club to be based on the simple objective of doing to the Party what we know has to be done – modernise and overhaul and make it a vehicle for progressive action in our society. We would include in it only those who were young and also had some contribution of a positive kind to make – by virtue of their position in the Party. It's a sort of colonels' revolt, with no objects save that of revitalising the movement.

We thought we might include in the Club: David Ennals, Peter Shore, Tony Howard, Ivan Yates, Gerald Kaufman, Shirley Williams, and Reg Prentice and Dick Marsh as trade union MPs.

Saturday 28 November – Labour Party Conference, Blackpool

Nye and Jennie came to dinner at our hotel with Shirley and Bernard

Williams. Nye turned to me most viciously at the beginning, attacking the campaign, TV, and the idea of surveys of public opinion. He was really a bit touched, thought Bernard Williams, who sat opposite me. Unfortunately I am like a red rag to a bull to him. Perhaps he knows that I don't trust him at all. Or is it because I am young and middle-class?

Couldn't sleep much tonight for nightmares about the National Executive election. I got elected to the Executive in bottom place – ousting Ian Mikardo. My vote had risen from 483,000 to 566,000 and Mikardo had dropped from 646,000 to 554,000. I am sorry it was Mik, and he said at lunch, 'I'm glad it was you', which was very sweet as he has lost the chairmanship, his seat, and this, all in two months.

In the debate Shirley Williams made a brilliant speech and won universal applause. Nye's speech this afternoon was witty, scintillating, positive, conciliatory – the model of what a leader should do. He didn't knock Hugh out but he gently elbowed him aside.

Monday 30 November
Heard from Sir Winston Churchill, to whom I wrote for added support in my latest plea to Macmillan for a change in the law to permit me to get out of my peerage. He won't write me a new letter but has given me permission to make further use of his earlier one written in 1953. Today is his eighty-fifth birthday. He certainly is a wonderful old boy.

Saturday 19 December
Dinner with Pam and Enoch Powell.

The Powells relaxed a bit about politics and I learned that they really cannot bear Macmillan, which is interesting. There may be more discontent with him in the Party than is generally realised.

Wednesday 20 January 1960
We heard that Nye is critically ill and it looks as if he may not last.

Thursday 21 January
To the House of Commons to talk to the 1944 Association – a group of Labour businessmen. It's also known as the queue for peerages. I gave them a talk on 'The Future of the Labour Party' and it really got a pretty frosty reception as they were all welcoming the spread of unit trusts. I'm afraid I didn't go down very well.

Saturday 23 January
To Bristol where I spoke at the Republic Day celebrations run by the India Society. There were lots of Indians there and lovely dances performed by dance groups and singing Hindu songs. There must have been nearly a

thousand altogether and it was certainly the most colourful and enjoyable do
I have been to in Bristol for ages. Britain is far too inbred and what we need
is some foreign influence to make us more interesting. American culture has
detribalised us to some extent and we shall be better off still when we get the
full blast from Russia and China.

Thursday 18 February
Had forty-five minutes' talk with Hugh Gaitskell this evening in his room.
He was very cordial and we discussed transport problems, for which I am
Front Bench spokesman, broadcasting, and then finally Clause 4. This
argument is raging in the Party at the moment as we approach the National
Executive meeting on 16 March. Hugh asked me what I thought about it
and I told him I was 100 per cent in favour of modernisation and additions
but I had a strong feeling we should not delete the famous phrase about
'common ownership of the means of production, etc'. He was a bit
surprised. I explained that I thought the whole thing had been represented
in a very negative way from Blackpool onwards. However, it was a perfectly
cordial evening.

Wednesday 16 March
Left early for Transport House for the long-awaited meeting of the National
Executive at which we are to rewrite Clause 4. Got there so early I had a
chance to look in and see the folks at the flat round the corner. It's so very
nice to be able to get Dad's advice with all his tremendous experience of
political rows over sixty years. Caroline said, 'Keep your mouth shut today.'
Dad said, 'Don't get involved.' I think it is all very sound.

Walking to Transport House I saw an enormous crowd of journalists and
photographers. There were even ten or fifteen Trotskyites carrying placards
announcing that they were from 'The Clause 4 Defence Society'. The
flashbulbs popped as I approached and it really was extremely funny to see –
I couldn't help laughing.

We were in the tiny committee room on the fourth floor and as I arrived
Bessie Braddock looked out of the window and claimed to have spotted a
journalist on the roof so we pulled the curtains.

There was some question raised about the leakages of Gaitskell's draft,
which had appeared in *Tribune* last week.

Finally Gaitskell opened. I kept my notes written at the time in my book.
He really went over the ground of his Blackpool speech again. In the
subsequent discussion it was clear that nobody wanted a great row. The tone
was extremely good and it was a very interesting debate. Walter Padley gave
an impassioned defence of Clause 4 as it stands and Sam Watson reminded
us of the two Irish labourers arguing about the ownership of a cow which
was standing quietly in the corner being milked by a lawyer.

It soon became clear that people were looking for some way of bridging the gap and Jennie Lee suggested that the words 'commanding heights of the economy' might provide such a bridge.

Dick Crossman suggested we wanted an amplification and somebody said surely it was a clarification too. Finally Charlie Evans of the NUR said, 'Why don't we reaffirm it?' So that's how the three key words – reaffirms, clarifies and amplifies – came into Gaitskell's draft. We accepted this by 22 votes to 1 with one abstention – Harry Nicholas of the TGWU on Frank Cousins's orders. I said it was like saying that we 'accept, reject and explain . . .'. We then paused for sandwiches before we went on to discuss the detailed amendments to Gaitskell's draft. This went through fairly smoothly with some toughening up. I tried to get World Government specifically written in. It was defeated. But I did succeed in getting in explicit repudiation of colonialism with the words 'rejecting the exploitation of one country by another'. This is in line with the Tunis Resolutions, and I felt was well worth while doing.

The press were still pouring round the building as we left it, catching us with movie cameras as we walked away. But news of the compromise had reached them and we were able to be all smiles.

Tuesday 29 March
Went to drinks at Mervyn Stockwood's – first time I have seen him since he was made Bishop of Southwark. He looked awfully pale and drawn. He doesn't enjoy good health. Had a long talk with Stephen Spender before I realised who he was. Also met John Betjeman, whom I felt I knew well through TV. He is terribly funny and, with that inane toothy grin, he talked about 'friends of friendless churches', and spoke bitterly about this and that bishop or rural dean who had ordered the closure of some 'lovely, Victorian, Gothic monstrosity'.

Afterwards persuaded Tony Crosland to come and have a meal in a pub and back for a drink. He is the most complex character and it takes half a bottle of whisky and immense tact to penetrate his susceptibilities. We had bucketfuls of self-analysis but finally did have a reasonably intelligent discussion about rebuilding the Labour Party and what Hugh should do now. I felt it had done something to bridge the gulf between us over the last few years.

Saturday 9 April
At home all day and David Butler to tea. South African Prime Minister, Dr Verwoerd, shot. The South African crisis is deepening.

Friday 6 May
Up early and by taxi for Princess Margaret's wedding. It was a glorious, hot summer day and we drove down Constitution Hill and past the Palace, down the Mall where the crowds had been sleeping all night and through

the Admiralty Arch into Whitehall. The Guards in full dress and the general
air of expectancy with all the decorations, and the streets empty of cars
reminded me of the 1937 Coronation. We were terribly early and sat on the
terrace of the Commons until we walked over to the Abbey.

Every pillar in the Abbey had a closed-circuit TV screen and during the
service we saw ourselves singing a hymn lustily. We also saw most of the
Commonwealth Prime Ministers and other visiting celebrities. Afterwards
we had lunch at the Commons and I went off to Bristol to canvass in the local
elections.

Tuesday 10 May
Met Jim Callaghan on the bus to the House of Commons. I think he has got
his eye on the job of Shadow Foreign Minister. He let slip some remarks
which made this very clear. The colonies are shrinking and he doesn't want
to shrink with them!

Saturday 11 June
The Party is in a deplorable state, Woodrow Wyatt's speech attacking Frank
Cousins as 'the bully with the block vote' has disheartened members.

Afterwards drove to Oxford for the Nuffield dance. Jim Callaghan was
there. Caroline has almost convinced me that he should be the new Deputy
Leader.

Wednesday 29 June
Parliamentary Party meeting this morning to pass a vote of confidence in
Gaitskell. The really important thing was the fact that all the trade unionists
who spoke in support of the motion were strongly critical of Gaitskell and
particularly attacked his assault on Clause 4 and 'his little coterie of friends'.
Manny Shinwell gave a tragic performance of senile egomania and Sydney
Silverman really lost his grip. Finally we passed a vote of confidence in
Hugh.

This evening we debated changes in the homosexuality laws. Kenneth
Robinson opened and I voted with the ninety-nine who wanted to legalise
homosexuality over the age of twenty-one.

Wednesday 6 July
Nye Bevan died this afternoon.

Tuesday 12 July
This evening to the dance at the American embassy. There were 700 people
there and we stayed until dawn was breaking. I haven't danced all night
since I was an undergraduate. It was without exception the most fabulous
party I have ever attended.

There were artificial trees with real fruit wired on to them. By using enormous plastic bags, four artificial swimming pools had been created in the garden which had been filled by the London Fire Brigade. Between and around them were gigantic candelabra wired for gas; from these tremendous candles burned continuous jets of flame.

The guests were the establishment *in toto*. We danced round beside the Armstrong-Joneses and saw the Queen Mother and Bob Boothby gazing at each other rather balefully across the champagne bottles. R.A. Butler, Lord Salisbury, the editor of *The Times*, David Niven, several dukes, Alf Robens, Frank Soskice, Osbert Lancaster, Joyce Grenfell, the Gaitskells, etc. etc. Name them and they were there. We had no really close friends but knew an enormous number slightly. Though we enjoyed every minute of it, we felt a bit like the Roman senators must have felt the night before the Huns and the Goths arrived to sack Rome. Such splendid extravagance carries with it an inevitable taste of decadence.

Wednesday 24 August – USSR trip

Boat train from Liverpool Street to Harwich where we caught the *Prinses Beatrix* to the Hook of Holland. The Moscow coach was in the siding – heavy with polished mahogany, bright brass, thick curtains and plush stuffed decoration.

Dinner in the wagons-lits as we passed through Utrecht and to bed as the train moved into West Germany. A Thermos, some Nestea, condensed milk in a toothpaste tube and saccharin provided that comfortable feeling of home as we headed for the Iron Curtain. We are the guests of the Inter-Parliamentary Group of the Supreme Soviet.

Thursday 25 August

Woken at 2.30 am by East German police and dozed till 7 when the train went through shining, flashy, opulent West Berlin towards the East Sector.

Tonight we went to bed in our clothes and at 11.30 the Polish police and soldiers called as we passed into the Soviet Union. At midnight two Red Army soldiers, a customs official, a girl from pest control, and an Intourist girl came in. Changed money at Brest and the wheels changed.

Woke late and had breakfast of ham and eggs and tea in the Russian restaurant car.

At 2 in Smolensk and rolling across western Russia all afternoon. At each level crossing stood a girl or woman holding a yellow flag in one hand and a silver or tin horn in the other. They were symbols of patient, loyal Russian people doing their duty and watching the great technology of Soviet power as it went on its way.

At 8.50 met by Nicolai Kutchinsky, who is to accompany us and translate for us. We went to the Sovietskaya Hotel and then drove round Moscow up to the Lenin Hills and on the Metro. We are definitely getting VIP treatment and will get on well with Kutchinsky. Comment on Russian society by him:

'I didn't want TV but my mother-in-law and the kids did. There's too much violence and shooting with all the revolutionary and wartime films.'

Breakfast in our room and drove to see new housing development. Big posters said 'Eat More Cheese'.

To Lenin's office and apartment and then to the cathedral in the Kremlin, the Armoury Museum and the Palace of the Soviets. It was all very beautifully restored and well kept.

Lunch at 4.30 at the hotel, by which time we were really knocked out. Kutchinsky is very anti-Molotov and we discussed the 20th Congress.

To the Park of Rest and Culture to see Obratsov Puppet Theatre. Lots of English and Americans in the audience. Dinner 11.30-12.30 in hotel; big lumpen Mongolian delegation at next table. Band playing in 1930 style with young male singer singing 'I Love Paris'. Discussed China, de-Stalinisation, Hungary and British colonialism. Kutchinsky is very agreeable and ready to talk frankly.

Monday 29 August
With Alexander Prosorovsky of the Planning Department to see a housing research project. Prefabrication is going ahead and we also heard about the operation of 'Comradeship Courts', which operate in blocks of flats and neighbourhoods to check bad behaviour by children, nagging wives, unfaithful husbands, etc. Sunday School has nothing to teach them!

This afternoon with Alexander Sirotkin to see the Moscow Metro, which is extremely impressive.

Russians are anti-American, to us anyway. Worried about China, pro-Macmillan, anti-Stalin and said the BBC is clever propaganda but its Russian Service is run by 1917 émigrés who are ignorant, or later émigrés who are hostile.

Tuesday 30 August
Woken at 5.45, breakfast at 6, and porter comes to collect baggage at 6.15. Caroline's in her nightie and I'm in underpants. No possibility of making myself understood. Porter withdraws and man in raincoat and trilby hat appears to remove baggage. He rings on the phone and has long talk in Russian to operator who understands him, but it doesn't help. I speak to girl with help of phrasebook but page flips over and I read the phonetic translation of phrases that have no meaning like 'I'm sorry your mother has been ill' and 'How many hectares of wheat are there on this collective farm?'

To Moscow Airport and by plane to Sochi, where we had a suite and balcony overlooking the incredibly beautiful Black Sea.

In a speedboat along the waterfront to see the enormous palatial sanatoria built by the trade unions for the workers. In the evening to the Opera with a stage the size of La Scala to hear *Traviata* sung by the Siberian Opera Company. It is all so fabulous and surprising.

Supper from 11 to 2 am in our room and a long and most intimate political talk which represented a complete breakthrough in personal relations. From then on we were on first-name terms.

Wednesday 31 August

Bathed before breakfast

A couple of hours of talk over supper in our room again: Kutchinsky says there are few political prisoners in Russia today and it is much easier than under Stalin.

'I would open the frontiers and prove Russia is confident of its system.'

Then he added, 'Collectivisation was a tragic error and Stalin a disastrous leader. If Lenin had lived it would have been very different. Khrushchev is absolutely honest and straightforward and gets no special privileges.

'The Labour Party needs discipline, should abolish the block vote, should know who it intends to represent, especially white-collar workers and technical people, and must be more concrete. The Campaign for Nuclear Disarmament is a protest but not a practical idea. It is isolationist, anti-patriotic and dishonest.'

Friday 2 September

By boat across the lake to breakfast in a restaurant and then drove through the mountains back to Adler Airport. Kutchinsky explained how the constitution of the USSR worked and how the CP representatives really controlled every organ at every level.

We flew to Moscow via Stalina and didn't get to bed till 2.30 am.

Saturday 3 September

We try unsuccessfully to telephone the British Embassy. The operator says it has no phone. Kutchinsky says it is very stupid and compares it with the refusal to publish a street map of Moscow as a hangover from Stalin.

To the Bolshoi Theatre to see *Ivan Sussanin* by Glinka – magnificent patriotic opera.

Sunday 4 September

To the Tretyakov Art Gallery: lots of socialist realism and rather dull.

Boris Krylov collected us by car for dinner at his flat. Mme Krylova and Krylov's mother-in-law live with the family – very crowded. Great family smiles and jokes and tremendous meal with enormous good will all round. They are so affectionate yet serious, good-humoured yet courtly and we felt immediately at home with them. Of course they retain the pre-revolutionary attitude to the outside world and look forward to the relaxation that they know is coming. But what a terribly tough forty years they have had.

Off to the Bolshoi again with Nick. But only stayed for one act of *The Taming of the Shrew*. Long talk over coffee at the hotel.

Monday 5 September
At 6 o'clock to the Praha Restaurant for a private dinner with Jacob Paletskis, a full member of the Central Committee. He is a rank-and-file leader and an old-guard Bolshevist. For an hour at dinner we have the most cordial talk, exchanging pictures of his grandchildren and our children, and I thought it was all going to evaporate like that. Then, all of a sudden switching to Russian, he turned to Kutchinsky, who later translated, 'Gospodin [Comrade] Wedgwood Benn, you have a very progressive record, except on one question, the question of Hungary.' It was a direct head-on challenge that I could ignore or take up and I decided to take it up. For an hour and a half we had a fierce argument through Kutchinsky.

Still, the conversation ended with many expressions of friendship. Paletskis pinned a medal on my lapel from the Supreme Soviet and I thanked him for the other presents of perfume, records, books and the Sputnik music box.

To the station to catch the Red Arrow to Leningrad. As the train pulled out, Caroline with a new bouquet waved goodbye and we settled into the comfortable sleeper to drink tea and eat biscuits while the bells of the Kremlin rang through the radio in our compartment, followed by the 'Song of Moscow', which traditionally followed them. As usual we had another talk with Kutchinsky.

'I hope that there is no war,' he said, 'because the Russian people have suffered so much and have worked so hard for so long that it would be very tragic indeed if they were, at the last minute, denied the fruits of their sacrifice.' And as he left he turned and said to me, 'You are an idealist underestimating the forces against you and you will be due for disappointments.'

Tuesday 6 September
Early this morning the woman brought us caviare and tea to wake us up. Met at Leningrad Station, and to the Astoria Hotel.

For a couple of hours we drove round Leningrad with an Intourist guide, who pointed everything out. We saw the Admiralty, the Winter Palace, the Kirov Stadium, the Aurora, and drove up and down the main streets. At lunch Kutchinsky said I should have been in the Tory Party, would have made better progress, and could have done more for my country. I said that he should have stayed an optical engineer – which was his job before he became a research worker in foreign affairs.

Just after midnight Nick and I decided to go for a walk and Caroline went up to her room. About thirty seconds after we had left the hotel we heard an enormous explosion behind us, turned and saw a column of flame rising thirty feet into the air right outside the front door of the hotel. We rushed back and saw a truck on its side blazing. Thinking of the man in there frying, and wondering if there was more petrol still to explode, we forced our way round it and into the hotel. Our room overlooked the site and Caroline, hearing me bang on her door, thought it was someone to say that I was in the accident. We watched the truck blaze until the fire brigade put it out with foam, and the ambulance – complete with a doctor, as is usual in Russia – had arrived. It was then that we discovered that no one had been killed. The truck had been stolen by a fifteen-year-old boy and it had skidded and turned over, leaving him a couple of seconds to get out before it blew up. Flash-photographers and police gathered, then the truck was towed away.

Not one word appeared in the Leningrad papers the next day. 'We don't believe in sensationalism,' they explained.

Wednesday 7 September
At breakfast Nick asked two personal questions. He wanted to know our family history and how rich we were. He had hinted that he will be making a report on our visit and these may be for inclusion in it. We answered both questions fully.

Caroline goes on to discuss anti-Americanism, which we have noticed in its most virulent form. We say that the propaganda goes beyond the policy differences, embracing all aspects of American life and constituting a sort of McCarthyism. Nick is very indignant but finds it hard to justify himself.

Thursday 8 September
We visited the Russian Museum and then at 12.30 went to the Cazana Cathedral which is now run by the Academy of Sciences. It is a museum of the history of religion. Our guide Nina Nosovitch, aged about twenty-five, was an atheist theological student, writing a thesis on reform in the Russian Orthodox Church.

The exhibits were designed to show that Christianity came from earlier cults. The Lamb of God, the cattle by the manger, Peter the fisherman and other symbols linked the religion with pagan faiths. A glass case contained extracts from Christ's teaching showing how it strengthened the slave owner by undermining the resistance of the slaves: for example:

'Turn the other cheek.'
'If a man takes your coat, give him your shirt.'
'Blessed are those who suffer.'
'Love thine enemies.'

As we left Nina shook us firmly by the hand, thanked us for being so interested, and said that the younger generation now didn't seem to care about anti-religious propaganda. Maria said afterwards, 'Unfortunately there is no systematic anti-religious propaganda except at Christmas and Easter.'

Kutchinsky realised that we didn't like the exhibition and couldn't understand why. We joked with him about items we would put in an anti-Communist museum. He said he would complain about its lack of objectivity.

In the evening attended a farewell dinner at the Restaurant Metropole. Everyone was so warm and friendly and they drove us to the dock and put us on board the *Estonia.* The wind was blowing and the rain bucketing down and we felt that winter was closing in on Leningrad and would hold it tight until the spring came to melt the ice. We had no real chance to say goodbye – just a warm handshake on the wet cobbles at the quayside. And then warm and comfortable in our cabin in this lovely new ship we edged out into the sea, our Russian trip over.

Tuesday 20 September
Dick and Peter to dinner and we discussed the Conference. The Left is determined to crush Gaitskell and the Right is determined to crush the Left on the defence issue. We represent the centralists and hope that the crisis can be averted by the Brown-Ennals formula which would allow the Executive to accept the TGWU resolution, instead of making a fight of it.

Sunday 25 September
Gaitskell's Battersea speech yesterday threw down the gauntlet. He is sticking firm. Cousins has similarly given a press conference.

Monday 26 September
I decide that it may be necessary to resign from the NEC at Scarborough in an attempt to make peace.

Thursday 29 September – Labour Party Conference, Scarborough
To King's Cross to catch the special train to Scarborough.

Caroline warned me last night that it would be fatal to resign. I thought her very unsympathetic indeed and we had rather a row. It seemed to me that the earlier I could resign the better so as to carry the fight to the Conference.

Dinner with Harold Wilson, Barbara Castle and Dick. Harold is busy composing his speech for Sunday night and frankly all he's interested in is turning the situation to his own advantage. He thinks Gaitskell can be dislodged. My opinion of him drops the more I see of him.

Phone Caroline and she's relieved that I am not resigning. Bed 10 pm.

Friday 20 September
Up early and breakfast at no fewer than four different tables in the hotel

trying to win people round to the benefits of peace-making.

This morning's NEC meeting was routine business in a jovial atmosphere. The Left have joined the peace-making moves with the *New Statesman* flat out for us and *Tribune* not against us. The *Spectator* and *The Times* are bitterly hostile. The real issue is that Hugh and Frank won't have it, each being anxious to destroy the other. We must try to strengthen the middle and make its pull irresistible.

Long walk and talk with Barbara Castle. Talk to John Harris, Hugh's adviser, who thinks a split is inevitable. Frank Barlow says to me: 'Being who you are, there is nothing you can do about it, old boy.' Jim Callaghan says, 'Don't worry, old boy. After this week we'll pick up the pieces.'

Despite this discouraging advice I decided I would have one more go, so I caught Gaitskell as he was going up the stairs to bed and asked if he would agree to meet me the following morning. He looked very wooden and gave me the wateriest of smiles but finally agreed and told me to come to his suite at 10 o'clock.

Saturday 1 October

For the last day or two I had been talking quite openly with the press about the peace-making efforts. John Cole of the *Manchester Guardian* had been interested but sceptical. My line had been one of unlimited optimism and I had claimed repeatedly that the centre was responding well to my peace-making approaches. I told them that everyone I spoke to wanted peace-making to succeed, even though many thought it was too difficult, too late, or hopeless.

Today I had planned my interviews with Gaitskell and Cousins to see what sort of reception I would get from the two extremes. At exactly 10 o'clock I knocked at the suite of room number 1 and Hugh opened the door and beckoned me in. He was wearing a dark blue shirt with no tie and blue trousers. He looked dejected and bored and had the longest face, which regarded me with intense distrust. I knew it was going to be a most unfortunate and unhappy interview – as it was.

I told him that I was very worried about the split, which I thought was unnecessary, and that he knew that I had worked to prevent it. I still thought there was time, with a little good will.

He replied most unsympathetically and said that under no circumstances would he be dictated to by Frank Cousins. 'Frank Cousins is *not* the only trade union leader,' he said. 'You seem to forget that.'

He then went on to attack Cousins in extremely personal terms and went on to say that Mrs Cousins was 'very left indeed' and to hint that she was a fellow-traveller. It was clear that on this point he was quite irrational. He said that he had underrated the strength of the campaign by the nuclear disarmers and the Communists and that it was clear that he would have to make a stand and fight on this.

He said, 'You are a very talented young man, but you have no political judgement and you don't realise that sometimes silence is golden.'

I left after fifty minutes, pretty despondent.

It was now pretty clear that my plan for a compromise had foundered. Over lunch the idea formed in my mind that if we couldn't get agreement between the official side and Cousins we might actually have talks to clarify the points of disagreement and invite Conference to accept a common interpretation of what these differences were and ask them to decide.

I drafted the memorandum along these lines, discussed it with Barbara Castle and got the Party office to type me out several copies. Armed with one of these I waited in the lounge for Frank Cousins to come in. He arrived with Harry Nicholas and some others and I was summoned over imperiously.

Frank was breathing rather heavily and was obviously on the top of his high horse. He said, 'If you think that you can save that man in this way, you've made the biggest mistake of your life.' It was clear he regarded me as an emissary from the Hampstead set, anxious to do anything that would save Gaitskell from defeat.

I tried again. 'Well, will you read my memo . . . ?'

'No, I won't,' he said.

'Well, how will you know what I've proposed if you don't read it?' I said bravely.

'I don't care. I won't agree. I won't read it,' he said. Harry Nicholas blushed scarlet at the way in which he was mauling me. I didn't give a damn, although it was a little disappointing. Frank seemed to realise that he'd gone too far; he grabbed the memo from my hand and looked at it. His eyes lit upon a sentence which said that 'when Conference has reached its decision the whole Party should accept it'.

'I certainly won't agree to that after the rigging and fixing of the vote which that man is out to achieve. If I defeat him, he must accept it; but I won't accept it whatever happens.

'I've always wanted to form a trade union political party and I've half a mind to put up against that man in his own constituency of South East Leeds. And as for you, you've burned your boats now and you've no future with that man,' he said menacingly, implying that I was finished unless I worked with him on his own terms.

Anyway he eased up a little bit after that and I explained that I would be putting this proposal informally before the National Executive tomorrow and that I hoped he wouldn't turn down the idea of talks out of hand. He stuffed the memo into his pocket saying, 'All right, all right, I won't say no now,' and with this half victory I got up and left him.

It was now pretty clear to me that both sides wanted a showdown and that

Cousins and Gaitskell were completely irrational about each other. Frankly, I agreed with both of them in their assessment of the other.

I ought to add a word about the atmosphere in the Royal Hotel among the Executive. For Harold, his speech on Sunday night at the Eve of Conference Rally was to be his great bid for the leadership and he had concocted a lot of phrases which were full of significance but took no stand. My contempt for him grew each time I met him and I don't think he has one-tenth the character of Gaitskell.

Just before going to bed this evening I saw Ray Gunter, who cursed me up and down in the sweetest possible way. 'You're crucifying Gaitskell,' he said. 'As you know, I'm no Gaitskell man but there are decent ways of doing this sort of thing.' I went to bed quite clear that I should resign tomorrow if the Executive refused my proposal for talks.

Sunday 2 October

I canvassed *the Times*, *Guardian*, *Herald* and *Daily Mail* correspondents this morning with my plan for talks and gave a copy of the memo to John Harris.

I also heard that Harry Nicholas would be authorised to accept the suggestion of talks if the NEC put it forward at this afternoon's meeting. I therefore went to the meeting waiting for the moment when I should have to make this proposal, having firmly decided that I should resign if it was rejected.

As we met, the CND parade led by Horner, Mikardo, Canon Collins and others tramped by the hotel shouting 'Ban the Bomb! Gaitskell must go!' It almost drowned our proceedings and introduced an element of mob violence into our affairs.

When we came to the defence resolutions, including the TGWU resolution, I moved that we initiate talks. My proposal was backed by Jennie Lee, Dick Crossman and a lot of others but was bitterly opposed by Gaitskell, Gunter and Sam Watson. After the vote on it was taken I raised a point of order. I said I had tried to bring peace . . . At this, the Chairman, George Brinham, interrupted me and said it was not a point of order. I raised my voice and shouted that he should hear me out and I then said I thought this was a disastrous piece of action and I proposed to resign from the Executive forthwith. I had got too excited and as I walked across the room to the door I heard George Brinham saying, 'Anyone can resign from the Executive, that is not a point of order.'

I went upstairs and saw George Brown. I told him what I had done and he said, 'Don't do anything else until you've spoken to me.' I summoned a press conference for 5.45 in the billiard room and telephoned Caroline to tell her the news. At 5.45 I read my statement to a gigantic press conference and answered questions.

I gather that I had caused some consternation after I left. I got some pretty grim looks from colleagues who later emerged from the meeting but Walter

Padley (who is not a unilateralist) clutched me warmly on both shoulders and said with tears in his eyes, 'What's your personal position now? Are you going to stand again? That's all that matters.' All the secretaries from the Party were also very tearful. They are CND and were very sorry to see me go.

I rang Caroline and my dad and he was wonderfully encouraging. Caroline was sweet as could be but she thought I shouldn't have done it.

To bed but couldn't sleep till about 3.

Monday 3 October
Very cold reception from colleagues and hardly anybody said they thought I had done the right thing. Someone quoted George Lansbury's advice: 'Never resign', and somebody else hinted that it was just a stunt to get re-elected on the Executive and avoid an inevitable defeat by Mikardo. Lots of other delegates were puzzled.

For the first time in my life tonight I had a sleeping tablet and it was a relief to get a few hours of rest.

Tuesday 4 October
The results of the election for the Executive were announced this morning and I have been knocked off by Mikardo. I rang Caroline to tell her and was very dejected indeed.

Wednesday 5 October
The long-awaited defence debate was opened well by Sam Watson and sustained a high standard throughout. George Brown recanted, Noel-Baker cheered for his Nobel Prize, declared himself a multilateralist, Denis Healey said Khrushchev used to murder cats when he was a child and Michael Foot shone like a torch of radicalism. Finally Gaitskell in a magnificent defence of multilateralism that captured the Conference threw the whole lot away in his final minutes with his attack on 'unilateralists, pacifists and fellow-travellers' and by his declared intention to 'fight, fight and fight again'. In the vote the platform was totally defeated but the Left was dejected and the right wing exultant at this 'moral victory'. Bob McKenzie, Ivan Yates and the rest are plotting the new non-socialist radical party that they would like to see emerge.

To the *Tribune* meeting to hear Soper, Mikardo and Foot and to bed very late, very depressed and feeling that I had made an absolute fool of myself by resigning. Caroline was comforting on the telephone.

Thursday 6 October
Still very depressed but was cheered up by the Chief Whip, who told me this story.

He said that after the result of the NEC elections had been announced in the morning session he was walking up the hill back to his hotel for lunch, feeling rather depressed at the state of the Party. In front of him were two old ladies with white hair – obviously delegates from their constituency Parties – talking keenly together. They walked rather slowly and he overtook them. As he passed by he could just hear one saying in a squeaky voice to the other, 'I just didn't know which way to vote. I wanted to kick that little shit Wedgwood Benn up the arse and then that bastard Mikardo got on.'

The Chief Whip is a great friend of mine and the tears rolled down his face as he told me.

Friday 21 October
Rang Audrey Callaghan. She said Jim was very depressed, but had come back from Czechoslovakia convinced that socialism does work.

Sunday 6 November
Hugh shouted down again at a meeting yesterday. The Party now at its worst.

Wednesday 16 November
To the Commons for a Broadcasting meeting. At 4.45 a messenger came in and said 'Lord Appleby' wants to see you urgently. I said I had never heard of him and was busy. Five minutes later the messenger came back with a note from Lord Amulree (who is a doctor): 'Sorry to bother you, but your father is in the House and not very well. I think he should be taken home and got a doctor. It is very difficult to decide what is wrong.' I left the meeting at once and met Amulree in the Commons Lobby. We hurried to the Lords' Lobby where Father had been sitting, but he was gone.

We found him in the Peers' Guest Room, lying down in a deep armchair. He said he felt dizzy and had a neuralgia pain. 'I won't talk,' he said, 'I'll have a bit of a rest. Ma's coming for tea.' His pulse was very weak and he was cold, sweating a little. I went to phone Mother to get Dr Pitts to come.

When I went back to Father he was almost unconscious and so we got a wheelchair and carried him down the stairs, where he waited in one of the little dining rooms in the Harcourt Corridor. He had his coat on and hat and began breathing very heavily so that I thought the end must be very near. We decided instead to get an ambulance to take him to Westminster Hospital. Finally this arrived and we wheeled him out into it. He was now completely unconscious and I held his head in my arms as the ambulance went out under the arches, through the courtyard, past the Speaker's House and through New Palace Yard.

It was very obvious that he was leaving the Palace of Westminster for the last time. The ambulance rang its bell to get through the busy traffic and at 5.45 we got to the Casualty Department of Westminster Hospital where Mother and Dr Pitts were waiting.

At 6.45 the result of the electrocardiogram showed that he had a coronary thrombosis. Dave and June arrived and we saw Dr Lloyd, the specialist, who said it was extremely serious. Lloyd said Father would talk but he didn't seem to hear when the doctor told him that he must be as quiet as a mouse. He said the next two days were the most dangerous and the question was, had he the reserves of strength to recover? Father said to me, 'What's the news? I'm not staying here, you know. You can't bully me.'

Thursday 17 November
Mother and Father's 40th wedding anniversary. News of Clark Gable's death. Mother phoned at 9.45 to say that Father's blood pressure was up above the danger level.

I went to the Commons for lunch and then to the hospital at 12.30.

Dave came to the hospital and at 2.30 the Sister told us that Father was very seriously ill and could go at any moment, although he was just holding his own. I looked in to see him and he said, 'Hello James. Where's Ma? I certainly did have a thump. I can't understand it. How's Caroline and the children?' He looked very, very pale.

At 6.45 Dr Lloyd said he thought Father was rallying a bit, but Pitts said it was touch and go.

I went back to the flat for a few sandwiches and then to the hospital, where I sat for half an hour holding Father's hand. He was pretty much unconscious. But his mind was going back. 'Father used to say "Boys, I never take an engagement on Sunday for money" ' and, 'That was in 1919' and, 'Old boy, you're absolutely right.'

He took my finger and tried to write with it as if it was a pencil. He was passionately keen to get on with his work, and that was always his character.

At 9.15 Mother was whispering in his ear, 'Don't worry' and he said, 'It's no good without breath.'

At 9.30 Dave and I were talking and the Sister hurried in and said, 'Come at once. He's very distressed and I'm very worried.'

At the moment of his death the only thing on my mind was all the arrangements that had to be made. One had to begin this job of fighting the peerage at the very moment when one was least inclined to think of anything else at all. But, as it happened, my mother found the battle the thing that really kept her going. The funny thing was I never had a chance to discuss the tactics with him as I'd always imagined I would. I'd always supposed he'd have an illness of a week or two, if not a month or two, and that he and I would have planned every stage together, which he would love to have done. But it didn't work like that.

As soon as Father died the escalator was beginning to move. The gates had clanged in the Commons and I was moved, against my will, up the other end of the building. Of course I was terribly sad and upset, and felt very lonely that the one man who could advise me wasn't there – Father. I plunged into the deepest, blackest depression, which really made it impossible to work.

3

1960–64

BIG BENN

LITTLE BENN

Return of the Prodigal Son

The death of Tony Benn's father led to the complete cessation of the diary for almost three years, during which time Tony Benn was engaged in the fight to prevent himself being removed for life from the House of Commons to the Lords. The commons voted to exclude him but although disqualified, Tony Benn insisted on standing as a candidate in his seat of Bristol South-East in the by-election of 1961. He won, creating an unprecedented constitutional situation. During 1962, David Butler interviewed Tony Benn extensively on the progress of the peerage campaign up to that point and it is from these interviews that the first extracts in this chapter are drawn. From January 1963, the diary becomes a continuous record.

I went to see Gaitskell. That was a very unhappy interview. Of course he was angry with me because of the row over defence. I've a very short memory and my father's death had obliterated from my mind all recollection of the row over the bomb and the Conference and so on. Looking back on it now, I realise that it must have been a much bigger factor in his mind than the peerage case. I had caused him a lot of trouble; he would have thought I'd stabbed him in the back and was now coming along and asking for a favour. So I must give him full credit for his understandable irritation with me.

I sat down in his room at the House and he said three things to me: 'Well, you can't expect the Party to make a fuss over you.' Secondly: 'We do need young peers very badly in the House of Lords, you know; all the peers are so old.' Thirdly he said, 'Meanwhile, in view of the fact that you're no longer a Member of the House of Commons, and you're not yet a Member of the House of Lords, you'd better not come to any more Party meetings.'

I was really knocked back by this because I had expected a rather different attitude. I think I got slightly angry. I said: 'It's all very well, saying you need young peers, but what am I going to live on?' 'Well,' he said, 'I hadn't thought of that. I suppose there is some difficulty in this.'

I'm afraid that, from then on, I never regarded Gaitskell as a particular friend. His attitude throughout the case has been very simple. When it's been in the news and leading articles have been coming out, then he joins in and makes a wonderful speech attacking the primitive tribal customs which hold back a Member, and all that. But as soon as the thing goes out of the headlines and becomes submerged, he forgets it. He thinks the public forgets it and he thinks there's nothing much worth doing about it.

On Friday 24 March 1961 there was a special meeting of the General Council in Bristol, an absolutely key meeting from my point of view. All these solid trade union chaps came out absolutely firmly in favour of fighting. Fred Newman of the Shopworkers' Union said that every house in Hanham had been canvassed and 2,000 had signed the petition; less than 1 per cent were not prepared to sign. They were fighting for a principle. They were certain of an overwhelming victory. Another chap said, 'Even if they do seat the Conservative this will only be confirmation of the privileges that we're fighting.' It went on and on like this.

Polling day in the by-election of 4 May 1961 was the usual awful business. I do dislike polling day. I was up at 6.30. I was at the office at 8.15 and I went round to all the polling stations and all the committee rooms. It's a killing job. I think in many ways it's a complete waste of time, although it does encourage the Party workers and that's the only case for doing it. There's no point in talking to the returning officers or the clerks. After all, you must look at it from a practical point of view and I suppose you have to get in and out of a car about a hundred times on polling day and this begins to mount up. Anyway, the turnout wasn't bad. We were quite encouraged in the earlier part of the day, although it simply poured first thing in the morning.

At 4 o'clock I went back to the hotel, and was told that Sara Barker from Labour Party HQ wanted to see me. By then I was tired and a little worried, because you never know till the end of the day how it will work out. I went to see her in the lounge of the hotel. She was sitting there with her lips pursed and she said, 'I've just come down to tell you that in your speech tonight you're to make no reference whatsoever to the future. I've been asked by the NEC to come down specially to say this to you. It's going to be particularly important if the result is better than we expect. The NEC will not support you, further, in any Election fight.'

I must say I was very resentful of this and the way in which it was done. First of all, she didn't wish me luck – a candidate on polling day is like a bride, he wants something nice said – there was no suggestion of good will about it. I said, 'You could have sent me a postcard to tell me that. I've no intention of saying anything about the future.'

But it did send me down to the absolute bottom of depression, the one thing that was unbearable at any stage was the feeling that my own people weren't with me and George Brown plus Sara Barker made me, at this stage, regret the whole business. I really did think that evening that I was an absolute fool. The whole thing had been totally misconceived.

We went out and did our last-minute knocking-up on polling day. It was still pouring with rain. The streets were absolutely empty. There simply was nobody who was going to vote from 8 till 9 – or so it seemed. The street lights shone yellow on the rainy pavement, and our voices echoed back from the loudspeaker. I raised my voice in an almost desperate way to persuade people to come out. I lost my voice completely between 5 and 9 that night; I couldn't speak at all. We came back to the hotel absolutely finished, thinking that possibly we'd get in with a majority of 2,000. We thought it quite possible that we wouldn't win at all, and that was just the end of the whole business as far as we were concerned.

After the polls closed Caroline and I went and had tea and apples at Temple Meads Station, where I ate most of my meals during the Election, because it was quick and easy. At 11 we went to St George's Grammar School to the count and we forced our way through a crowd of people who were beginning to form outside. The television lights were shining on the school on the main London to Bristol road and there was, of course, as there always is at the count, a great sense of excitement. But we were utterly dejected as we walked in. As soon as we got in people said: 'It's a landslide.' Our people came up and said, 'It's going four to one, it's fantastic.' All of a sudden, the thing changed. From 11 till the result was announced was the most splendid and glorious part of the whole campaign. The clouds had disappeared, our optimism and enthusiasm soared, we walked around. We saw votes pouring out of the ballot boxes; we saw the piles going up. We really thought at one stage that the Tory candidate, St Clair, had lost his deposit.

I think that was the very best part of the Election, just as two hours earlier had been the very worst part of the whole business. I sat on a child's desk in the corner and drew up a little statement of victory, which I hadn't given any thought to at all. All the press were there, and they were so friendly and, of course, the press reflects the current mood. Anyway, it was extremely enjoyable. Then we came to the declaration and the Town Clerk himself came and announced the results: Benn 23,275, St Clair 10,231.

Then we went out on to the steps at the front of the school where there's a little stone balustrade. There was an enormous crowd. I can't estimate the number, but it's a broad road, and I suppose there were 2,000 people there. And they were absolutely cheering their heads off. It was a wonderful moment. The only trouble was, I'd lost my voice so I had to shout hard to be heard. It sounded rather shrill. I went on from the uncontroversial bit that I'd said inside, to a highly political bit saying we'll go on from this till we've removed all privilege in this country. It was a fabulous scene.

After the speeches, we came down the steps. We got on top of a jeep and were driven very slowly from St George's Grammar School right up the hill along the main road to London, which was utterly blocked by people, to the headquarters. We went into the Walter Baker Hall and there were all these people gathered. It was a moment of great drama and great personal excitement. We were overcome with emotion and gratitude and I was unable to express it, of course, because I'd lost my voice. The result was a 13,044 majority with a 13 per cent swing. There were about 200 supporters in the main hall. This was about 1 o'clock; how they all got home I just don't know.

The following day we got up at 8.30 and, of course, the press was terrific. The headlines that day about triumph in Bristol completely wiped out the memory of the Committee of Privileges, the dull lawyers, the old nonsense. Here was the response from the people I represented. I was very arrogant at this stage, extremely arrogant.

After my election the *London Gazette* published a statement from the Crown Office saying 'Member returned from Bristol South East, Anthony Neil Wedgwood Benn.' I rang the Public Bill Office and arranged to collect the certificate. I phoned the Sergeant-at-Arms to tell him what would happen that afternoon. He said that as far as they were concerned, I was a stranger. I got five Gallery tickets, phoned the Speaker's Office and left at about ten to twelve for the House of Commons. There were four cars full of photographers chasing me there.

At 12.15 I went in to see Gaitskell, Brown, Bowden and Frank Barlow. They were very friendly, and extremely pleased with the result of the Election. Of course, I was full of excitement. They did really feel, then, that it had done the Party some good and this was the new factor: that the Party did recognise that a swing of that kind, and a humiliation for the Government, was a much bigger and better thing than they had previously realised. It did, undoubtedly, push into the background a lot of the doubt and even a lot of the hostility. Anyway, we discussed the tactics to be pursued in the afternoon. It was really that we should try to get me to the Bar and then, again, get me seated. We knew neither would succeed, because no stranger could be admitted to the Bar and the Speaker said I was a stranger.

I went to see the Speaker at 1.25. He had my letter and he said that he had ruled to debar me from the House. He discussed the procedure and said,

'You can't come beyond the door.' So I asked whether he had ordered force
to keep me out. He asked why I said that, and I said that I was not prepared
to stay out for any purpose other than to avoid a scuffle. He said he would
have to think about that. So I said, 'Well, this is quite clear. If you intend to
stop me you must give orders that force is to be used to keep me out. That's
the only condition under which I'm prepared to bow to your authority.'

He was very upset indeed. He said, 'I had no idea that you were going to
put it like that' So I told him he was responsible for keeping me out of the
House. I'd just been elected by a large majority and, 'If you're stopping me,
you must take responsibility for it.'

The Speaker was shaken by this. I also raised with him the question of his
ruling: his excluding me from the amenities of the House. Peers who have
been MPs are allowed to use the House of Commons. He said that because I
was not a peer yet, because I hadn't taken my Writ of Summons, I was not
allowed to use the privileges of the Commons. Well, he was rather upset, but
he said at the end, 'I know this must be difficult for you.'

At 2.15 I went out to St Stephen's entrance and there was Caroline and
Mother, and Stephen and one or two others. There were a lot of people and
a lot of photographers, and I had the return to the writ proving my election
to Bristol South East, which I held up. That was undoubtedly a key point – I
was approaching the House armed with the authority of the constituency,
and there's a certain dramatic excitement in it. Well, then came the scene at
the House.

I knew exactly what was going to happen; I'd even gone up that morning
and spoken to Mr Stockley, the doorkeeper, who was a distinguished old
naval warrant officer. I said to him, 'It's very important that this shouldn't go
wrong, or be in any way undignified,' which he appreciated, because the
truth was they were very scared. They were afraid that something would
happen. They didn't quite know what. It was, after all, quite a serious thing
to keep a man out who had a piece of paper saying he was elected.

It was the first time in history that this had ever happened. The Chief
Whip and I walked towards the door of the House. There were lots of
Members standing in the Members' Lobby and they formed a sort of 'V'
towards the Chamber. I suppose there must have been 50 to 100 there. I
came in from the Central Lobby and the journalists were all waiting there
too, although they're not allowed to report what happens in the Members'
Lobby. I went round and met Bowden and we walked towards the door of
the House and the people sort of came in on us.

When we got there Stockley came forward and put his hand up and said,
'You cannot enter, Sir.' I was very, very nervous indeed. It was a moment of
high drama, although the press said it was corny because everyone had
known what would happen. But I was relieved to get it over, because you
couldn't be quite sure *how* it would happen.

After the debate we went to the Strangers' Cafeteria, the only one we could use, and those dear women who worked there laid out a cloth on two tables so that my mother, Stephen, Caroline and I could have a meal. Now, my friends in the House when I go there are the police, the women in the cafeteria, who play a very big part in a Member's life, and some of the badge messengers, the ex-warrant officers who look after the Chamber. The idea that one had been thrown out by the Establishment, yet one was still a friend of the people who work in the Palace, meant a very great deal to me. They were so kind. Whenever I went to the Cafeteria, they always made a point of getting my meal. I didn't have to queue like anyone else. This matters when you feel you've been shut out. Anyway, at 10.30 the votes were over and we went out and went home and that was the end of the Election campaign. The next stage was the Election Court, at which I decided to represent myself.

It was on Saturday 17 June that I got a cheque for £500 from Mr and Mrs Edward Sieff of Marks and Spencer, who were old friends of ours. We were absolutely knocked sideways by this. They said that it was for us personally, to help us over this very difficult period without my salary. We wrote back and said we couldn't possibly accept it for ourselves, but that, if we lost the case, we would have to start a fund and could we put it into that? They wrote back and said they didn't really intend it for that, but if we wanted to, that would be all right.

On that day, which was also our wedding anniversary, Caroline and I went down to a social at the Corn Exchange in Bristol. It was a wonderful evening. All the people who helped in the Election came along and we had a splendid evening, with dancing and cheering and all that.

It was very interesting that the Lords are terribly pleased if you come in to prove a peerage. If I'd come in with string around my trousers and said that I thought I was the Marquis of Granby, they would have treated me with respect, because I would have been trying to get what they had to offer. But there was a feeling of resentment, because I was trying to get rid of it.

On 29 June we had this talk with Lynn Ungoed-Thomas and Elwyn Jones. I presented in outline, very quickly, in about ten minutes, the whole case that I would argue. They sat there with faces absolutely blank. They're great personal friends of mine and they didn't want to discourage me, but they simply said that it wouldn't wash at all. You start with a tremendous jurisdictional argument about whether the court has power to decide the issue, which was how we were going to start, and then go on to say you are not a peer. You have lost the ear of that court in half a day. They'll never go on listening. So we came home utterly crushed, feeling that it was completely hopeless. Then, of course, we took the argument and rearranged it in a new form.

I felt very much on my own after the early part of May, for about six weeks. Charlie Pannell did ring me up from time to time, and one contacted individuals when it was necessary, but I never felt that they were taking a continual interest. I had a few friends in the House. Lynn was one and Elwyn was another. There were a lot of people I could ring up if I wanted to or if I needed advice, but very few who took a lot of interest. The House of Commons isn't really like that. If you're sick, you probably get a letter from the Chief Whip and one or two friends may ring up. It's a community, but only in the building. The thing died a death after the Election and my barring from the House, right up until the case, because it would have been contempt of court to have referred to it in any way at all.

I was immensely impressed by the fact that the judges would listen to all I had to say. After all, I did talk to them for 22 hours and I gave them 135,000 words. They asked me 537 questions in the course of that, which kept it alive. There was no sign of impatience with me. I hope I didn't bore them. But, even if I did, they didn't show it. This made a very profound impression on my mind. On the first day of the case, the only thing we could do was to sit and listen attentively, and make notes to see if Andrew Clark raised any points we hadn't expected. He didn't.

On the second day, 11 July, we began to get into the routine of going to court. I got there early, with all the books, notes and materials. Clark went on all day. I ought perhaps, to say a word more about the court itself. It was crowded out almost all the time. Barristers were coming in and standing by the doors, or sitting. The Gallery was always full. There was a big crowd outside the court in the morning when we arrived, and quite a number of touching scenes. There was a woman called Mrs Belcher who lives in Shoreham. I had tried, unsuccessfully, to take up a point for her about her eviction from her house a year or two earlier and she came up from Shoreham every day to hear the case. Then there was a chap living in Westminster who was very keen on road safety; I had taken up a point for him and he came to the court every day. And one realised that there was a floating population of people who, for one reason or another, were interested and were coming in. Various other distinguished people looked in from time to time. It may have been a bit like the Christians and the lions in the local circus. But they were coming in.

Caroline sat beside me making notes of everything, and she was invaluable. Her natural pessimism matched my natural optimism.

By July I was very near the end of the case, and I had got everything prepared. We went out to dinner with the Sieffs. Well, anyway, the following day, Wednesday 19 July, I had finished my speech. The concluding passages, which I had polished with such care, really so moved me that I could hardly utter the last sentence because I was almost in tears. *The Times* reporter actually did, I'm told, break down at the end. Anyway, that was the end. Sir Andrew Clark got up, and I thought I had no right of reply, though I subsequently discovered I did have this, and did exercise it. But as far as I was concerned the main strain was over, and I felt very relieved. Clark droned on and on but didn't really take up any of the major points that I had made. He just dismissed them all. He didn't deal with them.

At any rate, it all finished, and when I sat down I think that was the end of the case altogether. The judges said they would reserve judgment, and I was still not sure, of course, what the result would be.

We went off early in the morning – it was another of the siege days – and sat in this packed court. It was fuller than it had been on any other day, and we heard the judgment, which was read by the judges alternately. I suppose the judgment took about two hours to read. I should think that for the first forty-five minutes it was just a recapitulation of the facts. There were some phrases like, 'we cannot allow our feelings or the feelings of the respondent to enter into our consideration.' Then one realised that it was lost. Then it all poured out in a most extraordinary form: that while the hereditary system is retained, it cannot in any way be modified. The phrase is there, and is the phrase which is quoted in the Soviet reports of the trial. The idea that the hereditary system was necessary took precedence over the democratic element in our constitution. This is a view of our constitution that simply doesn't fit in with the facts, because of course in no respect, except in this, does the hereditary system have anything but a very minor role to play in the government of this country. Any rate, that was the end of it and we kept our end up. It was a grim moment. It was the clanging of the gate. It was obviously the end of the first stage of the struggle, some eight or nine months after it had begun. But we were very cheerful and gave interviews.

I realised that I was faced with the absolutely crippling bill, and so simply made one submission to them. I said that I had tried to keep the case as short as I could. I'd represented it myself. I hadn't engaged expensive counsel. I had not contested any of the evidence. I had dropped several of the points that Clark had thought I might raise, and warned him in good time that I was going to. Clark jumped up and said, 'This is monstrous. Here are two men fighting, absolutely by themselves, one against the other, and the loser must simply pay.' All the costs were duly awarded against me. If no award had been made to costs, Tory Central Office would have paid his, and I would have paid mine.

The bill, when it came in from the other side, was £7,500 and our own was £1,000. We realised that a public fund was urgently needed, and we had various talks with people. Michael Zander carried on and we got a list of sponsors, including some fairly distinguished people who agreed to give their names. Attlee, Lady Violet Bonham Carter, Bronowski, Fenner Brockway, Jo Grimond, Augustus John, Elwyn Jones, Sir Compton Mackenzie, Christopher Mayhew, Gerald Nabarro, Harold Nicolson, Charles Pannell, C.P. Snow and the Bishop of Southwark all agreed to be sponsors of the Bristol Fund. We set up a committee of Ungoed-Thomas, Robin Day and Michael Zander who would be empowered to sign the cheques. Michael worked on this. It was difficult for me because I didn't want this presented as a hard-luck story; clearly that would have been wrong.

Macleod and Butler were both distinctly unenthusiastic about the case. I am afraid, frankly, that for reasons of crude self-interest neither of them wants Home or Hailsham to be able to come back to the Commons from the Lords. This is the only real explanation, because on grounds of principle you would imagine that both of them would side with the younger element in the Government who wants a new and modern image, and here is a way to be popular without spending any money.

David Butler mentioned that he had met Rab at a party, who had said, 'I don't think Macmillan is ever going to go. You know what he said to me last weekend? "I don't see why I should make room for you, old cock." '

I think that while Macmillan remains there, he might well think it unattractive to have Home back. Home would be a godsend to the Labour Party. His qualities are completely overrated by his own party and are preserved for the public mind by the fact that he is not subjected to cross-examination. So I would be very much in favour of him, but incidentally the Labour Party's attitude now is slightly altered by the fact that we might appear to be helping the Government to find a more effective leader, and quite a number of people have said to me, including Dick Crossman, 'Of course the price we pay for you is having Hailsham as the Leader of the Conservative Party.'

Friday 18 January 1963
Hugh Gaitskell died today after a terrific fight for his life over the last week or so. Nobody had realised how serious it was and it has dominated the press and television in an astonishing way. It is a terrible personal tragedy for him as he was closer to Downing Street than at any time in his life.

The odious thing about the obituaries is the way the Tories are building his death up with half an eye to suggesting that there is no possible successor. Macmillan's tribute was the most revolting, since he and Gaitskell hated each other. Indeed one of the curious factors operating to check bi-partisanship in politics has been this personal hatred.

For me, Hugh's death produced mixed reactions. I have worked closely with him for twelve years and when he was at his nicest he could be very kind indeed. After the 1959 Election he put me on the Front Bench as Shadow Minister of Transport, which was an extraordinary promotion.

On the other hand he was a divisive leader of the Party. He had a real civil servant's mind, very little imagination and hardly any understanding of how people worked. His pernickety mind always managed to engineer a confrontation of principles which he would then seek to resolve by brute force.

He never could understand the force or logic of views with which he disagreed. He projected the unilateralists as Communists and fellow-travellers and those who supported the Common Market as traitors to the Commonwealth and extremists. He thus isolated himself from an increasing number of colleagues as time went on. But his death seems a disaster because it looks as if George Brown will succeed him and for a number of reasons he is totally unsuited to be Leader of the Party.

Thursday 14 February

Tonight Harold was elected Leader of the Labour Party. It is a great shot in the arm and opens up all sorts of possibilities for the Party. I have known him well personally, have always agreed with his general line and voted for him against Gaitskell in November 1960. He is an excellent chairman, gets on well with people and has some radical instincts where Hugh had none.

Monday 25 March

This evening I had fifty minutes with Harold in his room. It was a delight to find him so relaxed and easy. Gaitskell used to be so tense and tired and often signed his letters while I presented my points to him. I gave Harold all the stuff I had prepared for the debate next Thursday and he seemed pleased with it.

Then he walked up and down beside the long table and talked in an expansive way about how he was going to run the Election. He plans to have a mobile headquarters of personal staff and writers moving from city to city with him and do a daily press conference and one or two major evening appearances. He's not going to hundreds of village courts and market squares.

He said, 'I'm not going to sit in my hotel room putting shillings in the gas and writing an article for the *Sunday Times* in my pyjamas as Hugh used to. If I have to do articles I'll have J.B. Priestley travelling with me writing them for me.

This is a most imaginative idea and we must gear our TV and radio to it. He seemed to want me to be with him all the time during the Election, which would mean even less time in Bristol than I had in 1959. He obviously expects me to do most of the working out of this.

Thursday 28 March

Had a long talk to Dick about the Profumo-Keeler scandal. He said that Dr Stephen Ward, the Harley Street osteopath procurer, ran a sort of brothel on the Astor estate at Cliveden. Profumo lied in his statement to the Commons and Wilson is putting a note of what happened to Macmillan with a warning that it will be raised if something isn't done about Profumo. I'm not in favour of private life scandals being used politically but it certainly makes the Government look pretty hypocritical.

Friday 10 May

On to Bryan Magee's party and then to Tony Crosland's for a couple of hours. I had a long talk to Tony about his attitude to Wilson, who he still thinks is a shit, but who he also thinks has done very well and would like to help in any way he could. I must try to pass this on to Harold since Tony is too good to waste. But the simple fact is that with Hugh's death his old courtiers feel out in the cold – exactly as I felt with Hugh. Roy Jenkins is bitter about it and jealous of what he conceives to be my relationship with Harold, which frankly is similar to his relationship with Hugh. Tony is getting nicer and nicer as the years go by and, as he is a very old friend, that is rather pleasant.

Monday 13 May
This evening went to St Mary-le-Bow, Cheapside, for a meeting of the Christian Agnostics to hear the Bishop of Woolwich, John Robinson, talking about his book *Honest to God*, which we had gathered to discuss. The Reverend Joseph McCulloch has organised this group, justifying its name by reference to the line (from Oranges and Lemons) which runs: 'I do not know – says the great bell of Bow'.

At this gathering were Canon John Collins of St Paul's Cathedral, Father Corbishley (a Jesuit writer), George Dickson (an industrialist), Duncan Fairn (who took the chair), Gerald Gardiner, Dr Graham Howe (the humanist psychiatrist), the Earl of Longford, Canon and Mrs Milford, Mrs J.B. Priestley and a number of others.

The Bishop opened by saying that secularism was not basically anti-Christian and that Christians must understand and even welcome the revolt against dualistic supernaturalism, the mythological view of the world and the religiosity of the Church. He said his book was designed to help those who were in revolt to see the basic validity of the Christian message.

Canon Collins asked whether Christ was perfect, for if he was he was then God. Woolwich replied that he wanted to write a book about Christ and that the Virgin birth made Christ seem unreal. Woolwich's interest in Christ lay in his normality, not his abnormality. He felt he could not make sweeping statements about Christ's moral life, for what was significant was his obedience. Collins replied that if you simply say Christ was 'the best man I know', Christianity could never get started.

We broke up for supper and resumed for another hour and a half. Later we had a much deeper discussion about the supernatural in which I had a long confrontation with Corbishley about whether the evidence for the supernatural came really from external manifestations or the discovery of hidden depths. Corbishley was splendidly Jesuitical in saying that you had to have mythology 'to get people to pray'. Here is the real nub of the question. Is prayer a duty or a need?

I attacked the double standards by which the in-group of Christians know that the mythology is bunk but they don't discuss it publicly for fear of offending the faithful. Moreover, if the maintenance of the idea of the supernatural is justified on the grounds of practical necessity, it must be judged by results. And by results it has failed to stem the rising tide of secularism.

Woolwich summed up briefly. He is really an academic with guts but he is coming under such heavy fire now that I wonder if he can stand up to the pressure. The Anglican hierarchy is beginning to sense that his vibrations may start an avalanche and ruin its plans for Christian unity. But then unity on those terms is death. I hope he has the courage to go on and see it through. *Honest to God* is certainly the most helpful Christian theology that I've ever come across and I'm sure millions of others feel the same.

Friday 17 May

Had to catch the night sleeper back from Teignmouth to London and got to Exeter station at 10.30 with three and a quarter hours to wait. The refreshment bar was closed of course. The waiting room was bare with a few hard-backed chairs, so I blew up a beach mattress, had a cup of tea from my thermos, set my alarm, stuffed the earpiece of my transistor under my pillow and went to sleep.

The alarm went off at 1.30 and I found the room full of football fans who had been eyeing me as if I was a drunk, or a crank, or both. The train was on time and I got to sleep quickly.

Saturday 18 May

Home at 8 am and off at 9.30 to Yarmouth for a Festival of Labour rally. It was so cold on the pier that the band was playing with literally nobody in sight. However, about a thousand people turned up for the meeting inside. I travelled back with Harold Campbell, the new Secretary of the Co-operative Party, and he explained to me the inside story of the London Co-op row in which John Stonehouse, a former director of the Co-op, has become involved. It is a complicated story but John doesn't come out of it very well. Also heard from him what a difference it had made to Labour's relations with the Co-op to have Harold Wilson in the job. Wherever you look his touch is evident.

Friday 24 May

This evening Caroline and I went to Mervyn Stockwood's fiftieth birthday party at Bishop's House in Tooting Bec. His chaplain, Mr Mayne, had organised it and it was a very amusing do. He called Mervyn 'My Lord', which was slightly overdone. Mervyn was wearing a huge purple cassock with a clanking pectoral cross.

The first people we met were the Attlees. Clem was sitting in the garden in an overcoat, looking terribly frail. He said my battle was a historic achievement and I thanked him for his support from the beginning.

Vi Attlee said what a great failure Herbert Morrison had been as Foreign Secretary – 'he just didn't understand it'.

Mervyn introduced the Archbishop of Canterbury to us at the end – the first time I have met him. He is a mountain of a man and so plump and smooth that he looks like some medieval prince of the Church. I thanked him for his kindly reference to my case and said I had never had any sort of Archiepiscopal blessing for anything else I had ever done. Ramsey gave a watery smile and indeed looked at Mervyn most of the time he was talking to me. He said that he had made five speeches in the House of Lords this year, two of them right, and three of them left. A very silly comment. Alas he is only fifty-seven though he looks seventy – so we shall probably have him for the next twenty-five years.

I also met a man called Oliver Cutts, the son of a costermonger who bought a lorry in 1946 and I imagine is now a millionaire who owns a chain of filling stations, a road haulage fleet and a great deal of land. He retained all his Cockney charm and obviously was a man of great drive. He's a friend of Bob Mellish's and shocked me by saying he hoped Bob would one day be Sir Robert Mellish, Bart, in view of his services to the Queen and Empire.

I said I very much hoped no such thing would happen and that Bob had been serving the people of Bermondsey and not the Queen and Empire at all. Here was a guy who left school at nine, licked the Establishment, and got to the top, and was now yearning to be a part of that Establishment. If politics is only about who is to get peerages and honours – our chaps or their chaps – then I'm not very interested in it. But I liked him all the same.

We went from there to Elwyn Jones's flat in Gray's Inn Square where he and Polly Binder live. He is a dear man and she is a tough and delightful woman. They had some Chinese author there and a few others. Elwyn is working with Gerald Gardiner on a book on law reform to be published soon. Apparently they have a scheme for appointing a vice-chancellor who would sit in the Commons as Minister of Justice responsible for legal reform. I hope they are getting this all through to Harold Wilson. If we are going to do the job that has to be done quickly, everybody must be ready to carry through some pretty fundamental changes as soon as we get into office.

Wednesday 5 June
This afternoon Profumo wrote to the PM, admitted that he lied in his personal statement to the House of Commons, and resigned. The BBC asked me to do a discussion about the political implications of this in their 10 o'clock programme but I refused. I can't think that the Opposition rubbing its hands in glee can do anything but political harm. It's a bit like wrestling with a chimney sweep.

This evening Caroline went to dinner with Lois and Edward Sieff and there she met a man called David Pelham who is making a film of Christine Keeler's life. She had a long talk with him and he said that Christine Keeler was absolutely determined to bring the Government down. She was 'a woman scorned' and felt bitter about being dropped by the top people. It is all a very murky world.

Thursday 13 June

I had to go to Leeds to speak for Merlyn Rees, who is fighting Hugh Gaitskell's old seat. The political situation is fantastic at the moment with the Cabinet deadlock and rumours rife that there are more scandals to come, and that Enoch Powell will resign. *The Times* is now leading a campaign to get rid of Macmillan and there is a real possibility of so many abstentions on Monday that the Government might fall.

The PM himself is almost bound to have to go. If I were a Tory I should insist on this just out of an instinct for survival. But they are such sheep that I do not expect a revolt and if Mac can go on I think he will be massacred in the Election. This cannot be buried, as Dr Stephen Ward will be on trial in October and there is bound to be a tribunal or inquiry. It is all terribly bad for politics and Parliament and is an indication of the decay of the old British Establishment. But in the long run it may do good by forcing us to re-examine some things we have ignored and creating the sort of crisis atmosphere which will make it easier for the Labour Party to reform.

Friday 14 June

We had a party this evening. Among those who came were Robin Day, Val and Mark Arnold-Forster, Liz and Peter Shore, Michael and Claudie Flanders, Simon Watson-Taylor with Carmen Manley and another girl, David Hockney, Shirley Fisher and a host of others.

Obviously the main topic of conversation was the Profumo business, which produces new sensations every few hours. Mark assured me that the Tories had decided that Macmillan must go but he would be given a majority in the House on the understanding that he would resign in August. Apparently the two main contenders now for the succession are Butler and Hailsham – with Hailsham edging ahead since his television broadcast last night when he slashed out at the decline in public morals and attacked *The Times*, the Bishop of Woolwich, the Labour Party and the Welfare State, which encouraged people to believe they could get something for nothing. This sort of maniacal outburst is exactly what the Tory rank and file want and no one can give it to them better than Hailsham.

By an extraordinary coincidence Hailsham is able to be considered for the premiership only because of my campaign which has led to the Peerage Bill at exactly the critical moment for him. All the Government have to do is to amend it so that it comes into operation immediately and Hailsham can then renounce next month. Mark Arnold-Forster has suggested to the Tories that Hailsham should then stand as Quintin Hogg for Profumo's old seat at Stratford-on-Avon. This is a master stroke that will provide exactly the sort of opportunity the Tories are looking for to obliterate the traces of the scandal. Quintin is then elected an MP during August and immediately succeeds Macmillan so that when the House meets in October, Mr Hogg is the Prime Minister of a new administration with twelve months to try to persuade the country that this is a new, forward-looking, vigorous, proud administration that will make Britain great again. Hogg is to be our de Gaulle. Of course, it may not happen but it is true that the only circumstances under which Quintin has any chance of success are exactly these.

Tuesday 18 June
Rang Dick Crossman and we agreed that we should try to plan a terrific thrust now to get rid of the Government. The important thing is to prevent them from having time to regroup under a new leader and present themselves as being 'under new management – no connection with the old firm'. All the papers this morning said that Macmillan was on the way out and so I wrote a paper for Harold, intended to suggest ways in which we could keep the pressure up and thus retain Macmillan or bring down the whole Government. Dick Crossman independently wrote a paper saying the same thing and we exchanged them.

Friday 12 July
If I dare confide an ambition to paper, the job I desperately want in the Labour Government is to be a member of the Cabinet as our permanent representative in New York at the United Nations; it would mean flying the Atlantic every week for Cabinet meetings. I believe it is the single most important job there is to do.

Monday 15 July
Wrote to the American Ambassador about the refusal of the American Government to grant a visa to Willie Gallacher on the grounds that he is a Communist. The old man is eighty-one and his sister is sick in Chicago. It really is heartless.

Lunch with Tommy Balogh at St Stephen's Restaurant to discuss his various projects. He is rather a nuisance in that he is always wanting to see me and it does take up such a hell of a lot of time. However, I am interested in what he is working on. He is jealous of the others who advise Harold and I think regards me as a useful link. He feels that his economic advice is negatived by the right-wing economists who advise Jim Callaghan. I can't help with that and I suspect that Harold deliberately keeps all his advisers, including me and Dick and Peter, at arm's length so that he is always in complete command. If I were him I should probably do the same, not wishing to be 'taken over' by anyone.

Tuesday 16 July
Drove to Northampton with Reggie Paget to speak at his Labour Women's Supper Club. As I entered the Mayor's Parlour, the Mayor handed me a card on which was written: 'House of Lords defeated Government by 125 to 25 in favour of amendment that the Peerage Bill should come into force as soon as Royal Assent is received.'

What a message to get from the Mayor of Northampton in Bradlaugh's own constituency! It represents a total breakthrough. The Government cannot resist this and their retreat has turned into a rout. I shall be back in the Commons before Christmas and maybe even sooner.

Thursday 18 July
To Bristol for a public meeting which was crowded. Felt rather funny during my speech but finished it and answered a couple of questions. Then decided to withdraw while they looked for a doctor. None was available so Herbert Rogers drove me to Cossham Hospital, where I was admitted to casualty ward. Various doctors examined me and decided to keep me in for a series of tests. I felt lousy and was very glad when they put me to bed and knocked me out. Decided to tell Caroline in case she heard from other sources. It must have scared her to get a phone call from the night sister and a Ghanaian doctor to say that I was in hospital.

Saturday 20 July
Caroline had cancelled most of my engagements for the next couple of weeks. It's so nice to have an excuse like this. She came down to Bristol yesterday and today stayed all day at the hospital and there were masses more visitors.

Dr Poku, at my request, took a hypodermic full of blood and put it in a test tube for me, as a reminder of the 'noble blood' which I shall lose in a few days. He mixed it up with some anti-coagulant so that it wouldn't clot and it turned blue most appropriately. He said he quite understood as his father was an Ashanti chief who had given it all up.

Monday 29 July
At 2.45 Mr Yavar Abbas of BBC Television News arrived to film us leaving for the Commons, and he then drove us to the Commons and filmed us greeting the coach party from Bristol (seventy strong) as it got to St Stephen's entrance.

It was a perfectly glorious, cloudless day and we stood and chatted outside St Stephen's and then poured in in a solid phalanx, led by Charlie Pannell, up through the central lobby to the Members' Dining Room. The Bristolians settled themselves down in the chairs all round the room and watched the other guests arrive.

Caroline and I stood at the door and greeted them all as they came in. We don't know exactly how many came but it was well over 300. Among those who were there were Clem Attlee (who had a talk to Stephen), Dora Gaitskell, Harold and Mary Wilson, Gerald Nabarro, Lady Violet Bonham Carter, Lynn and Dorothy Ungoed-Thomas, the Bishop of Woolwich, Arthur Lourie (the Israeli Ambassador), Messaoud Kellou, the Algerian Ambassador and two members of the Soviet embassy staff who had come to represent Mr Romanov. Also there were Canon Collins, Lady Jowitt, Cassandra, John and Patsy Altrincham, A.V. Alexander and a host of Labour MPs.

At 4.50, Charlie banged on the table and I jumped on a chair and made a speech that lasted about ten minutes. I summarised the history of the case and how long it had taken, and thanked the Party and especially Charlie Pannell. Also the Young Liberals like Lady Violet and Young Tories like Churchill. I also thanked the lobby and the lawyers, especially Michael Zander, and those who had given to the Bristol Fund, especially Lynn. I reserved the main bouquets for Bristol and for Herbert Rogers.

Finally, I thanked the family and said I wished Father had been there. Then I made a few jokes about the Peerage Bill and produced the test tube of blood taken in the hospital. I finished by saying that the time had come to put pomp and pageantry back in the museum and that this fight was the beginning of a much bigger fight which I was sure we would win too.

I walked back to the North Court Restaurant with the Bristol party, where Mother had arranged a sit-down high tea for them all before they drove back to Bristol in their coach. At the restaurant there was another round of speeches and bouquets were presented to Mother and Caroline. Those people radiated warmth and affection and it was quite an experience for us all.

To bed a very happy man.

Wednesday 31 July
The phone rang so incessantly that I couldn't even shave so we took if off the hook. CBS Television sent a unit to film the family and Hilary (aged nine) gave a sensational interview in which he said, 'The hereditary system is ridiculous and Britain ought to have a President who was elected instead of a Queen who was not.' The interviewer asked him if he had studied the American system of government and Hilary replied, 'Not in any detail, but I know what it adds up to.' We had no idea what he was going to say, but after they told him they were going to ask him some questions. Caroline found him in the bathroom washing his face, and saying, 'I am really nervous.'

I went to the Commons for the weekly meeting in Harold Wilson's office and then to Transport House for a broadcasting meeting. From there I picked up Mother and we met Caroline at 4.45 pm outside St Stephen's entrance. There were two film cameramen and about thirty photographers. It was another lovely day and I took off my coat while we were photographed with the Instrument of Renunciation. We went to have tea in the Strangers' Cafeteria, and then at about 5.50 we took our seats in the second row of the Lower West Gallery of the House of Lords. It annoyed me very much that the attendant kept calling me 'My Lord'.

There were fifty-seven Acts requiring the Royal Assent and the Peerage Act was somewhere in the middle. The ceremonial seemed awfully silly especially when the Clerk read out the names of some Bills like the 'Public Lavatories (Turnstiles)' Bill and the other Clerk said '*La Reyne la veult*'. As soon as the words of assent were given to the Peerage Act, we got up and walked out and Caroline accidentally banged the door of the Gallery which rang like a shot through the Chamber. *The Times* said we left 'as if a starting pistol had been fired'.

Downstairs a Badge messenger escorted us straight to the Clerk of the Crown's office, where one of his officials was waiting for us. Two *Daily Express* men were standing outside and asked if they could go with us. We said firmly 'No', and closed the door. By then it was 6.12 pm and just after 6.15 we were ushered into the office of the Clerk of the Crown, Sir George Coldstream. Sir George himself came in in his full-bottomed wig, took it off and put it on the table. I had a bag full of documents in case any of them were needed but none was asked for.

Sir George was absolutely charming and his face was wreathed in smiles. He said that he was glad I was the first to renounce and he showed me the Register of Renunciation which had been specially prepared pursuant to the Act, in which the names of those who had renounced would be written. My name will go as No. 1. Sir George then said to Mother how much everyone missed Father and what a popular Member of the House he had been.

At our request he let us out of the side door and we slipped down the stairs into the Chancellor's Courtyard and through the arches in the open towards the Strangers' Cafeteria, where the lobby were waiting. As we passed one of the Badge messengers of the House of Lords he said, 'Goodnight, Sir!' It was all over.

Caroline and I went over to Kenneth Rose's flat. Among his other guests were John and Patsy Grigg. John had renounced eight minutes after me and the Clerk of the Crown had said, 'I hope you don't regret it!' As he left, one of the secretaries in the office said, 'We have been dreading this day, but it hasn't been too bad.' I suppose this was a reference to my appearance. I must seem an ogre and monster to that department. Also there at dinner were Lord and Lady Freyberg. He is a major in the Guards, with special responsibility for ceremonial. We felt so 'one up' on him. If status symbols mean anything, far and away the best is to have had it and given it up.

Thursday 29 August
After lunch I went to the Commons – the first time for nearly three years as an MP. I wandered into the Chamber which was absolutely deserted – no

crowds, no messengers, no police, nobody. I just sat in my old seat on the back benches and looked around and thought. It was an extraordinary experience, incredible and exciting and vaguely unreal, like a man coming back from the dead. I stayed for about ten minutes there, then wandered around for a while and came home.

Monday 9 September
The Post Office telephone engineer came to the house this morning to discuss our new telephone system and I think there is one which will exactly meet our needs. Just after that, a man came and demonstrated the Ansafone. This is a tape recorder that answers the phone, repeats a recorded message, records an answer and signs off. Not only would it mean that the house was manned telephonically while I was out or away, but would also mean that I can monitor incoming calls to decide whether it's necessary to phone them back.

Saturday 21 September
Tony Crosland came in for a drink – self-invited. Susan is in Baltimore and we had a talk about George Brown and the state of the Party and our prospects – personal prospects – of office. He is busy preparing himself and I think would make an excellent Minister. We are very old friends now and although we don't agree about certain fundamental things I greatly enjoy talking to him, and after all these years it would be hard to have a serious cleavage.

Thursday 26 September
The Denning Report on the security aspect of the Profumo case was published this morning and is creating a storm. The confusion at the top is very evident. Denning skates over the other scurrilous scandals that have been circulating.

Caught the 1 o'clock train to Scarborough with Peter Shore, Barbara Castle and Tom Driberg. We stayed at the Royal Hotel and a whole flood of hideous memories of 1960 – when we had the nuclear disarmament clash – came back. What a ghastly Conference that was and how different this one is going to be!

Sunday 6 October
The boys are frantically tunnelling in the garden, following a film they saw about POWs escaping during the war. They are way under the concrete path and will be in the next garden unless stopped. It is a beautifully concealed tunnel with a wooden top covered with mud and can already hold two full-sized people. Joshua gives it away by removing the lid and disappearing himself when the other boys aren't there.

Thursday 10 October
Home to hear the news of Macmillan's decision to resign. At 9.30 Robin Day phoned from the Tory Conference in Blackpool to tell me that Hailsham had just announced his intention to renounce his peerage and could I let him have a quote that he could throw at Hailsham in a TV interview later that evening. I gave him one: 'It is a sad comment on Lord Hailsham's respect for the House of Commons that he is only prepared to give up his hereditary privileges when he stands to gain something from it personally.' Robin put this to Hailsham and I'd hoped he would explode but he is so determined to keep a grip on himself that he gave a pompous reply about 'my great sacrifice'. David Butler phoned to tell me that the Tories were so busy committing themselves to one or other candidate that when the choice was made it would tear them apart. Macmillan could hardly have done them a worse turn and there simply is no machinery for settling the leadership.

Monday 14 October
The correspondence in *The Times* is now well under way and it looks as if Lord Home may be the accepted third choice, able to unite the Butlerites and the Hailshamites. He will, however, be a dud when it comes to exciting the electorate and Wilson will run rings round him. The only men I fear – Macleod and Maudling – are both out of the race.

Friday 18 October
Macmillan resigned this morning and Home was asked to form a government. It is incredible that such a thing should have happened. From the Labour Party's point of view he is much less dangerous than Maudling but I am disturbed that my battle should have paved the way for a Conservative peer to come back to the Commons as PM.

Tuesday 12 November
To the Commons this morning where Parliament was opened for the new session. As the Queen is pregnant it was done by a commission – the Lord Chancellor read the Queen's Speech from the Throne – and I didn't bother to go along and hear it. In fact it is an Election manifesto and very thin in substance.

Friday 22 November
Just as I was leaving home to speak in Acton the phone rang and Hilary answered it and it was one of his friends. When he rang off he said that Kennedy had been shot and I didn't believe it. But we switched on the television and there was a flash saying that he was critically ill in Dallas. I drove to Acton and heard the 7.30 bulletin, just before going in to the meeting, which announced that Kennedy had died. It was the most stunning

blow and at the beginning of the meeting we all stood in silence for a moment in tribute.

I dashed home to watch TV and hear the details. George Brown was drunk when he was interviewed but everyone else who spoke was sensitive and touched and it was a most moving evening.

Saturday 23 November
Kennedy's death blotted out all other news and we watched a film transmitted via Telstar during the night. Melissa and Joshua drew the most wonderful pictures of what they had seen and it helped to get it out of their system.

This afternoon I took Hilary and his friends to a birthday treat to see *55 Days at Peking*. Caroline and I went to the Shores this evening. I heard from TV producer Jeremy Isaacs what happened when George Brown was on TV last night. He was so tight that he nearly got in a fight with someone else who had also come to pay tribute to Kennedy and they almost had to be separated. He is a complete disgrace and one day it will all blow up. One almost wishes it was more obvious so that Harold would have Party backing for removing him.

Sunday 24 November
Worked all afternoon and most of the evening. The papers are still full of Kennedy and today Lee Harvey Oswald, his alleged assassin, was shot while in police custody. The whole thing is so fishy and the shame of the Dallas police is complete.

Wednesday 27 November
Back to the House and worked on a speech on the Commonwealth Immigration Act. The debate lasted for just over three hours and although the Whips passed round a note asking us not to speak I was so provoked by Cyril Osborne and his racial venom that I launched into him. In fact, we were only defeated by fifty votes, which was very good.

Thursday 28 November
Looked in at the Party meeting, where George Brown made a brief statement apologising for his tribute to Kennedy last week. It was acutely embarrassing and there was no comment, nor even grunts of sympathy from MPs there.

Saturday 30 November
Home, preparing for a party. About thirty-five people came, including the Ungoed-Thomases, the Youngers, Anthony Sampson and Ivan Yates, Dave and June, Crosland and Susan Catling, Bryan Magee, Freddie Ayer

and Dee Wells, Jan Le Witt, Michael Flanders, Donald and Janet Swann, John Gross, Robin Day and Katherine Ainsley, and the Labovitches.

It went well though there was a tremendous row before the party broke up at 3 am about George Brown. Tony Crosland thought this was a left-wing plot to ditch George and it was all malicious and unnecessary. Unfortunately it is not as simple as that.

Tuesday 3 December
To see Harold Wilson at 6 o'clock at his request. Caroline had said some time ago that she thought Harold was anxious for people to advise him on what he should do and that I should think some things out in case I was summoned. In fact this was exactly what he wanted and I had some points ready. The Labour campaign has lost its impetus and must be begin again in the New Year, with a series of meetings that Harold is to address. I suggested that he anticipate our Election manifesto with one major keynote speech in which he outlines the programme of a Labour government. This programme must have a specific name like the 'New Britain' programme – an idea Caroline had suggested – comparable to Kennedy's 'New Frontier'.

Harold more or less asked me to become his principal speech writer and personal adviser. He said we should meet regularly to talk and I could consult with others like Peter Shore and Ted Willis in order to prepare and polish phrases for this great speech and others. I asked about using Dick Crossman but he said that Dick was 'going through one of his moods', which suggests there might be a slight estrangement there.

As I left he told me to keep up on transport, which suggests that I am going to get that, which is a most difficult job, posing problems that no Labour government can actually solve within five years. I would much rather be out of the Cabinet and in New York doing the UN job.

Friday 17 January 1964
To Kingswood Youth Club, Bristol. About sixty youngsters were there and I don't think most of them wanted to listen to me at all, but the vicar had invited me and they sat there while I talked. As soon as I had finished and the questions had stopped, they leapt up and got on with their dancing and I was sorry I had accepted. I sometimes wonder whether it is true that young people are supporting us. They were so defeatist about Britain and thought that nothing could be done to improve things.

Thursday 23 January
When I was in Wilson's room today, Marcia came in to say that Robert Carvel of the *Evening Standard* was on the telephone to enquire whether Harold had any speech writers. Harold said, 'No. I am working on a speech now, every word of which I have dictated.' Marcia looked at me and asked if

I minded. I said, 'Of course not.' The last thing I want is to be known as Harold's speech writer and I think it is the last thing he wants too.

Tuesday 25 February
To the Soviet Embassy for a farewell party for Romanov, the Minister-Counsellor. We chatted to Mr Ossipov who is the *Izvestia* correspondent. He was very critical of Wilson and I described Wilson's background and achievements as Leader of the Party. We ended with Trofimenko, who is the Radio Moscow correspondent in London. Harold Wilson had turned up at the party, which was decent of him as he is just leaving for America. He and Romanov have known each other for a long time. The Russians all think there will be no change when a Labour government is elected and indeed some of them are quite naïvely sympathetic to Home. This is partly because their philosophy doesn't allow them to admit that there is much difference between parties in a bourgeois state and partly because they would like the Labour Party to be much more specific about Anglo-Soviet relations and can't understand why we are not.

Saturday 29 February
Surgery in Bristol this morning and eleven people came with a host of problems. I have never known my constituency work heavier. About a hundred letters a week coming in and about two hundred a week having to be written.

Wednesday 4 March
To the Commons this afternoon and saw Harold Wilson with Peter Shore about Harold's speech in Liverpool this Saturday. He has just come back from America where he had got on excellently with President Johnson. I think they are both highly political animals and understood each other well. He was very worried about the report that had appeared concerning his alleged proposals to hand the Navy over to the United Nations. For my part I found it a very exciting idea and was rather sorry to see him backtracking so fast.

Thursday 19 March
Bought a second-hand photocopier this morning. It is the most fabulous machine and when I have got over using it as a toy I think it will be very handy. Caroline and I went shopping this afternoon and went for a meal.

Tuesday 14 April
Barbara Castle confided in me last night that she had grave reservations about Harold, and I have myself. He just doesn't like a showdown and yet until a political leader is prepared to fight a stand-up battle with his colleagues for the things in which he believes he can't be tempered by the

fires of controversy and win the dominance and respect he must have to lead.

Sunday 3 May
To Bristol this afternoon for May Day and back in the train with Jim Callaghan. Jim commented on Harold's technique of leading the Party by means of a succession of bilateral interviews – resisting committee discussions and not keeping people informed about where they stand. Jim thought this might make for admiration while it succeeded but would fail to build personal loyalty on which to rely in bad days. He thinks he himself will last about two years as Chancellor and is worried about the enormous bill he will have to meet. He told me he thought Frank Cousins would come in as Minister of Transport and asked me what office I would like. I said, 'The UN or the Post Office.'

Monday 11 May
To lunch today with Denis Healey in Highgate. It was for Mr Walter Lippman, the distinguished American commentator, and his wife, and George Thomson, Chris Mayhew and Roy Jenkins were also there. We had a long discussion which ranged round the situation in Vietnam. Afterwards I went up to see Karl Marx's grave in Highgate cemetery with the Lippmans and Roy.

Saturday and Sunday, 16–17 May
We spent three days at Stansgate. The sun was hot and bright all the time. I didn't do a hand's turn of work, just sat on the grass or on the beach, with the children playing about. They love the place.

Tuesday 9 June
To the Transport Committee joint meeting with the Science Group to hear Mr Duckworth, the managing director of NRDC, Mr Hennessy, his deputy, and Mr Kennington, the chief engineer of Hovercraft Development Ltd, describing their plan for the tracked Hovercraft as a means of 300-mile-per-hour inter-city transport, which offers higher speed, lower passenger costs, lower track costs, and lower fares than any other form of transport. It was an impressive presentation. It may be that this is the right way of tackling the London Airport link instead of monorail.

Wednesday 10 June
To the House of Commons this afternoon and took part in the debate on the Finance Bill on the fuel tax for public-service vehicles. It gave me an opportunity to make quite a serious speech about the need for developing public transport and the way in which we had to achieve a steady shift from private to rented vehicles.

Sunday 14 June
Hyde Park Corner to join the head of the procession to march to Trafalgar
Square about the Rivonia trial. Nelson Mandela has been sentenced to life
imprisonment with others. Most of the banners there seemed to be for the
Committee of 100 and the London Anarchists and the Trots and others.
That's the trouble about these demonstrations; they are always taken over
by those who are keenest. Anyway we marched to Trafalgar Square and I
took the chair. Among those who spoke were Bertrand Russell, the Bishop of
Woolwich, Elwyn Jones, Fenner Brockway, David Ennals, Angus Wilson
the author, Andrew Faulds, and someone called First, who had been the
editor of a magazine in South Africa. There were two or three thousand
people there and we collected £300 from them. Afterwards a few of us
marched to Number 10 and handed in a letter to the Prime Minister.

Wednesday 24 June
Up at 5 and worked until breakfast. Arriving at Transport House this
morning for the National Executive meeting, I heard a lot of chanting and
shouting and saw a number of people with placards outside the building. It
was a demonstration laid on because of the suspension of the Streatham
Young Socialists. I don't know how many of them had been whipped up by
the Socialist Labour League and its leader Gerry Healy. The place was
crawling with police. We did expel two Young Socialists and there was no
discussion of this at all. I would certainly have raised it but for the
demonstration.

    The only other thing of interest this morning was that we approved the
Ombudsman proposal, which I think is very important indeed.

Saturday 27 June
A lovely hot day and the family was in the garden most of the time. I spent
the afternoon working to get the basement kitchen organised. Caroline went
to the hospital to see June and her new baby, Frances. Every few minutes the
phone seems to ring with another American who's in town and hopes to see
us. We have almost got to the point of taking the telephone off the hook.

Tuesday 30 June
This evening Tam Dalyell and I wandered round the House of Lords' end of
the building to find out just what accommodation was available there if the
Commons were to take it over. We walked along deserted corridors, looking
in offices and making a note of the accommodation. We stumbled on the
Civil Defence Room and found on the wall huge charts showing the rooms
on each floor and roughly specifying their purpose. We were going to copy
them all down but it would have been too big a job. What is needed is a
photograph of them or to go along with a tape recorder and read off all the
names on to a machine. At one stage we were stopped by a policeman who

sent us away. Then we met a custodian – Mr Wilkinson, who used to be a dustman at Grosvenor Road when I was a child – and he took us and showed us many other rooms. I have arranged to go and see the whole palace one night with him. What is required is a blazing attack on the whole system.

Thursday 2 July
A huge row has developed about my nocturnal prowlings with Tam Dalyell around the Lords. The Lord Great Chamberlain wrote to the Serjeant-at-Arms and it was reported to Bowden, who went to see Harold. Harold said that we should apologise to the Lord Great Chamberlain. Bowden asked us to do so. Tam and I refused. We are circulating a motion as follows:

Control of the Palace of Westminster
That an humble address be presented to Her Majesty praying that the control of the Royal Palace of Westminster be transferred to a House of Commons Commission under the chairmanship of Mr Speaker; and to amend the powers of the Lord Great Chamberlain accordingly.

We plan to make this into a backbench revolt on 13 July, when accommodation is discussed. Harold takes no interest in this point and has got to be forced to realise that it is a live issue.

To the BBC this evening to do the debate with Eden. It was the usual predigested spot-timed cockfight.

Monday 13 July
This afternoon Dick Crossman went to see Harold and he told Dick that he was going to make me Postmaster-General, give me a chance there for eighteen months and then to the Ministry of Transport. I have no idea whether this is true or not (not Dick's story, of course, but Harold's intention). If it is, I don't think there's much point in sweating my guts out on transport policy between now and the Election. I'll borrow a book on the Post Office and take it on holiday instead. It would be a most interesting job to have and if I got it it would be attributable entirely to the memorandum I wrote to Harold last October. Such are the uncertainties of politics. But it is the first time that it has even been indicated officially that I am going to get anything.

Thursday 16 July
To the Commons and started looking through all the books on the Post Office. Most of the histories were written in the last century or the 1920s. It confirms my impression that the GPO has not (except possibly when Marples was PMG) been an up-to-date, go-ahead organisation.

Friday 17 July

Caroline and I went to Durham and attended the pre-Gala dinner. Also there were Harold Wilson, Frank Cousins, Will Paynter, Sam Watson and others.

At dinner I could hear Sam asking Harold who would be doing what in the Labour Government and I could just hear Harold giving some names. Afterwards when I was alone Harold came up to me and said, 'Tony, I thought it would be helpful if you knew that I want you to be Postmaster-General in the Government.'

I wasn't, of course, at all surprised, since Dick had told me this on Monday. It is a job I would very much like to have, but seemingly Harold thought I would be very disappointed at not being Minister of Transport to which I could reasonably lay some claim and which had confidently been expected by all the papers predicting the Government he would set up. He also knew that it was not a Cabinet job and therefore went out of his way to repeat what he had said before to me, that this was only for eighteen months. 'My real Cabinet will be made in 1966 – just as Clem's was made in 1947,' he said.

He told me that Frank Cousins would be Minister of Transport and he also told me the names of a number of other appointments. Frank Soskice for the Home Office (if he lives), Tony Greenwood for the Colonies, Sir Hugh Foot (with a peerage) to the UN, Gerald Gardiner on the Woolsack, Peggy Herbison at Pensions, Barbara Castle (in the Cabinet) at Overseas Aid.

I asked about the Assistant Postmaster General and he said that it would be Joe Slater, his PPS, who is very nice. Roy Mason is to go as Minister of State shared between Dick Crossman at Education and Science and the Minister of Labour to deal with retraining. Dick's other Ministers are to be Reg Prentice for schools and Lord Bowden for universities.

Harold stressed that I would be the only one of the newcomers to be head of a department, ie a departmental Minister of Cabinet rank, though outside the Cabinet, and that he thought that would be extremely important with University of the Air to launch and the Giro system to introduce. I reminded him that I had sent him a memo on the Post Office last November and he said he remembered it but had intended this earlier. 'I had thought of you doing a Bill Deedes – PRO for the Government – but decided against it.' I told him I was very glad he had as it is a job I would hate.

Wednesday 22 July

Caroline, Melissa and Joshua came to the House of Commons for tea on the terrace today. Afterwards they all went into the House of Commons just as Churchill was leaving the debate. It will be quite a thing for them to be able to say that they actually saw Churchill. If they live to be ninety – his age –

they will be saying in 2040 that they remember seeing a man who was elected to Parliament 150 years before.

This evening to Broadcasting House to help Denis Healey do a party political broadcast on Labour defence policy.

Friday 31 July – Saturday 1 August
To celebrate the beginning of the holiday I slept in the garden with Stephen and Hilary and we ate sausages and had a hurricane lamp. Tommy Balogh phoned. Ian Grimble came for lunch. The trouble is you can't cut the phone off. Started work on sticking in the family snapshots since 1959.

Monday 10 August
To Transport House this afternoon to see the set which has been prepared for the Election broadcasts. Then to the House of Commons to see Harold Wilson, who had flown back from the Scilly Isles today in view of the serious crises in Vietnam and Cyprus. He looked fit and well. We are saying nothing about Cyprus because there is nothing to be said, and on Vietnam we are terrified of saying anything that might upset the Americans. The British Government needs American support against Sukarno, who is attacking Malaysia and Wilson is particularly anxious not to upset Johnson at this stage. That is the way politics go.

Thursday 10 September
Valerie worked all day on Election preparations. She is checking through the list of Party members that I had, to see if they are still on the register and to put in Christian names and correct addresses. Meanwhile I have prepared a pile of material to go to them. The first is a letter telling them how important the campaign is and this is accompanied by the fact-sheet on conditions in Bristol, and a summary of the Election manifesto. Also going in is a Help card addressed to me for return and an excellent card on my advice service.

Tuesday 15 September
Worked in the office this morning. The first edition of the new *Sun* newspaper was published today – after a huge press and advertising ballyhoo build-up. It is appalling. It is slightly bigger than the *Herald* but basically the same – minus the limited *Herald* political content. It is a pale wishy-washy imitation of the *Daily Mail* and I don't honestly see how it can survive as a daily. It is the product of market research, without any inner strength and message. There is little hard news – pages of fluffy features and nothing hard to bite on. I am afraid that it may not be as much of a help to us between now and polling day as we had hoped.

To Bristol this afternoon and had a surgery and then went back to Unity House to discuss the Election plans with Herbert Rogers. The fact is that he has been able to do practically nothing and all the work on the Election which is being done in London by Valerie is going to be essential.

This afternoon the Prime Minister announced the date of the Election: which is to be Thursday 15 October, as we had all anticipated for so long.

This evening Peter Shore limped to Stepney again and was adopted as the candidate. I am delighted. Even though he is clearly a sick man and will need at least a month's complete rest he will be an MP at the end of it, whatever he does.

Wednesday 23 September
Harold Wilson phoned at 10.30 pm last night – and I was in bed – to say that my press release had been on the news and how effective it had been. He has never rung me at home and I have no doubt that he did it because I had been to complain yesterday about the broadcasting position, and he wanted to keep me sweet.

Dick and Tommy and I have to pretend we don't exist. Kennedy never minded it being known that he had speech writers and advisers, but Harold does. It's very silly but I know that my capacity to influence him depends upon total self-erasure. Dick finds this unbearable and is always leaking how central he is.

To see Harold at 11 and went over his future speeches. He couldn't have been more friendly.

Monday 5 October
To Lime Grove for the preparation of the Labour Party Election broadcast. It was an incredible afternoon. Dick Crossman, Michael Stewart and Kenneth Robinson were the principal participants. Shirley Williams was to link it. Everything went wrong and we had to reshoot many of the bits twice and even three times. Michael and Kenneth were delightful but Dick Crossman got into a tremendous temper and stamped up and down, shouting and swearing at everybody for having been kept waiting. He really is the most appalling prima donna. After he had recorded his piece he apologised, and then stayed for a drink and by the time he finally left, at 7.45, he had resumed his aggressive posture.

I went to Television Centre to be there while the editing took place and was then told that they had not had time to make the cuts and joins required and that it was quite possible that the film would break down. At 9.15 I returned to Lime Grove, was put in the set which was lighted and the whole crew was standing by. I had to watch the programme on a monitor and if at any point it broke, the camera was to come to me and I had to carry on as best I could until they could find a part of the tape which was good, in which case I was to hand back to it. It was the most appalling sweat and strain sitting there watching, expecting a break at any moment. In the event, one didn't happen and I got back home at about 10 o'clock, really washed out.

Friday 16 October

The result was declared about 1.15 and I had a majority of 9,800 – 4,000 better than last time. There were quite a few people in the street for the declaration and then we were towed in the traditional way, sitting on top of our car up to the Walter Baker Hall. After that we went to BBC Bristol for a television insert into the results programme. Then on to the TWW interview, followed by a radio interview and finally got to bed about 4.30. It is clear that Labour is winning.

Up at 8 and drove home listening to the results programme on the radio all the way. Lunch at London Airport and home by 2.30. There is an overall Labour majority of four only. Home has resigned the premiership and Harold Wilson has formed a government. We've waited thirteen years for this.

4

1964–66

Sunday 18 October

One of the oldest jokes in politics is about hopeful candidates for office who stay by their telephones when a new government is formed, just like husbands waiting for their wives to have their first babies. For both it's awful.

The TV and news bulletins kept describing people who were turning up at Number 10 and I was getting gloomier and gloomier and planning a completely new life. Then at 4.45 Number 10 phoned. Would I stand by for tonight or tomorrow morning. It was a great relief. I worked till about 2 am, reading all the Post Office stuff that I had collected and just couldn't go to sleep.

Monday 19 October

Up early and still waiting for the phone and still hearing of other people going down to Downing Street. I had completely given up hope again. Then at 10.55 am the phone rang and I was summoned.

There was a huge crowd of photographers outside and inside Bob Mellish and Lord Bowden were waiting. Finally I went in and there was Harold looking extremely relaxed. I shook him by the hand and we had a chat about the general situation and then he said, 'By the way, I want you to take the Post Office. I am giving you Joe Slater as Assistant PMG. Then in about eighteen months time I shall be reshuffling the Government and you will be in the Cabinet.'

Then he beckoned me over to the window, and pointed into the garden of No. 11. 'Look at that. It's the last of Reggie Maudling's luggage going,' he said with schoolboy enthusiasm. He told me he didn't know yet whether PMGs were Privy Councillors but that I would be one if it was customary.

I asked his Private Secretary to ring the Post Office and tell them I was coming. I told the press that all I could say was that I *hadn't* been made a peer. I then went to a call box and phoned Mother, came home and after lunch telephoned the Post Office and asked for the PMG's office. 'What's your name?' asked a gruff voice. I gave it and a few minutes later came a different and oily voice: 'Good afternoon, PMG. I think the DG wants to speak to you.' A minute later the Director-General came on the phone, said he had a lunch appointment and would come to see me at 3 o'clock. I said I would like a car to take me there immediately.

Wednesday 21 October

At 11.30 I had to go to the Privy Council Office for a rehearsal of the ceremony of admission into the Privy Council. We were greeted by the most awful stoogey-looking people, real Crown Office – House of Lords types. Among those there were Peggy Herbison, Kenneth Robinson, Roy Jenkins, Charlie Pannell and Elwyn Jones. I asked Elwyn if he was going to be knighted. He said yes, and I said, 'I'm sorry to hear it.'

We were summoned in one by one to the Queen's drawing room and she shook us by the hand. Then we stood in a row and the oath was administered to those who were swearing, whereas Kenneth Robinson, Charlie Pannell and I affirmed. I think they are atheists. I did it because I disapprove of a religious oath for any but religious purposes and because I wanted to pay a tribute to Charles Bradlaugh, who had fought four elections to establish this right.

We then went up to the Queen one after another, kneeling and picking up her hand and kissing it, and then bowing. I did the most miniature bow ever seen and returned to my line. When it was over she made a couple of remarks and we all walked by and shook hands. After that I had the oath of the Postmaster General administered to me. I left the Palace boiling with indignation and feeling that this was an attempt to impose tribal magic and personal loyalty on people whose real duty was only to their electors.

Thursday 22 October
Ron Smith, General Secretary of the Union of Post Office Workers, came to lunch.

We talked for nearly three hours, having lunched together in the staff cafeteria. I have met him once or twice but this was the first proper chance for a talk. He is a powerful man physically and temperamentally and one felt one was rubbing against granite. He wants me to meet the UPW Executive soon – with my wife – for lunch and an informal chat.

We had a completely informal discussion about pay and conditions. He said that the work conditions of postmen were very poor, especially in the older offices such as Mount Pleasant. All the capital investment had gone into telecommunications and the postal services were the Cinderella left to rot.

Friday 23 October
I am anxious to make some economies in the huge personal staff to offset the expenditure that the Office is going to incur in providing me with a dictating machine and modern office equipment.

I had a talk to my Private Secretary, Mr Tilling about this today and he told me that as we were in effect treated as a nationalised industry we were free from Treasury control and he was rather in favour of us organising ourselves along modern lines. There is no reason why the Post Office should be lumbering on using the techniques and filing systems of the Twenties. It is a modern communication industry and should reflect this in its practice.

I drafted a message to all Post Office staff which is to be circulated to them. This is really in the nature of an 'Order of the Day'. Tilling suggested toning it down slightly as he thought it too heady a draught of wine. I agreed. After three or four days I am getting to like Tilling. He comes from a Post Office family – like so many people who work here – is free from the usual Civil Service rubbish and has a very dry sense of humour. His caution is also a good thing in damping down my over-enthusiasm.

Saturday 24 October
Began sorting out all the papers in my office. I intend to bombard each department with a barrage of minutes and requests and questions and see how things work. I must also begin to do some serious basic thinking about major fields of policy – like broadcasting – for which I am responsible. Meanwhile I must somehow try to clear the tons of mail which are waiting for me to handle.

Saturday 31 October

Caroline and I went to Bristol this morning and Mr Tilling came with us on the train. In Bristol we were met by the Regional Director, Mr Scott, and spent the morning with him and his staff. At the end of this talk, after hearing all his problems, I asked Mr Scott, 'What would you like me, as Postmaster-General, to do?' 'Frankly, Minister, sit quiet,' he said. For about two weeks this has been hinted at broadly to me by all the people with whom I've come in contact and now at least someone has had the guts to say it out loud. It was a significant comment.

Wednesday 4 November

After a quick lunch I went to the Post Office for a meeting with the staff associations. This was instead of the sherry party which is traditionally held by an incoming Postmaster-General. I had written them all a letter explaining that I preferred to have a working meeting over a cup of tea. I gave them all a copy of our manifesto, 'The New Britain'. I told them I have presented each director in the Post Office with it as well and the meeting almost broke up with astonishment and suppressed laughter. But the reason for it is obvious and it was right to have done it.

Monday 16 November

To the Office, where I found an invitation waiting for me to a sherry party at Buckingham Palace. This is what I have been dreading and I have now got to find some way of establishing from the outset that I don't have to go.

Harold Wilson had asked me to lunch with him at the Commons. I think he had heard from Marcia, George Wigg and Tommy Balogh that I was feeling a bit lonely and we had an hour together which allowed me to talk to him about what I was doing. His Private Secretary had queried the reports that I had decided to ban cigarette advertising and I told Harold this was pure speculation. He is not against it and was only keen that I should follow normal procedures.

I came home to change and Caroline and I went to the Lord Mayor's banquet. It was a scene of splendid pageantry. Everyone is expected to wear a white tie but I went in a black one. The only other person in a black tie was George Brown and it established a warm bond of sympathy between us.

Before dinner Mountbatten came up and I had a long talk to him. It was the first time I had ever spoken to him and he spent the whole time name-dropping. His conversation consisted of a long list of well-known people whom he described by their nicknames and claimed to know very well. For the uncle of the Queen and an earl and Admiral of the Fleet, it was astonishing that he wanted to impress.

After that we went in to dinner and sat between Lord Chief Justice Parker and the President of the Admiralty, Probate and Divorce Division, and opposite a former Lord Mayor and Cecil King. Lady Parker, who was on my left, is an American woman from Kentucky. During the Archbishop of Canterbury's speech she wrote me a note on the back of her menu, 'When you are Prime Minister will you decree that there shall only be two speeches? I cannot bear another archbishop.' I wrote back underneath, 'By that time, you will need every archbishop you can lay your hands on.' She laughed – and handed it to the Lord Chief Justice.

Cecil King was completely lumpen and defeatist about the *Sun* and when we both tried to persuade him that its role was to criticise the Labour Government from the left, I don't think he understood what we meant.

As we left dinner, some City bigwig shouted, 'Why aren't you properly dressed?' I didn't hear him but he caught Caroline by the arm and repeated it to her. She was extremely angry. I had the opportunity for a word with the Lord Provost of Glasgow about the Post Office Savings Bank move.

Saturday 5 December
Surgery in Bristol this morning and home by late lunch. The telephone answering machine is an absolute Godsend. I sit in the office and hear the thing ringing and ringing and then the machine answers and the telephone stops. Without changing my number it gives me exactly the privacy that I need. I suppose one could just not answer the phone and it would have the same effect.

Monday 7 December
At the Post Office this morning an MI5 man came along to interview me about a political adviser who has given me as a reference for the positive-vetting procedure in order to work at Number 10. The chap was a real pudgy flatfoot police type, and very friendly. But it is an odious business being asked to answer personal questions about someone such as drinking habits, sexual deviations and private life.

I had the first of my informal lunch meetings with thirteen people from the Building, Welfare and Transport departments. They sat round my table drinking beer and eating sandwiches and apples like a lot of middle-aged bankers on a church outing. There was not a spark of enthusiasm, imagination or excitement of any kind to be seen. I am really talent-spotting and even a person of average intelligence would shine out of that sort of group.

To the Commons and Sir John Macpherson, the chairman of Cable & Wireless, came to see me. He is a retired colonial official and his company is progressively being squeezed out all over the world. He brightened visibly when I said that I thought perhaps he might be the instrument by which Britain sold satellite tracking stations round the world. But the DG was there with a million reasons why it couldn't be done. I have been PMG for seven weeks now and not a single bright idea has come up from below. It's like trying to resuscitate a dying elephant – tiring and almost hopeless.

Stayed at the Commons till 1 am working, voting and talking to the Serjeant-at-Arms about Commons postal, messenger and telephone services.

Monday 21 December
This afternoon we had the private office party with experimental colour TV laid on by the BBC and it went well.

This evening to the Commons to vote for the abolition of capital punishment – which was carried overwhelmingly. At last the gallows have gone.

Wednesday 30 December
I received a royal warrant giving me a quarter of a doe, shot in Windsor Great Park – one of the perks of Ministers. The only question is, what to do with it?

I did score one success today which gives me great pleasure. My scheme for using every post office as a mini art gallery has not presented the insuperable difficulties I expected and we are going ahead. It means that possibly 2,000 post offices will have pictures on display as a result of co-operation between curators of local museums and Head Postmasters. This is Arnold Wesker's dream – or part of it – coming about.

Thursday 14 January 1965
Defence, colour television, Concorde, rocket development – these are all issues raising economic considerations that reveal this country's basic inability to stay in the big league. We just can't afford it. The real choice is, do we go in with Europe or do we become an American satellite? Without a conscious decision being taken the latter course is being followed everywhere. For personal reasons, I would see much attraction in an English-speaking federation, bringing in Canada, Australia, New Zealand and Britain to a greater United States. But this is a pipe dream and in reality the choice lies between Britain as an island and a US protectorate, or Britain as a full member of the Six, followed by a wider European federation. I was always against the Common Market but the reality of our isolation is being borne in on me all the time. This country is so decrepit and hidebound that only activities in a wider sphere can help us to escape from the myths that surround our politics. I do not know yet what the answer is but I do know that the questions cannot be dodged.

Friday 15 January
To Bristol for an executive. There was a storm of criticism, both personal and political. On the personal level they complained that I had neglected the constituency since the Election, had sent the thank-you letters out late, had not sent them Christmas cards, and even that I didn't write to everyone who

was married or promoted, in the way that some Tory MPs do using the local press to keep them informed.

This was followed by an outcry of political protest. I could understand their terrific anxieties about the aircraft industry, which could acutely affect Bristol. But it was broadened out into a general attack on the bank rate, rising income tax, foreign policy and the lot. They are unaware of the critical economic situation, or of the achievements of the 100 days and emerged as a most short-sighted group. There must be much more political education and active campaigning. All in all, a discouraging meeting. My faith in democracy was a bit shattered.

Churchill is gravely ill and it looks like the end.

Tuesday 19 January
To the House of Commons this afternoon, where everybody was waiting to hear news of Churchill's illness. All major government policy statements have been postponed, the Prime Minister having cancelled his visit to Bonn. The crude fact is that everybody is waiting for the old man to die. Parliament will probably have to adjourn for five days when he does, since we can hardly meet while his body is lying in state in Westminster Hall. Yet he may well drag on for days, weeks or months. It is macabre and grisly.

Thursday 21 January
At midnight after we were both asleep, Peter Shore rang up to tell us the appalling news that Patrick Gordon Walker had been defeated in the Leyton by-election by 200 votes. This is a terrible shock to the Government and reduces our majority to three. It poses immediate problems for Harold. What is to be done with Patrick? He cannot be made a peer as Foreign Secretary, he can hardly be exposed to another by-election, and he cannot be left any longer as Foreign Secretary without being in Parliament.

My own feeling is that Gordon Walker's defeat is partly attributable to the crude manipulation of the honours list in order to make room for him. Quintin Hogg had a similarly humiliating result in his 1963 by-election. People who have elected a Member of Parliament whom they know and trust cannot like it much if he is bought off with a peerage so that the Prime Minister can impose upon the constituency someone else of his choice for reasons of his own. I put this to Peter Shore and it had never occurred to him that this might be the case.

Friday 22 January
The press this morning blew up the Leyton defeat – inevitably – as the Waterloo of the 100 days. There were urgent talks at Number 10 all day as a result of which Michael Stewart was moved to the Foreign Office and Tony Crosland to the Ministry of Education. I'm sorry that Michael has moved from a more important to a less important job and particularly that he has

given up education, where he was an anchor man who knew what he wanted. Also I have some doubts about Tony who has a middle-class obsession with the public-schools issue and may be weak on the comprehensives, behind-hand on the real issue of streaming versus non-streaming and too keen on extending the direct grant idea.

Sunday 24 January
Winston Churchill died this morning. I heard it on the news at 8.45. Thus ends the life of one of the greatest Englishmen of our time. Our family have much cause to be grateful to him. He it was who gave Father his extra twenty years of active life in the House of Lords. Also he was one of those who supported me so much during my long constitutional struggle and that support was of great practical value. Even with the many years of waiting for this moment it is nonetheless a shock.

The effect of all this is to put politics into cold storage for a week.

Monday 25 January
I had decided to write to Harold to get his general consent about a Churchill stamp and was told that his main anxiety was whether the Queen would agree to share a stamp with the face of Sir Winston. It's perfectly obvious that far from being able to get the Queen off the stamps, I'm going to fight like a tiger in order to get the right to put some other faces on. However, I happened to see him later this evening and I told him that the design would have to be approved by the Palace in any case and then he gave me the go-ahead. I suspect that the network has been feeding information to him to suggest that I want to get the Queen off the stamps and this has been reported tactfully to him.

Afterwards Caroline and I had dinner at St Stephen's Restaurant and as we looked out of the window we saw the coffin of Sir Winston being brought in and carried on the shoulders of the pallbearers to the catafalque in Westminster Hall where it is to lie in state tomorrow, Thursday and Friday.

Wednesday 27 January
Went to Westminster Hall to see the lying-in-state.

This afternoon I went to see the Attorney-General about the pirate-broadcasting Bill. Most of the discussion was about the title of the Bill, which is currently called the 'Suppression of Marine etc. Broadcasting Bill'. It is a massive document creating dozens of new offences, all designed to strangle the pirates. I have the greatest doubt as to whether it will be effective and the Government have no time to introduce it in this session. It is obvious that before this is done, an alternative of our own will have to be put forward. The pirates are establishing themselves firmly in public favour and if we killed them it would be extremely unpopular. I can see ourselves moving steadily towards the starvation of the BBC through a failure to raise the licence fee and ultimately capitulation in favour of commercial sound broadcasting. That is unless we permit the expansion of broadcasting on the basis of public service with advertising revenue to finance it.

Afterwards I took all the children to see the lying-in-state. They were much impressed except for Joshua, aged seven, who thought we were going to 'Lyons Steak' which he believed to be a restaurant. He declared that he was delighted as he was very fond of steaks. When he saw Westminster Hall he couldn't understand and said he knew there was a coffin under the flag, but he clearly didn't know what a coffin was or what it contained. The thing that made the biggest impression on him was the sight of the television cameras.

Monday 15 February
David Gentleman came to see me for breakfast this morning. He's about my age and is undoubtedly one of the best – if not the best – stamp designers in this country. He wanted to stress that it was impossible to get a decent quality of stamps in this country until the Queen's head was removed. We discussed it at great length and he had brought along an album of foreign stamps showing what was possible if the designer had a completely free hand.

Friday 19 February
I went to Number 10 with the car to bring Harold's personal secretaries Marcia Williams and Brenda Dew over to the Post Office for lunch. Joe Slater and I took them to the canteen and when he left for his train north they stayed for an hour's talk with me in my room. We discussed the network at great length. They hate Derek Mitchell, who is Harold's principal Civil Service secretary. We discussed in detail how these men operate, why their loyalty is to each other rather than to the Government, the techniques they use for evaluating the standing of Ministers and their power to undermine them and influence events. I mentioned the stamp business and the BBC lobby as examples. Marcia and Brenda are very nice and Harold leans heavily on them. No doubt there was a buzz of conversation in the Office to find out exactly why I had had the Prime Minister's personal secretaries to lunch and what we were talking about.

We discussed the honours list and I said what I had thought about it. They told me what a fantastic struggle Harold had had to get the footballer Stanley Matthews his knighthood. He is obviously in just as great difficulty as I am.

Thursday 25 February
I rang Marcia Williams at Number 10 and she told me that the Queen had readily agreed to give me an audience to discuss stamps, which is most encouraging.

To the Commons this afternoon and there was a deputation from the

Phonographic Society and the Musicians' Union brought by Brian O'Malley. They wanted to know how quickly I could kill pirates. Both are deeply affected. I told them that the legislative programme was congested and that there were political difficulties. We must have an alternative to propose.

I asked them to think hard about the problem of an alternative which would perhaps mean a national programme of light music made up of records and live orchestras, interspersed. This might be run by the BBC or possibly by a Post Office network called POP. It might be linked to local stations which could opt in and out of the network if their local resources were unable to fill the full day.

Wednesday 10 March

David Gentleman came to breakfast this morning at my request as today is the day that I am seeing the Queen about new stamps. He brought along the most beautiful designs for Battle of Britain stamps made up of silhouettes of RAF and Luftwaffe planes in combat, which could be sold in blocks of twelve. I didn't tell him I was going to see the Queen but I think he must have guessed it. He also brought along some models for Christmas cards and I shall take these into the Office and get them done.

Then to the House of Commons for an hour and at 12.20 to Buckingham Palace for my audience with the Queen. Yesterday I received a notification that the court was in mourning so I had to wear a black tie.

As my car arrived I was greeted by Sir Michael Adeane, the Queen's Private Secretary, and taken up in the lift to the private apartments. Adeane went out of his way to be friendly and was somewhat nervous of my arrival. He said, 'Don't you think our stamps need some new ideas?' and, 'There's a real danger we will get out of date, don't you think?' This was obviously designed to draw me out about the subject of my audience and also to suggest that the Palace was a great modernising influence. I nodded gravely, and agreed with him, and admired the view and looked at the paintings and then, at 12.40, one of the big flunkeys called out my name and I went in to the state apartment grasping a huge black official box, bowed, shook hands, the Queen beckoned me to sit down and I started on a carefully prepared speech.

I said that I was very grateful to her for seeing me as I knew the keen interest that she took in postage stamps. I said that I had some stamps for her approval but didn't want to worry her to approve them there and then. What I wanted to do was to talk about stamp design policy generally. I said that the new Government saw stamps in an entirely new context as part of the arts and not just as adhesive money labels for postage purposes. That was why we had set up a Fellowship in Minuscule Design and wanted to improve design generally. Miss Jennie Lee was greatly concerned, and the Prime Minister had kindly arranged this audience so that I could discuss it with the

Queen. There were many things about Britain that we ought to project abroad, perhaps through postage stamps.

Specifically we would like to have new definitives which would have a more beautiful picture of the Queen on them. She smiled graciously. On commemoratives, I said that we had broadened the criteria to many subjects that had previously been excluded and I thought this was the right technique. Also I said the designers were keen to produce pictorial stamps depicting perhaps our composers, our landscapes, our architecture, our painters, our kings and queens and this was a most exciting field that had never been explored.

'However,' I said, 'this raised the whole question of the use of the head on the stamps.' The Queen frowned and smiled. I said that there was a view held by many designers that the necessity of depicting the head on the stamp was restrictive and embarrassing. For example, the Burns stamp would be difficult to put out as a two-head stamp. Similarly, the United Nations stamp which the UN was trying to get issued all over the world in identical design would be excluded under our present rules. And even the Battle of Britain stamp might not be appropriate for a head. On the other hand, I added hastily, the Parliament stamp was absolutely right for the royal head and so of course was the Commonwealth Arts Festival and the 900th anniversary of the Abbey.

I said that the real difficulty was that, up to now, it had been understood in the Office that by the Queen's personal command stamps that did not embody the head could not even be submitted for consideration. I said this had led to a most unfortunate situation in which designers were full of new ideas but these were not allowed to be transmitted because it was generally thought that the Queen herself had refused to consider them. I said I didn't know whether this was true or not but it seemed to me the straightforward thing to do was to come along and ask whether this was as a result of a personal command of this kind. The Queen was clearly embarrassed and indicated that she had no personal feeling about it at all. I said I knew she wouldn't and that I knew this was all a misunderstanding but that it was rather ridiculous that there should be these lovely stamps available which she wasn't even allowed to see.

I thought in many cases the head would be right, but there were all sorts of other ways of doing it, such as embossing the head in white or having a silhouette, or a definitive stamp affixed to a commemorative or pictorial stamp, and that all I wanted – as I was not a designer or a philatelist – was the right to submit stamps of all kinds to her. She indicated that she had never seen any of these stamps and would be interested to see them. I said, 'Well, I've got some in my bag' (having brought David Gentleman's collection as provided this morning). The Queen wanted me to leave the new designs with her but I explained the difficulties and she agreed to see them on the spot.

This was exactly what I had hoped would happen so I unlocked my bag and spread out on the floor twelve huge design models of the stamps provided by Gentleman and also brought out his album of foreign stamps. I then knelt on the floor and one after the other passed up to the Queen the Battle of Britain stamps bearing the words 'Great Britain' and no royal head on them. It was a most hilarious scene because I had my papers all over the place and she was peering at something that had obviously never been shown to her or even thought about at the Palace before.

At the end I packed up and said I would take them away but that I was delighted to hear that she approved of a scheme under which we could submit things to her for her consideration. I said I hoped I might come back in a few weeks and that was the end of the audience. It had lasted about forty minutes instead of the expected fifteen.

As I was going out, Sir Michael Adeane – who I suppose might have been listening via a microphone during the audience – assured me that there had never been any indication whatsoever from the Palace that non-traditional stamps would not be acceptable. It was most amusing because of course it was quite untrue. But I said I was delighted to hear this and that now we could submit all sorts of designs. 'But I think the monarch's head has to be on the stamps, doesn't it?' he said. I replied that there was no rule about it but that it had always been done; but now that we could send in the new designs we could see where and when it was appropriate. He looked extremely uncomfortable.

So I went back to the House of Commons feeling absolutely on top of the world. The fact is the Palace is determined not to get into any controversy in which they might be seen to be responsible for holding back popular clamour for change. The real enemies of course are those forces of reaction – the Tory Party, the Civil Service, the Palace flunkies and courtiers – who use the Queen as a way of freezing out new ideas. No doubt she herself shares the views of the flunkies but the Crown has to be extremely careful. I had always suspected this was true but am now convinced that if you went to the Queen to get her consent to abolish the honours list altogether she would nod and say she'd never been keen on it herself and felt sure the time had come to put an end to it. Of course when you do that you have to be terribly charming and nice and I tried as hard as I could to do a little Disraeli on her with all the charm I could muster.

I went back to the Office and called the Director-General and Mr Wolverson in and told them about my visit to Number 10 and the Palace. They were a bit astonished I think that I had gone straight to the Queen and raised the question of the head with her.

To dinner with the Yugoslav Ambassador, Mr Prica, and his wife. Also there were Denis Healey, who told blue jokes throughout the whole of dinner, and George Thomson and one or two others.

Bed very late. It had been the best day since I took office with almost complete victory on the whole front. Now I must be sure to follow it up.

Thursday 25 March
At 10.30 this morning, Sir Kenneth Clark, Paul Reilly and James Fitton came to see me about stamp policy. I told them about my interview with the Queen and the new free policy for designers. They seemed excited by it and were not as critical as I had feared, but Sir Kenneth Clark said that George V had told him when he was a young man and first appointed to the Stamp Advisory Committee, 'Never let the sovereign's head come off the stamps.' Sir Kenneth had promised that he would not. At this stage I expected that he would announce his resignation. But he said that he felt that this pledge would be honoured provided they remained on the definitive stamps, which is perfectly agreeable to me. All in all it was a much more successful morning than I had expected.

Saturday 3 April
My fortieth birthday. The family came in early with gifts. Then we had tea this afternoon with Mother. It was a lovely day and we sat in the garden for a bit.

Friday 7 May
Tilling has been promoted to head of Organisation and Methods Branch and he wrote me this delightful assessment of my period as PMG to mark the occasion.

A new era was opened when Mr Anthony Wedgwood Benn became Postmaster General in October 1964. Mr Benn, young and forward-looking, was determined that the Post Office should become a science-based industry. He applied this principle not only to his department's services but also to his own post, and at the General Election in April 1969, the ancient office of Postmaster General was abolished and a 'Rapidec' Mark 999 computer was installed in Room G1 at Post Office Headquarters in St Martin's-le-Grand.

Meanwhile, the Post Office had undergone rapid expansion and change. Its capital investment rose to £ quinillions annually as its Headquarters, Regional Headquarters and local Telephone Area and Head Offices were all replaced by computers of increasing size and complexity. All the staff of these offices were retained as programmers, translating their previous work into binary code for the computers. Indeed, so great was the programming programme that the staff of the GPO had increased to over a million by 1 January 1984: 500,000 programmers and 500,000 engineers to tend the computers. All the staff had been transferred to the Central Organisation and Methods Branch on temporary promotion.

At their head was Sir Henry Tilling, GCB, who had been appointed head of the Central Organisation and Methods Branch soon after Mr Wedgwood Benn became Postmaster-General, and these revolutionary changes have been made under his baleful supervision. In an age dominated by machines, Sir Henry maintained the antiquated principle that machines existed to serve mankind, and, while he remained in office, the Post Office continued to serve the public's needs – unlike the rest of the public services which were run entirely for and by computers. Sir Henry, in his fortress in Stepney, retained not only these out-of-date principles but also old-fashioned habits which marked him as one of an earlier generation of administrators. He had his room heated by a coal fire and his tea served every afternoon from a silver teapot made 200 years before his birth. Needless to say, these unhygienic habits and his backward-looking, humanist-based policies caused resentment and discontent among his staff and the computers, and, when he eventually retired on 24 January, 1984, he was replaced by an Omniscient Mark 5 Computer.

By 1 February, 1985, there was a marked deterioration in the quality of the Post Office services, and with the collapse of the communications network in 1999, the world entered a new dark age, in which the darkness was more profound and prolonged than that which succeeded the fall of the Roman Empire.

Saturday 8 May
I wrote this verse today to celebrate Tilling's departure and promotion.

> A PMG's PS named Tilling
> To contemplate change was unwilling
> He'd detected decay
> Since Sir Brian Tuke's day
> And the future appeared to him chilling.
>
> The Department admiring this trait
> Picked him out for promotion one day
> Each new project he'd stop
> Brought him nearer the top
> Till as DG he had his own way.
>
> The savings in manpower he made
> Were a hundred per cent a decade
> He brought back the horse
> And the whole postal force

Were retired with their full pensions paid.

The most famous speech that he spoke
Was dismissed by the press as a joke
But ignoring their moans
He ripped out all the phones
And reverted to signals by smoke.

His achievements were legion I'm told
And historians now make so bold
As to claim he undid
Just to save a few quid
Innovations five hundred years old.

His knighthood he felt that he'd earned
By the millions of letters he'd burned
And he always did boast
That they played the 'Last Post'
On the day the PO Board adjourned.

His retirement to live in his den
Was marred by a fellow named Benn
For – still PMG –
He chuckled with glee
And built up the service again.

Wednesday 26 May

To the National Executive this morning, which was held at the House of
Commons. Only two things of interest came up. One was that the statement
on Vietnam which did nothing more than to explain the Government's
policy, including the reasons why we have supported the bombing of North
Vietnam by the Americans, which I found and find hard to take. Harold
explained the position and his general argument is of course that public
declarations are less effective than private pressure. I didn't feel it was the
time to say anything but I'm sure that a lot of people there, like myself, are
extremely unhappy about the way in which things are going.

Friday 28 May

To the *Daily Mirror* building to have lunch with Cecil King and Hugh
Cudlipp. I had apparently gravely upset Cecil King by not having attended
one of his functions earlier and the message reached Caroline through Lew
Grade that he was hopping mad with me and had said, 'I snap my fingers
and Harold Wilson comes to lunch but I can't get this man Wedgwood
Benn. Who the hell does he think he is?'

Cecil King is a big and rather grim man and Hugh Cudlipp, the ageing
boy genius, is not all that attractive. I decided to talk frankly about the Office

and how awful the civil servants were, how necessary it was to reorganise the whole thing, how the telephone service couldn't be be put right for a long time and how the postal services need to be reshaped, and to be forthcoming generally. I think I'm much too careful in talking to the press and probably most of my colleagues are much more free and easy and it pays off.

After lunch they got down seriously to the business of the fourth channel, in which they are vitally interested since they are majority shareholders in ATV, which is the one company that wants to take over the fourth channel. I told them that I would be sorry to see it allocated until I was absolutely satisfied that there wasn't some possibility of regional television performing a community function, buying programmes from programme contractors and broadcasting some University of the Air stuff. They didn't say much but were obviously disappointed and angry.

This highlights in my mind one of the great difficulties of being a socialist in the sort of society in which we live. The real drive for improvement comes from those concerned to make private profit. If, therefore, you deny these people the right of extending private enterprise into new fields, you have to have some sort of alternative. You have to have some body which wants to develop public enterprise but our present Civil Service is not interested in growth. It is geared to care and maintenance. The nationalised industries are not yet moving rapidly enough.

The thing to do is to find people who are keen on growth and give them the authority to grow on something other than a commercial basis. This seems to me to be the central problem of socialist practice today and I feel sure the answer lies in devolved authority. I don't believe that it is the drive for personal gain that makes private enterprise so energetic. I think it is the fact that when you are running your own show you have the authority to do what you want to do. And I'm sure the lesson for us is clear. We have somehow to create a multiplicity of public authorities and allow them to get on with the job. This is the case for splitting the Post Office up into its component parts as separate nationalised industries and for the progressive development of mixed enterprise where the state can work in partnership with those who are keen to break fresh ground.

Postal Controllers' dinner tonight. It was a real postal occasion. The whole general directorate were there together with postal controllers from all over the country. The first speaker, Mr de Grouchy, made a characteristic Post Office speech in which he poured scorn on the automatic telephones as if they were new-fangled devices. He said the Post Office had always been run by broad-minded ignoramuses at the top.

Replying, I drew attention to two occasions when the Post Office had been wrong in opposing innovation. One was the introduction of mail coaches in 1784 and the other was the statement in 1879 by Sir William Preece, the Engineer-in-Chief to the Post Office, when he said he saw no future for the telephone. I said we had a lot to learn from those who opposed change. Then I described the 'feasible service' and said we were considering it.

After me came Mr Jackson, who was eighty-two – one of the last surviving surveyors. He was a wonderful old man, upright, with a stern sense of duty, a good sense of humour and ready to argue all over again the case against mail coaches in 1784. He couldn't have done it better. I think I nearly overstepped the mark but I'm glad I said what I said. It was an enjoyable evening and it did bring a head the conflict between innovation and conservatism which has been rumbling along inside the Department since I've been there.

Sunday 13 June

I read yesterday morning that the Beatles had been given MBEs. No doubt Harold did this to be popular and I expect it *was* popular – though it may have been unpopular to some people too. The *Daily Mirror*'s headline was 'Now They've Got Into The Topmost Chart Of All'. But the plain truth is that the Beatles have done more for the royal family by accepting MBEs than the royal family have done for the Beatles by giving them. Nobody goes to see the Beatles because they've got MBEs but the royal family love the idea that the honours list is popular, because it all helps to buttress them and indirectly their influence is used to strengthen all the forces of conservatism in society. I think Harold Wilson makes the most appalling mistake if he thinks that in this way he can buy popularity, for he is ultimately bolstering a force that is an enemy of his political stand.

The other thing this week that's in my mind is the developing situation in Vietnam, where the Americans are now deciding to invade in full strength and we are left in the embarrassing position of appearing to support them. I believe this is an untenable position and sooner or later we shall have to come out and say what we really think. The argument that we are keeping quiet in order to retain influence is of course fallacious. The real reason is quite different. On Friday night there was the first 'teach-in' at the LSE in London on Vietnam. It was based on the 'teach-ins' that have appeared in the United States and which are an aspect of the non-violent movement. I think they probably will have an influence and I'm told that whenever Harold Wilson's name was mentioned at LSE people booed. It may well be that when the time comes the Labour Government will have been held to fail not because it was too radical but because it was not radical enough.

Wednesday 16 June

To the House of Commons where a Mr Sheppard came to see me. He had written to me eighteen years ago at Oxford asking if he could address the Oxford Union and I had written a non-committal letter back to say he couldn't but that if he would ever like to see me I should be glad to do so. He turned up last night at home saying he did want to see me and Caroline put him off. I rang him thinking it might be something important and he came this afternoon. He said that he had worked for twenty years on the greatest idea ever, which he'd written down on a piece of paper. He handed me this in an envelope and when I opened it, it said, 'Everything everywhere moves. It always has done and it always will. EVERYTHING EVERYWHERE MOVES.' He wanted me to take this to the Russians and the Americans so they could share the truth equally. He was a real nutcase but it was quite comic.

At about 5 o'clock this morning Raymond Fletcher collapsed in the Tea Room and it was a horrible sight to see three people holding him down and hear him groaning. Whether it was an epileptic fit, as was rumoured, or not, I don't know. But this is the price we pay for this late-night folly.

Tuesday 29 June
I have discovered that my instructions on stamp policy have simply not been followed. I asked to see the artists' instructions to those who were designing the stamps of the new Post Office Tower. I discovered that the instructions remained exactly as before and that no reference at all had been made to the fact that the Queen is prepared to receive non-traditional designs. The instructions all specified as usual, 'The Queen's head must be a dominant feature of the designs.' This is in strict contravention of what they know has been agreed and what I want. Unless you watch them like a hawk they simply don't do what they're told.

The same applied to the Battle of Britain stamps. I found that the stamps essayed by Harrison's at my request, incorporating six stamps in one block, had not even been prepared for submission to the Palace. I asked why and they said that I had agreed to a minute which had said this could not be done. I asked to see the minute and found that there was one tiny reference to the difficulty of producing 'multi-design' stamps in the time. This had been slipped in in the hope that I wouldn't notice it and would sign the minute and then it could be used to show that I had abandoned the idea. I found the letter to the Palace, rewrote the minute completely and recommended the stamps by Gentleman printed in a block of six with the Queen's head only on the top right-hand one. As second choice I suggested a block of six in which the Queen's head appeared in all. I don't know what the outcome will be but now that we have agreed that rejected designs are also to be made available to the press there will be some public discussion of the stamps. It may be that this is all risky politically but I think that I am covered by the agreement reached with the Palace in March under which non-traditional designs are able to be submitted.

To the House of Commons after lunch, where I heard Harold at Questions. He is fabulously calm and cool and the Opposition simply can't get at him.

Wednesday 30 June

To Number 10 at 10.30 to see Harold. He'd asked to see me about the appointments of the BBC and ITA governors. He wants Lord Annan as Vice-Chairman of the BBC and Asa Briggs on ITA. He thinks Professor Richard Hoggart at Birmingham might be unacceptable. But in fact, most of the hour and twenty minutes I spent with him consisted of a review of the general political situation. He feels that the decision not to have an Election this autumn despite our tiny majority has precipitated the Tory leadership crisis, which is true. There is also a row going on between Jo Grimond, who would like a Lib–Lab pact and Emlyn Hooson, Liberal MP for Montgomery, who is trying to wrest the leadership of the Liberal Party from the Bonham Carter dynasty. All this is greatly in our favour.

We had a long talk about the launching of a Vietnam initiative and he gave me the background to it.

Thursday 1 July

I told my office to ring Sir Michael Adeane. They did this, having discovered that he was at Holyrood House. When they rang he was actually with the Queen presenting my recommendations and when he came out he said she was prepared for most of them but was not too happy about the Battle of Britain stamps showing five out of the six in the block without her head. That is to say she had rejected the headless stamps.

I was anxious to do this by consent and so my office indicated to Adeane that I would be perfectly happy if she chose the ones with the head on each stamp. This will therefore be the stamp that is issued in September, but the press will be shown the stamps that were rejected. It will focus publicity on the machinery of selection and I shall explain that I make recommendations to the Palace including the Stamp Advisory Committee's recommendations but of course the final choice remains with the Queen. Once this has happened I think it will pave the way for further moves next year with the pictorial stamps.

Wednesday 7 July

Joe Slater came in to discuss the board minutes for tomorrow with me and then Joe, Wratten and I collected Caroline and we went to the GPO Interflora TV final. It was even worse than I expected, with a half-naked Hawaiian girl dressed in plastic flowers who insisted on putting a garland around my neck, although I had specifically asked that this should not happen. The thing was intensely embarrassing and I deeply regretted having agreed to do it. Caroline and I refused the dinner afterwards at the Beachcomber with all the gang of high-livers from the BBC, Interflora and the Post Office. Hilary's comment when I got home was the most revealing. He said, 'Dad, you didn't look at all authoritative, you were too eager, you were awful.' Thank goodness for one's children!

Wednesday 21 July

At 12.45 heard from Number 10 that the Giro was all right. It is a most interesting study of how a decision was made. Although this had been advocated by the Party in the past, nothing whatsoever had been put into the manifesto and it wasn't until two days ago that it first came to a committee of Ministers. Although Harold Wilson knew about it – because I'd kept him informed – and the Treasury had studied the paper earlier this year, the thing was carried through in two days without ever having to go to Cabinet.

From 3.30 to 7 we had the debate on Giro and I wound it up. To my astonishment none of the anxieties of the banks were expressed by Tories and it was almost universally welcomed. I was delighted.

I stayed until about 2 am working on a speech for tomorrow's debate on the Post Office services and kept in touch with the progress of the telephonists' strike. It is spreading.

Thursday 22 July

The *Daily Mail* today described the Giro as 'Benn's Bank'. This was taken from a suggestion Jeremy Thorpe made and it was rather pleasing.

Monday 26 July

Back to the Office and at 11 o'clock Sir Martin Charteris, the Assistant Private Secretary to the Queen, came to see me about the letter I had written to the Palace following James Fitton's visit a fortnight ago. Fitton wanted some designer-photographers to be allowed to photograph the Queen to help prepare the designs for the next series of definitive stamps.

I looked Charteris up in *Who's Who* and found that he was educated at Eton and Sandhurst and had been a Regular Army officer and he gave his relaxation as wildfowling. He was a tall, bony, bald man in his late forties. The Office was in a panic at his arrival and the staff were hovering around like a lot of birds.

Evidently the Queen was nervous at the thought of having a lot of photographers coming. I told him as much as I could about Fitton's idea and he suggested that Lord Snowdon should take the pictures. This suits me fine. The Queen doesn't like sitting for photographs and was doubtful about what I had in mind. It was agreed that Charteris would check with her that Snowdon could take the first series of pictures and I will arrange that some of the designers talk to him before he goes in so that he takes the sort of pictures in which they will be interested. The Queen is so busy that she can't have the photographs taken till October.

We also discussed the question of whether she should wear the crown or not. Brigadier Holmes said that the Garter King at Arms said she should either be wearing a coronet or have a crown over her head. I said that a stamp was not a heraldic emblem but a piece of modern design and I was sure the Duke of Edinburgh would take the same view. Charteris rather hesitantly agreed.

I also said that I hated using the word effigy as this suggested that I was asking for a death mask. All in all it was an amusing conversation because he had come suspecting foul play and I outcharmed him. It must certainly have relieved his anxieties for I'm sure the Palace is a lot more frightened of me than they have reason to be. The Office was also afraid that I would be rude to Charteris and were surprised to find that it was all butter. Anyway he went away perfectly happy and after I shook hands with him he turned and walked straight into the door which was rather comic.

At 4 o'clock I went to Fleet Building again for the press conference on all-figure dialling. O'Brien was in a complete tizzy and the general attitude of the Department was of baring their behinds for kicks from the press about this switch. I tried to take the offensive and to explain that this was inevitable, that it would bring advantages in terms of increased capacity, technical improvements by sectorisation, and open the way for direct international subscriber dialling.

Wednesday 4 August
Tam Dalyell told me that he and Eric Heffer had just been to see Harold Wilson to propose that the nationalisation of the docks should take place in the new session, following the publication of the Devlin Report on the ports and taking precedence over steel. I gather that Harold was interested in the idea and certainly with £150 million of public money about to be poured into the docks and the present labour dissatisfaction, I believe you could win public support for such a proposal. I said I would consider writing to Harold about this because there is a strong British interest and also there is a departmental interest in that the Post Office suffers from dock delays.

Friday 6 August
Parliament rose for the summer recess after the most gruelling session that I have ever experienced. But we have proved that we can govern and I think there is a reasonable chance that the Liberals will abstain in crucial censure debates, giving us another year at our job. Quite frankly I've got so much on my hands in the Post Office that I really would like one more year to finish it all off. My work will be done by the summer of 1966 and I should be happy then to move on to something else.

Tuesday 17 – Tuesday 31 August
The family spent this period in Bandol. We left by train and boat and hired a car in Marseilles. We stayed in a pleasant family hotel and we enjoyed the sunshine and the complete escape from politics. I was able to get an English paper of one sort or another every day but otherwise it was a complete and very welcome break from the Post Office.

Saturday 4 September

Hilary and I set off by train this morning to Bristol where Harold was speaking tonight. We stopped at Bath and saw the Roman baths and the museum of costume and then went on by car to Kingswood where I opened a fête for the Made For Ever youth club.

Then on to Unity House, where about forty people had gathered to see me in what Herbert Rogers had described as a deputation. In fact it was a gathering of Communists and others from all over Bristol who launched a most bitter attack on government policy covering Vietnam, economic policy and almost everything else they could think of.

After that I went to the hotel and then on to Harold's meeting. Hilary was allowed to sit in Caroline's seat on the platform and as the platform was introduced one by one to the meeting there was a round of applause for Hilary which absolutely thrilled him.

Hilary and I went back in the Prime Minister's motorcade to the hotel and Marcia said that Hilary could stay for dinner with Harold. At 10.45 we started dinner which went on till about midnight. Aside from Harold and Mary, Alf Richman, who is on Harold's staff, Marcia and two Bristol trade unionists, Hilary and I were the only others there. It was a delightful evening and we had a long talk about the Speakership. Marcia suggested we make Desmond Donnelly Speaker and we had an amusing talk about the possibilities. Harold is optimistic that a Tory backbencher might be induced to do it. Before we finally parted Harold gave Hilary an autographed photograph and Hilary went to bed in seventh heaven.

Thursday 9 September

Looking back on nearly a year in office, I think probably the only contribution that I have been able to make to the Post Office is to create an atmosphere in which people with ideas have felt that this was the time to bring them forward, knowing that they would be sympathetically considered. Brigadier Holmes, who is leaving headquarters to become Director of the London Postal Region, said to me today, 'Before I go, may I say as an individual, rather than as an official, that it has been an inspiration to work with you this year.' It was a decent thing for him to have said and if there is any truth in it I feel I have done my job.

Sunday 12 September

To Chequers all day for the Cabinet meeting which heads of department were invited to attend. It was my first visit to Chequers and it is a beautiful house. But the whole place is like a hotel and if any reminder were necessary of the fleeting nature of high political office, this gives it. Indeed even the bedrooms were like hotel bedrooms, with little brass squares outside into which names on cards could be dropped and with basins screwed against the wall like some one-star hotel in Blackpool. One could have a wonderful time

at Chequers, handing over the whole house to somebody who knew the
Elizabethan period and telling him to remove the excrescences of 1930s
modernisation and restore the place to a decorative style appropriate to its
age. He might at the same time add central heating, for I'm told that the
house is as cold as can be and those little brassy electric fires in every room
are also a real eyesore.

Sunday 26 September – Labour Party Conference, Blackpool
Peter Shore arrived in Blackpool this morning and I had breakfast with him.
Afterwards, Marcia brought us the first text of Harold's speech, which we
discussed. Then we went in to see Harold. I suggested that he should try to
draw a distinction between the Tory Party as the champion of those who
own industry and the Labour Party as the natural ally of the managers and
the people who run it. I also suggested that he should address the Liberals
over the head of the Liberal MPs.

The other most interesting argument was about whether we should
accept a resolution from the floor which rejected the idea that the
integration of public schools could be achieved by taking state places in fee-
paying schools. Dick Crossman said that if we accepted the resolution, it
would kill the Public Schools Commission stone-dead. Alice Bacon said she
would rather do nothing at all than do this. George Brown said that Dulwich
College had 90 per cent free places and surely we couldn't object to that.

In the end, with only George Brown, Dick Crossman and Eirene White,
from the Women's Section, against it, the Executive decided to accept this
resolution which effectively puts paid to what Crosland is planning. I was
delighted. We also agreed to accept a composite resolution in favour of
comprehensive education which included a reference to the active
discouragement of streaming.

Wednesday 29 September
This morning we had the foreign-affairs debate at the Conference.

Harold Wilson came to wind up. All I can say about his speech was that it
failed to rise to the occasion. He made jokes about the Tories, he was funny,
but also in a way cheap. He quoted himself several times and although there
was nothing in particular that you could put your finger on, and he did give
an effective answer to much of the criticism that has been directed against
the Government, it just failed to be more than a party answer. It didn't give a
vision or an analysis. The main resolution criticising the Government on
Vietnam was defeated by 4 million to 2 million after a card vote which Ray
Gunter tried to resist.

We had lunch at the hotel with Gerald Gardiner and Elwyn Jones and the
usual gang. Gerald was extremely funny. 'I was once told, years ago, that
Cabinet Ministers were allowed to see their own MI5 files,' he said. 'So I
asked my department to get hold of mine, thinking that this would give me a

good opportunity to judge the efficacy of MI5. After all I would be able to judge what they said about me in comparison with what I knew about myself. However, the civil servants hummed and hawed a lot and so I kept saying to them every week or so, "Where is my file?" In the end I said I wanted it by tomorrow and they said I would have to see the Home Secretary. Frank Soskice was embarrassed and said that he couldn't agree and that he wasn't allowed to see the files either. When they wanted to show him anything, they photographed a page and gave it to him but he never saw the complete file. He was so upset about it that I just let it drop.' Gerald went on to say that he had heard that someone who had insisted on seeing his complete file had been told that it had been destroyed the day before.

It was a most amusing story because not only did it reveal the essential naïvety of Gerald Gardiner but it was a direct confirmation of what one suspects: that there is no political control whatsoever over the security services. They regard a Minister – even the Home Secretary – as a transitory person, and they would feel under no obligation to reveal information to him. Indeed I do not know how the Home Secretary could physically get hold of an MI5 file short of sending a platoon of policemen along to take it out of the filing cabinet without the consent of those who were responsible for guarding it. It also said an awful lot about Frank Soskice as I can't believe that a Home Secretary could be fobbed off with just a page from an MI5 file if he insisted on seeing the whole thing. I had assumed that my difficulties in the Post Office were because I was not the person responsible for security. But I can see I would have a fight if ever I were sent to the Home Office. That is a job that does need cleaning up and where a tough Minister is required to take control.

Friday 1 October
Back from Conference. Caroline and I went out in the evening to the party given by Shen Ping at the Chinese Embassy to celebrate the anniversary of the liberation of China by the Communist regime. It was a splendid party and clearly the Chinese are moving more and more into the diplomatic world. I talked to the candidate from Luton, who told me that he had been in China and was much impressed by the genuine participation of people in the life of the community. He thought the rule that top management had to spend one day a week doing manual labour was a good one and I wish I could introduce it in the Post Office. But somehow I don't see myself as a cleaner or a postman without the thing becoming just a huge press gimmick. Certain techniques are applicable to a revolutionary society which are not applicable to an established society. But the idea is a good one and even if I didn't learn anything about the job it would certainly help to maintain a closer contact between top and bottom.

Sunday 3 October
Worked most of the day dictating, and writing to members of the Executive

to see if I can win some support for a new look at organisation, finance and publicity. I know Bob Maxwell is intending to do serious research and he is a potential ally. The big struggle with Maxwell is whether you allow him to use you or whether you use him. My firm intention is to keep some sort of control myself. But when you're wrestling with a millionaire you do start with something of a disadvantage.

Friday 8 October
Caroline and I went off by car about 10.15 and got to the Post Office Tower well before eleven for the official opening. Among the guests who came were Clem Attlee, who is our oldest and most senior ex-Postmaster General, Charles Hill, Lord Normanbrook, Sir Billy Butlin – who will be running the restaurant – and of course the top brass from the Post Office. Despite the grave Rhodesian crisis, which is reaching its climax today with Harold Wilson's last meeting with Ian Smith, Harold arrived with Mary Wilson, Sergeant Kelly (their detective), Marcia Williams and Brenda Dew, Peter Shore and Derek Mitchell.

Thursday 14 October
To the Aberdeen Head Office this morning about 9 after spending yesterday visiting Edinburgh.

In fact the real news today didn't come from my trip in Scotland at all but from a letter written by Mitchell at Number 10 to Wratten about stamp design. It was an astonishing letter for any civil servant to have written for it contains within it a clear statement that the Queen might under some circumstances 'reject the advice of her Ministers'. This of course does not come directly from the Palace but Adeane had conveyed this impression to Mitchell and Mitchell had conveyed it to the Prime Minister, who has decided to frighten me off by conveying it to me.

There are many angles of this letter which require a great deal of thought. The first is that it looks as if my new stamp policy has been torpedoed. Whether or not the Queen cares personally about it, Adeane and all the flunkies at Buckingham Palace certainly do. Their whole position depends upon maintaining this type of claptrap.

Realising that they were dealing with somebody who didn't intend to be bullied and couldn't be flattered, Adeane decided to get at me sideways by going to Harold Wilson and threatening political controversy, which he knew would be sufficient to effect an order by Harold to me to stop. This is exactly how the Palace works. It doesn't want to appear unpopular, yet at the same time it does not want certain things to happen and it uses the threat of controversy to stop any changes from going too far. Whether or not Adeane will go so far as to say to Heath or Salisbury or Home 'You'd better watch that Postmaster General, he's trying to take the Queen's head off the stamps', I don't know. They certainly aren't gentlemen when it comes to political in-fighting. But, at the present, Adeane obviously thinks this is the best way to operate.

For my part, particularly after all the unfavourable press comment that I have had, I am not sure how far I would want to go with the new stamp policy. It is only peripheral and I would be prepared to give it up if I could get out of the Palace an official order to stop it. For a piece of paper written in that way would be of priceless constitutional interest. What I am not going to do is to allow myself to be stopped without getting that particular order.

This evening I began to turn my mind to the best way of dealing with this letter. I do not intend to raise it with Harold Wilson. It is too unimportant to worry him with and I don't want him to give me orders to do anything. I want them directly from the Palace.

Sunday 17 October
A usual family day at home. I went to see Mother this morning. After lunch, we all went to the park and sat in the hot October sunshine. It was far better than days in June or July. The boys played football and Melissa played with a balloon. It was a lovely day.

Saturday 23 October
Surgery at Unity House, Bristol, this morning. It went on for two and three-quarter hours. There was a woman who'd had a miscarriage while on holiday in Austria and had had to pay the hospital bills; a philatelist whose first-day cover had been ruined; a Post Office engineer who said he had been passed over for promotion; an architect with a planning problem; an upholsterer whose factory had been burned down and who had now got into trouble for putting up a portable building one-twentieth of which was outside the building line and wanted help because he had an important export order. There was a manufacturer of ladders who was worried about rising British Railways charges; a woman who had fallen in the street and wanted to claim damages from the Corporation; a real working-class Tory who had come to argue about compulsory-purchase procedures; and there was a telephone call from someone who wanted to know whether educational welfare officers had any part to play in the new Home Office family service courts. In fact it was a perfectly representative surgery.

Tuesday 2 November
At 5 o'clock I went to see Harold in his room at the House of Commons, with my stamps. I thought he was a little uneasy to begin with and this was no doubt because Mitchell had told him I was being difficult. I opened all my stamps and showed them to him and he was absolutely captivated by them. The ones he liked best were of the old railway trains. I should have guessed this since he wrote his thesis at Oxford on the early days of the railways. In

fact he was absolutely certain that I had had these specially designed to win his support. He overrates my political sense. He also laughed very hard about the sporting prints, which he agreed were the best way of presenting new ideas to the Palace.

With regard to the Queen's head, he said that he had spoken to the Queen personally about it and that she didn't want her head removed from the stamps. 'She is a nice woman,' he said to me, 'and you absolutely charmed her into saying yes when she didn't really mean it.' He went on, 'I don't think you ought to go back and argue it out with her again because I'm sure you would win and she really wouldn't be happy.' He thus disposed of my claim that the network was operating to prevent this from happening. For my own part, I suspect that Harold more or less invited her to say no in order to keep in with the Palace. But, coming from him, there was no argument and I told him that it would create no problems as I could put a head on every stamp and showed him the cameos. He relaxed and realised that this would present no political difficulties for him.

Marcia came in at this stage and so did Brenda and they looked at the designs and were delighted with them, especially with the costumes. But when Marcia heard about the Queen's view she burst out and said it was a scandal that in modern England the Queen should have any say about anything at all, and why did she choose the stamps, what had it to do with her and couldn't Ministers reach their own decisions. I told her that I agreed with her entirely but if there was likely to be political trouble it wasn't worth it, and I would accept this. I do like Marcia, she's got all the right instincts and she does Harold a great deal of good.

Anyway, Harold said he would be seeing the Queen tonight at his audience and would tell her that we'd made great progress and probably the right thing to do would be to go along for another audience soon.

At 8 o'clock I went back to Downing Street for dinner with Dick, Gerald, Peter, Tommy and Marcia. Mary waited for us in the living room in the flat where they live and she was sad at having to live away from home. She really doesn't want to be the Prime Minister's wife and would love to be the wife of an Oxford don. This is not an affectation, it's perfectly genuine. She is a nice and unaffected woman. *Private Eye* are bringing out 'Mary Wilson's Diary' as a book and we discussed whether any action could be taken to stop it. Harold said that nobody had read *Private Eye* for over a year now as it was so scurrilous! It's one thing to run a comic column called 'Mary Wilson's Diary' and it's another thing to publish a book which many innocent people will think has been written by Mary Wilson. I think some legal action is called for and would succeed.

Harold came in straight from his audience with the Queen and told me that he had been there for an hour and a quarter. 'We spent ten minutes on Rhodesia, and an hour and five minutes on stamps,' he said. I'm sure this reflects the proportion of the Queen's mind which is devoted to Rhodesia as compared with stamps. He told me that she was perfectly happy to accept a silhouette, and to accept the rulers of Britain, including Cromwell and Edward VIII, but that her head had to appear on everything and the press was not to see any stamps without her head.

Anyway there it rests. The plain truth is that the Palace has won on the main point and I have been defeated by Palace pressure exercised through the network on me, using the Prime Minister as an intervening force. Harold, who is so busy using the Queen on Rhodesia and wants it to be known that he enjoys the closest possible relations with her, is prepared to sacrifice this for a quiet life, and freedom from political criticism. Within its limited power the monarchy and all it stands for is one of the great centres of reaction and conservatism in this country.

I heard a little bit more about Derek Mitchell's attempt to get Marcia Williams out of Number 10. There is a big tussle going on. Marcia is infinitely the most able, loyal, radical and balanced member of Harold's personal team and I hope he resists efforts to dislodge her.

Thursday 18 November
I worked over lunch and at 2.30 Dr Konrad came to see me. He is a psychologist who had done a report for the Post Office on alpha-numerical codes covering telephones and postal coding. The Office want to do a postal coding system which will consist of two parts: the first for despatch or outward sorting, consisting of postal districts in London and a simple extract code for other cities, the second part for inward sorting or despatch and they suggested that one digit followed by two letters would be best [eg W1A 4WW]. In my opinion this is confusing.

Downes and Wolstencroft had been at lunch with him and no doubt stoked him up on their side. In the end he was prepared to accept that it might be the subject of further research. Mr Downes said that if there was a change now it would set them back for six months and the coding in Croydon would have to be stopped, an argument that they had never used before, having previously told me that the coding could be organised in any way that suited Dr Konrad. I decided to drop my opposition to it.

Saturday 11 December
This evening Stephen had a party with his friends. They just bumped about and giggled like a lot of colts. The record player blared out and I could see my ceiling rising and falling by about two inches with the dancing above. Meanwhile I dictated letters and brought my diary up to date.

Wednesday 15 December
The pirate radio letters are continuing to flood in and there must now be 2,000 or more. I decided to make it clear that there would be a gap between the warning and the prosecution of the pirates and I think the prosecutions

cannot begin until after the White Paper on broadcasting. But it was necessary to make a statement about prosecutions in order to take the heat off the Foreign Office, which is under heavy pressure from European countries.

Wednesday 22 December
Back home about 7.30. The Cabinet reshuffle was announced this evening. Barbara Castle is to be Minister of Transport in place of Tom Fraser and Roy Jenkins Home Secretary. I am quite happy to be at the Post Office for a few more months to carry out the changes that I have started. Yesterday I sent a long letter to Harold reporting on the Post Office and giving him an idea of what was coming in 1966. It didn't call for any decisions but I thought there was no harm in making a private report to him.

Tuesday 28 December
Up early this morning and drove to Stansgate. The place was icy cold and within a few minutes of getting there the main electricity fuse went. So we had no light, heat or power. I rang the Electricity Board and they were there within three hours. After that we huddled round electric fires we'd brought from London and managed to get the central heating going, which gradually took the chill off the house. The place was in a terrible muck and we more or less camped but it was pleasant to get away from London and Stansgate is about the only place where I can relax and forget about the Post Office and politics and almost everything else.

Thursday 3 February 1966
To the Commons to see George Brown. He now claims that he is planning to settle the railway strike and is being stopped by Ray Gunter and Barbara Castle. He behaved monstrously to his officials, sending a senior civil servant out for bottles of gin and whisky and five minutes later ringing his own department in Storey's Gate to find out where the poor chap had gone. He really showed off. George is completely erratic and irrational and an impossible old boozer – rarely being sober after lunch.

Sunday 6 February
Peter Shore came to collect me to take me down to Chequers. If he hadn't done this I certainly shouldn't have got there.
    The place was crowded with the whole Cabinet and National Executive – about sixty in all. Harold started by saying that all options must be kept open. We were not there to discuss the date of the Election.
    Then George Brown gave a general introduction to the document that had actually been prepared by Peter but for which Terry Pitt was most elaborately praised. Tom Driberg queried whether there would be a statement on overseas policy. Then Jack Jones asked whether it would be

possible to cut defence costs and asked whether one could divorce defence and foreign policy from economic policy.

After that we came to part one of the document, which was on the state of the economy. Jim Callaghan said that the debt problem was not insoluble but he did not expect that the growth rate could be up to 4 per cent before 1968/9. He asked us not to be impatient and said we would have to have priorities within the public sector. He warned us that public expenditure was going up 9 per cent this year and we had to keep our promises in the Election within limits. He predicted that tax rates might have to go up and said that personal taxation was already too high. He rather pooh-poohed the idea of abolishing the rates because of the burden on the Exchequer.

We broke for lunch and I sat opposite Tony Crosland, who admitted that he now had some doubts about the binary system for higher education and rather regretted the philosophic speech he had made in defence of the binary system when he had only been at the Ministry a short time.

After lunch Dick made a most effective speech about the need for a policy covering the whole physical environment and the need to share social furniture between different groups. He thought it was ludicrous to have a large playing field for a school and then find the local authority wanted more open space for general recreation, etc.

Barbara then made a speech about transport in which she said that we must democratise car ownership and extend it more widely, spend more on the roads and get the physical integration of freight traffic on rail and road. She wanted to get away from the concept of paying our way in transport.

We then moved on to the social services, where Douglas Houghton talked about the need to re-examine family allowances and to rationalise social payments with fiscal policy. He warned us that social security – especially pensions – was mainly concerned with women, since 5.5 million out of the 7.5 million pensioners were women. Crosland said a word about school building and how difficult it was to provide new schools to replace old ones with his present budget. He broadened it out to say that we needed to have a poverty programme covering housing, social services and education under a separate agency – rather taking a leaf out of President Johnson's book. He went on to say that he was sure that there was more money that could be raised by taxation and that we were not at all at the limits of it as compared with other European countries.

Next came Kenneth Robinson, who again complained of the great difficulty in meeting needs under his present budget, which would have to be expanded two and a half times in order to provide for all the hospital beds required at the end of the century and to replace the pre-war hospitals.

We had tea and afterwards Jennie Lee spoke about the University of the Air and Peggy Herbison reported on pensions progress.

Marcia came round and whispered that Harold wanted 'the group' to stay behind – Dick, Peter, Gerald and myself. Tommy Balogh, of course, was not at Chequers. We had a meal with Harold and discussed the Election strategy. It is pretty apparent that the Election will come soon and we were told to come to Chequers again next Sunday by which time Peter Shore has to prepare a draft manifesto.

Home about midnight, feeling extremely tired and full of flu.

Sunday 13 February
Peter Shore turned up at 8.30 this morning and drove me to Chequers.

The manifesto should be a very good one. Harold was rather tired but we had an amusing time. I thanked him for bringing my Post Office reorganisation forward.

We talked at lunch about George Brown and Jim Callaghan and how both of them would like to be Leader of the House of Commons and got as near as we could to discussing various other changes. When the question came up of who would succeed Harold if he were knocked down by a bus, I asked Harold outright and he said that he would want to know who had paid the man who drove the bus.

Home in time for tea with the family.

Sunday 20 February
Collected Peter Shore this evening to go to Number 10 at Harold's request to go over the manifesto. It is obvious that the Election is imminent, although Harold pledged us to deep secrecy and didn't actually say so outright.

He began talking about his colleagues. Harold is terrified that if Jim Callaghan became Leader of the House of Commons he would conspire against Harold and weaken his position and we tried to reassure him that he was all right and had nothing to fear. It is extraordinary how a man in his position should have anxieties on that score.

He was incredibly indiscreet and it was interesting that every reference he made to his colleagues referred to their weaknesses. Caroline thinks, and I am sure she's right, that the way in which he manipulates people is by concentrating on their weakness. I must say I found the evening extremely unattractive. My opinion of Harold was lower tonight than it has ever been before. He really is a manipulator who thinks that he can get out of everything by fixing somebody or something. Although his reputation is now riding high, I'm sure he will come a cropper one day when one of his fixes just doesn't come off.

Thursday 24 February
To the Cabinet, where it was decided, after a short debate, to go over to decimal currency in 1971.

News from Ghana today that President Nkrumah has been deposed by a military coup. Everyone here is cheering because Nkrumah was such a hated figure. Much publicity is being given to the release of the political detainees. But of course they will soon be replaced in prison by Nkrumah's supporters. However wild and uncontrollable the cult of personality has become in Ghana I feel sure that history will treat Nkrumah much more kindly than now appears from the British press. It is hard to escape the conclusion that a newly independent country requires a tough leadership and a focus of loyalty, and although he has no doubt been corrupt and wasteful and has isolated himself from the people, I suspect that in terms of fundamental development Ghana has not done too badly.

Wednesday 2 March

One amusing incident today. I saw Marcia just before I went in to see Harold and told her that I had dreamed about her on the previous night. She told me that she had dreamed that Harold was dead and had not believed it until she had been shown the body. She said she hadn't dared to tell Harold this story. But then Harold had told her this morning that last night he dreamed that Hugh Gaitskell had been sitting in at a committee – all white. What an extraordinary combination of dreams.

Sunday 6 March

To Number 10 for a final look at our manifesto and also for a strategic discussion about the Tory manifesto, which was published today. This includes a great war on the trade unions, the remodelling of the Welfare State, strict control of immigration and pledges for greater increases in expenditure, coupled with the determination to cut taxation. We discussed the best way of handling this.

Monday 7 March

To Transport House this morning for the meeting of the Executive at 10.30 to go through the manifesto. We got through it quickly, with the minimum of discussion about the prices and incomes policy, which had been carefully worded to avoid trouble. There was some discussion about the nationalisation of the docks but the general view was that we should include a pledge on this. The only actual disagreement was over the phraseology of the sentence dealing with our entry into Europe. I voted with Mikardo and Tony Greenwood and Barbara Castle and one or two others against the firm commitment that 'Britain should be ready to enter Europe'.

Sunday 13 March

After having started extremely well in the Party and attracted people from left and right to his leadership, Harold has, since he's been Prime Minister, appeared to be too cunning and crafty and smart, and to be somewhat lacking in principle. It may well be that these are the qualities needed to be a Prime Minister – and to win Elections. I am not expressing my own opinion about this, but I think it's interesting to put on record that the more successful Harold Wilson becomes the less attractive he is to the sort of people who campaigned most actively for him as Leader of the Party when Hugh Gaitskell died.

Thursday 31 March
Polling Day. To headquarters at about 9 and from 9.30 am to 6 visiting all the polling stations and committee rooms. We had lunch at the 'Hole-in-the-Wall' and then went out again with our loudspeaker, doing final knocking-up. After the polls closed we cleared up the headquarters, went back to the hotel and began watching the BBC Election programme. It was evident that a big Labour victory was coming, although the size of the majority was predicted in the first place as 150 and began falling.

At 11.30 we went to the St George Grammar School for the count and wandered round. They count terribly slowly in Bristol.

Friday 1 April
From the time we got to the count till our result at 1.35, we wandered round with a radio and an earpiece hearing the victories pouring in. At 1.35 am the result was announced and my majority had increased by 1,600 to almost 11,500. But it was only a small swing to me because of all the new housing. Then we had the traditional ritual with the car pulled up to the Walter Baker Hall, where a television set had been installed. I met and talked to my supporters and then went off to do an interview for Welsh television. Bed at 4 o'clock.

Up at 8 and drove to London. The results continued on the radio in the car and it was clear that we had won the General Election with a majority in the mid-nineties.

One of the most interesting things about the new Parliament is the inrush of new Members, most of them young, many of them professional, and all of them keen and eager. They will be very different from the old Left and from the solid trade union members. The Labour Party is in the process of transforming itself into a genuine national party.

5

1966–70

'Give ordinary people more say in decision making'—WEDGWOOD BENN

FRANKLIN

In 1966 after the General Election of March that year, Frank Cousins, the Minister of Technology, resigned. Cousins had been brought in to the Labour Government from the leadership of the Transport and General Workers' Union, to give it strength, but resigned because he could not continue to support the Government's incomes policy. Thus Tony Benn became Minister of Technology, with, for the first time, a place in the Cabinet. Until 1968 however, because of qualms over the revelation of Cabinet discussions to secretaries to whom, at that time, he dictated his diary, he did not record Cabinet meetings in detail; in that year he began the practice, maintained ever since, of dictating direct onto a cassette recorder.

Sunday 3 April
Forty-first birthday and the children came in with gifts in the morning.

Mother came over for tea and we had a family party. No news yet of the reconstruction of the Government.

Monday 4 April
Just after lunch a phone call came, asking me to go and see Harold. I went across and had five minutes with him. After a brief exchange of congratulations he said, 'I'm going to offer you a Ministry but I rather hope you won't take it. It is the Ministry of Works, which is technically a little senior to the Post Office.' I asked whether it was in the Cabinet and he indicated that it was not. I asked whether he was reducing the size of his Cabinet and he said no. 'The Minister of Works is thought of as being marginally senior to the Postmaster General but its housing functions will be taken away and it would be left with Royal Parks and Government Procurement and the Palace of Westminster.' I thought quickly and decided that if I wasn't going to be in the Cabinet there was no point in moving. Anyway I didn't want to be under Dick Crossman as overlord of Works and Planning, and I wanted to finish my Post Office work. So I said, 'If you're not offering me a place in the Cabinet I think I'd rather stay where I am.' Harold looked uncomfortable and said, 'I have decided not to make many Cabinet changes and to try to get away from the idea of major reshuffles. Instead I will move people every year – one or two of them, like the Football League. The Ministry of Technology is the real glamour job and I can't think that Frank Cousins will stay long. He's not fit anyway. I'm not promising it to you but of course it would be easier to move you if you hadn't already been moved recently. Also you have a big job of industrial reorganisation with the Post Office and Arnold Goodman has told George Wigg that you are the only person who can really settle the television problem. The Cabinet is an ageing one and there will be room for you later on.'

I suppose I should have looked a lot angrier than I felt but I'm not sure that bullying gets you anywhere. Anyway I didn't conceal my disappointment when I said that I would rather stay where I was for the moment and finish what I had started. I told him that I was extremely interested in Technology and he said, 'You would have to learn the difference between a cyclotron and a megaton.'

Afterwards, home and picked up Caroline and we went to the party at Transport House to celebrate the victory. It was a pleasant evening though Harold didn't turn up. The next few months are going to be extremely difficult and are going to call for all my skill as a negotiator but I shall have a chance of modernising the Post Office along the lines that I know to be necessary.

Wednesday 6 April
Ioan Evans, my new PPS, came over. He suggested that I give two tea parties to meet the new MPs, which is a good idea.

At 5 o'clock I went for an hour's talk to Frank Gillard about broadcasting problems. I adopted the new policy of being forthcoming, on the understanding that it was entirely confidential. Frank told me about his plans to have Radio 247 run by the BBC to beat the pirates. It sounds as if he can offer a service from 5 am to 2 am with entertainment music on the medium wave band for the teenage audience, by opting out of the Light Programme, which would remain on VHF. His only problem is money. But it's mad to raise the licence fee to provide something that could be provided for nothing by advertising. All this points to a separate pop network which is used as a revenue raiser, where the Post Office rent the programmes, studios and transmitters from the BBC and pay them an enormous sum, thus ensuring that they are not corrupted by the advertising.

Tuesday 19 April

This afternoon Ryland and Lillicrap came and we had a long discussion about eavesdropping and the new menace of microbugs. I want a select committee to sit on this but apparently the Home Office are worried that if a select committee is set up, it will lead to awkward questions about the devices used by the security services. This seems to me to be just making a monkey out of the House of Commons and trying to preserve secrecy over an important area of public interest for one particular reason. I couldn't get Ryland or Lillicrap or Wratten, for that matter, to see the importance of a serious approach to this problem. For my part, I want regulations making it an offence to eavesdrop using radio microphones or to intercept telephone conversations and listen to and record them. But I can see that I shall have some difficulty about this. No doubt every other department will brief its Ministers against me and I daresay I shouldn't carry this through a ministerial committee.

Friday 29 April

I had a phone call from a man in Devon. He said that he had been unable to buy any 3d stamps the previous night, so instead bought 6d stamps and cut them in half with scissors and would I authorise them to go through the post. I was helpful but said that I had no authority to authorise this and that he should have put the 6d stamps on and then written to me for a refund. Later I discovered that in fact he was a stamp dealer and had not had thirty important bills to send out – as he told me – but actually sent out 600 of these half-stamps which he now claims are worth £15 a piece. I think he ought to be prosecuted.

Friday 13 May

To the Post Office Tower for a lunch for former Postmasters-General and senior Post Office officials. Of the PMGs five came – Billy Listowel, Ness Edwards, Ernest Marples, Reg Bevins and myself. The most senior former civil servant was Sir Donald Banks, who was the first Director-General of the Post Office in 1934. He told me that at that time the Postmaster General would come into the Office about twice a week when Parliament was sitting for a glass of port at noon. All the minutes for him to sign would then be laid around a long table in his office and he would walk round and sign them one after the other, have another glass of port and then disappear. In fact, he spent as much time on Post Office work as a Chancellor of the Duchy of Lancaster does on Duchy work. At that period senior civil servants worked from 10 am to 4.30pm, five days a week, and had eight weeks' paid holiday a year. Life was leisurely. At least it was in Britain. But it was during those years that the rest of the world caught up with and overtook us.

Billy Listowel told me at lunch that he had tried to get the Monarch's head off the stamps in 1945 but had been told that it was impossible and had dropped the idea under heavy pressure.

This evening to Ralph and Ann Gibson's together to read *The Importance of Being Earnest*, en famille.

Tuesday 17 May

Caroline went to the BBC today to record the second instalment of 'Charlotte's Web' in the Jackanory series.

This afternoon the Queen came to visit the Post Office Tower. I had to greet her at the entrance and we went up into the VIP lounge, where I introduced her to all the senior civil servants. Then she was taken through the apparatus rooms and up in the lift. I gave Wratten my movie camera to take some pictures on the observation platform as we walked round. Afterwards we went up and had tea with Billy Butlin, revolving in his restaurant. She was obviously not interested in the technical aspects but I think enjoyed seeing London from such a height. I suggested that there ought to be a state banquet in which all the guests went by the top table every twenty minutes.

As we came down she discussed the issue of bird stamps. She did not much like the six stamps put together and said she would prefer to have only four. I promised that this is what we would do. It was a minor concession but made me seem reasonable.

Friday 20 May

This evening Caroline and I went to the state banquet at Hampton Court for the Austrian President. I sat opposite Sir Michael Adeane and next to Mrs du Cann and Caroline was opposite Lady Adeane and next to Edward du Cann.

I spent most of the evening talking to Adeane and it was very amusing. I began by asking him about the effect the Conservatives' decision to elect their own leaders had on the Queen's prerogative in choosing a Prime Minister. He said that of course the Palace had had this problem three times in the last ten years and had hoped that the new Conservative system of choosing a leader would take the load off their shoulders.

I asked him about the official view of Anastasia, the daughter of the Tsar, and he said that he thought there was nothing in this. There was an old tradition of pretenders to the throne in Russia and that in any case there was no money to be picked up. I then asked him whether there would be any family embarrassment created if it was suggested that the Queen went on a state visit to the Soviet Union. He said that he thought the memory of the massacres at Ekaterinburg would certainly have prevented George V or VI from going and he thought it still might be difficult. I then asked why it was that there had been no embarrassment with the German relatives who had fought against us in two world wars. Adeane replied, 'Oh but the German royalty are all very decent chaps.'

Next we moved to Edward VIII and I said I thought it would be inexpressibly tragic when he died and his funeral took place. There would be a national sense of guilt that we were prepared to honour a man in his death but not during his life. Adeane hastened to point out that, certainly within the last few years, the Duke of Windsor's decision to live abroad was his own and he was happy in his house in Paris. He also said that experience in Belgium, where King Leopold continued to live, showed how embarrassing and difficult it could be to have a former king on the premises. I said I thought that there would be some feeling about the Duchess of Windsor when her husband was taken away from her in death and put back in his position in the long line of king emperors. He completely misunderstood my point and he said that there was a place prepared for the Duchess of Windsor as well in the vaults.

Then he raised the question of stamps and I asked him how he had liked the album. He said that the rule about having a monarch's head on the stamps had, he thought, always referred to the ruling monarch and he had some doubts about the use of previous rulers. I said that it would be easy to put the Queen's head on every single monarch's stamp although it might not look good. I asked him whether there would be any difficulty about having Cromwell or Edward VIII among the rulers and sounded so reasonable and earnest that I feel sure I disarmed him. So I sloshed him between the eyes by telling him that Archbishop Lord Fisher of Lambeth had written to me angrily about the removal of the Queen's head. This was a story that told heavily against what I was trying to do but indicated the grave and serious way in which I undertook my duties.

Afterwards we walked in the sunken gardens briefly and then came home.

Wednesday 25 May
To the NEC this morning where we got through the business in twenty minutes and George Brown introduced a discussion on the Common Market. It was highly geared to a Party audience and there were no trumpet

calls for European integration. He dismissed 'theology' and said the Government was only engaged in a probe. He admitted that the present French Government was opposed but thought that after de Gaulle died the position would change. Certainly we should do nothing to encourage de Gaulle's disruptive tactics against NATO. The whole thing was so anodyne that there was virtually no discussion.

Tommy and Peter and I had dinner together and Dick joined us later. I really let my hair down about my present frustrations and made it pretty clear that I thought Harold ought to give more support than he does. I agreed strongly when Dick said that it was only through being disloyal and leaking and making rows that you could get anything done. This rather shocked Peter, who still thinks that basically Harold is on the right side. I am coming increasingly to suspect that Harold doesn't want trouble and the person who makes the most trouble will get his own way. I think I went a bit far indicating this but it won't do any harm if it gets back to Harold. Indeed last Sunday's telephone call to Harold has already activated Herbert Bowden, and the broadcasting White Paper will be authorised next month. It is all beginning to prove Caroline right.

Monday 6 June
Today an invitation came in from Marcia Williams for me to go to Chequers on Tuesday for the night, to have dinner with Harold and then continue our talks the following morning. Harold realises, at last, that he is in real trouble and that is why he has summoned his old 'friends'. I think the time has come for a bit of frankness and I spent part of the evening drawing up a list of discontents so that the least I can do is to tell him frankly what people are thinking. There is an apparent loss of impetus by the Government. On key issues such as Vietnam, East of Suez and prices and incomes there is disagreement in the Party. There is uncertainty or inaction on other issues, notably Rhodesia and Britain's relations with the European Community, Britain's world role, parliamentary reform and Party organisation. There has been serious mishandling of the Parliamentary Labour Party since the Election, and, finally, our sense of purpose needs rearticulating.

Caroline had her Comprehensive Schools Committee meeting at home this evening and I worked late.

Tuesday 7 June
Left home at 8 o'clock to go to see Mother with a bunch of flowers from the garden for her sixty-ninth birthday.

I looked in at the Commonwealth Relations Office for twenty minutes to talk to Judith Hart who, like me, was invited to go down to Chequers this evening. Arrived there at 10.45 pm and found Harold, Marcia, Gerald, Peter and Tommy Balogh all comfortably settled in the white drawing room. Judith joined us at about 11.30.

We talked until well after 3 in the morning, ranging over the whole field of politics. Harold was badly shaken by the appalling press that he got over the weekend, suggesting that he had lost his grip on the Party. He had called us in because he felt the time had come to listen to his friends. I found a curious ambivalence in my attitude to him. If one wanted to talk as a friend it meant identifying every problem from his viewpoint and trying to help him to overcome the criticism to which he was subjected. But I am not sure that I am not one of the critics.

He began with his now famous theme that the British public was bored with politics and wanted him to be the doctor who looked after the difficulties so that it could go on playing tennis. I challenged that fundamentally and said I thought it was an élitist view of politics and was incompatible with a radical government. Maybe the public didn't understand economics and was sick of the abuse of party politics, but it was interested in real politics and it was our duty to pick those issues which related to matters we thought important and actually make then controversial. I cited the educational issue as an example and said that I thought the status of women in society might be another.

Harold didn't much like this but his idea that the public will go on comfortably enjoying rising living standards while the Labour Party worries about the affairs of the nation is getting dangerously close to Harold Macmillan's 'You've never had it so good' and that the Tories are the party born to rule.

On Vietnam, Harold indicated that he hoped at some stage another initiative might be possible but he was obviously not prepared to say anything whatsoever that might divide him from the Americans. About the only move he will make is to tone down the praise for American action which Michael Stewart is continually giving.

On East of Suez he was bitter at what he called the cynical coalition between the extreme Right represented by Christopher Mayhew and the pacifists and fellow-travelling Left. He was obviously worried by the Party meeting which is to take place next Wednesday and wants our advice on what sort of speech he should make. We all went as far as we could in pointing out that he must identify with the Left and articulate their anxieties.

He was optimistic that the situation in Rhodesia might be settled within two months. Since Judith was there and knew all about it, I didn't think there was much I could offer there.

On prices and incomes it appeared that he thought there was some solution which would enable Frank Cousins to stay on. Since he had more or less offered me Frank Cousins's job in October, I felt this was a hint to me that I wouldn't get my move.

We also discussed the seamen's strike which is causing him some anxiety, although he kept referring to it as a 'toothache'. In fact it is much more serious than that and with the cost of the sanctions against Rhodesia and the real difficulty in maintaining the prices and incomes policy, and the disappearance of the import surcharge in the autumn, the short-term economic position is very tricky indeed. Tommy Balogh kept referring to this.

I finally went to bed at 3.35 with the first light of dawn beginning to illuminate the distant Buckinghamshire horizon. My bedroom was the one that Harold Macmillan used throughout his period of office.

Wednesday 8 June

Up just before 8 and had a bath. Breakfast was brought into my room by the WRAF orderly. Then I went for a short walk round the house and took some movies. At 9.30 the same group gathered in deckchairs on the patio overlooking the garden at the front of the house. Coffee was brought and we talked till 12.

We ranged round the same subjects and it was generally agreed that this group should start meeting again so as to keep in touch with Harold and advise him. I think he still has the idea that he's going to be able to talk himself out of his difficulties. But I am not sure it will be as easy as that. One of the factors about being an isolated person is that your triumphs are personal and no one shares them, but your defeats are personal and there are not all that many people prepared to share them either.

Having said that, I must admit he was very agreeable and it was pleasant to feel that one had access to him over a wide range of subjects.

Tuesday 14 June

To Dick Crossman's house for an informal meeting on Party strategy. Tommy Balogh, Peter Shore and Gerald Kaufman were there, with Judith Hart joining us for the first time. She is very able and I like her immensely. Dick was utterly sunk in gloom and said he didn't care what happened to Rhodesia, he thought the incomes policy was nonsense and that unemployment was coming anyway and that it would be much better to have unemployment than to try to hold incomes down. It was Dick the teacher emerging, but it is wearing.

We were frank with Dick and I told him that he was a complete obstructionist on every reform other than his own. He glories in being a departmental Minister and is saving up all that he has to say about politics for his book, which he says he is going to start writing in three years' time. He keeps the most elaborate diary.

At the end of the evening, Judith and Peter and I agreed to start meeting regularly. Dick is profoundly defeatist and thinks that the Labour Government is really finished, and is getting to be more concerned about his book, explaining why it happened rather than how it can be corrected. Pen Balogh is the wisest of all and sees it clearly, more so even than Tommy.

Monday 20 June

One point of note today: in speaking about the seamen's strike, Harold referred to the Communist influence. This has caused a great deal of dissatisfaction among the Labour Left, and Peter Shore rang to tell me that he thought it was completely bonkers. I think I share that view. Indeed, I am beginning to wonder whether Harold Wilson is not becoming like Lloyd George. We shall have to see.

Tuesday 21 June

To the Commons and this evening to Number 10 for a buffet supper that Harold had laid on. Among those who came were Peter Shore, Ron Brown, George Wallace, Gerald Kaufman, Marcia, Percy Clark, and Dick's PPS, Geoffrey Rhodes, and members of the PLP permanent staff. Harold began by giving his usual analysis. The public 'are not interested in politics and want to play tennis and clean their cars and leave things to the Government. By contrast the Party wants to do things and change things, and the main thing is to keep it on the move like a caravan so that it does not have time to stop and fight'.

Tuesday 28 June

The House rose at about 8am and I came home for an hour: just time for a bath and breakfast.

Back to the Commons, where I sat almost through the whole debate on the seamen's strike. Harold Wilson began by naming the Communists who had intervened. It made me sick and reminded me of McCarthyism. The Left attacked him almost unanimously with powerful speeches by Michael Foot, Eric Heffer and Ian Mikardo. In a sense Harold said nothing that was new, since every trade union leader knew it and we were all afraid that by going in for these tactics, he would simply make the anti-Communist smear a weapon that every Tory could use against us in the future. All that can be said for his approach is that since the Communists are politically trying to use industrial discontent to break the prices and incomes policy, it is desirable that people should understand this. I am oversensitive because of the McCarthy period. I am not much convinced by this argument and still feel it was an undesirable thing to have done.

Home about 10.30 and straight to bed.

Wednesday 29 June

To the Office briefly and then to the Commons where Harold Wilson dissociated the Government from the American bombing of Haiphong and Hanoi. Heath criticised him for it and the Left was less than generous. Very few people realised the immense significance of this act of dissociation. From now on, things will never be the same, and we are perhaps witnessing the beginnings of the new policy.

Thursday 30 June

I dashed to Number 10 for the Economic Committee and afterwards I was asked to wait in Marcia's room as the PM had something he wanted to say to me. While I waited I read my horoscope in the *Evening News*. 'Follow your instincts. This is a lucky day for you.' At that moment Harold came in and I went and had a chat with him in the Cabinet room. 'Frank Cousins is resigning when the Prices and Incomes Bill is published this weekend,' he said, 'and I want you to take his place.' I did not react except to say how sorry I should be to leave the Post Office at this critical moment and on the eve of the announcement of historic changes. 'Well,' said Harold, 'that is always liable to happen. You have done an excellent job in modernising an old industry and few people know what has gone on. Now you must start learning and for six months you will have to keep your head down and read, and no gimmicks.' (That from Harold!)

So that is it. Unless Frank Cousins changes his mind the announcement will be made on Sunday and I am in the Cabinet with a chance to create a new department that can really change the face of Britain and its prospects for survival.

Friday 1 July

Up early this morning to the Post Office for the last time as PMG. I took my movie camera and got some photographs of Mr Parrot and Mr Rice in their red uniforms and top hats.

I spent the whole morning listening to the consultants McKinsey's presentation of their findings on the postal services. Roger Morrison and Alan Stewart spoke for about two hours and produced an enormous number of tables and charts, proving conclusively that the techniques of management used were totally inadequate.

I had a sandwich in the Office and then to the Commons where my parliamentary answer announcing legislation against the pirates came out. Peter Shore looked in at 11 o'clock and we talked for an hour and a half.

Monday 4 July

At 7.30 my driver, Mr Wilson, took me to the Post Office, where I arrived just before 8 and I handed in my keys and bag and collected my ashtray and mug and camp bed. Wratten was punch-drunk and said that he felt everything would stop now. Mr Atkins, my messenger, clutched my hand in both of his. It was all very sad and I felt the wrench of leaving.

At 8.30 I arrived at Millbank Tower and went straight up to my room. I was the first person to arrive and I had half an hour to get settled before the meeting at 9 am to discuss parliamentary questions. Peter Shore and Edmund Dell were there too. We went over questions for a time and then Frank Cousins came in to say goodbye. He was relieved in a way to have gone and yet obviously under considerable strain. I like Frank but I think that his heart is in the trade union movement. He really thinks the union movement is more important than the Labour Party or the Government, and that is where he wants to go back to and do his job. He reminded me that in 1960 he had said that my resignation would ruin my political career as Gaitskell would crucify me. 'I was wrong,' he said, 'and I'm glad that you've got this opportunity.'

It's funny to be on the site on Millbank where I was born and to look out over the same scene from a greater height. I can see the Post Office Tower in the distance and St Paul's. After lunch to the Commons, where Sir Otto Clarke, my Permanent Secretary, came to see me. He is one of the most brilliant Treasury men, rather erratic but exceptionally able. We discussed the amalgamation with Mintech of most of the Ministry of Aviation and the shipbuilding functions from the Board of Trade.

Thursday 7 July

At 11.30 I attended my first Cabinet meeting. I found myself sitting on the Prime Minister's extreme left in the corner with Douglas Jay on one side of me and the Chief Whip, John Silkin, on the other side. I had been to the Cabinet before but I was always called in to discuss something specific – and to be sitting in that room and feeling that I was now in the Cabinet was extremely exciting.

Then to the Commons, where I sat next to Ted Short. I asked him how things were going and he said it was difficult to take over the Post Office at that particular moment. The status proposals will go forward as before but the management structure would have to wait. This means that my plan to get rid of the Engineer-in-Chief and give telephones independence has been frustrated. Obviously the Office organised itself the very day I left and managed to stop it all. I'm not a bit surprised. This is the price you pay for ministerial changes. Power returns almost immediately to the civil servants and they see to it that projects they don't want advanced don't get advanced. Afterwards I dashed to Montague Burton's and got a couple of cheap suits off the peg.

Friday 8 July

At 11 o'clock I was called in to the Cabinet Room for the meeting between the French party, led by Pompidou, and the British side led by the PM.

I now have ministerial responsibilities that involve nuclear and other relations with France. I didn't have to say anything but it was interesting to see Pompidou, the French banker, looking shrewdly across at Harold, and Harold trying to be friendly by talking about technical co-operation. At the end Harold said that the Foreign Secretary wished to say something about the French nuclear tests. So Michael Stewart said how much the British Government regretted the fact that the French were testing nuclear weapons despite the Test-Ban Treaty. Pompidou said that his Foreign

Minister, Couve de Murville, would reply and de Murville said, 'I am grateful to the British Foreign Secretary for pointing out that now the British have completed their nuclear tests they think it is unnecessary for the French to complete theirs,' dismissing it with a touch of scorn. It was most amusing. Harold then said, 'Let's go to lunch,' and that was the end of the matter.

On the way out Eddie Shackleton called me on one side and warned me about Solly Zuckerman. 'Remember that he is a man without any sense of loyalty whatsoever,' he said. 'He wants to be loved and I'm sure there is a place for him, but if you encourage him do it discreetly.' This sort of high-level gossip is, I suppose, part and parcel of high politics. If I were C.P. Snow I would note it in my diary for my novel about Whitehall. As it is I find it rather unattractive.

At 1 o'clock I went to the Post Office where my old private office had laid on sandwiches and beer so that I could meet them all again. They presented me with a beautiful little reading lamp which will be just what I need for my bedside for reading official papers late into the night.

Don Wratten took me aside and told me what had happened in the week since I left. Wratten said that the DG was almost delirious with excitement at my departure and that Ted Short has asked him to delay his retirement for three months, which he was likely to do. This was so depressing that I really couldn't bear it and I was glad to hurry away after having said goodbye to all my friends there.

Saturday 16 July

Travelled up to Durham last night for the Miners' Gala. Breakfast in our room early and at 8.30 we heard the first bands approaching.

On the hotel balcony were Michael Stewart and his wife and George Brown. George beckoned me on one side and said he wanted to talk to me urgently. He was in a state of tension. In brief, he feared that the Treasury would come forward with major deflationary measures at home and he intended to resign from the Government tonight. He told me that he had only told Harold Wilson, Roy Jenkins and me. 'You may just as well make your speech under the same misery that I am going to make mine,' he said. I replied that if he did this it would mean the end of the Government – so I profoundly believe. The Cabinet simply would not have a majority in the House of Commons if George Brown had decided to opt out on these grounds. George's own remedy for the economic situation would be infinitely preferable.

Monday 18 July

I went to see George Brown and found him in a state of high excitement. Barbara Castle was with him. He repeated definitely that he was going. He said he had warned Harold a year ago that he was not prepared to put up with another episode of this kind and that Roy and Tony agreed with him.

Barbara said she thought there would be a majority in the Cabinet in favour of his view but George said that it was impossible that this could carry the day as Harold was so heavily committed publicly to maintaining the value of the pound. Barbara said she thought Harold would accept the majority view and George said, 'No, this involves his leadership. Do you want me as Leader, Barbara?' Barbara replied firmly, 'No.' 'Then Harold will win,' said George.

Wednesday 20 July

To the Cabinet again for another four-hour sitting on devaluation and inflation, ending at 1 o'clock. The question now is whether George Brown will resign.

Sandwich lunch at the House of Commons and then went to hear Harold make his statement at 3.30. George Brown was not sitting on the Front Bench and this became the subject of immediate comment. I had a word with Austen Albu and Bill Rodgers. Bill had just come back from seeing him and his eyes were red with tears. They all said what a tragedy it would be if he went and Austen said George had a death wish and somehow wanted to get out of politics altogether. A round robin of Members was quickly drawn up and conveyed to him.

This evening I had a talk to Peter and got home to bed after midnight. Caroline told me there had just been a news flash to the effect that George Brown had withdrawn his resignation and was carrying on.

Back to the Commons where I voted for the Abortion Bill, which was carried by 223 votes to 29 – a notable victory.

Then to the DEA where I sat in while George Brown interviewed the CBI about the wage and prices freeze. George put on one of his pyrotechnic displays against Sir Maurice Laing, John Davies, Sir Stephen Brown and other industrialists. He shouted at them, bullied them, wheedled them, giggled at them, but in a way – although it was a sensational performance – I felt they were hardened to it and am not sure that it was as impressive as George thought it was. He has not really got the stability to be Prime Minister, though he is in many ways an attractive and full-blooded figure.

Wednesday 27 July

Lunch with the leaders of the major machine-tool manufacturing companies. I found myself sitting opposite Sir Arnold Hall of Hawker Siddeley. He is an extremely able and cultivated man and I like him very much. A number of leaders of the engineering industry were there as well. It was my job to make a speech afterwards and I described the work of Mintech and the importance of the machine-tool industry and then went on to develop my thesis, which I am going to make a major theme throughout the coming months. It is simply this: what has gone wrong with Britain in the industrial field is not due to two years of Labour government, thirteen wasted Tory years, six years of socialist misrule, the War, the depression, the First World War. The origins of our difficulties go back much further. Germany overtook this country in the 1880s and indeed we began losing our lead in about the fifties or sixties of the last century.

The reason was that at that time we opted to become an imperial country instead of continuing as an industrial one. I recalled in my speech that in my childhood I had been taught a great deal about the engineers of the late eighteenth and early nineteenth century but that after that the school books concentrated on viceroys and generals, civil servants and diplomats, and this country had simply opted out of industrialism. Thus all the schools had geared themselves to producing the sort of people the Empire needed. When I said this there was a spontaneous burst of applause and one or two people came up afterwards and said I ought to publish the speech. In fact it was a pre-introduction model of a major speech which I intend to make on every possible occasion from now on. The truth is that Britain must now give up being an imperial country and become an industrial country again and only in this way can we reshape our society, and encourage people to regard work in industry as the most worthwhile job they can possibly do.

Friday 29 – Sunday 31 July
The whole family drove off to Stansgate, arriving at 10.30 on Friday. All day doing nothing on Saturday. It takes an awful time to unwind after a week's work and I have nightmares in which I am required to see General de Gaulle about the future of Concorde, or I arrive late in the office unshaven, not having read my Cabinet papers.

An old Post Office pillar box was delivered today at Stansgate – it weighs about half a ton. I had ordered it as Postmaster-General and it was to cost five or six quid. But as I had left by the time it was delivered they decided to give it to me as a gift. With a sledge hammer we broke off the bottom and gradually moved it over and erected it. I am very proud of it.

Pleasant sunny day on Sunday and we sat on the lawn. I didn't even open my red box. We drove home, getting back about 6.15. Parliament rises at the end of next week and I shall be glad of a break.

Saturday 6 August
Number 10 lives in an atmosphere of intrigue, encouraged by George Wigg, who is a completely crazy adviser, Marcia, who gets a bit hysterical and Gerald Kaufman, who just sits wisely and nods. What Harold needs is a frank talk from his friends, but at the moment he won't allow his friends to meet. He's afraid that if Dick, Barbara, Tommy, Peter, Judith and I meet, we may turn out to be against him. I find the upper strata of politics less and less attractive. It's not exactly that I'm naïve, but I really am only interested in politics in order to get my job done. Peter is of course a wise bird. He

suggested that I should go and see Harold soon, in order to mend my relations with Number 10 which are very poor at present.

Sunday 7 August
We had another pleasant day and Peter and I went over one or two joint projects affecting Mintech. I rang Tommy and he suggested I should ring Marcia, and he said, 'Harold was wounded, but is also very loving.' It was a typical Thomas remark. I rang Marcia and said perhaps I could come and see Harold at his convenience. She said he'd been waiting for me to come and see him ever since the crisis broke. I said I didn't want to bother him and wasn't at all sure what had gone on. Marcia said, 'At your level he expects you to bother him whenever you want to.' He would also like me to ring him before Cabinet when anything important is coming up to find out the line that he wants to take. On balance, I'm glad that I struck out on my own, since I had been Harold's adviser for too long and it is a good thing that he should see me in my own right.

Wednesday 10 August
George Brown has been moved to the Foreign Office. It is said that George made it a condition of his staying on at the time of the recent threatened resignation and that Harold acceded to it.

There is a great deal of dismay about the future of the DEA although it may be that Michael Stewart, with his quiet Fabian manner, will keep the thing going on a rather better basis than George could have done. There is some anxiety about George at the Foreign Office but he has always wanted the job and Harold presumably didn't feel able to stand out against him. I think Dick Crossman's appointment as Leader of the House is the best news of all as we probably shall get some parliamentary reform and he will now be acting as the liaison between the Government, the Parliamentary Party and the National Executive.

Thursday 25 August
The whole family – without Stephen – went to the Bradwell Nuclear Power Station this morning. They had laid on a superb tour for us and we saw the station which cost £58 million to build and is of a Magnox type, now obsolescent. We walked right into the reactor and saw the gantry that moved the nuclear fuel. We were frisked by Geiger counters, saw the heat exchanger and the turbines and then had lunch with the senior officials of the CEGB who had come to see us. It was altogether an enjoyable day.

The thing that interested me was the difference in attitude between Joshua, who is aged eight, and myself. I had to drive out of my mind all my primitive knowledge of how power stations worked – whereby you burned the coal, heated the water and the steam turned the turbines – and try to think of the implications of atomic energy. Joshua took it entirely for granted. It seemed natural to him that if you had a nuclear power station, you would be able to generate electricity and because he wasn't consciously thinking about the process, he got an awful lot more out of it than I did.

Tuesday 13 September
At noon Mr Webb, the Head of NASA, came to see me with Dr Draper, formerly of the Massachusetts Institute of Technology, who was responsible for the guidance system of missiles including the Polaris missile. Webb said the American space effort had reached such a scale that the payload they were going to put up could take over a number of scientific research projects which exceeded the capacity of American universities to provide. He wanted co-operation with us. I was extremely non-committal on the subject of expenditure but expressed a general interest in sharing the dissemination of information so that the technical fallout could be spread more evenly among the Western countries. Webb's main object of course is to build up a Western space capability in Europe to rival that of the Soviet Union and particularly to see that the French don't break away on their own and monopolise all the space technology in Europe. His first idea had been to suggest links directly with the Germans, following Chancellor Erhardt's visit to President Johnson last December when the joint space probe was proposed. He had then thought that it would be worthwhile looking in to see us and I tried to say enough to keep the options open without committing us to any expenditure which we couldn't afford.

Sunday 18 September
Lunch with Tony Crosland. Tony was in a very curious mood. He stressed how he was trying to cut down on the work he was doing and how important a complete holiday was. He said that he was devolving more and more work to his department, that the comprehensive battle was won and he was leaving it to Assistant Secretaries to approve the various reorganisation schemes that came up.

After lunch we sat and talked and I told him I did not like the idea of having to make every discussion in Cabinet a vote of confidence. I raised the question of the conspiracy and asked him if he had any knowledge of it and he denied it entirely. He said, quite frankly, 'I never was an admirer of Harold Wilson but I think he's probably as good a peactime Prime Minister as this country ever gets, even though over the last four months we appear to have been entirely without a strategy and I think he's been very bad. But in time he will learn to be less gimmicky.'

He thought that Jim Callaghan might conceivably visualise himself as Leader some time and he thought Roy Jenkins was ambitious too, but that none of these things was in sight over the next five years. I don't know whether Tony Crosland is discreet or not but there is always a certain risk in talking even to Cabinet colleagues. I don't particularly want this to get back to George Wigg.

Friday 23 September

To Number 10 for a discussion under Harold's chairmanship of the Productivity Conference and afterwards he asked me to stay. He said that his reshuffle in August had been the smartest piece of work he'd ever done 'as there are now six crown princes instead of just one'. This, I think, was his real motive and it confirms retrospectively what one has feared about his analysis of the July crisis. He also said that the only reason he had reshuffled on that day was because George Brown had told his press adviser and it had to be announced before it leaked. I asked if Mintech would have a new Minister of State in the next reshuffle and he said that it was very difficult, as he was up to the legal limit of Ministers of State and Ministers and he had to fit in Patrick Gordon Walker and he didn't intend to let Fred Lee go, and so on and so on. So it looks as if things are going to be delayed for a while.

Saturday 22 October

Driven to Chequers for the meeting on Europe at 10.45 am, which lasted until 7 pm. There were nineteen Ministers there, and numerous officials who left in the afternoon.

There was a great row in the morning when Sir William Armstrong, Joint Permanent Secretary at the Treasury, said that he didn't see any prospect at all of Britain being able to be in the Common Market unless and until we had devalued. George Brown got quite hysterical at this thought, because he knew that the Cabinet would be opposed to devaluation, George himself being in favour, and that this would affect our chances of entry. William Armstrong was really in the doghouse for saying this. We agreed that Harold Wilson and George Brown would visit the six countries of the Common Market to do a 'probe'. Harold was not prepared to let George go alone because he didn't trust George and he thought that George didn't trust him. I came to the conclusion that Britain would be in the Common Market by 1970.

Monday 24 October

In the evening we went to the Soviet Embassy and as George Blake, the spy, had just been 'sprung' from Wormwood Scrubs there were a lot of rumours around that he might actually have been in the Embassy at the time of the party.

Thursday 27 October

Caroline and I had dinner with the Gulbenkians at the Ritz. Christopher Soames and his wife and Sir Alec Douglas-Home and his wife were there. I sat next to Soames's wife Mary, the daughter of Churchill. She told me how bitterly angry and disappointed the family were that Lord Moran had been so unfair as to publish a book about her father's health. An enjoyable evening – Gulbenkian is an amusing man.

Sunday 4 December
Harold came back from HMS *Tiger* with a document half agreed with Smith. Wilson had been negotiating with Smith on board *Tiger* in the Mediterranean to try to end the Rhodesian crisis. We had a Cabinet specially summoned and everyone was there except Barbara Castle. I had great anxieties as to whether it was right to agree with what Harold had brought back, but I did.

Monday 5 December
Rhodesia rejected the terms agreed with Harold at the talks on HMS *Tiger*.

Tuesday 6 December
Lunch with Solly Zuckerman at London Zoo. We talked about nuclear weapons and he told me that he was keen that Denis Healey and the Defence staff should not be able to get away with further expenditure on nuclear weapons by hardening the Polaris submarine warheads. He said that he and Lord Rothschild were really at one on this.

Thursday 15 December
I called Donald Stokes and George Harriman in together to discuss the Chrysler/Rootes crisis. I put to them three simple questions. Do you want to see Chrysler take over Rootes? Do you think it is worth attempting a British solution – a regrouping that would include Rootes and British Motors and Leyland, in which there might be some government participation? Would you be prepared to bring about a merger between your two companies to try to absorb Rootes if the Government were prepared to help?

Thursday 22 December
At Cabinet I saved the Harrier vertical take-off jet, one of the most brilliant British aeronautical innovations, which Denis Healey always tries to cancel on every possible occasion.

The Rootes-Chrysler deal was approved by the Cabinet with general commendation. I tried to promote the idea of a special concession on electrical cars by taking off the tax and purchase tax so as to encourage their development.

In the evening I did a long and – given my limited knowledge of French – painful broadcast for the BBC French Service.

Thursday 26 January 1967
Had a row over Cabinet Ministers' memoirs. It had been reported in the

papers that Dick Crossman and Barbara Castle had signed contracts to write their memoirs and a Minister raised this at Cabinet on the grounds that it made some people very uneasy to know that their colleagues were keeping a record of everything.

Dick did admit that he had a contract to write and publish his diary. He had got a woman from Nuffield to edit it for him but out of respect to the Party he had arranged that they were not to be published until after the General Election. But there was still anxiety because if there had been a very narrow Labour or Tory majority followed by another Election, and in the interval between the two Elections, Dick Crossman's memoirs – with confidences about his colleagues – were published, it could have done enormous damage to the Party.

Barbara then admitted that she had also signed a contract to write her memoirs.

Harold declared that he intended to write three books. 'One,' he said, 'I will write immediately we leave office and that will be an absolutely factual record of the Administration. Later, when I retire, I shall publish a much fuller account in which I will give far greater detail – this is when I have retired from public life. Thirdly,' he said, 'I shall write a book about what really happened with instructions that it should not be published until after my death.'

I said that there were some of us who felt resentful that *we* hadn't been approached to publish our memoirs, and I said that I, too, was a diarist.

Monday 6 February
Premier Kosygin's visit to Britain, and his plane was diverted from Gatwick at the last minute so the whole Cabinet was diverted too. I drove at 110 miles an hour at one point to get there. Then to Claridges with Soldatov, the Ambassador, and Kosygin.

I might add here that the security services bugged Kosygin during his visit. I know this because I got a mysterious memorandum from the security services, reporting something they had picked up on tape that Kosygin had said about Pompidou. I didn't find it very useful, as it happened, except that it indicated how very close Kosygin and Pompidou were, due to de Gaulle's Eastern policy.

Wednesday 8 February
I went to Elliot-Automation with Kosygin and on the way in the car he kept looking out of the windows – I think it was the first time he had been to Britain – and asking questions, 'What is the cost of that house?' This was as we were going up through Hendon to Boreham Wood. 'How long would a man have to work as a worker to be able to afford one of these houses?'

In the evening we went to the Kosygin reception at Lancaster House, followed by dinner at the Soviet Embassy. George Brown got tight and kept shouting, 'I want to go home. Are they all Bolsheviks?' and similar remarks.

I received an invitation to go to Moscow for the May Day Parade and for talks. Sir Geoffrey Harrison, our Ambassador in Moscow, was absolutely opposed to a British Minister attending the May Day Parade because, he said, it would cause great political embarrassment.

Thursday 2 March

To Cabinet, where we discussed Party discipline arising out of abstentions on the defence debate. At the PLP meeting later, Harold made his 'dog licence' speech – that each MP is allowed to bite once like a dog but if they abstained or voted against the Government again they would be in trouble. This was a remark that he had thrown off at Cabinet in the morning and I must say that I didn't like it very much, and I liked it even less when he said it at the Party meeting. It caused tremendous offence because it was very insulting to imply that we were all dogs and he was our trainer. It also gave me a great insight into his attitude towards the Labour Party, namely that we were there to support him and that he licensed the Party, whereas of course we license him because we elect him.

Thursday 13 April

The GLC elections, and Labour were absolutely routed. We are losing support as a government, and this is rubbing off on Labour councillors who are very resentful against the Government. But there is a school of thought, of which Gerald Kaufman is one of the leading exponents, that the Labour Party doing badly has the great effect of sweeping out the most ghastly reactionary old Labour councils and bringing in new leadership – a very cynical view.

Monday 17 April – Ministerial visit to USSR

I went to the airport and flew on BEA to Moscow with Tommy Balogh, Ieuan Maddock, Harry Slater and William Knighton. Caroline was invited but Harold had personally vetoed it.

We were met by Kirillin and the Ambassador, Sir Geoffrey Harrison, and Gvishiani of the State Committee for Science and Technology and I was put up at the National Hotel. We had a short walk round the Kremlin – it was very cold – and we had dinner at the Embassy with Sir Geoffrey and Dr Alexander, who is the Science Attaché and generally thought by the Russians to be an intelligence man.

Then we had a meeting in the Embassy's secret conference room, which is in the basement and is suspended from the ceiling so that it does not rest on any foundations. From a corner of the room came the recording of a cocktail party playing continuously over our chat, and Ieuan Maddock worried them by saying that he could bug the room easily by stripping off the noise of the cocktail party and picking up the vibrations of the suspended room through the earth. But once you are in a room like that you can't honestly think of anything secret to say! We discussed our strategy until 1 o'clock in the morning by which time I was extremely tired.

Tuesday 18 April
To the Institute of the Tele-Mechanics where we were greeted by Academician Trapeznikov, a very distinguished man who was studying control theory and trying to relate cybernetics to biology and neurology. As we walked around his Institute there was a girl sitting with wires on her arms, picking up electrical impulses. She was opening and closing her hands and on the oscilloscope you could see the electrical impulses being recorded while people were trying to find out how the brain sent a message to the hand.

In the evening we went to dinner with Kirillin and his wife and daughter, Ola, at their flat, along with the Ambassador, and Gvishiani, Academician Artsemivitsch and Academician Keldersh. Madame Santalova was the interpreter.

I had been told by the Ambassador that Russian Ministers never invite British Ministers to their flats or homes and he was absolutely amazed when his invitation came in but it was, of course, because I had asked Kirillin to my home in London. It was lovely. We sat and talked in a tiny little flat where he and his wife and child lived. Kirillin is one of the Vice-Premiers of the Soviet Union and an eminent scientist. We sat in his little library while the meal was being laid and we ate together, then he showed us home movies of his trip to England and having snowballs thrown at him by the children.

It was a marvellous evening and afterwards he told us stories of Azerbaijan Radio, a great joke in Russia. Azerbaijan Radio apparently invites listeners to write in with questions like, 'Why do the Americans produce better automobiles than the Russians?' Azerbaijan Radio replies, 'Why do the Americans persecute the negroes?' indicating that there is no good answer.

Artsemivitsch, who is a leading nuclear scientist, was interesting. 'Science, we say in the Soviet Union, is defined as "Satisfying your curiosity at the expense of the State",' which is an amusing definition.

We talked about fusion. I had great anxieties as to whether we should go ahead with the huge Culham fusion programme which wasn't producing results. Artsemivitsch said, 'Well, ten years ago we said it would take us twenty years to make fusion work and we still say it will take twenty years to make fusion work, so we haven't altered our view in any way!'

Thursday 20 April
I went to the Institute of Cybernetics and met Academician Glushkov, one of the most brilliant cyberneticists in the Soviet Union and a member of the

American Computer Society. We had a Ukrainian lunch with them and at the Institute I was shown a computer they had built. I wasn't, of course, in a position to judge how good their technology was, but Ieuan Maddock, who was with me, said it was many years behind Western standards. They showed me one computer which had been specially programmed to put together every day of the week with every day of every year back to 1700. They said to me, 'Minister, tell us when you were born and we'll tell you what day of the week it was.' So I told them I was born on 3 April 1925. The computer creaked and groaned and produced the reply that it was a Friday. I said that was quite right, because I knew the day. So they asked, 'How do you know that it is correct?' and I replied very flippantly, 'Well, I don't remember 3 April, but I remember how excited I was on Thursday 2nd.' This was translated into Russian and then back into English and into Russian again and they thought it was rather a flippant joke for a senior Minister to make.

Sightseeing in Kiev and shopping with Mme Santalova. Then we caught the sleeper back to Moscow. On the train, sitting in the compartment next door was Academician Kornichuk, who is the President of the World Peace Council. I went in and introduced myself to him and Academician Glushkov, who happened to be in the train, came into the compartment and translated. We all sat and talked and I asked Kornichuk about the work of the Peace Council and how he was getting on in bringing the Israelis and the Arabs together. He replied, 'Ah they are impossible, impossible. We tried very hard but the Arabs walked out when the Israelis appeared.'

He was very drunk. He was on his way to Moscow to be given the Lenin Prize for a play that had made him famous, which he had written during the war. He was a sort of Kingsley Martin of Russia – an old intellectual on the left with an international reputation. He started attacking computers in exactly the way that John Betjeman might attack them. Glushkov translated, 'My comrade says that if computers are in general use they will destroy man's genius and his spirit and his imagination.' Glushkov, who was a young chap, laughed and was very amused by it. It was great fun.

There was a lot of champagne and singing in the corridors and Kornichuk and Glushkov and I ended up joining in, with some British songs included to make me feel at home. I was of course stone-cold sober and getting rather tired by this time.

Friday 21 April
The train arrived in Moscow at 9 o'clock and I had a very discouraging telegram, which I might have predicted, from the Foreign Office, signed by George Brown

Tommy Balogh was waiting at the hotel to see me said that we must have a discussion together before the final talks with the Russians. I said, 'Well, look, I am all tired and dirty,' so he came into my suite and sat on the bidet in the bathroom while I was quietly having a bath and he told me what he hoped to achieve and how we must plan it. It was only later that I realised we had disregarded all the warnings in the security briefings. The Russians would have photographs of me in a bath and the Government's economic adviser sitting on the bidet! We had a laugh about that.

Final talks and drew up the protocol with Kirillin. Then we drove to the airport and got back to London in three and a half hours.

Saturday 22 April
I went to see Harold about the Russian visit and he was very pleased with what had happened. I told him the story about my bath but he didn't think that was very funny.

Monday 24 April
I was debriefed on the USSR. Otto said to me, 'You must remember, Minister, that our trade with Russia is only 1 per cent of what it is with Denmark, and it is not an important market.' And that was the attitude of the Board of Trade people throughout – they never cared about this operation. Nor did the Foreign Office.

Sunday 30 April
I went to Chequers, where we had Cabinet all day on the Common Market and we voted by 13 to 8 for an unconditional application. I made a speech which created a favourable impression with the pro-Europeans, who thought me anti-European. I said we had to cut Queen Victoria's umbilical cord.

Those of us who favoured the application were not too worried about the conditions because we were a defeated Cabinet. Going back to the war, we had tried as a Labour Government to solve the country's economic problems and we had left in a balance of payment crisis in 1951. The Tories had tried and had left in the balance of payments crisis in 1964. We had tried and had had to put the brakes on in 1966, and we were now looking for solutions to our problems from outside and somehow we were persuaded that the Common Market was the way of making progress.

Wednesday 10 May
In the evening went to the State Banquet at the Royal Naval College, Greenwich, for King Faisal of Saudi Arabia.

Had to hurry back to vote in the Common Market debate in the House of Commons and there was a massive vote in favour of application. Almost all the Tories and the majority of Labour MPs were in favour.

Sunday 22 May – Ministerial visit to United States
To Washington and I met the Water for Peace UK delegation and said we
were here to describe our own achievements and to sell our products.

Then I went to talk to Sir Patrick Dean at the Embassy, a man I very
much dislike – a typical British Ambassador, arrogant and smooth.

I asked to see Robert McNamara at the Department of Defence and was
taken to the Pentagon. It is impossible to convey adequately the tremendous
respect with which McNamara is regarded in Washington. Here was the
great American defence establishment, overwhelmingly the most powerful
in the world, and McNamara, one of Kennedy's men, had come in and
established civilian control and crammed through programme budgeting. It
was like going into an emperor's court – the centre of military power in the
world.

I said that we in Britain knew of his military achievements but we didn't
know as much as we would like to know of his control of the Pentagon, and I
asked him whether he was interested in the Concorde or supersonic aircraft
for military purposes. He said he wasn't.

Tuesday 23 May
Caroline went to Capitol Hill to see the Senate and the White House.

It was the official opening of the Water for Peace Conference at the
Sheraton Hotel and Stuart Udall, the Secretary for the Interior, and
President Lyndon Johnson attended. President Johnson came round to
meet us. He looked absolutely drained of energy, totally exhausted. The
only other man I have ever seen who looked quite as white and tired was
Kosygin. The leaders of the US and the USSR really do carry a load far
beyond the capacity of a single person. What was interesting was the way the
American President moved, with no protocol but absolutely maximum
security.

He was surrounded by about five or six security men with their backs to
him, moving as he moved, and they had walkie-talkies into which they were
talking all the time, describing where he was, looking round, saying check
this and check that. It was like a Roman emperor with the Praetorian
Guard, only the Praetorian Guard was defending him with an electronic
network of security, rather than with actual weapons, though I have no
doubt the men were armed.

Wednesday 31 May
Melissa came to have a meal at the House and was kissed by George Brown
– she was thrilled. She met Barbara Castle, Douglas Jay, Elwyn Jones and
Jeremy Thorpe and she was as happy as could be.

Saturday 3 June
Went to the Farnborough Air Show. Met Pompidou briefly and Pierre

Messmer, the Minister of Defence, who was in charge of Concorde. Group
Captain Townsend, Princess Margaret's old boyfriend, was there.

It was a beautiful display. The French do these things in a fantastic way –
far better than we do. The Farnborough Air Show is just a pre-First World
War country cricket match compared to the Paris International Air Show.
Of course the French planes and French technology dominated. The F–111
came over, folding its wings. The paratroopers dropped, the French
Hovercraft was available for us to see, the Concorde was presented as a
French plane – it was a marvellous example of the glory of France being
exploited.

I came home and had my first ever automatic landing in a British aircraft.
I saw the pilot with his hands just by the stick but in fact it landed itself.

Wednesday 5 July
Bill Penney came in to talk about the centrifuge separation method for
producing enriched uranium. This centrifuge as a way of producing
uranium was based on a development by Dr Zipper, a German scientist,
during the war. In order to produce enriched uranium, centrifuges have to
turn at enormously high speeds, posing a mechanical problem rather than a
nuclear one, and once you have solved that, you can enrich uranium
without the tremendously expensive and bulky gas diffusion process.

Penney said that the centrifuge project has enormous military implications because the risk of the spread of nuclear weapons is much greater than
before. It means that countries like South Africa, which have natural
uranium, might be able to develop enrichment plants on a small scale almost
completely undetected, near their natural uranium field. I could see that the
effect on the Non-Proliferation Treaty and on other areas would be great.
Penney told me that all that had held up the centrifuge system from
operating was that there had been no parts able to rotate at the required
speed without breaking down. So the development of this use of centrifuge
was really a mechanical engineering refinement. Our fear was that if anyone
knew that the British AEA was using the centrifuge to enrich uranium, then
all the work that had been stopped or never started on centrifuges elsewhere
would begin with renewed vigour. We ourselves, after announcing that we
were going ahead with a bigger atomic programme for peaceful purposes,
had stated that we would be expanding Capenhurst for the purpose of
enriching uranium by gas diffusion, and everybody was waiting for the
second stage of the Capenhurst development to begin. In physical terms,
civil engineers and so on were all ready to move in and build it. But it was
now unnecessary to expand Capenhurst and we were afraid that the secret
would leak out simply because of the fact that Capenhurst wasn't going
ahead. Anyone who knew the score would be able to read into that the fact
that the AEA had the centrifuge. It would mean that Britain could meet its
own enriched uranium needs without being so dependent on the Americans

and that the big French plant at Pierre Latte would be the most expensive piece of junk ever.

The Dutch had boasted that *they* had found a better way of enriching uranium and that they were using the centrifuge, but the Dutch had no nuclear know-how and nobody believed them. The Germans were thought to be involved. When I visited the Julich reactor with Stoltenburg earlier in 1967, this was where the Germans were working on it.

It was so important that I went to see Harold at 11.45 that night to tell him the news, and explain to him the implications of it all, which he took on board. Then I went home and I worked till 3.30 am.

Wednesday 19 July
Cabinet meeting on public expenditure, during which there was a sonic boom. It was very funny. I told the Lightning jet crew to fly over London at 12 noon as we were sitting in Cabinet. It was a tremendously hot day and all the windows were open. I was afraid that there would be a frightful din so I passed a note to Harold saying that there would be a sonic bang at midday and should I tell the Cabinet? He said, no. So I sat there dreading it. At 12 o'clock, which we heard on Big Ben, there was a great sound like a clap of thunder. It did cause a shock, and was different from subsonic noise but it wasn't as bad as one had expected. But Miss Nunn, who was in the Cabinet secretariat, hadn't known what was happening and went very pale.

Friday 4 August
Because of unemployment in the North East, we were anxious that Swan Hunter should tender for two container ships which were on order, and I had had authority to offer a subsidy for this purpose to Sir John Hunter, who hadn't bid for it on the grounds that it wouldn't be profitable.

I called in the directors of Swan Hunter and as quick as a flash they realised that we had to give them the money for employment reasons, so they simply stuck out for more. I think originally we offered them half a million. They stayed for three hours and we tried to arrange it so that we could supervise the accounts. But in the end they went away with a million quid. Absolute bribery.

Saturday 16 November
Cabinet decided to devalue.

Spent all morning in a package of cuts while I had this terrible guilty secret, which I had to keep quiet until it was announced.

Saturday 18 November
Devaluation from $2.80 to $2.40 announced. A great moment of defeat for the Government but I felt cheerful about it as a matter of fact, because this was, after all, what we had tried to prevent for three years and this delay was

itself a great defeat for Harold. The following day he did his absurd broadcast on television saying, 'The pound in your pocket won't be devalued.'

Monday 11 December

To Paris in the HS125. Collected Sir Patrick Reilly, the Ambassador, in Paris and went to Toulouse for the roll-out of the 002 Concorde. It was icy cold.

Chamant met me and I made a little speech. I didn't speak in French, but I did say that as a tribute to this occasion we would now in future have a British Concorde which would be spelt with an 'e'. There was great cheering. I said, 'That is "e" for excellence; "E" for England and "e" for "*entente concordiale*".' This went down very well.

In fact, there was a hell of a row about this. The press said it was a capitulation to de Gaulle, whom had I consulted, and so on. When I sat and thought about it I realised that this wasn't taken as a joke. I had an angry letter from a man who said, 'I live in Scotland, and you talk about "E" for England but part of it is made in Scotland.' I wrote back and said that it was also 'E' for 'Écosse' – and I might have added 'e' for extravagance and 'e' for escalation as well! I then discovered that the British Concorde had always been spelt with an 'e', but after the French vetoed British entry into the Common Market in the early sixties, the Government gave an order that the Concorde was to drop the 'e'. So I had only reinstated the original spelling.

But it was a great day and, except for the icy cold, it was well worthwhile. It was nice to see Concorde out of the hangar. After worrying so much about Concorde, you wondered if you would ever see it.

The immediate problem confronting the Labour Government in 1968 following devaluation of the pound, was the mounting pressure for further public-expenditure cuts, and early in the New Year a succession of Cabinet meetings was held to find the money from different departments.

Defence expenditure was a target particularly the commitment east of Suez and the defence equipment budget, notably the proposed purchase of fifty American F-111 aircraft which had been ordered to replace the TSR-2 after Labour came to power. Concorde was also under threat.

In 1968 Tony Benn began the practice of dictating his diary on to a cassette and, for the first time, recorded Cabinet meetings in detail.

Wednesday 3 January 1968

To see Denis Healey, who was surrounded by some of his senior people who were in a very angry mood, and his language was full of f... this and f... that. He said that the defence cuts were mad; that they were just being done to make it possible to introduce prescription charges; that the whole thing was crazy. He did not intend to offer or accept any reduction in the F-111 commitment. He was also strongly in favour of retaining Polaris. I asked him about Concorde and warned him that if cancelled, this might lead to the cancellation of the Anglo–French military package. He thought that Concorde should go but if I supported the F-111, he was prepared to let others take the lead on the Concorde issue. This was really very crude politicking and I listened attentively and left without any sort of commitment.

In the evening we went to the Crossmans, where we had dinner with Tommy Balogh, Peter Shore and Barbara Castle. We started with a great gripe about the absolute exclusion of Cabinet Ministers from important decisions.

Barbara is very departmentally orientated and is terrified that her major road programme is going to be cut by Roy Jenkins. We managed to get her off that and agreed that a small group of five Ministers – that is to say Harold in the chair, the Foreign Secretary, the Lord President, the Chancellor and the Secretary of State for Economic Affairs – should form an inner Cabinet (which would be politically balanced, as it happens), and that other Ministers should be invited to come along as and when it was necessary to air their views on particular issues. But it is unlikely that Harold will agree to this, Harold now being full of euphoria about his success last December in preventing the South African arms deal and not feeling sufficiently threatened to call in his friends.

I am simply not prepared to accept the Treasury's right to dart into individual Ministers' departments and find savings to suit their particular policies. Whether or not this argument will survive tomorrow, I do not know. I put forward some powerful alternatives to the educational and health cuts proposed, and Caroline is working with her Comprehensive Schools Committee Group to give me an alternative list of proposals that would reduce government subsidies to private education and save as much without affecting the school leaving age, which is absolutely essential for comprehensive reorganisation.

It was an enjoyable evening but it became clear that Dick believed he had established a relationship with Roy that was as good as his relationship with Harold. This transfer of loyalty should make Harold pretty anxious. Roy is, of course, sitting pretty.

One forty-five, and all my red box still to do. What a life!

Thursday 4 January
The Cabinet met in an icy atmosphere, every Minister realising that he would have to defend his department estimates. The Chancellor opened with a severe warning about what could happen if things went wrong.

There had already been a general agreement that we should be out of our Far Eastern bases by either 1970/71 or 1971/72, and possibly earlier from the Persian Gulf. George Brown argued strongly in favour of 1972 and in this he was supported by George Thomson and Jim Callaghan, Fred Peart, Denis Healey, Cledwyn Hughes, Willie Ross and Michael Stewart. On the other side were Roy Jenkins, Dick Crossman, Barbara Castle, Peter Shore, Gerald Gardiner, Tony Crosland, Lord Longford, Patrick Gordon Walker, Ray Gunter, Tony Greenwood and Dick Marsh.

I said that I had never supported the idea of East of Suez very enthusiastically. I thought the Cabinet had not yet realised how isolated Britain was: we were locked out of the EEC, our US link was weakening and we would just have to look after our own interests. For my part I could see little credibility in a lame duck military presence on borrowed money and the best thing to do was to speed up the withdrawal.

We went on to discuss our military hardware. The Chancellor led in favour of a substantial cut and although he detailed the Phantoms and one or two other possible cuts, the whole debate centred on the F-111.

Here Denis Healey made the most formidable case in favour of the F-111, calmly and quietly, and with considerable power of argument. He said that our ground troops and our air force in Europe were much smaller than those of the French and the Germans and that the particular contribution we could make was strike reconnaissance by having fifty F-111s, which were the only aircraft capable of penetrating into Eastern Europe. He said this was the cheapest way of doing it and he drew attention to the offset purchases by the US in Britain which would help to meet the foreign-exchange costs.

After that the argument began building up for and against. Roy Jenkins was the first to speak and he said that here was a clear saving that could be made in foreign currency and he was prepared to accept the fact that the cancellation charges would be slightly more expensive in the coming year.

I was the last to speak and by the time I was called, the vote was ten in favour of keeping the F-111 and nine against, with mine really being the decisive vote. My heart was in my boots and I knew what this would mean in terms of relations with the Ministry of Defence.

I started by saying I found it an extremely difficult issue to deal with. Two factors inclined me strongly towards the Defence Secretary.

The decisive argument for me was that it was inconceivable that we could change our defence role and maintain the same hardware purchases. If the F-111 were to continue, we should have to knock off other bits of hardware: either the Polaris submarine fleet, the Harrier, which was the most advanced aircraft produced in Britain and had considerable export potential, or the British military capability to build complete aircraft on our own. If we abandoned this capability, it would mean we would be committed for ever after to buying American or French military aircraft. Therefore, if there was a hardware choice – and I thought there was – and if, as a responsible Cabinet Minister, I accepted that we had to make a choice, I had to come down against the F-111. It was the last contribution and it left the Cabinet divided ten–ten.

Denis Healey then wound up and he directed much of his speech to me. He said he thought my arguments were fallacious, particularly with regard to the alternatives, and he might be prepared to find other savings.

We were left with the Prime Minister throwing in his vote against the F-111, so that, seen one way, Harold Wilson and I decided that issue between us.

As soon as it was done, George Brown said it would make his job a great deal more difficult in talking about our maintenance of a capability to help Australia, New Zealand, Singapore or Malaysia and he thought that as it had been such an evenly balanced vote, the Defence Secretary should be allowed to produce a paper inviting the Cabinet to reverse its decision and to accept alternative savings. I strongly agreed that any Minister whose programme was being decided for him by the Cabinet should have this right. I must say Denis behaved with great strength of character and did not allow this critical decision against him – on the vote of the Prime Minister, who had supported him throughout – to affect his composure in any way.

The Cabinet broke up at 7.30.

I heard by indirect methods that George Brown had sent telegrams to all the Ambassadors in the Six, asking for an assessment of the reaction of the governments concerned if we did cancel Concorde unilaterally. Every single one of them reported unfavourably on the idea and the Ambassador in Bonn, Frank Roberts, said it would be the worst single blow short of withdrawing our troops unilaterally from Germany. He said it would confirm all the French suspicions about us being bad Europeans and would destroy our credibility as a technological partner.

Tuesday 9 January
Drove myself to the office in my own car because of the snow and from 10 to 11.45 we had a conference following up the Cabinet meeting at which it was decided to go ahead with Concorde but to try to get some agreement with the French on airline commitment by the summer of 1969.

After that, Ronnie Melville stayed on to tell me a bit more about the F-111 and the Ministry of Defence position. First he said that Sir James Dunnett, the Permanent Secretary at the MOD, wanted an opportunity to apologise to me for Denis Healey's behaviour at the end of last week.

I replied that I had known Denis for many years and neither his language nor his approach had in any way influenced me. But obviously it had greatly shaken the officials of the Ministry of Defence, and they were keen that I shouldn't have been so alienated that I would desert the F-111. Ronnie also told me that Denis is fighting for 100 per cent of his programme, and that the Ministry of Defence realised that there will have to be a fall-back position and are trying to persuade him to work one out.

I think what is really going on is an alliance between Ministry of Defence and Ministry of Technology officials to try to persuade Denis to recognise that he is not going to get everything he wants; and to try to drive me towards Denis, particularly in favour of a major purchase of the F-111, even if it is a little bit less than fifty.

At 4 the Cabinet met again for a further session on the survey of public expenditure. We began with roads and poor Barbara Castle was absolutely at the end of her tether. Her voice was rising with emotion as she explained the consequences of what Roy Jenkins was proposing and in the end a compromise which will affect a large chunk of her programme was agreed.

Then we had an amusing session on Home Office economies whereby Roy, because of his expert knowledge, has suggested a number of cuts which poor Jim Callaghan, his predecessor at the Treasury and successor at the Home Office, would have to carry out. Jim said, 'Now that Roy Jenkins has left the Home Office, he is proposing serious cuts, and I'm the one who has got to carry these cuts through so that the reforms which I, as Chancellor, financed for Roy will come to a stop.' This had a ring of truth about it. He stuck his toes in on the reduction of the strength of the police force and there was a flare-up in which Dick Crossman, always ready for a row, said it was intolerable that a Minister should decline to carry cuts through. The atmosphere was very unpleasant.

Monday 15 January
Cabinet at 10. When we got there, the Prime Minister handed round two telegrams from Lyndon Johnson about the current review of public expenditure. It concentrated on two things: first, our projected withdrawal from the Far East and the Middle East by 1971, which filled him with dismay; and second, the proposal to cancel the F-111. Johnson warned us in the strongest terms that this would be a catastrophic decision and would affect the offset arrangement that had been reached under the original agreement. I have often heard of American pressure upon British Cabinets, but this was extremely direct and it is much to our credit that we ultimately resisted it.

Then Harold reported on his talks with Harry Lee over the weekend. He said Lee had been almost hysterical and incoherent for large parts of the discussions, although he calmed down over dinner. He had threatened to withdraw the sterling balances and it had been very difficult to make sense of what he was saying. Lee kept repeating, 'This is the end of 150 years' association.' But he had left Harold in no doubt of his view.

Tuesday 30 January
Otto came in later about honours. He presented me with a very breezy list of people and I resented this for a number of reasons. First of all, I don't like honours. Second, they are always sent to me with a 48-hour deadline, so, in

effect, I really don't have any opportunity to change them. Third, my position is that of constitutional monarch – Otto will come in and explain why I can't do what I want. So when I saw the list, I said, 'Why don't we ever recommend trade unionists?'

'Oh,' he said, 'that's for the Ministry of Labour.'

'Why don't we recommend Dr Curran, the Vice-Chancellor of Strathclyde? He was on our Advisory Committee.'

'Oh, that's the Department of Education and Science.'

'Well then,' I said. 'On knighthoods, you've put down Sutherland, the rather mediocre Chairman and Managing Director of Marconi, who is also the Chairman of the Conference of the Electronics Industry. What about Arnold Weinstock? He's just done the GEC/AEI deal.'

'I assure you, Minister, I couldn't put that forward convincingly.'

'You put forward things that aren't altogether convincing to me,' I replied.

'Oh well, Helsby wouldn't have it.'

Of course it turns out that a group of civil servants crawls over this list and Ministers have no real say at all. John Stonehouse had put forward a private enterprise arms sales merchant-of-death type who handled the Saudi Arabian arms deal. Apparently the Ambassador in Jeddah thought he really *was* unsuitable! Of course the more Otto tried to justify his list, the worse he made it because I was clearly a very minor element in the decisions. 'I'll ask Helsby whether he would agree to consider Weinstock,' he suggested.

'That's no good,' I said, and he replied, 'If we put it in and it's turned down, we shall lose a knighthood,' as if somehow getting the ration was more important than getting the right person. But I didn't want to pursue it too much. It wasn't worth it.

Dinner with Verdet, Rumanian First Deputy Premier, at the Rumanian Embassy. The son of a miner, he had been a miner himself and had studied economics. We had a lot of jokes and fun and he said that the Rumanian Planning Committee had a saying: that miniskirts concealed the essentials but raised the hopes. I said that reminded me of a Five-Year Plan which also conceals the essentials and raises expectations.

Wednesday 21 February
Melissa, Joshua, Caroline and I went to the Mermaid Theatre to see a play organised by the Molecule Club about light. In the audience were hundreds of schoolchildren and Spike Milligan and a few bigwigs, including the Duke of Edinburgh. As Caroline and I talked to Spike the Duke came up and said, 'Sorry to interrupt your conversation.' We all went and had a cup of tea and Joshua and Melissa were introduced to the Duke: it was very funny because Melissa was sucking her hair and saying what she thought about education, completely unmoved, while Joshua kept interrupting his conversation to turn round and pick up more sandwiches.

Friday 23 February

Up very early and by helicopter to Winfrith with William Knighton for the opening of the Steam Generating Heavy Water Reactor. It was a tremendous affair which has received a lot of adverse press publicity because the whole day was to cost about £15,000 and 700 guests were to get lunch at £7 a head. At lunch I found myself sitting next to the Duke of Edinburgh.

We began by talking about Europe and it was evident that he was not a keen European and thought British opinion would be opposed to our joining now that the opportunity had passed. I said I thought this was perhaps inaccurate and that we would need a larger economic unit because industry was now on a bigger scale than national institutions. I explained that I was really a federalist. This worried him enormously, no doubt because the royal family wouldn't have much of a place in a federal Europe.

Then we talked about the institution of government and he said he thought it was a mistake to overcentralise, warmly supporting Welsh and Scottish nationalism; and so do I. But he did say he thought advice ought to be integrated at different levels. I asked him how he thought the monarchy would work over the next twenty-five years. His answers were rather interesting. He thought the first thing to do would be to get rid entirely of the Commonwealth angle by which he meant the Queen being Queen of Canada as well as of Britain. 'They don't want us and they will have to be a republic or something.'

He wanted to connect the monarchy more directly with Ministers and said he thought that Privy Councils were an absolute waste of time; that the Prime Minister's audience with the Queen should be broadened out to include other Ministers, who could explain things to her.

I said I didn't think that would help the monarchy at all because when this government got even less popular, which was possible, it would just identify the monarch more with us. He said, 'You wouldn't want the Queen to meet the *Opposition*, would you?' I said I didn't think that would help the monarchy. He said he wasn't thinking of the monarchy but of the national interest and he thought that if the monarchy didn't meet the national interest, he would opt out altogether. Quite what he meant by that, I don't know.

We went on to discuss the sort of people who were pro-monarchy. He said, 'Well, if you go to the East End they wave their little flags and they are very keen on the monarchy.' I said this sounded to me like a lot of Labour voters. But, he admitted, when people got cars and a bit more middle class, they weren't interested in or they didn't want to show their affection for the monarchy. I didn't disabuse him of this idea.

He then said he thought the Ombudsman should have been put into the royal household in order to make the monarchy seem closer to the people and to represent the nation. I said I thought this was nonsense. The Duke said that he acted as a sort of unofficial ombudsman and I think he does.

We went on to discuss ceremonial and the effect on it of television. He said that television really killed all ceremonial and I explained that was why Bessie Braddock would never appear on television. I don't think he much liked the comparison of Bessie Braddock with the Queen, though I am not sure there isn't something of a parallel.

I tried to point out that the monarchy was linked in many people's minds with a lot of reactionary forces. I said that during my peerage case I had had letters from many people who said that they had left Britain because they felt that the top jobs in industry or politics were reserved for those who had inherited their positions and that whenever I had tried to deal with the reform of the House of Lords I was always told you couldn't do this without threatening the monarchy. This sounded like loyalism, but top people were really leaning on the monarchy to prop themselves up.

He seemed rather shaken by this and he was very critical of our plans to reform the Lords. He said they were based on prejudice rather than on thinking and we ought to have an elected second house. I said, 'Well, yes, I rather agree with you but as you know we haven't got a very radical government. We are just doing what the British always do – adjusting – but we are getting rid of hereditary peers and I think that's quite right. If you do want a second chamber, I would rather get ERNIE, the Premium Bond machine, to give you one than have the hereditary House of Lords.'

That was how we left it. It was the first time I had had a proper talk with him and I felt as if he were a Tory MP, which is just about what he is. Altogether it was a revealing discussion: he is a thoughtful and intelligent person.

I caught the helicopter home and in the evening we all came down to Stansgate. It was quiet and Melissa and Joshua were excited, and Hilary very obligingly slept downstairs so that they wouldn't be frightened.

Thursday 14 March
To the House in the evening and settled down to do my boxes. At about 12.10 am there was a division, and while I was in the Division Lobby, George Brown called me over.

'You're a member of the Cabinet, come here,' he said. Then he told me he had just heard that Harold and Roy had decided to close the gold market in London tomorrow. He said he had not been consulted and it was an absolute scandal and didn't I think so.

I said, 'Are the Americans closing theirs?' He said he didn't know and I said that this would be the thing that would interest me.

George then called over Dick Crossman and said, 'Did you know this?' Dick said yes, and George blew up.

After the division, George gathered Tony Crosland, Dick Marsh, Michael Stewart, George Thomson and others in his room. What had happened was that Harold had been at a meeting all evening and had gone to the Palace for a Privy Council to get this Proclamation out to close the gold market, and George had not been told. While we were all sitting there, George picked up the phone and got through to Harold and exploded. He shouted at Harold and said it was intolerable and there were a lot of discontented Ministers. All we could hear at our end was George saying, 'Will you let me speak, Christ, Christ, will – you – let – me – speak. Now look, look, will you let me speak,' and so on. Then we heard George say, 'Now, don't say that: don't say in my condition. That may have been true some other nights, but not tonight. *Don't say in my condition.*' It was obvious Harold was saying he had tried to contact him but that George was drunk. I don't know whether or not he was drunk, because you can't always tell.

George continued to shout at him and Harold must have asked, 'Who's over there?' George told him and Harold said he had no right to call an irregular meeting of Cabinet Ministers, a cabal, and so on.

Finally Michael Stewart took the phone and said, 'Now, look, Harold, you must understand we are worried and we have just heard this. We really think we ought to have a meeting.' Harold than apparently said, 'Come to Number 10,' because Michael asked, 'Don't you think it would be wiser if you came over here?' George picked up another phone and said, 'Send my car and my detective to bring the Prime Minister to the House of Commons,' which didn't help.

There was another division and I went on to the Front Bench, told Fred Peart to be available and told Dick Crossman, who said he was busy and anyway he knew all about it. Barbara Castle was tied up in the all-night session on the Transport Bill. Finally, at 1.30 am, I went over to Number 10 with George Thomson. By this time Ray Gunter and all the other Ministers I have mentioned had been gathered, as had Peter Shore, who had been to the Privy Council at the Palace.

George shouted and Harold insisted he had tried to phone him and George said, 'I don't believe it.'

Harold said, 'I tried for an hour and a quarter.'

'I do not believe it.'

Harold got rattled and rather irritated and said, 'I am not going to be called a liar.'

George repeated that he didn't believe it and then demanded that Harold's Private Secretary, Michael Palliser, tell him how long the Prime Minister had tried to contact him. Michael Palliser, of course, wouldn't answer and frankly, I don't know whether Harold had tried or not. Maybe Harold did think George was drunk; he was certainly behaving as though he were. In the end George stood up and shrieked and bellowed and shouted abuse as he went round the table, then left the room.

Apparently, President Johnson had been closeted with his advisers all day, and in the course of the afternoon there had been a message from the Americans asking us to close the London gold market. We agreed as long as we were able to present the situation as done at the request of the Americans. I think we probably lost £150–200 million in reserves today and Harold thought if we hadn't closed, we would have lost £4–500 million. We are on the eve of the other devaluation that Cecil King predicted.

Harold and Roy had been going over this all evening, with meetings starting at 6, until finally at 11 they had all gone off to the Palace for the Privy Council and the order had been made. Tony Crosland and Michael Stewart were very niggled about not having been consulted. I said I didn't think a post-mortem would help and I wanted to know whether there would be a statement or not.

Then Dick Crossman came on the phone and said the news was all round the House and there would have to be a statement. At 2.15, Robert Armstrong, Roy's Private Secretary, began dictating a statement, which came at about 2.45 am. We went on arguing and arguing. By this time the press had gathered around Number 10 with flashing cameras.

Harold said that George would have to apologise or go. Peter said, 'Now, calm down. You did very well until you lost your temper with George. Just calm down.' Harold was very overstrained.

Roy's behaviour was very detached and strong and rather impressive. He's got his eye on the main chance and thinks Harold will destroy himself and that he, Roy, will then take over.

Afterwards Peter and I walked back to the House together. I talked to people; Judith Hart and I made a list of Ministers we thought would stick by Harold in a crisis.

George, meanwhile having stomped out of Number 10, sat ostentatiously on the backbenches and said he was now a backbencher. Of course, everyone left in the Chamber, including the Tories and the lobby, could see this and there he was shouting at everybody that he'd resigned. He behaved so disgracefully that under no circumstances should Harold take him back as Foreign Secretary. But I expect that in the morning Harold will think, 'Oh well, if George goes, there will be trouble on the backbenches,' and that'll be an end to it.

I talked to Ron Brown just before leaving; he said George was convinced that Harold had lied to him. George had checked all the switchboards to find out if any messages had been left for him and claimed that there had been none. So he was bitter as hell.

At 6 am I came home. I gave Tony Crosland a lift and he hotly denied that there was any alliance to replace Harold. He and Roy were at daggers drawn and there were great disagreements. But I'm sure Tony, in his heart, thinks that Harold will go. Tony took an optimistic view of our economic situation and didn't take too grim a view even of the gold panic. But with the Bank Holiday, the Cabinet split, gold suspended, and the pound in the front line to the dollar, I should have thought the possibility of the crisis which we predicted a month ago is very real.

When I got home I began dictating my diary. It's now 8 am on Friday 15, and I'm due back in the office at 9. But I must keep my diary up to date because if the Labour Government falls, as I now think quite possible, then at any rate I shall have documented the circumstances.

Friday 15 March
Just before I went to bed I heard that George Brown had resigned and that Michael Stewart had been put in his place. So that is the end of George Brown's tenure at the Foreign Office. It began with a threatened resignation because we didn't devalue and ended with a real resignation arising out of the consequences of devaluation. What George will do now is anyone's guess. He is a person of extraordinary intellect, courage and ability, but his instability is such that it is impossible to have him in a government. I wonder how capable he is of causing trouble from the backbenches. His resignation now as Foreign Secretary also raises the question of his deputy leadership of the Party. It is a major political tragedy.

Thursday 21 March
In the evening Caroline and I went up to Tommy Balogh's party. I had a long talk to Mary Wilson, who is very miserable, believing that if anything went right with the Government in the future, Roy would get the credit and Harold would get the blame. I think she may be right as far as the press is concerned. But there's no harm in bolstering her up and I tried to.

Wednesday 3 April
My forty-third birthday and the children came in with their presents in the morning, which was very sweet of them. But it was an awful day for a birthday because I had to go in very early and I was extremely tired, having been to bed so late.

Immediately after lunch Harold came down to my room and we talked for an hour. I pressed my claim for the leadership of the House if there was a reshuffle but he wanted someone who was a bit more genial and jovial and less worried-looking than me, someone with a trade union background who would drink in the bar all the time and be jolly. This was a requirement. So he's going to appoint Fred Peart.

Then he asked me, 'Were you serious about wanting Education?' (I had told Marcia this when rumours of a reshuffle were rife.)

'Yes, providing I could have an Education Act and make the comprehensive-schools thing a really living issue.'

He said he was thinking of Ted Short for it and that Denis Healey had wanted it. He went on to talk about his Inner Cabinet and I said I certainly didn't expect to be excluded for the rest of this Parliament. He had said that this Cabinet would be the first real 'Wilson Cabinet', that would last right through to the next Election. This of course is all bunk. I told him I didn't much fancy being outside the 'real' Cabinet and I raised the question of Peter – he is keen to move Peter from the DEA. I said I thought this would be disastrous; after all the attacks on Peter it would be quite wrong to move him. But Harold replied that Barbara had wanted to take over the DEA and Ray won't move from Labour.

He calmed me down and the Education thing was left as a possibility.

Monday 8 April
The National Executive Home Policy Committee gathered to consider a huge wodge of papers. George Brown arrived late and rolling drunk, and Alice Bacon, who had taken the chair, handed it over to George. He behaved outrageously and it was impossible to make any progress. Everybody was very courteous about it but the fact is he's a damned nuisance and I don't see any future in politics for him. I always knew that he would either get a new lease of life after his resignation or break up. I think he's breaking up.

Saturday 13 April
All day doing my constituency letters. Caroline worked in the British Museum. In the evening we went to the new Wimpy Bar at Notting Hill Gate and then watched television.

Monday 15 April
Caroline went to Trafalgar Square for the Aldermaston rally.

Sunday 21 April
Lazy start. It was a lovely day and Caroline sat in the garden. I mowed the grass and scrubbed the basement floor.

The news today is dominated by Enoch Powell's speech in which he raised the racial issue by saying that he thought this country had gone mad to admit so many immigrants and that it was like adding a match to a pile of gunpowder. Enoch is of working-class origins; he got a scholarship to a grammar school, did very well academically, became a professor at twenty-four and a brigadier at twenty-nine. But he has never been accepted in the Tory Party. He wasn't offered a job, for example, in the City after he left the Treasury with Peter Thorneycroft, and this obviously burned very much into his mind. He has got to have somebody to look down on and this is the way he does it.

Monday 22 April
Enoch Powell was sacked from the Shadow Cabinet this morning by Heath in a great and rather well publicised effort to reassert his leadership.

Wednesday 24 April
The press is still full of the repercussions of Enoch Powell's speech just before

the weekend. Yesterday 200 dockers came to the House of Commons and shouted obscene things at Labour MPs and called Ian Mikardo a 'bloody Chinese Jew'. He recognised some of the East End Fascist leaders among these guys. The white trash have picked this speech up. It has suddenly liberated them and there are strikes all over the place in support of Enoch Powell. He really has opened Pandora's Box. I should think Enoch Powell will get an enormous vote in his constituency, but from the Government's point of view the situation could be very dangerous and difficult.

Thursday 9 May

To the ITV studios at 11 for the discussion on the local government elections today. As I arrived at the studios one of Harold's staff was waiting for me and found a telephone and put me through to Number 10. Harold told me that Cecil King was coming out tomorrow with a tremendous attack on him in the *Daily Mirror* and he wanted to see me to build up the second stage of the campaign against King. But when I went into the studio the interviewer actually had the text of the article, entitled 'Enough is Enough', saying that Harold was no good and he should go. It said that Britain faced the worst financial crisis in its history and that lies about the reserves would be no answer. Quintin Hogg and Eric Lubbock and I were on and this was really all we discussed. I said that Cecil King was entitled to whatever view he liked about the leader of a political party, but it was a grave dereliction of duty to throw doubt upon our financial position in that way. Then Eric Lubbock commented that the attack was just because Cecil King hadn't got a job under Wilson, which was a bit cynical. I said that it wasn't surprising, that it was known he had been saying this privately for some time and all that was interesting was that it had come out. Then Quintin got terribly excited in the middle of the discussion and said, 'Get out, get out, get out. Everybody despises your government: get out, we don't want you any more.'

I just turned to him and said, 'Down, Quintin, down,' as if he were a great dog, which was the best I could do.

Saturday 11 May

I went to see Harold this morning. He was in his sitting room looking, I thought, awfully defeated and quiet. He said, 'I'm not quitting, you know,' as if I might have any doubts about it. I daresay he just suspects everybody, including me, and in the end he may just be left with Gerald Kaufman and Peter. I told him what I thought but he was absolutely opposed to saying anything to the Party. He was going to appear on television and talk to James Margach and release his speech to the PLP Trade Union Group of MPs next Monday. But he was not going to speak to the Party because he said he didn't comment on local government election results. I tried to persuade him that, as Party Leader, people wanted to hear from him. But it was no good; he wouldn't do it and so I decided to do it myself.

Thursday 16 May
Cabinet, and one of the first items that came up was votes at eighteen. Dick Crossman recommended that we should more or less have to accept votes at eighteen in view of our decision to give normal civil rights at eighteen. He made a play of regretting it but he was actually pleased.

Dick Marsh attacked it violently and said he thought we must have gone absolutely mad if we thought the working class wanted students to be enfranchised. When I was called, I said all that did was to make me wish they had raised the minimum age for entry into the Cabinet to forty-three, which would leave Dick out and put me in. But this was important and we had to accept it.

Peter Shore made a very good speech in favour and Gerald Gardiner was in favour. But there was great anxiety on the part of Willie Ross, the Scottish Secretary, and also George Thomas, the Welsh Secretary, for reasons of nationalism, and it may well be that this will bust us up.

Monday 3 June – Trip to Rumania
Flew to Bucharest, where we were met by dignitaries led by Alexandru Birladeanu, Chairman of the Science Research Committee, and by the Ambassador, Sir John Chadwick, and Embassy staff.

Dinner with the Ambassador and my staff (Ieuan Maddock, Harry Slater and Barry Smith). The Embassy staff were typical of a British embassy beleaguered in a Communist country, still fighting the Cold War hard. They made the point that Rumanians had never enjoyed any political freedom at any time in their history, that they had been under the Turks, under the Kings and under Antonescu, and they had not lost a great deal by having a Communist regime, although it was a rigid domestic regime which had not even been told about the position in Czechoslovakia. It was generally thought they were not wildly interested in Britain but did think that they had something to gain by establishing a partnership with us.

Tuesday 4 June
At 9 I was driven to the Council of Ministers for the first meeting with Verdet, the First Deputy Prime Minister. Around him at the table were a range of government people.

After the exchange of courtesies and inevitable television coverage of the opening session, we sat down and discussed practical issues. Our talks on computers developed into a general discussion about the COCOM embargo and we said that it was in the British national interest to develop as much independence as we could from the United States in the technical field. This point I had to hammer home again and again.

We finished at about 11.30 and at lunch I heard the news of Senator Robert Kennedy's shooting and it is depressing to think of the violence which makes democratic politics increasingly difficult. Not that the Americans are any different from the Europeans or indeed any other country, but it is more of a shock to discover that this can happen there in such a repetitive way.

At 4.30 I went back to the Council of Ministers for the first proper talk with Birladeanu who was accompanied by a number of others on the science side. When I commented that science was defined in Russia as 'satisfying your curiosity at the expense of the state', Birladeanu said that in Rumania it was said that if you want to spend money you could gamble, if you want to spend it enjoyably, you could spend it on women, but if you want to waste money, you have to go for science.

The Rumanians are pretty tough negotiators and this, I think, is one of their strengths. They are using their customer power in a way that we don't always do in Britain.

At 8 we went and had dinner at the Pascaras Restaurant overlooking a lake. It was a beautiful wooden structure with an orchestra playing on the ground floor and a tremendous gathering of people. Dragos, my interpreter, was there; he had guided me through all these discussions. We had a most enjoyable time.

Birladeanu had been in Russia in 1940. He knew Stalin, who he said was a highly intelligent man but had ruled Russia with oriental tyranny. He said Stalinism had paralysed economic science for thirty years and had prevented new thinking from developing. Birladeanu himself had been criticised in 1940 for saying that the factors of production were themselves a commodity.

He said he expected to see a two-party state developing in Rumania later and that no one had yet solved the problem of democratic political freedom in a socialist state. These were the things that interested him.

We sat down with everyone telling jokes and the dinner was just one long laugh. The first joke was about Khrushchev, who won the Nobel Prize for Science because he planted seed in Russia and got the wheat from Canada.

There was another story about Khrushchev coming to Rumania. Sitting down in the Council of Ministers' Room, the first thing he raised with the Rumanian Communist Party was, 'Why do you kill your pigs at only twenty kilograms' weight?' The Rumanians said, 'But we don't, except the little ones which we eat as suckling pigs.' Khrushchev said, 'But you kill them at fifty kilograms instead of 150 kilograms. What do you Rumanians think you are doing?' It was just this degree of authoritarianism that annoyed them.

Khrushchev asked them, 'Why do you Rumanians plant your maize in lines, instead of squares, which give you much better production?' Indeed, he referred to this at a major mass public meeting and the Rumanians very modestly did experiments in planting and found that you got better productivity from the rows. This just indicated Khrushchev's belief that he should be running Rumanian agriculture in the same way as he was trying to run it in the Ukraine and everywhere else.

This led them to ask me, 'Can an elephant get a hernia? Yes, if he's trying to lift the productivity of Soviet agriculture.'

They were also very funny about Mao. In China, they said, every television programme begins: 'Good evening, Comrade Mao. This is our television and we welcome you,' and ends: 'Goodnight, Comrade Mao.' Somebody asked, 'Why is that?' And the Chinese said, 'Ah well, you see, Chairman Mao is the only one who has a television set.'

They couldn't explain the Cultural Revolution and I was surprised they didn't have an analysis of it, because it is such an important development. I should think that, as Marxists, they would have, but if they did, they didn't want to tell us.

When de Gaulle came to Rumania, he went to visit a factory and asked one of the workers, 'How much do you earn?' The worker replied, 'I earn eighty lei a day.' De Gaulle said, 'How much does that buy?' So the worker replied, 'It buys you a cow.' So de Gaulle pulled out eighty lei, gave it to the man and said, 'Go and buy me a cow.' The man was absolutely paralysed and didn't know what to do, so he consulted the officials who said, 'You got yourself into this, you had better get out of it.' So he came back and said, 'Mr President, a cow would not be easy for you to take back on your aeroplane. Give me another twenty lei and I'll bring you a hen.'

I told a few jokes. They had a great sense of humour and it was altogether a superb evening. Afterwards, Birladeanu and I walked along the lakeside, over a little bridge and into a rose garden. It was a beautiful evening and everything was quiet except for the sound of orchestras from the different restaurants around the lake. I hadn't realised what a beautiful city Bucharest is.

Friday 7 June
Went to the Archaeological Museum, which was fascinating. We looked at the Roman port, where we saw old anchors and equipment just exactly as the Romans had left them. Visited the Mayor in his room, and had a short swim in the Black Sea.

Flew back to Bucharest and in the plane Dragos said he thought there would be two political parties in Rumania. He greatly admired the English. He was the son of a peasant and thought that collectivisation had gone too fast.

I went to the party offices for my meeting with Nicolae Ceausescu, President and General Secretary of the Party, and Maurer, the Prime Minister, and Birladeanu. The Ambassador accompanied me. I thought it would be a twenty-minute courtesy call but I was there for two and a quarter hours. Ceausescu is about forty-eight, grey-haired, modest mannered, very penetrating in his ability, and I liked him. Maurer is a big old-fashioned Labour stalwart, rather like a well-scrubbed railway guard who had become a Minister in Attlee's government, or even Ramsay MacDonald's in 1929–31, and Birladeanu, chain-smoking. The Ambassador was on my side of the table.

Ceausescu greeted me, and told me he had had a talk with Jennie Lee, which he had enjoyed. Then he said he wanted concrete results, and raised the whole question of computers and the need for a third generation. I explained the whole problem all over again, that this was of fundamental interest in the United Kingdom, that Rumanian independence and ours were not so very different, that we did not intend to be let down or scooped by others. I said we were frank, we told him the truth, that the French hadn't anything to offer that touched us. I hoped he hadn't been persuaded by the French that COCOM was some Anglo-Saxon arrangement that didn't apply to deals with France.

He said, 'Well, frankly the French do promise integrated circuits and the dates and deliveries are laid down.'

So I answered, 'Well, anything they can offer we can offer too, and I can offer it now subject to the same conditions.'

We got a bit further into this and Ceausescu told me that de Gaulle had said that embargoes were made to be broken. Ceausescu indicated that the French believed that the embargo was simply to preserve American economic interests until the Americans themselves could trade with Eastern Europe. I think the French are just about right.

We had a philosophical discussion which took up most of the time, about two roads to socialism. I cross-examined him about central planning. I said that when you do move towards a market-oriented economy, even under socialism, you are in effect leaving the decision about production to be made by those who are producing for the market and, therefore, it wasn't possible to have as much central planning as you thought. He wasn't able to answer this but he thought that central planning would still have a key role – and of course in some sectors it would, for example in the decision to buy and introduce computers.

We got on to the possibility of a dialogue between the Labour and Communist Parties. I said that during the Cold War, we hadn't had the opportunities for talks like this and I suggested that he might apply for the general secretaryship of the Labour Party, at which he laughed. They were saying that we had more or less sold out to private ownership, but the Ambassador chipped in and said that the Industrial Expansion Bill was an opportunity by which the Government could take shares in private ownership as a condition of making money available. I was a little surprised that he had realised the political and economic significance of what we were doing.

I raised the possibility that decision-making would break down in advanced societies, and talked about the way in which the institutions needed to be rebuilt to reflect modern power. I asked about the possible redundancy of the state, and when the 'withering-away of the state' might come.

Ceausescu contributed vigorously. He was strongly in favour of the acceptance of free will, he thought the withering-away of the state would be very welcome though he didn't quite see the withering-away of the Party. I discussed with him the possibility of us all becoming redundant. Finally, at 4.20 I left.

To the Ambassador's party, the British guests arriving early, at 6 o'clock, so that we could have a little ceremony of holding our glasses while the Ambassador toasted the Queen. The chap on the balcony played the National Anthem from an old gramophone record, and we all stood there. It was a most ludicrous, public-school, boy-scout event.

I talked to an enormous number of people. The staff of the Embassy said it had been very exciting for them having us there and we'd inspired them, and so on. But the real point about the evening was that Verdet, Radulescu, Birladeanu, and the Minister of Machine Building, the Minister of Justice, and the Minister of Mines – six Ministers – actually came to the party. It was the first time they had ever been to the Embassy and we sat at a special table and just told jokes about the Russians, the Americans and ourselves.

Radulescu said that mining mechanisation meant you had a lot of machinery and no coal. Birladeanu said the Ukranians were very lazy and he recalled a time when there had been a German bombing raid in the Ukraine. A horse had fallen into a pit and when the smoke cleared there was one Ukranian trying to help the horse out, and fifteen others advising. Radulescu said he had asked Castro about his beard and Castro said he was going to keep his beard until American imperialism ended.

Saturday 8 June
Got up at an ungodly hour. Left the hotel and met Birladeanu and Moldovan, who had come to see us off at the airport. Talked a bit about Stalin and they stressed again that he was very intelligent and decisive and had advised Rumania to slow down its collectivisation programme on the grounds that the Russians had no alternative as the Soviet Union was a pioneer; but that Rumania could do it in its own time in a more leisurely way.

Well, that was about it. They all waved and we got in our plane and we talked all the way back to London.

Wednesday 24 July
At the House of Commons there was a debate on Tam Dalyell, who had released information given to him as a member of the Science and Technology Committee on the Porton Chemical Warfare Establishment. I

went into the Lobby because I understood it was a three-line Whip. But I just couldn't face voting with all those Tories against Tam so I saw the Chief Whip and said 'I can't,' and he said, 'Well, don't bother,' so I went into the lavatory and I didn't vote.

Wednesday 21 August – Stansgate

A day that will not be forgotten. It was Stephen's birthday. That was the first thought in our minds when we woke up and then we heard the news that the Russians and the Warsaw Pact countries had invaded Czechoslovakia. My spirits sank, because, although we had half expected this might happen in the summer we thought it had all been patched up: this really takes you right back to Hungary in 1956.

The rest of the day was devoted to Stephen's birthday and, it being his seventeenth, he was able to drive on the highways. We went to Maldon together in the car, did some hill starts and then came back and had a lovely birthday party.

Cabinet has been called tomorrow on the Czechoslovakian situation.

Thursday 22 August

Up at 5.30 and to London for the Cabinet.

It was generally agreed that we didn't want to interfere with trade with the Soviet Union because, even in the height of the Berlin Air Lift or the Hungarian situation, we had still traded with the Russians. But there was a very strong feeling that ministerial visits and exchanges would have to be checked.

From my immediate point of view, of course, it has absolutely knocked every prospect of the computer deal completely out of the window because the Americans, who were bitterly opposed to my suggestion that we should supply computer technology to Russia and Rumania, will be adamant and Ministers opposed to it will have their hand greatly strengthened. So that is very disappointing. It also means my Russian visit is affected.

Dick Crossman thought we could do more, eg propaganda from the BBC. He is still the psychological warrior in moment of crisis.

Eddie Shackleton took a very strict defence view, saying that surely the important thing for stability in Europe was that each superpower should have its own sphere of influence and better that the Russians control Czechoslovakia than that there be any disturbance to the Western European status quo which might create a dangerous situation.

I did ask whether the hot line was being used and whether we had really taken into account the tremendous damage the Russians had done to the world Communist movement, which is completely split on this, with the British, French and Italian Communist Parties, and the Chinese, denouncing it.

But it was an unsatisfactory position. We agreed that Parliament would be recalled on Monday. There wasn't much we could do but we felt we owed to the Czechs to show that we did care.

Back to Stansgate.

Friday 23 August
Joan and Brian Simon arrived at Stansgate early this morning. Brian is Professor of Education at Leicester, the son of old Lord Simon of Wythenshawe, a former Liberal who became Labour. Brian is writing the book on comprehensive education with Caroline and is also a member of the Central Committee of the Communist Party. He had in fact just come back from a visit to Czechoslovakia in the course of the summer. They have many friends there and they were very upset indeed about what had happened.

Saturday 24 August
The Simons left at 6.30 this morning and they were due back tonight but phoned to say they couldn't return and we quite understood. I think he got deeply involved in the various meetings that were called, and we noticed that the statement the Communist Party issued was highly critical, so he apparently had won the day.

Sunday 25 August
Slightly better news from Czechoslovakia. The disappearance of Dubcek, First Secretary of the Party, has caused a great deal of anxiety but there are now rumours that he is in Moscow with General Svoboda, the President, and maybe something will emerge from it.

Thursday 29 August
Stansgate. I think it has been the worst August for years.

Stephen goes around with a camera and takes lots of sunset movies and Mother goes in every night and tells the 'babies' (Melissa and Joshua) Bible stories. Melissa is busy writing another 'novel'. She is always doing that.

Tuesday 17 September
This morning I went by helicopter to the Farnborough Air Show. At lunch I sat next but one to General Lemnitzer, the Supreme Commander of SHAPE, [Supreme Headquarters Allied Powers in Europe]. He told me an interesting and amusing story, although he didn't realise it. I had asked him about the Russian invasion of Czechoslovakia and he had said what an incredibly competent military operation it had been, how the Russians had maintained signal security and the Americans had known nothing about it in advance. Indeed, I learned later that Lemnitzer himself had been to Salonika the night before the invasion and clearly wouldn't have gone if he had had any forewarning. But he did tell me how the Russians had captured

Prague with an airborne division without any bloodshed. Apparently at about midnight, an Aeroflot airliner flying over Prague radioed through to the control tower saying it had a malfunctioning engine and asked if it could land.

The Czechs helped them in and on the plane were seventy security police and air traffic controllers who knew the layout of Prague airport absolutely perfectly. They simply overpowered the Czech air traffic controllers and took control with hardly any casualties and allowed the airborne division to land by dawn.

I was very impressed by this account and asked how he got hold of this story. He said Shirley Temple Black had told him. 'She is a very capable woman,' he said, which also gave away his political views as she is an extreme right-wing McCarthyite Republican. It fascinated and amused me that a five-star general, and the Pentagon and the White House, should have got the only information of any value about the invasion from a film star, a former child actress. But he didn't see the joke.

Monday 7 October
In the evening I went to a North Kensington Labour Party meeting, the first one held there, I think, since the '66 Election, and some Black Power people were there. They just laughed at the speaker before me. When I got up they began shouting. So I said, 'Look, I don't want to make a speech. I make about three a week and I would much rather listen to you.' So they came forward and sat in the front, a Black Power man abused me and said I was a lord and the British working movement was bourgeois and so on, and it became interesting after that.

Thursday 17 October
My speech on broadcasting policy to be made tomorrow came back from Transport House and I saw to it that it went round to Fred Peart, as Leader of the House, John Silkin, the Chief Whip, John Stonehouse, the Postmaster General, Gerald Kaufman at Number 10, and Charles Hill, Chairman of the BBC, with a little note.

Friday 18 October
To Bristol and Hanham for the meeting on the role of broadcasting. The local Party had got together a few more people than would otherwise have been there. The place was chock-a-block with journalists and television people. I had been on the phone during the day and discovered that Number 10 didn't want me to comment on it on any television or radio broadcasts afterwards. Harold is obviously rather angry.

This speech by Tony Benn was the first of the now familiar critiques developed over the years questioning the power and accountability of the press, television and radio – the 'media'. Part of the speech was directed specifically at the BBC:

'The BBC has assumed part of the role of Parliament. It is the current talking shop, the national town meeting of the air, the village council. But access to it is strictly limited. Admission is by ticket only. It is just not enough. We have got to find a better way and give access to far more people than now are allowed to broadcast.

'The trouble is that we have extended the overwhelming technical case for having a monolithic broadcasting organisation into a case for unifying programme output control under a single Board of Governors. Broadcasting is really too important to be left to the broadcasters, and somehow we must find some new way of using radio and television to allow us to talk to each other.

'We've got to fight all over again the same battles that were fought centuries ago to get rid of the licence to print and the same battles to establish representative broadcasting in place of the benevolent paternalism by the constitutional monarchs who reside in the palatial Broadcasting House.

'It is now a prime national task to find some way of doing this. It must be based on, and built around, the firm framework of public service control and operation, and not dismembered and handed over to the commercial forces which already control every other one of the mass media except the BBC. For in the BBC we have an instrument of responsible communication which is quite capable of being refashioned to meet our needs in the Seventies and Eighties as it did so brilliantly in the Twenties, Thirties, and Forties.'

Monday 21 October
There is a major row raging over my BBC speech. *The Times* led this morning with a heading saying that Gunter asked the Prime Minister to repudiate me so I am not out of the wood yet, but with all the other papers 'up against' me, I must expect a certain amount of trouble.

By and large, I am getting a very friendly reception from the Party, although some Labour Members have tabled a motion of support for the independence of the BBC: but then I don't disagree with that myself.

Sunday 24 November
The papers this morning are full of the news that de Gaulle has refused to devalue the franc. I must say I laughed myself sick all day. From all accounts at the Bonn conference last week the French threatened to devalue by 25 per cent and said they could not accept a devaluation of less than 11.11 per cent. And then in the event de Gaulle has refused to do it.

This afternoon Caroline and I went for an hour and a half's walk in Kensington Gardens. It was a very nice quiet day.

Saturday 30 November

Among my letters today was one from a man in Bristol who told me to keep away from the House of Commons for the next fortnight because he had sold some grenades at £3 each to somebody who intended to blow up the Houses of Parliament. Normally one would dismiss a bomb scare letter like that as a hoax but there were certain features of the letter which made it more interesting.

First of all he specified the amount of money he had been paid for each grenade in brackets; he was also concerned that I might be hurt and said that I had helped him once in Bristol, which made the thing rather authentic. He then went on to say that he had heard it was something to do with the Welsh nationalists, and the BBC in Monmouthshire. It so happened that the day after he had posted the letter the Welsh nationalists did stage a sit-in at the BBC studios in Cardiff, so there was enough to make it look quite serious.

I rang the House of Commons Police and got a phone call back, suggesting I take the letter to the local police station, so I sent Stephen round to Ladbroke Grove and he stood in line with a woman who had lost a handbag and a boy whose bike had been pinched. When the policeman asked what he wanted, Stephen said, 'It's about a bomb.' So they whipped him into a private room and he gave them the letter and told them the background. A few minutes later I had a phone call from Inspector Watts of Special Branch, who asked if I would let him have a note of the people I had helped in Bristol. I said that in eighteen years as an MP, I must have helped about 40,000 people, and he asked if I had any correspondence.

Tuesday 10 December

I went to Cabinet, where Harold began by 'Warning the Plotters'. He said that four senior Ministers had told him that one member of the Cabinet had been going round stirring things up, indicating conspiracy against Harold's own leadership, and that if this went on, within further ado he would simply reconstruct his government.

Denis Healey and Jim Callaghan are the obvious suspects, and they probably are doing it a little bit, but not as much as Harold thinks. I knew nothing about it one way or the other but I'm sure if there are conspirators that is about the worst possible way of dealing with them.

Wednesday 11 December

I went to Cabinet and the Falkland Islands was the only item; a long discussion. The general view was that the scheme that had been worked out and presented by Michael Stewart, ie signing a memorandum with Argentina saying that we would hand over sovereignty as soon as possible on a date to be fixed, but having a simultaneous document saying we wouldn't do it without the Falkland Islanders' agreement, gave an impression of deviousness.

Michael Stewart was very upset, understandably, but he had gone rather further than his brief and his paper was rejected. I think Harold was a bit embarrassed because he was pretty heavily tied up in this as well.

Friday 13 December
I went to Bristol and spoke at the Bristol Graduate Club about technology and politics. Just before my lecture there was a message from students at the sit-in in Senate House inviting me to go.

Yesterday I had made enquiries to Shirley Williams about what I should do and she told me the Vice-Chancellor was very worried and not prepared to negotiate with the students. She said I shouldn't go into Senate House and my office were so worried they arranged for a police escort to meet me at the station and at the university, which didn't please me very much because I don't need police to protect me in Bristol or among students. But I felt I couldn't visit the sit-in, so I wrote a little note saying, 'My meeting has just finished, I am going to have some food and I will be in the Grand Hotel later.'

I got back to the hotel just after midnight and three students were waiting for me, having been sent from Senate House. We talked for about two hours. I tried to be as sympathetic as I could. They said the writs against the six people the Vice-Chancellor had had to name were victimisation. I said the Vice-Chancellor is not going to abandon the writs and give up the fight against people who have taken over the building.

In a way, they sympathised with the Vice-Chancellor, Professor Collar – he is an aeronautical engineer – who found this problem on his shoulders and doesn't know what to do, while the other vice-chancellors are breathing down his neck. The pressure has built up, led by the *Western Daily Press* and the Right in Bristol, to use tear gas, smoke bombs and water cannon to get the students out of Senate House.

Actually the students are being very careful. They let the police in to inspect and have locked up documents; I don't think the Maoists are in control at all, but there are students there from other parts of the country.

Friday 3 January 1969
Up at 6 am to London where we had a Cabinet on Barbara's trade union White Paper. Barbara had rung me on Thursday night to discuss this because she'd decided to talk to the TUC before bringing it to Cabinet. This created a tremendous row. A lot of Cabinet Ministers bitterly resented having read in the press what the proposals were before any papers had been put to us. Dick Crossman was extremely angry, partly because he thought Barbara's White Paper was going to scoop his pensions White Paper, which he had been working on for eleven years, and partly because he thought it was sloppy work.

Jim Callaghan and others, Dick Marsh particularly, were entirely opposed to the idea of 'cooling off' periods or strike ballots. I joined in and said I was in favour. First of all industrial life is more complex now than it ever has been and you simply cannot have a disturbance in the system anywhere without us all suffering, and second, the democratisation of pressure groups, which is the case for strike ballots, seems right to me.

Friday 10 January
I got up early and spent the day with the Beagle Aircraft Company. I was flown up to Leicestershire in a 206, a beautiful aircraft, with the chairman, Peter Masefield. We saw a tatty little company producing these marvellous aircraft in a shed – just like building Spitfires during the war. I talked to the men in the shop and I told them why we had bought the company and how we were going to leave the management to handle it: we believed in them and hoped that they would support us.

Then in the plane down to Shoreham and saw the Beagle production going on, again talked to the workers from a platform they put up for me. It's part of my idea of talking to people directly.

I flew back to Gatwick in a Beagle Pup and Peter Masefield's son, Charles Masefield, who was the chief test pilot, let me loop-the-loop and do a slow roll which I haven't done for twenty-five years. I thoroughly enjoyed it.

Monday 3 February
I took Melissa and Joshua with me this morning to meet Colonel Frank Borman, the American spaceman, who's come to Britain on the first stop of a European goodwill tour. I met him at the front of Millbank Tower and he presented me with a miniature of the module which is going to land on the moon this summer, and then I took him up. I had the little ones waiting in the lift and he was awfully sweet with them. We had a most interesting discussion.

He said as far as spin-offs from the moon programme were concerned, the really valuable spin-off was management. Here was a programme that cost $40,000 million and involved 400,000 people. There were four million moving parts in the rocket spacecraft and they had got round the moon and splashed down within a few seconds of the computer predictions. This is undoubtedly a most important feature.

He told me one or two other amazing facts. For example, one thousand million people had heard him read from the Book of Genesis on the other side of the moon on Christmas Eve: 500 million on television and 500 million on sound – about one in four of the world's population. Borman himself said he thought the whole space programme had helped to unite humanity and to unite past and present and he gave a very interesting example. He said that during the flight the children of one of the other astronauts had sent a message through the space centre in Houston asking, 'Who's flying now?', and the answer was Sir Isaac Newton, because at that particular time they were operating without controls, just being carried towards the moon by the force of gravity. 'It united us with Galileo and we felt a part of history,' he said.

Wednesday 12 February
Up at 6.30 to go to the Babcock and Wilcox factory which is threatened with closure. Dick Mabon had come and together with the head of Babcock and Wilcox we went into the canteen to address the workforce. It was just like a pre-war scene of thirty years before, with the men in their raincoats and caps, all dirty and brown and no colour at all except for the bright lights of the television cameras covering the meeting. I said I had nothing to promise them but I would do my best. They listened very patiently and asked questions, and there was a cheer as we left.

We travelled to Scott Lithgow's along the Clyde in the ferry, saw them building their big bulk carriers, then to Upper Clyde Shipbuilders and as I went in I saw a tremendous crowd of people shouting and waving placards, 'Wedge Don't Hedge', and 'Let's Go With Labour But Not The Labour Exchange', and all that.

The shipyards were empty as I walked round with Tony Hepper. I slipped, through the gates and walked to a football field where 15,000 people had gathered.

It was a terribly cold day; my face was almost frozen with the cold. I could hardly smile, but I still jumped up on the truck and they listened to me. That was the main thing. I told them that it was difficult to get a match so that jobs were available in exactly the right quantities at exactly the right time. They were cheering and jeering and they didn't know quite what to make of it. They were clearly pleased I had come up to the Clyde to encourage them and I told them to keep their spirits up.

When I had finished my short speech, I jumped off the truck and talked to a few people. A woman came up and gave me a kiss and said, 'He's lovely': there was deep anxiety and criticism but also human warmth.

Tuesday 25 February
I had a meal at the House, changed into a black tie and went to Number 10 to meet President Nixon, who had expressed a desire to meet Cabinet members other than those who were going to dine with him.

The whole Cabinet was there, and so were John Freeman and the US Ambassador. John Freeman has apparently made a statement to the effect that he has ceased to be a socialist and to this extent has repudiated his past, but then again Nixon is supposed to have had psychoanalysis and repudiated his, so I suppose it is evens.

After introducing Nixon, Harold brought him round and described everyone's responsibilities. When I told him I was married to a Cincinnati girl, he said, 'Aha, Hamilton County,' which showed what a good politician he was, knowing the county pattern in a particular state. I told him about the Harriers we hoped to sell him and that I did a lot of business with America on aviation and nuclear energy.

Then we went and sat round the Cabinet table and Harold welcomed him formally. It was a rather agreeable atmosphere. Nixon said a word: how he was anxious that co-operation with Britain shouldn't only be about foreign policy but should cover the whole range of domestic matters. He laid great emphasis on the current problems of youth and protest and said that young people had nothing to strive for, and that there was no idealism left – or rather there was, but no scope for it.

Harold was quite contemptuous of the young and said they didn't know what to do, and all that. Judith corrected him and said the young needed to be inspired. One or two other people were asked to speak, then I said, 'Mr President, I spend five days a week trying to introduce technology and the other two thinking about the effect this has on society. Young people today are aware of this and they take it for granted; they have nothing to forget, as older people have, and they think we are suffering from acute institutional obsolescence – and I suspect they are right. It is all very well to mock them for not knowing what to do but I am not sure that *we* know what to do. They are international. Mr Borman spoke to one thousand million people when he read from the Book of Genesis orbiting round the moon: international technology has created a world youth movement.' I said I had a son of seventeen and had learned more from him than he had from me.

Then Denis Healey said something about young people not being interested in technology at all, but that wasn't the point I was making.

Dick Marsh said he had a son of eighteen and young people just liked making trouble, that was the important thing. There was really nothing in student protest to think about: it was just intellectual masturbation. It was a very crude and vulgar comment.

Dick Crossman said that all was lost, that De Gaulle was the silliest old man that ever was; that we were heading for an extreme right-wing period; that the Left had simply created a Gaullist victory in France, and had created Nixon's victory in America. It was a really *New Statesman* defeatist speech of the kind that Dick excels at. But there was a lot of laughter and at the end Nixon said, 'Why don't we have Dick Crossman, and we'll send you Marcuse!' That more or less ended the discussion.

Friday 14 March
Up very early this morning with Ivor Manley from my Private Office and Derek Moon, my press officer Gerry Fowler [Parliamentary Secretary] having missed the plane, and flew to Glasgow. This is my big visit to Upper Clyde to try to get over to the men that in fact there is no possibility of Upper Clyde being sustained indefinitely by a safety net. I had ten meetings, and I must have spoken to 7,000 or 8,000 men altogether. I began with the UCS

board, who conveyed their extreme anxiety and said they had been let down. They had all gathered there thinking they would get three or four years to prove the profitability of the company.

Then I had a general meeting of the shop stewards from the UCS group and I delivered my first talk and answered questions. It was pretty tough and there were a few shouts. One guy called Sam Barr, a Communist shop steward, said they simply wouldn't accept redundancy.

I remained in the canteen and the staff of John Brown at Clydebank had arrived, so I gave the same talk, and someone said that Hepper was much too remote in Fitzpatrick House and wasn't keeping in touch with the situation, which I am sure is true.

It was a very tough, very tiring day. But I think my trip to the Clyde created an impression that we are genuinely trying to help. And if you go there and see it for yourself, people relax. They know you know the problems and they don't get so intense.

Monday 17 March

Upper Clyde Shipbuilders is still a great anxiety and relations between the Shipbuilding Industry Board and UCS have completely collapsed because SIB are being obstinate rather than tough and UCS are just declining to pull their finger out.

There are so many people who want the whole thing to fail: Sir Charles Connell, the Deputy Chairman of UCS, who wants to punish Fairfields for their experiment and believes in the old idea of throwing men out of work to discipline them; Yarrow, the other Deputy Chairman, who is longing for the moment when he can pull out Yarrow's from UCS and make a profit and join up with his old friends in Lower Clyde; then there is Barry Barker of the SIB, who wants it to fail for rigid reasons; Victor Chapman and Cliff Baylis in my office, who think it can't possibly succeed; and Jack Diamond, who isn't prepared to provide Government money. There are a lot of enemies of Upper Clyde, quite apart from Lower Clyde, and others, so I am going to have a job propping it up. But I am going to go on trying because the industrial consequences of the failure of Upper Clyde would be tragic.

Wednesday 9 April

Having heard last night at Stansgate that Concorde 002 was to fly for the first time today I got up at 5, drove to London and caught a plane to Bristol.

We landed at Filton and it was an extraordinary atmosphere. There was this beautiful bird being pulled out on to the tarmac, the most advanced aircraft project anywhere in the world, and it was just like a sort of village cricket match. Juster, the President of Boeing, was there and Ziegler of Sud Aviation, and so on, standing about on the grass because there were no seats; and there was a buffet lunch.

Brian Trubshaw, the test pilot, dressed in his yellow flying suit, kept going backwards and forwards muttering, 'It's the paperwork that's holding us up, it's those chaps doing the paperwork.' As he left to get into his car everyone shouted, 'Good old Trubby, good old Trubby.' I thoroughly enjoyed it as a matter of fact, but I wondered whether the occasion reflected a degree of amateurism in modern technology that wasn't quite right. George Edwards, with his hands plunged into his pockets and his pork pie hat on his head, was walking about like a vicar at a country fête wondering whether everything would go well.

In the end, in the afternoon the plane was ready and I stood on the runway and watched the fantastic belching of black smoke, my backbone vibrating with the noise. Then it went along the runway for its final taxi and simply took off. I jumped into a helicopter with Ziegler and Juster and George Edwards and we flew to Fairford where it was to land, but we lost our way and we got there too late to land before the Concorde but we saw it on the ground and I took some movies. There was a fantastic scene of pressmen crowding and fighting all over the place; it was like the landing of Charles Lindbergh in Paris in the 1920s, or one of Amelia Earhart's flights. The crew came down very modestly and they were asked to wave and then there was a press reception.

I flew back in the helicopter to Filton and went to the presentation for the crew. Trubshaw was given a gold cigarette case and George Edwards made a speech in which he congratulated 'those chaps who did the steering. Your gang were very good, Trubby,' he said. 'I remember the days when we brought you in from the RAF; and I would like to say a word about the Minister who in my book is keeping a friendly eye on this in Whitehall', and all that. The whole thing was just like Biggles or Richmal Crompton's *Just William*; it had an entirely pre-war feeling about it.

Monday 21 April
In the evening I went to the London Chamber of Commerce banquet at the Mansion House for the International Chemical and Petroleum Exhibition. The first man I spoke to, who was from IPC, was criticising unofficial strikers and praising Barbara's Bill.

When I said to him, 'You look very brown, have you been away?' he said, 'I have just been to Majorca for two weeks but it was absolutely spoilt for me by all the Jews there.'

So that finished me. The sight of all these businessmen with their medals, sitting in that extraordinary Mansion House Banqueting Hall, just made me think that nothing at all had changed in one hundred years. Fortunately my speech was a summary of all that was wrong with British industry from 1850 onwards. It didn't go down very well but it was exactly what needed to be said.

Saturday 3 May
Melissa was on the 'Braden Show' and was asked about families she saw in television programmes. She said that they were very untypical because, 'we are just indifferent about our parents, we don't get excited about them because we know we have to accept them', and 'you never see people going to the lavatory on television'. All in all it was hilarious.

Thursday 8 May
A remarkable Cabinet. Jim got in again on the Industrial Relations Bill and more or less made an open challenge to Harold's leadership. Harold had been fiddling around with the constitutional issues raised by Douglas Houghton's speech yesterday in which Douglas Houghton warned the Government not to go on with the legislation, or else face the possibility of a parliamentary defeat.

Harold is a very small-minded man, he always gets to the least important part of the issue, suggesting ways of downing the Tories or embarrassing Heath or putting Harry Nicholas in his place, when events call for a higher degree of statesmanship. But the really significant thing was that Jim said that he thought that we had no chance of sinking or swimming and it was now a case of 'sink or sink'.

In the course of this discussion I absolutely went for Harold and said that what depressed me most was this view that we were utterly defeated. This was half our trouble. The Cabinet never discussed anything seriously, we were still tied up as if we were civil servants, calling each other by our official names, and I knocked Harold for six. He said we would have to discuss it later and it would come up again under the question of tomorrow's joint meeting with the National Executive.

Then we came on to Rhodesia and we killed the letter that was to be sent to Smith, who had overnight made a speech saying the whites would be in charge for a hundred years. So Barbara carried the day on that.

Monday 12 May
To the National Executive Home Policy Committee. Work was quite impossible because George Brown was totally drunk and Frank Allaun rebuked him for attacking Terry Pitt. The whole thing was a waste of time.

I rang Harold about my trip to Russia tomorrow. I told him that Michael Stewart had given me a very frosty interview, telling me to keep off politics, and I hoped I would do better than that, and did he have a message for Kosygin? He said yes, and then before giving me the message he asked, 'Is there anyone on the line?' and one of his Private Secretaries answered, so I knew the discussion was monitored, which was a comfort to me because, of course, what he said was totally contrary to what Michael Stewart had told me.

Harold wanted me to send his warmest greetings to Kosygin and to tell him that 'although we had had a difficult year, for reasons which we all understood' (referring to the invasion of Czechoslovakia), he now wanted the best possible relations. He told me to welcome the Soviet initiative in the Middle East and hoped we could make progress on it, and also hoped that in the new situation in Europe following the resignation of de Gaulle, the Russians would see the value of their links with Britain.

He asked me to remind Kosygin that when he had been at Chequers, Harold had told him that our membership of the EEC had as one of its objectives the containment of Germany within a wider community. This was all the more necessary now. I was also to tell Kosygin how much he still regretted the fact that the work they had done together on the Vietnam peace initiative in Chequers in 1967 had not come off.

Being in a position to pass on this message has put a completely new complexion on my desire to see Kosygin, which Michael Stewart was so much against. Harold said I should give this message to the Russians as soon as I arrived and asked for fifteen minutes with Kosygin and that I would probably get an hour.

Tuesday 13 May
A brief stop at Helsinki, and we picked up a Russian navigating guide and we got to Moscow at 10.15 pm (Moscow time), where we were met by Gvishiani and Kirillin himself, our interpreter Madame Santalova, the Ambassador, Sir Duncan Wilson, other Embassy staff and by Harry Slater and Cecil Timms, the head of Machine Tools who had gone on ahead of us.

Wednesday 14 May – Visit to USSR
At 10 I went to the State Committee and just before we began our discussion, Kirillin took me aside and said that Kosygin wanted to see me in the Kremlin at 12.

I told the Ambassador and this inevitably curtailed the morning meeting. At Solly Zuckerman's suggestion I also wrote out, on a piece of paper, what Harold Wilson had said to me and gave it to the Ambassador so that he would have something before him to set against Michael Stewart's guidance that I shouldn't talk to anybody about anything interesting.

At 11.45 we left the State Committee office and went to the Kremlin. There was a very modest entrance and a little lift. We went up two floors into a sort of waiting hall and then along a long corridor and turned left along another corridor, all on the inside of a quadrangle. There was a door marked 'Kosygin' in gold lettering on black glass, characteristically Russian. Inside were the Private Secretaries and press and television.

I had taken Duncan Wilson, Solly and Ivor Manley with me and the inner door opened and there was Kosygin at the end of a long table. He walked towards me and we shook hands warmly. Then we sat down at the far end of this long table, with him facing me and the interpreter in the middle, next to me the Ambassador and then Solly Zuckerman and Ivor Manley. On

Kosygin's side were Kirillin and Makiev from the Soviet Foreign Ministry and his Private Secretary.

Kosygin greeted me again while we were filmed for television. Then he started. He said that the technological agreement was going very well and that he was satisfied with it, as was Kirillin. Kosygin then reminded me that the Five-Year Plan was being approved next year, and that there was a lot of argument going on about what should and shouldn't be bought and he rather indicated that this was a factor we ought to keep in mind if we expected to boost our sales in the USSR.

Then he expressed considerable interest in atomic energy matters, saying that he had sent somebody to America who had come back and reported that the Americans were making good progress on this. He said he thought there might be scope for co-operation in this field in return for which we would get nuclear fuel.

I later discovered that this included enriched uranium as an offer, as well as natural uranium. So this was an indication that they might be interested in trying to provide an alternative source, other than the Americans or the new centrifuge plan, of enriched uranium for us.

After he had talked about the pollution of rivers in Russia I got in and conveyed Harold Wilson's greetings. I reminded Kosygin of the visit that he and I had paid together to Elliot-Automation in 1967 and I stressed our link with long-term trade and planning, referring to a speech which he had made on this subject when he was in London.

I moved on to fast reactors. I told him how very advanced we were in this field and how we had generated more nuclear power than the rest of the world put together, including the USA: our fast reactor would be on stream in 1970/71. He was evidently impressed.

Then we came on to the monetary situation and the behaviour of Germany. I said that the EEC provided an opportunity for us to supervise the Germans and I drew a parallel between this and the centrifuge arrangement with the Germans, where we were also supervising their work.

Kosygin didn't take up the question of the centrifuge although no doubt it registered in his mind. He did say that it wasn't just a matter of supervising the Germans, it was a matter of *controlling* the Germans and he greatly wished that we had co-operated on that many years ago.

I then congratulated Kosygin, in accordance with Harold's suggestion, on the initiative taken by the Soviet Government in the Middle East. Kosygin nodded his acknowledgement and replied that he wished that Britain was not so dependent on other parties who exercised a negative attitude, which I took to be a reference to the Americans.

He then went on to say that he would like to see the Prime Minister in Moscow in June or July for a day or two for talks 'on matters of common interest'. This proposal immediately gave a certain hardness to the talk with

Kosygin and enabled me to bring something back to London. Indeed it involved an immediate cable to London.

I said I would convey this invitation and said that the Prime Minister had made it clear that he knew that we, that is the British and Russians, had had a difficult year 'for reasons you will understand', but that he hoped for the best possible relations. To which Kosygin answered, 'We do not understand the reasons why we have had a difficult year but we would greatly welcome the Prime Minister in Moscow', and he repeated the invitation to Harold again when I said goodbye to him.

It was a very friendly meeting lasting for forty minutes and I had got across all the things that Harold had asked me to say. I was also reminded of what a very competent manager Kosygin is.

I went straight back in the car to the Embassy, drafted a telegram to the Prime Minister to be sent FLASH PERSONAL. Just as I left the Embassy a message came from Makiev, specially asking that 'I shouldn't make known one particular part' of Kosygin's proposals. This was obviously a reference to the invitation to Wilson and as I had no intention of making it public myself, because it would tie Harold's hands, there was no problem.

At 1.15 I went to lunch in the Kremlin and sat next but one to Miznick from Gosplan. He asked after Melissa, which warmed my heart to him. Elyutin, the Minister of Higher Education, was next to me.

I took the opportunity, since I was near Elyutin, of asking about their special schools. He said that about 1 per cent of the children in the Soviet Union went to the special schools and they were reserved for the most gifted children. 'However,' said Elyutin, repeating his observation of two years ago, 'I am very sceptical about special schools for gifted children, because I think they are really for the children of gifted parents.'

He said that they had been doing some tests on the amount of knowledge that was retained and after one year's gap 50 to 80 per cent of what had been taught at school had been forgotten, which was very worrying. On specialisation he said that there was absolutely no specialisaion at schools, except in the special schools, right up to university level.

Miznick told me that Kosygin had laid on a computer course for the top 200 people in the Soviet Government, including Ministers, Deputy Ministers, the chairmen of the State Committees and that, on a Tuesday and Friday in April, for three consecutive weeks, there had been ten lectures on the academic, hardware and application aspects of computers. I was impressed at this example of the professionalism of the Soviet Government. One of the most interesting things was that Kosygin had attended most of these lectures himself.

Thursday 15 May
Dinner at the Embassy. I tried to talk to Kozyrev, the Deputy Minister for Foreign Affairs, about the centrifuge. They were reasonably relaxed about

it, although they clearly thought it was part of the British tactic to bribe the West Germans to let us into the Common Market. They raised the Non-Proliferation Treaty issue and German power.

I just slogged it out by arguing our case. I stressed the importance of Anglo–Soviet links in the post-de Gaulle situation when the new Germany was getting very powerful, while France was rather weak and I thought that the Russians and ourselves ought to keep fairly close.

After the guests left, we went into the Embassy security 'Cage' at 10.30, and sent off telegrams about the Nuclear Policy Committee and the centrifuge. The Defence Department are being very difficult about the 'special relationship' and feel that our readiness to make our nuclear technology available to the Dutch and the Germans is likely to cause trouble with the Americans. A special memorandum is being written containing the whole nature of the Anglo–American nuclear relationship, and this is going to be submitted by the Foreign Secretary, who is also submitting my paper in my absence. It really is a very important meeting.

At 11.30 we went to the station to catch the Red Arrow, one of the marvellous trains still left in the world, to Leningrad.

Saturday 17 May
From 6.30 to 7.45, we went on a car tour of Leningrad in the rain, and I took a lot of movies.

In the evening we had dinner at the hotel with the Ambassador. I had a talk to Lady Wilson, who is an intelligent woman, about security and she said there was someone in the British Embassy who reports on them to the Russians and it was very unpleasant.

She said that anyone who has an affair, whether it's with a Russian or anyone else, is sent home at once, and that when she and the Ambassador had arrived, a couple of typists had been having affairs with diplomats from other embassies and had been sent back. It was known of course that people rather higher up also had affairs, and there was a feeling of discontent that the junior people should be picked on to return to London.

Sunday 18 May
We had a bite to eat in the Embassy, which Lady Wilson had provided, just cheese and apples and coffee, and at 10.30, Derek Moon, Ivor Manley, Ieuan Maddock and I walked in Red Square, then went back to the hotel where I found a radio, a gift from Kosygin and Gvishiani. I played it a bit, packed and went to bed.

Tuesday 20 May
I had a mug of tea made with my little boiler, which I plugged in to the shaver socket. This has made life tolerable this week.

At the airport I bought a few presents and had my last talk with Gvishiani, who had come to see me off, along with Kirillin, Madame Santalova, and the Ambassador. Then I thanked Gvishiani for the radio and he said, 'We know you listen to the radio a lot,' and with this inadvertent admission that my room was bugged, he added rather hurriedly, 'We remembered that you told us that you listen to the radio a great deal.'

The only other example of bugging that occurred while I was there was that the Ambassador had complained to his wife about the room which they had been given in the Astoria in Leningrad, and they received an apology the following morning.

Kirillin and Gvishiani examined the aircraft and we waved goodbye at 9.15 am and left for London.

There was a late night sitting and the Chief Whip wouldn't let me off, so I didn't get home until after midnight. I saw Caroline and the children and gave them their presents, including a balalaika for Stephen.

Tuesday 17 June
Our twentieth wedding anniversary, a day altogether spoiled for Caroline by the fact that she heard this morning that her mother had got cancer and was shortly going into hospital for treatment. She didn't tell me this all day and even in the evening when we had dinner together in the Post Office Tower she didn't want me to know it and only told me very much later, when we got home.

I went back to the office after Cabinet and had a meeting with UCS: Hepper and his people from Scotland told me that they were, after all, going to liquidate the following morning and I had at this stage absolutely no authority to prevent them from doing so. So I just listened very carefully and asked them to keep in touch with me.

There was a further Cabinet on industrial relations, which went on and on. Harold and Barbara became extremely bitter. Harold threatened to resign several times and said he wouldn't do what the Cabinet wanted him to do and they would have to look for a new leader, and so on; people were completely unmoved by it. His bluff was called and he just looked weak and petty, he spoke too much, he interrupted, he was angry. Barbara was frantic in the usual Barbara sort of way. In the end he said he would meet with the TUC tomorrow and he would tell them what he thought, do what he thought necessary, and the Cabinet would either have to uphold him or repudiate him. That was how it was left.

It was a very, very tense meeting and Harold and Barbara had evidently taken the future into their own hands, relying on the fact that we couldn't get rid of them. But I'm not sure that if it had come to a choice between Harold and Barbara and the survival of the Labour Movement and Government, people would not let them go; and I think Harold knew that and that was why he was so angry. But he did emerge as a small man with no sense of history and as somebody really without leadership qualities. My opinion of

Harold Wilson, if I haven't set it down in my diary recently, is very low indeed.

Wednesday 18 June
Cabinet was postponed and postponed and postponed, awaiting the outcome of Harold's negotiations with the TUC. We finally met at 5.50 pm. I went to see Peter beforehand, having told him that I knew Harold would climb down: and Harold and Barbara climbed off the hook and announced that they had found a settlement. Harold said that he told the TUC he had rejected their Letter and that if his demands weren't accepted, a Bill on penal sanctions would be introduced. He proposed that a solemn and binding agreement requiring unions to carry out this new arrangement should be taken by them and would have the same force as the 'Bridlington' Agreement of 1939 which regulated inter-union relationships.

He then went on to describe what a triumph he'd had, that it was a tremendous success. Judith Hart very foolishly suggested that there should be a dinner in honour of Harold and Barbara, which didn't go down very well because Harold was furious with Judith for not supporting him, and the rest of the Cabinet saw it as a complete climbdown. Harold was truculent; he had pulled it off again and this was his great achievement and nobody really felt disposed to disagree with him at that particular moment. He went and announced the settlement with the TUC at the Party meeting which of course was popular because it meant the end of the penal sanctions.

Monday 23 June
In the evening I had a talk with John Silkin, Peter and Gerald Kaufman, who was quite awful. I haven't talked to him for a very long time; he is completely cynical now, blown up with his own importance and feeding into Harold the most unsatisfactory ideas, which make Harold think that he is God Almighty and everybody else has got to fall into line. It was clear that John Silkin is in the doghouse and Peter is now hated by Harold for what he did on the industrial relations thing. Indeed last Sunday's papers were full of briefings by Harold on how certain Ministers had let him down.

Friday 11 July
This morning I went with Ivor Manley by helicopter to the Steam Generating Heavy Water Reactor at Winfrith for the Queen's visit. It was a most beautiful day and we had a lovely flight down. When I got there I had a talk to John Hill about the centrifuge and the reorganisation of the AEA and he wants to come and have a talk with me.

The Queen arrived and looked extremely angry. I think the truth is that she is bored but feels she has to look interested or something; anyway she walked round and I followed behind with the Duke of Edinburgh. Of course a Minister during a royal visit is just an office boy.

At lunch the Queen was really rather different, indeed she was very pleasant. First of all we talked about the television programme made about the royal family. She said it might have to be cut for showing in the United States; the American Ambassador had used very long words and made himself look rather ridiculous.

I asked her if royalty had to be so formal. The Queen said that it is just that you have to dress up and be told what to do for Privy Council. Obviously she did not much like the suggestion that the thing was more formal than was necessary.

We talked about the Commonwealth Prime Ministers' meeting and I asked her what impression she had formed of Trudeau. She said that he had been rather disappointing. I gave my view in support of disposable politicians – that, in fact, you could not do more than a certain amount of work before you had to go and refurbish yourself.

Then we moved on to the subject of the Royal Prerogative. I asked her whether, when there was a dissolution contemplated, she ever consulted the Speaker, because he was impartial. She said, 'I am supposed to be impartial but, of course, I can call in whom I like.'

So I asked her, 'Well, suppose, for example, there had been a row on the industrial relations legislation and the Prime Minister had come and asked for a dissolution. It was at least arguable that another Prime Minister would have held together a government without a dissolution.' She said, 'Well, we had to look up all the precedents on the dissolution,' and I pointed out that it might well have become real if the Parliamentary Labour Party had rejected an Industrial Relations Bill.

We got on to talking about the Lords and the Commons and she raised the redistribution of parliamentary boundaries. I think she wanted to provoke me into saying something but I didn't comment on it.

She told me that the royal train was bulletproof and had two diesels, which had its origins in 1937 when one diesel had broken down and the train had got stuck. That led to Concorde and she said how she wished Trubshaw had seen people applaud when Concorde went over on her birthday and I told her what I had told George Thomas, that if Concorde had crashed into the Palace that day, the occasion would have turned into a coronation.

She said, 'You *can't* cancel Concorde.' I pointed out the question was whether we could sell it: that was the real test.

We talked about the Civil Service machine and I remarked that a new Minister coming into a Ministry really was in a position to put the brakes on. 'Presumably,' I said, 'the machine thwarts you too?' I do not think that had quite occurred to her. I went on and talked about the desirability of having a longer government with Ministers who retired at a certain stage in order to cope with the rate of change.

She is not clever, but she is reasonably intelligent and she is experienced:

she has been involved in government now for eighteen years. She knew about the test routes for Concorde and that they would be going up the West of Scotland. So either she had been reading Cabinet papers or her Private Secretary had briefed her on this particular matter.

I proposed her health, having got my Private Secretary, Ivor Manley, to speak to Sir Martin Charteris, her Assistant Private Secretary, a typical pyramid operation, rather than asking her directly, 'Should I propose a toast?'

On the way out I had a brief word with the Duke who, as usual, was talking about high taxation as a major disincentive.

Friday 15 August
Pelting with rain all day. Caroline worked on an article on women's education and Stephen got his 'A'-level results envelope. He said nothing all day.

Today we heard on the news that UK troops had been committed to maintain law and order in Derry during the troubles that arose out of the Apprentice Boys' annual march.

We had discussed this in Cabinet before the end of July and agreed that troops could be used, so long as the Prime Minister, the Home Secretary, the Defence Secretary and the Foreign Secretary kept in touch with each other. So it looks as though civil war in Ulster has almost begun.

Saturday 16 August
Stephen woke us at 2.45, having finally opened his results, and told us he had got an A in History, a B in Music, and a C in Pure Maths.

Hilary went off to Scotland with his friend Alan Burton.

Sunday 17 August
I had a message last night from Ivor Manley saying there would be an emergency Cabinet on Tuesday to consider the situation in Ulster.

The crisis in Northern Ireland had been slowly building up with riots in July and August. On 12 August in Londonderry fighting broke out between Protestants and Catholics during the Apprentice Boys' march, and in the ensuing violence Catholics' homes were burned. Troops were moved into Londonderry, and then into Belfast, where the trouble had spread, after appeals to Roy Hattersley, the Minister of Defence for Administration, who was deputising for Denis Healey, from the Royal Ulster Constabulary and from Bernadette Devlin, Independent Unity MP for Mid-Ulster.

Tuesday 19 August
Ron Vaughan took me to London and Caroline came with me. We arrived home at 11 and found the Comprehensive Schools Committee, which uses my office in the basement, in action. I went off to the Cabinet.

I had underestimated the immense excitement over the Ulster thing. Downing Street was cordoned off and there was a mass of photographers and television cameras outside Number 10.

There were jokes in Cabinet about my new beard and Michael Stewart reminded me of what Attlee had said when Sydney Silverman, MP for Nelson and Colne, grew a beard. He had said, 'I move previous face' and indeed Harold began by saying, 'Motions to move previous face are out of order.'

We then settled down to discuss the Ulster situation. A paper by Jim Callaghan was passed around, which made five recommendations.

First, that the 12,000 B Specials [the Protestant Ulster Special Constabulary] should be disarmed; second, that we consider a Bill transferring some authority to Westminster; third, that there should be advisers attached to the Northern Ireland Government; fourth, that we might consider a coalition or, at any rate, more elements brought into the Northern Ireland Government; and fifth, that a Community Relations Organisation might be set up, possibly with a Minister on the spot, to examine complaints of discrimination.

Jim opened quietly and extremely well. He said he had been prescient in July in warning us that there was a very poor Intelligence Service in Ulster; he had seen Chichester-Clark and asked him about the demonstrations before they occurred and had not wanted them banned. He said Hattersley had done an extremely good job at the Ministry of Defence in Denis's absence, the troops had been welcomed by the people and indeed there had been many appeals for help at different stages.

The Stormont Govrnment say it is the IRA who are the cause of the trouble but this does not conform to British Intelligence. The Catholics were defending themselves with ferocity, as Jim put it, and it was really because of that fear that the situation had got out of control. Jim said we must remove the cause of the fear, ie get rid of the B Specials, and he would like to see Peacocke, the Inspector-General of the Royal Ulster Constabulary, replaced by a British Chief Constable. The Northern Ireland Labour Party agreed the recommendations in his paper but they fear that if the B Specials are disarmed, there will be secret arms caches kept and used. Jim pointed out that the B Specials got no police training, only shooting practice.

The meeting was quiet and Jim, I thought, did very well. Harold was all right except that, as usual, he was much too tactical and there was too little thinking about the future. Denis was realistic in seeing that he might find himself in a position of sending in the troops against all the Protestants. I wonder whether people understood how serious the situation was – whether, in fact, this was not the beginning of ten more years of Irish politics at Westminster which would be very unpleasant. None of us had thought it out very carefully.

I went home and waited and waited in case there was another Cabinet meeting but in the end Harold managed to carry Chichester-Clark on the proposals which were published this evening; not to disarm the B Specials but to bring them under the control of General Freeland the GOC, Northern Ireland. It is a compromise because he will actually collect their arms and keep them in armouries. That is the most effective way of dealing with them.

Caroline and I got back to Stansgate about 1 am, both pretty tired.

Sunday 28 September – Labour Party Conference, Brighton
Conference, and a late lie-in and after lunch we had the NEC. I moved that the press be admitted because everything had been leaked. This was very nearly carried.

I got as near as I could to proposing that there should be a referendum on our decision to go into the EEC. I had almost got it out when Harold realised what I was going to say, and stopped it: I didn't fight the issue. But I know perfectly well that no government will agree to go into the EEC if there isn't more enthusiasm than there is at the moment.

Saturday 4 October
To Number 10, where of course Ministers affected by the reshuffle had been coming and going all day. Harold told me he wanted me to remain Minister of Technology and take over the whole Ministry of Power, all the industry divisions from the Board of Trade and their industrial location work, and the industrial side of the DEA. I called Otto in and he knew exactly what it involved. This evening I had just a bit of time to think it all over. It is an enormous job that I have effectively been given and I must say I was staggered to find the whole Ministry of Power coming over to me but I couldn't ring anybody up to talk about it.

Sunday 5 October
I planned what I was going to do with this new huge department and at 6 the announcement was made on TV. The growth of the Ministry of Technology was *the* news; there was no question this was the main story of the day. Crosland has been given the job of Secretary of State for England, co-ordinating transport and housing and he is obviously very sick about it because he doesn't think there is anything in the job. I have been effectively given the Ministry of Industry job which is what I really wanted.

Wednesday 5 November
Came home for fireworks and worked late. Gradually emerging from a couple of weeks of real exhaustion.

I only had one bit of business at home tonight. I have been trying to put my oar in to be sure that the British don't join in the American underground tests of nuclear weapons without, at least, a meeting of Ministers to discuss it.

Denis Healey has been determined to get British nuclear weapons tested underground in the US, and since I put my foot down, he has been trying to get at me. In the end I decided to ring Number 10, and I put the points to a Private Secretary to pass on to the Prime Minister; I said I would abide by his decision, but I don't know whether Harold cares one way or the other.

Monday 17 November
At 11, I went to the Campaign Committee, where David Kingsley presented a report on the first round of the advertising campaign for the next Election, 'Labour has Life and Soul' and 'When it Comes Down to it Aren't Their Ideals Yours as Well?'

Denis Healey said we must present ourselves as a government that could govern. Jim Callaghan warned that people might not like change and might want a quieter life, which I thought was a bit of a dig at the dynamic Ministry of Technology! Generally there was a consensus and it was agreed we would do a television programme before Christmas and a party political broadcast at the end of the year, in which I would be the party spokesman.

Incidentally, *The Times* had an amusing two-column article by David Wood called 'Sandwiches with Benn'. It began by mocking me about my sandwich lunches, then said how industrialists were working happily with me and that the Tories were worried about it.

We had the Mintech board lunch. Harold Lever responded to *The Times* by producing some smoked salmon, freshly baked bread and cheese and some other things. It has become a bit of a joke. Next week I am going to take my sandwiches in a red handkerchief and see whether I can't lower our standards still further.

We discussed the need to ensure that there was adequate supply of stocks of fuel for the winter: corrosion in the bolts in the Magnox power stations has led to a 25 per cent cutback in their utilisation, and it is potentially a great tragedy if corrosion prevents these nuclear power stations from being used at all.

Wednesday 19 November
The Apollo 12 landed this morning and there was a moon walk, which, unfortunately, we weren't able to see because the television set had broken down.

Wednesday 26 November
To the Economic Policy Committee, where the Upper Clyde Shipbuilders problem came up. They have got into serious difficulty and want a substantial sum of money, and Jack Diamond was in favour of liquidating. In my paper I said we couldn't justify any more money on industrial grounds, but Harold chipped in and said that on political grounds, we couldn't have 8.5 per cent male unemployment on the Clyde – which I

agree with absolutely. So we decided to set up a committee to see what was the minimum we could give to keep them going.

Monday 1 December
I had a very sad and painful meeting with Peter Masefield and the board of Beagle to tell them that the Government was not prepared to continue to support them and there was no alternative but to ask the bank to set up a receiver and manager.

At the House of Commons for an all-night sitting.

Thursday 25 December
Melissa and Joshua woke up at 4.30 am and exchanged their presents. We had ours in the bedroom. It was a wonderful Christmas, Caroline having done all the work. After lunch Stephen, Hilary and Melissa played a madrigal, and we had the usual call from Cincinnati. In the evening Stephen and I took a bottle of whisky to the Mintech night guard, finished up with Mother and Buddy and finally got to bed about 1 am.

Wednesday 31 December
Went to Bradwell Power Station today and Sir Stanley Brown, and Mr Weeks, head of the CEGB study group on the Magnox corrosion, were there. I was met by the Station Superintendent and accompanied by people who had come straight down from London – Jack Rampton, who is the Deputy Secretary in charge, Trevor Griffiths, the Chief Nuclear Inspector, and John Bowder, my Assistant Private Secretary. I spent about an hour and a half with the working model, seeing exactly what the problem was, then went to have a look at the refuelling operation by closed-circuit colour TV, and to the control room. I saw a film of the removal of the sample basket which had taken place last year, and had lunch with the group.

I'm very glad I went because it indicated the real nature of the problem, which is seen by the CEGB not so much as a safety problem but as a problem that might affect the economics of the power station. The danger is that the very high temperature CO_2 gas which goes through the fuel elements has had the effect of oxidising or corroding the bolts holding the core restraint, and corroding all the other bolts in the reactor.

If, by any chance, there were any displacement of the graphite blocks in which the fuel elements run or, even more serious, of the channels into which the control rods drop, you might lose control of the reactor and it is possible that one of the fuel elements might melt. If there was at the same time a rupture in the head exchanger circuit you could get a tremendously overheated reactor with the fuel elements melting, causing a major nuclear accident that would kill many thousands of people in the area of Bradwell and would create a radioactive cloud that might kill people in London.

The real question is, do the control rods go in and out easily and could this be affected by further corrosion? They currently drop in 100 of them in 1.2 seconds and there's no reason to believe at the moment that this will change. But the position is being watched very carefully.

Mr Griffiths told me that he would keep an eye on the situation in order to lay down the rules about a shutdown for further inspection if he thought that the temperatures being operated were too high. The temperatue has risen progressively since the station's inception in the early Sixties, although recently it was reduced from 390 degrees Centigrade to 360 degrees. But in view of the problem of the fuel situation this winter, the fear of a power strike and the cold weather, the GEGB has decided to increase the temperature to 380 degrees, with the result that the old rate of corrosion, about twice the rate of corrosion at 360 degrees, has resumed. This is taking a calculated risk, so as not to dislocate industry.

I wrote a brief report on this and I am now trying to get an independent engineer to take on the job of reading all the documents and advising me.

Tuesday 6 January 1970
I went to the Campaign Committee this morning. Mark Abrams, chairman of Research Services Ltd, reported on the attitude of younger voters. I found one or two things interesting but also discouraging. For example, young people were not interested in education, that is to say they were against the raising of the school leaving age. This made a big impact on the Prime Minister and Jim Callaghan and one or two others who don't want to raise the school leaving age. All of a sudden one could see how very big decisions could be taken by government on the basis of the most inadequate evidence which confirms their prejudices. I realise we will have to fight very hard on that.

In the evening Caroline, Stephen and I went to Peter Townsend's party. Peter teaches at Essex and I was surrounded by three of his young sociology students who just called me a Fascist and called me it so often I got rather angry. A dull German professor linked me with a lot of other Fascists and when I said to him, 'Could you give me the names of any world politicians who disagree with you but are not Fascists?', he said, 'That is a Fascist's sort of question.' He defined Fascism as a belief in technology, and technology as a belief in the use of machines to change social values. Altogether I thought he was very poor stuff, of the kind you get among sociologists who don't study technology or industry or what is happening in the world. We very foolishly stayed till about 2, and I had to work on my boxes till 4.

Tuesday 17 February
There was a very significant development over UCS. In my diary last week, I referred to the fact that Jack Diamond went up to Upper Clyde. He found himself confronted by six chartered accountants and was very impressed by their figures so he agreed to pay the full £7 million to UCS, as authorised by

the Cabinet, Harold Lever having asked for £4 million and Jack previously being prepared to give only £2.5 million. In addition he has decided to dismantle the monitoring system because he is afraid that if you monitor you would have to pay the creditors.

Tuesday 24 February
Ivor said to me today, 'You are getting too many "Noes" from Number 10', which had a profound effect on me. I *have* had a lot of noes, so I tried to work out what they had been about; usually broadcasting proposals that Number 10 had turned down, my paper on government information services and another on persuasion in industrial disputes, and Ivor made the point that no Minister should have proposals turned down as often as that. So in the light of this, I didn't, for the time being, pursue another issue I had in mind.

Wednesday 25 February
Meeting with Yugoslav Prime Minister, Mr Ribicic, at Number 10. He said he was glad to see more and more people becoming involved in the problems of world peace and he hoped the interests of the superpowers would not dominate the world. He had got better relations with the Soviet Union because the Soviet Union needed Mediterranean friends and access to warm waters, and there were now closer economic and industrial links with the other Eastern Europe countries, except for Bulgaria whose claim for Macedonia had created a great problem. He also said he had good economic relations with America, but was critical of their policy in Vietnam, and their support of Israel.

He was afraid of great-power influence disturbing the Balkans, which was why he had opposed Israeli aggression and the invasion of Czechoslovakia. Relations with China were normalising because he thought the Chinese were settling down; he believed that Soviet–Chinese conflict was not really ideological but more a clash of interests and China was now actually preparing for a war with the Soviet Union.

Yugoslavia just wanted to be a European country, he added, but was not getting on very well with, for example, the Germans because of the problem of reparation and Yugoslavian émigré terrorism in Germany.

Harold then said he was glad relations with Russia were improving but we couldn't accept the Brezhnev doctrine. Michael Stewart made his usual negative speech, saying that we didn't really like the European conference proposal because our security was bound up with NATO, and this would have helped East Germany and underwritten the Brezhnev doctrine, though we hadn't rejected the idea outright.

To the Royal Society where I made my speech to the Manchester Technology Association on technology and the quality of life. I had worked hard on it and it got a very enthusiastic reception.

Thursday 26 February

To the Commons, where we held Auntie Rene's eighty-eighth birthday party and about fifty Benns of various ages turned up; Stephen came back from Keele and I had arranged for a cake. Margaret Rutherford – very depressed with two broken hips – was there. But Auntie Rene made a marvellous speech about how enjoyable life was as you got older. She had first been inside the House of Commons in 1892 when my grandfather was elected and she was a girl of ten, and Gladstone was Prime Minister – quite remarkable.

I had to go back to my office to meet Henry Ford II, who had come over from America at my request, following the announcement that Ford Cortina exports to America were to discontinue and the Capri was to be manufactured and exported from their German factory. Stanley Gillen, Bill Batty and Walter Hayes, Vice-President of Ford of Europe, were present. I put the case as strongly as I could, that this was an extremely important decision. We welcomed the size of the Ford operation in Britain and their investment and export record, but a decision made in Detroit which had led to the blanking out of certain British car exports to America was very serious, with damaging consequences for the British balance of payments and for Britain's reputation for exports.

I questioned him about the survey on which they had based their decision, and Ford said the reasons were much broader than that. British cars had a bad reputation for quality and reliability. I said, 'Doesn't this indicate some defect in quality control?' He rather agreed and said this was being looked at, and did say in the end that he would look again to see whether it was only in the first instance that the cars would be coming from Germany and that exports from Britain might not be ruled out. That was encouraging and it was well worth while having the meeting.

Ford went off but Stan Gillen, Bill Batty, Walter Hayes, Otto and others came and had dinner with us at the Café Royal together with Charles Smith and Ieuan Maddock. We had quite a discussion.

I am not very impressed with Batty. He just wanted to bash the workers – a typical British businessman. Walter Hayes is much more sympathetic. He has always been struck by my argument that the BBC and broadcasting is too important to be left to the broadcasters and we considered the whole question of how important issues could be seriously discussed on the air.

Sunday 8 March

At 9 I left for a meeting of the Inner Cabinet at Chequers with the Prime Minister, Michael Stewart, Roy Jenkins, Dick Crossman, Denis Healey, Barbara Castle, Jim Callaghan, Peter Shore, Bob Mellish, Tony Crosland and Fred Peart; Burke Trend and Michael Halls were present in the morning, although officials didn't come in the afternoon.

We sat in the library on the first floor and the first paper we considered was Jim Callaghan's on law and order, or what he preferred to call the 'war against crime'. This was split into three parts. First, the student question and Harold wanted to know why universities didn't take a stronger line and whether they could withdraw the students' grants. Michael Stewart was attracted to this idea. Dick Crossman said the situation was like the early days of the Weimar Republic, he could see democracy coming to an end, and we should have no hesitation in dealing with people who were destroying free speech.

I chipped in and said that self-discipline was what was required here; that on the merits of the issue students were very often right. I described my meeting with students at the sit-in in Bristol and how they had desperately been seeking a way out of it, and how the thugs – the extremists – had in fact been routed. It was important not to use police in the universities if this could be avoided. Barbara agreed with me, but there was a nasty touch of authoritrianism from other Ministers, which I found depressing. But we did agree that before Ted Short gave his response to the select committee report on student unrest, there should be a meeting for a few Ministers to discuss it.

Then we discussed the extremely difficult problem of the visit by the South African cricket team, and the fear that this would trigger off demonstrations all summer. Jim is going to see all the police chiefs to discuss it. He also said the Commissioner of the Metropolis had been invited to meet Ted Heath and that he hadn't objected, but he thought the Commissioner would tell Ted Heath that he didn't want law and order to be mixed up in party politics.

The third element in this discussion was crime and we all agreed that international comparisons would show how much better the situation was in Britain than elsewhere, although there is a rising tide of urban violence. Jim said he would discuss with Charles Hill and Lord Aylestone the crime and violence on television, on which I very strongly supported him.

Roy began the discussion by saying that he was fed up by the rumours that had appeared in the press that morning to the effect that the Chancellor was at bay and his colleagues were urging a soft Budget. Denis said he thought it was very damaging.

Tony Crosland went on to talk about an employment-generation programme, particularly in the regions where the construction industry is badly hit. Another £7 million was proposed for cleaning up our rivers. Harold thought there was a good political point here, since there were many Labour-voting anglers. In the end the choice is a political choice, not an economic one, and this was very evident as we discussed all the alternatives today.

After lunch I went for a walk with Barbara and Peter Shore. Peter is rather an authoritarian on student questions; Barbara is much more sympathetic – this is like the early days of industrial relations strikes in the ninteenth century. The temptation to take fierce measures is strong.

Then we really got on to the hard political stuff. Harold went round the room asking when we thought the Election should be and Denis said he was attracted by the 'long haul' – ie October – but that we should be ready to go earlier if things improved, and Fred said the same. I said, 'Well, if we are ready to go earlier, we had better be ready from June onwards. If it isn't right in June, we'll go until October, and if it isn't right in October, we'll go right through to the spring. But don't let's work on a date that is later than we think might be necessary.'

Harold gave his views. He said he had thought about the date for the Election for the last four years or more and the conflict with the World Cup had to be considered, and whether there might be strikes. He was a little afraid of a Tory campaign building up to the autumn and possible attempts to shake confidence in the pound: the weather would be better in the summer, the hours of daylight would be greater. I felt Harold was moving towards an earlier date.

Denis said he thought the expectations of better times to come would be greater than the reality, and so that was a sort of censensus that we should be ready for June.

The next question was what should we fight the Election on? Barbara said that people were bored with the balance of payments; they wanted better benefits and housing was important.

Jim said he thought the environment was too middle-class a weapon with which to attack the Tories.

Michael Stewart said that foreign affairs were going rather well, and emphasised the fact that no British soldiers had been killed in action.

Tony Crosland said he thought we ought to cut income tax or release people from the lower ranges of income tax and add it on to SET.

Dick said what he wanted was a working-class Budget, a real sloshing working-class Budget. People had waited a long time and they were entitled to it. He spoke about relief which would probably cost between £400 million and £600 million.

When I was called, I said I thought that fear of the Tories' right-wing policies would mobilise the faithful, win the middle ground and neutralise the Conservatives. The people would like us because we were a known team but we had to have confidence in ourselves and really believe we would win. If there was reflation to be done, let's do it selectively.

Then Fred Peart said that courage, competence, compassion and an egalitarian approach were necessary.

Denis said the public were bored with politics and would like a government that would relieve them of the responsibility for handling political matters. Then he went on to discuss in detail what he wanted to see in the Budget and at that moment, as Denis was describing in detail how he thought the Budget should be handled, what should happen to SET, income tax and purchase tax, with Dick chipping in, the Wrens came in with tea.

Roy was getting agitated at this open discussion of the Budget in front of the women, and so indeed was I. But Denis carried on and the risk of a leak from that, I thought, was enormous.

Looking back it was a very pleasant and informal day and much better than formally sitting round a table.

Sunday 29 March
Easter Day. Had a lie-in. Caroline is reading a book called *The Feminine Mystique* about the new Women's Liberation movement which is beginning to develop strongly in the States and even in Britain.

There was a power cut this evening which put us on candles and butane gas for the kettle.

Thursday 2 April
Interview with Michael Barrett on the BBC programme 'Nationwide' on the motor industry. There has been serious disruption and in particular a strike of 112 inspectors at Vauxhall which has thrown thousands of people out of work.

I was very nervous, curiously, and I didn't do at all well. When I got home Joshua said, 'It was terrible.' Caroline said the lighting was bad and I looked grim and uneasy. I felt grim and uneasy. I do so hate those BBC interviews where instead of talking to you about a problem, they are always aggressive towards you, which makes you defensive and not at your best.

Monday 6 April
Had a word with Peter Shore on the phone tonight. He is very pleased with the reaction to his speech on the Common Market which caused a lot of trouble, because he does believe, very strongly, that the Common Market is an illusion and politically it will be advantageous if it is clear that there are some members of the Government with reservations about entry. My view is different from this. I don't think economics are everything by any manner of means and if we have to have some sort of organisation to control international companies, the Common Market is probably the right one. I think that decision-making is on the move and some decisions have to be taken in Europe, some in London, and an awful lot more at the regional and local level.

Wednesday 8 April
Dinner at the Swedish Embassy given by Olaf Palme, the Prime Minister of Sweden who is over here. Caroline sat next to Tony Crosland and on his other side was Lady Greenhill, the wife of Sir Denis Greenhill, the head of the Foreign Office. Crosland said to her, 'I understand your husband is the head of MI5 or MI6 or MI7 or something.' Lady Greenhill said, 'Well, I've never heard of it.'

In fact Greenhill is alleged to be in charge of MI6 but it was the maddest thing that could possibly be said. Then Crosland didn't have a side plate and made a big fuss about that and pulled the waiter towards him and asked if he could borrow Caroline's side plate. The Ambassador got very agitated, as you can imagine, and asked Caroline, 'Is he always as rude as that?' She said, 'Yes,' and he replied, 'Well, I suppose now that George Brown has gone you've got to have somebody like that in the Government.'

I sat next to Dick Mabon's wife who is Jewish and very interested in Buddhism. She was really rather nice. Opposite was George Thomson: I asked him about his talk with Kozyrev and he said he hadn't made much of an impression.

I had to vote and missed Olaf's speech but I heard a bit of Harold's, which was odious. I can't quite say why but he is so conceited in his speeches and so ponderous.

I talked to Mrs Palme who is a child psychologist and very charming. Caroline said to Gerald Gardiner that the House of Lords was completely out of touch on education: he didn't understand but she made such an impression on him that the following day she got an invitation to go and have dinner with him at the House of Lords.

Friday 10 April
To Bristol. Mr Jeffries of BAC drove me to Filton where a four-engined Herald was waiting to take me up to Fairford. I got there and was kitted out in flying gear for my flight in Concorde 002. Brian Trubshaw, the chief test pilot, greeted me with the co-pilot and engineer and other members of the crew.

They had a suit all ready for me with W. BENN printed on the front. They gave me a parachute, strapped me into the plane and told me how to escape. It was an extremely uncomfortable seat; the poor navigator was sitting on an upturned bucket or something and trying to do his navigation in such a way as not to disturb me. I took a movie camera on board and they lent me a Sony VTR machine.

Finally we taxied away and began to take off. I was very tightly strapped in, my suit was too small and as we moved away I did wonder whether I wasn't being extremely silly; it would be ludicrous to be killed on a venture of this kind. It was only the fourth time that 002 was going to fly supersonic, so it was a genuine test flight and I had insisted that they treat it as such and take no notice of me. As we took off I was plugged into the intercom and could hear everything that was said. The only thing that went wrong was that the Nacelle doors around the undercarriage didn't close and they had to be put right.

Up we went, over the Isle of Man and Ulster and Stranraer, and then we turned and did a supersonic flight down the Irish Sea, but only at mach 1.05, so I don't think there was a bang. You couldn't feel anything. I took off my wristwatch and I thought I could just hear a faint tick even at supersonic speed. Then they did some tests. They kicked the rudder bar, rotated, turned, cut one engine right back, and so on. Then they came in and I heard a bump and thought they had put the undercarriage down but when I looked I found we had actually landed. I was unloaded, we got out of the plane and we found a mass of photographers. It was great fun. It took me back twenty-five years to the air force.

I changed and went to see the shop stewards from Filton, where there is an unofficial overtime ban over a £4-a-week increase. I got my first unofficial and somewhat unusual opportunity to try persuasion in industrial disputes. I told them how vital it was that Concorde should succeed and how awful it would be if I arrived in Washington for a meeting and somebody said, 'What about this unofficial strike at Filton?' They are going to consider what to do at a meeting on Monday.

Monday 27 April

Joshua went back to school today. Caroline wrote hundreds of letters; the typewriter is defective and the drying machine and washing machine are playing up. We are all a bit disenchanted with technology.

There has been a bit of trouble about whether civil servants are allowed to meet Tory Shadow Ministers. Otto has accused Harold of stopping them and Harold denied it but does want to know who is meeting whom. My view is to be very liberal about this but I had to fall into line and said that Otto was to notify Sir Burke Trend of any contacts that he or other civil servants had with the Tory Party.

Tuesday 28 April

We have all been worried about kidnapping attempts because Gerald Nabarro's daughter has been threatened, and so we told the children to be very careful going to and from school.

To SEP where we discussed the flood risk to London. Over the next seven or eight years there is a one-in-five chance that the river will rise one inch over the walls for one hour, which would cause the most appalling death and destruction. I suggested that there should be an emergency dam, some inflatable structure which would keep the water back while we were waiting for the major barrage to be completed.

Monday 4 May

After lunch Otto and Charles Smith and other staff came in to present the problems with Concorde, which are formidable – escalation of cost, delays, refusal by the firms to have any incentive contracts on production or to bear any loss, anxieties with the French, a strike which has delayed flights of 002, and so on. It is very worrying. Ronnie Melville, my Aviation Permanent

Secretary, has been indicating his anxieties in little minutes to me which I have begun to suspect are for the record.

Then he broke in to say, 'Well, Minister, I must tell you that my advice is that we cancel Concorde. I have come to the view we must cancel. It is not an economic aircraft' (of course it never had been), 'and unless there is some overwhelming national or prestige reason for us to keep it we should cancel.' He said that I was not to believe the figures that were coming from his officials. They always went up, and so on and so on – he really lost control.

So I said, 'Well, this is a very serious thing to state, and you will confirm, I hope, that this is the first time you have said it to me,' and he replied, 'Yes.' Ivor Manley noted that. Then I adjourned the meeting.

Afterwards I had a talk with Otto and told him I was very uneasy about this because it looked as though Ronnie had been building up to a break and this was the most embarrassing moment to do it: I didn't object that he had come to that conclusion, but he could have informed me in a different way.

Otto tried to defend him, saying that Ronnie was very upset and felt it was his duty to give me notice in advance of the report so that I didn't wait for the report to come. But I think Otto himself was pretty worried about what had happened. I said I thought this would make it very difficult for Ronnie to become Comptroller and Auditor-General, which was the job that had been set aside for him, because he would be investigating a project which he had himself masterminded and on which he changed his mind at a late stage.

Tuesday 5 May

A Cabinet on Cambodia and Michael Stewart began by making the most rigid speech. The decision of the Americans to march into Cambodia has triggered off the most tremendous demonstrations in the United States and here we are on the eve of an Election with the possibility of a revolt in the PLP.

There was in fact something of a consensus at Cabinet. I spoke and I said that I thought a formal statement would not be enough, that it wouldn't meet the public mood. We really couldn't support the Americans this time. Dissociation would mean washing our hands. The US policy had really failed. But for Nixon to admit this would be almost impossible because it would be the first US defeat abroad and it would look as though it were a surrender to domestic pressure. It could trigger off a great lack of confidence at home and abroad and therefore we must speak candidly to the US as a friend.

Tuesday 12 May

Caroline is writing an article for the *Sunday Times*. She is now on the ILEA and is being nominated also for the chairmanship of the board of governors of Holland Park.

I went to the Campaign Committee and the papers this morning described the new little plasticine figures of Tory politicians, called 'Yesterday's Men', which were designed by Alan Aldridge and taken on by David Kingsley and Peter Davies, for use on posters. They really are fantastic publicity people working for us.

In the afternoon I had an impressive deputation of trade union officials and local MPs from Jarrow and Newcastle, pleading with me to try to save the yard. I couldn't promise anything but said I would do my best.

Went to the House in the evening and the NOP today had a 7.5 per cent Labour lead, which has staggered everyone.

Sunday 17 May

Meeting of the Cabinet and NEC which had been planned some time ago. It was obvious as soon as we gathered at Number 10 that this was going to be the meeting for launching arrangements for the manifesto, and everyone there expected the Election would come on June 18. Harold opened by saying there would be an announcement soon.

Alice Bacon paid a tribute to Denis Lyons, Peter Davies and David Kingsley and described the 'Life and Soul' theme which began last September, and the 'Yesterday's Men' figures, and this idea is to be followed soon by the posters of 'Labour's winning team'. She said the Election publicity was more or less ready.

Roy Jenkins opened the afternoon session, saying he had had an easier job than he expected because he had been wanting to urge that we shouldn't put specific tax proposals in the manifesto. On the broad public-expenditure theme he said the Tories had lost credibility by their proposals. 'Don't let's rival them. Some of the proposals put forward in the course of the morning would cost a great deal of money. If we put in proposals we would have to cost them and that would put us in difficulty.' He said the position had changed because the economic picture had changed; only a year ago, in May 1969, the picture had been very grave.

There was a general assent to this and Frank Allaun said, 'If we don't make reference to a wealth tax, will it be ruled out?' Roy said, 'No, not at all.'

Then we had George Brown, and when he's good he's marvellous. He talked about the manifesto, and said it was a record, it described our aims, attitudes and intentions, and our intentions had to be spelt out. We must have some commitments. The activists must have meat and we had to get the themes right. The themes were social equality, the attack on poverty, quality of life and participation. The manifesto, when written into a record by the next Government, becomes the basis by which we are judged.

Harold agreed with George. He said we mustn't be guided by public-opinion polls (I must say that was a bit of a laugh because Harold lives by them), and we didn't have to prove ourselves this time. Prices were the biggest single issue and he thought we might deal with that by referring to the fact that the Tories have opposed us all along the line on our ways of controlling prices, that the Tories' present policies would lead to far higher prices, VAT and the end of council house subsidies. It was very important, he said, that the Tories shouldn't be allowed to forget Selsdon Park. Our manifesto must not be achievements plus promises: what we want is the idea of a developing government illustrated by what we have done, by what the Tories did, and by what we aim to do.

Mikardo, an excellent chairman, wound up, saying there would be no vote of gratitude, people wanted a sense of urgency and we would have to convey it.

Then we came to foreign policy. Michael Stewart began with a long speech in which he said we had to adjust to the real world; the Tory illusion of a world role for Britain was unrealistic; our approach to Europe was very important; Britain must neither be an aggressor nor a runaway; we wanted to conciliate and relax tension and defence was the key to relaxation of tension. We had played a large part in that relaxation, in disarmament and the NATO conference.

He said that race relations affected our relations with the developing world, and that aid was important. On the United Nations we had a good story to tell. Finally he said, 'If I may turn from foreign policy to the Party generally, our rock is the decent working man and he believes in less for the rich and more for the poor.' Then he produced a phrase which was pure Clem Attlee. He said, 'The decent British working man says to us, "We'll look after the underdog if you'll look after the dirty dog." ' By that he meant the criminals, and we must stand up for Britain and its fundamental decencies of democracy and freedom.

This was greeted with some applause because it was very straight and direct and it was Michael at his very best.

Denis Healey said, very crudely, that the manifesto didn't matter, we couldn't inject new ideas at this stage because it would have to be a book we were writing. We can't tax people for overseas aid. He had saved £3,000 million already on defence and £2,000 million on expenditure. Real cuts had occurred, people cared about security, the army was the most efficient and had the highest morale in the world, and the purpose of defence was to stop war and to stop people killing each other. He believed Britain was a country to be proud of.

Harold said he just wanted to let us know officially that he was going to see the Queen tomorrow and at 6 o'clock would announce the dissolution of Parliament. He gave us the timetable for the Election, with Parliament meeting the week after next and being dissolved on 29 May, polling day on 18 June. There would be no full Cabinet during the coming week. Jim Callaghan warned us that there was too much euphoria and we would have quite a battle ahead of us and it would start on prices and rents. Jim has this terrible problem of the South African cricket tour, where the Cricket Council have so far absolutely declined to change their attitude.

I went to see Mother after the meeting and came home to begin working on Election plans.

Monday 18 May
The Chairman of the CEGB, Sir Stanley Brown, came in to see me with the Chief Nuclear Inspector, Trevor Griffiths, for a very serious interview. The Hartlepool power station is to go nuclear and one of the consortia produced designs for an advanced gas-cooled reactor which Mr Griffiths, an engineer, thought were unsatisfactory; he thought the apertures were too great and if there was a serious failure the disaster would be calamitous. The metal doors covering the metal apertures were not sufficiently strong and he was in favour of a concrete pressure-vessel-type construction.

He had tried to get the consortium to change the design, but they had declined to do so, as had the CEGB, and he advised me not to authorise and approve the continuation of the work. Stanley Brown is a big, tough, straightforward engineer and I had to say to him, 'Look, you will appreciate that I have got a Chief Nuclear Inspector and I can't possibly disregard his advice.'

Stanley Brown said, 'Will you let us go on with the work and I'll review the problem later?'

'No, I won't,' I replied. 'If you go on now, the pressure to accept less than adequate safety standards will be very strong, because you will have got that much further with the project.'

So he asked, 'Will you get a second opinion?'

I said, 'No, I can't. If my Chief Nuclear Inspector had said he *thought* something was safe and *I* was uneasy I might get advice to cross-check what he says, but if he says it is not safe, I can't conceivably get somebody else in and then override his view.'

He then tried to get Griffiths to say what he would accept and Griffiths said, 'No, I am saying I won't accept this. You will have to put in other plans.'

So he left and then I did a run-round with Jack Rampton, my Deputy Secretary, and Griffiths. These are the nuclear problems in a nutshell: first of all, the corrosion problem of the Magnox stations hasn't been solved and it is not impossible that they may have to be closed down early; second, it now appears that there is corrosion in advanced gas-cooled reactors and we haven't got anywhere near a solution for that; third, there is the dissatisfaction with plans for the Hartlepool power station; and fourth, Dungeness B, being built by a consortium made up of Fairey Engineering and International Combustion, which has just fallen down on the job, is going to be three years late. All this constitutes a major nuclear policy problem. After the Election we shall have to re-examine the whole thing and see where we stand.

In the afternoon I drove to Bristol with all my Election gear. There was a local Party meeting, at which Herbert was appointed agent, and I was reselected.

Thursday 28 May
To Bristol, where the major political problem at the moment is that the envelopes for the Election addresses, which Herbert Rogers ordered a week ago from the regional organiser, have got lost on their way down from Newcastle.

Wednesday 3 June
Got to Transport House at 7.45 this morning and was there most of the morning for the usual meetings with the research people, the publicity people, Harry Nicholas and the Prime Minister.

In view of Enoch Powell's Election address which had raised the racial issue again, I decided that I would put out a press release on race relations for my speech at Central Hall Westminster tonight. So after the PM left for his press conference at 9.50, I went up to Gwyn Morgan's office and dictated a very violent attack upon racialism and I linked it with Heath's silence on Enoch Powell's position. I said that the flag that was being raised in Wolverhampton was getting to look more and more like the flag that futtered over Belsen. I showed it to Gwyn Morgan and I said, 'This is very strong stuff.' He replied, saying, 'Well, it has to be said.'

In the evening Caroline came with me to the meeting in Central Hall, where I was speaking with Jack Jones and others.

I spoke first. I delivered my speech on racialism – copies of it had been made available to the press and BBC television covered it very fully. The audience was quiet and, frankly, it was not a very good meeting. But, at any rate, I delivered my speech. It created tremendous press interest because of the strength of the language used.

Caroline and I came back home and I was immediately summoned to do a BBC television interview in the Election studio with Robin Day, who violently attacked me for my speech. He quoted statements that Heath had made condemning Enoch Powell and I said that if this was the case why did Heath recommend people in Wolverhampton to vote for Powell.

The NOP today showed a 5 per cent lead by Labour.

Thursday 4 June
Bristol. The Belsen speech has exploded across the Election. There is a tremendous row about it. Every paper is leading on it. Heath demands that Harold repudiates it and indeed demands my dismissal from the government on the same basis that Heath dismissed Enoch Powell.

Harold is furious about it and has left a message for me to keep off the racial question.

I was interviewed on Harlech Television. I went to Weston-Super-Mare to speak at the Tobacco Workers' Conference and then for a short sleep at the Grand Hotel. I had two meetings in the evening. I rang Caroline, who was a bit worried about the race speech. She thinks I went too far and should have consulted people and got advice before I issued the text. But Peter Shore was very reassuring about it on the phone so I have decided just to hold my ground.

Friday 5 June
I gave a press conference at my headquarters in Bristol for the local press and all they wanted to ask about was the Enoch Powell speech. I said I had nothing to add about it. The papers are beginning to report that Harold is angry, so the press men think I have been disciplined by Harold, which in a sense I have. The truth is that Harold had hoped to keep race out of the Election. But an issue as important as this can't be left out, because an election is a period when the public engages in a great debate about its future and as race is one of the most important questions in the future, it is quite wrong to try to keep it quiet. I am still a bit worried, however, and was encouraged that Doug Constable, whose judgement I very much respect, was in favour of the words I used on the grounds that if you were going to fight evil, you had to use fairly strong weapons. Indeed, he rather reflected on the speech and drew from it the conclusion that the Church was too quiet in its condemnation of evil.

Afterwards I drove to St Albans to take part in 'Any Questions' with Norman St John Stevas and Eric Lubbock. The first question was about the Powell speech. Norman St John Stevas who, in all fairness, is not at all a racialist, attacked me violently for it. I defended myself vigorously. Eric Lubbock supported me. I am very glad I did have the opportunity of speaking to a wider audience and giving the reasons why I made the speech.

Then I drove Eric back to London. He is an extremely agreeable man and could easily be in the Labour Party; I wish he were. We talked about the Liberals' prospects in Orpington, which he is hopeful of retaining.

Sunday 7 June
I got home from a meeting in Basildon and discovered that Joshua was worried about the tremendous controversy raging round my head over the race speech. One has to remember that children do find arguments involving their parents very upsetting.

Today, Brazil beat England in the World Cup: the political effect of this can't be altogether ignored.

Monday 8 June
Letters began pouring in on the Powell speech: 2:1 against me but some very sympathetic ones saying that my speech was overdue.

Saturday 13 June

Powell's 'enemies within' speech has now come out, in which he says that he suspects that civil servants have been faking the immigration statistics. He draws a comparison with Burgess and Maclean's unpatriotic behaviour, giving the impression that he really has gone entirely round the bend, and this has helped to blank out some of the criticism of me for having attacked him, because this is well beyond the pale as far as the British public is concerned. It is just not acceptable to say that sort of thing about civil servants. Enoch must be under heavy strain: he is calculating the Tories will lose the Election and people will then turn to him.

Sunday 14 June

At this moment I think we are going to win quite comfortably, though there are some anxieties in that the Tories *are* being extremely effective in their approach to women – their party political to women was a great success. They are hammering and hammering the economic theme and this is beginning to break the credibility of the Government's claim to have solved the economic problems.

Tonight England was finally knocked out of the World Cup which, no doubt, will have another subtle effect on the public.

Monday 15 June

The poor trade figures were hit by Heath and he made a really big issue of them, saying there was an economic crisis and that we had misled the public, that the situation was much more serious than we had admitted and that was why we had called the Election when we had. This was the first real breakthrough by Heath. He has concentrated in effect simply on two things – prices and the economic situation – and although he has been bitterly attacked by the press for his failure and scorned by Harold Wilson and the rest of us, he has stuck, in exactly the way that Home stuck in 1964, to his two themes. In 1964, Home was saying, 'Keep the deterrent' and 'Don't let labour ruin the economy'. Now Heath is saying, 'The economy is in a terrible state and only we can put it right' and 'We will tackle prices. The housewife should vote for herself'. These twin themes are the ones that are beginning to get through.

Anyway I did loudspeaker work in the evening in the pouring rain advertising meetings. I rang Harold up in Liverpool and said I thought the latest economic scare on the trade figures, and the fact that Heath had now talked openly about another devaluation, really was worth answering, but Harold was relaxed and said Roy was going to make a statement about it and there was nothing to worry about. He sounded as if he was just composing himself for another Election triumph. Having made my point, I left it.

Wednesday 17 June
My assessment is that we should win by a large majority, certainly with a working majority, and although I have some uneasiness, it is rather less than in previous Elections.

Thursday 18 June
Polling day. Caroline and I went round the polling stations. It is part of a ritual but it has to be done and it is very tiring. A journalist on *Time* magazine from New York looked in to see me for a short talk and wanted to know what our plans were for the future. I talked very confidently. This was for the *Time* cover story, I think. After we had completed the polling stations and committee rooms and loudspeaker work, we were pretty sure of victory by twenty or thirty.

Went back to the Grand Hotel, had a bath, tea and sandwiches and settled down to watch television before we had to go off to my own count. The first thing that came over the television that was slightly worrying was the result of a poll done by the BBC at Gravesend, in which they had interviewed people as they left the polling station. So this was the first poll, not of voting intentions, but of how people actually voted, and it showed a Conservative majority.

At 11.15 we got the first result and it showed an enormous swing to the Tories and, all of a sudden, there and then, we realised we had lost the Election. There was no question about it. There are regional variations and of course these came out. But the result in this first constituency was so overwhelmingly Tory that it was quite clear that we were out and the Tories were in, possibly with a tremendous majority.

In a fraction of a second, one went from a pretty confident belief in victory to absolute certainty of defeat. It was quite a remarkable experience. By midnight it was clear that they had won and we left in the most appalling fog to find Carlton Park School, where my count was being held.

At 2.30 in the morning my result was declared. My majority had been halved. I was able to keep abreast of what was happening elsewhere by listening to the results as they came out on my transistor radio.

Harold was not conceding the result but biding his time and I spared a thought for the poor man believing himself due to continue as Prime Minister and discovering he had been defeated. After the declaration I made a short speech and had a short interview with Jonathan Dimbleby, who tried to blame the Election result on my speech against Enoch Powell. At the Walter Baker Hall the Party workers were absolutely desolate. I told them not to worry – that we had been defeated but not routed.

I decided I would go straight back to London and clear right out of the office.

6

1970–74

Friday 19 June 1970

We left Bristol at 5 am with all our junk packed up: I began dozing off a third of the way home so Caroline took over the wheel. We got home at about 7.30, I unpacked the car and drove straight to the office. I just cleared everything out of my room, putting some personal things in my bag to take with me and leaving the rest in the waiting room next door, so that by 8.35 there was no sign that anybody had worked in my office. I thought this was the right thing to do and I couldn't have coped with any of my officials when I had been drained of authority in this way. It was a very emotional experience, a sort of bereavement. It wasn't that I particularly wanted to be a Minister, although the salary is useful, the car is nice and the authority is pleasant: it was this sense of being suddenly and absolutely cut off from work.

I went round and said goodbye to everyone and I must say I almost broke down. Jack, one of my messengers, said, 'I have never shaken the hand of a better man,' and that was really more than I could bear. I walked out and left the Millbank Tower never to return. Then straight to the House of Commons and I completely cleared my room there as well. On to Transport House and thanked all the people who had helped. They, too, were very upset and emotional.

When I got home I was told that a meeting of the Inner Cabinet had been called for 4 o'clock. I thought it was a bit much of Harold to have a meeting at Number 10 when we were so obviously defeated. But the Queen was at Ascot or somewhere and was coming back at 6, so Harold planned to resign then. I went in by the Cabinet Office door and we had a brief discussion about the arrangements. Harold said he was going to resign and thanked people. I said we were an ungenerous lot and nobody ever did say thank you in politics and I would like to say what a privilege it was to have served with him in his administration – which was a bit pompous but somebody had to say it. We agreed that we would have to think about the Parliamentary Labour Party and how we organised the Opposition, and that there should be no recriminations or personal attacks – all of which was kind of obvious. There was a shellshocked feeling to the meeting.

At the end I got my camera out and as Harold left it for the last time, I shot the only movie picture ever taken in the Cabinet Room. To Transport House again, where Harold appeared, having just been to the Palace to resign. We stood outside and cheered him – all except for Tom Driberg. He said, 'That man misled us all and picked the wrong date. Why should I cheer for him?' A very sour comment.

Meanwhile Heath had been leaving the Albany and going to Buckingham Palace to become Prime Minister – very exciting – and was seen entering Number 10. At the same time Harold's stuff was going out of the back door and into a furniture van. This was the beginning of Opposition. The thought that the Tories had won was very depressing; not just the thought of Tory Ministers in office but that their whole philosophy had conquered and that this would strengthen all the reactionary forces in society. I shall work very hard in Opposition and concentrate entirely on my political work.

Saturday 20 June
Heath's Cabinet was announced. Geoffrey Rippon has gone to the Ministry of Technology: he is a very right-wing figure, a member of the Monday Club, and a former Minister of Public Building and Works. I must say that depressed me a bit. I wrote to him but then I tore up the letter because it isn't normally done to write to one's successor.

For the first time in six years, I don't have a series of red boxes; I must admit that it is rather pleasant to be free.

Monday 22 June
I got up at 4.40 to get Stephen off to Keele University.

Lucille was very tearful at the result of the Election. When I dictated my goodbye letters, she wept over the typewriter and I must say I was sad myself. People came and collected the various keys that had to be returned to the office.

In the afternoon I went to Buckingham Palace for the audience with the Queen and I drove in my own car unlike some ex-Ministers who were still using their official cars, which I thought was slightly odd since we were clearly out. The courtiers could scarcely conceal their delight – Sir Michael Adeane, the equerries, the ladies-in-waiting – and were obviously thrilled at what had happened and were being polite to the 'little Labour men'.

I said to the Queen I had enjoyed office and she said, 'You will be seeing more of your family.' I talked about the stamps and thanked her for her help with them. Then she mentioned Concorde, so I said, 'Well, there are a lot of problems and I sometimes wonder whether it shouldn't just be kept to fly up The Mall on the royal birthday.' She laughed at that, and thanked me very much, as if I had somehow done it all for her. It was very courteous of her but I am sure that the idea that the Queen's Ministers are simply advisers, and that she is really the Government, in a position to thank them before they go, is deeply entrenched at the Palace.

Thursday 25 June
We had the last office Pink Shirt Club party at Holland Park Avenue. I bought blue and white striped tea mugs for everybody and put a pink handkerchief, pink tie, or a pink rose in each of them. They gave me a pink tie with the Mintech symbol on it. We had a lovely evening with all the old gang, and Kate Chaplin, Monty and Derek Moon from the Press Office were also there. We sat in the garden and played records. They left me a record of the theme song from *Dr Zhivago* which I had whistled up and down the Millbank corridors for years. This was effectively the end of my links with the Private Office after some very happy years.

Saturday 27 June
Slogged away, wrote sixty or seventy cards by hand. After just over a week I find myself slowly adjusting to the fact that nobody really wants to know you when you are an ex-Minister. It must be absolute hell if you retire or are fired and you are out while all your colleagues are still in. The truth is that it is almost rather comforting that everyone else is out as well.

Monday 29 June
Today Jeremy Thorpe's wife Caroline was tragically killed in a motor crash.

Thursday 2 July
Today was the Debate on the Address with Heath and Wilson speaking.
Harold is incredible, just like an India-rubber man, bouncing up again after
his defeat, completely unphased by the fact that he lost, and with the Party
just sort of accepting him again. I wouldn't have the strength to accept a
defeat of that kind. I think I would be very bad at coming to terms with it.

Wednesday 8 July
We went to the Home Policy Committee meeting of the Executive, where
Jim Callaghan got himself dug in as Chairman: he is building his power base
absolutely everywhere at the moment. Once in the chair he was very
reasonable, asking everybody to comment and complimenting us all on
what we said. Jim is a skilful politician, there is no question about it; very
skilful.

Thursday 10 September
In the evening I went and had dinner with Peter and Liz Shore and Tommy
Balogh, and his new wife-to-be Katherine Storr, who is a distinguished
surgeon. Tommy Balogh is leaving his current wife, Pen, to marry her. It is
really rather sad. I liked Pen Balogh very much indeed. Katherine Storr is
about the same age and looked rather similar.
    Caroline loyally went to hear Stan Newens, who lost his seat at Epping,
speaking to the North Kensington Labour Party. She is about to be made
Chairman of the Holland Park School governors.

Thursday 15 October
Six years ago today, the Labour Government won the 1964 Election.
    This afternoon Heath announced the abolition of the Ministry of
Technology. It is being merged with the Department of Trade and Industry,
with Aviation Supply going off separately.

Tuesday 3 November
Worked at the Commons. I circulated my draft letter to my constituents on
the Common Market referendum idea to Harold, Roy, Jim, Denis, Harold
Lever, Gwyn Morgan and Tom McNally. Shirley Williams drove me home
and I talked to her about it. I am hoping to get the support of one or two
people who are in favour of entry because it would greatly stengthen my
case.

Thursday 5 November
Harold Wilson came up to me and said, 'I understand you are suggesting a
referendum on the Common Market. You can't do that.' I said, 'Well, I sent

you the draft letter, Harold. Have you seen it yet?' He said, 'No. You had better bring it to the Shadow Cabinet.'

I discovered that it had not been drawn to his attention because he was too busy. I don't blame him for that but this is the moment when I am going to strike out on my own.

Sunday 8 November

This afternoon Mick Farren, a woman called Ingrid and a man called John Hopkins came for a talk. Mick is the author of the article 'Rock – Energy for Revolution' in the *Melody Maker*. What I didn't know was that last night these people, who are part of the YIPPIES (the Youth International Party) had been on the David Frost programme and had broken it up.

In the evening we watched Jean-Paul Sartre's 'Roads to Freedom' on television – a series that has been gripping us all autumn.

Wednesday 11 November

My letter to my constituents, 'Britain and the Common Market – The Case for a Referendum', was to come before the Shadow Cabinet today. But as Harold was in Paris for de Gaulle's funeral it was just noted and there was no comment. The only person who understood its real significance was Jim Callaghan, who said, 'Tony may be launching a little rubber liferaft which we will all be glad of in a year's time.' That is one way of looking at it. I am in favour of a referendum on constitutional grounds but even if there isn't going to be much support for those grounds clearly this is one way in which the Labour Party can avoid dividing itself into bits. So that is just about the best result I could have got from the Shadow Cabinet.

Saturday 5 December

I had a talk to Harold, who told me that had we won the Election he would only have continued as Prime Minister for three years. I have often suspected this but he has never said it specifically before. It is an interesting piece of information, because if we win the next Election he wouldn't continue the full term as Prime Minister as he is determined that he will never be defeated again. That means that the next Leader of the Labour Party will be elected within the next few years – that's my view. If I am going to make any sort of bid for the leadership at any stage, I shall have to begin preparing for it soon.

Monday 7 December

There was a power cut at 7.45 this morning because of the go-slow or work-to-rule by the power workers in pursuit of their claim. It lasted for two hours. Went to talk to Harold about the possibility of getting some proper meetings of Party officers every now and again to consider the running of the Party, giving the Party a higher sense of direction, which it entirely lacks. Harry

Nicholas is useless and doesn't see Harold often and the Executive is too big to do anything. The officers don't meet, and the Shadow Cabinet is just concerned with parliamentary tactics. And Harold is desperately busy writing his memoirs, or what he insists on calling his record of his administration.

We also discussed the question of the Common Market.

He doesn't understand that if he does come out against the Common Market it will absolutely wreck his credibility: the Tories will simply put up posters showing what he said about industrial relations when Prime Minister and then what he said when in Opposition under trade union pressure; what he said about the Common Market when Prime Minister and then when in Opposition, again under trade union pressure. And they will put on the bottom of the poster, 'Can you ever trust him again?' It is going to be much more difficult than he thinks.

Wednesday 16 December

Executive this morning and we came to my resolution advocating a special conference to be held before the Parliamentary Party had voted on the Common Market question. I moved this briefly. Denis said there wouldn't be time to organise a special conference and in any case we couldn't get a hall. Fred Mulley said that if the Tories hurried the legislation, the Labour Party in the House would simply abstain, as if somehow on the greatest issue of the century for Britain, Labour MPs could abstain on the grounds that they hadn't had time to consider it. Roy said something, and then I blew my top. I said this was a grave matter and I was not prepared to explain to my grandchildren that we hadn't voted on the question of British entry into the Common Market because we couldn't get a hall; I was not prepared to abstain and that those who were in favour of entry into Europe had better begin making the case for it instead of hoping to slip it through, which is what they are trying to do.

I carried my resolution on a special conference overwhelmingly, about 14 to 1, I think. Afterwards Roy, with his nostrils distended with rage, said to me, 'There are some of us who will never vote against entry into Europe.' I said, 'I am never going to urge you to do so. If there is a referendum you can vote for it then, but up till then we will argue that it should be put to the public.' Then Denis said, 'Your "support" for Europe is much distrusted. Why don't you make some speeches in favour?' Well, *he* doesn't make any speeches in favour. So my relations with those two are very poor at the moment. But this is a huge issue and it has got to be dealt with seriously.

Wednesday 13 January 1971

I invited Roy back home for a while. I explained the strategy for a referendum, which he was opposed to. But I think he is anxious to maintain some links with me. I asked him how he saw the future because, I said, I could see a possibility of the Labour Party actually splitting on this, resulting in a broad centre party which was European, flanked by a Powellite right and a Michael Foot–*Tribune* left. He said, 'I hope it doesn't come to that,' but he didn't rule it out. It was the first time he had been in our house for six or seven years or maybe longer.

Monday 25 January
Neil Kinnock told me today that he and about thirty others were organising a demonstration tonight against the guillotine on the Industrial Relations Bill and they were planning either to stand up in their places or to stand in front of the Speaker and try to get themselves or the House suspended. I argued with him for a long time, as sympathetically as I could, saying this would be a big step and it would annoy other members of the Party. I thought it worthwhile to go and see Bob Mellish, who was talking to Stan Orme and Callaghan about the same thing, and I did persuade Bob to call a meeting of the Shadow Cabinet in the evening to consider what to do. Michael Foot very sensibly said it would be stupid to make a big thing of this.

But it was agreed that some members of this group should come and meet Roy, Michael Foot, Bob Mellish, Douglas Houghton and Jim Callaghan. So we all dispersed but they failed to persuade the group not to demonstrate. So at about 9.45, they all got up, about thirty of them, including Eric Heffer and Reg Freeson, who are both Front Bench spokesmen, and stood in front of the table and shouted. The Speaker suspended the sitting, having said that this was all extremely boring, as boring as a standing ovation, which was quite a funny remark.

After the first suspension we had agreed to talk to the demonstrators in the Tea Room, but they were determined to go on and when the suspension ended, there they were standing in the middle again. The Tory Chief Whip, Francis Pym, got up and moved that the question be put, and it was put, and there was a vote and the Speaker declined to hear points of order. So that brought it to an end. It was rather surprising and there was a great deal of excitement.

Monday 1 February
I rang Clive Dunn, one of the television stars of 'Dad's Army', who has just had a tremendous hit record, 'Grandad', and he agreed when he was in Bristol next month to come and meet some old-age pensioners at Memory Hall.

Saturday 6 March
Went up by train to Newcastle and talked to the Northumberland Mechanics' Association and then to the dinner at which Vic Feather and Joe Gormley spoke. There were songs and bawdy speeches. As a result of the Tories' Industrial Relations Bill, the trade union movement, and the British

working class, have become proud of being the working class. Tory legislation has succeeded in shutting off the idea that somehow you can escape from your class and come up in a Davis Escape Apparatus, one by one, to join the ruling class, because the ruling class has let you down and is trying to suppress you. There is a tremendous self-confidence in being yourself and what you are. It is 'black is beautiful' applied to the working class, which is marvellous. It oozed out of everything Vic Feather said.

Just sitting and listening I noticed how much everybody made a reference to where they came from – 'He's from this part of Northumberland, or from Durham, of course, I'm from Yorkshire, you're from Lancashire.' I wonder whether we have given anything like enough importance politically to regionalism. I am sure we haven't. We have only looked at it technically and in terms of blueprints.

Wednesday 21 April
To the Education Sub-Committee of the NEC and got Joan Lestor into the chair. I thought she was preferable to Eirene White or Shirley Williams. While we were sitting there, Joan Lestor was opening her mail and she had a big fat envelope and she tore it open; inside was another envelope which fitted very tightly into the outer one, and as she began pulling the inner envelope out smoke began pouring out of the envelope. So she dropped it on the ground, and I poured water on it, dropped it in a wastepaper basket and called the police, who took it away. It was a homemade bomb of some kind and the man who had sent it had fixed some matches on the inner envelope and sandpaper on the outer one. If she had pulled it out quickly it would have burst into flames and blown up, and burned her face.

Thursday 20 May
Came back on the train from Southampton with Jeremy Thorpe, who really is a very nice, agreeable and kind person but has no weight as a party leader – just thinks of the House of Commons as if it were the Oxford Union Debating Society. Absolutely out of touch with modern trends and movements.

Sunday 30 May
The Party is heading for an extremely difficult summer. There is a small group of highly dedicated Marketeers led by Roy Jenkins, with Bill Rodgers as campaign manager, and including the old Campaign for Democratic Socialism types. They are genuinely pro-Europe (I give them credit for that), but they also see a last opportunity to do to the Labour Party what they failed to do over disarmament and Clause 4, namely to purge it of its trade union wing and of its Left. This group, working with the conservative Europeans, really represents a new political party under the surface in Britain. They

think a free vote would get them off the hook because they would be able to vote with Heath on the grounds that the question was above politics.

Of course the real crunch will come when specific legislation has to go through and any serious European would have to vote with the Government to bring British law into line with Community law. It is inconceivable that such a group, consistently voting with the Government, could do this without severing their links with the Labour Party, and to this extent it is impossible that the Party will do anything other than come out against Europe. But what the pro-Marketeers don't realise yet, though they soon will, is that if this situation becomes impossible for them, much better that they should be coming out against entering Europe without some consultation. This is what my referendum offers them, but a referendum is a difficult concept for them to consider and is a relatively novel idea, though Philip Goodhart, the Tory MP, has written a book on referenda which he sent me and in which he argues that it is a perfectly established constitutional principle.

The anti-Marketeers are annoyed that although I am not anti-Market I do see the possibility of optimising their support by using the General Election/referendum solution. So I think my role between now and the Conference, at which I become Chairman of the Party, is to present this proposal modestly and on my own. It is of constitutional importance but it also does have the great tactical advantage of keeping the Party united, and I think people will gradually come to see this.

Monday 14 June

UCS is in difficulty. Looked through my old files and came across a confidential memorandum written by Nicholas Ridley for Heath in 1969 about how to cut up UCS. I rang up Mark Arnold-Forster at the *Guardian* and gave it to him. I received it from Eric Varley – I don't know where he got it from – and I hadn't used it before because I was a bit worried about revealing a document which had been pirated in some way, picked up from a wastepaper basket or whatever. But with the possibility of UCS being knifed today – indeed the near certainty of it – I decided to let it come out.

I drafted a statement on UCS, calling for public ownership and workers' control in the yard itself, and went into the House of Commons. I had a filthy cold and felt terrible. I saw Harold Wilson and he approved the draft.

Davies made his statement in the House, that UCS would liquidate, and I attacked him violently, blaming him for it.

Had an urgent meeting with the Scottish Members and then decided to fly up to Clydebank with Hugh McCartney, the local MP. We went to Clydebank Town Hall where all the shop stewards were gathered and I reported what had happened in the House in the afternoon and what a betrayal it was. I was asked what attitude I would adopt to the workers taking control of the yard. I said if they felt this was right I thought their action was fully justified. This of course was encouraging or approving illegal action, but I had thought it all out some time before and I am sure it was the right thing to say. Then I asked them what they wanted me to say in the debate tomorrow. About an hour and a half later I caught the sleeper back to London and prepared for the debate.

Thursday 17 June

Our 22nd wedding anniversary.

'Yesterday's Men' was shown on television. This is the programme which was supposed to be a serious look at the Opposition and the makers had brought their cameras into the Shadow Cabinet. In fact it was a complete send-up. It was interesting because they had just taken the insignificant bits and strung them together, which made the whole thing trivial. They knifed Harold as hard as they could.

Friday 18 June

To Scotland by train, to the Clydebank yard with Frank McElhone to go over with the shop stewards what they wanted to do next. The workforce has theoretically taken over the yard today and, seen from the outside, this looks like a very revolutionary act. But when you get through the barricades and ask, as a friend, 'Well, what are you going to do?', they haven't a strategy, they haven't a plan, they haven't got anything at all. I probed how far they wanted workers' control to go, and they were very uncertain. But it helped me because I found a form of words for a statement that simply said that any management pattern would have to be acceptable to the workers as a whole.

Sunday 18 July

This evening I went to Geoffrey Goodman's home in Mill Hill for a gathering of the Left with Michael Foot and Jill Craigie, Peter and Liz Shore, Dick and Bridget Clements, Alex Jarratt who used to be an official at the Department of Employment and is now Managing Director of IPC, and Leo Abse and his wife.

At dinner Jill Craigie suddenly turned to Peter and me and said, 'I realise that the next Leader of the Party will be one or other of you and you will be getting the knives out for each other; but it's more likely to be Peter.' Peter was flattered but slightly embarrassed by this.

Monday 19 July

PLP meeting at 6.30 and Harold explained the procedure in the House for the Common Market debate on Wednesday. Norman Atkinson came out against Europe on ideological grounds and said that if we were taken in by the Tories, we should pledge ourselves to get out.

Barbara Castle made a speech for forty minutes saying that the party had been cornered by the Tories on the terms. She said there should be a select committee (which I agree with), devaluation would be necessary for entry, we would surrender our freedom of action, she had always been against entry even in the Cabinet, that when we had reapplied we were not committed to the Common Agricultural Policy and now the French had actually caught us out by entrenching the CAP before we were admitted. She said that the objectives must be to federalise but these were never discussed and if we supported entry we would be accepting a political coalition in this country. It was a powerful ideological case against entry.

Then Roy Jenkins said there was no great current of anti-Market feeling in the constituency Parties. He thought there should be consistency in commitment since the last Labour Cabinet, by a majority, voted to enter and the terms of entry would have been accepted by the Cabinet. If we didn't go in now, he said, it would be worse than if we had never applied. He didn't accept that we must reject entry because the Tories were in power. He attacked the negative insularity of the anti-Marketeers and said that socialism in one country was a slogan and not a policy and socialists in the other EEC countries wanted our help.

It was a powerful speech and the arguments carried a great deal of weight. But of course it was defiant – an arrogant and an élitist speech. A demonstration had been prearranged afterwards and people banged and hammered and shouted. Roy's speech was of course a direct attack on Harold Wilson and also on Healey and Crosland, who had climbed off the fence against the Market, and it changed the political situation in the Party at one stroke.

Afterwards I went down to the Smoking Room and sat with the Left, where Barbara was saying, 'We must organise, we must fight.' Michael Foot was shaken by it and I think it would certainly confirm Michael's determination to stand against Roy as Deputy Leader. It took you right back to 1951 or 1961 – the Party at its worst.

Tuesday 20 July
Went to the Trade and Industry Group meeting at the House, which had been summoned to consider the employment situation: while I was there a message was brought over to me to go and see Harold Wilson. So I walked over to his house, 5 Lord North Street, and found Harold in his shirtsleeves, pacing up and down the room.

He told me that he intended to make a statement at the Party meeting later today. He was extremely agitated about Roy Jenkins's great speech at the Party meeting last night. He said he was going to lay down the law and while he remained Leader he would handle the Party as he thought right: one of his real 'smack of government' or 'dog licence'-type speeches. Finally the text of his statement came over, he having written it and Marcia having made amendments. The first draft, which Marcia had cut down, was even more self-justificatory and obsessed with his leadership and referred to the number of weekends he had addressed meetings since the Election. He said to me, 'I don't know, I may just give up the Party leadership, they can stuff it as far as I am concerned. I pay out of my own pocket £15,000 a year to be Party Leader. I finance my own office. I have got an overdraft with my bank. All the money from my memoirs has gone. I don't know why I go on. But I'll smash CDS (the Campaign for Democratic Socialism) before I go,' and I'll do this and I'll do that. He was full of boasts but underneath was desperately insecure and unhappy.

I walked back from his house – I didn't particularly want to be seen with him in his car. But it was interesting that he called me in, which he only does when there is trouble.

I went over to the House and to the PLP meeting, where the statement was presented and it was received with acute embarrassment by the Party. One or two people at the end sort of pretended to applaud but it was very uncomfortable and nobody – except for a few middle-of-the-road people who thought it was necessary to straighten the Party out – could understand why he had made it.

I had a brief talk with one or two of the journalists, then had a meal in the Tea Room with Roy Mason and Frank McElhone. The position really is this: by making the leadership an issue and by using phrases like 'whoever is Leader after October', Harold has put himself in the most vulnerable position of all and I think it not impossible that somebody will stand against him: it might be Jim, it could hardly be Roy Jenkins or any of the others, but I think there is just a possibility.

I don't myself see much chance for the deputy leadership because I think Roy's honesty will win him support and the Left is almost bound to nominate Michael Foot, as the most direct attack on Roy that it can make. Michael is not an ambitious man. He is getting on himself (he is fifty-eight) and never having been in the Cabinet, he would be very much a stopgap candidate and would probably be defeated by Roy: so there may be some pressure on me.

I am almost ashamed to talk about this in my diary because it makes it seem that I am mainly concerned with that, which I hope I am not. But egoism eats up all politicians in time, which is probably the case for getting rid of them.

Thursday 29 July

The UCS statement, and the Government published a pessimistic White Paper by the so-called Four Wise Men, of which Robens was a member. There was extreme dismay in the House.

I ought to mention that Harold had called me in before the UCS statement was made and said that he would like to come to Scotland next week. He was particularly keen to do this because he wanted to expose Heath, who was sailing in the Admiral's Cup on Wednesday, and Harold had this idea, which he himself described as a gimmick, of sailing up the Clyde in a boat, visiting the doomed shipyards while Heath was yachting in the Admiral's Cup. He even suggested he might wear his outfit as an Elder Brother of Trinity House, which is the honorary title all Prime Ministers have. I must admit my contempt for Harold, which has been pretty high this last week, reached a peak. He said he would neither condemn nor condone the occupation. Well, that's no good, and I told him so. I was rather worried that he would wreck it all, but clearly he was getting on my bandwagon while being a bit more cautious about it.

Monday 2 August
I opened the House of Commons UCS debate which we had demanded, and my speech was perfectly all right. I got the case on the record but against bitterly hostile Tory benches and a certain amount of anxiety on our backbenches as to whether I had gone too far in my support for the occupation of the yards.

John Davies called me an 'evil genius'. Heath had cancelled his Admiral's Cup racing for the day and was sitting looking sour. It was a short debate but certainly worth while. There is no doubt that the press think the Government was right to wind up UCS and are critical of the line I have been taking.

Tuesday 3 August
I went to the House and saw the industrial correspondents on the workers' control issue, which I am going to write about in *Tribune* this week. Yesterday I talked to Norman Atkinson, to Johnny Prescott and one or two other young left-wing trade union MPs who are very much afraid, as I am, that I might appear to be misleading the men.

Friday 6 August
The papers carried a great deal about the *Oz* trial in which Richard Neville, the Editor, and two of his colleagues have been jailed for publishing an 'obscene' edition. Yesterday in the House, when the sentences were announced, Bill Hamling the Labour MP for Wolverhampton West, who is a member of the Humanists Group, handed me a motion condemning the sentences as being contrary to British justice, signed by Dick Taverne, who is a QC, Tom Driberg and Frank Allaun. I signed it too.

When I rang Frank McElhone today in Aberdeen, where he is on holiday, he was worried about this and said there had been a lot of criticism in Scotland of my signing the motion and I would lose fifty votes for the leadership. I said I felt deeply that it was wrong to jail these young people. This is the difficulty, if you are going to go out simply for high office, then you have got to be cautious and I am not sure that I want to be. I would rather stand up for what I believe. Frank was worried and I tried to reassure him.

Then I sat down and thought about how one would deal with criticisms of the line that I had taken. The truth is that middle-aged parents are the last to criticise the young because we were the war generation and the young are fighting against the obscenity of racial hatred and poverty and war. I jotted this down and showed it to Hilary but he thought it was too apologetic and I had better simply stick by what I had done.

In 1971, the Benns were invited to China by the Chinese Ambassador. The visit took place at the tail end of the 'Great Proletarian Cultural Revolution' which began in 1966 and raged on in different stages until 1969. The Revolution was actively supported by Chairman Mao Tse Tung and it brought with it fundamental changes and involved a period of turbulence and violence between the old regime and the forces of radicalism, which rocked the country.

Mao's famous 'big character' poster BOMBARD THE HEADQUARTERS *constituted official approval for the action of the young Red Guards who took over the universities, colleges, schools and factories and began a purge of the bureaucracy. The main objective of Mao and the Red Guards was to prevent the old functionaries from dominating the country, and to re-educate them by sending them into the countryside, in line with Mao's teaching that theory and practice must go together.*

This diary reflects the positive impressions of China and goes into considerable depth about life after the revolution, of which a glimpse is given here; it is a remarkable record of the aftermath of that extraordinary event.

Friday 10 September
We went by train from Kowloon to Lowu where we arrived at 10.26. There we got off the train, walked along the platform through the Hong Kong border post which didn't look, to me, to be under any sort of strain or stress and we crossed the border into mainland China. It was a very remarkable feeling crossing from one world into the other towards the Red Flag, with the Chinese soldiers standing there in their drab khaki cotton uniforms.

There was a health check carried out on the platform, then passports and tickets were inspected and we went into the waiting room, where we were invited to help ourselves to the works of Chairman Mao in several languages.

While we waited, we saw children coming back from school waving their red flags, and the big black steam locomotives with red painted wheels glistening with oil.

There were inscriptions on the walls of the station in Chinese and English. One particularly, which read 'The Japanese revolution will succeed if it follows Marxist/Leninist principles and pursues its own practice correctly', was put there at the request of the China Friends of the Japanese Workers' Delegation.

A Mr Sung, from the Institute of Foreign Affairs in Canton, arrived to take us to Canton. In the train he told us that Stalin had made mistakes but that today, the Soviet Union was, in effect, Fascist because it repressed criticism, Brezhnev was more cunning than Khrushchev. It was basically a revisionist regime. He stressed that the Chinese were only critical of the leadership and not of party members. He thought that even in Russia, they must be yearning for a Marxist/Leninist Party. He also said that 90 per cent of the world wants revolution and particularly Asia and Africa though circumstances in Western Europe and America were slightly different. He thought that Mao would be remembered mainly as a teacher, a poet and as a man of letters.

At 3, we arrived in Canton and were met by a member of the Institute of Foreign Relations. From 4.30 to 6.15 we drove around Canton, visiting the Yuesuh Park where we saw the old Krupps guns which had been used against the British in the Opium Wars. Over a stadium was the statement: 'Be vigilant – defend the motherland. Be prepared for war and other calamities.'

At the People's Hotel we met Mr Sun, the Chairman of the Revolution-ary Committee of the Hotel. He told us that the Revolutionary Committees were made up of members of the People's Liberation Army, the cadres and the mass of the workers. They had ten hours' study of Mao Tse Tung each week and three monthly self-criticism meetings. The hotel's Revolutionary Committee had removed the feudal decorations from the hotel; they had decided to admit workers and peasants, which the hotel had not done before; and they had 'put politics in command'. The Revolutionary Committee was selected by continuous consultation.

We had dinner with Mr Chen Yu, aged sixty-nine, the Vice-Chairman of the Provisional Revolutionary Government of Canton. He said that by coming we had contributed to understanding. When I asked him what his greatest problem was, he said that it was to learn to use the thoughts of Mao Tse Tung, that the masses were right and that science must serve the people. The Chinese intended to expand agriculture first, light industry second and heavy industry third, and then electronics. As we later learned, electronics had become somewhat controversial at the time of Liu Shai Chi and the idea that electronics could solve everything had been rejected by Mao during the Cultural Revolution. I asked one or two questions about China: whether the tactics of co-operation with the Kuomintang in the past might be used again to bring Taiwan back to mainland China and whether Mao could ever be wrong. I was told that he could not be because what he said came from the masses.

Saturday 11 September
At 9.30 we went to the 7th Middle School in Canton. Before the Cultural Revolution the school had been run according to the bourgeois intellectual

views copied from the old world but in the Cultural Revolution teachers and pupils had rebelled against this old line and had put 'politics in command'. We were told that the students were sent to factories and communes and railway workshops and had much to learn from the noble characteristics of workers.

The school had rejected the idea of marks and knowledge as a basis of selectivity.

The curriculum comprised politics, literature, maths, history, geography, revolutionary art, physics and chemistry. We were told that the main authors were Mao Tse Tung and Lin Piao, from whose work all literature was taught, and they also studied articles written by workers and peasants who had been learning Marxist and Leninist thought. They also studied military training and students went with the army units to learn how to fire guns.

An old teacher said that he preferred the new educational line and that in the old society, education had simply been taught to help pupils on step-by-step to university, to look for personal fame and glory, to put technology first. The exams were designed to catch the students out and really involved treating them like animals. Students didn't see their work as part of the general political development of society. But now they hoped they were more integrated with the masses. The leadership of the school was now under the firm control of the working classes and it was always asking, 'Whom do we serve?' Before, only 30 per cent of the places had been occupied by workers and peasants.

After lunch at 2.30, we went to the Canton school for deaf mutes. This had been opened in 1946 as a private, fee-paying school where there were forty students, and they were taught finger language. Now the school has been expanded and is based upon acupuncture. Nobody had cared much about deaf mutes, but in 1968 the People's Liberation Army medical team had come, having learned acupuncture and having first experimented on themselves, and began to deal with the problems of the deaf mute.

At the beginning of the treatment many of the children were able to hear but not to speak. But after three or six months' treatment some began to regain their power of speech quite quickly. The treatment consisted of starting and stopping the acupuncture over a period of six months. They had secured about an 80 per cent success rate in speech and within that a fairly high success rate with hearing.

Back to our guest house and had supper alone. Then to the huge airport and boarded the plane, an Ilyushin, which took us to Peking in three and a half hours.

Wednesday 13 October
Caroline's birthday.

I sent my Chairman's message to *Labour Weekly*, the new Party paper, in which I began spelling out the extension of Party democracy. We had the Shadow Cabinet meeting at 4 – the first meeting after Conference on the Common Market. The Chief Whip reported on the business of the House, telling us that the European Communities Bill would begin to be debated on 21 October. Harold moved that the PLP did not support entry into the Common Market on the present terms.

George Thomson then moved to enter the Common Market, after taking account of the resolution at the Conference. Shirley Williams supported. Jim Callaghan said if we flouted the Conference, we would immolate the Party and thoroughly upset the constituencies, which would have consequences for the Shadow Cabinet elections. Harold Wilson summed up against George Thomson's motion and it was agreed that the Parliamentary Party will be recommended by the Shadow Cabinet to oppose the Tory Government's proposal to enter the EEC.

Monday 18 October
We had the Shadow Cabinet at which we resumed the discussion on the Common Market. Roy put forward a resolution that we should have a free vote. Immediately after the meeting we heard that the Tories were going to be given a free vote – Heath had announced it himself. This was an absolute bombshell and so at 2.15 the Shadow Cabinet was called again. Harold said, 'If Heath gives a free vote, we shall have to have a free vote.'

I lost my temper with Harold, and I said, 'I don't know what game you are playing but we cannot have a free vote when the Party has decided its view.' I said, 'The line we take is that there must be a free vote of the *British public*. This is the right thing to happen, not a free vote of the House of Commons, which excludes the public from any right of choice.' The position was more or less held after that.

I was beginning to have second thoughts then about whether I would stand for the deputy leadership.

Tuesday 19 October
We had a Shadow Cabinet in the evening and Harold tried a new form of words. He said, 'This House, recalling the words of the Prime Minister in the General Election that no British government could possibly take this country into the Common Market against the wishes of the overwhelming majority of the British public, calls on the Government to submit to the democratic judgment of a General Election.'

Bob Mellish intervened to say, 'Look, Harold, it's all over. Leave it.'
Denis said, 'Leave it.'
Then Shirley tried to raise the question of the free vote and the argument started all over again.

By the end, the whole Shadow Cabinet was in a state of uproar and we were all set for a straight clash.

I had dinner with Eric Heffer, then phoned Judith, Joan Lestor, and Peter Shore to see how we could contain what had emerged, namely a European Social Democrat wing in the Parliamentary Party led by Bill Rodgers which was a minority but intended to defy the Conference decision. I stayed talking until 1 am and the atmosphere was tight. When I heard Charlie Pannell say that for him Europe was an article of faith, he put it above the Labour Party and above the Labour Movement, I was finally convinced that this was a deep split.

Thursday 28 October

The party is now on the eve of the great split when voting takes place and is absolutely dreading the situation. One of the factors that has made it a great deal worse is that Douglas Houghton, the Chairman of the PLP, has announced that he intends to vote for entry and this, of course, makes the revolt against the Whip respectable.

I received a letter from Enoch Powell – now that was a surprise – congratulating me on my Common Market speech yesterday, 90 per cent of which he had agreed with.

Harold opened the last day's debate on the Common Market and he hedged so cleverly that it was clear that if a Labour government was elected when he was Prime Minister, he would simply accept the Common Market. We had the vote and 69 Labour MPs voted for the Market, giving Heath a majority of 112. It was terribly tense and there had been rumours of people fighting after the vote; in fact, they were just shouting at Roy Jenkins as he went through the Lobby. It was awful.

Wednesday 15 December

The Jordanian Ambassador was machine-gunned near Holland Park School about three minutes before Melissa and all her friends were going down to get their fish and chips in the lunch hour.

Friday 31 December

Played pingpong and went out with the boys in the evening. Got home just as midnight struck and 1971 came to an end. It was the first full year of Opposition. As Trade and Industry spokesman I played a leading part in the big debates on Rolls Royce and Upper Clyde Shipbuilders, and the Government's industrial policy, which was very much the 'lame duck' policy. I was under heavy attack from the Tories: they wanted to make me the scapegoat for the failures at Rolls Royce and UCS and, although I fought back hard in the debates and won some support, undoubtedly the Tories and the Government did succeed in associating me with failure. In supporting UCS I came up against another group of people, namely the right wing of the Labour Party, which is opposed to my support of shop stewards, many of whom are Communists.

I got drawn closely into the Common Market argument and I spoke out frankly. My position on this was slightly ambivalent because I wasn't hostile to the Common Market, indeed I made speeches broadly in support of it as a Minister, but I did think there should have been a referendum and this was a difficult argument to get across. I certainly learned one thing – that the British public just isn't in favour of participation. It is told by its liberal élites that it shouldn't be interested in these things, and I am not sure how easy it will be to get people to accept participation at the moment. This intervention in the Common Market argument certainly cost me some support. I can't visualise myself having taken any other line because this is what I believed in, but it was a difficult period.

At the end of 1970 Frank McElhone had come to see me and had said that in his opinion I would be the next Leader of the Labour Party. For the first time I had a strong campaigner working for me. Frank McElhone is a very able political organiser, and without him I might have done much worse. But I think when it came to it, it would have been better if I hadn't stood for the deputy leadership; or, having stood, not to have spoken so frankly, been a bit more cautious. But that is contrary to my own instincts.

At the end of the year the bitter press attacks on me for standing had done me a lot of damage, there is no question about that, and they had affected my self-confidence. I felt I had had something of the stuffing knocked out of me.

I never remember politics being quite as unpleasant as this before; but maybe this is what life is like at the top.

I very much want to improve relations with the trade unions, where I think there has been deep damage done by the Common Market split, although the Government is so unpopular that the Party and the country don't want to see a split. We have got to handle this with great care.

The Party is in a bad way. I think the sourness left by the Common Market business, which is not by any means over yet, will remain for some time. I don't think Harold Wilson will ever be Prime Minister again, although I could be wrong. I have to improve my relations with the Labour MPs and with the Shadow Cabinet, and be a success as Party Chairman which is not going to be easy this year.

Friday 28 January 1972
Drove to Bristol on the M4 for the first time today. It took me two hours from home to the centre of Bristol. I must say it is a beautiful road and I began to feel that the whole geography of England had been altered by it.

Monday 31 January
There was a statement on the Bogside massacre yesterday in which thirteen Catholics were killed by troops, following the illegal march which had been undertaken by the Civil Rights people against a ban. I think it is the largest

number of people killed in the United Kingdom by British troops for 200 years or more. Bernadette Devlin was not called by the Speaker so she had to speak on points of order. At one point, she stamped down the gangway and went over and attacked the Home Secretary, Maudling, physically, an extraordinary sight. She smacked him and pulled his hair. People took her away and she was fighting with them. Poor old Hugh Delargy, Labour MP for Thurrock, is very shaky and sick, and being a devoted Irish Catholic he looked as though he would have an apoplectic fit and there would be a fight on the floor of the House. At any rate, she did withdraw. The Speaker, very wisely, didn't do anything about it.

Saturday 12 February
Tom Holliday drove me over to the Northumberland miners' meeting in the City Hall where Joe Gormley and I both had a tremendous reception. It was a very curious occasion because this huge hall was filled with working miners in their working clothes and the general impression was one of greyness and no colour, because of the dark browns and blacks and greys of their clothes, but they were in terrific heart even though beginning to experience some hardship themselves as a result of the strike.

The power cuts are now widespread and on alternate days we lose power for about three hours so that the whole economy is beginning to feel the effects of the strike. One aspect of this is that it set into being a tremendous emergency system of help for old people which had not existed before. I discovered that in my own constituency in Bristol, about 80 per cent of the streets are now covered by street wardens and street committees brought into being by the strike. The other remarkable thing about the strike is the extent to which the wives of the miners have supported their men and the extent to which the public – although gravely inconvenienced – are in sympathy with the miners.

Monday 14 February
To Transport House this morning, where we had a special meeting of the NEC on the miners' strike. Judith Hart spoke first and said we must support the miners without equivocation and she asked whether we should demand the resignation of the Government. She also thought it necessary to say something about the old and the sick and the need for local authorities and Labour Parties to help.

Joe Gormley pointed out they could have forced a general strike, but if they had had one, Heath would have gone to the country. 'We have never argued', said Joe Gormley, 'that we were a special case and we want a return to normality as soon as possible.

At the end of the meeting the resolution which I had drafted in support was accepted.

Tuesday 15 February
We had miners' meetings in the House this afternoon. A mass lobby took place. People were very critical of the previous Labour Government which, they felt, had let them down and I think that they were right. Looking back on it, I think our policy towards the mining industry was very shortsighted: stimulating nuclear power before we were really ready and running down the mines.

The theme of anarchy and unmanageability is beginning to emerge now in the Tory press and indicates that they may be thinking of turning this to political advantage. I think Ronald Butt in the *Sunday Times* began it, and Hailsham and others are on the same tack. The fear of anarchy is something that drives people to the right and this undoubtedly is what Heath wants.

Thursday 17 February
Today we had the vote on the second reading of the European Communities Bill. Heath won by eight votes with four Liberals voting with him. There were fantastic scenes in the House and great rage that some Labour people who had abstained would have carried Heath absolutely to the brink of defeat if they had voted.

I looked in afterwards to see Harold. He was immensely depressed. The fact that he had held the Party together right through to the second reading of the Bill was a great achievement and he couldn't understand why people weren't grateful to him. Of course, in practice, the situation is that everyone is thinking of Heath's humiliation, and nobody thinking of Harold's success.

But understandably, he being human, the terrible experiences he has had over the last few months on Europe have made him obsessed with his own position and he wanted a boost. I tried to cheer him up.

Monday 28 February
John Davies announced £35 million for Govan Shipbuilders at UCS.

Harold was on television tonight. He is going through a bad patch, though how anyone can tolerate being Leader of the Labour Party I just don't know. It is an almost impossible position. No one likes leaders, and though Harold seems unattractive, I can't think of anyone who would be better.

Friday 10 March
Up at 5.45 and flew with Frank McElhone to UCS. Jimmy Reid was away, resting after the strain of the last few months but Jim Airlie was there and so were some of the others. They told me that Marathon, who manufacture oil rigs, wanted about £12 million for Clydebank which would work out at about £4,800 per job. The shop stewards were quite prepared to support the Marathon bid within reason; the men would hold together even if Marathon fell through.

I had coffee with Jerry Ross, who is one of the old Communist shop stewards, Roddy MacKenzie, who has been the Treasurer, Bob Dickie and Willy McInnes who is a Labour Party shop steward. We talked about the next stage and in fact what these great revolutionaries want is simply joint production committees to share decision-making with the management. When I said, 'Surely you want more than this,' they replied, 'No – you must let the workers learn before you give them added responsibilities to carry. You must let them learn.' And so, far from this being a great Trotskyist plot (not that I ever thought it was), it turns out the most modest demands are being made by these people. I was much impressed to hear Jerry Ross, for example, saying, 'If we had a joint production committee, we should want to sit down when we made a profit and say "Now look, let's share some of it out in dividends, some to the state in payment of interest for the money they have loaned us, some in wages and some in investment." '

This is where you do have to rethink the propaganda that you get poured at you suggesting that the shop floor is irresponsible. In fact, the shop floor is not only responsible but painfully modest in the demands that it makes and I must try to get this point across in future speeches.

While I was with them, they told me that the 'David Frost Programme' had invited them to take part but in fact it was all planned to be a punch-up on the air. When they handed around a lot of drinks to the men before they took part, Jim Airlie had said, 'If anyone has more than a single beer, I won't let him on the programme.' Very impressive.

Wednesday 15 March
A big issue today was the Special Branch raids in Liverpool on the International Socialists: some friends of Stan Orme and Eric Heffer have been arrested and there is a great row about it.

Thursday 16 March
This afternoon there was an absolute bombshell: President Pompidou announced there would be a referendum on whether the French wished to have the Community enlarged.

At the PLP I spoke briefly and said that the implications of the French calling a referendum were important. It indicated a complete breakdown of confidence between Heath and Pompidou, since Heath had not been informed in advance. It was a continuing problem and we would *have* to look at the whole issue again. The Executive would look at it next week and the Parliamentary Committee would have to interpret it. I thought that a referendum would bring about Party unity. There was a general sort of air of congratulation and I was cheerful today.

I came home and worked on a paper on the referendum for the Executive.

Tonight Dick Crossman was fired from the *New Statesman*. I think they had hoped he wouldn't recover from his illness over the winter, but he did. They then tried to get him to withdraw on the grounds of health, and he wouldn't, so they just fired him.

Wednesday 29 March
By 8 to 6, the Shadow Cabinet voted for a referendum: Peter, Michael, Fred, Harold, myself, Jim, Ted, and Bob Mellish for; Roy (though mildly), Shirley, Harold Lever, Tony Crosland, Douglas Houghton, George Thomson against. So it was agreed to put a recommendation to the Party meeting that when the Market was debated again in April, we should vote on a two-line Whip in favour of a referendum.

Well, that was a tremendous victory.

Tuesday 4 April
Stansgate. Went shopping. Worked up in my little office. I was then diverted on to my carpentry. Mary Lou Clarke, my new secretary, started working at home today for the first time and we talked on the telephone getting everything straight.

I phoned Rupert Murdoch about the referendum, thinking it was about time I got some press support. Ian Aitken phoned and I tried to contact Alastair Hetherington of the *Guardian* to win him over as well.

Friday 7 April
Went to see Rupert Murdoch, who was with Larry Lamb, Editor of the *Sun*, and the Editor of the *News of the World*. Murdoch is just a bit younger than me. He is a bright newspaper man who has made a humdinger success of the *Sun*, which nobody else was able to do anything about, and the *News of the World*, although it has been declining in circulation, is now fairly stable. He was opposed to the referendum, because he is in favour of entering Europe, so his two Editors were opposed to it as well. But I used all the arguments I could and they asked if I would write about it.

Then I went to the Reform Club to see Hetherington to try to persuade him to change his opinion about a referendum and I said he couldn't refuse just on the basis that it would embarrass Roy Jenkins and Dick Taverne, as he had told me yesterday.

Monday 10 April
In the afternoon, just as I was leaving a meeting in the House, Peter Carver, the *Bristol Evening Post* lobby correspondent, caught me, saying 'Come with me', and began running through the corridors. I sort of pursued him. 'It's urgent,' he said, as he dashed downstairs and told me the rumour was that Roy Jenkins, George Thomson and Harold Lever were going to resign from the Shadow Cabinet because of the referendum. So I went to see Harold and he said that it was true. I think he was actually quite pleased.

Then we went to the Home Policy Committee and a statement was put out by Roy. As his attitude towards the referendum had been extremely relaxed at the second Shadow Cabinet, I don't believe it was that, but more the fact that he realised he couldn't go on as Deputy Leader of a party when he disagreed with a central part of the party's policy. I think that is really the position. Of course what he has been able to do is put the blame on me for the referendum.

I was interviewed in a hostile way on the 'News at Ten' by Douglas Stewart. Then I went on '24 Hours' with Harold Lever: he was most arrogant about the public and denounced the referendum. Although I like Harold personally, he really is a Tory – there is no question about it: a nice, kind, generous, humane, liberal Conservative. Brian Faulkner, the former Prime Minister of Northern Ireland, was also there, having been interviewed by Bob MacKenzie. He got entirely brushed aside by this row. I felt it was a bit discourteous until I remembered that the Prime Minister of Northern Ireland is just like the Chairman of the London County Council, nothing more.

All of a sudden, I realised that the referendum campaign had gone wrong on me because it made me out as a splitter, whereas it had originally been brought forward as a peace move. But you are judged by results and this is the price I'm paying for that.

Tuesday 11 April
The Labour crisis is the main headline news story. I got the blame, as I expected. I had to go off early to Dusseldorf for the International Metalworkers Conference: Olaf Palme, Prime Minister of Sweden was there; Bognar, Minister of Scientific Affairs from Hungary, and Ken Coates of the Institute for Workers' Control.

I flew home in the afternoon because of the crisis in the Party, cancelling a visit to Lausanne.

Wednesday 12 April
PLP meeting at 10.30. Bob Mellish introduced it and said he wanted to give the background to the Common Market debate next Tuesday. There would be a three-line Whip on our amendment calling for a General Election before entry; and the Shadow Cabinet had decided to have a two-line Whip in support of the amendment by the Conservative MP for Banbury, Neil Marten, calling for a referendum. He recommended support for this course of action. I detected a great deal of coolness by the Party and the general feeling was that the referendum should now be dropped as too divisive.

Tuesday 18 April
Worked all morning on my contribution to the European Communities debate in the Commons this afternoon. First of all we had the amendment

on the General Election – a very powerful speech by Michael Foot – then I interposed on the referendum by agreement with Michael and Peter Shore. I made my speech, which was detailed and long, and of course I got the absolute anger and hostility of the pro-Marketeers.

It wasn't a successful speech because frankly, every time I talk about the Market I just annoy people. The anti-Marketeers don't trust me because I am not anti-Market on principle, and the pro-Marketeers loathe me because I have pinpointed the thing that they find hardest to get away with, namely that they haven't got the support of the public for this. I do think I have suffered very much over the referendum argument. Anyway, a number of Labour people abstained on the referendum, enough for Heath to win the day. So once again, the coalition has worked and Labour MPs have saved the Government: everything the Government has done this year has been done with the consent of the pro-Market Europeans in the Labour Party.

Wednesday 3 May
I talked to Frank McElhone this evening. He was very candid and said 'Frankly at the moment, you have only got two friends in the Parliamentary Party – myself and yourself.' I think this is probably an accurate account of how things stand.

Thursday 4 May
The solemn conclusion I have reached is that my support for UCS and the shop stewards, and my support for a referendum and my line on the Common Market have really alienated everybody. Put quite crudely, I have got to mend my fences.

Monday 5 June
Went to the House of Commons, where there were tributes paid to the Duke of Windsor. I haven't referred in my diary to the death of the Duke of Windsor and the odious hypocrisy with which the royal family and the press and the Establishment handled it. Somehow, yesterday, this reached a peak. I didn't hear the debate but the government motion forgot to offer condolences to the Duchess and it was only as a result of a backbench enquiry that the amendment was made. The Trooping of the Colour was not cancelled and Parliament didn't adjourn on the day of the funeral of the former King. Tonight on television there was a marvellous programme about the Duke of Windsor which told his whole life story up to his abdication. Really, a lot of people are rediscovering how unattractive the monarchy is through the story of the Duke of Windsor.

Thursday 29 June
Caroline and I went to Number 10 for a dinner given by Heath for a

Senegali delegation including musicians. I was standing in for Harold. Caroline liked the music and talked to Heath about it. I find it difficult to talk to him, but I asked him about Sir Francis Chichester, the yachtsman. He told me that Chichester was dying from leukaemia and that was why he had had to come back from his trip. I did make him laugh by saying that at the Labour Conference, we sang 'The People's Flag is deepest red . . .' while the people at the back, the right wing, would sing, 'The People's Flag should be forgot, And never brought to mind again.'

Heath made a mad, impassioned speech about Europe and Africa and how now the imperial period was over, Europe was united and it could work with Africa to be an influence in the world. It was nineteenth-century imperialism reborn in his mind through status within the Common Market.

Caroline and I talked to Sir Patrick Reilly, the ex-Ambassador in Paris. He was the man who had written a sensational farewell despatch which was read everywhere in Whitehall and which included some frank comments on George Brown.

Wednesday 6 September
There was an awful massacre yesterday at the Munich Olympic Games – an appalling thing to have happened. Eleven Israeli athletes were killed by Arab terrorists from the Black September organisation.

Monday 11 September
Home Policy Committee. Another row over the Asians expelled from Uganda, although to be fair to him Jim Callaghan does recognise that we must have the Asians but just thinks we should limit the numbers. He was very open about it. I have some sympathy for those who say that it is easy for the people who live in Hampstead and Holland Park to say that the Asians should be admitted, but what are they themselves doing about helping the immigrants.

Saturday 30 September – Labour Party Conference, Blackpool
At 12.30 I went to see Harold. He was pacing up and down in his suite, in shirtsleeves. When I got there Marcia was with him. I hadn't seen her for ages. Her book has just been sent to me with two or three very friendly pages about me, and I said to her, 'How nice to see you – I haven't seen you for a year. Thank you for sending me your book: I must say your references to me in it were much kinder than in Harold's book,' pointing at Harold but not looking at him. As a matter of fact, it is a nice book. It recreates the confidence we had in 1964 when we all thought a great deal of each other.

We talked around a bit and then I said, 'You know, Harold, I have read all these silly things about a row between you and me but I'm the only one of your colleagues who came out publicly in your support in the summer and you know very well that I have never made things difficult. I was looking back over my papers for 1960 . . .'

'So was I,' he interrupted. 'I sent for photocopies of everything that happened in 1960.'

'Well,' I said, 'I had them in my files and I read your statement when you stood against Gaitskell, and I read my statement when I supported you and we have both been saying the same thing for many years.' We talked about the Common Market resolutions, and it was altogether a friendly chat.

Monday 2 October

We had the formal opening of the Conference and I made my Chairman's speech. It was thought to be a slight anti-climax. That is one of the difficulties about press coverage: the press had built it up as a challenge to Harold and were preparing themselves for Harold's great triumph, in which he would emerge as the man who saved the Party from extremism. So the Conference was worried because it had seen all this and began recalling the 1960 days.

Jim Callaghan, in a long and enormously boring speech, moved 'Labour's Programme for Britain' and took an hour and five minutes – he had been allowed about thirty-five. It was an absolute abuse of Executive privilege.

Went to the *Labour Weekly* reception and there was a big cake for their first anniversary. I said to Harold, 'You stick the knife in for a change, Harold.' Harold laughed, mainly because he thought it was an incredible piece of effrontery to make such a joke. At any rate, he did, and the story appeared in *Labour Weekly*.

Wednesday 4 October

We had the debate on the Common Market. I formally moved the statement and then we had Composite 43, moved by Clackmannan and East Stirlingshire, the Boilermakers' resolution, moved by Danny McGarvey, and the Engineers' resolution. The debate was thrown open and we got through it very well. I said at the beginning of the debate that I didn't intend to call many MPs but I knew that the Conference would obviously want to hear from Roy Jenkins and Michael Foot.

I had not actually had a 'request to speak' card from Michael Foot but I had had a handwritten note and I had not had a card at all from Roy; indeed, I had heard rumours that Roy didn't wish to speak. So I asked Gwyn Morgan, who was sitting next to me, whether he'd send a message to Roy. He said he didn't know whether he wanted to speak, so I said, 'Well, that's entirely up to him, but would you send a mesage, to ask him when he would like to speak, and I will call him.' A message came back saying he didn't want to speak. I said to the Conference, 'As Roy has indicated that he doesn't wish to speak, I will call Willy Hamilton to speak against the resolutions.'

Apparently at that moment people who were sitting near Roy shouted,

'Chicken, coward,' and he was absolutely furious. This became quite an
issue – had I done it deliberately or not? Well, in fact, I did decide in the
morning that I would do this because Roy had been attacking me all week
for new levels of censorship, for trying to shut him up and for intolerance. So
I decided I would put that to the test by making it clear that I had offered to
call him to speak and let him face the consequences of not speaking. I knew
his line – the 'low profile' which means you are afraid of the mass audience
and you just want to talk in private little groups about your principles and
integrity. Also Roy has been attacking me for a total failure of leadership. I
had failed, he argued, to give leadership to the Conference of the Party; he
by contrast was always giving leadership. The plain truth is that he hasn't
spoken at Conference about the Common Market for years, certainly not
since he got anywhere near the top, and whatever people may say about me,
I have certainly never lacked the guts to say what I thought. So, in fact, it was
a prepared manoeuvre if you like; it's a crude way of putting it but it was a
prepared decision – if he refused to be called – to expose the fact that he
wouldn't speak. I wasn't absolutely sure that he didn't want to; that is the
plain truth for the history books, in case anyone wants to know. And I am
not at all sorry.

Anyway, I called Willy Hamilton instead, and he delivered an attack on
me but it made a friend of him for life, so Frank McElhone assured me!

In the end the Executive statement and the Boilermakers' resolution were
carried and the AUEW was defeated. Jack Jones had been to see Harold and
Harold had given him some assurances about this and that, and no doubt
twisted his arm. So Jack had agreed not to vote for the AUEW, there being
no love lost between him and Hugh Scanlon at the moment.

I had a talk to Jimmy Reid and the UCS people who were down. They
were meeting Wayne Harbin, President of Marathon oil rig builders, that
night. I had an amusing exchange with them. We were talking and I was
advising them as best I could; they were all my old buddies. Then Jimmy
Airlie said, 'There's a photographer here, do you want a photograph?' So
Jimmy Reid said, 'We're seeing Chataway tomorrow and it might be
embarrassing if we were photographed with you.' I said, 'That's fine. A year
ago I was wondering whether it was respectable to be seen with you but if
now it's the other way round and you don't want to be seen with me, that's a
very great tribute that I shouldn't be respectable enough for you.' They saw
the point immediately and they laughed, and they got the photographer.

Friday 6 October
We had Harry Nicholas's farewell speech in which he meant to be friendly
but it came out in a way that revealed him for the male chauvinist pig that he
is – with all the cheap jokes about women. Made Caroline cringe.

I had heard rumours of Dick Taverne's imminent resignation as Labour
MP for Lincoln and so I had asked various journalists to keep their eyes open

and Mary Lou to feed me immediate information on the platform in case Taverne did make a statement before the end of the Conference. I waited anxiously all morning. Tony Banks, a Labour councillor, moved his point of order asking whether the changes I had made in Conference procedure would continue in future years. I said that was a genuine point of order but it was not for me, it was for the next Chairman. This was designed to boost my chairmanship, which had come in for a lot of criticism.

Then at about 12.15 I began getting news that Taverne had called a press conference. All the press lobby had gone to London to listen to it. He announced that he would be standing as a Democratic Labour candidate, and he attacked the Party. Mary Lou sent me a garbled typed account of what he had said but it was enough to indicate that his plan had been to see the Labour Conference end on a phoney vote of unity and then wreck it all by his statement. So I decided – without telling Caroline or anyone else – that I would make this the occason for a comment on Taverne and also on the role of the mass media; because last weekend *The Times* had published its survey showing that there would be tremendous support for a new centre-left-Liberal-type party, and I knew that John Torode was involved in helping Taverne in preparing a television programme this weekend.

So when it came to me to speak, I made my proper Chairman's remarks of thanking everybody and then I said the Conference had wanted socialism; wanted unity; wanted us to work hard together and wanted an Election. I said by chance, not of our making, the opportunity for the latter had come with the announcement this morning, a few minutes ago, that there would be a by-election in Lincoln. 'I say nothing about our departing colleague except for a tinge of sadness; but others have tried to damage us before and haven't succeeded.' They cheered and cheered at all this. Then I said, 'This is more than that because it is the first time that the mass media has actually put up a candidate in the Election. I wish the workers in the media would sometimes remember that they are members of the working class and have a sense of responsibility to see that what is said about us is true.' This led to another great wave of cheering. Then I went on to say that the mass media was difficult to deal with when it was selling their papers or producing their programmes but if they actually put up a candidate, then we should have a chance of defeating them. Then I brought the Conference to its feet to sing 'The Red Flag'.

It was quite clear to me that the people on the platform were absolutely livid at my speech. Harold apparently had been smoking his pipe furiously and everyone else was angry that I had raised the temperature by mentioning Taverne. What I gathered was that they still regarded Taverne as a member of the Party and an attack on Taverne was reopening inner Party splits, which they wanted to play down. Also they were annoyed about the reference to the mass media because they don't want trouble with the media and they are all gutless.

We packed up, and caught the special train home. When we got to London, the *Evening Standard* was already running my 'amazing' outburst against the press and my 'savage personal attack' on Taverne.

We were very tired. Caroline thought that a period of silence was required. She thought I had really perhaps made a mistake in ending the Conference the way I had done. I think that was also the view of Mary Lou, Frances Morrell and one or two others.

Saturday 7 October
There was tremendous coverage this morning of my Blackpool speech, the *Telegraph* charging me with inciting workers to strike against the press.

Sunday 28 January 1973
Ray Buckton drove me to Doncaster for a meeting on the railways. I like Ray: he is an interesting man, and a great friend of Clive Jenkins. Since he became General Secretary of ASLEF, he has been playing a very active part in trade unionism and is regarded as a great rather than a dangerous radical. He was cautious with me in the car – I suspect most trade unionists are cautious with all parliamentary people – but at the same time very friendly. He told me how the railwaymen had succeeded last year in helping the miners to prevent oil getting through to the power stations and, indeed, without the ASLEF ban on oil supplies he didn't think the strike could have succeeded. He also told me that someone from the Post Office Engineering Union had warned him that he, Ray, was having his telephone line bugged during the strike. These examples of working-class solidarity being used, tentatively, to defend people against the Government impressed me. I felt that they were preparing themselves, not in any sense for a revolution but for a transfer of power of an important kind.

Monday 29 January
Big news today arising from the Poulson hearing. A claim was made that Tony Crosland had been given a £500 coffee pot by Poulson. Tony, very sensibly, called a press conference immediately, produced the coffee pot, which he had had valued at £50, returned it at once and said he wished he had never seen the damn thing. By acting really quickly, he disposed of the issue straight away.

Saturday 24 February
I arrived home at about 2 am from Bristol to find the children still up and that Caroline had gone to Brighton because Hilary had been kicked in the back playing football there and had been admitted to hospital with serious kidney damage. Caroline stayed with him overnight. I had a few hours' sleep then drove down to Brighton, found Hilary in a bad way and we authorised an emergency operation. Rosalind his fiancée was very worried.

Wednesday 28 February
There was an all-day ASLEF strike today. The industrial disputes at the
moment – the gas workers, the hospital workers, the railway engine drivers
and the teachers – do represent a major government confrontation with the
trade unions, something which is creating a great deal of public agitation
and nervousness on the part of the political leadership.

Thursday 1 March
Geoff Bish, Stuart Holland and Margaret Jackson came in this morning to
discuss our Green Paper on the development of Labour's industrial policy
and the idea of a State Holding Company. I presented the outline I had
made of existing government powers and the new powers that we would
need in order to succeed. Stuart Holland is a very bright guy who worked at
Number 10 with Harold during the last period of government. He is
dissatisfied with Harold now and is rather attaching himself to me, though I
don't see much prospect at the moment of my own chances improving since
I am still living in the shadow of my year as Chairman of the Party and the
events of the Conference.

I went to Bristol for the AGM and afterwards watched the result of the
Lincoln by-election; Taverne won overwhelmingly. It was very depressing
because Taverne was cock-a-hoop and the TV coverage has been so pro-
Taverne, there was not even a pretence of being fair.

Wednesday 8 March
There were two bombs in London, one outside Scotland Yard and one in
Whitehall. The violence of the IRA appears to have come to the surface and
this has created a new political atmosphere in a way. It is frightening people,
and fear always turns them to the right.

Monday 12 March
At the Home Policy Committee of the NEC there was a discussion about the
next Labour Government. They all felt that the programme was so
complicated and full that it would take three Parliaments to implement. So I
chipped in and said I was uneasy about this; we really couldn't wait for
twenty-five years. What we wanted was a substantial and irreversible shift in
the balance of power and wealth in the *next* Labour Government and that it
wouldn't necessarily cost money if we were prepared to act swiftly.

Jim Callaghan said we should go more slowly and 'leave our humane
imprint on the social legislation of our time'. I declared that wasn't enough
for me and I would need an Industrial Powers Act if I was going to carry
through the sort of industrial policy a Labour Government would need.
This little clash was well worth having and I was much tougher than I have
been for a long time at that committee.

Thursday 5 April

Hilary came out of hospital and we are profoundly relieved that he will be able to get married on Saturday as planned.

Caroline was co-opted again as a member of the Inner London Education Authority.

At the House of Commons there was a meeting to discuss Judith Hart's document for a State Holding Company or National Enterprise Board.

Tony Crosland immediately raised three questions: were we clear about whether we wanted these companies to be profitable or not? Could we get efficient management? How would we justify the choice of companies for public ownership? He was in favour of a smaller experimental start.

Judith Hart said the Industrial Policy Committee had deliberately not revealed the companies they had identified. We said in the paper that twenty to twenty-five companies would be needed to yield significant control of the economy and she didn't think the management opposition would be an insuperable problem.

Stuart Holland emphasised that anything less than twenty companies would be a mere salvage operation. To be effective you needed a much larger number and Continental experience had shown this would work.

Edmund Dell said that by not naming the companies concerned, you are giving greater hostages to fortune. You could exaggerate the benefits against the cost involved; when you come to power there could be a crisis and this would all create short-term disruption. Management was a real problem that couldn't be brushed aside and it would be better to have a slow advance.

Eric Heffer didn't really like the State Holding Company and he would only accept it as a halfway house because we needed a better perspective. He was in favour of spelling out the names of the companies. Management problems couldn't be a reason for not going ahead and we may have to pay over the odds to get good managers. As to industrial democracy, he was in favour of self-managing socialism.

I said that the conditions after the next Election might be very serious with accelerated job losses as a result of EEC competition. If we were returned to power, since we have price and profit control in mind, we might as well develop a powerful capacity to increase investment. As to management, after my experience dealing with private management, I couldn't say I was very struck by it. Top management was not particularly efficient and the good management was just underneath it. On the choice of firms, we couldn't really make that selection now and this was inherent in the problem. On industrial democracy, we were waiting for the TUC to come forward. But certainly on the central question of whether the next Labour Government would introduce some control of the economy I am sure all Ministers would agree that bribing, cajoling and merging industry could not continue.

Judith Hart said that you couldn't extrapolate from existing experience of public ownership because conditions would be different. The Conference resolutions were our remit, and this remit required us to advance substantially; profitable manufacturing companies were the areas in which we should move. She thought the twenty-five companies should be named but we would be taking over going concerns and there were serious problems to be faced.

Anyway, the paper was more or less agreed after a good discussion. Crosland has got his eye on Trade and Industry in the next Labour Government and this is why he attends all these meetings religiously.

Saturday 7 April
Hilary and Rosalind married at the Kensington Register Office this morning with all the family there. We held the reception and they spent the night at our house after watching 'Match of the Day' on television!

Sunday 22 April
Easter Sunday. There is no doubt, looking back, that my chairmanship and my final speech at Conference strongly criticising the media did me a great deal of damage. In return, they attacked me bitterly for several weeks and then let me rot in silence for a time.

I go up and down, get depressed as things go wrong and then cheer up again afterwards. But I have got from now until the end of July, three months' hard work, to build up support in the House of Commons and make my Trade and Industry group work better.

I have written to Alastair Hetherington, Editor of the *Guardian*, Harold Evans, Editor of the *Sunday Times*, and Hugh Cudlipp, Chairman of IPC, saying I would like to see them again.

Friday 27 April
The Watergate scandal in America has reached astonishing proportions and today Patrick Gray, the head of the FBI, resigned. It is thought he destroyed relevant records in the case. This could well have a desperately damaging effect on Richard Nixon's last term and reveal him for what he really is, which we know from his early days as a muck-raking, anti-Communist McCarthyite.

Sunday 29 April
At noon Antonia Fraser came to see me about biographies. She has written a well received life of Mary Queen of Scots and of Cromwell, and has been invited by the BBC to do a programme in the 'One Pair of Eyes' series for August. In this programme she is interviewing the Conservative MP Nigel Fisher, who wrote Macleod's life, Macleod having left no papers when he died in 1970. She is interviewing Professor Hugh Thomas, who wrote John Strachey's life; James Pope-Hennessy, the biographer of Queen Mary, and

Michael Holroyd, who wrote the life of Lytton Strachey; and she wants to do some contemporary filming of me at a May Day rally in Birmingham in order to examine the possible role of film in biography.

As I sat and talked about it all with her it became quite clear to me that if one is going to record every minute as fully and completely as this, one does have to ask oneself the central question: 'Am I a participant in life and politics or am I an observer?' and if there is any conflict between the two, one must be a participant. It is rather like filling up the North Sea with oil instead of taking it out. One creates a great archive which may or may not be of interest to anyone else. What one is bequeathing is one's working papers and documents; watching life simply to make it interesting is not enough.

Antonia Fraser said that she had met Anthony Eden a couple of years ago in Barbados, and how pleased he was to talk to her. She described how her mother Elizabeth Longford, who lived in Hampstead and was a friend of Hugh Gaitskell's, bitterly hated Harold Wilson; how contemptuous she was of his style of life in Hampstead Garden Suburb. This explains a great deal of Wilson's dislike for that snobbish Hampstead establishment of upper middle-class socialists and Fabians.

Monday 30 April
Today the US Attorney-General, Richard Kleindienst and two of his closest aides, Ehrlichman and Haldeman, were sacked; tonight Nixon is due to make a great television broadcast about the Watergate scandal.

Tuesday 1 May
Nixon's address to the American public was awful, a speech in which he accepted responsibility for what had happened because he was at the top, his office had to be preserved, it would be cowardly to do otherwise and there could be no whitewashing in the White House – a really gimmicky PR phrase. But he didn't answer the fundamental questions and even defended the people he had sacked on the grounds that perhaps their zeal had been in a cause in which they deeply believed (namely his own re-election as President).

Wednesday 2 May
At the end of the Shadow Cabinet I raised the question of whether I should issue a statement drawing attention to our 'nationalisation without compensation' discussions in order to frighten off speculators from buying up bits of Rolls Royce, which the Government have put on the market. Shirley Williams thought this might be the occasion for redundancies, which the Government could blame on us. There was a generally discouraging atmosphere. Somebody said, 'Why do we always make Tony into a bogeyman? At any rate, he does draw these things to our attention.' So I let it slide. There is no point in going to the stake for one controversial statement.

Thursday 3 May
Coming back on the train from a meeting in Brighton, Ron Hayward told
me about how Marcia Williams was 'running Harold', how she and her
brother, Tony Field, and her sister worked with him, how Joe Haines was in
Harold's confidence, Alf Richmond, a press aide from the *Daily Mirror*, was
the baggage master, and Gerald Kaufman was round and about. This is the
kitchen cabinet – Harold's court. It has always been like that but it still
annoys Ron Hayward, who has not got a lot of time for Harold. But Harold
is a very shrewd political operator and one must not forget that.

Friday 11 May
The papers are full this morning of the total failure to float Rolls Royce.
Only £7 million was purchased by public subscription, only 360 of the 900
workers applied for shares and it was generally admitted that my speech had
played some part in stopping it, which is a great achievement. Even so, the
institutions have promised to pick up the remainder, so the flotation will take
place. The *Financial Times* reported the support given me by the TGWU,
and the *Daily Telegraph* had a fierce denunciation entitled 'Limousine
Socialism', saying that unless the Government adopted Labour's policy of
threatening to reverse existing policies, Labour would be in power whether
in or out of office – a marvellous comment in view of the fact that the House
of Lords and the City of London have kept the Tory Party in power in and
out of office for years.
    Clive Jenkins rang to say that the ASTMS Annual Delegate Conference
was going to have an emergency resolution along the lines that 'This
Conference welcomes the statement made by Tony Benn in support of the
defence of public assets and in defence of the security of the people whose
jobs depend on them'. This will be debated on Monday. Also next week is
the debate on Rolls Royce. So the Government are going to be in a real
difficulty.

Saturday 19 May
I should report that every day this week the Watergate hearings have been
on and are being shown simultaneously on television by satellite. It is
absolutely riveting. This is clearly going to bring Nixon down.

Monday 21 May
To the TUC–Labour Party Liaison Committee meeting at Congress
House, and in the lift I said to Jack Jones, 'We must nationalise the aircraft
industry, and I want a bit of help from you on this.'
    While we were sitting waiting for the meeting to begin, there was some
joking about what positions we would like to hold. Jim Callaghan said he'd
like to be head of the IMF. Douglas Houghton wanted to be General
Secretary of the TUC. Harold said, 'No doubt Tony would like to be the

Archbishop of Canterbury.' It was a very snide remark. But I said, 'Do you know, Jim, I had a dream about you that you *would* join the IMF' (these rumours have appeared in the last few days) 'and that you would come back on a mission when the next Labour Government was in power and wreck that government too.' It was going very near the mark but he did have the courtesy to laugh.

Thursday 24 May

The papers are absolutely crammed with the Lambton resignation; Lord Jellicoe, Leader of the House of Lords, has also resigned admitting that he had had affairs with call girls. It is astonishing when this happens. You get two Ministers resigning and the press behaves as if the whole world is coming to an end.

Sunday 27 May

Stansgate. Twelve hours in bed. The Lambton and Jellicoe affairs dominated the papers today – articles by A. J. P. Taylor and by Montgomery Hyde, editorials on private and public standards, historical parallels. 'Is it a Communist plot?' The Bishop of Leicester is sympathetic. Comments by the Chairman of the Church Committee for Social Responsibility, and so on.

Friday 8 June

Enoch Powell has made a great speech implying that he might recommend his followers to vote Labour in the next Election on the grounds that only the Labour Party would offer an opportunity to the people of this country to vote against the Common Market. This has created an enormous sensation: Will he be thrown out and what are his motives?

Sunday 10 June

Brian Walden, the Labour MP for Birmingham All Saints, came to the house at 11 o'clock and stayed until 3. I had asked him to look in. He drank quite a lot, and talked continuously but I learned a great deal. He told me that he had been Hugh Gaitskell's scriptwriter and that it was he who wrote 'Fight, fight and fight again', which was the speech that triggered off Harold Wilson's candidature against Hugh Gaitskell for the leadership in 1960. Also, in respect of the Common Market, Brian had invented Hugh Gaitskell's phrase about 'throwing away a thousand years of British history'. So these two phrases, for which Gaitskell is most clearly remembered, didn't actually even come from him. As one of Hugh Gaitskell's older scriptwriters myself, going way back to 1956, I was fascinated to hear this.

Anyway, Brian took it that I had wanted his advice and proceeded to give it me. He said he thought that I could possibly be the Leader of the Party and that I had to turn my mind quickly and carefully to the problem of why I wasn't getting across to Labour MPs. He thought the reason was that I was frightening them. They had their constituencies, a good job in the House of Commons and I disturbed them, disrupted life and made them feel they might lose. What they wanted was reassurance: Harold Wilson was always reassuring them and I was worrying them. This is not so different from what Frank McElhone says.

We went on to talk about economic policy and the mixed economy. He talked compulsively. 'Of course we want a mixed economy but a real one, in which the big companies and major corporations are either run or owned by the state; if people pay their taxes and are treated decently, and provided for properly, particularly with their pensions so that they are not humiliated in retirement, then we can have competition and capitalism at that level, where it really applies.'

Of himself he said he would never hold office and he intended to retire from Parliament when he was fifty. Although he wanted to go on with politics, it didn't pay enough. I urged him to think again but I think he was probably deeply hurt that he hadn't been given a job by Harold Wilson, just as Dick Crossman was that he hadn't been given a job by Clem Attlee in the 1945 Government. So Brian has compensated by using his natural brilliance in order to make money and to secure his own future.

Wednesday 20 June
Shadow Cabinet all day, where we had a full and important debate. Tony Crosland started by saying, 'What is the electoral strategy of the Left? The polls don't seem to imply any rise in militancy, and nor do the by-elections. There is no swing to the left, and, if anything, there is a swing to the Liberals. There is anxiety about undemocratic local Parties and trade unions. Labour MPs are more in touch with local Party members than members of the Executive. The trade union block votes are unpopular.' As a result, he couldn't either see or understand a lurch to the left.

Michael Foot said the 25-company proposal was crazy and he believed I had committed an error in submitting it. The Manifesto Committee was a joint body and not two bodies. He didn't want to have a vote on the twenty-five at the Conference and therefore we had to find a formula beforehand to avoid difficulties. Ron Hayward should start discussions on public owner-ship and we should put a statement to Conference that would wipe out the issue of the twenty-five companies, so that there would be general agreement. If we couldn't sort it out we were not fit to be here.

I said I wasn't prepared to go back and try to bribe businessmen to do what was not in the interests of their shareholders. As to Party democracy, I couldn't object to what Harold had said about the veto because he had only said publicly what had been said privately for years. But the case for taking some notice of the Conference was that when you looked back over the conflicts between the Conference and the Labour Cabinet in the years we were in office, the Conference had very often been right. But, I said, I thought there was a danger of double standards in saying some things privately and other things publicly.

Denis Healey blurted out, 'Well, Tony Benn has just advocated absolute madness – that we should debate this publicly – absolutely mad.' He was livid. Denis is a management man. He sees everything in terms of looking tidy and neat and efficient.

Then Michael Foot asked me, 'Are you *really* going for the twenty-five companies? Do you think we could win the Election? Do you *want* to win the Election? What are you up to? What are you saying?'

By the time I finished lunch, the rumour was already going round that Michael Foot had accused me of wanting to lose the Election, suggesting that I wanted to do it simply in order to become Leader of the Party. This story had been leaked immediately after the Shadow Cabinet and appeared in all the papers tonight: 'Foot Bashes Benn', 'Foot Stamps on Benn'. I declined to comment because I could immediately see the advantage of not trying to combat this story but to let it ride as having come from others. So I said nothing.

Collected the papers at midnight and cut out all the headlines. This is exactly what I wanted; leaks from the Shadow Cabinet that couldn't possibly have come from me and that will help me to put across my argument that the Shadow Cabinet proceedings should be made public.

Thursday 21 June
Jim rang up to tell me that I had been badly used and he said, 'You know, we could work well together.' He also told me he was writing a preface of a book on Giro and asked if I could help him with it. So I went back to my files and dug out my original article of June 1964 in the *Guardian* about the Post Office, Jim's letter to me when he was Chancellor, expressing great caution about it, and the text of my speech announcing it, and sent them all off to him.

Michael Foot came into my room at the House, very shamefaced because he has been described in the papers as the man who destroyed me at the Shadow Cabinet. He thought I would be angry but I wasn't. He didn't agree with it; he told me that Jack Jones was against the twenty-five, which I knew anyway. He said he had written to the papers saying the report that had appeared was inaccurate. He said, 'We can't have a confrontation over the veto and the NEC should submit a statement on public ownership which would ease the difficulty of compensation and the twenty-five companies.' I said I thought it was, in the end, a matter of honest politics, whether one was ready to say publicly what one said privately. I don't think Michael liked that very much.

Saturday 23 June
We prepared for a party today. About sixty people came, including Michael

Foot and Jill Craigie – both a little embarrassed – Dick Clements, Norman Atkinson and his wife, Eric and Doris Heffer, Ron and Phyllis Hayward, Frances Morrell, the Zanders, Robin Day, Margaret Jackson, Tony Banks, Alan Evans of the NUT, Peter Shore, Stuart Holland, the Harts, the Arnold-Forsters and the Meachers. It went on until about 2 in the morning, and it was jolly and friendly. We agreed to form the 'Twenty-five Club' committed to the nationalisation of the twenty-five companies.

Tuesday 26 June

I have been really absorbed by reading about the English Revolution and I asked Jack Mendelson, the Labour MP for Penistone, a former university lecturer, if he would give me a private tutorial. We had about an hour in the Tea Room on the Levellers and the Diggers or True Levellers, who comprised a radical group in Cromwell's army. It was fascinating. He gave me a reading list including Christopher Hill on Cromwell, so I have set aside Antonia Fraser's book now and am concentrating on the serious ideological and historical stuff.

All the parallels with the situation today are there. The argument with the King and his court: Heath and the City of London, with the big corporations. Then one can see the right wing of the Parliamentary Labour Party as the Presbyterians, rigid, doctrinaire, right wing, but officially on the side of puritanism or socialism. The Socialist Labour League and the International Socialists on the left are the Agitators. The Levellers are broadly the Labour Movement as a whole. There is the argument about the pulpit and who has access to it, which could be seen as the whole debate about democracy today. I had no idea that the Levellers had called for universal manhood suffrage, equality between the sexes, biennial Parliaments, the sovereignty of the people, recall of representatives and even an attack on property: concepts which later emerged in the constitution of the United States and indeed in the French Revolution.

Monday 9 July

John Poulson, the architect, and Andy Cunningham, who is on the NEC, have been arrested. At the House today, I spoke to John Cunningham, the Labour MP for Whitehaven, who is Andy's son, and I just said, 'If there's anything I can do, let me know because your father has always been very kind to me.'

Tuesday 17 July

Lunch at Quaglino's with the 1972 Industry Group of Labour businessmen masterminded by Rudy Sternberg, Sir Joseph Kagan, Wilfred Brown, Arnold Gregory, Derek Page and one or two others who have offered to advise the Labour Party on industrial matters. They are very close to Harold and hope to be put in positions of authority under a Labour government. I am rather cynical about them.

Thursday 19 July

Bill Rodgers came to dinner. Hilary and Rosalind had bought some strawberries and I gave him a good bottle of wine in the back kitchen of my basement office, where we talked for about three hours. First I tried to get him to assess the political situation – the prospects of winning. He thought there was a chance of winning but he didn't believe a radical change would be in tune with public opinion. On public ownership he felt that the case hadn't been made out and that we shouldn't really be doing it.

Then we got on to Harold and he said that Harold was a liability. He was meaner than he used to be, he hadn't matured as a statesman after he had been in power, that the middle of the Party was getting disillusioned with Harold. The new MPs had come into Parliament in 1970 thinking he was wonderful, and the more they had seen of him, the less they liked him.

Tuesday 11 September

Today there was a coup by the Junta in Chile and President Allende was murdered.

Friday 14 September

In the evening, Stephen and I went to see Alvaro and Raquel Bunster. Alvaro was the Ambassador in London for what was Allende's legitimate Chilean government. The Naval Attaché, an admiral, has thrown him out of the Embassy today. We went to see if I could be of any help. I took my tape recorder and recorded his account of what happened during the coup as far as it affected him, and an interesting record it is. Raquel has been ill and she asked me to get a message to her mother in Santiago so I spent most of the night trying to get through to Chile on the phone. The Post Office in London said they couldn't connect me; I tried a friend in Cincinnati who said he would try; finally I got through to ITT in New York and all their lines to Santiago were open, which in fact confirmed what Bunster had said, namely that ITT were in on the coup. I daresay we shall find out when the coup is over.

Wednesday 19 September

Jim Callaghan invited me to have lunch with him. It is all part of Jim's campaign for the leadership but still, I like him. We had a most pleasant time and talked about farming. He said, 'Of course, I am finished, past it,' and I said, 'Rubbish, we are moving into an era where much older people take over the leadership. Look at Churchill, de Gaulle, Mao and Tito.'

Friday 21 September

Peter Shore's pamphlet was published today recommending that an incoming Labour government should boycott all the institutions of the Common Market and discontinue all payments. I agree with this strong line.

I offered Frances Morrell a job as a political adviser in my department if we won the next Election.

Sunday 21 October
Nixon sacked Professor Archibald Cox, the Watergate special prosecutor, and Elliott Richardson, the Attorney-General, has resigned in protest: this gives the whole Watergate crisis a completely new impetus because Nixon has alienated the immensely powerful legal lobby, a sort of breach of constitutional rights.

Had a long telephone call from Stephen, who said he had been invited to St Antony's College, Oxford, for the weekend and since that is the great spy school, it wouldn't surprise me if they tried to recruit him.

Monday 22 October
Had lunch in the Tea Room with Jim Sillars, who brought me up to date on how wildly Scottish Nationalist the Scottish TUC had become, and how, if Britain stayed in Europe, he would become a Scottish Nationalist member.

At 5 we had the Shadow Cabinet and the Channel Tunnel came up, since it has now become inextricably linked with the Common Market. Peter Shore and Michael Foot are strongly opposed to it, as I am, with Tony Crosland in favour.

Saturday 24 November
Drove up to Ilkeston, Ray Fletcher's constituency, for a meeting. The local Party had laid on a bazaar and there was an old fortune teller, 'Madame Eva', in one of the side rooms with a crystal ball covered with a black velvet cloth (she was, of course, also an ordinary Labour Party stalwart). I was sitting in the hall working, having arrived early, and she came and sat down and began uncovering her crystal ball. I would *never* have gone to her for a prediction but I did talk to her, and after we had finished talking, she told me how she saw things in the ball, and how she had predicted various events.

As I left she said to me, 'You are going to have a great shock in February, a terrible shock. You are going to get the blame for something you haven't done. Then in September, it will all be all right again.'

Friday 30 November
Went early to see Harold Evans and Hugo Young of the *Sunday Times* and they listen attentively to my political analysis. I said, 'Look, both parties have failed. There is an energy crisis, and there may be a slump. The crisis is a crisis of confidence shared by the Establishment. It is not just a case of crooks governing morons. There is something else wrong. It is a crisis of consent as

in the late colonial period. We have got to convert negative to positive power and that means more equality and more democracy. You can have a right-wing dictatorship or a left-wing dictatorship, but we want more democracy and equality and not a National Government. A coalition government would be crazy.' Harold Evans, of course, has got his own candidates for a National Government and so have I. He asked, 'Why are you so unpopular with the press?' so I said, 'Because you write such unpleasant things about me. That's why.'

I don't know if I really made any impression but it was an attempt.

Monday 3 December
Dinner with Wilfred Brown, who also believes we are heading for a slump and food riots and there must be a National Government. If this is what the businessmen are saying, it is significant.

At the Commons I saw John Biffen, who told me, 'Enoch Powell is waiting for the call.' Also at the House, Peter Shore told me that Michael Foot – who he thinks is marvellous – must be the next Leader of the Party.

Friday 7 December
Travelled to Bristol and my election agent, Ennis Harris, warned me I'd lose the Election because my left-wing views were not acceptable. In the evening I went to Knowle Ward for a meeting where there were only four people, despite having distributed 700 leaflets. It really was awful. There is a great sense of crisis everywhere.

Wednesday 12 December
We had a joint National Executive/Shadow Cabinet meeting to finalise our Election manifesto in the event of a snap decision by Heath. We started by discussing the crisis, which gets worse every day. Jim Callaghan said that our policy was intended for the natural end of a Parliament but the present crisis meant that we should expect emergency Tory measures and we might ourselves have to move quickly in response to the situation.

'You can't separate our policy from the crisis and therefore we should appeal to the British people with our analysis of the crisis. Pensioners mustn't suffer,' I said.

Then on the manifesto defence proposals, Frank Allaun wanted £1,000 million cuts and the closure of the Polaris bases. Jim felt that this would break up NATO and create pressure for a German nuclear force. Judith Hart then said defence spending by a Labour government couldn't be sacrosanct. I argued that there was such a tough military-industrial complex in existence that we ought to be hard at this stage, or we never would be. Ted Short commented that the Tories would accuse us of leaving the country defenceless.

Finally, Jim suggested that Michael, Barbara, Tony Crosland, Terry Pitt and I draft the manifesto within a month.

Thursday 13 December
The trade figures came out with £270 million deficit. Went to the House of Commons and Heath announced a three-day working week to reduce energy consumption. There was a realisation of the great depth of the crisis.

Tuesday 18 December
IRA bombs in London.

First day of the economic and energy debate. Harold spoke and I wound up. Heath is beginning to crack. I felt somehow that there would be an Election and that this would be the last speech I would make for a very long time in Parliament. It was probably that silly old fortune teller in Derbyshire but somehow, the whole day I felt obsessed with the worry, which did nothing for my speech.

Sunday 23 December
I overslept and had a lazy day at home. Three more IRA bombs in London.

I tidied the office and wrapped Christmas gifts. We have decided not to go to Stansgate, because I felt I had to be ready for the possibility of an Election. The oil price was doubled again today, the second doubling since September.

Thursday 3 January 1974
I discovered that public meetings are not to be exempted from electricity restrictions, which will affect old-age pensioners' clubs and community groups, whereas cinemas, strip clubs, bingo halls and commercial entertainment are allowed to continue. So I wrote to Peter Walker demanding that these restrictions be lifted, so that democracy could function.

Went in to Transport House after lunch. Ron Hayward has agreed to run the energy Monitoring Service and the statements will come from Transport House, with Donald Ross publishing his information bulletins.

At the Drafting Committee, I asked whether Michael Foot was right to compare our attitude to the situation with that in 1940 and 1945 because in 1940 Britain had a coalition government, to which Jim said, 'Well, *I'm* in favour of a National Government.'

I repeated, 'A National Government?'

'Yes,' he confirmed, 'if it adopted our policy.'

'What – a coalition government?'

'Yes, but I know they wouldn't,' he said.

'What you are saying is that you would be in favour of excluding from the public the choice between two policies.'

'I think a coalition government, a National Government, would be a good thing if it would follow our policy,' was his reply.

John Silkin had said to me before Christmas, that he thought Jim might be won over to a coalition government; and John's theory was that Whitelaw – who had a great admiration for Jim – might offer him the premiership. I'd thought it a far-fetched idea, but this was a minor confirmation of it.

Monday 7 January

There was a cartoon in the *Daily Mail* depicting me as a stormtrooper with a swastika on my shoulder, ordering Joe Gormley and Ray Buckton to torture the British public, saying, 'We have ways of making you suffer.'

Went in to the Organisation Sub-Committee at 3.30, which was held by candlelight and camping gas because Transport House does not have light on Mondays. On the question of the 20 January meeting on the Common Market, the Poplar Civic Theatre was not available because of the electricity cuts and the Government's refusal to make an exception for political meetings, so the committee wanted to cancel the meeting.

'You must be mad,' I said. 'We must go ahead with the meeting, we must bring pressure to bear on the Poplar Labour Party.' John Cartwright, Director of the Royal Arsenal Co-operative Society, who was in the chair and who is the leader of the Labour Group on Greenwich Council, then said, 'We can't because the safety of the audience is at stake,' and Tom Bradley added, 'We might be breaking the law by having the meeting.' 'For God's sake,' I said, 'if necessary we'll have the meeting in the street and explain this is a ban on freedom of assembly. I have written to Peter Walker about it.'

Finally, it was agreed to issue a statement that we would go ahead with the meeting, but these chaps would capitulate on anything. If the Labour Party had been made illegal, they would have gone off to Wormwood Scrubs, mumbling under their breath 'obey the law' as they were bundled into the Black Marias. None of the top Labour leadership has any guts.

Wednesday 16 January

The main news today was a report of Enoch Powell's attack on Heath, Powell maintaining that an Election would be a fraud. The Governor of the Bank of England said we would have ten years of austerity. The pound dropped to its lowest level ever, I think, to $2.16.

To the Shadow Cabinet and Harold opened by saying, 'We won't discuss whether there is going to be an Election or not; but let's assume that the Cabinet is divided. Some Ministers are talking openly against Heath. If he fixes 7 February, it would be outrageously short, particularly with the printing difficulties and the three-day week. If it's 14 February, it's still an outrage because the electoral register used will be the old one within forty-eight hours of the new one becoming effective so we must make a maximum attack on that. The Government fear the worst now. The Governor of the Bank of England's statement was very important. I'll do a speaking tour: we must all speak with *one* voice on the basis of the manifesto when we agree it. No private enterprise and no gimmicks. I will be in London every day of my press conference and I invite colleagues to join me from time to time. We must make no Party capital out of the OPEC oil crisis.'

Michael Foot said we mustn't give the impression we could do nothing. 'As Tony Benn said at the Conference, we should not make the crisis we inherit the excuse for not implementing our programme but the occasion for carrying it through. We must convince people we will do what we say.'

Jim Callaghan wasn't convinced there would be an Election. He thought people would be nervous of voting if the street lights were out. What do we say to the miners? We must be simple and rather repetitive; don't broaden it out too far. 'Confrontation versus conciliation' would be one theme and 'Equality can't await growth' would be another. He hoped our party political broadcasts would be flexible.

Later, Harold said, 'Ignore Enoch Powell because last time, the attack on him lost five seats.'

I interrupted and said, 'Look Harold, I've heard you say this two or three times before and never contradicted you, but it just isn't true.'

'Well, I've said five times that you lost us five seats.'

'Let me deny it once,' I said, 'and then you can proceed.'

That was more or less it. But I did say to Joe Haines outside, 'I'm going to be the bogeyman.'

'Oh yes, they're expecting you to proclaim the revolution,' Joe replied.

'Well I'm tape-recording everything I say and every question and answer and every radio and television interview, so there will always be a complete transcript available: but I'm sure even that won't prevent me being misrepresented.'

Monday 21 January
To lunch with the Iranian Ambassador in honour of Harold Wilson. The Ambassador is a bit of a playboy, has racehorses and so on. At the lunch were Harold, Jim, Ted Short, Eric Varley, Gerald Kaufman, Lord Greenhill, the Permanent Secretary at the Foreign Office, Sir Martin Charteris, the Queen's Private Secretary, and others.

Sir Martin Charteris called me Tony, which I thought was friendly. I said, 'Oh, you're just the man I want to see to ask about dissolution and the rules governing it.'

He replied, 'Well, the Queen has absolute rights.'

So I said, 'Yes, of course, but I remember a discussion I had with the Queen's former Private Secretary Michael Adeane at Hampton Court in 1966 where I got the impression that the Queen was not anxious to get too involved in controversial matters and was therefore quite pleased that the

Conservative Party, for example, had chosen a system of election for their leader to avoid the invidious task of her having to make a choice.'

'Yes, that's right. But as to a dissolution, she has absolute rights.'

So I said, 'Let's discuss it hypothetically because I realise that we can't discuss the present position. But I take it the Queen would consult.'

'Yes, she has an absolute right to consult.'

'Well, I assume that she would consult former Prime Ministers. Does she consult the Speaker?'

'No, I don't think she does.'

'Well, the Speaker is a Privy Councillor. He's the man who knows about the House of Commons better than anyone else and from a completely detached position so, on questions of a dissolution, as to whether or not a man or a series of men might command a majority, the Speaker would be a very good person to advise.'

He said he had never thought of that and that it had never been done.

I said, 'I know it hasn't been done, but it would allow the Queen to distance herself slightly from the controversy by calling in the Speaker while preserving her absolute right.'

'Oh yes,' he replied. 'We must preserve her right because I think there has to be some risk attached in order to provide excitement for the monarchy. And, of course, in the end, the Queen's judgement would have to be tested by the events.'

He presumably meant that if the Queen refused dissolution to Heath, and then Heath was in some way defeated, this would be embarrassing to the Palace. So he said, 'In 1926, Bing, who as Governor-General of Canada was the Crown's representative, refused a dissolution to the then Prime Minister, Mackenzie King; King then resigned and got his government re-elected. The Governor-General's relations with him were much strained afterwards.'

Obviously the Palace has been busy thinking about dissolutions and how to handle them, and maybe my suggestion about the Speaker will be noted. I was particularly interested when he said there must be some risk for the monarchy to make it exciting.

Afterwards, Jim Callaghan drove me back to the House and expressed his anxiety about the power of the trade unions.

'Maybe, Jim, but look at the Government, run by the City of London, and nobody says the City is too powerful. It's a question of whose side you are on. It's a gut issue.'

'They're much too powerful,' he replied.

'Well, I don't believe in powerful leaders. I believe in spreading the power among the rank and file. Anyway, you were always pro-union when they supported your view.'

'Yes,' he said, 'but they are still much too powerful. This is our problem.'

Jim, in fairness to him, has always thought there wouldn't be a snap Election.

Monday 28 January

I think Jim is edging himself into position for a coalition government. Prentice has apparently attacked McGahey again and McGahey is in a difficulty because, on the radio tonight, he said, 'Many of the troops which may be mobilised are the sons of miners, and if they come to dig coal, we shall appeal to them and explain our case to them.' A perfectly reasonable argument, nothing revolutionary in that. But people are now talking about sedition. I think we're heading for trouble and I am tempted to make a speech in advance which warns that the full moral and criminal responsibility for what might happen will fall on the Prime Minister's head.

Tuesday 29 January

On the 1 o'clock news was a report of a statement drafted by Hayward and Callaghan which began, 'We speak for every member of the Labour Party as well as for millions outside it in sending the mineworkers our good wishes and support.' Then it went on '. . . But Communists and other extremist leaders of the NUM say they have wider political objectives . . . We utterly repudiate any attempts by Communists or others to use the miners as a political battering ram . . .' and so on.

Then came Wilson's Early Day Motion that had been put on the Order Paper signed by himself, Ted Short, Douglas Houghton, Bob Mellish, Eric Varley and others attacking McGahey by name. Jim was interviewed on the news and he attacked McGahey's reference to the troops. He said, 'Who would take notice of the miners appealing to the troops? It's rubbish', and that there would be a long and bitter strike. This was obviously designed to dissuade the miners from voting for a strike. Petre Crowder, Tory MP for Ruislip-Northwood, was asked about his proposal for the establishment of vigilantes and he said he hoped he would have the chance of driving a lorry through a picket line. Then Jill Knight, Conservative MP for Edgbaston, said strikers were the enemy of the state.

Went to the House for Questions and Norman Tebbit, the Tory MP for Epping, asked the Prime Minister whether he would arrange for the title of Lord Stansgate to be resuscitated. Another Member got up and asked whether Harold Wilson agreed with the statement I had made at the weekend, that it was not for Labour to instruct the miners on how they should vote. Harold got up and floundered a bit. I saw the Early Day Motion circulated by Harold Wilson attacking McGahey; indeed Harold said in the House that McGahey and Heath were the two extremists. I decided to do a bit of research and so looked up *The Times* for 1912; what was interesting was that in March 1912, the miners were balloting on a strike, the Government were rushing the Minimum Wages Bill through – which is like the

Relativities Report – and Tom Mann said the troops should assist the miners and was being prosecuted for sedition. Josiah Wedgwood, Bertie Russell and others set up the Defence of Free Speech Committee to defend Tom Mann. *The Times*'s leading articles were fulminating every day about syndicalist revolutions. And Ramsay MacDonald issued a statement warning against syndicalism but saying that the Labour Party wished the miners well. So there's been no real change in the Labour Party since 1912!

After dinner Michael Foot and I had a chat and he told me that Dick Crossman is dying, which is very sad.

Wednesday 30 January

This morning there were massive attacks on Mick McGahey, and the *Guardian* actually ran a leading article saying, 'Poor Mr McGahey, there's not much difference between him and Mr Benn.'

In the Shadow Cabinet, Michael Foot said he wished to refer to the Early Day Motion condemning Mick McGahey, and to Jim and Ron's statement. There had been no consultation on these. He said he disliked the attack on McGahey; McGahey might have been misreported, and anyway, he didn't like Jim's statement because it referred to extremists. Who were these extremists? Lawrence Daly?

Denis Healey said that the majority of the nation agreed with it and he was amazed at the naïvety of Michael Foot in not facing what he should have realised was a major threat to the social fabric of society. He wasn't so surprised at *my* naïvety.

I interrupted, 'Well, I, at least, am not an ex-Communist,' which shook the Shadow Cabinet.

'Well,' said Denis, 'perhaps it would have been better if you had been through these experiences when you were young.'

Douglas Houghton finished the meeting by saying that he was deeply troubled and the whole fabric of our society would be shattered.

It was a long, bitter and tough meeting.

Tuesday 5 February

Went to the House for Prime Minister's Questions. It was clear from Heath's answers that, with the announcement that the miners' strike would begin on Saturday night, the Cabinet had in effect decided to go to the country. Heath was busy burning his bridges and his boats and everything else. The whole atmosphere was of the hustings, no question about that.

Speculation is starting among MPs that Heath will now go for an early Election, possibly as soon as 28 February.

Thursday 7 February

At 12.40, the Secretary of the PLP rang me to say that the General Election was to be on 28 February and this was announced on the 1 o'clock news.

Tonight Enoch Powell decided not to stand as a candidate because he feels the Election is a fraud and he can't put forward a policy which he knows the Tory Government would break if they got elected. This is a very important factor. Many Tories will be extremely worried by Enoch's defection and it will do Heath an immense amount of damage; it is bound to have an effect in pushing us up in the polls. If only Harold would look and sound a bit more convincing, we might have a good chance.

Monday 11 February
After lunch I went to Stockwood, the most difficult area in my constituency. It was windy and cold and pouring with rain. What was worrying was that out of fifteen houses there were three women – housewives between twenty-five and thirty-five – who had voted Labour in 1970 but were impressed by the arguments about the unions, about the miners, about Communists, about militants, about strikes and about being fair but firm. So Heath's propaganda seems to be getting across and he is doing it on a big scale.

Came back absolutely persuaded that I would lose Bristol and that there would be a Tory landslide. Now, at midnight, having watched a lot of television and seen Heath doing a brilliant party political broadcast and Harold floundering away about the price of petrol, I am going to bed tired, exhausted and rather depressed.

Saturday 23 February
Today Enoch Powell made his big Birmingham speech – of which I have only heard the briefest reports – where he began to indicate that he would be recommending people who believed in renegotiation and the sovereignty of Parliament to vote Labour. That is going to be a major issue in this Election. The Common Market has come into its own in the last week. It is the big question because it touches at food prices, at Heath's misunderstanding of the character of the British people and also at the basic question of the freedom of Parliament and the people. Focusing attention on the Common Market is the main contribution that I have been able to make to Party policy over the last three years.

Wednesday 27 February
Later in the day, Hilary arrived from London with a copy of the *Evening Standard* containing an article by Kingsley Amis describing why he was going to vote Tory, and saying that I was 'the most dangerous man in Britain'.

Thursday 28 February
Polling Day.

We went to one polling station in Windmill Hill where there was a Young Socialist sitting with his YS badge and his Tony Benn sticker, and a boy taking numbers for the Tories. Later in the evening, we met the same boy in our Labour Committee rooms in Windmill Hill helping us to knock up late voters because he had been persuaded by the Young Socialist that he had gone wrong.

After that we went and had a meal at the Golden Egg in Clifton. Back to the hotel and I had a quick nap before going back out from 5 to 9.30, doing a final round of major committee rooms. Canvassers were pretty contented. There were thirty cars available in Brislington. The place was absolutely crammed with people, with very little sign of Tory activity.

At 10 pm we were back at the hotel and we had a couple of hours there. By then the first results were out and it was quite clear that the swing was not uniform, that the Liberals were doing well in Tory seats and knocking the Tories out but not having anything like the same impact in Labour seats. So it all looked quite encouraging.

At 12.15 we all went to the Brislington School where the count was being held, and found there two complete television crews. The media appeared to have taken charge, with gossip writers, etc, no doubt all waiting for my defeat. Harlech Television had taken the domestic-science room on the ground floor and had a canteen there with a big notice 'HTV staff only'. Caroline made such a row that we were allowed in for some baked beans and coffee.

The counting didn't begin until 1.35 am and it was 4.35 before the result came out. But well before then one could see that I was well in the lead, and in the end the result was dazzling – a majority of 7,914.

7

1974–75

Tuesday 5 March 1974

A week ago, I thought I might be out of Parliament altogether and now I am in the Cabinet as a Secretary of State for Industry. I feel I have to keep the hopes of the Left alive and alight. The job is enormous and the press is entirely hostile and will remain so. I have to recognise that in putting forward my proposals to the Cabinet, all will be opposed: but there are four powerful Secretaries of State on the left – myself, Michael Foot, Peter Shore, and Eric Varley – and we are a formidable team.

Wednesday 6 March

Frances Morrell, Francis Cripps, my secretary Mary Lou Clarke and my PPS Frank McElhone and I had a long talk about how we would use public ownership in the first instance as an ambulance for failed firms – because British Leyland and one or two other firms are in serious difficulties. Frances and Francis have both been appointed officially as my advisers; they are going to get about £4,000 a year and share a big office on the same floor as me.

The miners' strike is over with a settlement of £100 m, twice what the Tory Government offered but still about £25 m below their full claim.

Thursday 7 March
At 11.55 I was summoned over to see the PM, who said, 'About Ministers, I will let you have Michael Meacher as your Parliamentary Under-Secretary and I am giving you Gregor Mackenzie and Eric Heffer as Ministers of State.' Brian Walden apparently would not accept because he can't afford to take office and give up his other activities.

At 2 we had the Concorde meeting with David Jones, Deputy Secretary of the Department and Ken Binning, an Under-Secretary, both of whom I knew from my Mintech days. They told me in effect that there was unanimous official advice now throughout Whitehall for the cancellation of Concorde, and they had agreed that it was unsaleable in its present form. My own view is that we should continue with the present Concorde programme. This is one of the most difficult problems I have to tackle and I will have to fight it with tremendous care because it could be a disaster politically for me both in Bristol and personally.

Monday 11 March
At 10 o'clock we had a meeting about Norton Villiers Triumph at Meriden. Jack Jones came with Harry Urwin, Bill Lapworth (the Divisional Organiser of the TGWU at Coventry) and Dennis Johnson, the shop stewards' convenor.

I agreed that we would make expert advice available to the people in the factory – probably taking on consultants who would work for the shop stewards in preparing a case for viability. Second, if they needed any further information from the company, I would ask Dennis Poore, Managing Director of NVT, to make it available and I may even use my powers to put a director on the board. Third, I would ask Poore to desist from any attempt to harass the co-operative. Foruth, we would try to find some way of getting the bikes to America to meet the summer demand. This was the best I could do and we agreed to a press statement afterwards, stating that 'I had considered the position sympathetically and was helping the co-operative to get their case put forward in the best possible way'.

I agreed with my Ministers that I would leave home at 8.30 every morning, meet the press office advisers just after nine, and have a 9.30 'prayer' meeting with advisers and Ministers only.

Thursday 21 March

The Government is in an interesting position. Harold depends on Michael, Michael brings with him Jack Jones's loyalty and that triumvirate is *the* most important group in the whole Government. I think Roy Jenkins is being bought off. As to the rest, they are less important figures. Harold, of course, thoroughly enjoys this risky political position because it means he can do what he likes; so do the right-wing members of the Cabinet because they can always use the Liberals' parliamentary strength as an excuse for delaying any programme that they don't believe in. But this can't go on for long; there will have to be another Election – September at the latest.

Went over to the Cabinet at 10.45 and parliamentary affairs was followed by free family planning on the Health Service which Barbara got the Cabinet to agree to. Denis said it would have to come out of her budget.

Tuesday 2 April

President Pompidou has died. This is very important for Concorde, because French Ministers will now be unable to move until there is a replacement, so Achille-Fould will probably not come to London next week and the whole Concorde decision will be held up.

It is now 1.45 in the morning of my forty-ninth birthday. Just going to bed very, very tired with a tremendous weight of work on my shoulders. My goodness me, you don't have much time for thinking. But as Frances Morrell said to me, all Ministers have problems. Defence has got to make cuts, Crosland has to deal with mortgages, Jim Callaghan has to cope with Europe and Shirley Williams has got to deal with prices. Being a Minister is not an easy job.

Wednesday 3 April

Frank McElhone came to see me. The truth is that I have left him out in the cold and he was angry, like my secretary, Mary Lou, who feels isolated. He denounced me for ignoring the PLP, so I told him to fix things up, and he said, 'I have fixed them up and they have all been cancelled. You are devoting yourself to the wrong priorities.' So I have to placate Mary Lou and Frank; I have got to reallocate my work better so I spend more time with MPs; and I have got to keep the Ministers sweet, particularly Frank Beswick and Eric Heffer. I have got to be a better manager of people and I'm not very good at that, that's my trouble. I had a knocking from him for forty minutes.

I came home and there was a birthday cake for me, and then I settled down to my boxes.

Saturday 6 April

I wrote a note to Anne Crossman following Dick's death yesterday. Dick was a remarkable man, immensely intelligent and kind when he wanted to be but, of course, the teacher throughout his life – always preferring conflict, which cleared his mind. He was absolutely unreliable in the sense that he often changed his views, but he always believed what he said, which is something you can't say of others. He was also capable of being unpleasant and my friendship with him had deteriorated sharply in recent years. At any rate, he will be remembered through his diaries, which will be the best diaries of this period ever published; though I hope my own, if they are ever transcribed, will also turn out to be a reasonable record.

Tuesday 9 April

At Cabinet, the question of selling our warships to Chile came up again. Jim Callaghan reported that he had met a group of Labour MPs on the previous evening, half of whom had been in favour of releasing the existing warships. He said it would require legislation to stop the release, and how would you get the Chilean sailors off the ship already doing trials off the English coast, and so on and so on.

Michael Foot came out very strong against and I said, 'It is absolutely untrue that it would require legislation. What about the arms embargo against Israel during the recent war? What would we say if we discovered that the Russians had put in an order for some fighters from British Aircraft Corporation? Of course we can do it, it is a decision we are absolutely free to take.'

I raised the question of the repair and overhaul of Rolls Royce engines at East Kilbride for the Hawker Hunters which we had sold to the Chilean Government. I said, 'This is even worse because these Hawker Hunters may actually be used to strafe guerrillas with bombs.'

We lost. Only two of us spoke against, Michael Foot and myself. Barbara Castle was silent, so was Peter Shore, perhaps because, as Trade Minister, he was worried about the threat to copper supplies, which might be stopped in retaliation if we don't go ahead with the deal.

Wednesday 10 April

At 5 o'clock I went to the second Cabinet meeting, held for the first time in Harold's room in the House. Harold made a reference to Marcia and her brother Tony Field and the press allegations of improper land deals. He said he felt he had driven the press into a corner but he continued, 'I must tell you, there are two other members of the Cabinet, whose names wild horses wouldn't drag from me, who are being pursued by the press. One has been tailed for five years and on the other they have got a dossier two feet thick. They both would be regarded as being in the leadership stakes if I went. So I just want to warn you.'

This was Harold telling us that if any of us made a move against him, he might take action against the person. It was an extraordinary thing and showed him in the cheapest light because if he really had any information about two people in the Cabinet who were being tailed the decent thing would have been to tell them.

Northern Ireland came up next and Merlyn Rees reported that the situation was getting extremely serious; the IRA were involving women and using hostages to drive bombs into areas. Under a pledge of the utmost secrecy, we were told it was decided to surround Belfast and prevent any cars entering. This is to be announced soon.

It was agreed, again under the highest secrecy, that we would begin considering the implications of a total withdrawal. Of course, if that got out, it would precipitate bloodshed but we felt we simply had to do it. Roy took that view. Jim looked very doubtful but thought it needed to be done. Fred Peart, Peter Shore and Willie Ross are 100 per cent pro-Protestant. So the Cabinet would divide on Catholic–Protestant lines in the event of this happening.

Thursday 11 April
At 12.15 Sir Antony Part, my Permanent Secretary, came to see me. He hummed and hawed a bit and then said, 'Minister, do you really intend to go ahead with your National Enterprise Board, public ownership and planning agreements?' 'Of course.'

'Are you serious?' he asked.

'Of course. Not just because it is the policy but because I was deeply associated with the development of that policy.'

He said, 'Well, I must warn you, in that case, that if you do it, you will be heading for as big a confrontation with industrial management as the last Government had with the trade unions over the Industrial Relations Act.'

'I am not going to jail any industrialists. I am not going to fine them. We have just got to move forward.'

'I know,' he said, 'and I will try to lubricate things, if that's really what you mean.'

'Well, of course it is. I know I can't do it now but we have got to move in that direction.'

Then, blow me down, he put in a paper and tried to get me to agree verbally to a proposal that because of the extra burden on industry, which has reduced their liquidity position, we should allow them to put all wage increases through the Price Commission as an allowable cost which would give an extra £600 million to industry at the expense of the consumer. I said, 'That is an even more relaxed view of price control than the previous Government agreed.'

'It's the only way,' he replied. I refused. 'You can put your analysis of liquidity to the Treasury if you like, but I won't accept that.'

This is the way in which the Department of Industry acts, simply as a mouthpiece for the CBI, and that is what I won't have.

Sunday 14 April

Judith Hart rang me up to say she had been very worried by Eric's speech about warships for Chile because it had put her in a difficulty and she wondered whether *she* should make a statement, or resign. I told her to keep quiet, say nothing and leave it. Since I find myself saying to other people what Frances says to me, perhaps it would be better if I took my own advice and kept quiet.

Friday 3 May

Went over to Transport House and Jack Jones and the TGWU gave me, on loan, a beautiful old banner, 'The Workers' Union', about nine feet by nine feet. I'll have to give it back if there is a change of government.

Jack asked about Meriden and I said, 'I saw them and have told them to prepare a case against what officials are advising.'

He said, 'I know that and I appreciate it. What can I do to help?'

'You can press Denis Healey, Harold and Michael Foot at the critical moment when it comes before Ministers.'

Back to the office to see the Russian Ambassador, Mr Lunkov. I was just in the process of hanging up my banner and he took a lot of interest in it. My office is getting to look more and more messy, like my basement office at home.

Thursday 9 May

Peter Shore and I had a drink in the office and we talked a little bit about the EEC. He said that Helmut Schmidt, who is likely to succeed Willy Brandt as Chancellor, is much more Atlantic-orientated. He is a great friend of Giscard d'Estaing and the whole Community would take a very different direction than it had when Germany had been led by Brandt and France by Pompidou.

It is astonishing, the number of heads of state that have fallen recently. Trudeau, the Canadian Prime Minister, fell today and there is going to be an Election there. Brandt's resignation is an extraordinary one because it now contains a hint of scandal: an East German spy, Gunter Guillaume, had been to Norway on holiday with Brandt and has taken compromising photographs of him.

Sunday 12 May

Frances said this afternoon that she was convinced that the Department of Industry was sabotaging my industrial proposals. I feel the same. Sir Antony Part is making no progress, they just turf back things I want with their objections and I then have to force them to carry out my wishes – as I had to do with Meriden, with all the European questions, and so on. Frances says that on the planning agreements, the National Enterprise Board and the Industry Act, the officials are simply skating over the really difficult questions so they are never explored properly. It is as if I'm trying to swim up the Niagara Falls.

Monday 13 May

I had a sandwich lunch and asked Antony Part his view of whether there would be a slump. He said there might be. Then he added, 'We're reaching the point of the crossing of the Rubicon and your speech about workers' control will lead to tremendous opening of fire on us because industrialists fear you are going to establish it.'

'I am not trying to cross any Rubicon, I am sitting on the banks of the Rubicon, waiting for consultation before I proceed but if *they* cross the Rubicon and attack me that is a very different thing.'

Sunday 19 May

My relations with Harold are absolutely rock bottom. Tomorrow night there is a dinner at Number 10 for Academician Kirillin, and Harold hasn't invited me, though I am one of the principal Ministers (not that I want to go particularly). But I will have to consider how to improve my relations with him. He really does think that my public statements about 'open government' and so on, are destroying the Labour Party, whereas I think it is the only hope.

Monday 20 May

Dinner at Number 10 for Kirillin. I had queried the fact that I hadn't been invited so Harold put me back on his guest list. Harold spoke, beginning with a long, detailed description of all the negotiations with the Russians, describing dates, places, times, projects, what had happened. It was a display of his virtuosity of memory – amusing, though a bit egocentric.

As they were leaving, Peter Shore, Harold and myself stood on the steps of Number 10. It was a beautiful warm May evening and there were a few people watching from the other side of the road. Harold described how the Foreign Office had tried to get round the Cabinet proposals on the Chilean aircraft contract. He reminded us of a Ministry of Works memorandum to Attlee saying, 'We have read the Cabinet's proposals.' Attlee replied, 'The Cabinet does not propose, it decides.' So he has had a great fight with the Foreign Office and he is making a statement tomorrow on the Chile situation, which will be total victory. It couldn't be better. The Rolls Royce engines will not be overhauled and that is it.

Thursday 23 May

The amusing news tonight is that Harold has made Marcia Williams a peer.

Monday 3 June

I went to speak at Eastbourne to the National Union of Sheet Metalworkers, a very old union. My speech, which had been very carefully prepared, went down like a pancake on a wet pavement. No real response. Afterwards we sat round and talked about it to some of the men. They said, 'Workers are suspicious. They don't believe what's happening. They think all this involvement is a substitute for real power, and they know that they have real power, if they want to use it. They want socialism', and so on.

I think many unions are in a sense saying, 'We want the whole thing or we shall just use our veto because we can deal with management at any time we like so long as government keeps out of the way.'

Tuesday 4 June

There was an amusing incident today. The visiting Bulgarian Minister of Trade had given me as a parting gift a tablecloth and a little Bulgarian calculating machine, a tiny hand-held one in beautiful yellow, which had a memory. It was a lovely thing. The department that advises on gifts said I could keep the tablecloth but that the calculator was too valuable and it should be for office use only. I asked today what had happened to it and was told it had been sent away to be debugged in case it had a recording device in it, and when the technicians had looked at it closely, they had been enormously impressed by the quality of its circuitry, which they said was the best they had seen among American, German and Japanese examples. They were very puzzled by how the Bulgarians could have got hold of such marvellous technology. So it could be that Britain is reduced to copying the Bulgarians, though if that happens we really are finished!

A group of Scottish Labour MPs – Hugh Brown, Tam Dalyell, George Lawson, John White, Harry Ewing and John Robertson – came to see me at the House about the workers' newspaper co-operative in Glasgow. They were absolutely persuaded that the workers were serious people who ought to be supported. The most amazing thing of all was that George Lawson, who is a dour, tough, right wing, pro-Market MP and a stern critic of mine, said he believed the workers' co-operative was something that reflected the best in my ideas and he felt it was something we should support. It was like getting a kiss and a hug in public from Roy Jenkins. It did indicate that there has been a shift of opinion. I told them to go and canvass other Ministers and I would do my best.

Tuesday 11 June

There were three items on the agenda at the Public Enterprise Committee of Cabinet, first being the Meriden crisis. Joel Barnett and Harold Lever recommended that in view of what Geoffrey Robinson and Dennis Poore had said to them, the whole thing should be dropped. I fought like a tiger – I have never fought harder than I did there. To my amazement I got away with it. I have lost all respect for Harold Lever and Barnett too, the way they have handled this. If I had accepted their recommendation, there would have been endless trouble.

On IPD, I said I was very reluctant, but I felt you could not sack 1,200 people even though it was a bum firm. So it was agreed that the firm should go bust, that we should tell the Receiver we intend to buy the factory and set up a company for it, have a feasibility study and save the jobs as best we could. A sort of legalised work-in. That was not a bad conclusion.

I dashed over to the husbands-and-wives' dinner, with Barbara and Ted, John Silkin and Rosamund, Peter and Liz and Tony and Judith. I told them I have now declassified my Home Policy Committee document, and it will be available at the PLP for them to see tomorrow. I added that I was under heavy pressure and I wanted a bit of support.

Barbara turned on me. 'You with your open government, with your facile speeches, getting all the publicity, pre-empting resources – "I'm the big spender, I can't do it without money" – trying to be holier than thou and more left wing than me.' She was extremely angry with me. 'I know we can *only* get this expenditure if we go for a statutory wages policy,' she said, revealing once again her hatred for the trade unions.

I said, 'Look, Barbara, I haven't spent a penny, you've had pensions, the nurses' increase. I haven't been allowed to spend a penny. I'm thinking about future policy, and the only job I've been given is to sack 21,000 people in my own constituency working on Concorde. I have never said anything about pre-empting resources because I know that has got to be done collectively, but I am simply developing a case.'

But she retorted, 'How are we going to solve the problems?'

'We're going to solve them by trading off wealth for power,' I replied. 'We have got to admit it is an unfair society, and give people a perspective, and I am not prepared to accept that Britain is declining.' My God, Barbara's hatred really came out. I think she is feeling guilty.

Friday 14 June

There was a message from Number 10 that the Prime Minister has said I am not to make any more speeches on industrial policy until he has had the chance of a word with me, with no date fixed for that. So I said to Roy Williams, 'I shall take no notice of that whatsoever.' You can't tell a Secretary of State not to make speeches.

Then I had a candid talk to Roy. 'Look. This is what is really happening. All my industrial and regional policy in respect of Europe is being taken away and put under the Foreign Secretary's control. My Green Paper is being blocked by the Treasury, by the Chancellor's minute. My day-to-day business is now being watched by Harold Lever and Joel Barnett. All my speeches are controlled, and indeed I have been told by the Prime Minister not to speak or broadcast. And as regards appointments, the Prime Minister has said I am not to proceed even by letting it be known there are vacancies.

This is the position I am in and do you wonder that, frustrated within Whitehall, I turn outside, where my support is?'

Roy Williams, who is a shrewd chap, said, 'Well, you know, Secretary of State, having seen you at Blackpool at that POEU conference, I do realise what fantastic support there is and what a strength it must be.'

'Honestly, Roy, it is not that I want a boost, but that is where the support is and whether I am a Minister or not is of marginal interest to me because all of that will continue after I leave office. I will just have to run this as best I can. You mustn't worry and if the worst comes to the worst, I'll discontinue press releases and do street interviews instead.'

Tuesday 18 June
Went to London Airport and caught the plane to Brussels with members of my Private Office. We were met and taken straight to the Commission for a series of meetings.

This huge Commission building in Brussels, in the shape of a cross, is absolutely un-British. I felt as if I was going as a slave to Rome; the whole relationship was wrong. Here was I, an elected man who could be removed, doing a job, and here were these people with more power than I had and no accountability to anybody.

My visit confirmed in a practical way all my suspicions that this would be the decapitation of British democracy without any countervailing advantage, and the British people, quite rightly, wouldn't accept it. There is no real benefit for Britain. Though depressing and gloomy, I found it a most fascinating day.

Friday 21 June
We were defeated yesterday by 21 votes in a motion of censure against our industrial strategy, moved by Heath. But at least it forced Harold to defend the manifesto in Parliament. The papers of course were full of it.

Monday 24 June
To lunch with Jack Jones at Locket's. It was an interesting lunch because he was trying, as usual, to bully me. He began by saying, 'Harold Lever says Meriden isn't viable. They just want £7 million of public money. I am going to see him again in a couple of days.'

'Well, Harold Lever doesn't want this to work.'

'Oh, I'll have to see him about it,' Jack replied, making it quite clear that he is now bypassing me and going straight to Harold Lever.

We moved on to the general issue of companies that are going bust. 'Nationalisation is no good,' he said. 'People don't want it. Management in nationalised industries is very bad.'

'I haven't much faith in British management, but it's certainly no worse in the nationalised industries than in private industry.'

'But people don't want nationalisation.'

'Well, we may have no alternative if firms go bust.'

'What do you mean, "if firms go bust"?'

I gave him some examples – Fisher-Bendix, Beaverbrook's *Scottish Daily Express.*

'You don't want to support the Scottish newspaper workers,' he snapped.

I said, 'It's a very big political issue in Scotland whether they are entitled to have a newspaper of their own.'

'You don't want to do that. You don't want to save every lame duck.'

'What about British Leyland?' I asked.

'Why couldn't you sell it?'

I said, 'To whom?'

'Why don't you sell it to General Motors?'

When Jack Jones recommends that the British Government sell British Leyland to General Motors of America, there is an indication that the criticisms of him from the Left are correct. He was reinforcing everything Denis Healey says.

We moved on to the Common Market and I told him my view of the true position. He said, 'I have spoken to Harold and he says that the Common Market will never accept our proposals and that we will be out in six months.'

'You must be joking,' I said, 'Jim made one speech for domestic consumption and now he is in the process of selling out to the Market.'

Thursday 27 June

Antony Part came to see me at 4.10. He came on to my speech due to be made tomorrow at Buxton on regional policy. 'How did you get to see that?' I asked.

'The office here asked me to check the figures and they sent me a copy.'

I said, 'It's a political speech that's being made and the press release is going out through Transport House.'

'Well, Minister, don't you think that what you're doing is inflaming the North against the South?' That was a reference to the phrase 'industrial policies being discussed in the comfortable atmosphere of Westminster, Whitehall and Fleet Street' and to the fact that I describe other parts of the country, perhaps patronisingly, as the regions.

Well, I pointed to the map on the wall showing the assisted areas and I said, 'That's the most important map in Britain – that's where our support lies.'

'Well, you're inflaming people,' he said. 'You're raising temperatures.'

I said, 'Not at all – I'm using very clear language.' I went over and opened the manifesto. 'The first objective of the manifesto is about a fundamental and irreversible shift in the balance of wealth and power in favour of working people and their families,' I read.

'Well,' he said, 'I have never known a Minister in the whole course of my life in any party who has been like you.'

'Well, I'm sorry but as far as I am concerned my work as a manager or a Minister is nothing like as important as my work as an educator and spokesman – speaking for people.' Of course, Antony Part simply didn't understand that. He has a completely different way of thinking and just does not seem to be really trying to assist me in getting things done. He just comes along and warns me: that I've crossed the Rubicon, that I've done this and that. At a suitable moment, after the Election, I may ask for him to be replaced because of a breakdown of confidence between us.

Monday 15 July
Dinner with Jim Callaghan. He talked about how he didn't let the Foreign Office bully him, had only one red box every night and read the telegrams.

We discussed the Election, which he thought would be in October, and that we would win. He didn't think there would be an economic crisis between now and then.

We went on to the Party and the Left. He knows nothing about the Left at all. Never heard of the ultras, never realised that the Trotskyites were critical of Jack Jones and Hugh Scanlon, of Michael Foot, myself and Eric Heffer as 'fake' left. He simply knew nothing about it.

He was worried about Communists in the Party because 'I know documents pass across'. I was sure he, as a former Home Secretary, knew these things, but he said that it wasn't from being in the Home Office but from other sources. I said that I remembered him discussing with me the possibility of preventing Hugh Scanlon's election to the AUEW. I told him I wasn't worried about the Communists. They had no appeal whatever to the young, they were very bureaucratic and stick-in-the-mud.

Then he asked me about the industrial policy and how I felt about being a bogeyman. I said I didn't take it personally. He thought that if we lost the Election, people would blame me. I doubted that. Finally, he told me that he might give up next year, and I said, 'Now, look, Jim, you're sixty-two, Churchill became Prime Minister at sixty-four. You've got ten more years of political life in you if you want it. That's the decision you've got to make. You've got to keep yourself available.'

Well, then he declared that he didn't want to be Leader. He repeated it so many times that it was obvious that he did. He said he had told Harold that if Harold was going to retire, he must give Jim three months' notice so that Jim could retire before him.

I pointed out that we didn't know what was going to happen. I stressed that I knew that Jim disapproved of me very much and didn't agree with me, but nevertheless I liked him very much. I told him that I couldn't talk like this with Roy or Denis.

Returning to the theme of the General Election, he thought it would be a very bitter period if we were to lose. I said that we mustn't lose, but that it would still be a bitter period if we won. Jim wasn't sure he'd want to be Leader during such a period. Then he'd be sixty-six before the Election in 1979. He'd obviously worked it all out. I said that he must be available, that's all, like Cincinnatus.

Wednesday 24 July

At a meeting in my office of Eric Heffer, Frank Beswick, Michael Meacher and Gregor MacKenzie, I got Part, who has been made a Knight Grand Cross of the Order of the Bath, GCB, to bring out his ribbon and chain and cross which he had received this morning from the Queen. I took lots of photographs of him and somehow he looked so ridiculous taking such simple and innocent pleasure from it all, that it gave me a feeling of being one-up for the rest of the morning.

Hilary and Rosalind came over to the House of Commons and we had dinner together. Hilary came up to see my room and to use the lavatory, and there was Roy Jenkins smoking a big cigar, having forgotten to lock the door!

Thursday 25 July

At 12 I went to Cabinet. We discussed pensions, or rather Barbara spoke for twenty-five minutes. Then Denis made two points which Barbara answered. This went on for about forty minutes and in the end she lost. She should have simply said, 'Well, this is pretty non-controversial. I have no doubt everyone has read it; and it has been agreed by the Social Services Committee', and she should have left it at that. She really talked herself out, not for the first time.

I passed a lot of little notes to Bob Mellish during this carry-on. 'As Chief Whip, can't you move the closure?' and 'Perhaps she will have to stop for lack of food,' and 'It looks as if only the Dissolution of Parliament will stop her.'

Wednesday 31 July

Caroline and Joshua arrived at 12 and came over with me to the House. Jim Callaghan was making his statement on Cyprus and I followed with my statement on Concorde. I got some hostile questions, some friendly ones, and the Bristol MPs spoke. It was really exciting: I have saved Concorde and that is now off my chest.

The next statement on shipbuilding was also mine and I had the enormous pleasure of announcing the nationalisation of the shipbuilding industry. I worked so hard on the problems as Minister of Technology when I knew things weren't right, so I had given a solemn pledge that I would nationalise, a pledge which I was able to discharge. It gave me a tremendous thrill.

To the meeting of the Cabinet committee on my White Paper *The Regeneration of British Industry*, set up and chaired by Harold. The NEB's main strength in manufacturing would come from the acquisition of a number of key firms – that is to say, profitable firms, not just lame ducks. There was a great struggle but I think I got my way.

We came to future acquisitions and there was a real battle over whether or not we would say that if we provided regional grants, that would lead to public ownership. I said that when we were considering suitable firms for acquisition, we should add, 'The NEB will act also as a means to a further substantial expansion of public ownership through its power to take a controlling interest in relevant companies in profitable manufacturing industry.'

Dashed back to the office. It had been two and a quarter hours of absolute agony and bloodshed.

Thursday 1 August

Banner headlines attacking the nationalisation of shipbuilding in the *Daily Mail*, the *Daily Express*, *The Times*, the *Financial Times*, and so on. The employers are hitting back but the case is so powerful, I don't think we have to worry.

At 9.30 Part came to see me with two really tough items. First, the idea of a popular version of the Industry White Paper: I had said I wanted a million leaflets to go out to industry and he replied that, because it was near an Election and it would be controversial, we probably wouldn't be able to do it. I asked, 'Why not? There's either an Election or there isn't and it would certainly be no more controverisal than the White Paper.'

He said, 'I can only tell you that it would not be possible.'

Frances, who was sitting there, chipped in, 'Secretary, if you say that, that would be taken by people to be a political judgement by the Civil Service.'

Part picked up his folder, began to pack it and half stood up. 'Unless Frances withdraws that, I'm not continuing the discussion.'

'Half a minute,' I said. 'I'm not speaking for her, she'll speak for herself. But quite frankly what you said about the leaflet being controversial could only mean politically controversial. It isn't controversial for the Government, therefore it must be the Opposition who think it is. What is the Opposition objection? It's political.'

This went on for a long time and Frances said, 'I can't withdraw my comments. All I said is that your remark will be seen by others to be politically motivated, that's my best judgement.' In the end, she did say, 'It wasn't meant to be a criticism of you.' So then Part subsided.

The next thing he strongly objected to was my letter to the TUC in which I had offered them £20,000 to carry out research on job problems instead of giving the money to Cardiff University.

'You can't do that.'

'Why not?'

'The Department has decided to conduct a different sort of programme,' he explained.

'Who is the Department? It's me,' I said.

'But you can't give money to a trade union.'

'Why not? We give it to management, and to academics, why not to a trade union?'

He left and I must say it was exhausting. Part has been working to rule since we arrived and has done nothing to help me. He has just detached himself, and insofar as he has said anything, it has been completely obstructive. I think it all began when he asked me, 'Are you seriously going to try to implement your programme?'

Saturday 3 August

The *Daily Mail* said, 'Wilson Goes Cold on Benn', and every other paper took up the same theme on its front page or inside. It was a very, very dishonest briefing by Number 10 and Harold knows it.

Roy Williams, Ray Tuite, Caroline and I were flown in a Beagle to Fairford for the Concorde test flight, where we met Brian Trubshaw, the chief test pilot, who is an old friend of mine. We saw the shop stewards, all Labour, had a few photographs taken and then we had lunch with the executive management of BAC, all of whom, of course, are Bristol Tories, albeit friendly ones.

At 1.40, about sixty of us climbed into the Concorde, and the great plane rumbled to the take-off point. There were a couple of American Airforce colonels from Edwardes Airforce Base on board, and the plane was crammed with technicians, because it was being treated as a proper test flight.

Some of the shop stewards had never flown before, even one of them who had been in the aircraft industry for thirty-seven years. Another had gone to confession last night, and another had made his will. Some of them had been up during the war but not since. It was astonishing that in the aircraft industry, nobody had thought of asking them to fly. Indeed, they had themselves asked many times and the management had always turned them down, and I insisted on taking them all up this time.

The whole plane shook. You could see the front portion, because it is a very long plane, just wobbling. Then this roaring take-off. We climbed through cloud, not steeply but quite quickly. We went out to a point off the coast of Cornwall and down to the Bay of Biscay; we reached Mach 1 as we went supersonic at about 7-800 miles an hour. It rose to 2.02 which was something like 1,800 nautical mph. Absolutely no sensation in the plane at all. Somebody made a threepenny bit stand up on his table in front of him. We just behaved like people on a coach trip to Weston-Super-Mare or

Southend, taking photographs and talking. I did a radio interview for Bristol, introducing the morning show from the plane.

We came back over Bristol and turned and swung over the city, went to RAF Lyneham, flew over the airfield and landed at Fairford. I had another very brief interview with a couple of journalists about the flight. Then we went into the hangar and I thanked all the shop stewards and they thanked Brian Trubshaw.

It was an unforgettable day. I feel very pleased to have nursed that plane through its final crisis before its entry into service.

Friday 9 August
I stayed up to watch the special 'Midweek' programme and at 2am London time, Nixon gave his final broadcast as President. He made no real reference to Watergate and spoke as if he was a Prime Minister who had lost his parliamentary majority, full of the usual corny Nixon morality. An extraordinary broadcast. There was the fascination of seeing a great figure crushed; it was like a public execution.

In the evening I listened to Nixon's emotional farewell to the staff of the White House, and President Ford's inaugural speech, full of Midwest homespun philosophy.

Caroline and I went down to Stansgate. Very tired but awfully nice to be away.

Saturday 17 August
At 2 Caroline and I flew to Coventry, where we were met by the Lord Mayor. We were driven to the Triumph workers' co-op at Meriden. It was a fantastic spectacle. There was the freshly painted factory with an old picket tent and brazier on the gate and a couple of bikes out front, with Bill Lapworth of the T&G, Dennis Johnson, the chief shop steward, John Gratton from the AUEW and their wives to meet us. We went round the factory and talked to the men; the conveners and the stewards themselves took us round, and it was just like going round a Chinese factory – they were speaking with such confidence about their own skill and their work and how they wouldn't need as many supervisors and so on. Then we went into the canteen where tea was being served and Dennis Johnson introduced me briefly and I said a word; then Geoffrey Robinson spoke. There were one or two questions, and I described our industrial policy, and then they sang 'For he's a jolly good fellow' which was very touching.

Sunday 25 August
When the crisis comes, and it will probably be over a slump or Europe, a few people will go; Reg Prentice, Shirley Williams, Roy Jenkins and one or two others are bound to slip away into the centre ground, and the Labour Party will have to build itself up again.

Tuesday 10 September
Industrial Development Committee of Cabinet at 3. I asked the Committee
to note that the workers' co-operative at IPD was coming along well, and to
authorise money for the Receiver to keep it going until the end of
November. I was deeply committed to this and I believed we must succeed.

Harold Lever sat there bursting with laughter and Denis Healey thought
it was crackers. Harold Wilson said, 'It was in my last Election address; we'll
have to do something until the Election is over.' Utterly cynical. Frankly if
that little discussion had been recorded, it would have destroyed the
credibility of the Party completely.

Anyway, I said, 'Well, *you* tell me how you are going to get people to take a
£20-a-week wage cut, as is happening in Coventry now, to work for the co-
operative. And you tell me where you will get people to exercise the
responsibility that they are able to show. Merseyside is an absolute desert, a
battlefield, and we must deal with it.'

At 4.30 Sir Douglas Allen, the new Permanent Secretary at the Civil
Service Department, came to see me. He used to be at the Department of
Economic Affairs with George Brown and told some funny stories about
him.

Saturday 14 September
I am not sure about the Election – my thoughts go up and down. I must
record here too that Caroline is finding the strain appalling. She feels that,
being under the shadow of a Cabinet Minister, everything she does is
dismissed. I agree that this is a real sacrifice that the wives of politicians have
to make.

Monday 16 September
The Central Intelligence Agency, through William Colby, the Director-
General, has been giving evidence in Washington and has openly admitted
that the CIA spent $4 million undermining the Allende Government in
Chile. This of course is far worse than Watergate though it receives very little
public comment, and it is a candid admission of how they do it. One has to
keep an eye out for the role of British Intelligence here at home. Apparently
a man called Cord Meyer was sent to London by the CIA to work with the
British Labour Movement, and one would be foolish to underestimate the
extent to which American business is secretly mobilising in order to defeat
the Labour Government, and particularly policies on which we are going to
fight the Election.

Wednesday 18 September
A Cabinet had been called this morning and Harold said, very solemnly, as
if he were announcing a great event, 'Colleagues, I must tell you that Her
Majesty the Queen . . .' There was some chatting going on and he said,

'Silence, order. I am telling you that Her Majesty the Queen has assented that there should be a Dissolution of Parliament and an Election on Thursday 10th October, and that the announcement will be made at 12.45.' Well, since everybody knew quite well that that was what it was about, there wasn't much excitement.

There was some discussion about smears, and Barbara Castle said that she had heard that the *Sunday Times* was going to reveal that Ted Short owned six houses; and Harold said there was a rumour that his income tax returns had been photocopied, and so on.

Thursday 10 October
Polling Day. To Bristol Transport House, where the *Daily Mirror* was waiting – they photographed me at a couple of polling stations and on top of the car with my loudspeaker.

At 1 o'clock we had lunch and I made a further thermos so I could drink tea from my tin mug while sitting on top of the car. The seat was so hard, I got really sore. Fortunately, there was very little rain but it was cold up there and I had my anorak and blanket round me.

Josh arrived in the afternoon. He and Stephen went around together all afternoon and were terrific. We worked right through, had a cup of tea with George Easton, then finished at about 8.45 and went back to the hotel for a meal.

The results began coming in. The polls this morning were showing on average a 5.5 per cent Labour lead but it became quite clear that this distribution of our lead varied very much according to which part of the country it was, and in the Tory marginals, where they were fighting like hell, they did actually manage to hold their own. The computer began by predicting a 66 overall majority, but it narrowed and narrowed as the night went on.

To the count at about 12.10. BBC and ITN television said that mine was the only result they intended to show from the South West, and when I asked all the Labour agents who were gathered in the classroom, which we had booked and provided with a kettle, milk, teabags and sugar, there was an overwhelming vote against letting the cameras in to the declaration. ITN and the BBC were extremely angry. The result came out at about 1.15 am, a great deal earlier than in the last Election. My majority was 9,373 compared with 7,912 in February. I had a 17.7 per cent majority and my percentage of the vote rose from 47 per cent to 49.1 per cent. It was an absolutely superb result.

I went back to the hotel and watched the results until about 4 am. The computer prediction was of a Labour majority of five by the time I went to bed. In the event it was three.

Saturday 12 October
The *Economist* has demanded my dismissal as Secretary for Industry. Frank

McElhone rang to say he thought it was quite possible that Harold might move me – that is very much the rumour. But Jack Jones, I think, probably wouldn't favour that. Nobody can now claim that I did the Party any damage in the Election. Harold's own Election campaign was trifling and unimportant, with no real content; that man is capable of being Prime Minister four times without doing anything to change the structure of power in society.

Thursday 17 October
Caroline and I went to Tommy Balogh's house for the left-wing dinner. Judith Hart was upset and told me that Harold had called her in at 2.30 and had said, 'I can't appoint you back to your department because I understand you have got Communist connections.'

She said to Harold, 'I have never been a Communist.'

'No,' said Harold. 'But I understand you have been contacted.'

She said, 'Well, my son is a Communist.'

'It's nothing to do with that,' said Harold.

'Well, I did ring John Gollan, the Secretary of the Communist Party, in September to say I couldn't speak at the Chile meeting in Scotland because Jimmy Reid (a leading Communist Party member) would be there.'

'Oh,' said Harold, 'that's getting nearer the mark.'

She told me she got angry and decided that if she was sacked, she was sacked, and went back to her office to wait, but was called by Harold at 6 o'clock and told it was all right.

It is significant that the security services decided to pick off Judith Hart, very significant. And it is significant that Harold decided to take it up, having known her since 1959; he would have to pitch his judgement against the security services' judgement. It shows the sort of thing we are up against. It means the security services will pick me off if they have half a chance.

Judith said she was just angry with Harold but in fact she was weeping, she was so distressed.

Friday 18 October
I discussed Judith's story with Frances and speculated again as to why the security services had chosen this moment to go for Judith and why Harold had done it that way. I told Frances I had been very surprised that Harold had rung me up during the Election in Bristol and asked me if I knew anything about Bickenhall Mansions; had I been lured there to a flat to smoke cannabis? He had told me a story about Marcia's handbag having been taken and someone telling her to collect it from a certain flat, and she was afraid if she did she would be compromised in some way. I told Frances I had thought nothing of it.

She said, 'Oh yes, I heard that story during the Election.'

Saturday 19 October
Frank McElhone rang, shocked by Keith Joseph's speech in Birmingham, and saying that it would thoroughly upset the Catholic Church. Joseph's speech on 'The remoralisation of Britain' was an attack on permissiveness on the Mary Whitehouse model, and had advocated birth control for poor families so as to reduce the number of children they would produce, since the mothers were unfit to look after them. It was a complete master-race philosophy; the theory that the problem is the immorality of the poor rather than poverty is a most reactionary idea bordering on Fascism.

Sunday 20 October
The papers today covered Joseph's speech. The Churches have already attacked it and I must say it will do a great deal to repel people from the Tories; I think he may have thrown away the Tory leadership by being so explicit. His plan to deal with inflation by throwing people out of work, then when they are poor implying they are not fit to have children and that they are immoral, is so easy to destroy.

Monday 21 October
Went in to the office after lunch and I had a meeting with Secretary about advisers. Part treats me like a consultant psychiatrist would a particularly dangerous patient, and at any moment I expect him to ring a bell and a fat, male nurse in a white jacket will come and give me an injection.

Friday 25 October
Part told me that officials had been shocked that I had described the planning agreements as an extension of collective bargaining into bargaining for power. The officials who had been discussing this at the CBI now felt that they'd been engaged in a complete confidence trick.
    I said, 'I'm very sorry but what did you think the fundamental and irreversible shift in the balance of wealth and power was all about if it wasn't this? I've made endless speeches about this over the years and you must take them seriously. If people don't take them seriously and choose to present the argument in another way, well that's a problem for them. What I'm trying to do is to take the enormous power of the trade union movement and harness it to productive effort.'
    'Well, Secretary of State, the problem is that you are trying to proceed with seven-league boots, and we think you've got to go more slowly,' he replied.
    'Maybe seven-league boots,' I said, 'but I've been in the Department for seven months and I'm not aware of having done anything, made any progress at all. I've spent no money, got no legislation through, and I'm trying to get some indication that things are moving at all.'
    Then he said that other officials felt that I was difficult to work with, and

although they were absolutely loyal in interdepartmental discussions, officials in other departments had said on occasions that the Secretary of State for Industry had gone completely off his rocker.

'My view is perfectly straightforward. I try to say the same thing at the Conference, in Parliament and in the Department – and I don't agree that these ideas are so very absurd. Of course, I'm in a minority in the Cabinet.'

'Ah well, you're thought of as a devious Minister who mobilises people outside in support of your view in the Cabinet.'

Whether he was threatening to resign or not, I don't know, but there was a sort of vague hint of warning in the exchange. Part really is an impossible man, and I would get rid of him if I could. Roy Williams said it was quite untrue that officials found me difficult to work with. There were a lot of them who were extremely attracted by the ideas, and loyal to them. He thought that Secretary was speaking more for himself.

Tuesday 29 October
I heard that there is a plan to put armed guards to protect all Cabinet Ministers, after yesterday's car bomb in Dennis Howell's wife's car.

Friday 8 November
To the NVT motorcycle works at Small Heath in Birmingham for what turned out to be a very hostile meeting with about fifty shop stewards. I made a short speech and then they turned on me. 'You're just a tin-pot king thinking you can impose your will. You don't care about the jobs here. Why should the Meriden works have help? Is it really a co-operative?'

From there I went in to the mass meeting in the canteen, where there were two or three thousand workers. Not a single shop steward wanted to come on the platform with me so I climbed on by myself, sat on the table and picked up the mike. It was a pretty rough, hostile meeting. I described what had happened and that I would try to give them an assurance of their future if we could get an expansion programme going.

Poore had clearly recognised that the feelings of the shop stewards and of the workers at Small Heath were against the Meriden co-operative. He had said this to me many times and I hadn't believed him, but it seems that he was to some extent right.

After that, the Meriden shop stewards Bill Lapworth, Dennis Johnson, John Grattan and Geoffrey Robinson and I talked until 9. Broadly the strategy we worked on was this: we would get the shop stewards from all three plants together, and work for the objective of public ownership for all three plants in a British motorcycle corporation.

Caught the train back to London and got home exhausted.

I did get a clear feeling from today's events of an alarming situation; there was the militancy of people sticking to their jobs, which I fully support, but at the same time, the fear of slump means that workers will turn against workers and working-class solidarity will be strained to its utmost.

Friday 22 November

I walked through St James's Park and got to Number 10 at 10.30, where the joint meeting of the Cabinet and NEC was taking place up in the State Dining Room.

Harold began by announcing that owing to the bombing in Birmingham last night, he wouldn't play much of a part in the discussion but he hoped to look in and out. In fact, he disappeared altogether and except for one walk through the room later, he kept himself absolutely clear of the whole business.

The bombing story is absolutely dominant with anger rising, a petrol bomb thrown into a Catholic church, some factories in Birmingham refusing to work with Irish workers. The damage done to Irish people here, even though they may be Protestants, is terrible, every one a victim of this same awful process of escalating violence.

Monday 25 November

Walked across the park again this morning. The John Stonehouse drowning is a bit mysterious. Bob Mellish had dug out a Hansard text of the last written question John Stonehouse asked before he disappeared, requesting the statistics on death by drowning. It was a most extraordinary coincidence – or else very mysterious. People don't believe he's dead. They think that with the financial trouble that he's in, he's just disappeared. Coastguards on the Florida coast say that he certainly didn't swim out more than fifty yards because they monitor all swimmers who go out that distance. I can't bring myself to write to his wife, I don't know what to say.

Cabinet met at 10.30 and the first item on the agenda was the report from the Home Secretary on Northern Ireland. His paper outlined the measures he proposed: to outlaw the IRA and other organisations, to provide for closer border checks with the Republic and to take powers to deport certain Irish people in Great Britain who had lived here for less than twenty years back to the Republic or Northern Ireland. The main provisions were to be temporary and would expire after six months unless continued in force by an order.

They were emergency powers of a pretty Draconian kind, including the power to extend the detention period from forty-eight hours to seven days on the Home Secretary's instructions.

Harold Wilson asked, 'I take it we'll include other terrorist organisations' and Roy replied, 'Yes, but not the Palestine Liberation Organisation – or the NUM, no matter how difficult they get!'

Later, I saw Don Ryder and I offered him the chairmanship of the NEB, which was a bit of a formality since he already knew about it through

Harold. He is very managerial, rather conceited and he thinks he is the cat's whiskers. But he will carry a degree of confidence and that's about as far as I need to take it. I think if I give him a couple of strong union men he'll be under a bit more pressure than he might expect.

I talked to Frances about the whole impact of the civil war that has begun. Three postboxes were blown up at Victoria, King's Cross and Piccadilly today. It is very alarming and one doesn't know what's going to happen but I suppose we'll have to learn to live with it like the Irish do in Northern Ireland. There's no doubt in my mind that we shall have to get out.

Monday 9 December

Frank McElhone arrived and I took him home for a meal. As he spoke to Caroline and me, it all came out again, his absolute disenchantment with my performance. He said that the Parliamentary Party remains centre and left, and that if I didn't give some attention to the centre of the Party, I would never have any chance whatever. He still had great faith in me but he said I really did have to take this seriously now; even the Market was going to slip through, with only the Left voting against it.

Obviously, he was sick of the fact that I haven't made much use of him over the last seven months, haven't listened, and that there've been no perks of office. Then he said, 'Look, I've got ten premium bonds in the bank. I haven't got a penny behind me. I've just put a new loft in the house and I've told the children that if the Scottish Nationalist advance goes on, and I lose my seat, we're back to a council flat, in the ghetto. We'll just go back to where we started.'

He made it clear that his work with me made him hated both in the Lobby and the PLP, and he now feels that this makes life too difficult. I think he suspects that his chances of becoming a Minister would be greater if he severed his link with me, and he needs the money as a Minister. I think that's it, and I've done nothing for him: it's very human and understandable. So, he actually wants to break the link as my PPS. He says that we'll still be friends and that he'll do what he can for me, but he does not want that organic link.

Saturday 14 December

Rang Joe Ashton and asked his advice on who I should appoint as my new PPS. He agreed to do it himself, saying, 'I wouldn't do it for anyone else, and I wouldn't do it for you for a long period, but at this particular moment you need your friends around you, so I'll help.'

That's settled then. I'm very pleased because I like Joe; he gets on well with the media people, he has a good solid trade union background, he's a journalist of note and linked very closely with the trade union movement, and as he is Chairman of the Industry Group of MPs we shall work very closely together.

Thursday 26 December

Boxing Day. Continued the draft of my letter to my constituents on the
Common Market. I identified the five changes that would occur as a result of
Common Market membership, stressing that I was writing as an MP and
not as a Minister. I was not dealing with the arguments for or against entry. I
added that I was ready to accept the verdict of the referendum but that we
should respect each other's views, and so on.

Saturday 28 December

Up early and stapled the copies together then sent them round to all
nationals, to the Press Association, to the *Western Daily Press*, to the *Bristol
Evening Post*, to Harold Wilson, to Joe Ashton, to the office, to Michael Foot
and to Peter Shore. The copies went out at 12.30 and that was the die cast,
though the release time is not until 1 pm on Sunday. I sat tight and waited to
see what would happen. Sure enough, at 6.20, one of Wilson's Private
Secretaries rang and said the Prime Minister had received the text of my
letter and wanted to know whether the copies have already gone out to the
press. So I said, 'Yes, they have, but if you are speaking to him, you might
draw his attention to the fact that I do not deal with the renegotiation at all,
simply the constitutional change that has occurred.' He told me that I would
be receiving a personal message later tonight from the Prime Minister. Then
I did begin to think that he was going to make this the occasion for firing me
and I became slightly anxious.

On the other hand, the issue is so crucial that I couldn't possibly withdraw
this one to please him. I rang Peter, who asked if there was any reason why I
shouldn't hold it back for a bit if the Prime Minister asked me to. It would be
almost impossible to ring round all the papers and cancel it and I didn't
intend to do that. But it would be very disappointing to be fired at this
moment.

Left for Stansgate at 7.30, and within a few minutes of arriving there, the
phone rang and it was Roy Williams. He had had a telephone call from
Stewart, one of the Prime Minister's Private Secretaries, with the following
message:

'We spoke earlier this evening about a statement which your Secretary of
State is releasing to the press tomorrow morning in the form of an open
letter to his constituents about the Common Market. I understand that
the text of this statement is already in the hands of the press with an
embargo for midday tomorrow. The Prime Minister, who has seen a
copy of the statement, has asked that what follows should be conveyed to
your Secretary of State tonight as a matter of urgency:

'The Prime Minister considers that this statement contravenes the
Cabinet decision of 12 December as minuted in the confidential annexe

sent to all Cabinet Ministers immediately afterwards and summarised in the Prime Minister's letter to the Secretary of State for Employment and copied both to the Secretary of State for Trade and to your own Secretary of State in reply to their letter on the proposed agreement to differ.

'The Prime Minister trusts that your Secretary of State will recall that on the meeting on 12 December it was agreed that the Cabinet should meet early in the New Year to discuss all aspects of the handling of the problem, including the issues raised in the letter from the Secretary of State for Employment, and it was agreed that no one should be involved in private enterprise on these issues until the Cabinet had collectively discussed how the matter is to be handled.'

I said to Roy Williams that he should ring Stewart to say he had transmitted the message to me and that I did not believe that I had contravened the decision of 12 December; indeed, I did not recall having received the letter Harold referred to, responding to our joint request that Cabinet Ministers should be allowed to differ over the Common Market. Roy Williams couldn't recall having received it either. So if the Prime Minister has made an error and this letter did not reach me, that puts me in a slightly stronger position.

But I emphasised he should say to Stewart that as the Prime Minister's message contains a reference to documents, I would have to wait until Monday until I could have access to those documents and then I would send a minute in reply. This means that on Monday, in a fairly leisurely way, I can get the documents and study them and compose a very short response. I am not going to get locked into a long correspondence with the PM. He's a very curious man; he simply won't talk to any of his colleagues, he has to communicate by correspondence which creates an arm's length relationship that is entirely artificial and unreal.

Sunday 29 December

Very nice to be away from the rush and furore. Joshua was busy with his car.

Came upstairs and began listening anxiously to the 1 o'clock news, which contained a reasonable summary of my letter. 'The Secretary of State for Industry has made an attack upon the Common Market and said the British people would be signing away their democratic rights if we remain in the Common Market.' They went on to list some of the democratic rights that I had said would be affected. There was no comment and there was an interview with Harold which had obviously been recorded before he went to the Scilly Isles.

So it has got the best possible start and we shall just have to see what happens. Nothing further has come from Number 10.

Thursday 16 January 1975

At Cabinet we had a brief report on John Stonehouse as to whether he should be unseated from the House of Commons and I asked, 'May I say something that I know won't be very popular. I think we've got to be very careful about this. I'm the only man sitting here who's been expelled from the House of Commons by a House of Commons committee, and that's wrong. The electors put us here, and once we start arranging that people can be dismissed by the House of Commons, that's a very dangerous precedent. Stonehouse hasn't been convicted of any offence, you can't pre-empt that. When Peter Baker, the Tory MP for Norfolk South, was in jail in 1954 for nine months awaiting trial, he didn't resign. You say Stonehouse has been absent from the House for two months, that's true, but Francis Noel-Baker was absent from his Swindon seat for *three years* after the 1966 Election. You say that he's let his electors down, but then Chris Mayhew changed parties. The Chiltern Hundreds is not for nothing because an MP *cannot* actually resign from Parliament.'

To my amazement I got a bit of support. Roy Jenkins and one or two others agreed. Bob Mellish just took the lynch mob's view. 'The Party's angry, we want to get him out.' So we agreed to set up a select committee.

Tuesday 21 January
Cabinet, where the entire morning was devoted to Europe.

First Harold said that he thought an agreement among Ministers to differ would be acceptable from the moment of the Cabinet decision. We would need guidelines to ensure that we all behaved in a comradely way, and there should be no personal attacks.

Barbara Castle thought that the freedom we were being invited to agree followed from the referendum. Of course, in the end, the renegotiated terms we got would not necessarily meet with the requirements of the manifesto. There would be a messy middle-of-the-road muddle.

'You talk about a messy middle-of-the-road muddle, but if the Cabinet understands what I mean, I'm at my best in a messy middle-of-the-road muddle,' said Harold.

Everybody hooted with laughter; it was a very revealing comment, and Harold is at his best in those circumstances, laughing at himself. Bob Mellish passed a note across to me: 'He's like a hippopotamus who likes flopping about in the mud.'

Thursday 23 January
In the afternoon, I heard Harold make his historic statement, that there would be a referendum and that Ministers would be free to speak and to vote – a notable constitutional change. I am intensely proud to have been associated with it.

Dashed over to the office where Gregor MacKenzie was giving a party for Burns night. He asked me to propose a little toast to the immortal memory of

Robert Burns. I said my mother was a Scot and I therefore spanned the
great border. I had as Postmaster General instituted a stamp for Robert
Burns, though when I suggested it, my officials were very much against it.
They warned me that Robert Burns's private life had fallen below the
standard that would be accepted by Her Majesty for admission to the
enclosure at Ascot.

Wednesday 29 January
I have been told that the Foreign Office will stop the Industry Bill if I don't
give a pledge to the Commission that it will conform to Treaty obligations. I
am bloody angry and this is the real crunch, revealing the Foreign Office at
its weakest. All these promises that are given that you wouldn't have to
bother about the Commission, that British interests would be safeguarded,
are absolutely false.

Tuesday 4 February
The great event today is the Tory leadership election and I heard Heath
make what turned out to be his last intervention as Leader of the Opposition
when he asked about the risk of a war in the Middle East. He was pretty
confident against Mrs Thatcher.

Made my statement on steel and there was a bit of a hoo-ha in the middle
of Questions and Answers because the result of the first ballot for the Tory
leadership was spreading round the benches. It was Mrs Thatcher, 130;
Heath, 119; and Hugh Fraser, 16. So Heath resigned and that's the end of
him. Very sad in a way. Politics is a brutal business, and I think we would be
foolish to suppose that Mrs Thatcher won't be a formidable leader; and
Harold couldn't pour scorn on a woman because people wouldn't have it. I
think the quality of the debate will be raised because the Tory Party will be
driven to the right and there will then be a real choice being offered to the
electorate.

Wednesday 5 February
Willie Whitelaw, James Prior, John Peyton and Geoffrey Howe announced
that they were standing against Mrs Thatcher in the second ballot. But I
guess that she will sweep the board, because the opposition has become a
completely negative 'Stop Thatcher' campaign, which I think will bring her
tremendous support.

Saturday 22 February
Mrs Thatcher has been mobbed in Scotland. She's like the Queen really;
she looks like her, talks like her and is of the same age. I don't know whether
she will be able to survive after the honeymoon but she is a popular figure.
Heath is being forgotten and is being sloughed off just as Eden, Macmillan
and Home had been.

Sunday 23 February

Frances Morrell told me that she had heard from the journalist Patrick Cosgrave that Tory Central Office had prepared a tremendous campaign in favour of Britain remaining in the Common Market and constituency parties were being asked to work flat-out to get a 'Yes' in the referendum. But when Mrs Thatcher was elected she told them to drop the whole thing – this was the price demanded by the anti-Marketeers for their support. So Tory Central Office has shelved it. It is a most interesting story.

Meanwhile, Heath is to head the pro-Market campaign around the country and if he becomes the hero of the Tory press, that will undermine the position of Mrs Thatcher. On the other hand, if Wilson is supporting Heath then it will do enormous damage to Wilson. Heath's support won't help anybody!

A telegram arrived last week from Bristol saying, 'Get out if you value your life.' It had been passed to the security people, who sent it to Canon Row police station, where a Superintendent Harden had asked Mary Lou to go in and see him tomorrow to discuss it. It is slightly odd that they should take so much notice now. I have been getting letters every month saying, 'You have six more months to live,' '. . . five more months to live', '. . . four months', and so on, posted in the Reading area and nobody seems to have taken any notice of them. But this telegram apparently interests the police. I am surprised that the Post Office agreed to send such a telegram. Perhaps they reported it to the police in Bristol; perhaps they know who sent it. I am slightly irritated in fact that Bristol should be the source of the message because I have always rather prided myself on never getting any threatening letters from the city of my own seat.

Tuesday 25 February

To Ministerial Committee on Economic Strategy this morning, where we dealt with the paper I had submitted, called 'A Choice of Economic Policies', outlining Strategies A and B. Strategy A was the strategy which had been discussed fully in the Committee so far. In consisted of three aspects: tax increases and public-spending cuts; some form of enforceable pay restraint; and further transfers of cash into the company sector. I thought it would be very serious to adopt this strategy, which I feared would lead to heavy deflation, rising unemployment, cuts in real wages and the withdrawal of support from the Government by the TUC and the Labour Movement.

In outlining Strategy B, I warned that this strategy might strain international relations possibly including retaliatory measures, strengthen middle-class opposition and impose some stress on relations between the Labour Movement and the Government. Finally, if the Government continued on its present course, there might be severe confrontation which would merely deepen the existing social divisions. When I had finished,

Denis came back, saying that we mustn't panic; that the situation wasn't anything like as bad as was suggested; and that we must switch to exports and investment. He was against import controls, because it would mean that we were failing to expose British industry to foreign competition.

I came away exhausted. It is getting awful tough now.

Thursday 27 February

This morning Jack Jones came to see me at my request. I told him everything was all right with Meriden, and then I asked him if he would like to serve on the NEB. 'No,' he said. 'I am a General Secretary of a major union and I can't do that too.'

'Could you be pressed?'

He said, 'No.'

Then at 4.15 I went over to the Department for what I thought was a final round of talks with the Meriden people. I reported what had happened and said, 'We have cleared the sum for export with the Cabinet. Now I am hoping we can make progress. Are there any problems?'

So Poore said, 'There is a little problem. You want an annual review of the figure and I must have a guarantee for five years.'

I said, 'Look, the Cabinet wants this to come off. It must come off. We have got to find a way.' I banged the table and I was a bit rude.

He then added at the end, 'And I want an inflation guarantee.'

'Come off it,' I said. 'Well, that's it, you'll have to close your factories. Every time anything is agreed, you want something else.' He left the room at this point.

It is this kind of thing that makes me a socialist. If you take the Meriden situation, why should I have to deal with one man about the jobs of 2,000? Caroline put that to me and she is absolutely right. It is an extremely primitive way of dealing with industry.

Friday 28 February

I went off to record an interview in a video studio near Moorgate. I arrived there just as ambulances and fire engines were pouring by, within a few minutes of a crash at Moorgate tube station in which between fifteen and twenty people were killed, an appalling tragedy.

Saturday 1 March

Today I got a letter, posted in London, written in purple felt pen to Mr Wedgewood (spelt wrongly) Benn, House of Commons. It read, 'You rotten traitor. Thank God you have only 7 more weeks.' I don't take much notice of death threats, I think because nobody has been murdered in the Palace of Westminster since Spencer Perceval, in 1806. But you never know, with George Brown's attack on me as an enemy of democracy, a good citizen might feel it is his public duty to polish me off. I will just have to take reasonable precautions.

Sunday 2 March

I had a telephone call from Allister Mackie of the *Scottish Daily News*. He told me that just before Bob Maxwell went to Moscow two days ago, he made a bid for the whole of the paper, insisting that in return for his £100,000 investment, he should be made Chairman and Chief Executive and the whole co-operative structure should be wound up, leaving him in charge. Allister said it was a terrible bombshell.

I said, 'Look, there are two points. First of all, remember that if Maxwell wants to take it over, it is the first real independent proof of viability because he wouldn't want to take over a dead duck. Secondly, call his bluff, don't change the prospectus because if you bring it back to Ministers, they will kill it. So issue the prospectus as far as you can, as it is.'

He said he had a telephone call through to Maxwell in Moscow. An hour later he called me back saying he had made it clear to Maxwell that they were not prepared to accept his conditions and Maxwell had backed down, so it looks as if they are safe. I was delighted.

Tuesday 4 March

Frances Morrell had rewritten the text of a talk I am giving to American press correspondents, leaving out all the good bits. So I lost my temper and stamped and shouted. She said, 'Well, we have got to be careful.' I said, 'Yes, but this won't help.' I cooled down and apologised. It is becoming clear that I can't make the speech I wanted to at all.

Wednesday 12 March

To the House of Commons, where Harold made his statement on the Dublin summit of the heads of the EEC governments to finalise British terms. It was really rather sad to see the Tories waving their order papers and Labour people silent, except for the pro-Market group. It is all over bar the shouting. Shirley Williams reiterated on the radio today that she would resign from the Government if the country voted to leave the Common Market. So, in fact, she has now established freedom to dissent.

Tuesday 18 March

A momentous day in the history of Britain.

At Cabinet we had before us the papers detailing the renegotiation package, and for the first time the issue of sovereignty was discussed properly. The crucial question was whether the Community was to be a supranational structure or a community of sovereign states.

Harold brought us on to the main question. Should we accept the terms or not? 'I recommend that we should stay in and that is the view of the

Foreign Secretary, though he will speak for himself. We have substantially achieved our objectives, the Community has changed *de facto* and *de jure*. The attitude of the Commonwealth has changed too. The Commonwealth wants us to stay in, and the Commonwealth trade patterns have regrettably changed. If we had a free trade area for the UK, the conditions upon us would be stiff or stiffer. I am only persuaded 51 per cent to 49 per cent, indeed I had anxieties right up to the last few days, but I now recommend that we stay in.'

Jim Callaghan followed, 'In supporting you, Harold, I would like to say something about the development of Europe. I am unashamedly an Atlanticist, but we are living in a regional world and we must use the regional organisations. The Soviet Union does not find our membership of the EEC a hindrance to détente. Indeed, I believe that secretly they might like us in, to control the Germans. The seventy-seven non-aligned countries which are now banded together at the United Nations have the potential to destroy the UN and we are better able to withstand them in a regional group. As to the prospects for democractic socialism in the Community, four of the countries are Labour, or have Labour representation in the Government: Holland, Denmark, Germany and the Republic of Ireland, and now Britain. The market economy as an idea is quite flyblown, and the withdrawal of Britain would strain our relations with Ireland.

He quoted Benjamin Franklin: ' "When I first looked at the terms for this Constitution I was not persuaded of it. As wisdom came, I came to see that I was wrong." '

In the end, it was sixteen to seven for staying in. Harold then said, 'I hope that nobody will think the result has anything to do with the way I composed the Cabinet because when I formed it a year ago, there were eight for Europe, ten against and five wobblies. Now, of those who have expressed their view, who intends to take advantage of the agreement to differ?'

Six of us said Yes – myself, Barbara, Michael, Willie, Peter and Eric.

Thus it was that the Cabinet reached its view to stay in the Common Market.

We finished and at 1.30 I walked through Downing Street, back to the office. After that, I just needed to unwind.

Thursday 20 March
Cabinet at 10.30 – and it turned out to be most acrimonious and dramatic. Peter had told me that there had been a tremendous scene last night and when we got into Cabinet, Harold began to speak.

'I've pulled you in without officials because a very dangerous situation has developed. When I gave permission for an agreement to differ, I assumed that the anti-Market people would appoint a spokesman to speak for them. Instead I find that there has been a press conference, a statement by dissenting Ministers, an Early Day Motion, and an NEC resolution in circulation asking the special conference to fight against a government decision. I know one or two pro-Market MPs may be campaigning but this is an attempt to bounce the NEC and it's dangerous.

'I cannot lead a Cabinet when its members mobilise outside agencies including the NEC. It is impossible for me to keep the Cabinet together on this basis. One Minister offered to resign last night, but I don't want to lead a rump. It has been a field day for the Tories and I have got to face Parliamentary Questions today. We must face it, it could be 1931 all over again. If we get disorganised, there are members of the Party who would put the Common Market before the Party. What I'm afraid of from this polarisation is a pro-Market coalition, a Tory-dominated coalition with perhaps a titular Labour leader – and it would have much worse relations with the trade union movement than even Heath. Indeed, I doubt if democracy could survive, and I'm not going to play it this way. The Cabinet should discuss it and find a solution by 12.30 today.'

Shirley Williams said, 'I will never join a coalition. I had hoped that the Party would show the same charity towards dissenters as the Cabinet.'

Michael Foot, who had spoken to Harold about this last night, thought the problem was not insoluble but we couldn't have a cut-and-dried solution by 12.30. He said to Harold, 'It's no good saying you can't tolerate members of the Cabinet heading a campaign against the Market. We are entitled to head a campaign. We're not prepared to engage in a charade. We are going to make our view effective like you. It is the only dignified basis on which to proceed.'

'The most intolerable thing was the Early Day Motion, and the National Executive resolution,' Tony Crosland chipped in.

Denis tried to lower the temperature of the debate. 'The solidarity of the Cabinet is what matters and the Party must be as tolerant. The bulk of the activists don't even think the Common Market is important. Ministers on the NEC must not establish a collective decision, it would be damaging, it would go to the Party Conference, and therefore I want to ask those Ministers concerned to withhold their support for anti-Market campaigns. It would split us deeply, worse than it did when we were in opposition.'

Willie Ross added, 'We are all collectively responsible for the well-being of the Labour Movement. I opposed the Referendum but the Leader is now being tied. We have no one else to rely on but Harold Wilson. We must limit the damage and drop the campaign against the Leader because the logic of it is only too clear. Ministers ought to be a bit busier in their own offices.'

Barbara said, 'The accusation then is about the press conference and that it is intolerable to campaign against the Cabinet.'

'I never said that,' Harold interrupted. 'I shall apply for legal aid if this sort of thing is said.'

'Well,' said Barbara, 'if it had gone the other way, I'm sure the pro-Marketeers would have campaigned for the Market. I have followed the guidelines, I refused to debate with Shirley Williams on television. But you're also saying we shouldn't embroil the Party. That's naïve, and the guidelines didn't cover the Party anyway.'

'I sent *instructions*, not guidelines, to Ministers when they were appointed last year, that they were always Ministers first.'

During coffee break, Harold slipped away up to his study. We met again at noon, without Harold, and with Ted in the chair.

Bob Mellish began by saying, 'We have underestimated the strength of the anti-Market vote. There are about 160 pro- and about 140 anti-Market MPs, and a split would damage the Movement. The London CLPs are broadly anti-Market but they don't really care. We could make the Prime Minister look a laughing stock. I plead with the Ministers on the NEC not to use their power. And as for Harold, I hope he will not overreact because this is a test of his leadership.'

Crosland thought we'd got off to a bad start. 'The people in Grimsby don't worry and I shall persuade them not to take a view.'

Roy Jenkins said this situation was endemic in a referendum, which is why he was against it, but he didn't want to make too much of that. He didn't think the press conference or the Early Day Motion were important, but freedom for campaigning must be absolute. Ministers on the NEC had not considered these matters. The Leader's position would be impossible and we must have symmetry all round.

Roy Mason argued that the PLP was bitter because of the acts of a minority. It was all planned before Tuesday – the Motion, the blackmailing of MPs to sign, and the NEC round robin. As for television, Michael, Peter and Tony Benn had all been on, and it was a devious and clever conspiracy.

'We're on the brink,' said Elwyn, 'the Prime Minister's near to resignation. It could be a disaster for social democracy if he went. The NEC resolution will tear the Party apart. Other Ministers might resign.'

'Well, if the Prime Minister resigns, we'd all be out anyway,' said Jim.

'Withdraw the motion then,' said Elwyn.

Michael suggested that the matter be deferred. The talks should go on for the next day or two, maybe Ron should put up a statement to supersede the NEC resolution.

Jim endorsed Michael's proposal for more time, and Ted said that it looked as if we were going to have to rely on Harold to get us off the hook once again.

It was, without doubt, the most extraordinary Cabinet meeting I have ever attended.

Friday 21 March
To Meriden in the West Midlands. There was no one to meet us at first because they were all so busy, which was good. There are about 170 people working there now, at a flat-rate pay of £50 a week – a dream for them after

eighteen months of privation. They have 2,000 applicants to work at what is £20 below the going rate in Coventry. No supervision, and no clocking in. They have elected organisers in each shop and they've managed to cut out a lot of the paperwork.

Thursday 27 March
I had a runaround on the *Scottish Daily News*. I had told my colleagues that the Action Committee were £40,000 short and recommended that the Government put in the difference, but I had had no favourable response at all. I asked Roy Williams to ring the Prime Minister to fix for me to see him this afternoon to discuss the NEB appointments and the *Scottish Daily News*. Roy set that up but Harold later cancelled the meeting. So I was just about to send a bitter minute around to the Prime Minister and everybody else saying, 'You have now killed the *Scottish Daily News*' when I thought I had better ring Allister Mackie first. I apologised for not succeeding and he said, 'I never thought you would. Maxwell is going to put up the extra money.' I literally leapt for joy.

At 3.30 Bob Wright of the AUEW and Jack Service came to discuss Ferranti. They said the Ferranti brothers, or Basil at least, had tried to persuade the unions to agree to just a 25 per cent government holding so that the family interests in the firm could be preserved. In fact, we are going to have to go up to 75 per cent or 85 per cent holding as a result of the need to put in large sums of money and to value the shares correctly.

Sunday 20 April
Willie Whitelaw has made a statement that the Tories would not feel bound by a negative referendum vote and Frances advised me to involve Mrs Thatcher over this. So at 1.30 I rang the Press Association and dictated this letter, embargoed until 5 am.

Dear Mrs Thatcher,
Mr Whitelaw has predicted a constitutional crisis if the British people vote No in the Referendum.
As the Labour Party is pledged to accept the result, this could only happen if the Conservative Party in Parliament used their votes to block the people's decision.
Will you please – as Leader of the Conservative Party – say whether or not the Conservative Party in Parliament will consider itself bound by a majority vote for British withdrawal from the Common Market?
Everyone is entitled to have a clear – and immediate – answer to this question.
Yours,
Tony Benn

Tuesday 22 April
The papers this morning reported Mrs Thatcher's reply to my letter, saying that the Tories would not be bound by the Referendum, basing herself on what Harold Wilson had said about a referendum not being binding on Parliament.

After Cabinet I sat and talked to Joe Ashton. He told me that Dennis Skinner and others had asked when I was going to make my bid against Harold. Right-wingers were saying that I was so active that it must mean that I was going to challenge Harold.

'For God's sake, Joe, damp that down. I'm doing a marvellously interesting job and I've got the Referendum on my plate.'

'Well, don't forget that if you lose the Referendum and we stay in Europe and have a million unemployed in November, Harold will have some questions to answer.'

I said I knew that.'

Friday 25 April
I learned from Ron Vaughan that Harold Wilson had arranged that in future all former Prime Ministers were to have their own car and chauffeur for life. That's never happened before and indeed until 1970 even the Leader of the Opposition didn't have a car and a chauffeur. It was Heath who agreed that for Harold. Of course now Harold has returned the favour, but he has also given a car and driver for life to Home and Macmillan. The drivers in the car pool are saying, 'The crafty bugger must be preparing to get out, and then *he'll* have a car for life.' That's the conclusion to be drawn, because when he does go, he'll never be made Leader of the Opposition again.

Wednesday 30 April
A journalist from the *Daily Mail* turned up at home and asked Caroline how Joshua was in hospital. She said, 'Joshua is not in hospital' – thank God, he was home at the time, so she knew nothing had happened to him at school.

Then the reporters went to the school and asked the same question. They went to Hilary's house, and even tried to get in touch with Stephen at Keele University. It was hysterical harassment.

Monday 19 May
At 9.45 pm there was a bombshell. It was announced that Monty Finniston had dropped the redundancies and that the BSC and TUC had reached an agreement on other ways of tackling the steel industry's problems. It was a complete victory and I don't think I've gone to bed happier for a very long time. It was the workers who had done it, not me.

Thursday 22 May
In the *Socialist Worker* today was a piece saying that what really terrified the

Establishment was that I was fighting for jobs, while they were trying to sack people and this was the real offence, together with workers' participation and public ownership.

So for the first time, the ultras have had to take on board my strategy and to identify the divisions between Healey and Thatcher, who are the monetarists, Heath and Shirley Williams, who are corporatist coalitionists, and myself.

Friday 23 May

Harold was on television tonight. He was questioned about the economic situation and the Common Market. He just waffled. Then they asked him about me and he said, 'Oh well, Mr Benn is a bogeyman like Lloyd George and Churchill and Bevan.'

Robin Day said, 'But you've attacked him yourself, called him an Old Testament prophet.'

'Well, he dreams about the future but what he says isn't government policy,' Harold said.

'Are you going to dismiss him?'

'When I make my ministerial dispositions, I shall see you get a copy.'

That was a clear indication that he intends to get rid of me; actually it gives me a marvellous feeling of liberation.

Tuesday 3 June

Neil Kinnock picked me up and drove me to Cardiff. He thought it was essential to keep together all the people who had come to work in the Labour Movement against the Market. Two thousand people were waiting, an enormous meeting. Michael Foot turned up, the first time I'd seen him since he had come back from Venice and he looked pretty old and tired.

There were a few 'Keep Britain In Europe' people waving their banners, which helped to make it interesting.

Thursday 5 June – Common Market Referendum

Up at 6 o'clock and back to London. Melissa and I walked to St Peter's Church Hall, Portobello Road, where we cast our votes – the first time Melissa had voted.

Back to Bristol, where Caroline met me and we drove around in a lorry for four hours with the loudspeaker simply shouting, 'No to the Common Market.'

The ITN 10 o'clock news predicted a 69 per cent Yes vote and a 29 per cent No vote, so it looks like an enormous majority for staying in.

I rang Frances. She's realistic about it. 'Oh well, people are sick of elections, they are glad it is settled. Harold has scored a tremendous triumph, but it's over and done with now. The Left has played its trump card and been soundly defeated. This is the moment really to fade out.' If that is the case my inclination is to get out and work on the sidelines.

I worked out a draft statement on the referendum. I would say that it had been a good debate and that I accepted the verdict. It is half past midnight, I am desperately tired. It looks as if in this great referendum, the British people have overwhelmingly voted for Common Market membership, but it may be that even the leaders of the three parties and the entire press have not been able to secure more than 50 per cent of the vote, and that is less than wholehearted consent. I must not be resentful but that might be worth pointing out.

There is a swing to the right, which I think one has to accept will continue for the remainder of the 1970s. The 1980s may be different but it is going to be a long hard wait.

Friday 6 June
Got home from the POEU conference at Blackpool to find a dozen journalists gathered in the front garden, plus a television unit. I said I would make a statement when I had seen the complete results.

Stephen and Hilary were in the house with Dick Clements, then Frances and Francis arrived, followed by Michael Meacher and Joe Ashton. It soon became clear that there was a Yes majority everywhere.

Jack Jones was on the television, saying that if Tony Benn was moved from the Department of Industry it would be a grave affront to the trade union movement. He was serious, strong and principled.

To the House of Commons at 6.15 to the National Referendum Campaign party. Neil Marten was host, Douglas Jay, Enoch Powell and many more were there. Enoch came over to me; I don't think I've spoken to him properly since I attacked him in the Election for his rascist views.

'Well, Enoch,' I said, 'you certainly got your case across clearly and concisely, and the great merit of it all was that it was good political education.'

'The great political education is only just beginning,' he replied.

'What do you mean?'

He told me that he'd just come from the ITN studios in a taxi, and the taxi driver had asked him, 'Are you Mr Powell?'

'Yes,' said Enoch.

'What attitude are you adopting towards the Common Market, Mr Powell?'

Enoch was much humbled by this and said to the taxi driver, 'Do you remember I used to be a member of the Conservative Party?'

'Yes,' the taxi driver said.

'Do you remember why I left the Conservative Party?'

The taxi driver said no, he had never heard the reason. So Enoch asked how he had voted in the Referendum.

'I voted No.'

'Oh, did you?' said Enoch. 'Why?'

'Well, I heard there was some talk of a European Parliament and I was not prepared to see the British Parliament put under a European Parliament.'

The point Enoch was making to me was that the campaign had not gone on long enough for people to understand exactly what everybody was saying, but they had picked up the gist of it.

At the end of the day, we heard that 17 million people had voted to stay in, and 8.5 million to come out, which was some achievement considering we had absolutely no real organisation, no newspapers, nothing.

Monday 9 June

Harold made his statement on the Referendum, and afterwards, in the Tea Room, I heard he wanted to see me at 6. I walked over to Number 10 and went into the Cabinet Room, where Harold was waiting, looking very brown and relaxed. I sat some way from him and he said, 'I'll come straight to the point. I'd like you to take Energy.

'It is a very important department, dealing with North Sea oil; the negotiations with the oil companies are under way with Harold Lever and Edmund Dell. It involves the miners, who you know very well, it involves nuclear power which you know inside out, and that's what I want you to take. You've got lots of energy, if you know what I mean,' he said smiling.

I didn't smile.

'You'd enjoy it,' he said. 'It's a very important job.'

I said nothing.

'Well, haven't you got any questions?'

'No,' I replied, 'except how long are you going to give me to think about it?'

'I must know soon. Two hours.'

'Overnight.'

'Oh no,' he said. 'Got to know by 9.45.'

'Well, my wife is away till 10 and I want to discuss it with her, so what about 10.15?'

'Nine forty-five,' he insisted.

'I'll see you in the Lobby at 10. All right?'

I picked up my coat and Ron drove me back to the House.

I said to Roy Williams, 'Clear up my office, remove my banner, take everything out as if I had never been here.' I invited Stephen and Hilary to come to the House because I wanted their advice. I rang Caroline but she was at a governors' meeting at Holland Park School so Melissa, bless her heart, went all the way to the school and pulled Caroline out. Caroline's first thought was that I had been assassinated, which in a way I had.

She came to the House and the evening was spent in endless discussions with a succession of colleagues, with Joe bringing up trayloads of grub from the Dining Room (which I really must pay him for).

The general opinion is that I *should* take Energy, because there is no principle involved in being offered another job in Cabinet.

Ten o'clock came and went, and I heard Harold had called Michael in again before 10 and said he'd decided to postpone the whole matter. That was a good sign.

But after the division, Eric Varley rang and I went down and had a word with him. He is very close to Harold and he told me what had happened. 'I think Harold entered into some commitments with the City or somebody, and he has to get rid of you.'

Tuesday 10 June

To the House of Commons at 11. Judith Hart told me that although she had been reinstated as Minister for Overseas Development by Harold, her office had been told that she would not be allowed to go abroad.

Michael Foot came in, having just spent forty minutes with Harold. He told Harold that he thought I wouldn't take Energy. Harold was very cross and said he was sick of personality politics and all that went with it. Michael said that Roy Jenkins had withdrawn his threat of resignation, which had only been made to protect Reg Prentice.

Harold had told Michael that Fred Mulley would be going to the Department of Education and that Judith had been offered Transport, outside the Cabinet. Reg Prentice was to have Overseas Development, in place of Judith, under the aegis of the Foreign Office.

At 6.10 I was summoned to see Harold in his room in the House of Commons. I had to run the gauntlet of Bernard Donoughue and Joe Haines outside his room. Harold looked at me intently with his piggy little eyes.

'What is your answer?'

'Well, Harold, I have been thinking very hard about it. I am concerned about two things. One, the possible humiliation or downgrading of dissenting Ministers, and two, the implementation of the manifesto.'

'On the manifesto,' said Harold, 'as far as industrial policy is concerned, you know I am as keen on it as you are.'

'Well, I don't accept that, but if you say so the manifesto will go ahead.'

I continued, 'The third thing I'm concerned about is the Party. We've had two General Elections and a referendum which has been a great strain. You yourself said we should all buckle down and you have now created this terrible uncertainty and alienated everybody. The Industry Bill is in chaos because you've taken me off it. With Eric Heffer and myself gone there is nobody to run it. What you are doing is simply capitulating to the CBI, to the Tory press and to the Tories themselves, all of whom have demanded my sacking.'

He said, 'Well, I am not taking Jenkins's advice.'

'I don't give a damn what Jenkins says, you are capitulating and if you think this is going to save you, you've made a great mistake because they'll be pleased for twenty-four hours and then they'll turn on you.'

'They'll turn on me anyway,' Harold said. 'I am just a captain of a cricket team wishing to make changes, and it has got nothing whatever to do with the referendum. I am entitled to make changes.'

I said it was difficult to know when to go, and he had never understood me, always thinking that I was after his job when all I wanted was to see the policy implemented. 'Of course,' I went on, 'this now has to be seen against a much wider background. Michael Young is calling for a statutory pay policy and we are heading for a coalition.'

Harold insisted that that had nothing to do with him. I pointed out that the Movement would interpret it that way.

'You don't speak for the Movement,' he said. 'I know as much about the Movement as you do.'

He pushed me for my decision about the job. Looking back on it, it is possible that if I had refused Energy, he might have kept me in Industry. But as he was going to see the Queen at 6.30, and I am sure she would have had to have advance notice, perhaps he wouldn't have. Indeed, later tonight, I heard that he had said that if I had refused to go to Energy, he would have taken over the Department of Industry himself as he did the Department of Economic Affairs in the 1964–70 Government.

Anyway, I accepted the job. I think he was quite surprised. I walked out and banged the door.

At 7.30 I went over to the Overseas Development Ministry, where Judith was giving a party for her staff. She was almost in tears. I gave her all the arguments for not resigning and told her that we'd both been humiliated, but one couldn't resign because of personal pride. She refused to accept it, saying how close she had been to Harold, how she had helped him in the campaign to become Leader. Now she believed he hated her. I suddenly felt that we had to save her. I decided to ring Number 10 and ask Harold if Michael and I could see him. We went over to Harold's. Michael began, 'Now look Harold, we have come to see you because we want to be constructive. We are very concerned about Judith. It is quite reasonable to offer her Transport, it is a very important department and Tony and I have urged her to take it. But it must be in the Cabinet.'

'Oh,' said Harold, 'we can't do that. We would have to introduce a Bill to increase the size of the Cabinet.'

'You've done it before, you can do it again,' said Michael.

'I can't have people arguing, we don't change the Cabinet to fit people.'

Michael was warning Harold of the unsettling effect all this was having on the Party, when I came in. 'Now look, Harold, let us be quite plain about this. It is victimisation, either because of the referendum –'

'It is nothing to do with the referendum –' Harold interrupted.

'You now offer her a Minister of State's job, number three in the Department of Environment, with the first two – Crosland and Silkin – in the Cabinet.'

Harold said he couldn't discuss it but I added that he appeared to be making a clean sweep of everyone who had ever had anything to do with industrial policy. Judith had gone, Eric had been sacked, I had been moved, Michael is being moved –'

'Who told you that?'

'That's what Barbara told me,' I said, realising I shouldn't have.

Harold insisted that Judith's had been a sideways move, and that, in fact, I had accepted a bigger demotion than her because of my attachment to the Industry Bill.

'Don't reopen that, I've said what I have to say.'

'Judith would not take the job, unlike you Tony. You very bravely did.'

'Look Harold, you say it is suicide but there is no doubt that you gave her the knife.'

'Well,' he said, 'she shouldn't have taken that attitude. We can't have prima donnas.'

Then Barbara turned up. I do admire her for that, it was nearing midnight and she had got dressed again after a heavy day, jumped in a taxi and come all the way to the House to save Judith. She fought her corner and even said she would accept being replaced by Judith at the DHSS.

By now it must have been becoming clear to Harold that we were not prepared to serve if Judith was not put in the Cabinet. He said that he had made his position clear. 'I've got to do this,' and looking directly at me he said, 'when you have my job, you'll have to do it.' That was intended to annoy Michael and Barbara.

Barbara described Judith's contributions with great affection, and Michael was very courteous. But it was left to me to say time and again, 'It is a basic trade union principle that you do not victimise people after a strike; we will not have it.'

At this point, he began to realise how serious it was and looked a bit shaken. We left saying that we'd be back tomorrow morning to give Harold some time to reconsider.

We went to Room 18 in the House, which was crowded with people – Barbara and Ted, Tony Banks, Frances Morrell, Norman Buchan, Neil Carmichael, Judith and Tony Hart, Margaret Jackson, and John Grant whom I don't trust. I described what had happened and said that Barbara was great and Michael was courteous.

Later Joe said, 'Tony, if you are going to become Leader of the Party, and you now stand well above anyone facing Harold, you have to fight that man, get into the ring like Cassius Clay and knock him out or be knocked out. The Party and the Tribune Group think that you should have held out longer on Energy.'

I took his point. I will have to fight but it will be at a moment of my own choosing, on the cuts or the statutory pay policy, or the reactionary economic policy.

If Harold goes, I should think Denis Healey would take over as the strong man in a crisis, or perhaps Jim. Roy would not get it and I certainly would not because the PLP would be too nervous that I would lose them the Election. I suppose I have a vague interest in Wilson going on, but what we have seen today is a completely new procedure for dealing with reshuffles. The Left must organise and advise those people offered a job or pressured to move out of a job as to what they should do. Wilson has made a fatal error and he will not be Leader of the Labour Party by the end of the year.

8

1975–76

Wednesday 11 June 1975
The press were outside our house again by 7, three cars filled with reporters, poised with telescopic lenses. Ron Vaughan turned up at 7.30 with all the morning papers. The *Guardian* had it right: 'Wilson gives Benn's head to the City'. By the time Josh left for school, there were about fifty journalists, two television units and three or four radio interviewers with microphones standing outside. We had decided not to say anything at all to the press, so when they confronted Josh, he ignored them. One of them shouted, 'You fucking well answer my questions.' Josh took no notice so they said, 'You push off, you little shit.'

Now Josh, at sixteen, is perfectly capable of exchanging harsh words with anybody of his own age, but when two or three grown men who, in a sense, are symbols of authority, swore at him like that, it really worried him.

Ron walked ahead of me with my bag and Caroline, Stephen and Hilary watched me as I left. I walked out slowly and as I opened the front gate, the television cameras turned, the flashbulbs popped and the mikes were pushed menacingly at me. 'Do you regard your job as a promotion or demotion?' 'What do you think of Mrs Hart?' and so on.

I just walked through them as if they weren't there and that made them wild. They had dehumanised me in the press, now I was dehumanising them by not acknowledging their existence.

Monday 30 June
I found in my red box a farewell letter from Sir Antony Part. It read:

Personal, 29 June

Dear Secretary of State,
It was sad that, for whatever reason and perhaps due to a misunderstanding, we did not say goodbye to each other when you left the Department. At any rate I want to write now on behalf of the staff of the Department as well as myself, to thank you for all the many courtesies you displayed towards your civil servants, and so far as I am concerned, the sympathetic consideration you showed to me during my recent illness.

It was especially kind of you to find the time to come and visit me in the hospital and write as you did to my wife with your programme of radical change. Granted the political balance within the Cabinet, you were bound to face your senior advisers with some difficult problems, but whatever our professional anxieties were from time to time, we enjoyed the challenges and the stimulation, and you were generous in your appreciation of the support that you received on such key subjects as the Industry Bill and the Post Office.

We admired your outstanding skill in communication (even when, occasionally, we were worried about what you were communicating!) and the deftness of your drafting. But, important though these are, they are less significant than the general thrust of your philosophy, so clearly illustrated in its many facets in the book of speeches (and it is characteristic I know that they were speeches and not private memoranda) that you kindly gave me.

In our different careers we have both sailed through rough waters and, indeed, I expect we should each be surprised if the waters were ever to become smooth, and possibly not know what to do with ourselves if that were to happen! For the marriage of ideas and reality is unending and fascinating, and the responsibility for the fate of others is an unremitting burden for people who are in positions of leadership.

But where would either of us be without such challenges – and how would either of us fare without the imperturbable and invaluable help of such people as Roy Williams?

I send you from myself, Peter Carey and all those who served you in this department, the most sincere salutations together with my own warm thanks for your personal kindness.

Yours sincerely,
Antony Part

No one can resent a warm letter; in the end I sent the following reply:

Dear Sir Antony,

It was very good of you to write and I appreciated it. I well realise that my brief period in the Department of Industry imposed a heavy strain on you and your officials arising from new policies and initiatives which in turn aroused a major public debate.

Throughout all this I received every possible personal help and I hope you will convey my gratitude to all those involved at various levels, from your own throughout the Department, and including the Private Office.

I am sorry that the pace of the reshuffle made personal farewells impossible, but that is one of the hazards of political life. I do hope you are completely fit again and that the anxieties of the winter will never recur.

With kind regards,
Tony Benn

Wednesday 2 July
At 9.15 I saw Bernard Ingham, my new press officer, who asked me about my personal position. I told him I was strongly opposed to the proposal for public expenditure cuts and that there were four options: to put up with it, to oppose it from the inside, to come out and oppose it constructively, or to come out and oppose it destructively. I thought opposing it from the inside was perhaps the best thing to do.

He asked if it would be a good idea to brief Ian Aitken of the *Guardian*. I arranged for this to be done later.

Thursday 3 July
At 7.30 a group of Ministers gathered in my room – Peter Shore, Michael Foot, Stan Orme, Albert Booth, Joan Lestor, Michael Meacher, and Barbara Castle. Frances Morrell joined us. At the prospect of resignations by the Left, Barbara began shouting, 'The Left, it is always the Left, you always lose. Why don't you fight? Why don't you put up an alternative?'

Shirley Williams has the room next door and the walls are so thin, she probably heard every word.

I said, 'I put up an alternative months ago on import controls.'

'Oh, that's no good,' she said. Barbara thinks socialism is about the social wage, which of course is based on the expenditure of her own department. Although she argues against a statutory policy, she would accept it if it would prevent public expenditure cuts in the DHSS. Actually she's not on our side at all, she's on the other side.

Boy, was she shrieking, throwing her arms in the air. 'All right, you say I am not fair, but nobody has ever been fair to me.' That revealed the burning sense of personal injustice which makes Barbara tick. She is a tough woman and she certainly fights for what she gets, but she is very cynical, and she hates my guts. One thing's for sure, all of this will get back to Harold. If Barbara tells him we are thinking of resigning, that will really worry him.

Sunday 6 July

The *Observer* had a huge two-page spread on the government U-turn. It included a leading article praising Wilson for adopting the Heath policy, and a piece on Jack Jones describing him as the Godfather, privy to everything that was going on and supported by Michael Foot.

Tuesday 15 July

At 3.30 Sir Eric Drake of British Petroleum came to see me and I went out of my way to be charming. He said that government holdings of British Petroleum shares must be kept below 50 per cent because it would destroy the credibility of the company in the United States, in New Zealand and elsewhere – BP operates in eighty countries. Therefore, he wanted the BP Burmah shares sold off in the open market but not to foreign governments. Well, I'm not accepting that.

I had contemplated giving Drake the chairmanship of BNOC but he was so negative and hostile that I changed my mind. I'm glad I saw him and it is probably a good thing to be on reasonably good terms with him, though he is the most Tory of Tories.

Spent most of the afternoon on the Petroleum Bill Committee.

Spoke to Gerald Kaufman, who told me that, at a meeting in Oxford, a man had got up and said, 'The only reason that Tony Benn didn't nationalise Westland is that he has shares in it.'

Well, that's an extraordinary story. I was grateful for him telling me.

Thursday 17 July

The papers over the last couple of days have reported the news from New York that Exxon has openly admitted to paying $51 million (£20 million) to Italian politicians and political parties over the last nine years. That's over £2 million a year flowing from a single oil company into Italian political funds. The number of people who could be bought, corrupted, suborned, diverted, blackmailed and assassinated with £20 million defies the imagination. One shouldn't be in any doubt at all as to what we're up against and I shall use this if necessary to defend the development of BNOC.

Saturday 19 July
Went shopping with Melissa and we walked up Kensington High Street. We went into Biba's store which really is the end of a dream. You can see why it failed really because it was the final fling for the excrescences of sixties fashion, now all gone bust.

Tuesday 22 July
I heard today that the problem of what we would do with oil off the Falkland Islands has been settled by the Foreign Office. They have insisted that we agree to discuss with Argentina joint exploration of the South Atlantic, and this is intended to get us off the hook.

Lunch with Frank Kearton at Courtaulds headquarters in Calenese House. I have known Frank now for nine years and he is resigning tomorrow as Chairman of Courtaulds.

We talked about Harold Wilson and he said he had met Harold recently and Harold had told him, 'In politics, timing is everything,' and compared himself to Stanley Baldwin. Harold has compared himself to all sorts of people in his Walter Mitty life. He was the Kennedy figure in 1962 with 'Let's get Britain moving again'. Then he became a bit of a Macmillan figure. Then he and Lyndon Johnson were the greatest pals. Now he's Baldwin. That just about sums him up.

We discussed Jack Jones, for whom Frank has enormous respect because he's a great statesman. We talked about worker participation and economic policy and I mentioned the co-operatives. I said that the Treasury was now running things.

'I don't think the Treasury has a policy,' he said. 'They stumble along from day to day. When William Armstrong resigned from the Civil Service, he had a little dinner party at Sunningdale and I was invited. He just kept saying that all was lost, and there was no hope for the country and he couldn't see his way forward at all. I have never seen a man so utterly defeated.'

I said, 'That's because he was the one who persuaded Heath to drop the Party's objections to the prices and incomes policy, and then he saw the policy crumble in the face of the miners and I think he was utterly demoralised.'

Melissa came into the House and everyone admired her out on the terrace, saying she looked like an actress from a television programme, 'The Main Chance'. She was shy as the MPs came up to speak to her but I was so proud of her.

Tuesday 29 July

Yet more strange goings-on with our rubbish. For some time it has been collected very early each morning, whereas before, Kensington Borough Council only collected it once a week. We wondered who was taking it and, as we read recently in the paper that someone had bribed the trashmen in Washington to give them all the rubbish from Kissinger's house, it occurred to me that this might be happening to me. So I decided to buy a shredding machine and also Joshua fitted up a wire leading from the rubbish area at the front of the house to a bell in the house.

Talked to Bernard Donoughue, who was interested in the fact that officials were mainly concerned to protect the confidentiality of official advice to Ministers, which is why the Crossman *Diaries* worried them so much.

At Cabinet we talked about Meriden and the future of the co-operatives, and the discussion threw light on a number of things. First of all, it was absolutely clear that both Court Line, and Meriden, which is Eric Varley's razor job, are being used to discredit my period at the Department of Industry. They are trying to make out that it was incompetence on my part, and linking it with Rolls Royce, Upper Clyde Shipbuilders and Concorde.

Secondly, Harold's strategy in moving me from Industry is not only to reverse the policy, but also to ensure that I get the blame for the troubles that come when the policy *is* reversed. He is hoping to chip away at my standing within the Movement at the same time as the new policy is being prepared – a Treasury policy under which people will not be able to go to the Industry Department for money because there will be no money, no help, no tea and no sympathy. Gerald Kaufman is certainly in there digging around seeing what he can find that might be damaging to me.

Friday 5 September

Got to the House of Commons at 12.10 and missed the bomb at the Hilton Hotel by about ten minutes. It killed two people and wounded sixty-nine.

Thursday 25 September

There were more reports in the press on the hearings in Washington which have revealed that the CIA was opening the mail of senior politicians, including Nixon before he was elected. One really is indebted to the American investigative process for bringing things to light. No doubt similar things have happened here and exactly on the same basis, but they are kept completely secret.

Caught the train to Blackpool and checked into the Imperial Hotel.

Friday 26 September – Labour Party Conference, Blackpool

The papers today reported the admission by the FBI that they had engaged in over 250 domestic burglaries for political and other purposes. There was also a report in the *New York Times* that the CIA was again giving money to West European socialist parties to intervene in Portugal.

Just before the Executive at 10 I had a word with Bryan Stanley of the POEU and I mentioned my concern about telephone-tapping.

'Oh yes,' he said, 'there's no question about it. I believe that the Tories were engaged in a widespread surveillance campaign involving the telephone-tapping of activists in the trade union movement and the Labour Party, as well as in the Communist Party. The aim was to prepare a general dossier and, in the run-up to an Election, blacken the character of political opponents.

'Whenever I tried to find out anything about it from my own members, I discovered that this telephone-tapping is done by specially recruited people who, though they may be members of my union, are not prepared to say a word about it. There is tight security amongst them. It goes on on a more limited scale now, but during the referendum campaign, for example, people in the anti-Common Market groups on one or two occasions picked up their telephones and found recordings of what they'd just said coming back to them.'

Sunday 28 September
When we were last at the Imperial Hotel two years ago, Tony Wilson, a seventeen-year-old who worked in the hotel as a sort of page boy, told us that he earned only £14 for an eighty-hour week. I suggested he form a union. Well, he knocked on the bedroom door and there he was with his little spectacles and his cheeky manner, and he said, 'Oh, Mr Benn, I formed that union. When they heard that Mr Benn had suggested it, it spread like wildfire. We've got the TGWU here – and we're 60 per cent unionised – and we've now got £20 for a forty-hour week.'

I was invited to the POEU/UPW dinner and was asked to speak. Afterwards Bryan Stanley paid a tribute to Roy, Denis and Jim, and said, 'I want to say a word about Tony Benn. I'm very sorry that he was moved from the Department of Industry and from Telecommunications. It's not for me to comment on the circumstances but he was the best Minister the Post Office has ever had because he identified himself with our members. We were very sad to see him go.'

It was a courageous speech and Jim and Denis looked absolutely sick. I wish Harold had been there but he arrived later, just as we were thanking and leaving. I tried to avoid him but he saw me through the door.

Wednesday 1 October
I worked till 3 in the morning on my speech for the industrial policy debate today. Judith presented the industrial policy statement in a very academic way. There were various other speakers. A Young Socialist from West Stirlingshire made a marvellous speech. It was the youngsters in many ways

who stole the limelight. One man got up and said, 'I cannot let this occasion go by without saying plainly that the removal of Tony Benn from the Department of Industry simply for implementing our policies has created a deep mood of cynicism and despair.'

I spoke for about fifteen minutes and it was very effective. I got a rather different sort of standing ovation from Michael, Denis and Harold, in that it began on the fringes and moved into the middle. I don't think Jack Jones stood up and I know he was reading his newspaper throughout my speech, as he had through Eric Heffer's and Judith Hart's.

I had been asked to go with Jack Jones to see a delegation from the TGWU about offshore oil workers, so I left the platform and Jack walked out with me. Well, he turned on me and I hope I can be forgiven for repeating what he said.

'What's the fucking use of talking about redundancies in that general way when I've got these fucking workers and you have done fuck all about them?'

'The offshore oil workers?' I asked.

'Yes, these people at Graythorpe. I don't suppose you've ever been there.'

'Not only have I been there, Jack, but I've been trying to get new orders for them from the oil companies for the last two months. Indeed, yours is the one union that hasn't taken any interest whatever in this issue.'

He said, 'Well, what about getting union recognition on the rigs?'

'I'm working on that too.'

'The National Union of Seamen have done a deal on their own in which the men on the rigs are members of the NUS, not the TGWU.'

I said, 'You've been slow off the mark. They've done it and it's nothing to do with me. I'm not in charge of the National Union of Seamen.'

He was boiling with rage. 'Who do they think they are, all this criticism of the Government?' and he referred to the Tribune Group. I told him I wasn't even a member of the Tribune Group.

We arrived at the Planet Room, where all these awfully nice guys – shop stewards and one full-time official – were waiting in the hallway. I shook hands with them and in Jack's presence I told them what I had done.

'I've been up to Scotland. I've been to Graythorpe and Nigg, and I've seen the union committee and the Scottish TUC. I've written to the oil companies, and the OPEC oil prices will help. I've also arranged a new licensing round. I'll continue to help in any way I can. I'll keep in touch with Jack Jones. If you want to come to London you can see me. Jack has been pressing me on this.' This was quite untrue and he knew it, and when I said that I think he felt guilty.

Friday 10 October
I had a dream that Harold had called me in and said, 'I want you to be Vice-Chamberlain of the Royal Household with a seat in the House of Lords in charge of boxing under the Minister of Sport.' He told me this in the great

Cabinet Room, which was full of people. 'I'm afraid this doesn't mean a place in the Cabinet for you,' he said. I replied, 'Harold, I must think about it,' and Sir John Hunt said, 'Boxing is very important. We must preserve the quality and excellence of the Lonsdale Belt.'

Tuesday 21 October

The *Daily Mirror* ran a story under the heading, 'Britain to become the nuclear dustbin of the world', by a Stanley Bonnet. In fact, the man behind it was Bryn Jones from Friends of the Earth, who is the industrial correspondent on the *Mirror*. It was about the BNFL contract under which we would reprocess 4,000 tons of irradiated fuel from Japan and would then have the problem of disposing of the toxic waste. I decided to go on the 'World at One' so a chap came along to interview me. I think I put the case across and I told the Department to put out a background note.

I rang Marcia and invited her for a sandwich lunch. She came in Harold's car and gave me a message from Harold, 'Tell him to keep cheerful.' I asked how it was going at Number 10 and she said it was awful. 'In the old days I had Gerald Kaufman to work with but now it's Haines who's the official man and Bernard Donoughue,' whom Marcia thought was just feeding Harold's insecurities.

'I have good personal relations with Harold but I'm shut out completely.'

She said that Harold sometimes nearly gives up and she was sure that one day he'd resign.

Well, that's a load of rubbish! She asked what I thought about being moved. I said, 'It was like moving Nye Bevan from the Health Service. It was a complete capitulation.'

'Harold was under heavy pressure,' she said, 'not just from outside but from inside too.' Well to hell with that. 'Harold reported that you had lectured him more than he had ever been lectured before. He does have a difficult time and he thought it best to move you, and he found a way which both met the criticism and annoyed the others.'

I said we should keep in touch because I like Marcia. If she went it would be awful.

Thursday 23 October

At 8.50 this morning, just before I went off to work, Caroline and I were in the bedroom and there was the most enormous explosion. I thought it was a bomb in Roy Jenkins's house near by. So I dashed down the stairs and opened the front door and I saw there were a lot of people about 150 yards down the street. Then, through the trees in Campden Hill Square, I saw flames licking up twenty-five to thirty feet and realised that the explosion was over by Hugh Fraser's house. Indeed, it turned out that someone had put a thirty-pound bomb near his Jaguar.

The street was in a tremendous state of uproar with police cars and fire engines all over the place. There had been a bomb just up the road at Notting Hill when the Jordanian Ambassador was hurt, but this was the closest to home and it absolutely shook us. A friend of Josh's, who comes up the hill every day to meet Josh, said the boy just in front of him had been blown off his bicycle. Some of the windows in the house next to ours had been blown out.

The press turned up in their hundreds and Caroline went down and asked whether any schoolchildren had been injured and when they said no, she went up to the school and told the headmaster, so that when anxious parents rang up, he was able to tell them that everything was all right.

Monday 3 November
Arrived at Aberdeen at 8.30 for the landing of the first oil from the Forties Field. After breakfast at the Skeandhu Hotel, a film was shown of the Forties Field and then Harold Wilson arrived with Jim Callaghan, Sir Eric Drake of BP and a lot of others, and we all drove to BP's headquarters at Dyce.

The first thing I noticed was that the workers who actually bring the oil ashore were kept behind a barbed wire fence and just allowed to wave to us as we drove by. We arrived at a huge tent, constructed at a cost of £40,000, and laid with an extravagant red carpet. The tent was about the size of two football pitches and held 1,000 people, most of whom had been brought up from London. We were given a cup of coffee as we waited for the Queen to arrive.

Eventually we were taken out on the dais to watch the Queen's Rolls Royce approaching. Out came the Queen in a green dress, followed by the Duke of Edinburgh and Prince Andrew. She shook hands with all of us, and we went back into the tent and had drinks, and the Queen circulated. Then she went into the computer control room and we followed. She pressed a few buttons I believe before going outside for her walkabout. There, behind another fence, were about 500 Aberdonians waving Union Jacks, and the Queen and the Duke of Edinburgh walked in front of them as if they were animals in a zoo.

At lunch I sat next to Mrs Steel, the wife of David Steel, who is to succeed Drake as Chairman of BP. Jim was on her other side and he said how much he enjoyed the Foreign Office and it wasn't like the Treasury. 'You know, you would enjoy the Foreign Office, Tony.'

I said, 'Well, Jim, perhaps in your second administration that will be possible.' He laughed.

To be frank, the day was a complete waste of time and money, and when you see the Queen in action, everything else is just absorbed into this frozen feudal hierarchy. All the old bigwigs are brought out into the open as if they were somehow responsible for a great industrial achievement, while the workers are presented as natives and barbarians who can be greeted but have to be kept at a distance. It is a disgrace that a Labour government should allow this to continue. I know there is a security problem but there was no need for this. I also felt that this great Scottish occasion was just an opportunity for the London Establishment to come up and lord it over the Scots.

Saturday 8 November

On the train back from Bristol, a nervous, rather weedy-looking buffet car attendant came round with coffee. He told me he served in the army but after four or five stints in Northern Ireland, he had a nervous breakdown. 'It was terrible,' he said. 'The children spit at you, the grown-ups throw stones at you and shield behind the children. My friends were blown up, but what really upset me was that I used to go out with a Catholic girl who was going to be teacher. Her brothers found out and shot her through the knee caps as a punishment for going out with a British soldier. She had to have both legs amputated.'

It was a most brutal story. My God, we have to get out of Ireland.

There was a programme last night about the Orange Order in Glasgow marching through Catholic areas to provoke them. We will have to get out because the English cannot solve the Irish problem.

Tuesday 11 November

The *Scottish Daily News* died yesterday.

Cabinet at 10 and there was an oral report on Chrysler. I had stayed up till 3 am going through all my papers on this. Eric Varley told us that American-owned Chrysler had been in difficulties earlier this year and that 25,000 jobs would be directly affected. Chrysler have said that if the UK took it over, it would have losses of £55 million and another £80 million would be needed for investment. The alternative would be to let it go into liquidation in three months.

I said, 'Prime Minister, this is the biggest collapse in the industrial history of this country, twice the size of UCS, involving perhaps 67,000 people at a cost in unemployment pay of about £70 million. It is a disaster. This is a repeat of the motorbike industry, and it is happening year after year.' Harold Wilson said it wasn't a lame duck, it was a dead duck. '138,000 working days have been lost in disputes in the motor industry this year and the report must go forward and be agreed.'

That was the end of that discussion and we went on to devolution. Had a most fitful night just lying on the couch with the light on and my door open so people could see me. Every time the division bell rang I went to vote – I have no idea how many times.

Thursday 13 November

Cabinet at 10 and the much delayed discussion on public expenditure.

Harold opened by saying this was the hardest of all decisions for any government to make and he hoped there would be no recriminations.

Denis Healey began, 'We are talking about the period when we are returning to full employment. Output will be rising from 1977 to 1979. There will be a shortage of resources and money. We must make room for investment and exports. A 10 per cent increase in investment is expected in 1977–9. We must aim at a balance of payments surplus in 1978–9 or else the debt repayment will burden us and mortgage the North Sea oil. The Crosland proposals for lower cuts would pre-empt resources and would be a recipe for disaster. We cannot escape these cuts. We cannot borrow unless we make the cuts now or within the next six months. We are already borrowing 20 pence in every pound. The only alternatives to public-expenditure cuts are to print money or raise interest rates and a quarter of the PSBR is now due to the recession.

'As for taxation, some increases are inevitable which will undermine the £6 pay-limit policy. If company tax is raised it will either cut jobs, investment or prices: on income tax you might go up by between 5p and 9p in the pound, which will cut take-home pay and the unions will then start bargaining on post-tax income.

'At the Labour clubs you'll find there's an awful lot of support for this policy of cutting public expenditure. They will all tell you about Paddy Murphy up the street who's got eighteen children, has not worked for years, lives on unemployment benefit, has a colour television and goes to Majorca for his holidays.' If that's the case, I'd be interested to know how many people who frequent the Labour clubs actually vote Labour.

Wednesday 19 November
Lunch with the Japanese Ambassador, Mr Kato. His wife was most amusing, very beautiful, and had been brought up in America. We had a long talk about acupuncture – the Ambassador has arthritis and he has had fifteen injections at £20 each which have done him no good at all. Madame Kato said, 'I could have bought a new outfit with that.'

I said, 'Look, I have some acupuncture needles and I'll come and stick them into him any time you like. Then you can have a new outfit.'

Madame Kato asked me if I had heard of pressure points. I said I hadn't and the Ambassador told me that it was part of Zen Buddhism. Madame Kato began to press my hand and pull my fingers, saying, 'This will help your heart, this will help your stomach, this will improve your eyesight,' and we had a good old laugh. It was most unusual because the Japanese are generally rather formal.

Jack Rampton came to see me and we had a helpful talk. I said, 'While we're on staff matters, I'm a bit worried about Bernard Ingham.' He told me Bernard had gone to see him, saying he feared that he'd lost the confidence of Ministers. I said, 'I think that's true but it's a much deeper problem. He doesn't seem to take an interest and isn't very helpful.'

'He's an energetic chap,' Jack said. 'He has an idea of what a Minister should do and he bullies him until he does it.'

I said, 'On the principle that everybody does best what they most enjoy doing, wouldn't it be a good idea to give him a full-time job on energy conservation?'

'That might be one way of doing it or else I could have a word with Douglas Allen of the Civil Service Department and see what can be done.'

Wednesday 26 November
Hilary's twenty-second birthday.

The *Western Daily Press* had a marvellous headline, 'Benn and Son Lead New Market Attack' and said, 'Mr Tony Benn, Energy Secretary, and his son Hilary, together with other Cabinet Ministers . . .' It was because Hilary was on the list of sponsors of the Common Market Safeguards Committee. I was really pleased.

Thursday 27 November
The press reported that Reg Prentice had been rejected by the NEC on his appeal but that some attempt at conciliation was going to be made; Reg has now said there are a number of Trotskyite Labour MPs in the House of Commons. He is doing himself terrible damage and I think his prospect of recovery is slight.

Cabinet, and the first item was the problem of pay beds in the NHS. Barbara Castle said she was faced with militancy by the consultants and the unions and she wanted the Cabinet to agree that she could legislate to phase out pay beds and establish control herself over all private hospitals with more than seventy-five beds in case there was a flood into private hospitals.

Harold Wilson said he didn't mind that (though he had doubts about it) but there would have to be real consultation and there were some things he couldn't say now because they would leak. I guessed that, for the first time, he was talking about Harold Lever leaking to the doctors. On every issue Harold Lever always supports the Right, the rich and the powerful against the Labour Party and all it stands for.

Harold Lever himself said he was against a general holding power, and he thought there was great danger in putting such power in the hands of a Minister. There was a risk of bringing the Government down because there would be a Labour revolt in the House of Commons on private pay beds, and he said there was a lot of Trotskyite pressure on the Health Service.

At the end, Harold Wilson said, 'Don't let's decide anything today. Just empower Barbara and me to see the doctors and we'll have a little miscellaneous committee of Ministers to consider it.'

Listening to the discussion, which could in a way herald the end of the

Health Service, I was reminded that the key question is: Whose interests are you looking after? As a Cabinet it is our job to look after the 90 per cent of the population who use the Health Service and not to worry about the 10 per cent who don't.

Friday 28 November
Up at 6.30 and with Caroline to visit the Bedwas Colliery.

After lunch we headed off down the pit. There had been a great fuss about whether Caroline could come. Ronnie Custis had told us that superstition prevented women being allowed down the pits. So I made the most scrupulous enquiries and could find no trace of this.

Anyway, they decided to send a young nurse from the pit hospital down with Caroline and a party of about twelve of us set off in all the gear – woolly underpants, a blue shirt, a great orange boilersuit, a donkey jacket, socks, boots and a scarf. It was an old pit opened about 1912. We went down about 2,500 yards into the roadway below and sat in a little train which took us up the roadway. Then we walked in the dark with the lamps on our helmets to guide us. We had to crawl about 300 yards along the coalface to see the coal-cutting machine in action.

One of the dangers pointed out to me by the manager was a break in the chain pulling the machine along, and in fact it did break. We could hear a lot of talking and shouting over the loudspeaker system but they were all very polite. Later I realised the reason they didn't want Caroline to come down was because they were afraid of the bad language. In the social club later in the evening, I said, 'That explains why when the chain broke, I could hear the miners up and down saying, "Oh bother it, dash it, golly, it's broken!" ' The miners roared with laughter.

We were underground for about two and a half hours. Then we came up and had a shower and a cup of tea. The characteristics of the mining industry that make it so remarkable are that most of the colliery managers, under-managers, overmen, deputies and shot-firers all started at the pit and worked their way up and therefore there is no management brought in from the outside. There is no real parallel with the rest of British industry in that sense.

The nation is not remotely interested in the mining industry. If there is a pit disaster, they are heroes; if there is a wage claim, they are militants, but as to the rest they simply don't want to know.

Afterwards at the social club we met Neil Kinnock and his wife Glenys, a sweet woman. Arthur Hayward, the chairman of the Lodge, welcomed us. 'Tony, we greet you as a friend. Many of us came over to help you last year because we felt you were a good man and we wanted to assist you during the Election; and we want to make a presentation to you. We want to make you an honorary member of our Lodge in the NUM.'

1 (above). 'The Prime Minister (Attlee) made a long awaited statement on the new defence plans . . . It was received in glum silence on our side of the House.'
2 (left). President Roosevelt, d. 1945. 'Everyone was hushed for some minutes . . . without a doubt everyone was as shocked and as sad as if Churchill himself had died.'

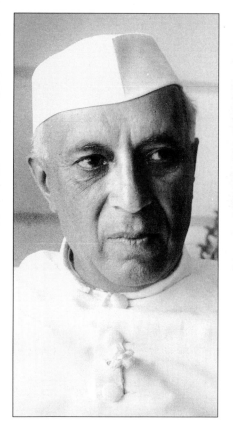

3 (above). 'Denis Healey said Khrushchev used to "murder cats" when he was a child.'

4 (left). 'Nye described his talks with Nehru and the significance of the Communist victory in Kerala.'

5. Baby Joshua with his siblings, (clockwise) Melissa, Stephen and Hilary.

6. 'I took all the children to see Churchill's lying-in-state. They were much impressed, except Joshua who thought we were going to a Lyon's Steak House.' Churchill is seen here with Eden.

7 (above). 'Macmillan's tribute was the most revolting since he and Gaitskell hated each other.' January 1963.

8 (left). 1961 by-election congratulations – a family victory over the Lords.

10 (above). 'Home was asked to form a Government. It is incredible that such a thing should have happened.' 18 October 1963.

9. 'Today Kennedy's alleged assassin was shot while in police custody. The whole thing is so fishy and the shame of the Dallas police is complete.'

11 (below). 'I then knelt on the floor and, one after the other, passed up to the Queen the stamps bearing the words "Great Britain" and no royal head on them.'

12 (left). 'De Gaulle has refused to devalue the franc. I must say I laughed myself sick all day.' November 1968

13 (below). 'We agreed that Heath was not as formidable as we had feared at the time he was chosen leader.'

14 (below). 'I said to the Director General and the Chairman of the BBC "I hear from everybody that you are very worried about my appointment." They both looked rather sheepish.'

15. 'To Chequers this evening
. . . Harold had called me
because he felt the time had
come to listen to his friends.'

16. TB with Old Bristolians,
1974.

17. 'Mrs Thatcher was
reported as saying that two
more terms of office would
exterminate socialism . . .
She'll have a job to outdo
Kinnock.' November 1986.

18. 'Like many rows with Jim, it blew up and blew over and blew out. He couldn't have been nicer.'

19. 'At Cabinet . . . Michael and I were arguing that we should peg top salaries for both civil servants and nationalised industry chiefs.'

20. Snookered in Chesterfield, 1983.

21. Office politics – TB's basement in 1985.

22 (right). 'The streets were packed for Reagan's visit. He began the day by riding round Windsor Great Park in a coach and four with Nancy . . . a movie star acting the part of a King.'

23 (far right). 'People were singing and waving their arms and kissing and hugging. Someone had draped on Nelson's Column a banner with the words Nelson Mandela's Column.' 11 February 1990.

24. 'Neil Kinnock yaps like a little dog at Thatcher's heels and she kicks him aside.'

25. TB with radical, no gimmicks singer and song writer, Billy Bragg.

26 . 'Gorbachev is going flat out to endear himself to the establishment in the West, and I suppose he's gaining a worldwide reputation which he can use for domestic purposes in the Soviet Union.'

27. Last of the Summer Books. With Claire Rayner and Bill Owen on a literary tour.

Afterwards, I was given an overman's stick and all the miners signed it for me – a lovely reminder of the day.

Thursday 4 December

When we came to Foreign Affairs and the EEC, I said, 'Can I ask one question about passports? On television I saw a picture of our blue British passport disappearing and a purple European Community passport being substituted. That really hit me in the guts. It is quite unnecessary. Everybody knows that Britain is in the Common Market. You could put European Community on the back of the existing passport, you could stamp on page 3, "This man is a European whether he likes it or not." But we have got to be careful: like metrication and decimalisation, this really strikes at our national identity and I don't like it.'

Harold Wilson said, 'I don't need to be lectured on Kipling.'

I said, 'Well, Harold, if you can talk to the Commission and keep the common touch, I shan't worry.' Everybody laughed but it is a serious concern.

Saturday 6 December

There was a very funny item in the *Guardian* this morning called 'What Makes Tony Benn Run?' by Martin Walker. It estimated that on my eighteen pints of tea a day for forty years, I would have drunk 29,000 gallons, used 20,000 KW hours of electricity and a ton and a quarter of tea, etc. It quoted what doctors said, what the Tea Council said: that the Jockey club would argue that this was a higher rate of caffeine addiction than was permitted for racehorses.

Tuesday 9 December

Ron Vaughan told me this evening that government drivers had been told to take Ministers a different route home tonight because with the Irish terrorists holding two hostages in Marylebone (the Balcombe Street siege), there is a real fear that the IRA might try to kidnap Ministers to trade them off. I spoke to Stan Orme, who said that his government detective is desperately worried. I rang Caroline to tell her to bolt the front door and close the shutters and not let anyone in. What an extraordinary time.

Tuesday 16 December

At 4, Arthur Hetherington and Denis Rooke, the Chairman and Deputy Chairman of the British Gas Corporation, came about appointments to the Gas Board and I agreed to Don Ryder and the three industrialists they wanted. Of the trade unionists, I wanted Hugh Scanlon and Terry Parry of the Fire Brigades Union. Hetherington said, 'Well, as far as Scanlon is concerned, I want to be sure that the man we have is loyal to the country.'

The background to this is that Rampton has written a note that security would not allow Hugh Scanlon to see any documents that are Confidential or above – in effect saying he's a security risk. I had this with Jack Jones, and the NEB last year. So I insisted that I see the security report which led Rampton to write that minute because unless good evidence is produced, I'm not prepared to rule that he's ineligible. But I've no doubt that Number 10 will ban him anyway.

The truth is that Hetherington just does not want Hugh Scanlon appointed to the Gas Board at all.

We came on to the appointment of a woman member. I said I wanted Marjorie Proops from the *Mirror*, a very tough, down-to-earth woman. 'Oh,' they say, 'let's have the Duchess of Kent.' That really summed it up. They wanted the Duchess of Kent, a Tory industrialist, and two right-wing trade unionists. I wasn't having it, but was good-natured about it all.

Monday 22 December
I had a brief word with Rampton, cleared the BNOC appointments, agreed to put Brian Tucker on the board of the AEA, then we went on to the Gas Board appointments. Rampton told me that I couldn't see the security services report on Scanlon and it would have to go through Number 10. Well, this is the first time I have ever been denied information from the security services. I am now (and perhaps all Ministers are) in a category that is not allowed to see security reports. Since Committees of Privy Councillors are supposed to be able to interrogate security officers about these matters, it is an astonishing drift away from accountability. Anyway, I sent a minute to Harold setting out the details and said that, subject to his approval, I thought Scanlon should be appointed.

When I think of all those bloody businessmen on nationalised industry boards who hate nationalisation and, if they are merchant bankers, invest their money abroad, and these guys have the cheek to say that because Scanlon is a bit left-wing, or for all I know he may have been a Communist at one stage of his life, that his loyalty is in some way suspect, it makes my blood boil. What they are really saying is that Scanlon might convey information to enemy forces; of course there is nothing secret in the Gas Corporation except the laying of pipelines and the idea that Scanlon is a sort of pre-war traitor with blueprints is ludicrous.

Thursday 25 December
Stephen and June, Hilary and Rosalind and their sheepdog, Wellington, came round and we all exchanged presents. Our home is a great family centre and it is all a result of Caroline's love, her care, her attention to detail. She is a remarkable woman. No man is more fortunate than I.

Monday 5 January 1976

We left this morning for Tehran and in the party were Peter LeCheminant, my new Private Secretary, Frances Morrell and Bryan Emmett.

The visit is becoming an interesting one because the Shah is in financial difficulties as a result of the liftings of oil having fallen, so he's now pushing us to increase our purchases.

Tuesday 6 January

Tea at the Residence and at 4 I went to see Jamshid Amouzegar, the Minister of the Interior. He was involved in the hijacking by Carlos of the OPEC Ministers in Vienna. He said that Kreisky was weak and that Carlos had boasted that Kreisky would certainly concede to the demands of the hijackers, which he did of course.

Carlos had apparently talked completely openly and indeed boasted his view. He had broken with Arafat and had expressed his hatred for Yamani, who he claimed had sold the Arabs down the river. He had remained calm and collected throughout, although for forty-four hours he didn't sleep at all. Carlos said that sometimes he had gone for seven days without sleep. Amouzegar asked him how he managed it and Carlos said he had ski-ing holidays and that he only did a job like this every six months.

Amouzegar said some of the young terrorists who were with Carlos were very nervous and their hands were shaking. They sat facing the Ministers, with machine guns in their shaking hands. He thought Carlos was a split personality, a Jekyll and Hyde. He gave autographs, asked the Venezuelan Minister to post a letter to his mother, waved to the crowd, and when I suggested that he was a bit of a Robin Hood, Amouzegar agreed that was a fair description. He wanted to be loved, and he felt that he was doing it for the poor.

Wednesday 7 January

The Charge d'Affairs George Chalmers took me in his car to see the Shah and on the way he said to me, 'I suppose the Shah is really like Mussolini in his early days – with a vision and an idea – before he became involved with Hitler.' He also said the previous Empress had been completely corrupt, she'd had affairs with young men and with women. She'd done terrible damage but the Shah had been infatuated with her. He said the new Empress was liberal and popular and one had to take this into account.

We were met at the Palace by Vahidi and Etemad, and shown to a waiting room lined with photographs of Podgorny, Brezhnev, Mao, the Queen with Prince Philip behind, and various other heads of state – almost all of them signed To His Imperial Majesty. Then at 11.30 we were shown into a beautiful room with marvellous arms and glittering crystal decorating the walls, and an exquisite view of the snow-covered mountains. There was the Shah looking neat and well groomed. He is fit and well preserved but of course he does look older than he appears in photographs. Every office has an oil painting or a photograph of him and the Empress. He beckoned me towards him and someone with a movie camera took pictures. George Chalmers, Peter Le Cheminant and Bryan Emmett were all present, Bryan sitting writing notes.

The Shah greeted me and said that Britain was learning what Iran had learned about oil in the past, and that Iran was playing a world role and had to consider the developing world and the maintenance of the Iranian way of life. He said there were two countries in the world that had to maintain their own standards, Iran and possibly the UK. There were dangers but we had to succeed. We needed each other, we had a common philosophy and a common interest in the Persian Gulf. He said our boys in Oman were fighting 'side by side'.

He talked about the oil companies, who were trying to get a few cents off the barrel and said that if Iran collapsed, they wouldn't be able to get the oil out and the companies must understand that. He thought some oil should be used for exchange and some sold on the market, but for exchanged goods Iran needed other revenues. He had said earlier that they had to replace their oil revenues with other revenues and were concerned that food-producing countries shouldn't raise food prices.

Then he described the Iranian nuclear power programme and he said he was getting the technology from the French and the Germans, and he might even take it from the Soviets – why not? But he was happy to co-operate with everyone. I described our programme and said we had made a lot of mistakes and we were happy to make our knowledge available.

Then he went on to talk about other sources of energy – solar energy in the South, geothermal, electric battery cars. He told me he would be ready to contribute immediately to this latter development because he saw a time when every family in Iran would have two cars – an electric car for the town and an automobile for getting about. The country's annual per capita income had risen from 200 dollars to 1,500 dollars so they could well afford this. I said Walter Marshall, the Department's Chief Scientist, might come to Iran to discuss these matters with him.

He asked about the North Sea and I described how profitable the BP Forties Field was. He said that the North Sea would transform our prospects if we were not imprudent. It depended on our not sitting back and assuming it would solve our problems. I mentioned NIOC and he said the oil companies must learn the lesson that capital could not interfere with the national interest.

Then I asked him about the 'white revolution' of 1963 when he introduced his reform programme, and he was most interesting. He told me that during the war Iran had fallen very low, and even as a boy in Switzerland he was already 'thinking about the peasants'. During the war Iran was, of course, a victim and all the people could do was hold together. They had very serious problems with their oil and after the war, a madman (that was a reference to the Prime Minister, Mossadeq) did them great damage. Khrushchev had believed that Iran would fall like a ripe plum into his lap but he had been proved wrong. He said that another country (meaning the US) had thought it could control Iran and that too was a problem. All these factors led to the white revolution – Iran had to be free of foreign influence and modernise but maintain its independence, its national identity and cultural heritage.

In fact, he said, there were so many reforms over the years that they didn't have much to destroy – just 'landowners and priests'. There was no great gap between rich and poor and even in the old days, when Persepolis was built, Persia had no class system and tolerated different religions. Persepolis he told me was built by paid labour.

He is a man for whom it would be impossible to have affection but who would count historically as having been a 'good king'.

Saturday 10 January
Finally left for the airport and we began the long flight home. I did a lengthy TV interview at London Airport, arriving home absolutely exhausted with a hacking cough and bronchitis after a most thrilling week in Iran. The regime is hateful and I can dictate this openly now on to my diary tape; in Iran I always feared my rooms were bugged. It is the most royalist, repressive, absolutist National Socialist regime, but that isn't to say it isn't going to grow and be important, so we have to have some relations with it.

One of the most unattractive aspects about politics is that whatever your own aspirations may be, you have to work with others who are repressive. That is certainly true of the Soviet Union and now we know more about America, it is certainly true of the US. But our own record in Northern Ireland, and in bolstering up the Sultan of Oman's corrupt regime, is also quite appalling.

Wednesday 21 January
The press gave the latest unemployment figures – 1.4 million – and Mrs Thatcher is now referring to us as the natural party of unemployment.

Sunday 25 January
To Chequers in the evening for a meeting with BP about their relationship with BNOC. We had drinks in the Great Hall with a huge log fire. The place does look lovely. Harold asked endless questions about Alaska, Iran, Canada, and David Steel of BP was uneasy because he didn't really know the figures. Monty Pennell, the Deputy Chairman of BP, was full of facts and Frank Kearton didn't say a word.

Afterwards Harold showed everyone round. He took us to Churchill's room, which has been left untouched, and pointed out the little mouse which Churchill had added to a picture. We went into the Long Gallery and he showed us Elizabeth I's ring, with its little cameo of Anne Boleyn, which on Elizabeth's death had been carried all the way to her successor, James VI, in Scotland. James rewarded the courier of the ring by making him the Earl of Home. He showed us Cromwell's death mask lying on silk and his swords on the mantelpiece, Napoleon's red despatch case and the records made by the British soldiers who guarded him on St Helena.

Harold described how the swimming pool at Chequers had been built by Walter Annenberg, the former US Ambassador, to commemorate President Nixon's visit to Chequers and I suggested the pool should be renamed 'the Watergate'.

Then we sat round the log fire with coffee, brandy and cigars and Harold Wilson said, 'We take no decisions at Chequers. This meeting didn't take place. Tony has explained your position but I didn't understand a word; will you tell me?'

David Steel then launched into BP's objectives: independence; cash flow from the Forties Field; North Sea operations and international operations to be preserved. He said, 'The BP shares owned by the Bank of England are a problem. We can offer you help but no more.'

When the question of independence came up, Harold got into a long, rambling metaphor about the virginity of BP, how the original marriage had not been consummated because the bride was frigid and how rape was involved – how would they cope with a more randy customer, in the person of Frank Kearton? It was vulgar and thoroughly embarrassing.

His performance tonight was pretty disrespectful, slighting and crude. Harold never rises to the occasion but he was very relaxed. Steel was friendly but difficult. Pennell is a Tory industrialist and basically hostile. Frank seemed rather less than full-sized because BNOC is so weak and there was no indication of support from the PM.

Monday 26 January
The newspapers are still reporting the repercussions of Mrs Thatcher's attack on the Russians last week, and their retaliation, describing her as the Iron Lady or Iron Maiden, has absolutely delighted the Tory Party.

Saturday 31 January
At 1 Caroline and I went to lunch with Nikolai Lunkov, the Russian Ambassador, and his wife at Kensington Palace Gardens. They had asked us through the Private Office and the four of us lunched alone at his flat. He has been here two and a half years. He's a 55-year-old, rather dull, ponderous Russian bureaucrat and his wife is a nice middle-aged mum type. He told us how upset he was that when he had written to object to Margaret Thatcher's speech, the press here had called it 'an outburst from Moscow'. The 'Iron Lady' tag, which appeared in the Red Army paper *The Red Star*, contrasted sharply with what Mrs Thatcher had said to him personally.

'When you meet her she's so charming, she wants better relations with the Soviet Union.'

'Her aggressive stand is just for internal consumption,' I told him, 'for her own rank and file.'

He said, 'Julian Amery was even worse. Do you think we should have responded?'

'It's pleased the Conservatives very much,' I said and left it at that. I didn't want to be drawn into discussions about Mrs Thatcher with the Russian Ambassador.

Monday 2 February

The papers are full of Jeremy Thorpe, who is in real trouble over this man Scott, who has claimed a sexual relationship with him: it looks as though he's on his way out.

I talked to Frances and Francis about how we should cope with the mounting press campaign on fuel bills and hypothermia in the elderly.

Friday 6 February

Meeting in the office on fuel disconnections, and I have decided to suspend disconnections of pensioner households temporarily and set up an inquiry under Peter Lovell-Davis to consider problems of payment and collection.

Thursday 12 February

John Biffen, the new Tory Energy spokesman, came at 10 and I had literally five minutes with him. I said perhaps we could establish what the options were so that our discussions in the House would be more sensible. He said he would like that. I commented that I didn't enjoy the bashing by Heseltine particularly, though I did admire him for making the headlines in Opposition which is a very difficult thing to do. I have high regard for John.

Friday 20 February

Arrived home in time to wish Melissa a happy nineteenth birthday.

To the office and found that the new miners' banner with a plaque presented by Arthur Scargill had already been screwed up on the wall next to my desk. It is a most beautiful banner, a gift unlike the T&G one, which is only on loan.

Saturday 21 February

Joan Lestor resigned as Under-Secretary in the Department of Education and Science because of the cuts in education, but the most exciting news is that Hugh Scanlon's appointment to the Gas Coporation has been accepted by the Prime Minister – so that tremendous battle has been won.

Sunday 22 February
We had a lovely birthday party for Melissa. Then at 6 Ken Coates, Joan
Lestor, Judith Hart, Tony Banks, Michael Meacher, Dick Clements and
Frances Morrell arrived. We discussed the present economic situation and
Ken came back to his theory that I should resign. Judith said, 'Why keep the
Government going?' and Tony asked why I didn't vote against the
Government as a Minister.

We had to dispose of this argument not because it wasn't a good argument
– it is a good argument – but only when you hear it deployed can you give
the proper counter-argument which is that the Movement wants three
things. It wants the Government sustained; it wants loyalty to the Prime
Minister and Ministers; and it wants a different policy to be pursued. If you
resign, you'd get the blame for undermining the Government. If you attack
the Prime Minister or other Ministers, you simply get into a position where
you are deflecting people from real issues on to personalities.

At the end of the evening Joan asked me what she should say about her
resignation and I suggested she make a speech in the House of Commons. I
found Nye Bevan's and Harold Wilson's resignation speeches and we read
them. I told her I'd see her tomorrow and advise her. When I sat down, I
realised that here was a priceless chance for Joan to get across what the
whole problem was. So I wrote a resignation speech for her and she can do
what she likes with it. It is an attempt to try to get the argument aired in the
Commons in a way that would be hard to contradict: it would hoist up a real
flag.

Monday 1 March
Went to the House and couldn't decide whether to vote for compulsory seat
belts. I thought it was a form of tyranny that would make me look a Stalinist.
But I rang Caroline and she said, 'Think of the babies, the children would all
want you to, and lives might be saved.' So I voted in favour and it was
carried by a huge majority.

Tuesday 2 March
The only really good news today is that George Brown resigned from the
Labour Party. Most people thought he had left years ago but he finally
resigned and was on the radio tonight – drunk as ever, giving the most
muddled reason why he resigned. But there will be real pleasure inside the
Party. If the right-wingers would slip off one by one, that really would be a
gain.

Wednesday 3 March
George Brown claimed in the *Daily Mail* today that his resignation had been
triggered off by listening to Alexander Solzhenitsyn. There were some sad,
indeed absolutely tragic, pictures of him, falling over by his Jaguar car and

being helped to his feet by journalists. One is torn between pity and loathing for a man who is ruined. I can't put it differently – for someone who has played such a savagely right-wing role in the Labour Party. He began to come to prominence with his attack on Cripps and his motion to get him expelled from the Labour Party; then he tried to get Bertrand Russell expelled and generally speaking he pursued all the wrong courses on everything, trampling on everybody who got in his path.

Saturday 6 March
Went for a long walk with Melissa and we visited Westminster Abbey, the first time Melissa had been inside. Of course the whole of Westminster is my village. That's where I was born, went to school, where Father and Mother were married, where Father died and where his memorial service was held, and where I work. It is a strange place, Westminster, very dull in the sense that there are no natural centres or shopping areas but I've been around there for fifty years.

Sunday 7 March
Dinner at the Foots. There is a very strong rumour that Harold Wilson is about to retire. Nobody knows where it comes from except some funny things have evidently been happening. There is a possibility that some papers which were stolen from Harold's desk may envelop him in some way in a scandal. Jill is very much in favour of Harold going and I have little doubt that she, Michael and Peter would all support Denis as leader. But if Roy stood, as I think he would have to, and Denis, Jim and Tony Crosland, but Michael *didn't* stand, then it would be a very curious line-up. Whether I stood would depend on whether I was nominated and by whom.

Saturday 13 March
The Thorpe story is moving to its climax. On the news tonight, it was reported that he had made a statement to the *Sunday Times* denying seven allegations made by this decrepit, sad, blackmailing, former male model, Norman Scott. I think that the press have decided to destroy the Liberal Party because it is now an embarrassment to the cause of building up Mrs Thatcher as an alternative to Wilson, and they are doing it by releasing information about Thorpe which they have had for years. Some Liberal MPs, like Steel and Richard Wainwright, are concerned about this, and then there are some inconsequential ones like Pardoe and Cyril Smith – absolute cynics and opportunists – who are trying to seize the leadership; the Young Liberals are trying to get rid of Thorpe because they think he is not left-wing enough. So we are witnessing the crumbling-away of the Liberal Party but it will recover when the Tories come back to power and people don't want to vote Labour. It is going to be round the mulberry bush as with everything in British politics.

Sunday 14 March
Quite a chilly day, and Caroline and I went for a lovely walk in the park,
round all the places we used to take the children. We felt like an elderly
couple, which I suppose is what we are at fifty.

Tuesday 16 March
A day of such momentous news that it is difficult to know how to start.

After a meeting with Frances and Francis, I went to Cabinet at 11. Harold
said, 'Before we come to the business, I want to make a statement.' Then he
read us an eight-page statement, in which he said that he had irrevocably
decided that he was going to resign the premiership and would stay just long
enough for the Labour Party to elect a new leader. People were stunned but
in a curious way, without emotion. Harold is not a man who arouses
affection in most people. I sat there listening quite impassively and although
other people were shocked and surprised because nobody knew it was
coming, there was still a remarkable sort of lack of reaction. But when he had
finished speaking and thanked us all, Ted Short said, with visible sorrow –
his eyes were filled with tears and his face was red – 'I think this a deplorable
event and I don't know what to say except to thank you.'

Bob Mellish said, 'I take it we'll proceed straight away to the election of a
new leader.'

Jim Callaghan, who found it hard to conceal his excitement, said,
'Harold, we shall never be able to thank you for your services to the
Movement.'

Then Harold got up to go, because he had to see Len Murray and
Cledwyn Hughes to tell them. He walked out of the Cabinet and that was it.

When he had gone, Shirley said, 'Don't you think we ought to formalise
our thanks?' Barbara agreed, so the two of them began to draft something.

After a rather odd Cabinet, I left Downing Street at about 1. By then there
was a huge crowd of people, hundreds of television cameras. Over my
ministerial lunch, we discussed why Harold had done it. Alex Eadie said the
Movement would be shaken and we had to protect against fears of a
coalition. Then the question of who would stand for Leader arose. Everyone
had left except Frances, Francis and Joe, and Joe said, 'You must stand.
You'll get a lot of votes.' Frances and Francis agreed.

I called Bryan Emmett in and I said, 'Now, look, you mustn't say to
anybody that I'm standing because I haven't made up my mind yet but I
want the decks completely cleared of all engagements. Just tell Bernard
Ingham that you don't know what I'm doing.'

Went over to the House and into the Chamber. I sat on the Front Bench
and Harold came in at 3.15 for Prime Minister's Questions and a question
on the Royal Commission on the press provided an opportunity for
everyone to pay tribute to Harold. Margaret Thatcher wished him well and
suggested a General Election. Jeremy Thorpe joked, most inappropriately,

how nice it was to hear Harold was going on the Back Benches because it was such a comfort for a leader to have his predecessor beside him. Heath congratulated Harold on joining the fastest growing political 'party' in the House of Commons. Enoch Powell congratulated him for bringing peace to Ireland in contrast to the appalling policies of the previous Government, which was an absolute hammer blow.

Had a cup of tea and saw Stan Orme who said, 'Tony, you shouldn't stand. I'm a friend and I admire you very much but Michael Foot has got the best chance – Eric Heffer and Dennis Skinner feel the same.' I said, 'Thank you. I fully appreciate it. There's a big difference in policy between Michael and myself and I think if I stood it would have to be on that.'

Ernie Fernyhough came up and said, 'Tony, you know how I feel about you but I am supporting Michael Foot and I have told my local paper.'

I said, 'It's entirely up to you. I'm not campaigning or canvassing in any way but I should be fighting for policy changes.'

Frank McElhone told me that the Scottish Members were divided between Jim Callaghan and Michael Foot, and therefore I hadn't any support whatever from them.

Then I saw Mik and he said, 'I argued on the radio that I would support you. I don't think you'd win, and I'd support you against Michael if the two of you ran together. But I think Michael has the better chance.'

I said, 'Look Mik, there's only one case for standing and that is to campaign for a change of policy.'

Went back to my room and Joe and Maggie Ashton came up, then Barbara Castle, followed by Ted. Barbara had come in to say how we must get a 'Stop Jim' movement going – a typical defeatist view – how she thought Denis was good and how Michael should stand. I said I was going to see Michael so I didn't let her guess anything. She began by saying 'Wedgie, we all agree the future is yours.' That's a load of nonsense really, the question is what does the Party do *now* to avoid a collapse?

Michael Meacher came to see me and asked if he could help in any way. I said, 'Yes, take soundings and help me draft a statement saying we should campaign for a change of policy.'

At about 8 Joe and Maggie came home with me, where Stephen and June, Hilary, Mary Lou, Frances, Francis and Melissa and Caroline were all waiting. Almost everyone there thought I should stand. Frances had her doubts. 'You might be badly defeated and humiliated,' and Francis (who takes his lead from Frances) then added, 'Yes, it might damage the policy if you didn't get any support.' Joe Ashton said, 'You could always withdraw if you weren't getting the support.' Well, you can't do that.

Hilary thought I should throw my hat into the ring first because 'if Michael comes in later, he is theoretically splitting the Left vote, not you'.

I listened and set all the arguments down on paper. The case for standing is winning, or to win next time, to get an alternative policy across, to influence other candidates, to establish a power base. The case against is that people will say you're frightened that you might be humiliated, attacked by the trade union leadership, massacred by the press.

In the end I decided I would stand.

Wednesday 17 March
I didn't get to bed until 2 and I was up at 6.50. Joshua went out and bought every newspaper which reported in full Harold Wilson's resignation statement and a list of possible candidates. It confirmed my view that I must move very quickly indeed to implement my decision to stand. I rang Michael Foot and told him, and he said he might stand, and would like to see me this morning at 11. I then rang Herbert Rogers to tell him I had decided to stand on policy and asked him to arrange a special meeting of the GMC for 7.30 on Friday.

Stephen picked me up at 8 and took some equipment to the House of Commons for Mary Lou who is going to set up her office in Room 18 on the ministerial corridor for the duration of the leadership election. From 9.15 until 11.15 Frances and Francis, Joe and I hammered out my initial statement, explaining why I was standing; I had three points: industrial policy; open government and parliamentary democracy; and industrial democracy. I heard that Jim Callaghan had declared and Michael had indicated that he would stand. At 11.15 I went to Room 18 and was told Michael had been in several times but I decided not to go to see him until after my press conference because I didn't want any one to be able to ask me if Michael Foot had requested me to stand down. At 11.30 I met the press, and then had an interview with ITN and the BBC. At 12.15 I heard that Crosland had indicated he would stand. Crosland said on the news that he was a radical moderate who stood on his record.

I had a prearranged lunch at Locket's with Danny McGarvey and I went back to the House at 2.40 and saw Michael Foot and said, 'I'm fighting purely on the issues,' and he said, 'I think you are wrong to campaign in the open, for a new policy.'

'Michael, I think the moment has come. You know my views, you have heard me in the Cabinet and I have told you privately. I think I must do it this way and, as you know, I will support you in the second ballot if I drop out as I probably will.'

He said, 'Well, we have been friends for many years and we always will be.'

Caroline arrived at 4 to give advice and help. Then Judith Hart turned up and I took her into the office next door, which was empty, and she put her hand on my arm and said, 'Tony, I love you dearly. I greatly admire you. You must be the Leader of the Party one day but not now.' I took her hand gently off my arm and said, 'Judith, no emotion and no feeling. You must do what you think is right. I am fighting on a policy and I have no option. I am doing what you did last summer – and I supported you – because I must now bring out the truth.' She agreed with everything I said and at the end she said, 'I hope you know I'm very fond of you.' I gave her a big kiss.

Frances and Francis said to me, 'Look, you are not going to get many votes' – I agreed with that – 'so you ought not to be saying you are going to win.' I said, 'I understand that, and I'm not fighting to win anyway. But I don't want to give the impression that I'm a minority, that I'm a loner, because, after all, I am carrying the banner for the TUC Economic Review.' We had a lot of strategic discussions about all this and Joe Ashton kept popping in and out. He was marvellous.

Joan Lestor was in my room using the typewriter. She didn't know I was standing. I told her, 'It's like your resignation. I have got no choice. I have got to do it.'

She asked if it would damage me personally, and I answered, 'Nothing could damage me or humiliate me save something dishonourable. I must put this forward. I am not going to ask you to vote for me because I am not asking anyone. But this is what I am doing and why.'

Thursday 18 March

Cabinet and we discussed the Falkland Islands, a paper from Jim pointing out that there were thirty-seven marines there and 2,000 islanders and the Argentinians were being very difficult. There was possibly some oil there and we couldn't hold the islands against an attack. He had two suggestions, one of which, rather tougher than the other, was to consider a condominium or to let sovereignty pass to the Argentinians and lease the islands back and develop the oil jointly.

I had a short nap in the afternoon and at 3.15 I went into the Chamber where Harold Wilson was doing his last Questions. He was very relaxed. Peter Shore sat next to me and he said, 'By the way, I'm backing Michael Foot.'

'I knew that. That's why I didn't tell you I was going to stand.'

'I hope one day I can vote for you,' he added.

Friday 19 March

To Bristol by helicopter for the special General Management Committee and rang London to see what was cooking. Frances came on the phone and said, 'Have you thought about it? Don't you think you should stand down now?'

I said, 'I won't discuss it, Frances.'

'No, Your Majesty.'

I said, 'It's no good saying that. It's no good saying to a candidate in the middle of a campaign, "Won't you withdraw?" I won't withdraw.'

The GMC was held in the very room in which I was selected twenty-six years ago. It was crowded. I said, 'I'm going to be rather formal', and I read them the three statements I had issued: on why I was standing; on parliamentary reform; and the text of my letter to MPs. It was a highly principled, intelligent meeting. They accepted the resolution after a long discussion about whether other candidates should be asked to announce their adherence to the policies adopted by the Labour Party Conference.

Monday 22 March
To Number 10 for Harold's farewell Cabinet dinner and arrived to find a tremendous gathering of cameras in the State Drawing Room. Harold had organised the dinner so that we would all be sitting in our usual Cabinet places around the big table, so I was between Michael and Peter. We had a marvellous meal. During the second course, of poached salmon, the hollandaise sauce slipped off the tray, dropped on to Denis's plate and splattered him: he was in a very jolly mood and laughed loudly.

At the end of the meal, Ted Short got up and he made a boring speech, followed by Harold who was even more boring, describing how he had avoided giving any indication of whom he would vote for, that he knew how every member of the PLP would vote, and so on. As Harold sat down, Michael said across the table, 'Harold, Tony wrote an obituary of you ten years ago and I think you ought to hear it.'

So I got up and said, 'I foolishly told Michael about this obituary, but as a matter of fact, I happen to have it with me! When I was young and naïve many years ago, I asked you, Harold at Chequers what we should do if you were run over by a bus and you said, "Find out who was driving the bus," ' so Harold interrupted and said, 'What do you mean *when* you were young!' and we all laughed. I said, 'This was in the good old days before you had to ask Joe Haines's permission to broadcast and what Joe would have said if he had had a request from the Secretary of State for Energy to do an obituary of the PM, I don't know! Anyway, I won't embarrass you by reading it though I wouldn't change a word of it all these years later and it was very nice. But I will read you the last question Kenneth Harris asked me. "Mr Benn, you have said some very nice things about the Prime Minister. Have you any criticisms?" I said. "Yes, he was never a backbencher."

'Harold, the Party, if the press is to be believed, is about to elect a very senior politician to be its new leader and in a few years' time there will no doubt be a demand for a younger man. All I hope is that when you stand again, you won't split the left-wing vote.'

Jim was friendly to me, and cheerful. He said, 'I had given up ambition years ago but when the opportunity to become Leader comes your heart is bound to quicken and I am really fighting to win.' I said, 'I know that.' Of course he wants my vote in the second ballot. I can get on well with Jim Callaghan though he is a tough politician and wouldn't let you get away with much, probably less than Harold.

Michael Foot said he didn't think Harold was going to retire at all. He said he thought in a few years' time there would be a national clamour for him to come back and take charge again.

Spoke to Marcia, who said she couldn't understand it and that Harold had said the other day, 'I suppose Paddy', (that's his labrador) 'is going to be replaced by an older dog.' So there is no doubt who he thinks is going to win and who he wants to win – Jim Callaghan.

'By the way, Harold, I'll tell you who knew your secret before anyone else,' I said.

Harold had been boasting how it had been a well kept secret, and he said, 'Who?'

'The Government Car Service.'

'What do you mean?'

I said, 'As far as I remember, Ted Heath provided you with a car when you were Leader of the Opposition, the first time that had ever happened, and you gave him a car when you won in 1974. But last year when Ted Heath gave up the leadership of the Tory Party, you made a ruling that *all ex-Prime Ministers* would have a car. I gather you foisted a car on to Sir Alec Douglas-Home, who didn't want one, and Lord Avon, who didn't want one. Well, the word went round the Government Car Service that the reason you'd done this was because you were going to retire.'

I said this jokingly, but Harold began looking very sick. He said, 'Not at all, it's for security reasons.'

Marcia was just smirking and it was obvious Harold didn't like it. She said to me, 'You are a naughty man – of course that's right!'

So Ron Vaughan had been absolutely bang on.

Harold said, 'Well, you'll be here one day.' There is no doubt that Harold has a deep personal dislike of me and I don't know what it is. The pathetic thing about tonight was that nobody was sad that he was going. He hasn't inspired any affection, he's just done his job like a Civil Service Prime Minister for years, fudged every issue, dodged every difficulty, but kept us in power, kept us together, ground out the administrative decisions. It is difficult to feel warmth for him though, as a matter of fact, I get quite soft when I think of his kindness.

Thursday 25 March

A remarkable and dramatic day. Today was the first ballot in the leadership. Caroline, Josh and Stephen came over to the House of Commons. Mary Lou and Joe were there, then Frances, Francis and Mik arrived. He is a scrutineer and I told him I had decided to announce my withdrawal immediately from the second ballot at the Party meeting even if I got through to the second ballot. Mik said, 'I think that is right.' I asked if I was in the second ballot and he said 'Yes', and then I asked if I was ahead of Healey and he said, 'You are, quite clearly, though you haven't got as many votes as I would have liked.'

I had a tremendous row with Frances, who has changed her view, and Caroline was on her side, saying that I shouldn't withdraw immediately but should think about it.

Then I went to the committee room where the PLP was gathered for the result, and sat on the back row just behind Cledwyn Hughes. The results were announced by George Strauss, the chief scrutineer. Foot 90, Callaghan 84, Jenkins 56, Benn 37, Healey 30, Crosland 17. Foot did extremely well, Jim less well than he expected, Roy Jenkins got twenty less than he expected, I got twenty more than many people thought, Healey did very badly and Crosland did marginally better than the disastrous result that had been forecast. When Cledwyn announced, 'In the second ballot Crosland goes out and the candidates are –', I got up and said, 'Cledwyn, I have decided to withdraw my name from the second ballot in favour of Michael Foot.' However, the Party was so stunned by the surprise result, that they didn't really notice what I had done.

As I was walking down the corridor I passed Michael Foot's room and it was jammed with people including Neil Kinnock, Judith Hart, John Silkin and I said, 'Good luck'. They said come in and I said, 'No, I just want to wish Michael luck.' I went to the lavatory and when I got back to my room Neil Kinnock and Judith were there, both feeling guilty, I think. They again asked me to go to Michael's room and join the campaign. I said, 'I am going to support Michael, you needn't worry about that. But I am not going to sit in as a sort of Back Bench member of Michael Foot's campaign committee. I'll talk to Michael privately.'

Did several TV and radio interviews and came back and talked to Joe. I must say a word about Joe. Not only was he my PPS for just over a year but he has been my friend and as campaign manager has been absolutely brilliant. Every time he is on television, his whole presentation has a completely different flavour from that of the other po-faced campaign managers.

Friday 26 March
Cabinet at 10.30 and as I sat waiting with Michael outside the Cabinet Room Jim came up and he said, 'Well, Michael, I just want to tell you that if you win on the next ballot, I shall have twenty-four hours of disappointment but after that I shall be completely all right.' Jim was trying to be friendly but it wasn't terribly convincing.

Saturday 27 March
Slept until midday, then Caroline and I went to the Holland Park School Fair and had a lovely day. Gradually began sorting out the backlog of work.

Monday 29 March
Went over to Number 10 for Harold Wilson's farewell party. I thought it

would be for Transport House people but when I got there I found it was a typical Harold party with all sorts, including the two policemen from Number 10, with their wives, Wilfred Brown and his wife, the Baloghs, David Frost and his latest actress girlfriend, Morecambe and Wise, the Judds, Ron Hayward, Marcia.

Marcia was very miserable. I saw Mary Wilson and said she would be able to have a quiet life now. 'I have done my best,' she said, 'but I now just want to slip back into obscurity again.' I asked Ron Hayward, 'Why do you think Harold has retired?' He said, 'Things got too much for him, and he's lost his nerve.' I don't think that's true, but it is an interesting thought.

Tuesday 30 March
The results of the second ballot were Jim Callaghan 141, Michael Foot 133, Denis Healey 38. I must say the fact that Denis only got one more vote in the second ballot than I got in the first gave me great pleasure; he was utterly rejected really. It looks as if Jim is going to make it, but there are still uncertainties one way and the other.

At 10.15 I went and voted for Michael Foot in the final ballot.

9

1976–79

Thursday 1 April 1976

The HS-125 was waiting at Prestwick Airport with my old friend Captain Dan Thomas, and I flew with John Hill, Bryan Emmett, and Bernard Ingham to Dounreay, where Dr Blumfield, the Director, met us. I had a chance to look at the new security fence and perimeter track. I pursued with John Hill and with the Deputy Director exactly what the fast-breeder hazards were and the answer is simple: if the sodium pool in which the reactor is situated ran dry or if the control rods could not be inserted and the reactor went critical, then you could get a melt-out through the metal chamber and possibly, though John Hill denied this could happen, through the concrete emplacement: you would have what is called the China syndrome – where the thing would simply burn its way down through the earth and come out in China (that's a ludicriously extreme reaction).

In Dounreay, the scientific élite have assumed the role of the lairds and treat the local people as the hoi polloi, although their high level of skill means there is an element of mutual respect.

Monday 5 April

The Wilson era has ended and the Callaghan era has begun. I would say that Jim will prolong this Parliament as long as he can because it may be his only period as Prime Minister. If he loses the next Election, in due time he too will go.

Tuesday 6 April

I went into the House for lunch and who should wander in but Harold himself, puffing his pipe and looking frightfully well.

Harold told us that, walking his dog at Chequers last night, he had decided he was going to sit on the Front Bench and listen to the Budget debate. I must say, my heart warmed to him a bit.

I am going to have a talk to him once the tumult has died down. There are a lot of things I'd like to know – particularly about the security services and I am sure he would be prepared to talk to me.

I sat through Jim's first Prime Minister's Questions and number one led to twelve minutes of congratulations. The second was directed at me. 'Did the statement made by the Secretary of State for Energy about import controls represent the policy of the Government?'

Jim replied, 'No, Sir. My Rt Hon friend was giving reasons why he was putting himself forward as candidate for the leadership of the Labour Party.'

Then Norman Tebbitt got up and asked, 'Is it right for the PM to keep in his Cabinet somebody who hates the policies of the entire Government?'

Jim replied, 'I read my Rt Hon friend's statement carefully and if there hadn't been a better candidate standing, I might even have voted for him myself,' at which the whole House broke out in laughter.

Wednesday 7 April

Had a long talk to Francis Cripps. I don't know if I will ever be Leader of the Labour Party but I don't fit the specification for the job as it now is. If I were Prime Minister I would divide the job into three: there would be the Leader of the Party in the Cabinet, with the power of appointment. Then I would have a Chairman of the Cabinet to see that government business was carried on in an orderly way. And I would have a leader of business whose job it was to turn the manifesto into the statute book.

It may be that after five years of Tory Government we may come back in the Eighties. I am sure that the time for all this is the Eighties. It is not now.

Thursday 8 April
Bryan Emmett and Bernard said they would like to take me to lunch. So
Francis and I went with them to the Pimlico Bistro and had a meal. At ten to
two Bryan was called away by the waiter. When he came back he said, 'The
Prime Minister wants you to phone. There's no security problem about
ringing from the restaurant.' So I went downstairs in this little cubby hole of
an office, surrounded by dirty cups and bills, I phoned back and was put
through to Number 10. Jim came on the phone. 'I want you to stay at
Energy.'

I said, 'I think I have more to offer in terms of democracy and Devolution
and Parliament, so I'd like to be Leader of the House.' I said I would phone
back with my answer but I would also like to see him.

We jumped into the car and I went to see Michael Foot. 'Michael, what's
going to happen to you?'

'I am going to be Leader of the House.'

'Well, in that case, I would like the Department of Employment.' Michael
said Albert Booth had been offered it and accepted.

'Well,' I said, 'he could change. He would be a marvellous Secretary of
State for Energy, but on merit, seniority and capacity to pull the trade union
movement together, I would do a better job at Employment. You know I
could, it would be difficult but I would pledge my support. I could do it.'

'Well, I am afraid Albert has already accepted.'

Of course, the truth is that there has been a double deal – that Jim would
block Roy Jenkins from going to the Foreign Office by putting Crosland
there, on condition that Michael would not press for me to get Employment.

Friday 9 April
The Roy Jenkins faction are hysterical that Roy hasn't been given the
Foreign Office in the reshuffle.

Monday 12 April
I had a message to go over to see Jim Callaghan and he said, 'I will tell you
frankly, they say you don't take an interest in Energy.' This is interesting
because this must have come from Sir Jack Rampton straight to Sir John
Hunt – the network at work.

'You have great ability,' said Jim. 'I think you could be one of the greatest
leaders this country has ever had but I am not sure that you are not aiming to
go out and be the darling of the Left. Well, I can be a very hard man and I
shall call you in one day if it goes wrong and maybe I shall sack you.'

Jim is handling me skilfully because I am somebody who needs to be at
least thought of as not destructive, if not appreciated. I assured him, 'I am
not sitting waiting for the revolution to march on London, I live in the naïve
hope that one day you will accept the policies that I advocate.'

'When they make sense, I will,' he replied.

'That's fine, that's all I ask. Incidentally,' I said, 'I won't resign unless I think the Government is destroying the Movement, and I can't see that happening.'

'Not under me,' he said.

I saw Harold tonight wandering round the House and he has absolutely shrunk; it shows that office is something that builds up a man only if he is somebody in his own right. And Wilson isn't.

Tuesday 13 April

Jim's first Cabinet. The order of seating was changed. Jim opened by saying, 'I would like to thank formally the retiring members – Barbara Castle, Willie Ross, Ted Short, and Bob Mellish. I would like to welcome the new members. I have changed the seating and perhaps you ought to look where everybody is. I hope you will look at my Minute on Procedure very carefully and ensure that your junior Ministers get it.'

When Foreign Affairs came up, Tony Crosland just said, 'Nil.' His idea of being clever is to pretend there is nothing that should be brought to the Cabinet. He once boasted he had had no debates in the Cabinet about Education, but he's not going to get away with it on Foreign Affairs.

In a moment of undue goodwill today, I decided to send a letter to Jim with my book of speeches, so I wrote him a note in my own hand saying:

Dear Jim,

This is strictly for your bookshelf and not for the Prime Ministerial reading list. These speeches chart a sort of Pilgrim's Progress which may be a better guide to what your Secretary of State for Energy really thinks than can be gleaned from Lobby or Whitehall gossip. It comes inscribed with genuine affection and respect, deepened by your personal kindness over these last few days and combined with heartfelt good wishes.

Yours, Tony

I inscribed the book, 'To Jim, with affection and respect, Tony Benn.'

Wednesday 21 April

A box was delivered this evening and there were one or two interesting things in it, including a most friendly note from Jim.

My Dear Tony,

I did appreciate your letter and the inscription in your book.

And I want to say your good wishes are totally reciprocated – and don't let either of us believe all we read about the other in the newspapers!

Audrey has brought the speeches to the farm to read this weekend – despite my remonstrations!

Let us meet after Easter and have a talk about the way you see things going, not just in your department but more generally in the Party. Please ring my office.

Yours ever,

Jim C.

I haven't had a letter like that from Harold Wilson in the whole of my life, and it really helps.

Thursday 29 April

Quite a day! At 7 the doorbell rang and it was a journalist. Then when the papers arrived, the *Daily Telegraph* had a headline, 'Benn Set on Collision Course'. This referred to my abstaining at the NEC on a motion of censure attacking the public-expenditure cuts instead of voting against the motion. The *Daily Express* had a huge banner headline, 'Benn Rats on the Cabinet', and I must admit it worried me because I thought it was an awful start with Jim, with whom I was establishing a good relationship.

On the way to Cabinet I asked Crosland how he was enjoying the Foreign Office and he said it was boring, which is typical of Tony. I said, 'I presume you are thinking about nothing but the Treasury.'

I had a message from the PM's office that he wanted to see me this afternoon so I went into Jim's office and he said, 'I had a question in the House today about collective responsibility and I gave the only answer I could, that collective responsibility includes all Ministers, who must be expected to defend government decisions at all times. I don't want to be emotional but we can't have this. If somebody wants to take over this job and do it better than me, I am happy to give up but while I am in, you've either got to be with the National Executive or the Government. You may have to choose. There are five Ministers who are also on the Executive and I think we should meet.'

'That's fine. I'll write a paper for it if you like,' I told him.

'No, don't do that. It must be absolutely secret.'

So Fred Mulley, Shirley Williams, Jim Callaghan, Michael Foot and I are going to meet for a discussion and I think that's very important.

I commented, 'There were more Ministers on the Executive at one time.'

'Yes, well, some went, some Harold got rid of, and I had to end Barbara's career. Harold used to keep a big majority in order to have a tame vote there and I haven't got it now.'

'I know, but I think we had better discuss it because I don't like hearing the Executive attacking the Government, or the Cabinet speaking with contempt about the Executive. Actually, I think the NEC wants to make a go of it.'

Jim said, 'I don't know. There are certainly three of them in continual contact with Communists. It's not "reds under the bed" or that sort of stuff' (which of course it was) 'but I know that everything that goes on in that Executive goes straight back to King Street. I have ways of knowing.'

'I suppose as Home Secretary you know how these things work, but I don't actually see it that way.' I presume he was saying that the telephones at the Communist Party HQ are tapped.

Then he said, 'You have got to accept our policy. You have a lot of ability. You are a young man.'

'I'm not a young man,' I said. 'I'm fifty-one. I've been here twenty-six years and the NEC wants to make a go of it. But I appreciate the way you have handled the situation, the problem created by my views.'

Monday 10 May

The big news is that Norman Scott, that awful male model, has finally succeeded in dislodging Jeremy Thorpe, who resigned today as Leader of the Liberal Party. It is terribly sad for Jeremy. Maybe this is a great victory for the South African security police, against whom Harold Wilson railed again yesterday. It makes you wonder whether he is the next one for some scandal of a financial kind, linked to the burglary of his papers. Very strange, I must say. I still can't understand why he has gone.

Sunday 23 May

The scandal of Harold Wilson's resignation honours list is still exercising the press. The whole thing is utterly corrupt. What we need at the moment is a great attack on the power of patronage that is given to the Prime Minister. It is much too much for any one man to have. We would never give a king the power to do all that a Prime Minister can do – far more than an American President, and far more than is desirable.

Monday 24 May

Had dinner with Frances and Judith and we talked about how to deal with Thatcher's argument, which is that the Labour Government are doing to the trade union movement what the Tories could never do; that in doing it the Labour Government are getting profits up and holding prices down and therefore restoring vitality to the capitalist mechanism; and that by doing so they will disillusion their own supporters and make it possible for the Tories to return. Hence when the Tories do return they will find the Labour Movement broken and divided and demoralised, with capitalism booming.

Thursday 27 May

Harold Wilson's honours list is still the big news item today. It is unsavoury, disreputable and just told the whole Wilson story in a single episode. That he should pick inadequate, buccaneering, sharp shysters for his honours was disgusting. It has always been a grubby scheme but the Establishment never reveal the grubbiness of their own peerages and honours. Still, we've never had anything quite like this in the Labour Party and it has caused an outcry. It will clearly help to get rid of the honours system.

To Locket's for lunch with Roy Hattersley. We had sort of committed ourselves to having a meal together and I enjoyed it. He is an attractive guy and we talked about Tony Crosland and Jim; he prefers Tony. He thought Tony trusted him more whereas Jim wanted to run everything himself. He found Crosland amusing and civilised and of all the people in the Labour Party, Crosland was the one whose views he shared most completely.

I said how pleasant life was without Harold and Roy said, 'Yes, but it is an appallingly pedestrian government under Jim.' He described the junior Ministers' meeting on Monday. 'Of course,' said Roy, 'I take the view, as you know, that freedom is what matters. I've never been a member of any group.' I pursued that with him and we talked about education. He takes an absolutely hard line about banning all private education. On health, he's in favour of banning any private health provisions because it will destroy the Health Service. I said from these issues which he cared passionately about – and I didn't blame him – it could be inferred that he *wasn't* in favour of freedom. He said he knew that, but we had to carry out these policies.

Roy also said that when he had stayed in the Shadow Cabinet in 1972 after Roy Jenkins and David Owen had resigned, all his friends had cut him off – Bill Rodgers, David, John Harris – and he was absolutely isolated and pilloried and was always described as 'that rat' by Bernard Levin.

It was a very enjoyable talk.

Thursday 3 June
Jack Rampton came in and told me that Sir John Hill wanted to see me today to tell me he wanted to cancel the steam-generated heavy-water reactor. An absolute bombshell. So Hill and Walter Marshall came to see me, with Chris Herzig, Rampton and Alan Phillips present. John Hill sat looking shifty, watching Rampton most of the time, and said, 'I have been in Russia and in Finland [or Sweden] and I've been thinking; I have come to the conclusion that we should cancel the SGHWR.' He then gave all sorts of reasons – it was expensive, there was a small market, the customer didn't want it, the American light-water reactor (PWR) had been proved safe – and it turned out that he wanted the development of the fast breeder to be accelerated.

I let him finish and then I asked, 'What view did you take two years ago?'

'I was in favour of the advanced gas-cooled reactor,' he said. 'The customer has to decide.' He couldn't really give me a clear answer.

So I asked Walter Marshall what his view was two years ago. He said, 'I had only just joined the board. I didn't know much about it but I had doubts.'

I think there is now a plot to kill it off. They see it slipping, costs escalating, they want to save money and get on with the fast breeder without delay.

I said, 'This news is tremendously important. It's the AEA deserting its own child. We developed the Magnox and the AGR ourselves and we are proud of it. This will come as a real shock. Moreover, it is bound to throw doubt on the fast breeder because if you are not going to build the system, the SGHWR, which you designed, people will say, Why not buy the fast breeder from abroad?'

As a matter of fact, I am not sorry. I personally don't want the SGHWR but I shall fight like a tiger against the American light-water reactor.

Marshall was very uncomfortable, even though for him it was a triumph. Rampton was looking quizzical because he never liked the SGHWR. I think they all reckon on my going quickly and then they'll get the American reactor. But I'll be absolutely opposed to that and I might have some influence over the decision wherever I am in Whitehall.

Tuesday 8 June
Didn't get to bed until 4 am, up at 7.30 and another all-night sitting tonight. I brought my car in so Ron Vaughan doesn't have to wait up again.

Wednesday 9 June
Had lunch at the Foreign Office with Tony Crosland. He was in that great room overlooking the park. Anyone working there would be quite paralysed and incapable of challenging the existing authority in any way. He had his jacket off and was in his blue and white striped shirt with his shoes off, his specs on his nose and a cigar. For him, informality is a sort of substitute for radicalism and it amuses him. He brought with him to the Foreign Office his diary secretary from the Department of the Environment and she obviously acts as his personal friend. I took some photographs of him. He is enjoying it enormously though he says it is a bore having to go abroad so much.

We gossiped about Roy Hattersley. Tony said that although Roy was very able, he was unsuccessful politically because he angered people. He had angered the Jenkinsites and the Left and generally speaking had isolated himself. Tony does love gossip – mind you, so do we all.

Friday 11 June
We had an amusing lunch in the State Drawing Room. Peter said that in 1968, presumably when he was Secretary of State for Economic Affairs, he had attended a dinner at the Royal Academy and sat next to Mrs Thatcher when she was Opposition spokesman on Economic Affairs, and he had tried very hard and very non-politically to get on with her (he said she was the most unpleasant woman he had ever met) but she had an absolute thrusting ambition and reflected the most odious values, of everyone doing well for themselves. Shirley Williams recalled sitting next to Ted Heath at a dinner and when she tried to speak to him, he declined to answer – simply didn't reply. She had turned to the man on her left and asked, 'Does Ted Heath not

speak to women?' and he had answered, 'He doesn't speak to many people at all.'

Shirley thought Mrs Thatcher would be out by the end of the year, that the Tories simply would not accept her. That is interesting, but I find it difficult to imagine.

Tuesday 15 June

At 3 we had a meeting on the fast breeder – Arthur Hawkins and Robert Peddie of the CEGB, Frank Tombs of the South of Scotland Electricity Board, Peter Menzies, Brian Tucker, Alex Eadie and Rampton. I began by saying. 'I am committed to looking at this again and there are a lot of general questions – safety, time scale, methods. Will you give me your comments?'

They told me that the fast breeder just wasn't safe. I think the phrase was that it was in some way 'physically unstable'.

'You mean because of the problem of the China syndrome?'

'Yes,' they said. 'The core might melt through the container and go right through the earth.'

'Well, if it's unstable at present, what about the reactor at Dounreay?' I asked.

Peddie said, 'Don't ask me about safety at Dounreay,' and everybody laughed.

I said, 'I have to ask.'

They told me that in fact the AEA have different safety standards to the Nuclear Inspectorate because they are doing research and development. I suppose the plain truth is that Dounreay isn't safe and that's why it was originally situated there.

Sunday 27 June

Still boiling hot, I think 95 degrees yesterday. The *Observer* had a piece on the Energy Conference, the first time they've seen any merit in what I have been doing since about 1970.

Tuesday 6 July

Cabinet spent three hours or more discussing the papers that had been submitted by Denis Healey and Joel Barnett calling for a cut of £1.25 billion in public expenditure to produce a cut in the PSBR to £11 billion; and secondly, calling for the abolition of the contingency fund by reabsorbing all the extra bids back into the main programme and making cuts elsewhere.

I had two briefs with me, one from the Department resisting what was being suggested, and the other – an excellent paper from Francis Cripps arguing his case even more strongly and effectively on general economic grounds – linked to the paper at last Friday's Committee. I was therefore in the formidable position of being the only other Cabinet Minister with a view to put before the Cabinet.

We sat round the table in our shirtsleeves on a very hot July day and it reminded me of my first meeting as a full Cabinet Minister ten years ago when we were in exactly the same position.

I pointed out that the size of the cuts demanded was much bigger than it appeared – £1.25 billion, plus £1.6 billion that would flow from absorbing the claims on the contingency fund into the main programme – nearly £3 billion of cuts. I didn't want to worry the Cabinet at the moment with my departmental arguments but the damage would be irreparable to our policy on oil and other areas. If we did have to make economies, they should be done on a different basis.

After everyone had contributed, Jim summed up by saying there was a majority for the cuts. So he suggested bilateral talks between various Ministers to sort it all out, and we would consult with the Neddy Six and the PLP.

Saturday 10 July

To Stansgate. Still unbelievably hot. It's been in the eighties or nineties for about a month now and the grass is absolutely brown, like Cincinnati grass.

Wednesday 14 July

My first appointment was with Dunster and Gausden, the Nuclear Inspectors from the HSE, about the fast breeder. They told me that past experience was no help in considering the safety aspects of the fast breeder. Sodium-cooled systems were different from gas-cooled ones, and plutonium, which was dependent on sodium-cooled systems, raised special problems. There were two basic safety issues. One was the mechanism of a whole core accident which might derive from an escalating sub-assembly accident, perhaps a local blockage of fuel, though the Americans and the French were less concerned about this. As to a whole core accident itself, the core would disintegrate, melt and vaporise or collapse and perhaps explode the reactor, and the whole core would be released into the containment, which could fracture; there was no agreement about the extent of the release of energy into the atmosphere, nobody could calculate it. I asked why they hadn't tested it at a nuclear testing ground. They said, 'The United States was to have tested the energy release but they found it too expensive, and then their fast-breeder programmes were set back.'

'How many people would die?'

'Thousands would die over ten to twenty years, as well as those killed in the explosion.' They did say, however, that the commercial fast-breeder reactor is licensable subject to conditions. After a long discussion I came up with the idea I would send them questions and publish their replies, and they were quite taken with that.

Thursday 15 July

Cabinet at 9.30. On public expenditure, the main item on the agenda, Jim said, 'We have got to decide today what to do.' Denis then outlined his objective, to reduce the PSBR to £9 billion by 1977/8, to reduce money supply by 10 per cent and the domestic credit expansion to £8 billion.

There were two general papers, one from Peter Shore and one from me. Peter was called first and he said tax was the right solution, and he warned of the terrible dangers of making cuts in his particular field. He rambled a bit. I must say I am lucky in having Frances and Francis. I do sound more coherent when I am called. I spoke and summed up by saying: 'Prime Minister, I think the Treasury have won the battle and lost the war because they will never ever be able to come back and argue this again; the Cabinet won't have it, the Movement won't have it, the Party won't have it, the unions won't have it and the public won't have it. Can I finish with one point which I put without offence or discourtesy. I think that the British Establishment is now infected with the same spirit which afflicted France in 1940, the Vichy spirit of complete capitulation and defeatism. It is that which is going finally to destroy us. I hope nobody will take this as being offensive but my Privy Councillor's oath requires me to disclose my opinions in the Council and this is what I have done.'

Denis sat there scarlet. He always blushes when he is in difficulty and the argument is gaining force. A year ago, I was alone and now I am in a minority of five or six.

After further discussion Jim Callaghan said, 'We must now move to a decision. Is it agreed that we exclude making cuts in social security benefits – because I think that would be impossible.' That was agreed. 'Is is agreed that we exclude cuts in overseas aid – because I think that would be very unpopular.' I think the report in the *Observer* that Reg Prentice might resign over such cuts had influenced him. So that went through.

Later, I had a talk to Peter Shore, who said to me, 'Do you know, I would either like to be entirely free of responsibilities or Prime Minister.'

'I feel rather the same,' I replied, 'but as my ambition is to be Leader of the Party, it is not incompatible with your being Prime Minister!'

He said, 'I would also like to be Foreign Secretary because so much could be done. If only this country would mobilise all its assets, its defence assets, its oil assets, which you are trying to get hold of it, its goodwill assets, it could do so much.' I agree. I get crabby with Peter in my diary from time to time but I like him enormously.

Monday 26 July
I came home and talked to my driver Ron. I tell him everything. It is a day when politics was perfectly bloody and I have a thumping headache.

Thursday 29 July
I visited three desperately sick MPs who had been brought in for the vote on

the Aircraft and Shipbuilding Bill. Alex Lyon, the MP for York, looked as if he was about to die – old, thin and weak; Frank McElhone was flat on his back on a stretcher in a massive spinal carriage with Helen beside him; and Alec Jones from Rhondda was recovering from a serious coronary. Sir Alfred Broughton from Batley and Morley was brought in on a respirator. It is quite criminal but we needed those votes to win.

Friday 6 August
John Stonehouse was convicted yesterday of fraud and sentenced today to seven years in jail.

Thursday 12 August
Stansgate. I'm reading a remarkable book by Milan Machovec called *A Marxist Looks at Jesus* which the magazine *Theology* has asked me to review. It is a translation of the German book *Jesus für Atheisten* and it is fascinating.

Wednesday 8 September
Went to the dentist who has just moved into a new surgery in Westbourne Grove. All his new equipment is imported – Italian X-ray machine, Japanese light, German drill, and so on. This is what one sees everywhere, the decline of our manufacturing industry and floods of imports.

Thursday 9 September
First Cabinet since the summer recess. Tony Crosland said, 'I expect you have heard, Chairman Mao is dead.' In fact, I hadn't heard it on the news. He didn't say much about it. 'I don't suppose there's much point in my trying to assess Mao Tse Tung's role in the world,' and he just passed over the event. Somehow I did feel that Mao merited a moment of reflection in the British Cabinet. In my opinion, he will undoubtedly be regarded as one of the greatest – if not the greatest – figures of the twentieth century: a schoolteacher who transformed China, released it from civil war and foreign attack and constructed a new society there. His influence throughout the world has been immense, based to some extent on power I suppose, but also on his tremendous achievements. Whether history will just put him among the emperors or whether he will be seen as having a quality distinct from them, I do not know, but he certainly towers above any other twentieth-century figure I can think of in his philosophical contribution and his military genius.

Friday 10 September
There is going to be a reshuffle triggered off by Roy Jenkins, who has finally left the Government. Merlyn Rees becomes Home Secretary; Shirley is diverted into Education, where she will have to carry the can on all the public-expenditure cuts (although she does fully support them); John Silkin

has been kept in, which surprised me, to become Minister of Agriculture, and there are three new members of the Cabinet – Roy Hattersley, Stan Orme and Bill Rodgers. Fred Peart is now Leader of the Lords – how he survives, I don't know.

Roy Jenkins came into politics on the coat tails of Attlee, as the son of Attlee's PPS, and never shone individually while Gaitskell was alive because he was one of his principal lieutenants. When Gaitskell died, he emerged with full force as the leader of the liberal right of the Party who believed more in Europe than in the Party, ultimately sacrificing the deputy leadership in 1972 over the Referendum. He came back into the Government in 1974 as Home Secretary, desperately wanting to be Foreign Secretary. He has now accepted the presidency of the European Commission as a way of getting out of British politics and can never return except possibly in a coalition government. He is a charming man really, an Asquithian Liberal I suppose – not Labour in any significant sense.

Tuesday 21 September
At 9.30 Michael, Ron Hayward and I saw Jim at Number 10 to discuss some of the conflicts between the Government and the Party which will arise at Conference. He was really worried about the bank and insurance nationalisation demands and he read out letters that he had received from the clearing banks and the insurance associations asking for a view. He said he and Denis agreed that if it were passed at the Conference the pound would fall: it would be a disastrous policy, though he had no theological objection to nationalisation, indeed he served on the Italian nationalised bank as a director. But, listening to Jim, I realised that if the crisis is so great that you have to postpone socialism, and that even mentioning socialism brings down such a bitter attack on you, you really are up against powerful forces that you don't control; if anything, that makes you more of a socialist. Jim says we'll be defeated by the banks and the insurance companies, but if that is the case, all the more reason why we must tackle them.

Tuesday 28 September – Labour Party Conference, Blackpool
I retained my place at the top of the NEC, picking up 4,000 more votes, with Michael in second place. Norman Atkinson became Treasurer, knocking out Eric Varley. Joan Maynard told me that Jack Jones had been trying to get her knocked off the NEC and have Margaret Jackson elected instead.

There was a debate on devolution, and Neil Kinnock made a speech attacking the statement, to which Michael replied. Neil Kinnock is not a substantial person. He is a media figure really: I have suspected it for some time and he knows I know it.

Joe Ashton told me there was a resolution calling for a working party to examine new methods of electing the Leader. This had been tabled by Ken

Coates, seconded by Joan Maynard's constituency, Sheffield Brightside, and accepted. So that is a historical event.

The pound has dropped to $1.63.

Wednesday 29 September

On the way to Conference a delegate came up to me and said, 'Have you heard about the loan? I hope you're not going to guarantee it and accept it.' It was the first I had heard but apparently Denis had gone to the IMF and borrowed £2.5 billion and the conditions won't come out until after the Conference.

Went over to the *Mirror* party with Frances, and Jack Jones said amiably, 'You know, young man, you'll be Prime Minister next.'

I said, 'I have no ambition and I've seen too many who have.'

'I'm not talking about that sort of ambition. You will be if you play it right.' A bit patronising. He said Jim was out of his depth and didn't know what was going on, and he made a very offensive remark about Denis Healey.

Then Joe and Maggie Ashton, Frances, Caroline and I went over to the *Tribune* meeting, where Eric Heffer made a most principled attack on Callaghan for his speech, and Neil Kinnock did a brilliant bit of fund-raising.

Thursday 30 September

News of the IMF loan filled the papers and there is much confusion. The smell of 1931 is very strong in my nostrils.

Denis had arrived during the banks and insurance companies debate with a terrible flurry of cameras. There were hisses and boos when he came forward to speak and he said, 'I have come from the battlefront.' He then went on to shout and bully and rule out all alternative policies, saying this was the only way forward.

Jones, Scanlon and Basnett looked very uncomfortable. The Conference was pretty hostile but when he finished, it having been such a bold and vigorous speech, parts of the Conference cheered him – the PLP, the Post Office Engineers, I think. I couldn't even clap him, his speech was so vulgar and abusive.

Denis went back to his seat and held up his hands in a sort of Mohammed Ali victory salute, suggesting it was a great triumph. Tonight the media presented it as Denis having won over the Conference to these tough new measures, and so on.

I think we'll probably have import controls by the end of the year.

Friday 1 October

Joe Haines wrote a piece in the *Mirror* about the bully boys and the Trotskyites in the Party and how we must clean it up. It reflected the pit of security service paranoia that was epitomised by Wilson's kitchen cabinet in its later years. Thank God that man has gone, and Haines with him.

Tuesday 5 October
Had a brief talk to Frances about Enoch Powell's speech yesterday on repatriation in which he suggested that £1 billion be spent to send home one million immigrants with £1,000 a piece in their pocket. It developed into a tremendous argument. Frances said, 'Of course it would help unemployment.' I said, 'That is a Fascist argument.' 'You're saying the working class are Fascist,' she said. 'I am not saying that. I am saying that is a Fascist argument which, if it were accepted, would divert from the real issue – how to get full employment, and so on – to the idea that the blacks are responsible for unemployment, and because workers are divided, one among another, the Tories would go in and clobber them.'

William Rees-Mogg came to lunch. I have known him since 1947. He was then a pompous young man with a gold watch and rather fancy waistcoat.

I asked what policies Mrs Thatcher would pursue. 'She believes really, and so do I, in a monetary stabilisation. That is to say you would have a sudden attack on money supply and it would be like Schacht in Germany or Poincaré in France after the First World War or de Gaulle and Erhardt after the Second World War; this would lead to a temporary substantial increase in unemployment but then it would settle down, confidence would return, people would wake up and find they had a hard currency instead of a soft currency in their hands, though less of it of course. That, I think, is the right policy.'

Then we talked about the collapse of Keynesianism, the collapse of the Beveridge idea and when the consensus died: was it during the Wilson or the Heath Government? In fact we both agreed that the Centre had collapsed under us and that there was now a pretty basic choice to be made.

After lunch we sat in armchairs and he said, 'Let me ask you one thing. I can never understand how the Left of the Labour Party, which is always talking about democracy, reconciles this with state centralisation.' I said, 'I agree with you. I'm part of the democratic Left. I believe in dispersing power and my answer is that you have got to get investment into industry somehow, which will require state planning, but then you have got to break down the great big state bureaucracies.'

Then he said, 'Have you seen the figures we published in today's *Times* showing the decline in the rate of profit?' The profit at replacement cost had shrunk from 18 per cent in 1960 to 4 per cent in 1975. 'Those figures are awful and maybe Marx was right in saying there will be a historic decline in the rate of return on capital,' he said.

I asked him, 'To what do you attribute that? To Keynesianism, to trade unions, to socialism, or to the ballot box?'

He said. 'I don't know.'

'I wonder whether the capacity of poor people to buy hospitals and schools and pensions using the ballot paper when they haven't got any money doesn't put a spanner in the works,' and I quoted Bagehot. 'What I feel is that we have got to find a way of getting investment, preserving democracy and maintaining liberty and it is in this area that we are really discussing what the new consensus is to be because you can't have a society without consensus.'

Thursday 7 October

At 5.30 I went over to Number 10 for the meeting with the miners. Afterwards Jim said, 'Joe Gormley's a very skilful negotiator, much better to appear to give him nothing at this stage.' Jim's a pretty dab hand at negotiation too! I had asked for five minutes with him, so we sat in the Cabinet Room for an hour and a quarter and had a lovely talk.

'Well, what do you want to talk about?' asked Jim.

'First of all, I appreciate the very open discussion in Cabinet this morning. I want to make three concrete and helpful suggestions. One is that we might consider having a committee of Ministers responsible for the industrial strategy, that is to say Industry, Trade, Energy, Employment, to monitor the industrial strategy, checking how we are getting on, but it must be under non-Treasury chairmanship.'

'Denis won't like that,' he interjected.

'I am simply saying that industrial strategy ought not to be under the Treasury. Next, on the City side, I have been giving consideration as to whether we shouldn't have the Governor of the Bank of England attending the Economic Strategy Committee, just like the Chiefs of Staff attend the Overseas and Defence Policy Committee.'

Jim replied, 'Oh no, that's the Chancellor's job, to represent the Governor's view, the Governor is just an instrument of government policy and it would weaken the Chancellor.'

I said, 'I'm not so sure that is a bad thing because at the moment, we don't consult the Governor. The Governor ought to be able to convey to us the reality as he sees it and hear our argument.'

'Before the First World War, of course,' said Jim, 'the Chiefs of Staff were members of the Cabinet, the First Lord of the Admiralty sat with the First Sea Lord, and so on. You probably know that as you are a historian. That's why they still come to the Overseas and Defence Policy Committee.'

He didn't like the idea.

Then we came on to Conference and he said, 'I thought it was awful, sour, bitter and I had a lot of letters about your behaviour, which was seen on television, sitting there grimly during my speech. I've had the letters set aside and I'm going to read them later.'

I said, 'Well, Jim, it would be very nice if every morning I woke up and found that everything I did was sweet and reasonable and sensible like Shirley Williams but it isn't like that. It is pretty rough, you know, when even the *Financial Times* prints a picture of Michael and me side by side looking glum with the caption "Two unenthusiastic members of the Cabinet during the PM's speech", when we weren't even sitting together during your speech.' He hadn't seen it and I told him there was an apology in today's *FT*. 'Now look, Jim, you know that in every article about you that has appeared since you became Leader I have stressed how well I get on with you. And there's not a morning I don't wake up and thank God that you are Leader and Harold Wilson is gone.'

Then he said, 'There is another thing about the Conference. What about all these Trotskyites – and I get my information from a source I can't disclose.'

I said, 'I presume it's the intelligence services.'

He said, 'Fifty-seven thousand votes were cast for Trotskyite candidates for the NEC. That must be a substantial number of constituencies under Trotskyite influence.'

'Jim, I hope the intelligence services understand all this. I read all the left press. Trotskyites are youngsters and if we get them into the Party, we'll win them over.'

'You're too optimistic about it. I think Conference has lost us the Election. When do you think they will wish to have an Election?'

'I haven't thought about it very much but I presume that you want to leave it a bit. We must win the next Election, and I think we can.'

'As to you,' he said, 'I can see you as Leader of the Party in Opposition and ten years in Opposition you will be.'

'I will never be Leader of the Party.'

'Yes, you might and I'm trying to give you a fair do.'

I said, 'I know that the PLP as it is presently constituted will go for somebody else. I am not going to wreck my life by ambition.'

'Now, about this alternative strategy of yours, you were very honest this morning in saying it would involve sacrifices, but could we sell it to people?'

I said, 'Yes Jim, I'm sure we could.'

He replied, 'I think more public-expenditure cuts are coming. Denis hasn't told me but I think it is going to happen.'

'I should think there are because that is the policy and we'll just have to stay glued together. That's all.'

Then he said, 'You know I mentioned that Helmut Schmidt was coming to Chequers this weekend.'

I said, 'Yes, I heard it from my office.'

'What do you mean?'

'I heard it from my driver, who heard from the car pool that there was a meeting at Chequers and he wondered if I was going. The car pool is the source of all information.' I told him how Ron Vaughan had heard that

Harold had introduced the rule that all former Prime Ministers should have a car and that was how we knew Harold was going. Jim laughed.

We had got down to gossiping by this stage and he said, 'I'll tell you a thing about Harold. When we were at a summit just before Harold retired, Aldo Moro (the Italian Prime Minister) was delivering a seventeen-page written speech on the international monetary system, and Harold took one earphone off and I took the one off my good ear, and Harold leaned over and said, "When I go, Jim, shall I take the Garter, the OM, or go to the Lords?" So I said what I always say in those circumstances – "What would you like for yourself?" – and Harold said, "I think I'll take the Garter", which he did.'

I said, 'Well, old Clem took all three – a Garter, the OM, and the earldom.'

'Yes, I remember in 1955 when Clem went to the Shadow Cabinet and said, "Just to let you know, I'm resigning and shall I take an earldom?" Edith Summerskill said, "Of course you must take it, Clem", and he took it.'

I came home scribbling all the time in my notebook so that I didn't forget a word.

Monday 11 October
I went to hear Thatcher in the Commons. Her speeches are solidly argued, like an *FT* article, but don't carry conviction, have no depth, don't look into the roots of the problem. Jim made a bold and human speech which went down well and had more substance to it.

Tuesday 12 October
It is 2 am and today is Caroline's birthday. We have had such a marvellous life together and her radicalism and support and determination have really kept me going. I couldn't have managed without her.

Tuesday 26 October
Sat and talked to Frances. I am utterly depressed and dejected. I have absolutely failed to persuade the Government not to do what it is about to do. It would be better if we were defeated now, I am persuaded of that, but I mustn't bring the Government down because if I do the responsibility will be put upon the Left, rather than on the Right where it really belongs. Somehow the whole world is whirling and it is having a physical effect on me. I actually feel physically ill.

Wednesday 27 October
Had David Owen to lunch in the office. I don't really know him well: he worked with Barbara when she was at Social Services and she had great admiration for him, and he for her, and he is trying to be friendly. I asked him about his family and one of his grandfathers had been a clergyman, the

other a miner. His clergyman grandfather had originally been a Methodist but as he was blind he couldn't go round the circuit so he transferred to the Church of Wales and David had been brought up in that tradition. He felt it was getting weaker in the Labour Movement.

He was tremendously critical of the Treasury which he feels is determined to encourage the IMF to demand cuts from the economy. They are just out for our blood, and were furious with Jim for trying to negotiate with Helmut Schmidt for a Common Market loan to fund our sterling balances over a long term to avoid the rigours of the cuts.

David Owen was one hundred per cent in support of planning agreements and particularly of the NEB and industrial democracy.

I said, 'Of course, it has all now been dropped really.'

He said, 'I am sure industrial democracy is right.'

Then, indicating his personal support, he said, 'You have more influence in the Labour Movement than any other man at this moment and we have got to fight for these things.'

We got on to a curious discussion about élites. He said, 'I believe in élites, that élites have to lead and that you have got to have men of intellect and ability.'

'I agree you have got to have ability,' I said, 'but I believe that it is *will* that really matters, a power of concentration and determination.' That more or less wound up the discussion.

Friday 29 October

Up at 6.30, and Caroline and I flew to a little airport and were driven to Selby for the opening of the new coal mine. There was the Lord Lieutenant, the Duchess of Kent and the High Sheriff of the County, who was a landowner owning 10,000 acres on the Selby coalfield. Derek Ezra and Joe Gormley and others represented the Yorkshire mining establishment.

Joe was called to speak and he had a few notes and he began in a measured way and then somehow he forgot that he wasn't at a pithead meeting and started to talk about productivity and the role of the miners – he appeared to be rebuking the Duchess for implying the miners were barbarians being brought into these villages. It was a marvellous speech, absolutely political, and might have been made at a miners' rally. As Caroline said afterwards, the two establishments were there, the old feudal Establishment – the Duchess, the Bishop and the Coal Board – and Joe, me and the miners representing the new Establishment, with so much more confidence than the old. Amazing that the old feudalism still survives.

Lunch was hilarious. The Duchess sat next to me and Joe leaned across and said, 'What's your name, love?'

She said, 'Katharine.'

He said, 'I'm Joe.' Then he held up his glass and said, 'If you can't be good, be careful.'

Then Arthur Scargill came up and had a word with Caroline and I took him over and introduced him to the Duchess. It must have been an extraordinary experience for her, meeting this guy who is regarded as the most revolutionary miners' leader in Britain.

Tuesday 2 November
Went off to Carlisle feeling pretty unwell. Dale Campbell-Savours is the Labour candidate for the by-election here, a tall, rather elegant mixture, I thought, between Bob Maxwell and John Lindsay, the Mayor of New York. Afterwards I had a cup of tea in a little hotel, then went to the Labour Club. It might have been from that programme 'Days of Hope', and a real 1930s working-class club. The warmth, friendship and loyalty were there but it made you realise how little the post-war capitalist recovery in Britain had reached beyond the South and the Midlands.

Tuesday 9 November
Brian Sedgemore agreed today to be my PPS. I went to Jim's room to tell him and he was having a sandwich with his PPS Roger Stott so I put my head round the door and said, 'Only thirty seconds. You took away my PPS and I'd like to appoint a new one, Brian Sedgemore.'

He asked Roger Stott to leave the room and said, 'I think you have made a great mistake. He is very uncouth with Mrs Thatcher. You ought to have somebody else more in the Centre of the Party.'

I told him, 'I think I ought to pick from one of the thirty-seven who voted for me. There weren't many of them.'

'Will he support us on the IMF?' he asked. I didn't know so he followed, 'You had better ask him. I can't have you appoint him now and then find he resigns in six weeks.'

'I'll put that to him if you like.'

He said, 'If you insist on him, I'll accept it.'

Thursday 11 November
Before Cabinet, I talked to Merlyn Rees, who said, 'I have never seen the Party in such despair. People think the Government might fall by tonight, the Opposition may defeat the Aircraft and Shipbuilding Bill.'

In the meeting, Jim said, 'It is going to be extremely tough from now until Christmas and I don't want to carry on leading a government that is divided. I don't want to give up, or anything of that kind, but we have got to be united. We have got to make that clear.'

We went on to the Queen's Speech, which is to be delivered on 24 November. There was a reference to the 'unacceptable level of unemployment' and the point was made that we couldn't go on talking about it as unacceptable, so that was deleted. The reference to replacing the Official

Secrets Act by some new legislation was omitted and the general point was
made that the less Parliament did this coming year the better.

Jim said, 'We have just got to axe some Bills,' and he went through the list
trying to get some of them chopped. Stan Orme suggested that the
European direct elections might be deferred. Stan said, 'It looks as if the only
Bills we can bring forward are those the Tories and the Liberals will accept.'
I was nodding in agreement and Jim said, 'It's no good Stan saying that. It's
no good Tony Benn nodding sagely. We have got to face the fact we are a
minority government.' In the end, nothing in terms of legislation was
actually cut.

Friday 12 November
Stayed at home all day. Julie Clements, my new secretary, came in, a very
nice woman. I like her very much.

Monday 22 November
Before lunch I sat in on the Aircraft and Shipbuilding Nationalisation Bill in
the House of Lords, on which they were solemnly deciding, by 190 to 90
votes, that they would delete ship-repairing. They knew they were engaged
in a major constitutional crisis by rejecting such an important Bill and I
heard Fred Peart saying that it was inadvisable to do this. My presence at the
bar was noticed by some Tory peers; they must hate my guts.

I went over with Caroline to Number 10 for a dinner for the President of
Venezuela. Talked a bit to David Steel. Jim made a good speech. I told him
that he looked very boyish and he said he'd washed his hair for the occasion!
I also had a long talk to John Biffen, whom I really like. He said he spent a lot
of time defending me and the idea that I was an authoritarian was a load of
old codswallop.

Caroline and I enjoyed it very much. When we arrived home, the paper
that is being discussed at Cabinet tomorrow was in my red box. It is
absolutely terrifying. £1.5 billion cuts, including the sale of BP shares and
delaying the upgrading of pensions. I just feel that it is unacceptable.

Wednesday 24 November
Decided to dictate a Cabinet paper, with Francis by my side, to be classified
as Top Secret, in which I spelled out the choices facing the Cabinet, the
dangers of the IMF route and the alternative strategy, ending with a long
passage on the problems of implementation.

To the Energy Committee chaired by Merlyn Rees, where the first item
was Windscale. A year ago we agreed to the siting of a thermal oxide
reprocessing plant for Japanese nuclear waste. I had held it up for some
months to allow public discussion, as a result of which it was alleged that the
French had been offered the contract. I held inquiry hearings in Windscale

itself, and in London, and finally recommended to the Cabinet that we go ahead with it.

It is of course a major planning issue and the Cumbrian Council, who are interested in the jobs, approved it, but Peter Shore as Minister of the Environment had the right to call it in for a decision by himself. He wrote a paper for today's meeting calling it in, although the whole of Whitehall had briefed their Ministers against doing this because it would involve delay.

I described how, on a visit to Tokyo a year ago, I was told that Windscale had had a fire in 1957 and that part of it was not operating yet, something I had never been told by my officials. I said it was not a problem of middle-class cranks versus solid workers. It was the scientific community trying to get its way with political Ministers.

We were discussing the statutory rights of people to have such matters properly looked at, and we should be very careful before we tell a Minister to blank out these statutory rights.

Peter got very hot under the collar and said he was calling it in anyway. Anyway it was agreed that it would go to Cabinet and meanwhile Peter would extend the decision time.

When the history of nuclear power comes to be written, I think this discussion will turn out to be a significant one.

Thursday 25 November
Lazy start. First Cabinet at 10.30. *Tribune* came out with the 1931 Cabinet minutes which I had dug out in preparation of my case against the IMF loan. The *Guardian* had a full story indicating that Jim had withdrawn his support from Denis. Things are very difficult at the moment and I'll keep my head down at Cabinet. I'll put in my paper and leave it at that. The *Guardian* story by Peter Jenkins about Callaghan taking over the helm from Denis probably came from Harold Lever, who is a close friend of Jenkins. Peter Jay had an article in *The Times* based on the 1931 minutes.

When we came to the IMF, Jim said that after the Cabinet on Tuesday, he and Denis had carried out the necessary action. He had sent messages to President Ford and Schmidt, Denis had personally seen Alan Whittome, the head of the IMF's European Department, then Whittome had been to see the Prime Minister and the Chancellor together. Jim said that the IMF knew about our fear of deflation and we faced a serious dilemma between retaining on the one hand the confidence of the TUC and, on the other, the confidence of the markets. He said that Ford and Schmidt did not want a decision today.

He went on to say that he had met Len Murray on another matter but since Len was a Privy Councillor, Jim felt able to tell him about the situation and the dilemma. Whittome had asked us to look at three scenarios for 1977/78: one was the PSBR at £8.5 billion, another at £9 billion and a third at £9.5 billion.

Jim stated that none of these measures were going to be attractive. All the packages before us would be unpopular but he took the point about extra time for discussion and agreed that we should have two Cabinets next week, using Wednesday for discussion and Thursday for the final decision.

I hoped the real options would be before us on Thursday and not just a Yes or No to the IMF proposals. We had to have broad discussions about the political implications of various courses of action. There were things that the IMF could do to us which we might accept but would involve taking away our seals of office, we would be a government without power. Thatcher would then get in and the people we look after would suffer terribly.

Monday 29 November
Tea with Brian Sedgemore and I told him about the refusal by Jim Callaghan to let him be my PPS and he agreed to let it rest till after Christmas. I'll get back to Jim then.

Tuesday 30 November
To Michael's Foot's room. Jill was there, with Albert, Stan Orme, Peter Shore and John Silkin. We talked about tomorrow's Cabinet now all the papers have come round, fourteen of them including mine. We talked things through in depth, agreed on tactics and decided to meet again tomorrow night.

Wednesday 1 December
Francis and Frances came for breakfast and I spent from 8 till 9.30 going over the papers for the Cabinet.

We agreed that I must be careful to distinguish myself from Crosland and Healey, hoping that I wouldn't be called till later in the morning, by which time Crosland and Healey would have knocked each other out, then I'd come in with the alternative strategy, saying what we needed was reflation instead of high unemployment. So we sketched out a line of approach.

Frances came in the car with me to the Cabinet, which was delayed from 10 till 10.30. This made us a bit suspicious. You don't normally delay a Cabinet of that importance unless there's some hiccup, and we wondered whether Jim and Denis were having a set-to; in fact when we went into the Cabinet Denis was just coming out, so I think they must have had a talk. Whether it indicated a row or a make-up I don't know.

When the Cabinet met finally at about 10.40, there were no officials present, a thing that hasn't happened since Jim has been PM. He said, 'I want to draw special attention again to the need for secrecy. Some of the press reports have been very damaging and very accurate, for example, the blow by blow account in the *FT* last Friday called "An Honest Man in a Labour Cabinet".' (That must have been a reference to Healey.) 'I know who gave it to the *FT* and I shall take the necessary action to deal with the matter when I next have a reshuffle.' He went on to say, 'We are in a position where we shall have to rally to the majority view, whatever it is, or it will not be possible for me to go on. We have to remember that we have some critical by-elections coming up.'

Denis said, 'I'm glad you've said what you've said because I've been the victim of many of these leaks and colleagues who have tried to make themselves out to be heroes at my expense have done themselves, as well as me, a lot of damage.'

At that point, officials were brought in, and Jim called me, shrewdly concluding that it would be better to get me disposed of first. He said he wanted to conclude the general discussion today.

'Prime Minister, I think we're all aware that this is a political decision as grave as any in our history, that we cannot really rely on others to help us, particularly Ford, who is a lame duck, or Schmidt, whose view is pretty monetarist in character. I base myself on the telegram that came in after the Socialist Congress in Geneva in which our officials there said that Schmidt had warned about inflation and said that public expenditure not properly financed had been the cause of unemployment. I assume that represented his view. Carter wouldn't want to get too involved until he becomes President, therefore we have to rely on ourselves and trust our judgement. I entirely share the view that the survival of the Government is in the national interest, but in this context we must consult our partners – the TUC and the Labour Party.'

Jim interrupted me, 'I perhaps should tell the Cabinet that I have seen Len Murray about something else last Tuesday and I also keep in pretty close touch with Jack Jones.'

'Well, that's better than nothing,' I said, 'but I want to emphasise this very much indeed, because they've put their reputations at risk in supporting us and if we take decisions unacceptable to them, it would not be fair. There are two alternative strategies, the Chancellor's and mine, and there is a very big choice to make. My paper warns against deflation of any kind, imposed or self-imposed. I have been driven to the conclusion, very reluctantly, and I hope the Cabinet will believe me, that expansion requires protection.

'In 1974 when we were elected, I was very keen on our industrial policy, which I played some part in formulating, but I did come to the conclusion that this would not work while our industry bled to death. I simply do not believe that it cannot be made to work. In 1931 the Chancellor warned the Cabinet that import duties or revenue tariffs were not acceptable, and that if we came off the Gold Standard, the standing of living of workmen would fall sharply. Yet two months later, both were done. Someone from that Labour Cabinet subsequently said that we were never told we could do it. Peter's paper draws attention to the fact that all import controls are legal under the General Agreement on Tariffs and Trade and under the EEC and I think we should seek international support on that basis for that alternative strategy. It would be inexplicable to our movement that we had never even tried on our alternative strategy with the IMF and yet more inexplicable that in order to get the loan we have promised not to undertake that alternative strategy.'

I was subjected for about half an hour to the closest cross-examination. First, Jim asked, 'Do you think we need the loan?'

I said I would prefer to have the loan rather than not. I reminded the Cabinet of the famous cartoon in 1940 of a soldier after Dunkirk waving his fists and saying, 'Very well, alone!' I said that I thought the IMF would help us because it would be in their interests to do so.

Bill Rodgers asked what my policy would do to unemployment, and I replied that although I hadn't got a Treasury computer to mislead me the one thing that was absolutely clear was that unemployment would rise under existing policy and would get worse under extra cuts. Import controls would substantially improve the unemployment situation. The big difference now was that with unused resources we would not need cuts on the scale forecast by the Cambridge School, of which I am not a member, in order to go for the alternative strategy because these resources could be brought into play.

Harold Lever wanted to know why I thought we could survive politically. If we could get it through the Cabinet, could we get it through the House of Commons? What would our stance be electorally?

My opinion was that nothing would be more fatal to our electoral chances (and I had no crystal ball) than the Party going to the country having laid off employees in the manufacturing industries and in the public-service sector on the grounds that the bankers wanted unemployment to restore confidence. I said it would be much better to present this in a vigorous way. I thought we would get support nationally, even in the House of Commons, and have a far better chance of winning.

I was also asked about exchange controls by Harold Lever. I said I knew very well that the Treasury had a secret emergency plan. I didn't know the details but it was there and we would need it, certainly in the short run.

Denis said, 'Yes, but where would you get the foreign currency to fund us immediately if we had exchange controls?'

Jim replied that it could be that new sources of money would become available in the short run for that purpose.

I mentioned the export of capital being on a large scale but they disputed that, saying these were profits made by British firms abroad.

Shirley Williams asked if my strategy was a threat or a real policy. I answered that I'd adopted it reluctantly, I would much rather we didn't have to do it but I thought it was inescapable. Mrs Thatcher would do it and in a way she would probably find it easier because no one would suspect her of wanting to make it an entry point into a full siege economy. We had to make it clear that we would be prepared to adopt this strategy in order to release the money. It would be absolutely inexplicable if we didn't try it out.

Peter was called next. He said we had two alternative strategies: the earlier policy had failed and we could either go for deflation or import controls. Denis was for deflation, which would encase us in a two-year tomb. The IMF tranches would come bit by bit; we would be drip-fed to police us and it was all very well to tease and hound Tony Benn, but the alternative policy needed to be looked at properly. Jim wouldn't accept that I was being teased and hounded – I didn't think so either – but I suppose that's how it looked.

Peter's position was slightly different from mine. He believed we were not paying our way and the easiest way to deal with that was to control imports. As to retaliation, we would have to look at our rights. The GATT and EEC provisions allowed any country to take these protective measures where there was a risk to its currency or to forestall a fall in its monetary reserves – they had almost been written specially for us!

Jim said the fear wasn't exactly of retaliation but of a possible trade war.

Peter Shore believed the Italians would retaliate, the Americans and the Germans would have no grounds, nor would the Japanese, and he wasn't sure about the French.

'What about the small countries? Would they follow suit?' asked Shirley.

She pointed out the risk of emulation by, for example, Australia, New Zealand and Canada if we took the GATT line and Peter didn't rule that out because there would have to be another world economic conference quite soon. The world system was seizing up.

Elwyn asked about the mid-term position. We had to return 1.6 billion dollars to the central bank on the 9th, we had to finance the external deficit and we had a £2.5 billion deficit expected next year. How would we deal with the immediate borrowing or were we prepared to risk the bankruptcy of the UK?

Peter said the current account would be closed in 1977 under his proposals. Second we could push forward the impending dollars repayment for three months. Thirdly we would get the IMF's backing, but if we didn't we might have to mobilise our assets and then release them in an orderly way. We would have to guarantee the sterling balances as we had done before.

Jim said he was particularly worried about these survival problems, and Bruce Millan couldn't understand why import controls were on the basis of now or never.

The third gladiator in the ring, Tony Crosland, began with marvellous arrogance. 'I think the proposals I wish to put forward will command more support than Tony's or Peter's. I want us to stick to our existing strategy. We have had deflation, we have had devaluation, we've got a wages policy and it will work. There is no case for a change. New cuts would have a disastrous effect on investment because they'd damage wages policy and destroy confidence.

'But we live in the real world of expectation and there are two scenarios to consider. One is the £1 billion net cut which is unacceptable, and the IMF won't really press us for it. If they do, we should resist and threaten a siege economy, or talk about our role in Cyprus or our troops in Germany, or our position in Rhodesia, membership of the EEC, etc. Schmidt and Ford would soon give way.

'The other alternative is tolerable: to get £1 billion off the PSBR by selling the Burmah oil shares, having import deposits which are a bit deflationary and have political advantages, and to do a presentational job to the IMF by announcing now the cuts we had decided on in July but which have not yet become known, and possibly some extra cuts.'

'What if the IMF say no?' I asked.

'We won't accept it.'

Denis pushed him. 'But what if they stand firm?' Tony believed that they would, but that we would have to defend ourselves.

Stan Orme thought that the market might require even greater cuts than the IMF.

'They will be real cuts,' said Tony, 'but we are going to discuss all of that tomorrow.'

We had a tremendous speech from Roy Mason. He thanked Denis for his courage and imperturbability, his intellectual resilience, his strength and moral fibre, at a time when the country is bankrupt and the Party is at its lowest ebb. He said we'd had the militants of NUPE, the disastrous Labour Conference, the NEC, which was the laughing stock of the country, Transport House, which some people seem to think has 2,000 employees because it writes so many embarrassing reports. There was no buoyancy in the Party.

'We have to keep the Cabinet and the Party together and Tony Benn at least has a clear alternative. But we can't survive alone. How can we finance and support ourselves? Peter Shore and Tony Crosland are looking for a painless way out.'

On quotas he reminded us of the wrath of the European Free Trade Association when he was President of the Board of Trade. We were the biggest fish in EFTA at that time. Now we were very small fish in the Common Market. Threatening was no use to us now because it would put a brake on world trade and there would be no lubrication to keep it going.

GATT was sympathetic, he thought, but the EEC would react to Tony Benn's measures by saying they are subsidising us. They would not allow the green pound to remain at its present level, we would lose £500 million a year, inward investment particularly in semi-manufactured goods would be threatened, the protection in inefficient industries would go on and managers don't want a siege economy. Import deposits were not on, unemployment would rise anyway because of our strategy. 'After all, why did we nationalise the aircraft industry, the shipbuilding industry, the car industry, if it wasn't to rationalise them and cut jobs? As to the mining industry, we have put in tons of money to make it efficient and we have to go back to pit closures. Steel was the same. We've taken the misery out of unemployment but we're not taking the credit. What we need are selective investment measures and we try to eliminate the balance of payments deficit, we rally round the tax cuts, we rally round a cut in inflation for our wage policy. We should be emphasising these things.'

I went back to the office, and Frances and Francis and I went over it all.

Thursday 2 December

Slept late, because I didn't get to bed until 2.30 in the morning.

Cabinet at 10. Parliamentary business as usual, followed by Foreign Affairs. Tony Crosland reported the Geneva Conference on Rhodesia saying that a date for reconvening it in January had been agreed.

We came to the IMF negotiations. 'We now come to a decision on the quantum,' started Jim.

'Can I ask a procedural question?' I said. 'Are you going to decide things bit by bit *ad referendum* at the end; or are we going to have to reach a final decision today?'

Jim replied that he would be dealing with that in his summing-up. Then Peter Shore said, 'Are we going to be discussing a paper from Shirley which has just come round?'

Jim said, 'Well, I should never have yielded but I did to a woman. She said she would do a one-page paper but in fact it is longer than that.'

Denis opened today's discussion, which lasted throughout the whole morning. He said there had been a general feeling yesterday in the Cabinet that had led to a rejection of the alternative strategy and the siege economy, and therefore we would have to seek agreement with the Fund. We only had £2 billion left next week and if we failed to agree with the Fund, it would be a disaster. Then much more drastic measures would have to be taken, and there would be higher unemployment. The question was: what adjustments should we make and would they satisfy the Fund and meet criticism at home and abroad?

He said the PSBR must be cut below the forecast of £10.56 billion because otherwise we would either have to print money or we would have to have higher interest rates. Denis said, 'I now recommend that we go for a £500 million sale of Burmah shares; for a net reduction of £1 billion in the PSBR in 1977–78, mainly by cuts, with another £1.5 billion reduction in 1978–79. Unemployment would rise by 30,000 by the end of 1977 and by 110,000 by the end of 1978; but these would be offset by micro measures of a kind that Albert Booth has suggested. Anything less will not restore confidence even if the IMF accept it.'

Jim Callaghan then said, 'I think the time has come for me to give my view. I read the Hansard on the Tuesday debate in the House and I noticed the speeches by Heffer, Maudling, Oonagh McDonald, Enoch Powell, and Eric Ogden, which were very interesting and well informed. I must admit, I am not sure about what to do, but I think the time has come to make my position clear.

'I want to look at it from a political and economic angle. It is very hard to jduge what will happen. These measures could have an adverse effect on the PLP and the unions but the public may take a different view. The Chief Whip sent me a minute to say that there is an absolute need that, whatever we do, we must avoid any legislation following from this package because it is not possible to rely upon the Parliamentary Party support to carry it through. But Denis's proposals do need legislation and the Cabinet had better face it. The PSBR approach alone is not enough and my view, therefore, is as follows.

'Denis has fought very hard and I must tell the Cabinet that there is no agreement with the IMF yet. I must also tell you very confidentially that the Managing Director of the IMF, Johannes Witteveen, came to London yesterday and I had a long meeting with him. I read him Article 12 of GATT, which provides for exemptions; it amused me yesterday, when I was told by Tony Benn that we had never put the possibility of import controls to the IMF. So I read it to him and he was very unyielding and he wants £2 billion of real cuts. Schmidt was going to phone me this morning but it was an abortive call. But I had a word with President Ford yesterday on the telephone and he said that if the Fund came through he would try to help with the safety net. He said he felt sure that it would be acceptable to the Congress.'

Then Jim read out – because Prime Ministers like to show how well they get on with Presidents – the last few words of his exchange with Ford which ran something like this:

Jim: Sorry to bother you, Gerry.
Ford: Well, don't worry, Jim, I expect you're busy.
Jim: Well, it's just a question of which of us remains in office longer.
Ford: Well, I sincerely hope you succeed. When will the Cabinet decide?
Jim: By 1 pm.
Ford: You might be out of office first . . .

An almost exact reproduction, of course, of the telephone call on 23 August 1931 in which the Prime Minister announced that he had had a call on the phone from our Ambassador in Washington. That stuck in my mind as I listened to Jim.

Denis said, 'Congressman Henry Reuss will help.'

The Prime Minister continued, 'What I said to Ford is this. I would like to propose a three-legged stool: a cut of £1–1.5 billion in the PSBR; a safety net; import deposits on the same basis as Italy. I might be able to sell it.' Ford said their attitude was to be firm but fair.

Jim then added, 'I have also told Schmidt this, but if we can't sell it then we have a completely different perspective. I support this policy because: first, it will allow lower interest rates; second, the uprating of benefits will be reduced in a way that will be sensible; third, we will be reducing tax at the margins: fourth, we will perhaps be dealing with indirect taxation; fifth, our industrial strategy will be strengthened. But we do put our lives to the test and our life as a government could come to an end. We must all understand that if we reject this, our overseas friends and critics will bring the life of this government to an end and the tremors will shake us.'

Then Michael Foot spoke for the first time this week. He began very quietly by saying he was grateful to the Prime Minister, 'But I must tell you that your proposals are not satisfactory. £2 billion cuts and all the consequences that will flow from that, are inconceivable. The whole position has been changed by unemployment rising to 1.75 million in the forecasts and we would be accepting an increase in that. As to pay arrangements, the Party believes in egalitarian approaches to pay and you can't unscramble that. If you tried to deal with benefits by statute, it would destroy TUC support. The legislation would not be passed and we would be in a position where, if the Government was defeated, Labour candidates would be fighting an Election in favour of cuts in social benefits. The Party and public opinion can't be divided in that sense.'

He said he recoiled in horror from the unemployment effects and the cuts in benefits. 'If we followed this course we would forfeit our agreement and our association with the unions and would be ground to death. We must connect what we do to our own beliefs. We may not get the loan but we have better prospects than a course that would be a disaster for the Government. We need more time; we want to sustain the Government; or, if forced into Opposition, sustain ourselves in unity rather than be split into snarling groups.'

Crosland said that the Prime Minister's statement was a very grave one. He had thrown his judgement in with the Chancellor and this was a completely new factor. He thought it was wrong economically and socially, destructive of what he had believed in all his life. Also it was politically wrong. He doubted the judgement of the Cabinet and what was proposed was wrong. 'But the new factor is your view, Prime Minister. What would be the consequence of rejecting the Prime Minister? The unity of the Party depends upon sustaining the Prime Minister and the effect on sterling of rejecting the Prime Minister would be to destroy our capacity. Therefore I support the Prime Minister and the Chancellor.'

Then I spoke. 'Yesterday, Prime Minister, one crisis plan was put to the Cabinet and was rejected. Today another crisis plan – the true nature of which is now advancing on us – is before us; and it is based on the fact that we throw more people on the dole, and we then cut the dole but give tax remissions for people who are better off.

'This plan is based on two things: on Treasury forecasts that have been systematically wrong and on a monetarist theory that we don't, for one moment, accept ourselves and are only having foisted on us by others. Denis tells us now that if it is worse than we think it is going to be, we'll ease it up later. But it is already much worse than we thought it was going to be in July and the Treasury remedy is to increase the cuts. I therefore don't believe that we will ease up.

'Second, we are told that the trade union movement will welcome the cuts in benefit in order to help to reduce the pay differential for their workers. But they won't do anything of the kind. They will say, "If you bust your side of the Social Contract, we'll bust our side." And what they will say is let's go for big wage claims because that way we can keep the benefits up and we can reflate the economy to correct the deflation that the Government has imposed upon us.

'Then there will be only two weapons left in our armoury. One is monetary policy, where you don't have to bother with what the trade unions say, Mrs Thatcher's view, because you turn off the taps of money and leave them without any power; or a statutory pay policy. Those are the only two things left. There is an eerie parallel with 1931.'

Jim interrupted and said, 'There is no such parallel. I don't accept it. I have been reading the minutes you have been circulating, every one of them, and I don't accept it.'

'I am very sorry but if I am in the Cabinet I must say what I think and I think there is a parallel with 1931 because then, too, the loan hinged upon cutting the benefits.'

Jim interrupted again and said, 'Well, I lived through it. You didn't.'

'Well, my dad was in that Cabinet. They voted for the cuts in benefits, and I won't accept them and I make that absolutely clear.'

Michael Foot made one final point. 'We have had a discussion. Only a majority is for this view, it is not unanimous, and the Cabinet minutes always say, "The Cabinet noted with approval the summing-up of the Prime Minister." Well, we don't all approve of the summing-up of the Prime Minister.'

Jim said, 'My summing-up will say that a majority of the Cabinet agrees and therefore surely you could "note with approval that a majority of the Cabinet agrees".'

Michael came back to the point I had made at the very beginning and said, 'Is it clear that the Cabinet can suspend its final judgement until the very end of this whole business when we know the quantum, we know the response, we know the allocation, we know whether we can get import deposits; we know the whole acceptability?'

'Yes,' said Jim, 'I agree with that.'

With that the Cabinet adjourned at 1.15.

The foregoing diary was actually dictated in my room at the Department of Energy directly afterwards. Frances came in and wanted to know what happened so she sat while I dictated it. It is the moment of defeat and we have to recognise it. She said the *Titanic* was going down.

At 4.15 I went over to the House and thought it would be nice to have a word with Joe Ashton. Now he is a Whip I'm able to be a bit more candid with him. I told him, not in great detail, that the forecasts on unemployment and inflation were very high, that in fact the Government was going to go for cuts and deflation and was attacking benefits.

He said the truth was that the Party was absolutely punch-drunk now on anxiety and had been conditioned to what was likely to happen. In effect he was telling me to relax and not to get steamed up. It had all happened before. Eric Heffer had written an article today also saying that whatever happens, the Goverment had to be sustained.

At 5.30 I saw Michael Foot, who was distressed about this morning's Cabinet, and hoped he would have an opportunity of a word with Jack Jones, whom he hadn't actually seen for two or three weeks.

I'm thinking hard about how to handle the situation. It is most important not to get it wrong and go out on a limb but at the same time to try to bring the Movement in.

Wednesday 8 December
I got the report on the Windscale incident. On 10 October, nearly two months ago, there was a leak of high-activity waste material at Windscale which I was not told about. I wrote on Peter Shore's report that it was inexcusable and I would make a parliamentary statement tomorrow.

Monday 13 December
At 2.30 the two Nuclear Inspectors came about the Windscale episode. It was horrifying that neither of them had actually been up to Windscale to have a look, even though 100 gallons a day is seeping out. I was totally shaken and they were acutely embarrassed.

Went into the House, which was pretty full because of the Devolution debate, and I played it very low key. Just as I was leaving, Nicholas Ridley, Conservative MP for Cirencester and Tewkesbury, raised a question about the surveillance of trade unionists by the secret services, which must have severely embarrassed the Front Bench.

Wednesday 15 December
Today I had a report to the effect that some tritium had been found on the beach at Windscale a year ago which had not been explained. There didn't appear to be any link with the recent silo seepage but now they have

discovered that there could be a connection and so this raises the question of how long the leak has been going on. Was it reaching the beach?

I asked for all the details and tonight I had a note in my box that a man had inhaled some plutonium a year ago at the radio-chemical centre at Windscale and was now being watched. Now that I have demanded that all nuclear incidents be reported to me, I realise I shall be absolutely swamped by them. I have to find a way of revealing them without causing a scare but in view of the fact that tomorrow morning Peter is going to try to get a Cabinet view on Windscale, I'm hoping I can use some of the information to good effect.

Friday 17 December
There was an article by Peter Jenkins in the *Guardian* saying Jim Callaghan should sack me and get Joan Maynard, Lena Jeger, and Judith Hart removed from the Executive at next year's Conference.

Saturday 18 December
John Cunningham came to see me. He is desperately worried about Windscale because the plant is in his constituency.

Sunday 26 December
Caroline gave each of us a copy of the *Communist Manifesto* in our stockings, published in English in Russia, and she gave Josh a book called *Marx for Beginners* and gave Hilary Isaac Deutscher's three-volume biography of Trotsky. I read the *Communist Manifesto* yesterday, never having read it before, and I found that, without having read any Communist text, I had come to Marx's view. It is some confession to make in a diary but the analysis of feudal society, the role of the Church and religion, the class struggle, the impact of technology in destroying the professions, the cash society, the identification of monopoly and the internationalisation of trade and commerce, all these things had been set out absolutely clearly by 1848 by Marx and Engels. It is a most astonishing thing and I feel so ignorant that at the age of fifty-one as a socialist politician in Britain I should never have read that basic text before and I am shy to admit it.

There is no doubt that in the years up to 1968 I was just a career politician and in 1968 I began thinking about technology and participation and all that; it wasn't particularly socialist and my Fabian tract of 1970 was almost anti-socialist, corporatist in character with a democratic theme – management and labour working together. Up to 1973, I shifted to the left and analysed the Left. Then in 1974 at the Department of Industry I learned it all again by struggle and by seeing it and thinking about it, and I have been driven further and further towards a real socialist position, not a Marxist position particularly; in reading about the Levellers and our own heritage I realise that so much of British socialism goes back quite independently into our history. But, except for the fact that the *Communist Manifesto* wasn't written with an understanding of British history and British society, it is a most amazing summary of the impact of the Industrial Revolution – Marx was writing within seventy years of Adam Smith. So the Industrial Revolution gave rise to capitalism, socialism and trade unionism at about one and the same time.

I record this now while I am reading all the basic texts in order to try to understand what is going on.

Tuesday 28 December
It has been a very remarkable year really in the aftermath of the Referendum when the Party was in a terrible state of depression and the Government appeared to be going forward with its own right-wing policy unchallenged.

I must think about Europe. My concerns at the moment are how the Party should react to the Common Market and I think we should call for major reforms in the Treaty of Rome committing us to a democratic socialist association of states which will bring about a fundamental and irreversible shift in the balance of wealth and power in favour of the working people of Europe and their families. And it should be open to all countries and aim at dismantling all the federal parts so that it becomes an open association with none of the present centralisation and bureaucracy.

Next year I also want to try to restate the case for parliamentary democracy and democracy against capitalism in the very strongest way possible, to show why it is that the Labour Party is committed to democracy and free speech.

I say little of the family in this diary. Caroline is terribly busy. She has got two or three major projects on all the time and is highly respected and regarded by all the people in the educational world. Stephen has just had three months in America working with Senator Eagleton and has to finish his thesis, which is a big strain for him, particularly coming back to England after the glamour of Washington. Hilary is well established with Rosalind and his job with ASTMS will last as long as he wants it. Melissa has three years at LSE and Josh is kicking around until he goes to his polytechnic next year.

I'm very richly blessed with an extremely happy family life and could not be more content. I've had as much happiness and comfort and sustenance in my fifty-one years as any man could expect to have in two or three lifetimes, so even if things go wrong and I lose my seat – as I might well do in the next General Election – I have plenty to remember and a role to perform even if it isn't necessarily in the House of Commons.

Sunday 16 January 1977
Amazement of amazement, the *Sunday Times* had two leading articles today,

one saying that the motorcycle co-operative at Meriden must be saved, and the other singling me out for favourable mention for my open-government policy at the Department of Energy.

The background to this is that I had called in the Nuclear Inspectorate to ask them questions about the fast breeder, like 'What would happen if a fast breeder blew up?' They had answered, Well 10,000 (or whatever) would be killed, and I had stopped the discussion and said, 'I really cannot be told this in private, and know it privately; do you mind if I put the questions in writing to you and publish the answers?' So the answers were published this week.

It must be the first time in history, I think, that the Nuclear Inspectorate have been cross-examined by their responsible Minister, or indeed that the Minister has ever revealed in public the interrogation of his officials about nuclear policy, or about anything.

Monday 17 January
With Caroline to *Tribune*'s fortieth birthday party at Number 10 – it was immense fun. Jim was charming and had baked a cake which said, 'Happy Birthday *Tribune* – Life Begins at Forty', with a red ribbon round it. He made a little speech saying he read *Tribune* and had done for years, and yearned for the day when he would agree with it.

Then Jim took us down to the Cabinet Room, which I wanted Caroline to see. We all stood there – all the wives and Dick Clements, the Editor of *Tribune*, and his staff. Jim told me to stand behind my usual seat. 'Now, where do we all sit?' he asked. So I began going round and we could remember our side of the table, but when it came to the other side Jim couldn't remember. I went through them. 'There's Harold Lever, and next to him Fred Peart. Next to him David Ennals, then John Silkin . . .' When we got to the end we couldn't think of anybody else. So Jim pulled out his diary and said, 'Well, let's look it up and see who else is in the Cabinet.' 'Don't tell me,' I said, 'we forgot Edmund Dell.' In the far corner was Bill Rodgers's seat. We'd all forgotten about him. There was a great deal of laugher, and it was very agreeable.

We had a word with Denis and Edna Healey. Denis gave a good imitation of Mike Yarwood. He was full of *bonhomie* and goodwill.

Tuesday 18 January
I worked until 2, then up at 6.30 to go off to begin my tour of European capitals as President of the Council of Energy Ministers.

I took my own mug and lots of tea bags. When we arrived in Paris we were met by the Ambassador, Nico Henderson, a tall, grey-haired, scruffy man, almost a caricature of an English public schoolboy who got to the top of the Foreign Office. I don't think I had ever met him before; he was rather superior and swooped me up in his Rolls Royce.

The end of a day of negotiations, and I enjoyed it very much. In a way it's very relaxing not to be a British Minister, just a European one.

But I must admit that the standard of living of, for example, the Ambassador – a Rolls Royce, luxurious house, marvellous furniture, silver plate at dinner – is indefensible. Ours is a sort of corporate society with a democratic safety valve. What a long time it will take to put it right. And how do you get measured steps of advance? Undoubtedly openness is one, and negotiations and discussions with the trade unions is another. Nobody should have power unless they are elected.

Wednesday 19 January
At 7 in came the butler and the sub-butler with the silver salver and silver teapot and China tea and lemon, scrambled egg, crispy bacon, toast and marmalade.

We flew off to Brussels and went to the international press centre.

They hadn't really opened by 10.30 but we found a little corner in this lush building, had a cup of coffee, and who should buzz in but Sir Donald Maitland, our Ambassador to the EEC, who always looks very busy.

We sat and talked for a bit and the journalists, who had arrived by 10.45, were drinking at the bar. I had been warned that not many people would come to a press conference but about thirty-five journalists, French and British and from all over the Community, turned up. I simply told them what I had told every Minister.

Maitland looked terribly agitated. I think it was partly at the idea of the Community having an Eastern policy, which has terrified the Foreign Office – because they know nothing about it. I asked permission from nobody to broach the subject.

We went off from there for a lunch with the Belgians, given by Sir David Muirhead, our Ambassador to the Brussels Government, who lives in another of these great fancy houses with a butler, a sub-butler, a log fire and God knows what. I found the Belgians terribly funny, by which I mean that they laughed at my jokes.

The truth is that everyone who works at Brussels, be they Ministers, bureaucrats, representatives of the delegations or the press, have just got used to the fraud of it all, the muddle, the confusion and the obscurity. So, when someone comes along and says Ministers must be in charge and they must meet a directive and do things openly, then it is like saying the emperor has no clothes on. That is really the reaction.

We flew to Luxembourg, a ghostly airport which was absolutely empty. A snow plough or something had been along the runway, a large wartime runway built for the B52 Flying Fortress bombers. Gradually we saw these tiny figures in the snow waiting for us. It was like an exchange of prisoners in a spy story.

The Ambassador, Antony Acland, a relation of Richard Acland of the famous Devon family, was there and we drove off, together with the Permanent Secretary, into this idyllic little town and up to the twelfth floor of a tall office block. There was Monsieur Mart, who is actually called the Minister for the Middle Classes, Economy, Transport and Energy! He is a jolly man, and I liked him.

Luxembourg would really like to be a province in a bigger Europe. The people don't like the way the big nations fight for their own interests. Mart interpreted my informality and particularly my external perspectives as being farsighted and bold and leading only to common policies. Although I wasn't really deceiving him – I don't believe in a federal Europe – I do believe in harmonising our approach one way or another by agreements, as long as we don't get all these directives and regulations; that is what I object to, the power of the Commission and the law-making. But as to agreements – I'm all for those.

Back to the airport and flew back to Northolt in the snow. Lovely to be home.

Thursday 20 January
I got into the office at 8.30 this morning. Brian Sedgemore, whose appointment as my PPS was announced today, was there; we had a talk and went over a speech I am giving at a Tribune Group meeting tonight.

Cabinet. We came to Devolution and I raised one point – that in the provision for a referendum there should also be a referendum for electors in England. I said I forecast that we wouldn't get through a Bill under which the English were not also allowed to vote.

At the end of the Cabinet I passed a note over to Jim. Yesterday he had sent round a minute to all senior Ministers:

10 Downing Street

19 January 1977

BREVITY

The papers which I see – memoranda and reports addressed to me personally, as well as papers for Cabinet and its committees – are too long; and they seem recently to be getting longer. . . .

We cannot afford inflation in words and paper, any more than in our currency. It is often harder work to be brief – but only for the writer. We shall all benefit as readers. Let us adopt again in our ministerial papers the habit of setting out in plain words, and in short paragraphs, the main points (detail in appendices, if need be) and the recommendation. The same discipline should apply to memoranda etc addressed to the public bodies outside government and to the public. Please take any necessary action in your department to achieve this. Your Permanent Secretary

should inform the Head of the Civil Service of what has been done and he will report to me.
     L.J.C.

So in reply my note said:

PM
BREVITY
OK
A.W.B.
19.1.77

and I attached to it an extract from Mao's collected works which began: 'Let us now analyse stereotyped Party writing and see where its evils lie.'

I feel my relations with Jim are improving. I think maybe he needs me on the industrial democracy front, and now that Sedgemore is appointed I feel more cheerful.

After lunch I had a meeting with Friends of the Earth, and we had a fascinating discussion about civil liberties and nuclear power. They put a lot of questions to me; I said I would get them answered and write to them.

Saturday 22 January
Up early for my surgery all morning, then to the hall where the all-day policy conference of Bristol Labour Party was being held.

I stayed for about three hours, shivering in this icy-cold, bare hall.

But the meeting was a display of basic democracy and basic decency. There was the Chairman sitting on the platform entirely by himself and a chap sitting at another little table who was the head of the standing-orders committee. He had a little handbell which he announced he would ring after three minutes, and twice after five minute if the speaker didn't stop, then he would blow his whistle. Everyone laughed.

Most of the people were delegates and the agenda dealt just with Bristol issues. The first part was housing and the homeless, then direct labour, then resolutions about the Lord Mayor's office, and so on.

It was a mixture of socialists, Marxists and Christians, with powerful speeches about the immorality of evicting families: seven families have been evicted in Bristol, they said. One was an old man dying of cancer, another was an old man with asthma, another a battered wife with two children.

Tuesday 1 February
At 9.30 this morning, Frances Morrell's daughter Daisy, who is three and a half, came to the office. She had her hair done in little bows, and a red coat and a red anorak, and she was all shy. I showed her round the office and took lots of photographs of her and Frances.

Thursday 3 February

To Cabinet at 10.30. It was pouring with rain and there was a big traffic jam, due I think to a bomb scare in Whitehall. I had to run the last couple of hundred yards from Birdcage Walk to Number 10.

Unfortunately I have lost the notes I made at Cabinet – whether I left them at the Cabinet Office or dropped them somewhere I don't know. Anyway I shall have to dictate it from memory.

First of all next week's business, then a long discussion about how to handle the Scotland and Wales Bill because the Chief Whip reported that on his best estimate, after a great deal of lobbying and canvassing, we would be defeated by 39 votes on a timetable motion (guillotine). Michael Foot said it might be better to advance the referendum issue in the Bill and get that out of the way, and then proceed to the guillotine later.

The draft wording of the question which would be on the ballot paper for the Referendum was read out: 'The Government has suggested the establishment of a Scottish Assembly under devolution proposals contained in the Scotland and Wales Act, under which Scotland would remain a part of the United Kingdom. Are you in favour of the implementation of this Act in Scotland?' And the same for Wales.

Lunch with David Wood of *The Times*. He was born in Grantham, I think, and knew Margaret Thatcher's father, a local shopkeeper who became an alderman; he remembered the daughter when she was a little girl. We had a long talk about the Samuel Smiles Victorian ideals of self-help, duty, etc, which David Wood believed in.

He remarked, 'Margaret Thatcher's a very cautious woman, you know, very cautious. She will have to get rid of Airey Neave and George Gardiner and broaden her base; she may be bold in thought but in action she will be very cautious. She wants to get on with the trade unions very much and thinks she can: she sees no reason why she shouldn't. She knows they are powerful and she has got to learn to live with them. That's the way the Tories operate.'

Friday 4 February

I had to deal with Amoco. On Monday night there had been long discussions with Amoco which went on until midnight and which were supposed to be concluded on Tuesday but had foundered on the simple point that the President of Amoco Europe, Mr Aune, the Amoco executive, Norman Rubash, and the lawyer, Ed Bissett, had declined to accept the form of words that Shell and Esso had accepted: namely that they would have a statement of intent as to their refinery policy in Britain and their readiness to try to optimise the use of North Sea oil; and that they would conduct their trade in a way that would maximise the benefit to the United Kingdom. They would not accept this because they claimed it would commit them legally to a £100 million investment in the Milford Haven refinery and they were not prepared to do that.

So I said to Frank Kearton, 'Will you stick with me if I am strong?' Frank was terribly keen and the officials did in effect agree, so I called in Aune and Rubash at 11.15 without any of the others. They had been warned of the attitude I would adopt and I think they wanted to test it.

With me I simply had James Bretherton (taking notes), Frank, and John Liverman, and I asked Aune and Rubash what had gone wrong. They produced a long explanation about how the whole thing had changed, they had never understood that what was wanted was this, and they had produced another draft. I said, 'Look, I am not negotiating it. We were going to settle the whole thing on Friday and we went through the words very carefully.' They said that the board of directors would never yield their powers over investment.

So I said, 'You told me you were fully authorised to discuss it.'

'Well,' they said, 'will you look at this new draft?'

'No. I cannot go beyond the Shell–Esso arrangements.'

Rubash looked absolutely white. Aune looked shifty.

I continued, 'That is it. You are dealing with Her Majesty's Government and these participation talks are intended to make a real difference. We are not prepared to be pushed. You are not dealing with a sheikh in the 1940s, you know, you are dealing with the British Government in the 1970s.'

'Well,' they said, 'This hundred million clause . . .'

'I never mentioned a hundred million,' I said. 'You invented it and then you say it is a barrier. We have never asked that, but it is intended that there should be deep discussions about your market-policy – that is what the whole thing is about. You have to value the goodwill of the host government, and, if you don't attach importance to that goodwill, that is a matter for you. Will you please let me know by tonight.'

While we were talking, messengers came in with tea, so I turned round and waved my hand and they took the tea away. I was just coming to the end of the discussion and inside I was boiling with rage – I felt like the president of a banana republic dealing with a multinational company. I'll never forget that experience with Amoco. If they won't co-operate they won't get participation, and they won't get the licence, and that's it.

Saturday 5 February
I got home and worked like a fiend from about 1.30 to about 7.30, did my red box, signed all my letters, then put a few things in my satchel, put on my anorak, went to Liverpool Street and caught the train to Southminster, not having told Caroline, Lissie and Joshua, who were at Stansgate for the weekend, that I was coming.

I thought I would walk all the way to Stansgate but it would have taken about an hour and a half and I didn't think I would make it so I rang

Caroline from a call box. Actually she had been asleep for an hour but wouldn't hear of me walking all the way and got out of bed. I had got about a third of the way to Stansgate when they picked me up. It was lovely, and I would have been absolutely miserable at home on my own.

Monday 7 February
Joe Haines's book, *The Politics of Power*, is being serialised in the *Daily Mirror* and included a slashing attack on Marcia Williams. Marcia, who is in bed with a slipped disc and can't get up, issued a statement saying that Joe Haines had once had a whisky bottle broken over him and she had had to sponge his coat. So it looks as if the gang has fallen out. Apparently this afternoon Harold went to visit Marcia at her bedside.

Thursday 10 February
Cabinet, and Jim said, 'Before we start I would like to mention the Silver Jubilee; the Cabinet ought perhaps to consider giving a gift to the Queen – a token of some kind.' So Shirley Williams suggested a saddle, because Jim had said we want to give her something she would really use. Someone else said don't forget that Parliament gave Charles I a saddle, at which there was a lot of laughter.

I said, 'We are a Labour Cabinet, so if we are going to give her something shouldn't it be uniquely Labour?' I added, 'I am not suggesting a leather-bound volume of our constitution' – at which there was a sort of groan around the whole Cabinet. Fred Peart put his head in his hands and Jim said, 'Let him finish.' I continued, 'Well, I think we should perhaps give her something that comes out of the Labour Movement. I have got in my office a vase, given me by the Polish Minister of Mines, carved out of coal by a Polish miner. What about that?'

Elwyn Jones said, 'Well, in Wales we have beautiful clocks set in carved coal', so the suggestion wasn't entirely ridiculed. But I was interested in the reaction to the idea that we should give her something representing the work of working people.

Peregrine Worsthorne came to lunch; he is the Associate Editor of the *Sunday Telegraph*. I asked him about his work. He said he wrote on a Friday, and tomorrow he was going to write about Marcia and Joe Haines, and that the whole story reveals how corrupt government is, and why it should not have too much power. His article will show in effect how unfit for government Labour is, that respect for authority has been eroded by it, and this is damaging.

I told him my theory of the forty-year cycle: that there have to be real radical reforms about every forty years – 1832, 1867, 1906, 1945, 1980. He said, 'Yes, but next time they will be right-wing. Mrs Thatcher will tear up the Welfare State by its roots, and the health service and education. That's how the radicalism will manifest itself.'

I said, 'Maybe you are right, you know. It is going to be pretty disruptive.'

He added, 'She is prepared to deal with the unions as a power but with no social contract or wage control – she doesn't believe in all that; she will just deal with them as a power in a monetarist society.'

So I said, 'Well, you know Heath tried that with his monetarist policy, but he had to reverse it, and I think she will have to reverse it too.'

He asked me, 'Aren't you worried about the power of the unions?'

'I know what you mean – the middle class is worried – but if I look at the powerful groups I have to deal with, the unions are only a part. All right, Jack Jones is powerful, but that's nothing compared to what Fleet Street can do – it pillories you, holds you up to excoriation, Bernard Levin says you are mad. I feel like poor old Solzhenitsyn in Russia, except that Fleet Street can't actually put me in a lunatic asylum. There is the power of the big oil companies who operate here, and are bigger than nation states. There is the IMF, which forces us to cut the Welfare State. In that jungle of power I don't see the unions as being dominant.'

Worsthorne told me, 'I am not in favour of a further stage of reform. I think that the Establishment now needs to be defended, needs to have some backbone put in.'

I said, 'In 1970 the Establishment thought: when Heath comes in he will know all the answers, he'll take us into Europe and discipline everybody. But by the time we came to power in 1974 the Establishment was totally demoralised.'

Monday 14 February

This morning the papers reported that Tony Crosland was in hospital having been taken ill yesterday, and as the day proceeded it became clear that he was critically ill.

He evidently had a stroke and is deteriorating. Later in the day Bob Mellish came up to me and told me he was not expected to live. I asked Roger Stott, Callaghan's PPS, and he confirmed that in fact he might well die tonight, but that in any case he could never come back to work. I must say, looking back on it all – though I mustn't assume the worst – he really is my oldest political friend. I have known him since 1943 when he came back to Oxford on leave from the paratroopers and we spoke together in a debate. That is an enormous length of time and, although he has been arrogant and on the Right of the Party and difficult and supercilious and so on, I recognise that underneath it all there has been a kindness of heart and gentleness of manner and personal sympathy which I found immensely comforting and helpful. He supported me on a number of occasions, although we have been on entirely opposite sides of the Party. I really feel very sad for him, Foreign Secretary for less than a year, at the peak of his parliamentary career at fifty-seven.

More revelations in the papers this morning by Joe Haines, including that the CBI and the City demanded my dismissal as Secretary of State for Industry: this is not anything new, but just confirming it.

Tuesday 15 February
During lunch I phoned the Administrator of the Radcliffe Infirmary at Oxford and there is no doubt Crosland is dying – they don't know when. Later I heard from David Owen that he had never heard doctors so pessimistic about a stroke patient. Susan is with him and apparently is all right unless she meets friends and then she breaks down.

It's 2am and I am going home. I forgot to mention that at 7.30 for half an hour Frank Muller, from the Australian Labour Party, came to see me. He's an environmentalist and he told me briefly about the Australian Labour Movement's growing determination to stop uranium mining in Australia. He said the mining is of no particular benefit to Australia, it benefits the international uranium companies, and he thought there was a possibility that those interests had contributed to the overthrow of the Prime Minister, Gough Whitlam, in November 1975. He knew something that indicated that the companies were discontented with the Labour Party and the trade union attitude towards uranium before the election following Whitlam's removal.

It was a bit conspiratorial, but it was interesting, and I described the position here frankly – the enormous power of the nuclear lobby in Britain and my fear that we would go under to it. I wondered if Australia would be able to hold out so long on uranium that it could impose a moratorium worldwide. It has opened up as a left–right issue in Australia.

The facts are fascinating and I do find it one of the most interesting arguments at the moment. He was a serious, bearded, sensitive guy, a zoologist by training, employed by an environmentalist group financed by the Government. It gave me a new dimension to it all. There's a lot to be said for not being dependent on officials.

Wednesday 16 February
First engagement was at Number 10 for a joint meeting of the Cabinet and the NEC. Tony Crosland absent of course, and the latest news is that he has died mentally. He is really a breathing corpse. It's tragic.

One of the advantages of doing a diary is that when you dictate it from notes at night, or in this case the following morning, you do get a slightly different feeling about it. I came away feeling that Jim had absolutely clobbered the Executive and that there had been a lot of ill will, but it was just a debate, a regular old Labour Party discussion. The fact that we met together I think was worth while. I've been through so many periods when one thinks there is going to be trouble but in the end there never is.

Anyway I went back to the office and Robin Day came to lunch, the first meal with him for ages. I have known him for years, since 1945.

Over lunch he said he didn't like Mike Yarwood imitating him because Mike Yarwood had him on TV more often than he was on himself. I asked him what he would like to do in the future. Apparently he applied for the job of Director-General of the IBA and of the BBC and was turned down. He said he thought there was too much trouble whenever he got involved in anything.

I asked him if he would like to go into the House of Lords, an idea which excited him very much. He is fifty-two or fifty-three, a year older than me, and we all have to begin looking forward. I think Crosland's illness and impending death is making everyone think a bit about the future.

Then he talked a little bit about politics, about how Mrs Thatcher was a radical, that John Biffen would probably be Chancellor, Howe would get the Woolsack and that she would be a great reformer. This is the Tory line now. He didn't think there was a shift to the right at all, and of course he is the great architect of the notion of 'left-wing extremists' and all that. In all his broadcasts it is always the left-wing, the left-wing, the left-wing.

I didn't try to be provocative and it wasn't a very memorable lunch, but an agreeable one.

Brian Flowers came at 6.15 and stayed for an hour and a half; I really enjoyed it and I somewhat poured my heart out to him. 'Look, I really want your help because the whole nuclear thing is getting out of control. The lobby has got me by the neck; I don't know what to do about it. But I do want a new scientific adviser.' He said, 'You're right to remove Marshall – you can't have Marshall as both scientific adviser and Deputy Chairman of the AEA.' He suggested Sir Hermann Bondi from Defence, who would like to come, but Rampton doesn't want him.

We talked about civil liberties, the way in which the lobby was working, and how it might be checked and watched. It was candid and extremely friendly.

Thursday 17 February
Cabinet began at 10.50. On foreign affairs, David Owen sat in for Tony, who is lying literally on his death bed in Radcliffe Infirmary. David said that messages had reached him that Vorster, the South African Prime Minister, thought that Smith would accept black majority rule in Rhodesia in two years.

On President Idi Amin of Uganda, Peter Shore asked for more information about the killing of an archbishop and two Ministers, in effect by Amin. The men had 'confessed' to plotting against Amin, and I think he had then arrested the three men, and said later they had died trying to escape.

Peter asked, 'Do we have to have Amin at the Commonwealth Prime Ministers' Conference?'

So Jim said, 'Well, there is not much we can do. We are not the ones who invite people to the Conference. It is the Commonwealth Secretariat.'

Of course in the back of our minds is the possibility that if we did keep him out, which I suppose we are entitled to do, he might kill every English man and woman in Uganda as a reprisal. He is a brute.

Saturday 19 February

Heard on the 7 o'clock news that Tony Crosland died earlier this morning. It is extremely sad. He was so very good to me, taught me economics, helped me get a seat, was kind to me in Parliament, and under that gruff and arrogant exterior he really had a heart of gold. I liked him very much. I know other people didn't, and I was often critical and scornful of him and thought all this intellectual stuff was much overdone, but he did, through his book, have a profound influence. He was the high priest of revisionism or social democracy in the Labour Party for a generation, and the book will be studied and read long after his death.

Sunday 20 February

Melissa's twentieth birthday, bless her. She is such a lovely girl and she is a great source of pride to the family. She got all her presents and was thrilled.

The papers today are jam-packed with obituaries and tributes to Tony Crosland.

Roy Jenkins rated him above any living socialist philosopher. The rest of the papers went into an emotional spasm about him. I must say when I read it all it struck me that, all right, he was a very nice guy, he wrote a good book, but if I look back over his political career I can't honestly say his judgement was particularly good. Certainly *The Future of Socialism* misread the underlying crisis in a capitalist economy.

And, I had better be candid, I felt a twinge of jealousy at the thought of the guy who was going to be appointed to the Foreign Office tomorrow by Jim Callaghan. I suppose like anybody else I am ambitious and feel it is a bit hard to take if others are jumped above me.

Monday 21 February

To the House, and heard that David Owen had been made Foreign Secretary at the age of thirty-eight – a fantastic promotion. I must say it entertains me slightly that Roy Hattersley, David Ennals, Eric Varley and even Merlyn Rees and Shirley Williams have not got that job. Jim has created a new star in the Labour Movement and he has got another twenty-five years to go. If you begin as Foreign Secretary at thirty-eight you are an absolutely dominating figure.

Well, had a chat in the House of Commons, came home. Judith Hart has been brought back in as Minister of Overseas Development, and Frank Judd has been moved to the Foreign Office as number two to David Owen, which was quite a skilful move, and Joel Barnett has been put in the Cabinet.

I saw Merlyn as I was leaving and he said, 'What do you think of what Jim has done? Don't you think it proves that foreign affairs don't matter any more, compared to the economy?' I said, 'Not at all. Of course they're important. First of all, economic problems are now very largely seen as international, and secondly the Foreign Secretary has got an absolutely crucial job to do in setting our relationship with the Common Market. Are we to be a major nation or are we going to be submerged into a federation? These are crucial questions.' Merlyn was taken aback a bit, and I said I was delighted for David.

Tuesday 22 February
In the Commons there was the vote on the guillotine motion to limit the time available for the Scotland and Wales Bill and we were defeated by twenty-nine. Twenty-two Labour MPs, I think, voted with the Tories, quite a number abstained, and we were absolutely smashed.

It is a very big political event because we won't get the Bill through now. The Government will have to think about what it is going to do. It is a major defeat. The Scottish Nationalists are absolutely furious. Quite what will happen in Scotland and Wales I don't know. It could become a nasty situation, very quickly.

Wednesday 23 February
Caroline and I went to dinner with the Speaker. First time I had ever been to the Speaker's flat in the House of Commons – you go up in a little lift above the state rooms. The other guests were Bill Rodgers, Merlyn, Cledwyn Hughes, Joel Barnett and wives. I felt a terrible sense of gloom. There were all the pro-Market people, all Cabinet Ministers, and I didn't enjoy it; I don't think Caroline did much either. I do like George Thomas, and I get on well with Joel and the others, but I felt the one thing you couldn't discuss was politics. Here we were at a political dinner and there was no possibility of a really political discussion between us. I was very quiet.

Thursday 24 February
After the Cabinet I went straight to Broadcasting House to make a programme with Keith Joseph. Keith is an absolutely tortured soul – he was in agony, his face twisted in anxiety, his head in his hands. He was scribbling notes, and worrying; he really is a sick man. We talked about Heath, and the U turn, and what Heath's Cabinets were like; Keith said most discussions took place in Cabinet committees, there was a sort of Inner Cabinet and the Cabinet as a whole did not discuss very much. Keith Joseph himself realised his mistake about policy and now favoured more open government. I tried to be jolly and cheerful. Then we went and recorded a 45-minute discussion.

Sunday 27 February
London, and Caroline and I went to the Foots' for dinner. The Baloghs were there, and Judith and Tony Hart, welcome back after Judith left the Government nearly two years ago. The Shores came in later.

We talked over dinner about Ministers dying early, about abortion – it was a morbid discussion, really.

Monday 28 February
Did my box, and found a letter from Sir Peter Ramsbotham, our Ambassador in Washington, to Sir Jack Rampton, saying he had seen Schlesinger, who stated that the fast-breeder programme would be sharply cut back. That is really very important, marvellous news. So I might win.

Tuesday 1 March
To the Cabinet Economic Committee, and we came to a paper on unemployment. The paper described a 300,000 increase in unemployment this year.

I should add that Rampton, my Permanent Secretary, had written on my brief in his own hand, 'Why don't we have national service? We are the only country in the whole Community who don't have a year's national service.'

Wednesday 2 March
Frances Morrell had been to Number 10 yesterday or the day before and she told me that the only thing worth my doing was to become Leader of the Party. I said there was another choice, to influence the Party, and she said there was no real influence except as Leader. But I've seen so many lives wrecked by ambition and I don't intend to do that.

Thursday 3 March
The Editor of the *Daily Telegraph*, Bill Deedes, came to lunch. I've always liked Deedes. He told me that F.A. Hayek, the author of *The Road to Serfdom*, had come to see him the other day, and Hayek had said, 'You know, my view is that Britain ought to pursue an effective monetarist policy – but I'm very worried about unemployment; it's on such a scale now.'

Well, if Hayek is worried about unemployment, and the Editor of the *Daily Express* is worried, and Bill Deedes is worried, why isn't the Government worried?

At the very end Bill said, 'You know, you are a very thoughtful guy, you've a lot of experience, you can obviously manage your department, and you have got a lot more supporters in the *Daily Telegraph* than you might think.' He was frightfully nice.

Monday 7 March
Tony Crosland's memorial service was held in Westminster Abbey. It was a

tremendous event, as you would expect for a Foreign Secretary dying in office. The Abbey was packed, the Cabinet in the choir stalls on the left, where as a Westminster schoolboy I used to sit every day for Latin prayers. Opposite were all the other Ministers and Ambassadors. There were three former Prime Ministers over on the right – Heath, Wilson and Home – and Princess Alexandra was there representing somebody.

It was the Establishment recognising and at the same time burying the idea of social democracy. First of all we had the Dean saying a few words about Tony's incisive and lively mind, about his passion for a just and equal society, his unfaltering desire to raise up the underprivileged and to care for the less fortunate. Then we had the national anthem, then Derek Gladwin, southern regional secretary of the GMWU, described in the programme as Grimsby-born, who read Ecclesiasticus, 'Let us now praise famous men.' Of course we had the hymn 'Jerusalem'. Then a reading by Dick Leonard, a past PPS of Tony's, from *The Future of Socialism*, in which the first passage read was as follows:

> It is not only dark satanic things and people that now bar the road to the new Jerusalem but also, if not mainly, hygienic, respectable, virtuous things and people, lacking only in grace and gaiety.

The most astonishing thing to read, that the only bar to socialism was now hygienic respectability and virtue. Later came a passage attacking the Webbs and continuing:

> Today we are all incipient bureaucrats and practical administrators. We have all so to speak been trained at the LSE, are familiar with blue books and white papers and know our way around Whitehall.

An absolutely élitist view of politics; then finally the famous phrase:

> Total abstinence and a good filing system are not now the right signposts to the socialist utopia, or at least, if they are, some of us will fall by the wayside.

After an address by Lord Donaldson, his old friend Jack Donaldson, we had the prayer for Parliament, which contains these words –

> That thou wouldst be pleased to direct and prosper all their consultations to the advancement of thy glory, the good of thy church, the safety, honour and welfare of our sovereign and her dominions.

and so on – the parliamentary prayer which of course is absolutely pre-parliamentary, let alone pre-democratic.

That memorial service really could be published as a Gaitskellite pamphlet. It was the Gaitskellites mourning their dead.

Saturday 12 March
I had a bath and Caroline and I went and bought a couple of vases and drove to Woolwich Town Hall at 10.30 for my driver Ron Vaughan's marriage to Peggy. It was a lovely day and we went to the reception in the Star Hotel.

Sunday 13 March
Caroline and I picked up her cousins, Jean and Dudley Bahlman, and drove to Number 10.

We looked at portraits of all the Prime Ministers, which Hamilton, Gladstone's secretary, had arranged would be put on the stairs. I had my polaroid camera and took pictures of Dudley beside Gladstone's portrait and sitting at Gladstone's desk.

I should think Heath had spent millions redecorating the place – a fantastic amount of redecoration. We looked into the 'Garden Room' and there was one of the famous Garden Girls, high-society typists and secretaries who work for Number 10. There are thirteen of them and one is always on duty. She was working at a Singer sewing machine. It was just like drifting into a country house, the last remnants of Edwardian England. These girls are from 'good' families, having been to Roedean and other girls' public schools, because class is seen as the ultimate safeguard of national security.

Then we went into Number 11 and Number 12 Downing Street and in Number 12 we saw pictures of the government Whips in 1910, including Father, who was then in the Liberal Party.

Monday 14 March
John Hill came in to talk about Windscale. I asked 'What are the real hazards there?' and he told me something extraordinary. 'Well, there's activity everywhere you dig on that site. Don't forget that after the war Windscale started as a weapons site. We would be pushed to produce 20 kilograms of plutonium before the Russians marched on Berlin; Windscale was given top priority. Whenever we had a spill we just covered it up. For example, in 1957 one of the reactors caught fire and we simply poured in 300,000 tons of water which went right through the plant and into the ground. You can't dig anywhere without the soil producing a radioactive response.'

He said the plant itself was built to two standards of containment: there were the double-clad, no-leak tanks; and there was the low-activity waste. There was always some seepage from all of it but there were inspection checks.

Tuesday 15 March
Cabinet discussed the proposed sale of BP shares which had been agreed as part of the IMF deal in December and I was called on to speak first. I said that, as the Cabinet would remember, I was strongly opposed to the sale of shares and the public reaction had also been adverse; 100 Labour MPs of the Left, Right and Centre, including John Cartwright, Phillip Whitehead and Jeremy Bray, had signed a motion against it, and Len Murray had reminded us that it would be a breach of the Social Contract.

Then I read the paragraph from the Public Accounts General Purposes Sub-Committee criticising the sale of the shares.

Going round the table, Harold Lever and Edmund Dell were of course in favour of selling the shares. Denis Healey said it would cost us 2p on income tax if we didn't. Peter Shore wanted to leave it a bit and Bruce Millan said something helpful. I said at the end that the argument that it would damage BP if we had a big shareholding was nonsense; they had always complained about it, but no one had ever mentioned it to me. If we did reduce our holding and a foreign government bought the shares, it would be awful. People said that the North Sea was in hock and mortgaged up to the hilt and this would reinforce that view. Why not defer it?

But I was defeated. Denis said we had to know today in time for his Budget.

Thursday 17 March
Cabinet at 10. The first thing was that Jim said, 'I told the Cabinet I would buy a gift for the Queen and I asked her what she would like and she said she would like something she would use personally, something she really could use herself.' So Peter asked, 'Well, what is it?' He said, 'A silver coffee-pot.' Everyone laughed, because the one thing she must have a million of is silver coffee-pots. So anyway, Audrey Callaghan had gone out and found one and it was brought in and put on the table. It is Victorian and, since it will cost each member of the Cabinet £15, it is worth at least about £370.

I said, 'I assume that as it is a Cabinet coffee-pot it won't leak?' Jim said, 'You can say that to the Queen yourself.'

We went on to Carter, and Jim reported on his trip with David Owen to the United States. He said Jimmy Carter is a very fast reader, has an amazing capacity to absorb his briefs; he reads at something like 3,000 words a minute. 'About the same speed that Harold Wilson writes his books,' I said. Jim went on to say Carter was a great supporter of the Labour Party, and when Jim had told him, 'Well, we may save the country but lose the Election', Carter had replied, 'Well, I hope you succeed with both.'

Friday 18 March
To Bristol, and was met at Temple Meads by someone from the Independent Businesses Association. I had geared myself up to sympathise

with small businesses and at the same time I was rather nervous of them because I thought they would all be potential National Front people.

Well, I couldn't have had more of a surprise because Mr Tucker, who met me, a man of about sixty-five, born in Bristol, couldn't have been nicer or more politically sympathetic. He hated the Common Market and had been Labour all his life. We and his son, who looked like a really tough self-made Tory businessman, drove in a Rolls Royce to Transport House, Bristol, where I met the small businessmen in the company of Harry Wright of the CSEU. It was an absolutely fascinating hour.

They talked about being inadequately represented. Their voice was not heard. They can live with a lot of legislation, but, said Mr Tucker, the big firms control the paper-money empires and they want recognition of their role.

A printer who employed thirty-five people said, 'I may look wealthy on paper with my premises and plant but I work very hard. I want to pass it on to my sons, but the business would have to be sold to pay for death duties.' He stated that half the people in this country are employed by small businesses; but corporation tax, VAT, PAYE, CTT, CGT, masses of civil servants and a huge inflation of tax levels made things very difficult.

Then Mr Tucker's son said, 'Equality and fairness are not the same. We are not speculators or big businessmen, we are all professional managers, and we are oppressed by the weight of the legislation. We want to be reasonable but it is a weight, and we would rather employ more people than pay more tax.'

It was a very useful meeting; I thoroughly enjoyed it.

Monday 21 March
The papers are full of Election fever. Everybody is steamed up about it but I am rather calm because I am absolutely sure a deal will be done with the Liberals (Michael made it pretty clear last night) and because if there isn't a deal and there is an Election we won't do all that badly.

Also in the papers today, the *Cambridge Review*, to which Francis Cripps contributes, forecasts a rise in unemployment to about two million; and the press has given it very little coverage.

The Labour Party–Trade Union Liaison Committee met at 10.30. It was agreed we would set aside the agenda and discuss the current parliamentary situation. Jim was asked to speak, and began, 'Well, Chairman, I think . . .' And Barbara as usual said, 'Would you speak up, Jim.' Barbara's a bit deaf, I think.

So Jim continued, 'Well, I was trying to think of what to say!'

Listening to the discussion, I came to this conclusion. David Basnett, Len Murray, Hugh Scanlon and Jack Jones all want the Government to survive and would be perfectly content to do a deal. They are critical of the Left because they think the Left would bring the Government down. So the trade union leaders ask what is the lesser of two evils in the present situation. Well, the Labour Government is the lesser of two evils compared to the Tories, and Labour with a bit of Liberal support is still the lesser of two evils. No doubt they would carry it further and say, 'Look, if you put up with the Common Market, which limits the freedom of action of the Government, and with the IMF, which limited the freedom of action of the Government, then clearly the Liberal limitation on freedom of action will be less.'

If you take that view – that Jim must be kept as Prime Minister (which is different now from having a Labour Party in power) – that is the only conclusion you can reach. I might add that the trade union leaders are terrified that their own position will be put at risk, if their members say: Well, you delivered us tied hand and foot into the hands of the Tory Government.

Tuesday 22 March

I had a morning at home till 11.30. More speculation about the deals that are being done, and I am quite clear in my mind that one *is* being done.

At 12.40 Francis and Frances came in and we had a blazing row because I said I thought that in my speech to the trade union group of MPs this evening I should say something that bore upon the current political situation. Frances disagreed. She was going to have lunch, so I worked in my room and wrote a few things and had some sandwiches, then she came back and we went over it again. She said, 'Let them discredit themselves. Just sit back and do nothing, say nothing.'

'That's very cynical,' I replied.

'Well, being in this place has made me cynical.'

So I said, 'Well, surely we must sustain the government campaign for our policies and get re-elected with a big enough majority to implement them?'

'No, no, if you go along with this, you are going along with a coalition.'

'Well, shall I resign?'

'No, don't resign. Just stay there.'

It was an awful meeting, and she was very upset and left the room.

Francis Cripps stayed and I talked to him, probing him. He said, 'You can't put it right with a speech. You have got to quietly make contact with all the people in the Labour Movement who are thinking it out for themselves and support them and encourage them and gradually re-create a new Labour Party from inside the wreck of this one.' He was quite sensible. I'm sorry I was cross with Frances Morrell, but she is a difficult woman and I am a difficult man, and when I think I am right I am usually wrong.

Caroline and I went together to the Waldorf for the annual party given by the Thompson brothers, the Labour Party's solicitors. The general rumour is there is a deal and we heard on the 10 o'clock news that Pardoe had said there would have to be a written deal.

Wednesday 23 March

A momentous day. As you might expect, the press was full of rumours of deals and talks. I thought about it again this morning, and after talking it over with Caroline I decided I would oppose any long-term deal with the Liberals. I had a message before I left at 9.30 to say that the Cabinet had been called for 12.

I went to the Cabinet at 12 and there were crowds of people in Downing Street, including hundreds of photographers.

Jim opened the Cabinet absolutely red-faced. I have never seen him so red. It was strange; he was scarlet. Michael was white and drawn.

Jim said the Cabinet would recall that last week the Chief Whip reported we would lose the vote of confidence tonight, and that at the TUC–Labour Party Liaison Committee last Monday it was clear the trade union leaders did not want an Election. They had encouraged us to hold discussions with other parties while preserving the integrity of our party. 'In the last two days,' he said, 'I have been engaged in talks and plans, including contingency plans for an Election on 5 May and the Budget problems associated with that. I am grateful for the forbearance of colleagues and I will now report the result of these discussions.

'We began with high hopes for the support of the Ulster Unionist MPs and it is not clear yet what they are going to do. Jim Molyneaux and Enoch Powell would like to support us, and in these discussions we have not neglected the interests of Gerry Fitt and the SDLP. The Ulster Unionists have proposed that we recommend to a Speaker's Conference that there should be more Ulster Members, and legislate to that effect.

'Now,' said Jim, 'I won't take the Cabinet through the long discussions which took place, but last night an agreement was reached with the Liberal Party which I will read, and will circulate. I would ask members of the Cabinet to return their copies.' He said the documents would be signed by himself and David Steel; then he went through the details of the agreement.

By 20 votes to 4 – the four being Peter Shore, Stan Orme, Bruce Millan and myself – the Cabinet consented to the Lib–Lab Pact.

It was now about 1.20 and Jim said, 'I must now ask those who have voted against it if they are prepared to go along with it.'

Stan Orme said, 'Yes, Prime Minister.'

I said, 'I can't answer that question because, despite Denis's comment that the Prime Minister speaks for the Party, all you can do round this table is commit the Cabinet. You can't commit the Party. The Cabinet does not control the Parliamentary Party, or the National Executive, or the Party in the country, and therefore the best I can say to you, Prime Minister, is that there will have to be consultations with the PLP, with the Executive and, in my case, with my own constituency Labour Party, and I am afraid I cannot answer your question until those consultations are complete.' He didn't press me.

That was it and, feeling very sick, I went over to my office. Frances was in the canteen and I scooped her up before she began her lunch and we had a talk. She was immensely agitated about the whole thing. 'This is the Left losing again and we must do something immediately,' she said.

So that is it. Without any consultation with Cabinet colleagues as a whole, Jim and Michael have negotiated something absolutely contrary to what Michael had told me on Sunday night.

Thursday 24 March

On the way to the office I went to Metyclean, which is one of my favourite ports of call when things are going wrong. I bought myself a Casio quartz clock computer which has the most fantastic facilities – gives you the time, works as a stopwatch and as a calculator, and has four alarms. It weighs four ounces and fits into your pocket. I was thrilled with it.

Got back to my room at 7.40 and the phone rang. It was Jim. 'There's a letter going round criticising the arrangement with the Liberals,' he said. 'I just want to tell you that, if you sign it, it will be incompatible with your membership of the Government.'

So I said, 'Well, I've already signed it.'

'In that case I want your resignation.'

'I had better think about it,' I replied.

'You know you have been sailing very close to the wind.'

'Jim, all it says is that we should have a special meeting of the Executive. It doesn't comment on the Liberal thing.'

'Yes, but it has been started by Mikardo, and anything Mikardo does is bound to be damaging to the Party.'

I said, 'Actually Eric Heffer asked me to sign it at the Party meeting.'

'Well, that's it,' he said. 'I want your resignation.'

I told him I wanted to think it over and he continued, 'I know you saw Mikardo yesterday and it was a pretty uncomradely thing to tell him what went on in the Cabinet. And it was pretty uncomradely to tell the newspapers.'

I said it wasn't a very comradely thing for me to hear about the deal with the Liberals from Pardoe forty-eight hours before the Cabinet was told.

'Well, we were very busy,' said Jim.

'Maybe you were. If you want to get rid of me I fully understand; perhaps having done a deal with Steel you don't need me any more.'

Jim insisted that that wasn't the case but he wanted an answer by tonight, as he was leaving for Rome in the morning.

After 11, I rang Number 10 and asked to speak to the duty officer. After a long pause, Jim came to the phone.

'Oh, Jim – Tony Benn. I've withdrawn my signature.'

'Well, I appreciate that very much,' he said. 'If it comes out that your name was withdrawn, will you say it was a mistake?'

Then I rang Frances and told her it was all over. 'You should never have signed it,' she said. 'It has weakened your position.'

'Don't attack me, please, Frances. Don't criticise me.'

Actually she is under pressure at the moment. She told me this morning she couldn't go on, the strain was too great.

That's the end of another immensely eventful day.

When I reflect on it, I probably should not have signed that letter.

Sunday 27 March

Caroline and I decided that we would not attend any more of the Sunday night dinners. I'm not saying some of the participants couldn't be brought in in some way – Stan Orme and Peter Shore certainly could – but it must be on the basis that we really are trying to work out how to re-create the Party and not just stumbling on.

Tuesday 29 March

Brussels for the meeting of Energy Ministers of the EEC. I had breakfast in my room in Donald Maitland's beautiful house. The room had heavy shutters which opened on to a balcony, overlooking a lovely garden bathed in bright spring sunshine. It was very cold, however, and flurries of snow were settling on the frozen grass.

We sat from 7 in the morning until 5.30 the following morning, but frankly I don't think the discussions were interesting enough to relate in detail. I took my white mug and got tea brought to me throughout the day.

I took the chair, and the first thing I did in the session was to ask whether Ministers would agree to having the Energy Council conducted in the open. I went round each representative in turn and every one of them found reasons why it couldn't be done – except Dick Mabon, bless him, who said yes. So that disposed of that idea.

The French are so good at Europe. I do admire them. They are clear-headed, logical, quiet, and they present their arguments in a Community spirit. The Germans, on the other hand, are blunderers and end up banging the table. The little five hate the big countries and band together to keep us in order, but they are frightened of the industrial and economic strength of Germany, whose geographical position allows her to dominate Denmark, the Netherlands, Belgium and Luxembourg. Everybody worships France because of her skill in diplomacy and her grandeur. Italy is just a beggar on the southern flank, a transparently devious beggar.

I'm being very blunt because I'm angry! The Irish are trying to be helpful, but they don't want to be thought of as an appendage of Britain. Indeed, to be lined up with the British all the time is a slight embarrassment for Dublin on the Continent, and so we can't really rely on them for support.

Anyway, bed at 5.30 am.

Saturday 9 April

Slept till after 10, had a mug of tea and dictated my diary for the last four days.

I should mention that on Thursday night President Carter announced that the Americans were going to wind down their reprocessing operations and stop work on the fast-breeder reactor because of the risk of proliferation from the manufacture of plutonium. It was a tremendous statement, and the BBC took it up immediately. John Hill attacked it on Friday's 1 o'clock news, while Brian Flowers welcomed it.

I had a message from Number 10 that I was not to comment on it, which made me very angry – a British Energy Minister forbidden to comment on American energy policy! The nuclear lobby has obviously got at Jim, saying it will wreck our relations with the Common Market and upset the French and the Germans.

So I sent a message back saying that I wouldn't comment on the non-proliferation aspects but I would like to comment on the energy implications. I got a message back that I wasn't to do that either. It really is insulting, and I'm beginning to wonder whether Energy has now become far too important for me to remain in charge, and whether Jim might not try to move me to another department.

Saturday 23 April

James Bretherton rang to say there had been a blowout in the Ekofisk field and 4,000 tons of oil had bucketed into the sea in just twenty-four hours. I said I might go up there, and much of the morning was spent on that.

Jim rang me. 'Your phone has been off the hook.'

'I was just using it.'

'Well, it was,' he said. He was very shirty. 'If you are going to look at the blowout, why don't you go to Norway?'

I decided I would and sent a message.

Apparently the blowout is huge, there's a force 10 gale and low cloud, but aircraft can't fly lower than 5,000 feet in case there is an explosion, and ships have been banned for 25 miles around. I shall fly over the field and then go on to Stavanger or Oslo.

Sunday 24 April

Up at 6.30, and left for Northolt. I boarded an RAF Andover with James Bretherton, Bernard Ingham, Henry George, our Director of Petroleum Engineering, and a guy from the Board of Trade Marine Division, and we headed for the Ekofisk field.

We were kept at 3,000 feet and five nautical miles and it was a most remarkable sight – a great jet of oil and spray and the slick spreading a sheen over the water. A number of vessels were standing by, including a warship.

We cruised around for about half an hour, before going on to Oslo to

meet the Industry and Foreign Ministers. We talked for two hours at the
airport hotel and they reported what had happened and went into all the
other aspects – terrorism, fire, cost, fisheries and research.

Flew back, gave some more interviews at Northolt and came home.
There was some coverage on the news but not much.

Thursday 28 April
Cabinet at 10.30. David Owen reported on Pakistan and the Middle East.

David Ennals interrupted in his odiously helpful way. 'I would like, Prime
Minister, if I may, to intervene for a moment to say how well I feel David
Owen has done in his recent visits to Africa and the Middle East, and
perhaps it would be in order, since we don't thank each other very much, for
this to be said.'

So Jim observed, 'Well, I said how well David had done last week. I can't
say it every week.'

I said, 'I take it this is the equivalent of Idi Amin eating his Cabinet
Ministers' – referring to a story in today's paper from a Ugandan defector
that Amin had killed a member of his Cabinet, had his liver cut out and
mixed with his lunch.

'If I started eating my Cabinet I don't know who I would eat first,' said
Jim, looking around the table and settling on me.

The rest of the Cabinet was devoted to the direct elections issue.

I had a meeting to review the case of a Mr Gillen, who died in the early
Sixties of leukaemia, having worked for three years for the AEA. His widow
was claiming that his illness was due to his work.

Jack Jones had written to me several times about it, so in the end I called
this meeting with the AEA legal, professional and medical staff, and the
Department of Social Security sent their administrative and medical people
along. Alex Eadie was there with me – which was a great comfort because,
having been a miner, he was familiar with the whole question of
compensation cases. I didn't have much of a leg to stand on, to be candid,
but I went into it very carefully. At the tribunal in 1964 the whole thing had
hinged on whether it was probable or merely possible that this guy had
contracted leukaemia from his work in the AEA. The judgement had been
that it was only possible.

But on questioning them I was told that Japanese survivors from
Hiroshima and Nagasaki had suffered this particular type of leukaemia;
secondly I drew out that there had been some marginal change in diagnostic
and analytical skills since 1964; thirdly, that the National Radiological
Protection Board had been set up since 1964; fourthly, that an appeal had
actually been heard since 1964.

I decided to write to David Ennals and ask him to get the matter looked at
again. I have never seen so many glum faces in my life.

Monday 2 May
First meeting at 10 was to prepare for the Downing Street summit with Carter.

The second item on the agenda was the implication of President Carter's statement on energy, and David Owen had presented a paper which had been written by his officials. David declared at the beginning that the paper was too complacent – which it was.

I said, 'I wasn't consulted about this and my officials tell me they weren't fully consulted. It is based on the assumption that there are no defects in our policy. We ought to be a bit more modest. What is happening now is the first serious re-examination of nuclear power; there are problems of plutonium loss and uranium loss, of toxic waste, the destination of which is undecided, of large-scale plutonium handling, of uranium supplies, of what to do about the fast breeder and about the export of sensitive technologies. We ought to have considered all this.'

David Owen thought we should welcome the Carter proposals and study them, we should link up with the USSR, and we should have some links with the IAEA and the nuclear suppliers group.

I added, 'We are highly trusted in the United States through our scientific knowledge and technical capacity in nuclear matters, but we are not America, we are independent, unless we upset the EEC countries.' All the officials nodded because they are determined that Britain must not alienate the French or the Germans. That is the main concern of the British Establishment – to bow and kowtow to Europe.

Thursday 5 May
Cabinet began at 10.30. As we were sitting down, Shirley said to me, 'Your paper on nuclear policy was the most brilliant paper I have ever seen' – referring to the one we discussed on Monday. So that strengthened my feeling that the social democrats are potential allies against nuclear power.

Jim referred to the summit of the industrial nations in London at the weekend and Carter's visit to north-east England tomorrow. Carter would be tremendously well received, but he hadn't realised what a row there would be over which colliery band should be chosen to play!

Saturday 7 May
At 12 Ron Vaughan came and drove me to Lancaster House to meet President Carter at his drinks party. It was absolutely jam-packed with journalists and Ambassadors wandering about, but I went through to the little room where we normally receive guests. Carter's son Jeff was there; he is twenty-one, doing Geography and Geology at Washington, and wants to get involved in the International Geophysical Year. He was a real Southern lad from Georgia and he looked a bit awkward, yet you could see he was

having the time of his life. He was obviously very proud of his dad and I rather liked him.

Well, I had to catch a train to Swindon at 1.20, and Carter still hadn't arrived at 1 o'clock. It was clear that I wasn't going to see him and I asked the people there whether I should go or stay. Some said I should stay, and that it was a great opportunity. But I decided to go and do my May Day meeting. Someone else said, 'I am sure the President would expect you to keep in touch with the grass roots.'

So I said to young Jeff Carter, 'Well, as I am going to miss your father, can I give you a message? I am the Secretary of State for Energy and, first of all, I hope he won't be pressured into giving up his nuclear policy.'

'Oh no, he won't,' he said.

'And, secondly,' I went on, 'tell him we are old family friends of the Niebuhrs' – at which point he interrupted and said, 'Ah, my father has read every single word that Reinhold Niebuhr has written.'

'Well,' I added, 'we used to stay with him in New York', and I quoted Niebuhr's remark that man's capacity for evil makes democracy necessary and man's capacity for good makes democracy possible. 'Remember two Ns,' I said. 'Nuclear and Niebuhr.'

I had brought a copy of my Levellers pamphlet to give to Carter, so I put on the front 'To President Jimmy Carter from Tony Benn' with a little note saying that this traced our common heritage from Amos to Micah through the English Revolution and the American War of Independence and so on. I scribbled on the back, 'Sorry to have missed you and I have sent a message through your son.'

Had a mug of tea and some sandwiches on the train and arrived in Swindon just after 2. We marched through the town with the band, and I made a speech in the park. Afterwards I was driven to Reading, and then I came home, so exhausted that I couldn't work, so I watched the Eurovision Song Contest and went to bed.

Monday 9 May
Arthur Hawkins from the CEGB came to say goodbye. I have had some tremendous clashes with him, he is such a difficult man, and I thought it would be rather a painful goodbye. I asked after his health, and then blow me down if he didn't say how much he enjoyed an article on Father which I had written. He said Father was an old Victorian Nonconformist and that I was a chip off the old block. So that was a nice surprise.

Then he mentioned by name one civil servant in my department and suggested I get rid of him. He said that this man was disloyal to me and could not be trusted. 'He said to me once, "Arthur, I would very much like a holiday. Can you arrange a trip?" ' Arthur said he wouldn't do it. 'You check the contracts he awards,' he told me. It was really rather frightening but I didn't pursue it further.

Sunday 15 May

I lay in bed till 12. There is a huge row about Peter Jay's appointment as Ambassador to Washington. It will weaken Jim's position on the direct elections issue and make it harder for him to sack me.

Monday 16 May

At last Thursday's PLP, Jim had apparently threatened to resign if he didn't get his way on Peter Jay. The fact that there is so much bitterness over this does suggest that Jim's spell is broken now.

Later I had a deep discussion with Frances and Francis about the whole affair. Sir Peter Ramsbotham has made a skilful statement in Washington saying what a brilliant and imaginative choice Jay was, how the handover would be smooth and so on. It is ironic that Ramsbotham has come out of this so well while Jim has been made to look an absolute swine. As somebody said, why didn't Jim just appoint Ramsbotham as Governor of Bermuda and *then* replace him with Jay, instead of the other way round?

Wednesday 18 May

I had a curious nightmare last night. I was standing by a deep concrete pit in a prison with a noose round my neck. I swayed over this pit, looking down and knowing that with the drop the rope would break my neck, and there was this tremendous compulsion to jump, but I didn't. I woke up in a sweat and found it was 3.50. Perhaps it meant that I have managed to control my self-destructive urges; or maybe I was visualising in dramatic form the problems of resignation or dismissal from the Cabinet over direct elections.

Friday 20 May

I went straight to the House of Commons for a meeting of the GEN 74 Committee. We had a couple of papers before us: one on how we should handle the follow-up to the summit on proliferation, the other on the transportation of plutonium. On the latter, I asked three questions.

'How is plutonium actually moved at the moment – is it by sea, land or air?'

I was told that it was moved by sea in steel canisters actually welded to the side of the ship, transported by land in this country, and that small quantities were moved by air.

'What protection is given, particularly as it crosses from one country to another?'

'We protect it till it passes out of our hands and then another country takes it in.'

'What effective safeguards are there that the plutonium we send abroad, for fast-breeder reactors, research or whatever, is actually used for the purpose intended? For example, do the French account for the use they make of our plutonium?'

I was told that under the Euratom Treaty they didn't.

I think I put my finger on three important questions that officials, technicians and scientists – but not Ministers – have considered.

Peter Shore mentioned the possibility of our dumping at sea and Fred Mulley talked about 'silly pressure groups'.

Sunday 22 May
Melissa and I went to Hyde Park. It was a beautiful day and we walked for an hour. We paid 75p and took a boat out on the Serpentine. It was marvellous.

Monday 23 May
President Carter made a speech at a university yesterday declaring that American foreign policy was going to be reshaped on the basis that the Cold War was over. America, he said, was no longer prepared to support any dictatorship that called itself anti-Communist, because America was no longer frightened of Communism and wanted a new international system based on confidence and faith in free societies.

It was a most important statement. It goes far beyond anything Nixon has done and puts Mrs Thatcher completely out in the cold on rearmament.

In the afternoon I went over to Number 10 for a meeting with Jim that I had requested, and I stayed for forty minutes. He said, 'How are you?'

'I said, 'I'm fine, very well indeed: I got up yesterday morning and went for a row on the Serpentine and a three-mile walk with my daughter. How do you feel, Jim?'

'I'm fine.'

'You always look so cheerful.'

'Under the surface it isn't like that.'

I said I knew how he felt; I was the same. Then he half apologised for having been rough with me. I said, 'Well, I much prefer working with you than with Harold – I must make that clear.'

He then asked if I wanted to talk about energy, and I replied, 'No, I don't want to bother you on that question, but can we talk about the political situation?'

'Do you mind my writing this down?' he asked.

'Not at all. I won't even say to you, "If you weren't writing down so much you would listen to me" ' – which is what he had remarked to me in Cabinet.

He said, 'Well, it is not for my memoirs.'

I went into the direct elections to the European Parliament. 'You know my view, but I am not making a case on the grounds of personal passionate feeling; I am saying that you will split the Party on the vote, and you will split the Party in the direct elections themselves, and after all this pulling together to survive you will find that you have destroyed yourself when it comes to the General Election.'

'What do you suggest?'

'I think you should defer the decision as long as possible, perhaps wait till Conference, and let the French take the brunt with the Germans.'

He was happy to postpone it till 1979 or 1980.

'You know you have a much better chance of being Leader if we win than if we lose the Election. I am not saying you will be Leader, but I shall certainly give up a year after we win.' I told him I didn't believe that. 'Oh,' he said, 'I shall certainly give up after a year and there will be a chance for you.'

'Well, if we are defeated I won't be there anyway. I shouldn't bother about me. The PLP would not elect me as Leader, you know that. I am not going to ruin my life by worrying about that; I have got a different role.'

Thursday 26 May
At 9.30 we had the Cabinet committee which deals with Common Market issues (CQM), and pig-meat was on the agenda.

The Commission had appealed to the European Court to rule out of order the pig-meat subsidy that John Silkin had agreed, and the court had ordered that this subsidy cease forthwith. John Silkin reported that he had met Gundelach, the Commissioner for Agriculture and Fisheries, to try to get him to prolong the subsidy till 11 June to give time for it to be phased out.

Frank Judd intervened to say that Foreign Office advice was that 'forthwith' meant at once. The Attorney-General (Sam Silkin) thought it would be wiser to stop anyway now, because we had to challenge the court and if the court thought we had been dilatory in obeying their interim injunction it might damage our case.

I asked whether this was the first time that a European Court decision had been taken against the British Government, and I was told it was. Then I asked what would be the political effect of this on pig producers in the UK. John Silkin said it would mean in effect the destruction of our industry, the mass slaughtering of pigs and the abandonment of our processing plant in favour of the Danes. All in the name of free competition!

I just wanted to be told explicitly – as I was – that I was a member of the first British Government in history to be informed that it was behaving illegally by a court whose ruling you could not alter by changing the law in the House of Commons. That was an absolute turning point, and of course it could happen on grants, on oil policy, on intervention to support industries and so on. At a moment of great excitement, with the Tribune Group coming out against the Common Market and the direct elections brewing, here was an example of direct Community damage to a basic British interest.

Wednesday 8 June
At 9.30 we went off to Buckingham Palace. I suppose Caroline and I have been invited to evening parties there before, but we never actually went to

one, though I have been to a garden party and to audiences of the Privy Council over the last thirteen years.

The Commonwealth Prime Ministers were there and we went into one of the reception rooms overlooking the garden, where we were offered drinks. I fell in with Paul Martin, the High Commissioner for Canada and a former Foreign Minister, who is always terribly friendly.

By this time we were beginning to string out and we formed a receiving line to be introduced to the Queen and the Duke. I gave an inclination of my head and shook the Duke's hand.

We were ushered into another long chamber and there were the people who had had dinner – Prince Charles, Princess Anne, the Duchess of Kent, the Duchess of Gloucester, Princess Margaret, Mountbatten and the whole royal family, along with Macmillan, Wilson and Home. We saw the Harts, the Booths, the Healeys and the Owens but I didn't see any others.

As we were talking to Kenneth Kaunda, one of the equerries came up and said, 'Princess Alexandra would like to meet you.' I think she must be the daughter of the late Duchess of Kent.

But fortunately, or unfortunately, as we were moving in that general direction, someone told us that Princess Anne wanted to meet us. So we went over to her. She is interested in anything to do with horses. So I asked her about royal carriages and how they were built, and their springing, and whether they made you travel-sick.

We slipped away, avoiding Prince Charles, and sat on a couch, and at that moment we saw the Queen and the Duke just talking to each other. Caroline thought they were going to come over but the equerry swooped on them with Judith and Tony Hart.

Audrey Callaghan came up and had a long talk with Caroline. Then Mary Wilson came up; I gave her a big kiss – I do like Mary. She said, 'I am so pleased about your speech on the Common Market; the one hope for Labour in the next Election is if we fight against the Common Market.' So I said, 'Don't tell Harold that', and she announced she had told Harold what she thought of my speech and he didn't mind at all. She looks so happy since Harold has given up the premiership, and somehow the fact that I am in a continual struggle, even now, with Harold doesn't really affect our relationship. She is an extremely nice woman.

Audrey invited Caroline for lunch at Chequers on 26 June while the Cabinet are there for political discussions.

We slipped out of the Palace. They hadn't given the drivers anything to drink and Ron had just been sitting in the car for two and a half hours. Very inconsiderate.

That reminds me: one of the flunkey equerries in uniform was bowing and scraping as he brought us in and Caroline said, 'It is awfully cold in here', to which he replied, 'I am afraid the temperature of the boiler is set by those who work here and they wear a heavy uniform of livery and they think it is too hot.' So Caroline said, 'Well, that's all right because I am all for working conditions being determined by the shop floor. If that's what it is about, then I understand.'

Saturday 11 June

Edinburgh. At 9.45 we went down to catch the bus to the Miners' Gala. It was about 34° Fahrenheit and pelting with rain; we froze for most of the day.

At 11 we marched out with Mick McGahey, Bill McLean, General Secretary of the Scottish Miners, Peter Heathfield, Secretary of the Derbyshire Miners, and Ray Buckton of ASLEF, and several pipe bands. We marched through Edinburgh, down the Royal Mile, through the courtyard of Holyrood House and the beautiful park overlooked by rocky high hills, and finally on to the stage. We were covered but there was no shelter for the audience; it was still freezing and raining, but it didn't deter them. The people gathered out there, many of them old retired miners, must have had an agonising time.

After a thrilling morning, despite the weather, we were picked up and driven to Bannockburn for tea with Dennis Canavan, the MP for West Stirlingshire. We arrived early, so we went to the Golden Lion Hotel in Stirling and looked in vain for a warm radiator.

We rounded off the evening in the Thirteen Fourteen pub, within a stone's throw of the site of the Battle of Bannockburn, where Robert the Bruce beat Edward. I went into the lavatory and an old man came in, a bit the worse for drink, saw me, poked his finger in my chest and said, 'You're bloody like Benn.'

'I'm not surprised – I am.'

He shook me by the hand, pumped it indeed, and limped off.

By God, we were tired by the time we caught the sleeper, but it was warm.

Sunday 12 June

One interesting thing at the moment is the way the flamethrower of the press is being turned on me again as it was during the Common Market referendum campaign. They have five lines of attack: that I am mad, ambitious, incompetent, a hypocrite and a red. This week I appear to be all of them at once. Alan Watkins describes me as a boy inventor – the next thing to a mad professor.

Monday 13 June

At 2 Red Adair came to see me – the great Red Adair from Texas who handled the blowout at Ekofisk. He was a modest guy, and with representatives from the UK Offshore Operators' Association (his biggest customers) also present he was not prepared to be too critical of their standards. He said, 'Minister Benn, they are doing the best they can, and I don't want to tell them what they ought to do.' Unfortunately he declined to have his photograph taken with me!

Thursday 16 June

Cabinet, and another discussion on the direct elections Bill. Then foreign affairs, and David Owen paid a tribute to Jim's brilliant chairmanship of the Commonwealth Conference, at which point David Ennals said, 'I met twelve presidents and heads of state recently, and I must say it was absolutely brilliant, absolutely brilliant, your leadership, Prime Minister.' I do really dislike David Ennals. He is so obsequious.

Came home and worked late. Caroline came down at midnight precisely and reminded me that it was our wedding anniversary.

Friday 17 June

Yesterday Julie brought in the most fabulous birthday cake in the shape of an 80 for Mother, who is having a party at the House of Commons this afternoon.

Steve and June, Hilary and Rosalind and Melissa and Josh, who by the way has passed his driving test, all turned up and went off in the car with Mother's present. Got to the House and about 180 people turned up for the party. It was pouring with rain, and cold as anything, so there were heaters in the marquee on the terrace. Elsie Chamberlain, whom Father appointed as first woman chaplain to the armed forces, was there, and the Chief Rabbi, the Lord Chancellor and his wife Polly Binder, friends from the Council of Christians and Jews, the Council for the Ministry of Women and the Congregational Federation; really it was so friendly and Mother was marvellous. Father's old secretary, Miss Knox, came – I hadn't seen her since I was six.

Monday 20 June

At lunchtime we had a Private Office party financed by what is loosely known as the slush fund; when I travel abroad I get a living allowance but I never spend a penny of it – I never buy a bottle of whisky or cigarettes or anything. So the allowance goes into the Private Office fund. There were about forty people there.

Wednesday 22 June

At the House this evening, Audrey Wise told me all about the strike of the women workers at Grunwick. She had been down there supporting the strike and she saw a policeman pulling a girl's hair, so she put her hand on the policeman's arm. He immediately released the girl and said to Audrey, 'You'll do, love', bundled her into a Black Maria and charged her.

She was shocked; she had never been in an incident like that in her life and she didn't know what to do. She was discussing how she should handle her defence, and I said, 'Why don't you try saying you were arresting the policeman for assault and battery?' Brian Sedgemore is helping her to find a good lawyer.

I should mention that the fighting this week on the picket line at Grunwick has been on a massive scale. The police have been behaving abominably, plucking people out of the crowd. It has attracted thousands of people from all over, including five MPs today. Roy Grantham, General Secretary of APEX, thinks it is getting out of control. Some of the police are just National Front men, and it is alarming because it is reminiscent of the 1930s.

Then Jim Sillars came up for a talk. I hadn't spoken to him for a long time. His Scottish Labour Party in fact is a non-event.

Sillars is a proud man with charisma and appeal; he knows how to use the press, and of course he has been taken up by the media. He thought he would be Prime Minister of Scotland, but actually the press are only interested in him because he split the Labour Party. It shows how easy it is to go wrong, mainly by being misled by a sense of your own importance.

Friday 24 June
Home, and I found that the BP share offer had been oversubscribed within one minute of opening because of the discount. Every single BP share could be sold in Britain. This means we don't have to sell them in America, but of course we feel committed, so the jobbers will be refusing British bids for BP in favour of New York. The National Iranian Oil Corporation, ie the Shah, is trying to buy 1 per cent so he can get a foothold in the North Sea. We have handed some of the most valuable assets of this country to the Shah, to the Americans and to private shareholders, and I am ashamed to be a member of the Cabinet that has done this. I am going to put in a full report to the Cabinet so they know exactly what we have done. We have provided a blueprint for selling off public assets in the future and we will have no argument against it. It is an outrage.

Wednesday 29 June
Had a long talk to John Davies, my predecessor at Industry – the 'lame duck' Minister, as he was known. John told me that even during the last Tory Government of 1970–74 Maggie Thatcher and Ted Heath loathed each other – so the hatred is not born out of her becoming Leader but is deep-seated. I daresay Heath doesn't like women and she probably doesn't like men who don't like women.

Sunday 3 July
Dinner with the Baloghs, the Shores, the Harts and Jill Foot. Judith was very sharp, directing criticism, I thought, at me.

We talked about Tom Driberg's book, *Ruling Passions*, for which Michael Foot has written the Postscript. Tommy Balogh said one night when he was in Malta he stopped in a club for a drink and there was Tom Driberg chatting up a sailor at the bar.

Monday 4 July
To a meeting on the Falkland Islands at Number 10 after Questions. David Owen has suggested a sellout because of our great defensive weakness: ie give Argentina an economic zone of 200 miles around the islands, and keep the islands on a three-mile fishing limit. Then we would just hope that the problem could be resolved peacefully.

My department has briefed me strongly against this on the technical grounds that, if we concede a difference between the economic zone of 200 miles and the land mass of the Falkland Islands, that could be used against us in our median line disputes with the French and the Irish over the Scilly Isles and the Channel Islands.

But the plain truth is that if the Argentinians wished to attack the Falkland Islands they could easily crush them. Fred Mulley pointed out that the Argentinian Government, a ghastly Fascist military dictatorship, had ordered £700 million of warships from Vosper Thorneycroft, so they would be crushing the Falklands Isles with British warships.

The Argentine Government is determined to get hold of the islands, even though they are 400 miles away, and the arms trade, the total spinelessness of the Foreign Office and the general decay of Britain will have combined to put us in a position where we will be unable to do anything to defend the 1,950 people who live there.

Tuesday 5 July
I went over to the Palace for the coffee-pot presentation. It was a beautiful sunny day, not a cloud in the sky, and we drove through the Palace yard while the guards in their red jackets were conducting their manoeuvres. There weren't as many soldiers as there used to be, but it was fun. There are tourists all over London and it makes the centre of London impossible for ordinary travellers.

We gathered and talked a bit, then we all lined up in a great semicircle and the Queen and Duke of Edinburgh came in. The coffee-pot was on the table and Jim stood there and said, 'Ma'am. The Cabinet considered how we should record your Jubilee with respect – and affection, if I may say so. We decided to give you a gift and I looked up the precedents, and on Queen Victoria's Golden Jubilee in 1887 the then Prime Minister, the Marquis of Salisbury, decided to give her a portrait of himself.' Everyone laughed.

'This time,' he said, 'we thought it would be better to give you something useful and although Tony Benn wondered whether the coffee-pot would leak, unlike the Cabinet' (laughter), 'we thought this would be what you would like.'

The Queen, who can't say good morning without a script, referred to a bit of paper and said, 'Prime Minister, thank you very much indeed. I feel sure the coffee-pot will be more useful than a picture.' More laughter.

We had all been correctly positioned in strict pecking order – that is to say Foot, Healey, Elwyn Jones, David Owen, Shirley Williams, myself and so on. In the Palace protocol is everything. Shirley gave a low curtsy.

After the presentation we were chatting, when Jim came up. 'Come and have a word with the Queen.' He ushered Shirley and me over to her. She didn't look frightfully well; her face was pale and she said she had a cold, possibly pneumonia. Roy Mason was also standing there and, in a booming voice, he declared, 'Ma'am, the whole of Yorkshire is looking forward to your visit.'

I said, 'Do let me ask you this. When were Privy Councillors' uniforms last worn at Privy Council?' Well, she didn't seem to know much about the Privy Council. I added, 'I think they are the House of Windsor uniforms, Windsor jackets and livery with knee breeches and a sword and so on.'

'I don't think my father wore it,' she said. Well, of course her father wouldn't have worn a Privy Councillor's uniform. But in the Thirties Ramsay was always photographed at the Palace wearing it with a cocked hat and a sword.

Then Shirley said, 'Ma'am, I have often thought that, in addition to reading the papers, which we know you do so carefully all the time, you might occasionally have audiences with Ministers, say two or three Ministers every few months, and then you would understand Ministers' policies. Because of course, Ma'am, you are so much closer to the people than we are, you know how the people feel, and you may like to know how Ministers feel as well.' The Queen said she read the papers very carefully.

I remarked jokingly, 'The only interest my officials seem to think you take in our activities is when we leave the country – because Private Secretaries always come in hot foot and say, "The Queen has given permission for you to go to Brussels." ' I said she must be frightfully busy. She told me that she did take an interest.

Then the Duke of Edinburgh joined us and I told him that Shirley Williams had been persuaded of his idea, which he had voiced ten years ago at a lunch at Winfrith, that the Queen should attend Cabinet and that the Ombudsman should be a member of the royal household.

'Oh yes,' he said, 'a very good idea.' Well actually it was a lousy idea because, as I had said at the time, if the Queen attended the Cabinet, when the Cabinet became unpopular she would become unpopular, and she didn't want to be mixed up with us. Secondly the idea of an aggrieved citizen writing to a member of the royal household was absurd.

'In Saudi Arabia, you know, King Khalid holds court every day. People come and say, "Your Majesty, I haven't got a telephone", and he raises it with his Ministers. That is what the monarchy should be like,' said the Duke.

The Queen did make one interesting comment. 'We had the heads of the

Common Market here to dinner the other night, and Helmut Schmidt was so rude.'

I said, 'He always is.'

'Yes, but they were all so cynical and disillusioned and he was so rude and unfriendly.'

That confirmed what I have long suspected: that the royal family loathe the Common Market because they have no role in it. There is no European President's Council in which Queen Juliana can meet the Grand Duchess of Luxembourg: they have no forum and therefore are driven back into a quaint tourist role.

Wednesday 6 July

I should mention that Jack Jones was defeated overwhelmingly at the TGWU Conference. They voted for no pay restraint or limitation on free collective bargaining whatsoever in the coming year. Jack took it well.

Tuesday 19 July

I had a talk with Harry Evans of the *Sunday Times* in the evening. He thought the Government would fall this autumn and that Thatcher sensed power; without Phase 3 there would be nothing to keep Labour in power. There was a chance Thatcher would be in power by Christmas but he wasn't sure whether she would win if we stayed in for another year. He thought the Lib–Lab Pact might fold. We are in difficulties over wage claims: there is no doubt about that.

After he had gone I saw David Owen about breaches of sanctions of BP in Rhodesia. He wanted to know whether it had been brought to me personally; I said it had and I had asked for names.

Wednesday 20 July

This evening I saw Bill van Straubenzee, the Tory MP, walking by Mother's flat. We had a chat and he thought there would be an Election this winter. 'Mrs Thatcher is much better than people imagine. Now there is no pay policy and she has nothing to lose, she will be dead set on being Prime Minister, and the City and the businessmen will support her in that. She is a very competent woman indeed.'

I asked him if he thought Ted Heath would get a job under Mrs Thatcher.

He said, 'No, he has behaved very badly.'

'If Thatcher were defeated in an Election, would you get rid of her?'

'Oh, yes,' he said, 'we are much less generous than you are.' He was certain that Ted Heath wouldn't succeed her but Willie Whitelaw might. 'The man to watch,' he said, 'is Francis Pym.'

'I presume that if Carrington were in the Commons he would get it?'

'Yes,' he said. 'But Francis Pym is a quiet chap coming up.'

Friday 29 July

Today the *Daily Express* had a fantastic story – Chapman Pincher saying that MI5 had bugged Harold Wilson. The whole security story is now breaking, and this was bound to come to the surface one day.

The Cabinet met at Number 10 for a discussion on Europe which I had suggested at Chequers, and it was one of the most remarkable Cabinets I have ever attended.

I took my cameras because I do feel at this period in my life that I should go on recording various events. So I was feeling cheerful, but we'd only just sat when Jim said, 'Well, I think it's hardly worth having this meeting at all. The whole document that we are discussing today has been leaked to the *Financial Times*, clearly by a member of this Cabinet. And there is an article in today's *Guardian* in which John Silkin has said that the Common Agricultural Policy proves that crime does pay.'

Just at that point, when tempers were at fever pitch, somebody came in and said there was another closure vote at the House. So we all scooped up our papers and leapt into our cars like a lot of Hell's Angels to go over to the House of Commons.

I talked to David Owen there and he said, 'I don't take this very seriously. I think this is psychological warfare by Jim to get us all to pull together.'

I went back to Number 10 at about 11 and sat around with the rest of the Cabinet. Then I realised that Jim hadn't arrived yet and I had a supreme opportunity. So I took my first movies and a few stills in the Cabinet Room.

It soon became clear that we were not going to meet again in Number 10, so we were all moved back to the House and finally began at 11.30. Jim opened by saying the most important thing was Party unity and that we must preserve our internationalism.

At one stage Jim had to leave because Mrs Thatcher had demanded an immediate statement about the bugging at Number 10. Jim said, 'I don't want any of you to come to the House – it will make it too big an event. I want to go in alone, deal with the question and leave.'

So the rest of us went over to Number 10 for drinks, and I had a word with David Owen and Merlyn Rees about the bugging. David controls MI6 and Merlyn MI5 and they both said, 'We control the security services completely; the people at the top are very decent; you would be surprised about how good and decent they are. Some of them you would know, but of course you wouldn't know what they did. It is quite untrue and Harold Wilson is absolutely paranoid.'

'Of course,' said Merlyn, 'there is electronic surveillance at Number 10 but that is so nobody can get in.'

'How did the story come out?' I asked.

They said MI5 were angry that Harold Wilson appeared to be going to dinner parties, getting tight and telling people that MI5 had muddled up David Owen with Will Owen and Judith Hart with Mrs J. Tudor Hart. 'It's quite untrue,' said David Owen. 'They never muddled us up. They are getting back at him to frighten him by saying they bugged him.'

I said, 'I hope you do keep them under control. I was at a dinner in 1971 when Harold told the CBI that the Government bugged the TUC.'

'Oh,' said Merlyn, striking his head with the palm of his hand, 'how awful; he should never have said that' – which indicated that Merlyn knew.

I went on, 'Bryan Stanley told Ray Buckton in the 1972 strike that the ASLEF locomen were bugged.'

'Well, it may be true that at some periods in industrial disputes that does happen,' Merlyn replied.

'Yes,' said David, 'I always thought during the seamen's strike it was done.'

So I pursued it. 'Take another case. When I wanted to appoint Jack Jones to the National Enterprise Board, I was told he was a security risk. When I asked to see the report they withdrew their objection. And in the *Sunday Times* the other day it said all the trade union leaders are bugged. You've got a lot of experience of it, Merlyn, you have been in Northern Ireland, where the situation is kept under very tight control. You must know how these things happen.'

'Yes, I am sure I am told.'

David added, 'I have been through it very carefully, and nothing would be done without my knowing.'

Of course I don't believe that, but I wouldn't have dreamed of mentioning my own experience to them.

Cabinet resumed at 2.45 in the PM's room and we were told to limit ourselves to three minutes each. I said, 'Here we are meeting to consider a paper by David Owen on the Common Market, yet we do not have before us the NEC documents which were cleared on Wednesday and on which they have worked for a year. We are not even considering what they said. Similarly, David Owen's paper has not been made available to the NEC.'

Jim said, 'Well, the Government must govern. I can't have government papers put to the Executive.'

'But, PM,' I said, 'when the 1972 Industry Group of sympathetic industrialists prepared a report on industrial strategy, you set up a Cabinet committee to look at it. Never in my whole life do I remember the Cabinet ever taking NEC documents seriously or setting up committees to look at them. They just don't come to us.'

Jim, red-faced, pointed his finger at me. 'You are working against us.'

'That is a very serious thing to say. I have been in the Cabinet over many years and I don't remember a Prime Minister ever saying such a thing to a Cabinet colleague. If you believe that is the case, you have the remedy in your own hands.'

'Well, maybe I shall have to take the necessary action,' Jim replied.

I said, 'You have the power to decide who is in and out of your Cabinet and, I promise you, if I personally were your only problem, you wouldn't have a problem.'

'You are leading a faction against us,' Jim retorted.

'If you want my honest opinion, I am quite happy to go along with David Owen's general approach, but I want to see this country restored to itself, with the right to govern itself by its own legislation. That is what I think is important. You hear all this about our parliamentary democracy being undermined by Marxists or by extending the public sector, but the plain truth is that it has been undermined by Brussels. It may take twenty years to do it but I want to work to restore to the British people the power to govern themselves and then to work for others.'

The tension was electric. Bill Rodgers said, 'If others are going to speak on the Common Market question before Conference, then I am going to speak.'

'We don't want any more speeches,' said Denis, and David Ennals wanted an assurance that everybody would shut up.

I came in again. 'I remember well during the Referendum of 1975 that Shirley Williams said that if the vote went against the Market she would withdraw from public life.'

So Denis chimed in, 'You promised to abide by the Referendum and you have broken your word.'

All of a sudden a wave of hatred engulfed the room. It turned into a personal clash between Jim and me with odd interruptions. Stan Orme interjected, 'I won't have Tony Benn pilloried in this way; he is quite entitled to his view', and Michael Foot remarked, 'Tony reflects a very important element in the Party's thinking which has to be taken into account.' It was an amazing scene.

Jim finally said, 'I don't know what Tony Benn intends to do. We've had no clear answer from him as to what he intends to do.'

Harold Lever said, 'On the limitations of European legislation on the British Parliament, this situation is no different from the IMF or NATO or GATT.'

'But it *is* different,' I argued, 'because those bodies do not have the power to change the laws of this country. I sat at a committee the other day with John Silkin when we were told that the Ministers were behaving illegally and that is a complete change. My advice, PM, because I don't want a confrontation any more than you do, is to let the Party and the Government decide their respective views and then reach a compromise. If you force the NEC to climb down it will lead to a confrontation.'

Well, that was it, and the Cabinet adjourned. I had a word with Michael and Stan and John Silkin and they said, 'For God's sake, keep your mouth shut!' We walked back and I told Stan that I was surprised more than angry, genuinely surprised, because I thought it had been a constructive meeting up until the row. I was a bit shaken, and David Owen said, 'Well, you did go a bit too far, when you held the press conference on the Common Market Safeguards Committee.'

Saturday 30 July

To Bristol for my surgery, which lasted five and a half hours. There were complaints about Hell's Angels; parents from a Catholic school whose headmaster had been suspended by the Avon Education Committee, who thought he was mad and wanted him to see a psychiatrist; an old man of eighty-two who took down his trousers and made me examine the shrapnel wound in his hip from 1916, and so on.

The news tonight reported that Harold Wilson has demanded an inquiry into Chapman Pincher's statement that MI5 bugged Number 10. That means we are going to have a tremendous silly-season debate about something of crucial importance.

Sunday 31 July

In the afternoon Caroline and I went for a lovely three-mile walk right round Shepherd's Bush and back.

Monday 1 August

The story of the Wilson bugging was still running in the press. Chapman Pincher had commented that the security services were perfectly entitled to bug even a Prime Minister if they thought he was engaged in a Communist conspiracy. A most interesting admission.

Tuesday 2 August

This morning Frances Morrell rang to say that the *Evening Standard* had asked her which of my children was having treatment in the private wing of the Radcliffe Infirmary in Oxford. It turned out that in today's first edition of *The Times* the diary column had contained a report to that effect and that we were using Caroline's maiden name. I must say I blew my top.

I rang *The Times*, made them read me the first edition, and wrote it down. Then I wrote a letter after about a dozen drafts. Arthur Davidson, the Parliamentary Secretary to the Law Officers, assured me the report was defamatory, so I sent the letter round to the Editor and rang up to be sure it had arrived. Rees-Mogg came to the phone and said he would publish the letter and a retraction and apology tomorrow. I let it go at that, but, I must say, this really stirred me. It's the third absolutely blatant lie this year.

Frances was most helpful. She's at her best on these occasions and suggested I prepare a dossier and send it over to Stuart Weir, the deputy editor of *New Society*, who promised to do a piece on it. So this I did. It's not possible to convey my anger adequately.

The *Evening Standard* and the *Daily Express* rang up during the day to ask if the story was true. I mustn't get obsessive about the press, like Harold

Wilson, or paranoid, saying Smear, Smear, because that's destructive. But I won't let them tell lies.

Anyway at 3.30 Dick Clements came over for a talk. He mentioned that the *Tribune* correspondent, on talking to one or two of the police at Grunwick, had received the impression that in arresting Scargill and Audrey Wise they were punishing the Labour Government for holding their pay back. That was an interesting story – quite a new dimension.

Wednesday 3 August
At 6 I went to see the PM. While I was waiting outside, Beaumarchais, the French Ambassador, scurried out. I spent about an hour with Jim. He was red-faced – with embarrassment, I thought. I said, 'It is very nice of you to see me. I felt somehow it had all gone wrong last Friday when we discussed the Common Market. I know you think of me as Dr Jekyll and Mr Hyde, but really I am Hyde, Hyde and Hyde again!'

'But looking like Jekyll.'

'Maybe,' I said. I told him I didn't think the Conference was going to be destructive; there was a way round.

So then he apologised. 'Do you know, to be perfectly honest, I was very rude to you, and I think I was unfair. I told Ken Stowe at the end of the day that I had overdone it, and I worried about it all weekend.'

'For Heaven's sake, don't apologise, you had a hell of a day. Anyway, I was a bit worried and I wanted to come along and have a word with you, motivated by the same spirit.'

So, like many rows with Jim, it blew up and blew over and blew out. And I am awfully glad I went to see him because he couldn't have been nicer. I wanted to make peace with him and retreat a bit.

He said, 'I thought you were really trying to wreck the whole Government and withdrawing as leader of the Left in order to take over.'

'Look, it isn't like that. I am trying to persuade people, and I think if we get the framework of the Conference right then we can have a meaningful debate.'

'Of course,' said Jim, 'there are people on the Executive who just want to wreck the Government. I know there are.' He does have an obsession about this but I didn't pursue it.

I described the outline of what I would like to say about Europe. He said, 'Well, if you were to admit that the debate isn't an in–out debate, that would revolutionise the Conference.' I said I'd think about it.

He was very friendly and I told him I much preferred dealing with him than with Harold. He half repeated the apology and I felt embarrassed. I did tell him that I was glad that none of that sensational Cabinet had appeared in the Sunday papers. I had quivered as I opened them.

'Well, thanks for coming. I appreciate it very much.' And on that note I left.

Tuesday 9 August
Spent the morning working on the false private medical treatment story.
Dick Clements had sent me a copy of a franked postcard conveying the
inaccurate *Times* story which had been sent to the *Tribune* office, and we also
discovered that *Labour Weekly* had received one as well.

I could just see the number of the frank so I rang up the Post Office and,
believe it or not, it turned out to be the European Movement frank. So it was
from their office that these postcards had been sent, which may mean that
they were the source of the story in the first place, though I can't prove that.

Wednesday 10 August
Stansgate. Caroline went shopping. I had twelve hours in bed, which is my
way of recovering. Later Caroline and I went for a jog in the lovely warm
weather.

Monday 15 August
Damp, misty and sunless but quite warm. Red box arrived. Melissa wrote
from Italy. Joshua rescued an injured baby rabbit and has put it in a box
until it recovers.

Tuesday 16 August
Little bit of sunshine. Went shopping. The rabbit died.

Wednesday 17 August
Thunderstorm, and a really wet day. Red box arrived. Elvis Presley died.

Thursday 18 August
I should mention that over the last two weeks there have been clashes
between the racialist National Front and the ultra-Left in Lewisham and
Birmingham, and the papers have been in a frenzy. The press is doing its
best to put all the blame for the violence on the ultra-Left and then use the
National Front as an excuse for banning demonstrations.

Monday 3 October – Labour Party Conference, Brighton
Conference opened. Denis was called in the economy debate and spoke for
ten minutes, then Barbara wound up. She may not be at the next
Conference and won't be in the next Parliament so it could be her last
Conference speech. She was so keen and spoke skilfully, with passion and
fire, but it didn't lift the Conference – I don't think anything could have
done. Ted Castle is dying, I'm afraid – he looks terribly ill.

After lunch I dealt with the Chancellor's dilemma. He was in effect saying
that under capitalism you couldn't do better than we had done. I argued that
we needed structural change if we were to make progress.

But it didn't come over well. I must record that Hilary was shocked,

Stephen didn't like it and Caroline was appalled, so I can't pretend it was a success. The fact that Jim came up and said, 'Congratulations, that was a real leadership speech', didn't exactly please me. I think the Left were very disappointed.

Friday 7 October
Last day of Conference. Apparently Edna Healey and Evelyn Jones had a discussion on Monday – which Caroline heard – over the fact that Jack Jones had criticised Labour Ministers for expensive living.

Although on the face of it Jim has got his way, in fact he has failed entirely to change the Executive. Radical motions were carried, and the vitality of the Party is phenomenal.

Sunday 9 October
There was an account in the papers of how Henry Ford agreed to Jim Callaghan's request to site Ford's engine plant at Bridgend, South Wales – which explains why the pay policy could not be applied to Ford.

Melissa and I went out for a two-hour walk and we had a lovely talk. She has terrific admiration for Caroline: Melissa is a serious feminist.

To the Harts' for dinner with the Foots and the Booths. Judith described her meeting with the Cabinet Secretary, Sir John Hunt, held at Jim's request, about the security services' supposed confusion between her and Mrs J. Tudor Hart. Sir John Hunt confirmed that there had been a mix-up, and I said I didn't think that likely because the security services did a very thorough job.

Michael said, 'I sat with the Prime Minister when Judith was reappointed in March, and the security services did raise some objection.' He said Jim was good on security matters; an inquiry into the Wilson bugging story would not be helpful, but Jim was not against a general look at the problem at an appropriate time.

After dinner we discussed pay policy and I said I thought that the proposed sanctions on firms to restrict wage rises were illegal, that they were acts of impropriety, that they were not effective or credible and would be politically dangerous.

Michael just blew his top and shouted, 'You just want us to go back to inflation. Face the real problems – you have got to help the lower paid.' He was red with anger.

Judith mentioned our industrial policy.

'I'm not against that,' said Michael. 'That's different.'

'It isn't different,' I said. 'If you want to get pay agreement and understanding about pay, you have got to implement the industrial policy.'

Jill rebuked Michael for being so excitable.

Monday 10 October
Reg Prentice had wide coverage for his attack on the Labour Party and his decision to cross the floor to the Tories.

Saturday 15 October
Mrs Thatcher's speech at the Tory Conference yesterday was reported in the papers. She had attacked me, and others, for having attended a public school and said that it was the direct grant schools that had given people of her class an opportunity which they would not otherwise have had. It was a very subtle argument. She did well and encouraged the Conference, though the reality is that the Tories are deeply worried that they might not win the next Election.

Caroline's birthday, and we had a lovely tea party at home.

Bing Crosby died today.

Tuesday 25 October
Luxembourg. The Research Council began at 10.15 and after long discussions Henri Simonet, the Belgian Foreign Minister, said, 'I ask you to take note of the fact that there is a 5 to 2 preference for siting Jet at Culham, with two abstentions, one of which will rally to the majority. Accordingly the Jet site will be in Culham.' So that was satisfying.

I loathe the Common Market. It's bureaucratic and centralised, there's no political discussion, officials control Ministers, and it just has a horrible flavour about it. But of course it is really dominated by Germany. All the Common Market countries except Britain have been occupied by Germany, and they have this mixed feeling of hatred and subservience towards the Germans. It is such a complex psychological relationship. But our self-confidence is flowing back now.

Friday 4 November
This morning the headlines were hysterical. The *Financial Times* had 'Callaghan Warns of Winter Strikes; Labour Ready to Fight Unions on Pay'. The *Guardian*: 'PM Appeals for Restraint through Hard Winter'. 'I'll Stand up to Miners Says Jim' from the *Sun* and 'Lights Stay Off; Blackout Threat to Kidney Patients' in the *Daily Mirror*. The *Morning Star*: 'Power Peace Hope Fades'. The *Daily Mail*: 'We'll Fight the Strikes'. *The Times*: 'Prime Minister Appeals to the Nation for Support in Winter of Dislocation'.

Monday 7 November
The papers are full of attacks on the firemen's strike and the power workers' strike. Yet the *Daily Mirror* carried a report that Princess Anne has spent £100,000 on new stables with a swimming pool to clean her horses and special lighting and heating in the stables so that they dry off immediately after a race. This is the Britain of Jubilee year.

At 5 we heard that an 84-year-old woman had died in hospital shortly after having an operation which had been interrupted by a power cut. In fact, she had had three heart attacks, one before, one during and one after the power cut. The operation had taken place in a high-risk warning period, the standby generator had failed, and she had been resuscitated and died after the power had been restored.

Tuesday 8 November
Over to Number 10 for EY Committee. Jim took me aside before the meeting. 'I hear you're saying this is not a problem for the Government. You're not suggesting the power workers be paid?'

'Well, it wouldn't present a problem for the Government,' I said.

'But this is unofficial action.'

'Jim, are you after winning the pay policy or grinding every shop steward's face into the mud? You must leave me with some discretion on how I handle this matter. I'm trying to improve the Government's position.'

I had a message from James Bretherton that John Lyons, General Secretary of the Engineers' and Managers' Association, had rung with regard to my favouring the unofficial strikers' demand that they shouldn't lose any pay. His men have been helping to cover the strikers' work. Lyons said that, if such payments were made, his members would withdraw their support. I must say his influence throughout this dispute has been entirely unhelpful and negative.

Ronny King Murray, the Lord Advocate, had some urgent news for me. 'You are shortly going to get a memorandum on a proposed change of policy on AEA guards. It will suggest that people holding plutonium should be shot on sight. I want you to know because this will be presented to you as the view of all the law officers, but it is not my view.' I was grateful for the information.

Monday 14 November
On my way to work this morning, it made me sad to see the firemen picketing outside the fire station just behind the Army and Navy store in Victoria. These men of such courage, who lose a man a fortnight in fires and are paid below the national average income, are now being put in the dock. But the ones who appeared on television today, the first day of the strike, came over very well. They were asked about their consciences and they replied. 'We have got consciences but a conscience can't pay the mortgage.'

Every time they show soldiers fighting fires, it draws attention to the tremendous dangers that face firemen. I don't think the Government is going to win on this.

Tuesday 15 November
At 10.15 I went to the Defence and Overseas Policy Committee [DOP] of Cabinet at which we were discussing the Falkland Islands. I am not a

member of DOP as a whole and I am involved only with respect to the oil in the region. All the Chiefs of Staff were there. Before us was a secret Joint Intelligence Committee report marked 'Delicate Source – UK Eyes Only' which pointed out that the Argentinian forces were strong enough to take over the Falkland Islands, with their population of 1,950, without a shot being fired. David Owen reported that the Argentinians were likely to be very tough if the negotiations scheduled for December in New York fell through.

When I was called I said I appreciated the gravity of the situation but to divide the sovereignty of the islands with a three-mile limit from the sovereignty of the areas outside, where the oil is, could have tremendously damaging implications for us. It might be better to be defeated on this point than to concede it now. Going to UN arbitration was ruled out because world opinion was against us.

Jim, in a very John Bullish mood, said, 'World opinion may be against us, but they might feel differently if the Argentinians attack the Falklands.' So he asked the navy to send out two frigates and possibly a nuclear submarine *before* the negotiations began. A very tough line.

We were all sworn to secrecy about the military operations. I don't like secrets.

To the Friends of the Earth reception to celebrate the end of the Windscale Inquiry and had a long talk to Walt Patterson and Tom Burke, the director. They are a great crowd. They've done very well, and gradually their view is beginning to be taken seriously. I must get them into the Labour Party.

Tuesday 22 November
This evening I was handed a letter from Number 10 referring to a meeting I had arranged with colleagues to discuss the Europe direct elections Bill.

Dear Tony,
I am attaching a copy of a letter which was found by a Conservative on the top of the copying machine and handed to my office. You will see it says there is to be a meeting of Ministers in your room tonight and is signed by Michael Meacher, the Parliamentary Under-Secretary of the Department of Trade.
As you are aware, no meeting of Ministers should be called without my knowledge and agreement. I do not know whether you are aware of this letter but I am sure that now you know about it, you will cancel the proposed meeting.
Yours sincerely,
Jim Callaghan

The pressure is building up, and if this continues I am going to be in deep trouble. I don't believe for a moment that Michael left a copy on the copying machine. Anyway, it's out now, and I should think it will be all over the place. I decided to do nothing about it. Why should I cancel the meeting? I meet Michael and Peter and John every week – have done for years – without the Prime Minister's permission.

Later I went to see Michael Foot in his room, and Peter Shore and John Silkin were there. Michael was red and angry. 'What's this about this meeting you're having with the junior Ministers tonight?'

'I told you this morning.'

'Well,' he shouted, 'I think it's bloody crooked that you should hold it.'

'What do you mean?' I asked.

'We agreed we would do nothing and keep in touch and meet early this week,' said Michael.

'Fine, I've never said we wouldn't. I haven't made a statement, I'm just consulting people. I'm not going to be told I'm bloody crooked. The only other time that has ever been said to me was in this room by Dick Crossman, who called me a bloody twister, and I walked out. I won't be called bloody crooked. I am entitled to consult whom I like.'

'You've no business to do that,' said Michael. 'You know very well how it will be interpreted.'

'Michael, I am awfully sorry, but, if Ministers are not allowed to meet, who authorised *this* meeting?'

He withdrew his remark about my being 'bloody crooked' and I said we'd leave it at that.

Then we began arguing about how to vote in the direct elections Bill. Michael started on me again. 'You just want the Tories in, and then we will be in the Common Market for life.' He says that every time, before every Election: do everything he tells you or the Tories will get in. 'You, with your halo of martyrdom,' he grunted. 'I've been anti-Market longer than you.'

The fact is, they are turning the flamethrower on me, and I have no doubt whatever that if I did leave the Government and then we lost the Election the defeat would be attributed to me. I said surely there was room for one person in the Cabinet who actually believed in the Party's policies. Michael did at least apologise, but my links with him are severed completely.

Went back to my room and at 9 Brian Sedgemore, Michael Meacher and Margaret Jackson came for the meeting. I told them about Jim's letter and said, 'If you want to slip off, now's the moment to do it.' Michael Meacher was horrified by the story about finding his letter on the photocopier. Then Bob Cryer joined us and we talked for an hour.

It was quite clear that none of them wanted to go as far as voting *against* the Bill so we left it at that.

Tuesday 29 November
After lunch Brian Sedgemore and I went for a walk round St James's Park with Dennis Skinner. I have a lot of time for Dennis.

Wednesday 30 November
After lunch I began the campaign to defeat the guillotine which is being imposed on the European Elected Assembly Bill. Dennis Skinner said his contact was Norman Tebbit, who is very anti-Europe.

Monday 12 December
Press conference in the Department, Bernard Ingham's last, as he is leaving to take over as head of the Energy Conservation Department, something I suggested to Jack Rampton when I was getting on badly with Bernard, but I'm sorry to see him go now.

Frances and Francis came in all excited because Kenneth Berrill has submitted his paper on nuclear reactor choice, on which the final decision is to be made next Friday, and he attacks the paper Bruce Millan and I have jointly submitted. Berrill says we should start series-ordering of PWRs. Astonishing! I asked to see the PM to discuss it.

Here is the head of the CPRS (the Think Tank – none of whom is an expert in nuclear matters) writing a paper flatly contradicting the two Secretaries of State responsible. This is a big constitutional point. The CPRS is now the Cabinet Office voice, with full membership of the Cabinet. It's the imposition of a sort of unelected European Commission on to the British system.

Sunday 18 December
Something I forgot to record. The other night Caroline came to dinner at the House, and we met Harold Wilson in the corridor. It was the first time I had spoken to him since his farewell dinner in 1976. It was clear that we couldn't avoid saying something to him, so as I passed I remarked, 'I saw your programme on Gladstone.' 'Yes,' he said, 'but they cut out a lot of what I said about his sex life.' He's a lonely, isolated figure now. Caroline has a theory that he stumbled on a security plot against himself and that those responsible were now trying to discredit him in order to prevent him from ever speaking out about it – an interesting thought.

Monday 19 December
At 9 I had a meeting on the safety of oil rigs with Frank Kearton and John Archer of the Department's Marine Division. Frank warned that rigs were desperately dangerous installations because they compress gas at 6,000 atmospheres in confined spaces, and that a leak would cause a massive explosion killing up to 200 people. The proposal was that I press ahead with

an inquiry into the safety of the rigs using two engineers and two trade unionists.

John Archer, who is Chairman of the Marine Safety Committee – an interdepartmental committee – said there were uncompleted reports on fire, the safety of cranes, rigs and platforms under construction, and divers and standby vessels, and he hoped to have these reports in six months. He didn't want anything superimposed.

I reserved the right to take the matter to Cabinet colleagues.

Sunday 25 December
Christmas Day. Although our eldest child is twenty-seven next year, they all turned up at home at 8 am to exchange presents and came into the bedroom to give us ours. The children love Christmas, and Caroline makes it such a marvellous occasion. Thirteen of us sat down to lunch.

Wednesday 28 December
I rang the manager of The Clash, a political punk rock group, because there had been a suggestion from the BBC Television Community Programme Unit that I have a four-minute discussion with the group. I have grave doubts about a Cabinet Minister appearing with a punk rock group, given what the media would make of it, and he agreed with me that four minutes was not enough for a serious discussion. But what he said was interesting. The Clash are apparently very popular with working-class youngsters, who don't find anything in our popular culture that meets their needs or reflects their feelings. He told me the group were not really concerned with being commercial and refused a lot of television because it put them into an artificial setting when they were really a live group. They are popular in Sweden, France and Yugoslavia. He said that to get any attention at all you had to be absolutely bizarre, but to understand what The Clash were trying to say you had to work really hard because the lyrics were in pidgin French.

Saturday 31 December
In my heart of hearts I believe the country is moving sharply to the right. The trade union leaders are so enjoying their corporatist relationship with the Government that they don't want to hear anything about socialism. The real battle is within the Labour Movement now and it is a struggle for the soul of the Movement. Jim Callaghan is riding high. The press loves him because he's openly right wing in the Cabinet, at public meetings and in the PLP. The Executive is hanging on to what remaining influence it has. It may be that one has to lengthen one's timescale – the whole of the 1980s may pass before we see a change.

Dictating this now, on the last day of the year, I feel depressed about it all, but I know that when we meet and start working on the General Election, which is likely to be in 1978, then the vitality will return.

The major issues of the 1980s will be the battle against federalism in the Common Market, the struggle to get back to full employment and to sustain the Welfare State, and the question of civil liberties and the role of the security services.

Monday 9 January 1978

Chaired the NEC Home Policy Committee, where we passed a resolution condemning Judge Neil McKinnon. He had discharged Kingsley Read, a leader of the British National Party, in a case where Read had referred to 'coons, wogs and niggers'. McKinnon had actually wished him well, saying this had been a free country until the Race Relations Act had been introduced. He even ignored Read's comment on the death of an Asian – that it was 'one down and a million to go'.

Tuesday 10 January

The *Mail* had a front-page spread drawing attention to my role in the unanimous resolution denouncing Judge McKinnon. The *Sun* had a headline, 'Wedgie in War on "Coon" Case Judge'.

Gladys Spearman-Cook, who runs a paper called the *Occult Gazette*, wrote to me saying I was a disaster, and God would strike me down. She was previously a great supporter and had described me as a reborn King Arthur, at the time of the Referendum!

Sunday 15 January

In the evening I reluctantly went to the Foots' house and I found it very depressing. For the first time I felt I had nothing in common with any of them. Tommy Balogh is a thoughtful, independent chap but Peter Shore has moved to the right in a really tough way that makes him another Callaghan. Michael is just lost.

The whole Labour leadership now is totally demoralised and all the growth on the left is going to come up from the outside and underneath. This is the death of the Labour Party. It believes in nothing any more, except staying in power.

Saturday 28 January

At Temple Meads Station in Bristol waiting for the late train back to London, I went to the buffet on the platform and bought a sandwich, a Fry's chocolate bar, some Wrigley's spearmint gum and an apple. I was about to pay when an old man in a raincoat pushed forward and thrust a pound note at the girl. I thought he was trying to get ahead of me and I was going to say, 'Excuse me', but it turned out that he was paying for my food, which came to 54 pence. He turned to me and said, 'I know you, I know who you are', left the money and disappeared. I did not know what to do, but thought it was very touching.

Tuesday 14 February

Neil Kinnock came to lunch, and Caroline advised me to let him talk. Well, there was no problem there because he talked for an hour. He hadn't really thought deeply about the political situation and his conclusions were incredibly non-radical for a member of the Tribune Group. He believed that 'Emperor Jim with his quiet-life policy' was right for the Party and that this would be more comforting than Thatcher's divisiveness. We couldn't defeat right-wing populism, and his recommendations were so modest that they might have emerged from a latter-day Liberal. He often gave me the impression that he is not altogether serious. Not that he made jokes, but his arguments were just not convincing, and I found it rather depressing because I had looked to Neil for some sort of cutting edge.

Brian Sedgemore told me later that Neil was playing it long and didn't believe anything would happen until the late Eighties. But on his present performance I'm not sure he would have much to say even then.

Sunday 19 February

Caroline and I left for Chequers with Ron at about 9.45. It was a rather nice idea of Jim's that we should bring our wives, and Caroline had a swim in the heated pool.

We went up for the Cabinet at 11 and Jim said he would like to begin with a few items that weren't strictly related to the Budget and the pay situation. First he had some evidence that Margaret Thatcher was going to make a speech about law and order this weekend to try to influence the Ilford by-election, and Roy Hattersley had confirmed this because she had talked about nothing but muggings recently, no doubt to prepare the way. Jim said we would have to pre-empt that. Merlyn is going to make a statement this week.

Then he said he would like Ministers to make more speeches on Saturdays and Sundays. 'I know that Ministers don't usually make speeches over the weekend, not that I tap anyone's telephone' (which I thought was a strange comment), 'but we must now broaden the issues on which we speak beyond departmental interests.'

Jim went on to say that Thatcher was moving further and further to the right and it was something we hadn't seen before in a Tory leader, but that left us to occupy the centre ground.

'There are other factors here that we have got to take seriously,' Peter Shore argued. 'Mrs Thatcher is beginning to reflect a genuine English nationalist feeling, a deep feeling about the English and how they see themselves in terms of their own history.'

I said, 'What she is doing is long-range shelling deep behind our lines, attacking things we had assumed were already part of the consensus. There is a danger she will be political and we will be managerial, so I welcome what the Prime Minister has said about speeches being broader.'

Roy Mason commented, 'Thatcher is deliberately highlighting the security of the state, and stimulating fear, with talk of hooligans, rearmament, defence, and more money for law and order.'

From that little discussion I had a deep feeling of anxiety that we were being told we would have to move towards Mrs Thatcher on these issues.

We adjourned for lunch at 1, and as we left the room Sir John Hunt thanked me for sending my paper 'Accountability in Labour Politics'. 'I read it with great interest and I would like to talk to you about it.'

I said, 'Of course, it was written very much with you in mind because it's up your street.'

He gave me an impenetrable look. I'm glad I sent it to him. I don't want anyone to think I'm doing it under cover.

To sum up the day, there was a lot of goodwill but I feel isolated because I am in a minority. Jim is avuncular, calm, quiet, a Herbert Morrison type, always with an eye for what the man in the street will think and without much time for the rank and file of the Party.

Wednesday 1 March
Dashed over to the weekly PLP meeting and I'm glad I did because I heard about forty minutes of the debate on reselection of MPs.

Joe Ashton said he wanted to be practical; a local Party general management committee must be able to sack an MP – that was what democracy was about – but we must get it right, otherwise we could have twenty-five deselected Reg Prentices and it would be impossible for the Parliamentary Party to discipline them for the remainder of the Parliament.

Then came one of the most remarkable speeches I have ever heard in my twenty-eight years in Parliament. John Golding, who is a real tough cookie, got up and said, 'I was adopted as a candidate because I could organise the selection conference via the union. I got forty-six votes: it was a disappointment because fifty votes had been promised to me and I lost four votes in the course of the selection conference. I could hold that seat by organising the GMC any time I like, by packing the delegates in. I have organised more selection conferences, and seen how they are packed, than anyone in this room excepting Ron Hayward and Reg Underhill. The ideal method of selection under which people are chosen by the GMC is pure cotton wool. It doesn't happen like that at all.

'Now, if we choose to reselect MPs, it will be a traumatic experience because we shall start packing GMCs to see that our people get in. The Party would take two years to recover and it would be disastrous. The Parliamentary Party is already divided into factions and we must not translate that situation into the constituency Parties.'

He added, 'I protect the trade union seats from the media men, from lecturers and lawyers, and if reselection is to take place it must be reselection by *all* the members of the Party.' Well, by this time people at the meeting were laughing at this extraordinary declaration of truth by a right-wing organiser. If it had been a left-winger who said this – Eric Heffer or Neil Kinnock or worst of all Andy Bevan – the place would have been in uproar. But the cynicism was such that the Party just took it. Michael Cocks said, 'He's right, you know, that's what actually happens.' I felt utterly sick.

Bob Cryer said, 'As a point of order, I hope that speech is not reported.'

Audrey Wise spoke next, and in a typically democratic way she said she very much regretted that Labour Party members *couldn't* hear that speech. It is indeed *because* you can pack one selection conference that reselection is necessary.

I had to leave then, but I am awfully glad I went. It was the talk of the day.

Monday 6 March

At the Home Policy Committee, which wasn't terribly exciting, we agreed in principle that the Party should commit itself to opposing blood sports; we will also look at factory farming, the protection of the environment, vivisection and cruelty to animals.

Tuesday 14 March

As I was sitting outside the Cabinet Room waiting for a meeting Jim came up. He was very agitated about something. He heard me cough and said, 'Nothing trivial I hope.'

Over lunch Frances gave me a great lecture and made a list of my strengths and weaknesses. My weaknesses, she said, were that I was thought to be fanatical and humourless, and that I was building on too narrow a base in the Party. She advised me, 'You must be more human and more relaxed. And you must go for more support in the PLP and TUC General Council.'

Wednesday 22 March

At 9 I had my first meeting with Ian Gillis, my new Chief Information Officer, who is replacing Bernard Ingham. I miss Bernard.

Saturday 25 March

I'm reading E.P. Thompson's *William Morris*, which is a marvellous book. It gives me an insight into his relationship to the Romantic poets of the 1830s, influenced by the French Revolution. I found it a little difficult understanding the link between the Romantic movement and the Pre-Raphaelites, but I was more familiar with William Morris and the Social Democratic Federation. He opposed the parliamentary socialists in the first instance and was contemptuous of the Fabians.

Monday 10 April

Organisational Sub-Committee at 3.30. There was a long discussion about the National Front. Frank Allaun believed they should be banned from TV and schools, and should be treated as pariahs. I said it wasn't their appearance on TV that gave them publicity so much as the press. You couldn't stop TV covering their meetings during the Election, and I thought it was better to argue it out.

Frank and I don't see eye to eye on this. I can understand his point. He thinks that, if Hitler had been crushed early on, the holocaust would never have happened.

I take a rather old-fashioned liberal view, but I didn't win. Advice is to be given to local candidates and I think I shall be able to justify whatever the Party decides.

Snow fell today. Unbelievable. It isn't quite frozen but it is very cold and the trees are bending with the lovely snow on their boughs. Caroline went out after midnight and I took a photograph of her with my polaroid against the white background.

Saturday 29 April

Caught the 88 bus to Trafalgar Square for the Friends of the Earth Windscale demonstration. There were about 10,000 people, mostly young, and it reminded me of the CND marches, with a combination of right-wing and rather prim ecological people and left-wing commune types with beards and babies.

I climbed up the steps of St Martin-in-the-Fields and sat on my portable seat facing the square. There was a group playing and then the speeches began. I couldn't hear very well so I went round and took a few pictures.

Friends of the Earth are not politically strong enough to stop nuclear power but they are hoping to check the mad rush towards the fast breeder, and I think that's an extremely powerful counter-pressure to have.

The 6 o'clock news reported Arthur Scargill's call for civil disobedience to stop Windscale, and Caroline remarked that he was really a general in the field – indeed, she had seen him recently in a television interview with General Clutterbuck talking about the army's role in civil disturbances, Clutterbuck having written on the subject.

Anyway Arthur came to dinner at 7 with his wife Anne, and some sympathetic journalists. Stephen looked in momentarily.

Arthur told me it was rumoured that I was there in the crowd, but I couldn't possibly have spoken because I am the Minister responsible for Windscale.

Throughout the evening, Arthur talked most of the time. He is about thirty-eight, a remarkable leader, tough, perky, amusing, with lots of personality, a marvellous mimic of all sorts of accents.

Arthur thought that, if we lost the Election, I would become Leader of the Party.

'I'm not so sure,' I said, 'because a lot of left-wing MPs would be defeated and the PLP could drift back to the right. Also the trade union leaders would have to work with the new Government and wouldn't want a critical left-wing Labour Party which might embarrass them in front of their own rank and file.'

'The miners would support you,' said Arthur.

Saturday 6 May
Melissa is in bed with flu. Rosalind came out of hospital; she has a growth in her lung but it's not clear yet what it is.

Saturday 20 May
The doctors opened up Rosalind yesterday and found that the growth had developed so much that they just closed her up again. Most of the morning was spent on the phone to Hilary, who has been fantastically courageous. Rosalind's parents, Peter and Lesley Retey, were obviously very distressed.

I rang Liz Shore, who gave me some information, then Hilary arrived. As soon as he saw me his face crumpled in tears – he towers over me now – and I comforted him. I can hardly bear thinking about it.

Monday 22 May
At 10.15 I had a word about Rosalind with Dick Mabon, who was a physician. He said, 'You must get a second opinion, find out what the chances are, and how long she has. You must find out how much pain is involved because if she is going to have a long treatment she might not be able to take painkillers – that could be agony for her and it might be better not to try to prolong it.'

I did tell my driver, Ron Vaughan, about it and he said, 'It's turned summer into winter', which I thought was touching.

Saturday 3 June
Rosalind is not at all well and Caroline was distressed about it. Hilary is marvellous – in a way too strong. Joshua is staying with him, which is a great comfort.

I sat downstairs in my office trying to work and I found myself sobbing at the thought of that young couple being broken up by illness, and of all the agonies to come to her and Hilary.

Friday 9 June
A visit to Windscale with Caroline.

Windscale was originally an army ordnance factory called Sellafield before the war, and after the war it was used to develop our nuclear weapons programme and its name was changed to Windscale. John Hill, who was present today, reminded me that he worked there in 1950, probably at the beginning of the civil programme. There is still a military operation there.

They store spent fuel elements from nuclear-powered submarines and process the plutonium that's needed for the country's hydrogen bombs.

We were greeted by John Hill, Con Allday (Managing Director of BNFL) and others. We had coffee and then went round together.

We toured the oxide storage ponds, and I must say they are very mysterious, those deep indoor swimming pools with their dark green water. They are lit up underneath and you can dimly see these fuel elements that are used in nuclear power stations, vaguely threatening, though the water is apparently a complete shield against any radioactivity that gets out.

Then we went to the chemical separation plant, where they break the fuel elements down into depleted uranium, plutonium (which is the most deadly substance of all) and highly toxic waste. They showed us what they called the Harvest demonstration rig where they take these highly toxic wastes, which have been evaporated down to about a tenth of their volume, and mix them with ground glass, put them in a furnace and fuse them into a glass bottle which permits the heat but not the radioactivity to be released. This is placed in a metal flask and left to cool for twenty years, when they believe it will be ready to put in geological formations.

From a roof we had an immensely impressive view of the site. I remembered John Hill telling me last year that in the early days they didn't really understand what they were handling and the whole site was soaked in radioactive toxic wastes.

I comment on this because when you see this vast complex you are struck, on the one hand, by the skill and scientific knowledge of the people who run it and, on the other, by the exceptional vulnerability of such a complicated system. Nobody can truthfully say that this whole project can be handed over to future generations to look after safely when they've no idea whether future generations will be faced with invasion, earthquakes, floods, strikes or plagues. It is a tremendously risky thing to do, and the duration of the risk, 10,000 or 15,000 years, is enormous.

We were taken downstairs along a corridor, and it was something like the vaults of the Bank of England. There was a door about two feet thick and inside that another door with circular panels either side, each padlocked, through which the plutonium was placed and stored.

The whole thing is electronically monitored of course, and it would be impossible for terrorists to get through the door and into the safe and then remove the plutonium – although there's no question whatever that, if the country was invaded, a hostile scientific team could get the plutonium out in a jiffy.

Two years ago I had to introduce legislation to arm the AEA guards, but in fact I think there are military forces there, out of view, protecting the military establishment.

We went back and talked to the employee representatives – the staff and unions. They raised the Windscale planning inquiry and were in fact now persuaded that it had been well handled. The debate was broadcast in full last month from Parliament, and many of them had listened to it. It had given them the feeling that the work they do was explicitly endorsed by Parliament.

Lunch was a tremendous buffet with prawn cocktail and a decorated salmon, and turkey and strawberries and cream.

Drove to Newcastle across Cumbria and Northumberland. It's an area I'd never been to in my life, full of Roman forts and a bit of Hadrian's Wall. Arrived at the Park Hotel in Tynemouth for the NUM dinner.

Saturday 10 June

Came back on the train. Caroline and Judith Hart went to dinner in the dining car, and Caroline told me afterwards that at their table was another diner who had been shooting a bit of a line about the wine, complaining and generally showing off to them.

At one point I walked up to the buffet, not seeing Caroline. As I went by, the man had apparently said, 'Who's let that bloody twit on the train?' (I hadn't heard this.)

Caroline had replied, 'That's my husband', and for the rest of the meal he hadn't said a word.

Sunday 18 June

Went to visit Rosalind. We hadn't seen her for a week and she looked paler and thinner. She had that slightly translucent skin tone which is the sign of a sick person. But her eyes were bright and she smiled.

I heard today that the Top Salaries Review Body chaired by Lord Boyle has come up with proposals for increases of 30 per cent for senior civil servants, chairmen of nationalised industries, senior forces officers and all the rest. That will mean another £8,000 for Permanent Secretaries. It's unbelievable, and obviously causing a great deal of embarrassment.

Wednesday 21 June

Brian Sedgemore, Frances and Francis and Michael Meacher came to lunch. To be perfectly candid it was a leadership planning meeting. Michael offered to draw up a list of people from the PLP who might be prepared to vote for me as Leader in the event of Jim leaving. He said we should start work on it now. Michael is very devoted and willing to do a lot of work on this. Obviously I found it encouraging.

Sunday 16 July

Chris Mullin came to see me. He is about thirty, fought North Devon in 1970, works for the BBC and writes for *Tribune*. Anne McDermid, my literary agent, has persuaded him to turn my speeches into a book. I liked him. He's just written a book called *The Manifesto of an Extremist* in which he

discusses various themes – the press, the Cold War, and so on. It's an
arresting title, but it may do him some damage.

Thursday 20 July
Cabinet, and we came to the very important White Paper on pay, *Winning the
Battle against Inflation.* Jim began by indicating that the Liberals would not
support us on the control of dividends, and Michael called for it to be
published on Monday.

We dealt with percentages and what we should do about low pay.

Denis said, 'We should accept the 5 per cent limit recommended in the
paper. The unions won't endorse any guidelines but they do accept that the
Government has a responsibility in this field and are only really expecting 5
per cent. The CBI can't give a commitment but they like it very much.'

David Owen favoured the 5 per cent, as did Roy Hattersley, who said that
7 per cent would be too high and would mean higher inflation.

Stan Orme was absolutely opposed to a norm.

I suggested we put in an amendment, as we had last year, to the effect that
the Government's intention was to retain the level of real incomes in the
current pay year.

Jim said, '5 per cent it is, and I have told the unions that they have all the
weapons. We are naked in their presence and we need their co-operation. I
said that at Durham and got a warm response.'

Sunday 30 July
The big news today is that the Attorney-General has announced that
charges in the Jeremy Thorpe affair are imminent. The whole of British
politics may now erupt over this. It will certainly affect the Liberal Party's
Election prospects.

Since there is no certainty that the Liberals are going to put up a
candidate against me, I may be fighting a much harder battle with the
Tories. I shall appeal quite openly to all the radical Liberals in my
constituency to vote Labour, and I'll just have to hope that enough of them
do.

Wednesday 2 August
Caroline came to dinner at the House – the anniversary of the day we met
thirty years ago. We went up to sit in my room for the last vote before the
recess was called: maybe the last vote of this Parliament.

Friday 4 August
Jeremy Thorpe was arrested today, along with three others, and taken to
Minehead police station, where they were charged with conspiracy to
murder Norman Scott. They were released on bail of £5,000 each, put up
by Eric Lubbock.

All the rumours that Thorpe is implicated have turned out to be correct. It is the most tragic story. Here is a well-connected, brilliant, amusing man who won North Devon from the Tories in 1959, became Leader of the Liberal Party when he was in his thirties after Jo Grimond retired, and who in February 1974 carried the Party to its greatest electoral achievement since the war. And he has had this terrible anxiety on his mind, being blackmailed by this male model. The man is completely broken. The charge of conspiring to murder is obviously very serious, and if he is convicted there can be little doubt that he will go to prison. Inexpressibly sad.

The question now will be how much did Harold Wilson try to cover it up to protect Thorpe for political purposes?

Wednesday 6 September
Joan Lestor rang and told me that, at Brighton yesterday, Jim Callaghan had asked her where she was going to be over the next few days. She's convinced an Election is imminent and thinks 28 September is a possibility, in which case the Election timetable would be very tight.

Thursday 7 September
Went into the office and found they were re-laying the carpet, which seemed very significant.

Cabinet at 10.30, and I was sure the Election was going to be announced. We met without officials present. Jim said that there had been much speculation and he had consulted his Ministers, especially Michael Foot and Denis Healey, but the responsibility was *his*, although it affected all our fates, and it was an enormous responsibility. He had considered other factors such as the Devolution Referendum, and the fact that according to most opinion polls Labour voters do not want an Election – though our activists do – and he announced that he'd written to the Queen last night to say that he did not propose to seek the dissolution of Parliament.

I was most surprised, and indeed angry that the Cabinet had not discussed a decision of this magnitude. The letter to the Queen had been sent, and that was it. I later discovered that he had decided this course on 17 August, so when he asked for our opinions last week, as a result of which I wrote to him, it was already a *fait accompli*.

He thought we might get a majority in Parliament on the Queen's Speech debate and we would fight when we could see the prospect of outright victory. We could win now, but he said the position would be clearer once the improvement in the economy was felt more fully. He wanted to disprove the idea that governments just go for an Election at the first sign of a blue sky and he intended to make that point in his broadcast tonight. There would be difficulties ahead in the winter, but he wanted the electorate to see the full picture and not just the first stage of our recovery, because the real question was whether an early Election would help with unemployment, pay, or any of the problems facing us, and the answer was no. He said he would prefer that there be no discussion of this matter because he could not unwrite the letter to the Queen.

Sunday 24 September
To Hyde Park to address the Anti-Nazi League rally. There was a lorry with a steel band playing, and there were tens of thousands of young people. The average age was about twenty to twenty-five, and there were banners and badges and punk rockers, just a tremendous gathering of people. It was certainly the biggest meeting that I had ever attended in this country – bigger than the Upper Clyde Shipbuilders demos in Glasgow.

A speaker from the Socialist Workers' Party spoke from the platform first, followed by Arthur Scargill and me. Tom Robinson, a gay pop star and a committed socialist, sang. Bill Keys, General Secretary of SOGAT, and Dennis Skinner were there. As far as I know, Dennis and I were the only two Labour MPs. Multiracial rock music has given the movement leadership and it is a tragedy that the Labour Party can't give a firmer lead, but it has never done so.

Tuesday 26 September
Moss Evans and I talked for an hour and a half; considering he has the Ford pay claim and a national Ford strike on his hands, it was amazing that he could come at all. I asked him how it was going. 'I notice Terry Beckett (Chairman of Ford) got an 80 per cent pay increase today,' I said.

'Oh,' he said, 'we've known that was coming for ages – profit-linked of course. It just isn't on; Ford have made great profits and our people have contributed to it.'

Moss told me it would cost the union a quarter of a million pounds a week to keep the Ford strike going, and they could borrow more money, interest free, from other unions.

He looked out of the corner of his eye to see my reaction to all this. I was quite impassive, and I said, 'I just want to know how we're going to get out of it without being painted into a corner like Ted Heath was. Jim feels that reducing expectations is the right thing to do.'

'Yes,' said Moss, 'when you talk to Jim he says, "The mass of the people are with us and will continue to support us", but, you know, the rank and file of our people are the public too. We have a million and a quarter T&G workers and we are just as much members of the public as those who don't want wage increases. You can't re-create the Social Contract, you just can't do it. You've got to have flexibility now, we've got to be able to renegotiate in industry.'

Friday 29 September – Labour Party Conference, Blackpool
Sir Fred Catherwood, Chairman of the Overseas Trade Board, Terence

Beckett, and today Joe Gormley and Ray Buckton have all been attacking the rigidity of the 5 per cent pay limit. Jim is digging his heels in and Denis Healey had been in Washington saying the same thing to the IMF.

Saturday 30 September
Pope John Paul died yesterday after only thirty-three days as Pope.

Barbara Castle is extremely keen to have a vote tomorrow, though she herself intends to abstain. She is anxious to crucify the Executive over the very issue on which she was crucified in 1969, when she was forced to drop *In Place of Strife*.

Sunday 1 October
To the National Executive to consider the motions to Conference. Barbara Castle had an emergency resolution opposing the EMS but she took twenty minutes to speak on it. She quoted Harold, Jim, Roy Jenkins, the Party, the TUC and so on. She doesn't know when to stop.

Anyway, we voted, and Barbara's motion denouncing and rejecting the EMS was carried by 16 to 9 – a tremendous success.

There is great excitement and there is no doubt it is the Left's Conference. Jim can't ignore that completely.

Monday 2 October
Joan Lestor delivered her Chairman's address, ending with a quote from Tawney, and that was followed by an overwhelming vote against smoking at the Conference, so that was the end of my pipe.

Denis Healey breezed in and made an awful speech about how we must all support Jim and so on. After Michael had wound up with a call for loyalty, to everyone's amazement the motion against the 5 per cent was not remitted but carried by about 4 million to 1 million, and the alternative strategy motion was carried without a vote. The Right tried to be clever by endorsing the Government's stand on economic and monetary policy and calling on the Movement to support it, as part of a general vote of thanks to the Labour Government. They thought they'd get it through but it was actually defeated by 3 million to 2.8 million. The result was dazzling, and Jim's whole position now is endangered.

It's hard to know how to react, because the IMF and the City of London may withdraw their support from the Government, and Heath and Steel might offer to back Jim up. The trade union leaders will be embarrassed by all this, but their rank and file had to be allowed to speak. We can't do anything without the support of the whole Labour Movement.

I refused all requests for interviews because it only makes trouble.

In the evening I went with Caroline and Stephen to Tiffany's Ballroom for the Labour Agents' Ball, where the big news was that Jim had decided not to attend – the first time in years that he'd missed it. The agents, who are mostly right-wing machine men, were utterly demoralised by the vote.

Tuesday 3 October
Yesterday's vote against the Right's motion in support of the Government was significant because it prevented the Conference from facing both ways, as it did last year.

So Jim started the day with a handicap, though I must say he went on to make the best speech I had ever heard from a Party leader at Conference. He was modest and fair, and he said that nowhere else could such an intelligent debate about pay policy be held. Yesterday's debate was outstanding for its relevance, and for the experience of those who argued the case.

'But the White Paper stands,' he said, 'and we have to prevent inflation from rising. Conference defeated the Government's pay policy yesterday and that was a dramatic moment.'

He went on to talk about the Government's achievements, about the caring society and participation and pressure groups. I sent him a little note, which I heard later was well received.

Wednesday 4 October
Dennis Skinner was fresh from his NEC victory and looked slightly manic and aggressive. Eric said, 'That man frightens me. Is he really democratic?' Dennis is a pyrotechnic; he isn't frightening at all. He's just pleased because it's another left-winger on the NEC.

Monday 9 October
It is a fortnight tomorrow since I last wrote to Merlyn Rees reminding him about my question of whether my telephone had been intercepted, so I decided to write again.

Dear Merlyn,

I wrote to you on 12 September to ask you if my telephone calls are or ever were tapped by the security services. Having received no acknowledgement or reply I wrote again on 26 September and asked if you had received my earlier letters. Your Private Secretary telephoned my Private Office the same day. The message did not, however, confirm that you personally had received or even seen my letters.

I enclose copies of these letters and of your office message. Two more weeks have now elapsed without any word from you. The questions I put were quite straightforward. When may I expect your personal reply?

Tony Benn

I don't know why I have plucked up my courage so much, but I have no intention of being diverted from it now.

Tuesday 10 October
Anthony Tucker of the *Guardian* came to see me, and I told him that I believed he was right about being victimised over his stand on nuclear issues. He said, 'It's not just me. Professor Lindop of Bart's Hospital, who is a member of the Flowers Commission and is a well-known expert on radiological protection, wrote an article for a paper in the East of England. She was violently attacked in a letter from Michael Michaels.' (Michael Michaels was my Under-Secretary at the Ministry of Technology.)

He also pointed out that there was a Euro-nuclear link, in that pro-Common Market people were also pro-nuclear, as I am well aware. He maintained that John Hill, Chairman of the AEA, had complained to the Editor of the *Guardian* about what he, Tucker, had been writing. As a result, Tucker had been undermined. He gave me a copy of a memorandum that he had written to the Editor and I drafted a minute saying that I would not have the Department penalising journalists because they were critical of our policy. When I showed it to James Bretherton afterwards, he advised me to consult Bernard Ingham, since it did imply a criticism of him.

Wednesday 11 October
As I was about to go to a press conference at 5, I saw a brown envelope marked 'Personal' in my tray and, though I yearned to open it, I went to the press first.

Back upstairs I read the letter, which was from Merlyn Rees, and it was astonishing. He apologised for the delay, said that he thought the acknowledgement made it clear he *had* seen my letter, but that I could not be told whether or not my telephone was being intercepted. That had been the practice and he was not prepared to vary it in respect of a Member of Parliament. The fact that I am a Privy Councillor, a Cabinet colleague and a senior member of the Government made no difference to him.

He pointed out that, in respect of West German telephone-tapping, the European Court of Human Rights had not ruled that this was an infringement of human rights, and he mentioned that the Machinery of Government Committee of the NEC had not suggested that these matters should be covered by a Freedom of Information Act.

I should add that Merlyn mentioned that he had sent copies of the correspondence to the Prime Minister.

I came home and wrote an eight-page memorandum on the security services and the case for an inquiry.

Tonight, addressing the Tory Party Conference, Ted Heath pledged his full support to Jim Callaghan on pay. That can't be right.

Monday 16 October

A new Pope was elected today – Cardinal Wojtyla from Cracow. He's taken the title of Pope John Paul II and he is the first non-Italian Pope since 1522, so it's quite an event. He was in a German POW camp or concentration camp. I think he's a good choice.

Wednesday 25 October

Lunch with Frances, Geoff Bish, Francis, Michael Meacher and Bryan Gould. Frances Morrell and Brian Sedgemore think I should be quiet now and just drift into the leadership of the Party by doing nothing. That may be the right tactic, but I just feel we are fighting a battle and I am impatient to be in it. They don't understand my attitude on this. We analysed Jim's views on the EMS and drew some interesting conclusions as to what he must be thinking: that Britain was ungovernable and therefore we needed a federal European government; that there was great political value in being associated with Schmidt; that there would be a fear of a run on the pound before the Election. He didn't really have any faith in the pay policy, so international monetarist disciplines would be the best way of holding the unions in check.

At 5 I, went to see Jim alone in the Cabinet Room about my paper on reform of the security services, which I had put to the Home Policy Committee.

He said, 'On this business of the security services. Why did you ask whether you were tapped?'

I told him about the delay in Merlyn's reply to my note.

'That's because it came to me,' he said.

'It's a serious issue, Jim.'

'It is all under ministerial control,' he replied. 'We hardly bug anybody. Incidentally, your telephone isn't tapped.'

'I didn't say it was. But my son picked up my voice on the radio the other day, and my daughter made a call and heard a recording of what I had just said.'

'It's all under control,' he repeated.

'But how do we know that?'

'Look,' Jim replied, 'there must be an element of trust on this.'

I assured him I wasn't suggesting that I distrusted him, but you had no idea what the secret services were up to.

'Well,' he said, 'I have just changed the heads of MI5 and MI6, as a matter of fact. I have appointed Sir Howard Smith as head of MI5, and I have known him for years.'

'So have I.'

Jim told me that Howard Smith had just come back from our embassy in Moscow, and Jim had informed him, 'Say goodbye to Gromyko – tell him you're coming back to take charge of MI5.'

'Well, if the Russians can know who the head of MI5 is, why can't it be published here?' I asked.

'He might be a target,' Jim said, 'an IRA target.'

'Lots of people are targets.'

He didn't tell me who the head of MI6 was, so I said, 'I heard from an American, who was on President Carter's Commission, that a man called Sir Leonard Hooper was head of MI6. These names ought to be known.'

'Just makes them targets for the IRA,' Jim muttered. 'The whole thing is under control.'

'Well, you say that, Jim, but I heard of a WEA course on William Morris, in Wales, where the police wanted to find out who had enrolled because they thought that Morris was a Marxist.'

'Well, let me give *you* an example,' Jim replied. 'Two MPs went to some Anti-Apartheid meetings and they complained to me that they had been followed by plainclothes men. I'll tell you why the men were there – to keep an eye on BOSS, the South African secret service, and to find out which meetings they were attending.'

I didn't say, but I found that hard to believe because Special Branch and MI5 work together with BOSS.

'Let me give you another example,' I said. 'Harold Wilson, in my presence, told the CBI at a dinner in March 1971 that the TUC were bugged. I didn't learn *that* as a Minister.'

'Oh, Harold is just a Walter Mitty. Once, in his study upstairs, he turned round the picture of Gladstone and there was a hole in the wall. He called Ken Stowe in and put his hands to his lips and said, "Shhh!", pointing to the hole. He's just a Walter Mitty.'

'Well, maybe, but the *Pencourt File* stated that he thought he was being bugged; and Chapman Pincher was certain Wilson was bugged.'

'Pincher's links with the services ended five years ago,' said Jim.

'Well, he has just published a book, *Inside Story*, saying that five members of the Cabinet are Communists and one is in touch with Moscow. Presumably he thinks it's Michael Foot.'

'Oh, that's all stopped. Chapman Pincher has nothing to do with the security services now.'

I reminded Jim of my efforts to appoint Jack Jones to the NEB, and that I was told he was a security risk, at a time when he was carrying the whole Government on his shoulders. I was told I couldn't have Hugh Scanlon on the British Gas Corporation because we needed somebody who was loyal to the country. How did we know security was under control?

'It is. And your telephone isn't tapped.'

'How many telephones *are* tapped?'

'139,' he replied, 'and each one has to be authorised by the Home Secretary on a warrant. Every three months the Permanent Secretary and the Home Secretary go over the list and discuss whether or not to continue tapping individual numbers. Not even all the foreign embassies are tapped.'

'Well, the POEU are of the opinion that between 1,000 and 2,000 phones in London alone are tapped.'

'That is not so,' said Jim. 'It has got to be a question of trust.'

'But a lot of people are worried, and I think we ought to have an inquiry.'

Jim said, 'I am not making available anything that is secret.'

'I didn't expect you would, but we should get some high-powered people to look at it and put some guidelines down. The Solicitor-General supports me on this.'

'He knows nothing about security.'

'Nobody does,' I said; 'that is the whole point.'

Jim continued, 'Now, on this freedom-of-information business. There's a committee looking at it – GEN 29.'

I replied, 'Yes, I read that in the papers too.'

'Would you like to be put on the committee?'

I said yes, so I was put on it.

I think Jim was sorry he'd blown up at me on Monday and I told him I understood; we were all under great strain. He admitted to having a very low boiling point.

I had the impression that he wanted to find out what I knew about the security services. I said I wasn't being paranoid; there was a big civil liberties issue here, and had been for many years. I was an old-fashioned radical liberal and I didn't believe in all this secrecy. He remarked that if I started inquiries I'd only drive the intelligence service underground. Well, that was rich, given that they were already underground.

Friday 3 November

The Ford workers voted overwhelmingly today against the Ford pay offer. The BBC television coverage deliberately created the impression that motor car workers are dangerous and violent, while the BBC is the voice of rationality. It is disgusting.

Thursday 16 November

Jim Callaghan had some of his grandchildren in the Cabinet Room before Cabinet began and some photographs were taken. I must say the Cabinet gets more and more like the royal family.

John Silkin was congratulated on his recovery after being knocked down by a moped, and John Smith was welcomed as the new Secretary of State for Trade in Edmund Dell's place.

Tuesday 21 November

The papers are full of the Jeremy Thorpe case. On the face of it, it would appear that he had a homosexual relationship with Scott – though that is no longer a crime – and that there was a plot to incite people to murder Scott. It's tragic for Jeremy.

I wrote today to the Redgraves, enclosing £20 towards their libel costs against the *Observer*. I composed the letter with care to make it clear I wasn't supporting the Workers' Revolutionary Party, to which they belong.

Wednesday 29 November
Had a meeting with Jim Schlesinger, the US Energy Secretary, who is over here. He was once Secretary of State for Defence and was sacked by Ford because of a disagreement he had with Kissinger, and he has also headed the CIA. He is a tough Republican intellectual, lives an austere life, in line with the Presbyterian faith to which he was converted from Judaism, and is a very dour man. He doesn't believe in publicity or any of that stuff, and is not gregarious at all. When I took him upstairs to my room, where a huge crowd of people had gathered, he just sat down and stared at everyone. He doesn't suffer fools gladly.

Anyway, I welcomed him and said I'd been looking forward to his visit. 'I hope it's OK if we do our business in this order: your energy policy/our energy policy; the world energy scene; Iran, Mexico; OPEC and oil prices; UN international energy; coal policy; fast-breeder reactors; and anything else you might like to raise.'

'Fine.'

'How would you like to start?'

'Up to you.'

Tea was brought in at that point and he said, 'Is that your mug? If it were any bigger you wouldn't be able to lift it!' I told him I had a two-pint mug at home but I didn't bring it to the office. It was a sign of friendliness on his part after a slightly tense beginning.

'Tell us first how your energy policy in America is going,' I said.

'Well,' he replied, 'politics is like ju-jitsu. We asked for more powers than we got, but we got more than they realised, and we are now going to use them.' He went on to give a very tough presentation of their policy.

I said, 'My assessment is that we have to think long-term and that is beyond the range of market forces. I don't worship market forces, though I am not being completely ideological about it. You've got these great big companies and you've got to keep an eye on them.'

What followed was a very informed discussion between two experienced people – he with far more power and experience, but it did range over everything and I must say I enjoyed it.

He looked at my Workers' Union banner and said it was beautiful. I said, 'You see the religious themes depicted in it – trade unionism grew out of the chapels in this country.'

'It could have come from the Soviet Union, with those realistic figures,' he said, to which I replied, 'Socialist realism is very much the same as capitalist realism.'

'What do you mean?'

I said, 'Developing societies with a lot of self-confidence and thrust go for realistic art. It's only in decaying societies that you get all this decadent stuff like the Impressionists. That's why Khrushchev and Eisenhower agreed about chocolate-box art.' He laughed.

I asked him if he knew where the hammer and sickle were to be found in London and he didn't, so I promised to show him.

We walked out to my car to go to lunch at the Dorchester Hotel; he had no security guards with him, and when I asked he told me that he never allows them.

I got the driver to pass by St James's Park because Schlesinger is a great birdwatcher. I asked him about the CIA and he said, 'I was there for five months at a difficult time, right in the middle of Watergate when we had done some terrible things.' He said the CIA got up to some funny things but at least they tried to maintain some standards and co-operate up to a point with the White House. But Nixon had just expected them to do anything he wanted and that wasn't on.

'I am puzzled about Nixon's departure,' I said. 'I never could quite understand it.'

'Nixon lied to the American people and they wouldn't have that. If he had said, "Yes, there was some funny business for which I take full responsibility", his popularity would have risen enormously, but he looked the American people in the eye and he lied to them.' Schlesinger thought Nixon had behaved stupidly and could otherwise have survived. Also, he thought a Democrat could have got away with it because of their majority in Congress but, as a Republican, Nixon had miscalculated.

As we passed the imposing Victoria Memorial in the middle of Buckingham Palace roundabout, I said, 'There's the hammer and sickle.' There were the two lions, and a man holding a hammer aloft and a girl carrying a sickle. He laughed.

I told him I admired Carter and that he struck me as a sensitive guy. 'Do you know that Jim Callaghan is very attached to him, and when the dollar was in difficulties I think Jim called in the American Ambassador just to express his support for Carter,' I said.

'Yes, the President knew that and was pleased.'

At lunch were Frank Kearton, Derek Ezra, Moss Evans, John Hill, Dick Mabon and others.

After lunch I said to Schlesinger, 'I am not going to make a big fuss so I am going to ask you just to say a word.'

Schlesinger replied, 'I have enjoyed today very much but I never thought I would be taken by a British Secretary of State for Energy to see the hammer and sickle outside Buckingham Palace!'

So Dick Mabon turned to Frank Judd sitting beside him. 'Tony's done it again!'

'My God,' I said to Schlesinger, 'if you go round telling that story, I'll be in trouble with the CIA.'

I think he took me literally. 'Oh, don't bother about that,' he said. Everyone laughed and it was fun.

Thursday 30 November
Before Cabinet, Merlyn Rees came up to me and said, 'By the way, Tony, I want to make the point again that I control all the security services personally. I check and review everybody whose phone is tapped and I assure you it is completely under my control.'

'Well,' I replied, 'Chapman Pincher's recent book claimed that you weren't told anything.'

'That's absolute rubbish,' he said.

Thursday 7 December
Cabinet, and on the EMS summit Jim had little to say. Sterling was firm and the final decision of both the Irish and the Italians on the EMS had been deferred. At Brussels Jim had stated our unwillingness to join the exchange-rate mechanism to be set up on 1 January 1979, while being prepared to participate in other aspects of the system.

He then said that a proposal had come up that there should be an informal summit meeting between Schmidt, Giscard, himself and President Carter on the island of Guadeloupe to discuss political and security developments.

'Where is Guadeloupe?' asked Peter.

'It's a French island in the Caribbean,' said Jim, obviously pleased that he had been included, because it showed he was still part of the big league. 'But keep it very quiet because the French don't want it to get out.'

A few minutes later someone came in and handed Jim a note. He then announced, 'I can tell you that the *New York Times* have published the news so we can now refer to it.'

Jim's psychology is quite extraordinary.

Then we discussed the issue of low-paid workers, and Albert Booth said it was a real problem. 'I would like a £3 minimum rise, that's to say nobody who is low-paid should get less than £3 as a result of the 5 per cent. Some of the lowest-paid will get only £2.15 or £2.25 on the present guidelines. The poorest people in the community are no better off now than they were in 1949; indeed, the lowest quarter of all are worse off.'

Michael Foot supported Albert, and Jim said, 'It's just a moral issue.'

Denis intervened, 'Child benefit and other assistance of that kind have helped the low-paid. Employers in the private sector couldn't afford to pay £3.'

Monday 11 December
I had a report from my Under-Secretary, Robert Priddle, about the oil-tanker drivers' dispute, for which the Civil Contingencies Unit had produced Operation Drumstick. There are two options: to mobilise troops before Christmas, which would of course be very provocative to the unions; or wait till after Christmas, which might be too late to prevent a serious oil shortage. I decided to go for the slower option and try to get the guidelines slightly fudged – which the Prime Minister would endorse. If an emergency arose, we would then ask the unions themselves to maintain essential services, thus avoiding the use of troops.

Tuesday 12 December
The press attacks go on. The *Daily Mail* wrote an article implying that when the House of Lords was abolished we would have no more Elections in Britain – a scandalous comment.

EY Committee began at 10.10 with Gerald Kaufman reporting on a recommendation from a study group that we accept BSC's proposed closure of Shotton steelworks. This would be a direct breach of a clear pledge given by the Chairman, Charles Villiers, and by Eric Varley last year that Shotton would not be closed until 1982–83.

Kaufman said there was substantial overcapacity in the steel industry and the situation would deteriorate further with the coming on stream of the new integrated steel plants at Ravenscraig and Redcar. 'BSC now proposes major closures at Corby and Shotton in 1979–80. These are the best closures to choose if we are going to follow this course. It would involve 5,000 redundancies at Shotton in North Wales, affecting Merseyside, and 5,500 at Corby. Male unemployment in Shotton would double, and at Corby it would increase from 20 per cent to 28 per cent. But the failure to close Shotton would cost £29 million and defer the viability target for BSC beyond 1980 to 1981.' He said the Foreign Office and the Department of Trade feared that keeping the plants open would give rise to American and Common Market objections.

Eric Varley said it would be very difficult for him because in Merseyside Dunlop were about to announce another 3,000 redundancies.

Jim asked, 'Why, with all these redundancy announcements, are the figures for unemployment going down?'

'Because the service industries are picking up redundant workers,' said Denis.

Friday 15 December
The Government was defeated in the Commons over the use of economic sanctions against Ford, following their settlement of 17 per cent with their workers last month.

Sunday 17 December
Worked at home this morning, and in the afternoon Lissie and I sat and watched the end of *The Railway Children* and I had a good weep.

I must say, the more I think about the political situation, the more it looks as if the whole atmosphere is clouding over. I can see a series of disputes starting in the early part of the year. The oil-tanker drivers' dispute could drag on, and then we go into the spring with a deepening world recession as a result of the impending oil price rises.

Monday 18 December
At 4.30 I had what turned out to be a very useful meeting on the dispute with Albert, Moss Evans and Jack Ashwell, national officer of the TGWU. I explained the problems if the strike started on 3 January and we had to call the troops in, we would have to put people on alert immediately. I told them I would like to get the goodwill of the T&G.

Jack said, 'That's OK.'

Moss Evans asked Jack Ashwell if the strike could be deferred and Jack said no.

'Of course,' said Moss, 'we don't want the troops used.'

'Neither do we,' I told him, 'but if I need to use them I will have to declare a state of emergency.'

Tuesday 19 December
To Cabinet, and Jim was in a frightfully cheerful mood and joked, and the atmosphere was very jolly. The first item was the tanker drivers' dispute, and I had to give a report. 'Prime Minister, I shall have to carry the can – the only one with petrol in it!'

Cabinet ended at about 12.20, and I had a drink with Peter Shore and Stan Orme. Jim came up to us and said, 'Do you know, I just feel that 1979 is going to be my year. I think everything is going to come right.' I thought for a moment he was joking, but I am sure he was serious. I nearly asked, 'Have you tried walking on water, and will you rise on the third day?', but thought it irreverent.

Saturday 30 December
Got the train to Stansgate and joined Lissie, Caroline, Stephen and June.

I sat down to write a memorandum called 'The Maintenance of Essential Services during Industrial Disputes', urging that the trade unions take on responsibility by agreement with the Government. If I write it as a Cabinet paper, it becomes classified, and nobody will ever know about it. However, I think I will send it to Len Murray, and if the TUC is favourable put it to the TUC–Labour Party Liaison Committee.

Monday 1 January 1979
Snowed in at Stansgate. Melissa is writing something called 'Fight Sexism in

the Benn Family' in which she denounces the men for leaving all the work to
Caroline.

Thursday 4 January

At 8.30 this morning I had a phone call from Bill Burroughs, my Private
Secretary, to say that Texaco drivers had gone on all-out strike.

Frances Morrell has been invited to a nomination meeting as Labour
candidate at Birkenhead, Edmund Dell's constituency. It would be lovely if
she could get selected there; she has certainly earned it.

Friday 5 January

The Texaco strike is worse, and Manchester, the North East and parts of
Scotland are running out of oil.

Sunday 7 January

As a result of Melissa's campaign, I cleaned the house from 10.30 till 7 and
did five loads of washing. In the *Observer* there was a complete account of the
paper I am presenting to a Cabinet committee tomorrow on miners' pay.

There was a most interesting radio phone-in programme about Iran.
That terrible Tory, Michael Charlton, was the presenter and he interviewed
a close colleague of Khomeini, the Muslim leader who lives in Paris. It was
extremely good; an Iranian woman caller asked if women would have rights
in an Islamic republic. He said, 'Yes, absolute full voting rights, but we are
not prepared to have women turned into sex symbols.'

On 'The World at One' Mrs Thatcher was reported calling for a state of
emergency and saying she would take away social security payments from
strikers.

Monday 8 January

At 1.30 I went with Robert Priddle to Shellmex House to the emergency
committee which Dick Mabon has been chairing. As I entered the room, I
couldn't but remember that these were the biggest companies in the world
and any common interest that a Labour government might have with them
at this moment is strictly temporary. John Greenborough, the President of
the CBI and Chairman of Shell, was present.

Well, the new year has begun with a vengeance. I would like to believe
that, if a left-wing policy were being pursued, we wouldn't be having all this
trouble with the unions. But the truth is that our society is so vulnerable
through its centralisation and interdependence, that whatever policies you
pursue you can't avoid problems like this. Having said that, the situation is
made worse by the Government's philosophy, which is still basically anti-
trade union. There will have to be a fresh deal with the trade unions to
involve them more closely with the business of government because, frankly,

they have got too much power to be excluded – thank God. That's what the planning agreements and industrial democracy were all about, and we've done nothing about implementing them.

Thursday 11 January

At 10.40am Jack Cunningham came to report on the emergency situation. The oil-tanker drivers' dispute is resolved, and there is no point in having a state of emergency for the road haulage drivers because the troops couldn't provide emergency coverage of that magnitude.

Cabinet, and there were Jim and Sir John Hunt, all bronzed.

Jim reported on Guadeloupe. On the SALT talks, Schmidt and Carter had drawn attention to the fear of Russian domination in the grey areas of strategic arms limitation.

Elwyn Jones said, 'I wish the importance of these Guadeloupe discussions could be understood and explained to the public because you, Jim, had a very bad press when you were away.'

'I expected that. I tried to explain that I didn't think there was a crisis when I got back but I got kicked on the shins for it.'

I realise that Jim felt guilty about being in Guadeloupe. He had had a bad press and had done poorly on television, and he was worried about the situation. But at the same time it was a historic Cabinet at which we were warned of a higher level of defence expenditure and of a possible break with the TUC. A Cabinet to remember.

Sunday 14 January

In the evening we had a party with about thirty people, including Chris Mullin, Eric and Doris Heffer, Frances Morrell, Michael and Molly Meacher, Albert and Joan Booth, Bryan and Gill Gould and others. It was the first party we had ever given where everyone was on the left. It was a great liberation really.

Monday 15 January

At Cabinet Jim asked what was the case against having a state of emergency. Clearly that was what Jim wanted, but Merlyn said the Tories were only demanding a state of emergency for cosmetic purposes. Denis Healey said we would only need it if we required extra powers, which we didn't at present.

'Well, is there a case for having a cosmetic state of emergency?' asked Jim.

'It's too early,' muttered Shirley, and Roy Mason said, 'No, because it raises false expectations that we can solve the problem when we can't.'

'When should we have it, then?' asked Jim.

Elwyn Jones advised us to consider very carefully whether the Prime Minister wasn't in fact right, but John Morris thought it would do us damage.

Joel Barnett was against it. 'The tanker drivers' dispute proved that we can get out of difficulty without a state of emergency.'

Bruce Millan remarked, 'The TGWU could do a better job than the troops, and the General Officer Commanding Scotland thinks that the use of troops would worsen the situation.'

Jim said, in a very threatening way, 'The key to all this is trade union power. They have got us and themselves into a real difficulty. Thatcher, trade union power, secondary picketing: these are the real issues. The trade union solution of their moving emergency supplies doesn't help. It is having a very strong effect on the middle classes and many of our own people. This is a setback, but we must not desert our policy now.'

He went on, 'How should we cope with the matter? I would like a new deal with the TUC but they must face their responsibilities or the Tories will mangle them. The 5 per cent policy was right; Methven, the Director-General of the CBI, said so last night.'

I tried to make a speech but was cut short by Jim. 'I don't want to hear all that,' he said.

It was an exhausting Cabinet.

Tuesday 16 January
Today I began a regime which will probably last for twenty-four hours. I jogged in the bedroom for about twenty-five minutes and did some exercises. Resolved not to eat any bread, potatoes or sugar, and to stop smoking. It's terrifying the extent to which one is dependent on drugs. If I tried to give up tea as well, I think I would go mad!

Heard Mrs Thatcher in the debate called for by the Opposition on the industrial situation. She launched into an attack on the trade union movement, and Jim then paid a warm tribute to her speech. He offered a few sops to the trade unions on low pay and comparability but basically he stuck to the pay policy and tightening the rules on picketing.

It's 10.45 pm and I still haven't smoked.

Sunday 21 January
Had my first pipe for about five or six days. Somehow the pressure of not smoking made me think of nothing but my pipe.

Wednesday 31 January
Brian Sedgemore came up to me in the Lobby and told me that John Biffen had warned him that someone from the BBC was spreading a story that I had two children in nursing homes in London. It was decent of Biffen to tell Sedgemore, and it indicates that the scandal factory is beginning to go into full production again.

Thursday 1 February

The local-authority workers and the Health Service unions are out on strike and the manual workers in the water industry are engaged in spasmodic disputes. There is a general sense of unease all over the country. We are in an atmosphere of siege and crisis which the media are continuing to play up.

Cabinet at 10.30, and it was one of the best discussions we've had in a long time.

School caretakers and maintenance workers are out on strike now, and Shirley Williams said there were picket lines outside many schools, in some cases supported by the teachers. The unions were saying that children and teachers could cross the picket lines but that no effort must be made to carry out the caretakers' work. The strike of the maintenance men meant that temperatures in schools were falling below the 60-degree legal minimum, making it impossible to keep the schools open.

'This is fantastic,' said Jim. 'When I was at school there were days when you couldn't put your pen in the inkwell because the ink was frozen. What nonsense.'

Shirley pointed out that the Health and Safety regulations required it.

Jim asked how the Cabinet was going to survive. We had got to the point where indiscipline was threatening the life of the community and the Government must have a clear line. The situation was extremely grave and the Tories could win, giving Mrs Thatcher a mandate for the most violent anti-trade union policy. But at least the trains would run on time, he said.

He praised Peter for his speech in the Commons yesterday when he urged us to spell out that what was happening in this country was a threat to democratic society.

I didn't believe that. 'I have always worked on the principle that, where large numbers of people behave irrationally, something else is usually wrong. People feel a deep sense of injustice and they don't feel properly represented. We have to be careful not to fall for this idea that everybody has just gone mad. David Owen says that what is happening is pure thuggery, but I doubt that. It can't be easy for people to go on strike. They lose their income and they have a deep feeling of anxiety. When I was in Newcastle recently, I heard an NUJ man deliver the most violent attack on the management of his paper and he swore that he would die in the last ditch with the printers. I discovered that he was a Tory candidate for a north-east constituency.'

I said, 'Look, PM, before we go any further, you have made many references to an Election but we're not being asked as we go round this table to agree to an Election if this policy fails. That raises quite separate considerations.'

'Well,' Jim replied, 'I am not ready to carry on. I am fed up with the NEC and a defeat this way would at least be an honourable end to this Cabinet. I'll tell the TUC that I've had enough because when I read their document, it really filled my cup of disillusionment to overflowing. Someone else can take up the leadership because I am not going on.'

Denis Healey said, 'We all understand the strain you're under as the "youngest" member of the Cabinet.'

'All I can say,' Jim replied, 'is that if we have an Election we are likely to be defeated.'

I said, 'I very much hope the minutes won't record that', and Sir John Hunt shook his head.

As we left the Cabinet, I was so annoyed with what Denis had said earlier about middle-class guilt and so on that I said, 'Speaking as a peer of the realm, I hope nothing I have said will be attributed to middle-class guilt.'

Thursday 15 February
The Gallup Poll puts the Tories 20 per cent ahead.

Thursday 1 March
Cabinet at 10.30 and the first item concerned the devolution referenda in Scotland and Wales which are taking place today. Jim suggested we react slowly to tomorrow's press stories. We had given people the choice and the Government must not rush to a decision.

Then Jim went on to the claim by nurses in NUPE, COHSE and the Royal College of Nursing, saying they were the 'heroines of the hour'. But Denis felt it would be difficult to give the nurses more money even on the basis of the RCN commitment to no strike action.

At this stage Jim and Denis got engaged in a nasty exchange, with Jim pressing for more money for the nurses and Denis resisting. What would be the repercussions on the Health Service and the Civil Service?

'Denis is trying to put me in the dock,' said Jim. 'I spend 80 per cent of my time on pay and I shall decide how to handle this.'

Friday 2 March
Today the results of the referenda were announced. The Welsh voted about 4 to 1 against devolution, and the the Scots 32 per cent in favour of the Assembly and 30.8 per cent against. So the Yes vote in Scotland was well below the requirement of 40 per cent of the electorate. Now the Government's life is at risk.

Sunday 4 March
Referenda results in the papers – lots of speculation. Will it bring the Government down? etc, etc. I rang Jim at about 11.45 and offered to go in if he wanted to have a chat.

We talked over the phone about how to win the Election, about the women's vote, and so on. He was sure we could win, and we couldn't just walk away from the devolution issue. We would discuss it with the PLP. He thanked me for ringing and I said I didn't want him to think his old friends were deserting him in his moment of need.

Thursday 8 March

Cabinet, where Jim pointed out that the Thorpe trial would start on 13 April and the Liberals wanted an early Election to avoid all the embarrassment. We should lay the order for repeal of the devolution legislation and offer all-party talks with the Liberals and the Tories on the future of devolution.

At 12.35 Jim sent the officials out and we had a talk on the timing of the Election.

Jim said, 'Mrs Thatcher – and don't ask me how I know this – wants May because she thinks she will be able to exploit pay problems in the local government elections campaign that month. She's going to campaign against bureaucracy, for the restoration of freedom, the reduction of direct taxation and an increase in indirect taxation. And she's going to ask for power to clip the wings of the unions.'

Wednesday 14 March

EY Committee at Number 10. Jim warned us to expect another vote of confidence in about two weeks' time. If the worst came to the worst, said Jim, we had better leave Thatcher to inherit the situation. If prices rip, the Tories will have to cope with it and then we'll get back in again because of their inability to cope.

Sunday 18 March

Had a call from Bill Burroughs to say there had been a terrible mining disaster in the Golborne Colliery near Wigan. He arranged for an RAF plane to fly me and Colin Ambrose to Manchester, and we drove over to the colliery.

We waited with the Mining Inspectorate people and rescue teams and others till Sid Vincent, the Regional Executive member of the coalfield, arrived. Three men had been killed and eight badly burned. It was really very distressing. I asked if I should go to the hospital but I was told the relatives were too upset. That's the third big colliery disaster that I have been to, one in 1975 and then Bentley Colliery last year.

Came back in a raging blizzard about 9.30 pm.

Thursday 22 March

Cabinet at 10.30, and Jim told us that Richard Sykes, our Ambassador in the Hague, had been shot dead along with his footman. Nobody knew why.

Jim handed round the table his statement on devolution, which we discussed at great length. It is clear that we might buy a month of support but, when we come to the end of the talks with the Tories, Liberals and Nationalists, we'll be voting on the orders to repeal the Scotland and Wales

Acts, and on that we can't survive. So the Election will have to be in May, though Transport House and Jim and all the pro-Europeans want it on 7 June.

Sunday 25 March
Hilary told me that Rosalind had asked her doctor how long she had to live if she took no further treatment. She was told between three and six months – maybe longer. She doesn't want any more treatment. She is on a grape diet and looks frail but is active. She's spending a lot of time at Stansgate now, alone, thinking and walking. A most courageous girl.

Wednesday 28 March
To the vote of no confidence in the Government. Roy Hattersley, it was said, tried to get a couple of Scottish Nationalists to support us by promising an inquiry into prices in Scotland and Wales, and had given Frank Maguire, the Independent Member for Fermanagh and South Tyrone, three bottles of whisky and offered an inquiry into food prices in Northern Ireland, to try to gain support. I sat on the Front Bench next to David Owen and Roy, and it looked as if we might have won at first because one Member came from the Aye Lobby and put his thumb up. He apparently thought we'd won by one vote – 312 to 311 – but actually we had only had 310 votes. As the tellers came in, Spencer Le Marchant, the Tory, took his place at the right of the table facing the Speaker and we knew that they had won.

So at that moment the Labour Government ended. Jim and Thatcher made short statements and as we walked out Labour Members sang 'The Red Flag'.

That's the end of a memorable day in British politics, the first time for fifty-four years that any government has been defeated on a vote of confidence.

Thursday 29 March
I heard today that KME had finally gone into liquidation on Tuesday – symbolically, the day before the Government was defeated.

Cabinet was advanced by half an hour because of our defeat. Downing Street was jammed with photographers behind the crush barriers. Jim announced the date as 3 May. Parliament would end next Wednesday. The new Parliament would meet on 9 May for swearing-in and it would be officially opened on the 15th. We were then given a long list of Bills that the Tories agreed should complete their passage, because after losing the vote of confidence we can only legislate with their consent. It didn't include the Education Bill.

On procedure, Jim said Ministers would receive word about the use of official cars, writing articles for the press and so on, which he was sure we'd treat 'with our usual regard for instructions'.

On the manifesto, Jim emphasised, 'I want to make it absolutely clear I am not prepared to be worn to a frazzle by an argument with the NEC, and I hope other members of the Cabinet will take up the battle and not leave it entirely to me. The Cabinet will have a meeting with the NEC later, but I am not prepared to see the NEC give instructions to Ministers in a future Labour government because the purpose of the manifesto, if it has one, is to appeal to the public and to give the general direction of policy. The NEC wants detailed commitments and I shall resist that.'

Friday 30 March

Ron Vaughan picked me up from home at 3.30 to take me to Paddington and told me that a car had blown up at 3 o'clock in the House of Commons car park. We later heard that the car belonged to Airey Neave, Conservative MP for Abingdon and shadow spokesman on Northern Ireland. It exploded as he drove out of the car park, causing the most terrible injuries. He died later in Westminster Hospital, after being cut out of the car with an oxyacetylene lamp.

He was a very courageous man who had been a prisoner of war at Colditz, but he took a hard line on Ulster and that presumably was why he was killed – by the Provisional IRA or another splinter group. But this does introduce the possibility of tremendous police protection and pressure for a toughening-up of security measures. I am sad and sorry at what has happened but it confirms my belief that we must have a new look at Northern Ireland.

Sunday 1 April

Hilary gave me for my birthday (on Tuesday) a long stick with a mirror and torch attached so that I could look under my car for bombs. Joshua had given me exactly the same. So touching.

Monday 2 April

Half a million civil servants are on strike.

To the National Executive at 11 to discuss the draft Election manifesto. Jim Callaghan said it was well rehearsed and we'd had more democracy than before, but the Tory manifesto would be very general with a few major themes: to reduce taxes, to cut the power of the unions, and to assert law and order. We should do something similar – to focus on cutting unemployment, getting lower inflation and dealing with union unrest by negotiation. Jim had produced a draft of his own.

He continued, 'On a quite different matter I must warn you that with the political assassinations that have taken place, particularly Airey Neave's, there is a risk to NEC members. Therefore on the issue of Northern Ireland and terrorism we should have as little difference as possible between

ourselves and the Tories. I think there should be talks with both parties to
discuss it.'

We stood for a moment in Airey Neave's memory and Shirley Williams
suggested sending a letter of condolence, which was agreed.

Joan Lestor asked what was meant by an agreed response to terrorism.
Did it mean capital punishment?

Jim said no.

After some argument, Eric suggested that a small group should be
established now to reduce the manifesto to the right length, and Jim then
asked, 'What about *my* document?'

So by 17 votes to 6 it was agreed that a sub-committee be set up to
consider the two documents. A long discussion then ensued about who
should be on it. In the end it was agreed that the members would be Jim
Callaghan, Frank Allaun, Eric Heffer, Denis Healey, Tony Benn, Michael
Foot, Lena Jeger and Russell Tuck, to meet at 6.15 tonight at Number 10
and no doubt work through the night on it.

As we were leaving, I told Jim that I had been asked to do an interview on
the Harrisburg nuclear accident, and he said that was all right so long as I
was at the manifesto meeting tonight.

Over to the House through the civil servants' picket lines. There was a lot
of security at the House, as you'd expect.

Then the drafting group which had been set up this morning met at
Number 10 for the manifesto discussion. It was a dramatic evening. Jim
Callaghan took the chair in the Cabinet Room, which was overawing for
NEC members who hadn't been there before. Apart from the members
agreed this morning, there were David Lipsey, Reg Underhill, Ron
Hayward, Joyce Gould, Jennie Little, Geoff Bish and Tom McNally.
Because of the strike of civil servants there were no Number 10 staff but a
Private Secretary brought in a plate of sandwiches and drinks at 8pm. I had
about four ginger ales but there was no tea. At midnight the messengers
appeared and brought refreshments, so the old 'family retainers' formally
made their protest and came back on duty.

Anyway, we had two drafts – a shortened version of the original one by
Geoff Bish; and Jim's, drafted by Tom McNally and David Lipsey, a
meaningless document half the length.

After a tussle we took Jim's draft as the basic manifesto and I raised every
single point from our original draft.

The toughest battle came on economic policy, since Jim had left out full
employment and concentrated on inflation. But of course if you go for
inflation targets it is just a green light for the Treasury to go on with its
monetarism. Denis and I had some sharp exchanges; in the end we included
something on employment, but it was pretty meaningless.

We got commitments to increase public expenditure and then discussed
industrial policy – whether planning agreements should be statutory, and

whether the NEB would include investment in profitable manufacturing industry.

We kept jumping from text to text, from past manifestos to the TUC–Government *Into the Eighties* document and so on. It was really a very tiring meeting. One thing became clear: we should have got a set of points solemnly agreed between the Government and the Party, even if they weren't published; the detail may not matter to the reading public but it does matter as far as the agreement between the Party and the Government is concerned. It was also clear that the whole thing was about Party democracy, because in effect Jim was purporting to speak on behalf of the Government, yet none of Jim's proposals had ever been before the Cabinet and he was just speaking for the whole ministerial team without consultation. He felt that he had the final word.

We came to the House of Lords, and I said that the Party had believed for a long time, and it was unanimously accepted at Conference, that the Lords held back our legislation, there was too much patronage and we should state that.

Jim said, 'I won't have it, I won't have it.'

Eric lost his temper and banged the table. 'What do you mean you won't have it? Who are you to dictate? Who do you think you are? You are just a member of the Party.' He banged the table again.

'Well,' said Jim, 'I won't have it.'

I said, 'You can't do that.'

'I can.'

'No, you can't. What are we to say to people who joined the Labour Party to have some influence on our parliamentary system? They will say, "We joined the Party, we got this through, we've elected a Labour MP and we want him to implement our policy." '

Jim said, 'You'll have to change the Leader.'

I said, 'That's making it into a personality issue, not a political issue at all.'

'Well, I won't do it. I am the Leader of the Party and I have to decide what is right. I have responsibilities that I have to take and I won't do it.'

So in the end we decided to put the House of Lords on one side.

At one stage Denis leaned over and said, 'You're being very helpful. Why are you so cheerful?' I said it was my birthday in half an hour, so, as midnight struck, Denis announced, 'It's Tony's birthday', and Jim started singing, and then everybody joined in: 'Happy birthday to you, happy birthday to you. Happy birthday, dear Tony, happy birthday to you.' I said thank you very much and that I wished I had my tape on to record it! The whole evening was a funny mixture of table-banging, shouting at each other and slightly nostalgic sentimentality. There was a lot of conning and overawing going on.

I shall have to think very carefully about future manifestos. Of course the real answer is for the Government and the NEC to meet regularly instead of once every five years.

At 3.15 am, as we left, Geoff said we'd given away a lot tonight.

I had a terrible aching headache that went right down to the base of my skull. I'm not feeling too well at the moment; I'm puffy, my ears need syringing, I have the most ghastly piles, and my eyes are burning. Generally speaking I feel absolutely whacked.

To bed at 3.45 am and Caroline, bless her heart, wished me happy birthday, my fifty-fourth.

Wednesday 4 April
Jim held a party at Number 10 for the end of the Parliament. He and Audrey received us and we all went upstairs possibly for the last time as a Labour government. Jim made a speech standing on a chair.

'It's three years tomorrow since I became Leader and I want to thank you all and I hope you all enjoy the campaign. We went through the manifesto the other night, and because it was Tony's birthday he was very nice to me!' (Actually *he* was a little bit nicer to me because it was my birthday.) He thought we'd win. Mrs Thatcher was worried and he said he was going to enjoy the fight. Whatever the outcome, we'd meet again in a month.

Thursday 5 April
Farewell party with the Private Office and Press Office. Bill Burroughs made a little speech and they gave me a Wedgwood mug. I thanked them all and said this was my third farewell party – the first was when I thought Jim was going to get rid of me, and the second when I thought there was going to be an Election last year!

Saturday 28 April
Up early and prepared for a visit at home by John Hill and Dr John Dunster, Deputy Director-General of the HSE. On Monday I had been told that at Windscale, 2,200 gallons of unconcentrated high-toxic liquor had escaped over the years and was in the ground ten feet below the soil with only the clay separating it from the water table. When you hear all the warnings about how dangerous nuclear waste is going to be – with its 30 years of half-life, 500 years of danger and for centuries beyond – it is horrifying to think that this was just ten feet below the soil.

My impression of Windscale is that it is a very dangerous site indeed. I discovered that the evidence which had been analysed in March had come from borings taken in November. So it was three months before anyone knew about it. Of course, BNFL are absurdly reassuring. Once again my confidence has been shaken by the behaviour of the nuclear industry. John Arnott from my Private Office was present, and Frances Morrell also came at my request. I'm glad she did because it was one of the most remarkable meetings I think I have ever experienced.

Hill was embarrassed and Dunster was uneasy. I said, 'Thank you for the report on Windscale. I have arranged for it to be published today.'

Earlier John Arnott, who is one of my Private Secretaries, had told me that it wasn't possible to publish anything on a Saturday. I said it was, and he said the Press Office advised that it wouldn't get much coverage. I then said I didn't care what they advised, I wanted it out as soon as possible, and then he told me they couldn't do it in the afternoon. I had to be sharp with Arnott. 'Type out a note saying that I am releasing the report from Sir John Hill, that the HSE will report later, and send it round to all the newspapers, the BBC and ITV and the Press Association.'

We began the meeting and Sir John Hill argued there was nothing in this leakage.

I said, 'This is the most deadly toxic waste there has ever been.'

Dr Dunster asked, 'What about these chemical factories where the soil is absolutely sodden with toxic waste?'

In effect the Nuclear Inspectorate, which should be an independent watchdog, is in cahoots with the AEA and this is the great problem. The nuclear fraternity feel they know each other very well, they trust each other as being united in disliking a Minister, particularly a lame-duck Minister who they think will be out of office in four days and to whom they therefore have no further obligation.

I went over what I'd been told by the Inspector on Monday.

That was how we left it, and I insisted I'd put out the reports and that there would be a public inquiry. They were horrified by that; they just didn't think it was serious.

Then towards the end I looked at the note I had sent to Hill instructing him to stop work on the PWR pending the Harrisburg report, and I found the original was in my file. I said to John Hill, 'Why is that here? Have you seen it, John?'

'Yes,' replied John.

Then I realised that the letter had already been folded, and when I get letters for signature they are always flat. I asked, 'Why have *I* got it?'

John said the Department of Energy office had asked him to return it.

I turned to John Arnott. 'On Monday I want the names of the people who recalled this letter – which was done without my authority – and the reason why they recalled it.'

On this note we closed the meeting.

John Arnott asked to use the telephone and then he came back into the room and announced, 'I think I should tell you that I recalled your letter.'

I said, 'Thank you very much indeed; that is the end of the matter.' He left.

I talked to Frances. This was an act of open defiance and I am absolutely determined that I will not leave office until I have got across to the public that there must be a public inquiry. I will not be prevented from doing my job on nuclear safety just because there is an Election.

The real anxiety about nuclear power, of course, is the bomb – civil power is only a cover for that. Windscale is a military as well as a civil establishment, and that is what frightens the Civil Service, the Cabinet Office, the military and so on.

At 4.45 I had a message to ring Bill Burroughs. He said the PM had seen the text of my press release and thought it was alarmist. There should be an investigation, not an inquiry, and there was to be no reference whatever to the military aspect. As far as the Atomic Weapons Research Establishment (Aldermaston) was concerned, if asked I was to say that Sir Edward Pochin of the NRPB had settled the matter – a reference to the information I had received from the scientist at Aldermaston about health and safety hazards. I had asked some questions about this and received factual answers from Fred Mulley, but every month Fred has prevented me from publishing them on the grounds that it would lead to difficulty in getting a pay settlement at Aldermaston.

I told Bill that I couldn't accept that an investigation was the same as an inquiry. But the Cabinet Office had obviously advised the PM on what he should say and they'd concentrated mainly on the military aspects; this confirms my view that the main anxiety is military. The fact that the PM was wheeled into play in the middle of the Election on what was a fairly harmless press release I thought was very interesting.

I decided I'd write to Jim.

Thursday 3 May – General Election
For eleven hours Caroline and I drove around the constituency, in cold weather which turned to hail and snow. I sat on the roof of the car in a blanket with rubber overtrousers, wearing a woolly cap and anorak. It was freezing. We went round every single ward and it was terribly exhausting.

The first result was from Glasgow Central, where there was a Labour swing, as expected in Scotland. In the North West we didn't do too badly but it became clear that in London and the Home Counties and the Midlands we were going to lose heavily.

At midnight we went to my count. The result was finally announced at 5 in the morning – scandalously inefficient. I was fed up and our Party workers were a bit depressed. To cut a long story short, the Returning Officer gave the result without inviting the candidates on to the platform. My majority went down from over 9,000 to 1,890; the Liberal vote slumped and the Tories picked up the extra votes. I felt mortified, although I'm in for five more years. I made a speech outside, as dawn broke, to a crowd of supporters. I declined steadfastly to go on any of the Election post-mortem programmes. The media were utterly corrupt in this Election, trying to make it a media event.

Tragically Ron Thomas was defeated in Bristol North East. David Owen held his seat at Devonport but the West Country as a whole was disastrous for us.

Friday 4 May
It was a warm day and we got home totally punch drunk.

Shirley Williams was beaten, and the media treated it as if it were a state funeral – this remarkable, able, brilliant girl – whereas for me it was 'Benn beaten back by poll'. The difference in treatment between the Right and Left of the Party was unbelievable.

Watched all the rituals on television – Jim going to Number 10 and to the Palace, and Mrs Thatcher at Tory Central Office, then at the Palace and to Number 10, surrounded by great crowds.

We lost Audrey Wise, Tom Litterick, Doug Hoyle – such excellent people. John Pardoe was beaten; that gave me a lot of pleasure, I confess. Thorpe was beaten in North Devon and was interviewed in the most cruel way, looking absolutely ashen.

Stephen looked in. We lost Kensington, for which he was agent, by 5,000, but he did a grand job.

Bill Burroughs and Ron Vaughan came over from the office with my possessions. I gave Bill the key to my red boxes and my pass and seals of office. Ron was near to tears. I gave him the oil painting of autumn which was a gift to me from the Russians.

Julie Clements was in doing champion service. I don't think I'll have any of the withdrawal symptoms I had in 1970. It's almost unbelievable that there are no more red boxes.

A dramatic day in British politics. The most right-wing Conservative Government and Leader for fifty years; the first woman Prime Minister. I cannot absorb it all.

I have the freedom now to speak my mind, and this is probably the beginning of the most creative period of my life. I am one of the few ex-Ministers who enjoys Opposition and I intend to take full advantage of it.

10

1979–81

Wednesday 9 May

Went into the Commons for the meeting with the ex-Cabinet at 10, and there were four policemen checking each car. The meeting was in the Leader of the Opposition's suite overlooking New Palace Yard.

The first item was the leadership. Michael Foot suggested Jim be elected unanimously and that was agreed. Michael said all the other officers within the PLP would have to be elected and we settled dates for that.

I asked when we were going to talk about what had happened in the Election.

Jim said, 'I'll tell you what happened. We lost the Election because people didn't get their dustbins emptied, because commuters were angry about train disruption and because of too much union power. That's all there is to it.'

I insisted, 'I think we ought to go back over what has happened.'

Jim said, 'No inquests', echoed by Roy Hattersley. 'We must maintain collective Cabinet responsibility, and I don't want anyone to table a motion in the PLP without first clearing it with the Chief Whip, and I don't want any member of the Shadow Cabinet to speak without consulting the appropriate spokesman.'

That was just amazing – collective Cabinet responsibility in Opposition!

Thursday 10 May

I put out my press statement that I wasn't going to stand for the Shadow Cabinet and, as a courtesy, I rang Jim immediately afterwards to let him know. I think I woke him because he sounded very gruff.

At 1.45 I went to see Jim in his room. He said, 'If I'd known you were not going to stand for the Shadow Cabinet, my decision might have been different.' I presumed he meant his decision to stand again. When I asked why, he said, 'I'd like to go back to my farm.'

I told him, 'I think you're right to stay in, and I am pleased you've said there isn't a vacancy because we can debate the issues without the leadership question interfering. There has to be a debate because some very important themes will arise. You've had me in the Cabinet a long time, you know what I think and what I'm going to say.'

He said, 'You talk about the Party but there are two Communists on the NEC.'

'Who?' I asked.

He named them.

'Are you saying that they are members of the CP?'

'No,' said Jim, 'but they are in continual touch with King Street.'

'Well, all that tells me is that MI5 bug their telephones, and that worries me much more. When I asked whether my phone was bugged, I didn't get an answer.' I said I honestly didn't think he knew what went on, and that was worrying too.

At 2.20 I went into the House and sat two rows behind the Front Bench, just like a new Member, and I realised that for years I had paid no attention to Parliament whatsoever.

Mrs Thatcher came in. MPs were being sworn in, and I joined the queue to affirm, after all the Ministers had been through.

Tuesday 15 May

State Opening of Parliament. Seeing the Lords and Ladies in their finery made me realise how little we did in power to make the country look more democratic. We are such a disappointment in office.

Jim looked old and bent and sad and tired. Mrs Thatcher made a most impassioned speech, from notes, except for one passage about Rhodesia which had been typed out no doubt on the insistence of the FO – the most rumbustious, rampaging, right-wing speech that I've heard from the government Front Bench in the whole of my life.

Afterwards I saw Ted Heath and told him, 'I've never heard a speech like that in all my years in Parliament.'

He said, 'Neither have I.'

'I suppose this really was what Selsdon was all about.'

'Oh, there never was a Selsdon policy,' Heath replied. 'It was invented by Harold Wilson. Look at our 1970 manifesto; it wasn't there at all.'

I went on, 'Well, Keith Joseph, when he was Shadow Minister of Technology in 1969–70, made a lot of similar speeches.'

'Quite different,' he responded.

I said I had some sympathy with Thatcher – with her dislike of the wishy-washy centre of British politics. He gave me such a frosty look that I daresay I had touched a raw nerve.

Sunday 17 June

Our thirtieth wedding anniversary, and a marvellous thirty years we've had together. If the next thirty years are as happy, I will be richly blessed.

Took breakfast to Caroline and read the papers. The *Express* had a piece about the great struggle for the future of the Labour Party between Callaghan and Benn, Heffer and Atkinson. It is right in a way.

Wednesday 27 June

Just after midnight (of 26 June), the phone rang and it was Hilary. He said he thought Rosalind was dead. We took a taxi to his home in West London.

Caroline felt Rosalind's pulse. Hilary rang the doctor and he came and declared her dead. Rosalind's parents, Lesley and Peter Retey arrived. Gradually our whole family arrived and sat in the bedroom and talked and talked. It was all very painful.

Thursday 28 June

Condolences came in from Dennis Skinner, Frank McElhone, Dick Douglas, from a Tory MP and many others. The Labour Party sent a telegram to Hilary, and that sort of sympathy and support is a tremendous comfort.

Thursday 5 July

Rosalind's funeral. The family have rallied round wonderfully. Hilary's front garden was covered in wreaths; the one that touched me most was from Dave, the milkman. Hilary's workmates at ASTMS had sent white roses. There were masses of flowers. It was a boiling hot day.

At precisely 10.45 the hearse came. On top of the coffin was a lovely wreath of red roses from Hilary.

When we got to Chiswick cemetery the chapel doors were open and the organ was being played by the head of the music department of Holland Park (Rosalind and Hilary's old school). Mother read from the Bible, and Peter Retey read a poem by Hartley Coleridge called 'Early Death'. Ann Morrish read the sonnet 'Shall I compare thee to a summer's day'. Stephen played a piece he had composed on the organ. Then Hilary got up and, a few feet from his beloved Rosalind, delivered his beautiful address, without a tremor in his voice. It was perceptive, sensitive, tender and amusing but at no stage was it sentimental.

Six men including Joshua, Stephen and Hilary and Rosalind's two brothers carried the coffin to the grave. Mother said, 'Ashes to ashes, dust to dust', Hilary tossed some soil in, and we all threw in red roses. It was terribly, terribly sad.

Thursday 19 July

Heard that Melissa got a First Class degree from LSE. As soon as the House had voted against hanging – by a majority of 120 – I dashed home and gave her a hug. She was told that she was the first woman for twenty years to get a First in history at LSE, and there had not been a First Class in history there for seven years. She was so excited, we stayed up till 3 in the morning talking.

Tuesday 31 July

After a meeting of the Fabian Society Executive, Michael Meacher, Larry Whitty of the GMWU, Brian Sedgemore and I went and bought hamburgers at McDonald's and sat in the piazza outside Westminster Cathedral. Dusk was just falling, the cathedral was beautifully illuminated and a half-moon rose above it. One felt one was in Istanbul.

Larry Whitty described the trade union leaders' attitude. The general line was going to be that all these constitutional questions should be postponed at this year's Conference and referred to an inquiry.

Thursday 23 August

Eighteen copies of the book Chris Mullin has been working on with me, called *Arguments for Socialism*, arrived today. It is a great moment seeing for the first time a book one has written.

The *Economist* had their cover story on me: the article inside said that the Labour Party was bankrupt and that I was filling the vacuum with new ideas (dangerous ideas, of course).

Sunday 26 August

Stansgate. Hilary and I had a day out. First we drove to Hatfield to see Ray

Buckton, who lives in a delightful 400-year-old thatched cottage which he has renovated.

Ray told me about the threats to his life during the 1972 and 1974 miners' strikes (when ASLEF was providing industrial support), and inevitably we went on to talk about the security services. He said that as a result of the threats a chap from Special Branch was attached to him, and he turned out to be the son of a Welsh miner and got to know Ray quite well. He more or less told Ray that some of his telephone calls were being bugged. Ray wondered whether some of the death threats hadn't been engineered to provide an excuse for his being under surveillance during the dispute.

He told me there was a right-wing group – including Bill Sirs and Sid Weighell – working hard to gain control of Trade Unionists for a Labour Victory.

On to Harlow, to Clive Jenkins's house, where we had arranged to meet Caroline and Stephen. Clive was wearing an apron saying 'YOU CAN'T BE TOO THIN OR TOO RICH'. His house consists of four cottages knocked into one, in which forty-one people lived before the war. Now it is just he and his wife Moira, and his two children.

There were guns on display, two wagon wheels at the front and a commemorative plaque of John Milton that he had bought. He was barbecuing sausages; we sat down at 2 and got up at 4.30 after a fantastic lunch of five courses.

He told me that David Basnett wants Jim to give up the leadership, and in conversation David had asked Clive, 'Who do you want?' Clive had replied, 'Tony Benn.' On David's list of candidates are Owen, Healey, Shore and Merlyn Rees. Clive said, 'David is nervous of you because you are serious', and implied that David was offering me support for the electoral college if I drop everything else. But what I really care about is the manifesto and accountability: the Party Leader issue won't make any difference.

He told me *en passant* that Tom Jackson had once been in the CP. Clive is full of lots of little stories – he loves exchanging gossip.

He has been offered a year's scholarship in Washington, which he can't take, but he has accepted a six-week stay and they have laid on facilities for him. His attitude is: if it is going, take it.

Monday 27 August
Drove to Southend to see Bill Keys of SOGAT. Bill is a nice guy: I don't know him well but he is passionately in favour of racial equality; he said his experience in the East End of London as a kid had really converted him to that view.

Bill was terribly friendly. There is no doubt whatever that the trade union leaders, even those who don't like me very much, see me as a factor in the situation that they have to take seriously.

Drove home. On the news we heard that Lord Mountbatten and his grandson had been killed in an explosion on a boat off the Sligo coast, close to the border with Northern Ireland. It may have the most tremendous repercussions: the murder of an international figure, the Supreme Allied Commander in South-East Asia during the war, a Viceroy of India, a member of the royal family, is going to make people think again about Northern Ireland. The whole world will discuss this particular event and I think it may be a turning point.

Tuesday 11 September

Went up to Corby by train for a demonstration by steelworkers. Before the war, Stewart and Lloyd, the private steel owners, discovered low-grade iron ore in Northamptonshire and built Corby up over twenty years into the biggest steel plant in Europe, attracting people from all over the world; 72 per cent of the workers were from Scotland. The workforce lived in camps until about ten years ago when they started building up the new town. But Corby was always a one-industry town. Now the plant, at least the iron- and steel-making part, is under threat of closure.

I couldn't tell them, but the Labour Cabinet had decided in February this year to support the closure of Corby. These guys are now faced with the possibility of 30 per cent male unemployment, and they have called in the Labour Party to help them fight. An awful irony; I felt tremendously guilty.

Wednesday 12 September

At 3.30 I went to see Jim Callaghan; I had suggested we had a word before Conference. He's in his new room, in the Serjeant-at-Arms's old flat.

I tried to be friendly and said I hoped he would be safe when he goes to Ireland because I had read that he might be in danger after the Mountbatten business. He wasn't too concerned but he said, 'Poor old Roy Mason is deeply worried; he has absolutely maximum security but still he's afraid of what they'll do to him.' I sympathise with him.

I had decided that I would talk about how we could make Conference the launching pad for the Party's winter campaign against the Tories. We had to have a really good programme with the TUC for economic and social advance and jobs. I didn't want him to think I was concerned only with the internal Party democracy issues.

'Well,' said Jim, 'we have to be realistic about public expenditure; we do need more productivity in British industry.' He just gave the old Thatcher/Healey view.

We came to the question of Conference's power over policy, and he said the Party would split over it. I declared, 'Jim, you've had more experience of this than I have but the situation is nothing like 1951 or 1959.'

'For the first time in my life,' he said, 'the trade unions are openly talking about disaffiliating from the Party. And take this Militant group. I am very worried. If you saw the reports I am getting' (presumably security reports) 'you'd realise what a danger it is.'

I remarked, 'Is it any different from the Bevanites, or the Tribune Group, Victory for Socialism or CND? I don't think so. No one group has ever got hold of the Labour Party.' I was more concerned with the Reg Prentices and Dick Tavernes.

'It is very regrettable what they've done.'

Jim is obsessed with the Left. On the Conference, he agreed that reselection could be discussed. He had an open mind on the question of the electoral college – of course Healey wouldn't become Leader if there was a college. On the drafting of the manifesto, he would not accept the proposed changes. 'I must warn you I have a quote here on the subject from Keir Hardie that I shall use. If you press this today you'll be in real trouble.'

'You know my view, Jim. Conference must be free to decide.'

'Maybe I didn't handle the NEC very well on the manifesto issue but I will not allow this to happen. I may have been obstinate but the Lords issue was absolutely wrong.'

He told me he had seen my picture on the front of the *Economist* and had thought to himself: There's a man who has really got a great section of the Party behind him; why doesn't he use his influence? and so on. He accepted that I didn't want to be Leader, and I said, 'If I did, I'd be a bloody fool to be saying what I'm saying now because it's alienating a lot of people.'

There was one amusing exchange. Jim said I was more devious than I admitted. I reminded him that he had once told me he wasn't as nice as he looked, and I said I wasn't as nice as I looked either.

Wednesday 26 September
Julie and I are absolutely swamped by letters – they are just pouring in. I don't know how to cope with it all.

Tonight is 'The Parkinson Show', and Caroline and the children gave me lots of advice about how to handle it.

I was picked up at 5 by Anne McDermid and Chris Mullin and we went to the studio. I had never met Michael Parkinson before and I liked him immediately. He's a very agreeable and intelligent guy. The actor Stewart Granger and the showjumping commentator Dorian Williams were the other guests.

We did a run-through and then I was interviewed alone for half an hour. It was a delight; Michael was so friendly. He asked how it felt to be the bogeyman, and I said it had nothing to do with me. He asked about the Conference amendments and resolutions and I explained them. Would there be a split? No. Then he asked about Father and the peerage case and I dealt with that. He finally came back to the Conference and asked if I thought we'd win. I said yes, I thought this view would prevail.

In fact it was the best TV interview I have done. About 8 million people watch it, I believe.

Eric Heffer, Frances, Mother and Dave all rang later to say how good the programme was.

Sunday 30 September – Labour Party Conference, Brighton
Press coverage very hostile to me. Hilary arrived from London and I gave him a big kiss.

At lunch, who should Barbara Castle bring along but Janet Brown, who does the brilliant impersonation of Mrs Thatcher. She was all dressed up like Mrs Thatcher, and a lot of photos were taken, including one with me.

Mik said today, 'I expect a thousand people have told you but you were brilliant on Parkinson.' I felt that programme was a turning point.

Hilary went off to the Common Market Safeguards Committee AGM. He was introduced as a councillor and got a tremendous reception. Afterwards I was told by Jack Watson, who clutched me by both arms, that Hilary had made a great impression, and Ron Leighton told me that he eclipsed me. I was so proud.

At 2.30 I went to the NEC meeting to consider our position on the resolutions to Conference.

After some attempts to muddle the issues, I won the vote 15 to 11 recommending Conference to take the constitutional amendments.

I then moved the Coventry South West resolution from Victor Schonfield and the Campaign for Labour Party Democracy on mandatory reselection of MPs.

Shirley said, 'This removes all safeguards for Members – an MP isn't even given notice if he or she is removed.'

'Shirley is absolutely wrong,' I insisted. 'She doesn't understand it. If you have a selection conference you are not removing any safeguards because there are none.'

Jim said, 'I can only tell you it won't stand up, it won't last. MPs do a job of work. What about the Militants who are taking over the management committees in the small inner-city constituency parties?'

A vote to accept the resolution from Coventry South West was carried by 15 to 9.

On the manifesto there was a long and complicated discussion, but in the end the constitutional amendment to Clause 5 that I had drafted and moved (and that had gone through the July Executive by 9 to 8) was defeated by 14 to 12 because Alex Kitson voted against it on behalf of the TGWU, and Doug Hoyle voted against it on behalf of ASTMS. So two important unions defeated us.

The composite resolution calling for an electoral college in principle was carried by 20 votes to 3.

We won on six out of nine votes. A marvellous success for us.

The NEC considered the rest of the composite resolutions, and then I caught a taxi to the Institute for Workers' Control fringe meeting on accountability versus patronage.

Tuesday 2 October
It was Jim's speech today, and he was quieter than I expected, amusing and light-hearted. It was effective, to be candid. He robustly defended the Government's achievements and attacked those who had attacked him. He warned against the constitutional changes, and talked about international-ism and compassion. No socialist content whatever, of course.

But it was warmly received, and I did get up for the standing ovation at the end. Joan Lestor turned to me and said, 'What a scandalous thing to do', and I said, 'Not in the slightest. I served in his government and I respect him.' I am rather fond of Jim anyway.

In the afternoon Conference debated the constitutional resolutions. On the election of the Party Leader through an electoral college, the AUEW had split and voted against. It made all the difference, because with the AUEW vote we would have passed the resolution. But the fixers won't win. We'll come back next year and put it right. I went out while the result was being read out; I didn't want to hear.

I came back in for the debate on the mandatory reselection of MPs. Mik made a good speech, and Eric Heffer wound up, with quite a lot of barracking from the floor. It was an angry Conference, with the PLP and trade union sections pitched aganst the constituency Labour parties. When the vote was taken it was 4 million to 3 million for composite 33, which instructed the Conference Arrangements Committee to put immediately to the Conference the amendment to the Party constitution. This amendment provided for reselection of MPs once in every Parliament and this was carried by a majority of 2 million.

So the efforts of the Right have failed. It has been the most amazing campaign, and after five years of hard work we've carried it through. The MPs will just have to accept it. It means there are 635 vacancies for candidates in the next Parliament. MPs will have to take notice of their GMCs.

Wednesday 3 October
Frances and Francis and I went over my speech to Conference for this afternoon. It didn't look very good on paper, but then they never do.

To the conference hall, and the first debate was on the manifesto – the composite resolution calling for constitutional amendments to be put before the 1980 Conference to give control of the manifesto to the NEC alone. It was proposed by Stuart Weir of Hackney South and Shoreditch CLP, and we won by almost a million votes. Amazing when you think the matter was first raised by me only in June at the NEC's Home Policy Committee.

Although we didn't get the constitutional change itself through, we got a clear statement of how it was to be organised.

Friday 5 October

A month ago I never expected we'd achieve any of these things. The PLP is absolutely furious. There will now be a major attempt by the Right to oust Jim Callaghan, partly because they'll say he wasn't strong enough to beat the Left, but also because they only have a year to get Denis Healey elected by the PLP before any rule changes occur.

Thursday 15 November

To Bristol and in the hotel I heard the most sensational news bulletin. Sir Anthony Blunt, the Adviser for the Queen's Pictures, knighted in the 1970s, was revealed as the 'fourth man' in the Burgess/Maclean/Philby spy ring. He confessed in 1964 to having been a Russian spy and was protected, and knighted *after* that. Now he's been stripped of his knighthood and he's left the country.

All this came out in the Commons in a written answer from Mrs Thatcher, but that means it was known to the 1964–70 Labour Government, the Heath Government and the 1974–79 Labour Government. If Andrew Boyle had not given this away in his book *The Climate of Treason* it would have never been revealed. Amazing. It shows again that the British Establishment trusts the upper class to be reliable without vetting, whereas Philip Agee or Aubrey, Berry and Campbell are outlaws, hounded and treated quite differently. Incidentally, had the Official Secrets Act been amended as is now proposed, Andrew Boyle would be liable to prosecution for publishing this.

The minimum lending rate has gone up to 17 per cent; this will lead to bankruptcies on a large scale and unemployment.

Friday 16 November

It appears that Prime Ministers from Home onwards were *not* told by the security services about Blunt, and therefore the key question is whether there was a secret state within a state which was not under democratic control.

Tuesday 20 November

Blunt is to give a press conference today. When you consider that his 'offence' ended in 1945 it is hard to see him dragged through the mire.

On the 1 o'clock news Blunt was shown being cross-examined by a small group of journalists on behalf of the BBC and ITN. He came over with some distinction really. He said he'd put conscience above the law and his loyalty to his country, and he regretted it, but that was his explanation. Nothing had happened since the war, he claimed, and all he'd done was to hand over military intelligence about the Germans to the Russians – nothing that put our own security at risk. It's a very interesting story and I asked the Speaker this morning if I could speak in the debate tomorrow. Mrs Thatcher announced that business would be postponed to debate the Blunt affair.

Tuesday 4 December
At 12.10 I was taken to the Cartoonist pub in Shoe Lane to receive the Golden Joker Award. I was uneasy about going but the atmosphere was jolly – all the cartoonists were there. I mustn't impute to everyone who works in the media the hostility that one gets from the proprietors and Editors. I was presented with a gold tie-pin and I made a speech about the important role of the cartoonist in society.

Appearing in a human guise from time to time is quite useful – Mrs Thatcher and Enoch Powell have both received the award. Vic Gibbons told me he was a socialist; his grandfather, John Burgess, was a founder of the ILP. He gave me two original cartoons. Mac, the *Daily Mail* cartoonist, presented me with a cartoon showing me walking along the street smoking my pipe and a lot of flies buzzing round my head, while round the corner Jim Callaghan, David Owen and Denis Healey were wielding great clubs, one of them saying, 'Remember, if we're asked, we were just swatting the greenfly!'

Friday 14 December
To Bristol for my surgery. Surgeries do bring MPs up against the harshest and saddest aspects of life. One woman who came to see me was a widow of about seventy living on a pension. A year ago she took into her house an elderly disabled man whom she had befriended, a bachelor. So the local DHSS had stopped her widow's pension on the grounds that they were cohabiting and would have to be treated as a single unit and receive social security as a married couple. The man would otherwise have to go into a home (at a great cost to the ratepayers). She had appealed to the tribunal for the restoration of her pension and she said that the head of the tribunal had asked her whether they were having sexual intercourse – she broke down and wept because of the shame of it. Having met them together, I knew it was an absurd idea. They have separate rooms. But even if they were cohabiting what does that have to do with her entitlement to a widow's pension? I promised to write to the DHSS and get the matter reviewed, but I know I won't win.

Walked in the pouring rain to the hotel and got soaked to the skin. Had a hot bath, dried my trousers on the radiator and slept until the Party GMC at Unity House.

The GMC went on for three hours and was entirely dominated by Bryan Beckingham, Pete Hammond and others from the Militant Tendency. They moved endless resolutions. Their arguments are sensible and they make perfectly good radical points but they do go on interminably in their speeches.

Friday 21 December
To Bristol, and on the train were a lot of slightly drunk business executives in their late thirties singing in the buffet car. One was wearing a paper hat.

I queued up to get my tea and bacon and egg and they were saying, 'There's that f . . . . . g extremist, Mr Benn', and they sang bits of 'The Red Flag', and kept up an absolute barrage of insulting remarks.

As I went by carrying my tray they opened the door with elaborate and false courtesy and bowed and said, 'Happy Christmas to you, Sir', and I said, 'Thank you' and went on.

I think that was the first experience of real whipping-up of feeling by the press against the Labour Party. After the victory of Mrs Thatcher, the old Establishment is now wildly self-confident – the Civil Service, the military, business, bankers and so on.

Monday 31 December
Stansgate. In the evening, after the meal, Mother sat and talked; she is fascinating. She is eighty-three next year, and first came to London in 1910 when Edward VII was on the throne. She knew Asquith, Lloyd George, Ramsay MacDonald, Arthur Henderson, and so on. She has a wide theological knowledge, and to hear her describing the various meanings of the immaculate conception, the physical ascension of Jesus and all that is so interesting. She reads the Old Testament in Hebrew and the New Testament in Greek and so she knows the nuances of translation.

Looking at the Thatcher Government, it has begun implementing its reactionary policies with great vigour. Of course, it is a unifying force for the Labour Movement at a time when our debates are inevitably internal and divisive.

Tuesday 5 February 1980
20,000 people, mainly young women, crammed into Central Hall for a rally against the Corrie Bill, which would restrict a woman's right to an abortion. I spoke briefly to offer my support, and said there should be no restrictions of a woman's right to decide within the provisions of the present law. This was one of many attacks on women's rights – the Employment Bill, the sexist and racist immigration laws, child benefit cuts, the tax laws – and women must organise; it was the only way to win. In calling for the right to choose and the freedom to control their own bodies, these women are rediscovering what the whole trade union movement has been fighting for – the right to choose, the right to decide how our own bodies are going to be used.

Wednesday 6 February
I had an incredible message from the BBC asking if I would join in a

discussion on monetarism and government intervention, following the showing of a series of six half-hour talks by Milton Friedman, the American monetarist economist, called 'The Right to Choose'. I would be in discussion with the Deputy Governor of the Bank of England and Roy Jenkins, under the chairmanship of Peter Jay.

I rang up the producer and said that six programmes of Milton Friedman was more than all the party politicals put together during an Election. I had never known the BBC give so much time to this particular religion. The woman I spoke to said, 'Well, we are going to balance the discussion.'

I told her I was prepared to do half an hour with Friedman, but I would not be a token left-winger with three monetarists. She went off saying they would rethink it.

Thursday 7 February
The PLP was interesting. Mik asked, 'Could I please have a clear account of the Front Bench attitude towards repeal of the Tories' Employment Bill and Education Bill.'

Eric Varley made a short statement saying we would repeal the former, but might reintroduce passages about ballots. He was a bit evasive.

Then Neil Kinnock got up to speak. 'Well, I can't give an assurance we will repeal the Education Bill. We are committed to ending the assisted places scheme, but we cannot pledge reinstatement of school meals and milk because of the economic situation we shall inherit.' He sounded just like a Minister, indeed like the Chief Secretary to the Treasury, and it went down very badly.

Reg Race, the MP for Wood Green, and Kevin McNamara, the MP for Hull Central, were alarmed at Neil's statement. Other Members spoke, and it was clear from the shouting that Neil had dropped a clanger.

Up jumped Neil again and made it worse. 'It could cost many millions to restore cheap school meals and school transport.'

People were aghast at his second attempt.

Someone brought up the defence vote, but then Jack Ashley got to his feet – being deaf he had only just been informed in writing of Neil's comments – and said it was the most staggering statement that he had heard at a PLP meeting.

Afterwards the Right was laughing itself sick that a left-wing Front Bench spokesman should have made such a statement and the Left was saying, 'That is what happens when you become a Shadow Minister.' Poor old Neil has taken a knocking.

Friday 29 February
Leap Year. Went into the House early for the Corrie Bill debate.

Jo Richardson and Joyce Gould, the National Women's Officer, who was sitting under the Gallery, are really masterminding the campaign in the House. Joyce had written to every Labour MP who had voted against Corrie last time to thank them and to guide them through the next stage of the debate. For the first time I thought the PLP was doing its proper job. Why don't we have Labour Party officials sitting under the Gallery in the civil servants' boxes when the Labour Government is in power?

It looks as if we have defeated the Bill by talking it out.

Tuesday 25 March

Joan Lestor told me that Neil Kinnock is now canvassing for Michael Foot as Leader. I am terribly torn because I don't actually know whether my prospects are at all good.

The position on the leadership at the moment is like this. Healey is obviously the front runner, and he has Barry Jones of East Flint, John Smith and Dick Mabon all competing for the privilege of being campaign managers, with Joel Barnett really doing the work.

Then to the right of Denis you have Roy Hattersley. I suppose he is a serious candidate of a kind – he does lots of meetings around the country and projects an impressive image and has a group working for him in the PLP.

Then other possible candidates on the right are David Owen, Eric Varley and maybe Merlyn Rees.

Then there is Peter Shore, a right-wing, anti-European figure; and John Silkin, who allegedly has received £10,000 from the TGWU to run his leadership campaign.

Eric Heffer I know has been going round seeking support.

Finally Michael Foot, on whom there is heavy pressure to keep Denis out.

Wednesday 2 April

During the evening Caroline came into the basement office and said the news bulletins were full of rioting going on in the St Paul's area of Bristol. Apparently the police had decided to make a major drugs raid on the Black and White Café in Grosvenor Road and had arrived in force, with dogs. A tremendous confrontation developed between police and young blacks and young whites, many of them unemployed. To cut a long story short, the police were not there in sufficient force, so they withdrew from the area for four hours, during which looting and burning occurred. By about midnight it was over.

Friday 11 April

Chris Mullin came to see me; he had just come back from Vietnam and Cambodia. He described how the Chinese had invaded Vietnam on a punitive mission, dynamiting all the schools, hospitals and factories in the towns they occupied. They removed all the equipment from factories and sent it to China, leaving the Vietnamese nothing. An astonishing story of brutality.

Sunday 4 May
President Tito died today. He had been in intensive care for such a long time that his death had in a sense been forgotten about, but it was a great event, and a man of his magnitude in world history will not easily be replaced. He is the last of the great war leaders, the only one left being Hirohito, the Emperor of Japan.

Monday 12 May
Home Policy Committee at 5.30, with lots of resolutions. The most serious one was an attack upon the Government for contemplating the break-up of the ILEA. We agreed to propose its reinstatement if that happened, but Neil Kinnock as Shadow Education Spokesman didn't want to commit himself. He really is behaving like a Minister already, without ever having held ministerial office. Eric Heffer attacked him and said, 'You really worry me, Neil.' But Neil believes this demonstrates that he is responsible.

We went over the draft rolling manifesto, and Neil again opposed our commitment to restore the school meals, school milk and school transport services. It is a gross misjudgement of the mood of the Party at the moment. Neil's argument is that if you pledge to do something in an immediate response to a situation, and then you fail to keep that pledge, people are disappointed.

Wednesday 28 May
Willy Brandt was giving a lecture at Chatham House, and had asked if while he was in London he could visit me. I must say I was very honoured. He came to see me at home, after he had seen Jim, accompanied by Jenny Little and his own Private Secretary, and stayed for an hour and a half. I have known him since 1957, though I don't suppose he remembers that I met him when he was Deputy Mayor of Berlin. Then I met him again in Bonn in 1975. When he is thoughtful and relaxed, as he was today, he couldn't be nicer.

He thought Schmidt would win the elections in Germany, and that the SPD should open up to absorb the Green Movement in Germany. He talked about his famous North–South report and said Olaf Palme was initiating a disarmament report similar to his.

The thing he really wanted to discuss was the Common Market. He wondered if an initiative by the German SPD would help the Labour Party.

I said, 'For many years our socialist friends in the Community thought that Roy Jenkins spoke for the Labour Party – which he didn't – and we have had to fight to get across our view that there has to be some constitutional change. But we are not behind Mrs Thatcher with her nationalism and the

Budget and the CAP. Our concern is a broader one, and I think the way to deal with it is to recognise that the Treaty of Rome has caused a log-jam, and that we have to get round it by initiatives on East–West relations, on disarmament, on the Third World and on energy.'

Then we talked about East–West relations. He thinks the Russians are not planning an advance into Western Europe but a strong military directorate is growing up in the Soviet Union. He said that low-level détente in Germany means that families who couldn't meet when the Berlin Wall was put up can meet now.

I said I welcomed the fact that Giscard had gone to see Brezhnev.

'Yes, so did we, but Giscard did insult Schmidt.'

I asked, 'What do you mean?'

He said, 'Well, he advised Schmidt not to go, and then he went himself!'

We laughed; that was typically French.

I told him he mustn't think that the Labour Party was inward-looking about Europe; we were struggling to fight off the most right-wing Government we have had, and it will take us a decade to put it right. I think he understood that.

Altogether, Brandt is a wise man, and what I like about him is that he is past the management stage and is now the father of his tribe, in a way.

Friday 30 May

Frances Morrell rang to tell me about the Rank and File Mobilising Committee, which is working to get together the CLPD, Labour Coordinating Committee, Institute for Workers' Control, the Independent Labour Publications and the Socialist Campaign for a Labour Victory, to agree on a programme of Party democracy.

In the evening we had a party, a sort of new left gathering, with Frances, Ken Livingstone of the GLC, Victor Schonfield, Audrey Wise, Tom Litterick, Chris Mullin, James Curran, a lecturer, his wife Margaret, George Osgerby, one of James's students, Dick Clements and Biddy, Geoff Bish, Dawn Primarolo, Jon Lansman of CLPD, Peter Hain and others. These are the people who have formed this Rank and File Mobilising Committee and, when the time comes, they will be the people who organise the Benn election campaign.

Friday 6 June

Had a cup of tea at the House with Joan Lestor and Neil Carmichael, and Joan asked, 'How are we going to get you as Leader of the Party when the press hates you so much? People think you would lose us the next Election if you were Leader.'

I said, 'I think the real issue is this: that if the press is to choose our leader it will also choose our policy, and, once you accept that, then you are saying there can't be a Labour Party.'

Caught the shuttle to Edinburgh for the Scottish Miners' Gala tomorrow. At dinner I sat next to Mick McGahey, the President of the Scottish miners, who is exactly my age, a very principled guy.

Mick's father was a miner and founder member of the Communist Party and had not worked from the General Strike of 1926 to the Second World War: a tremendously scholarly man who when he retired read Gibbon's *Decline and Fall of the Roman Empire* and Churchill's history of the Second World War. Mick is also highly knowledgeable. He had read E.P. Thompson's biography of William Morris. He said he had read *Arguments for Socialism* and, though he didn't agree with everything I had said, at least I was getting back to fundamentals. He couldn't have been nicer.

Friday 13 June
Set off with Caroline and Hilary for Whitehall College, the ASTMS country club, for the Commission of Inquiry weekend. It is a most beautiful place, built at the turn of the century for the Gilbey gin firm. It has now got a swimming pool and sauna, and beautiful lawns. Hilary told me that Clive had actually bought some goldfish for the water garden especially for this weekend. In each room there were drinks, and in our room a kettle and two ASTMS mugs – and two penknives with ASTMS inscriptions!

The whole of the Labour Party's Commission of Inquiry was gathered for its final discussions: David Basnett, Eric Heffer, Michael Foot, Jim Callaghan, Terry Duffy, Moss Evans, Bill Keys, Norman Atkinson, Frank Allaun, Joan Lestor, Jo Richardson and myself.

Saturday 14 June
I had a troubled night; I worried that we were going to waste all our time on the preliminaries and never get to the main decisions. I woke at 6.30 and got up and went through all my papers again looking out of the window on a tremendously rainy day, unlike yesterday's beautiful sunshine. Four policemen were walking in the gardens, and I must say the whole thing is rather absurd.

After the afternoon session we were summoned up to Jim Callaghan's room for a party to which Clive had contributed some bottles of champagne. It was very jolly. I had a quiet word with Moss, Clive and Bill Keys. I think they have tried to get a compromise which they think will get them through, but they are not prepared to say what it is.

Back into the Commission at 8, and reselection of MPs was the key question. Eric Heffer moved, straightaway, that the Commission adopt last year's Conference decision on mandatory reselection; Frank Allaun seconded Eric, David Basnett in the chair accepted it, and the debate began.

Michael Foot was opposed to it. Clive Jenkins said, 'Reselection should be mandatory unless 60 per cent don't want it.' This was very complicated, and Jim argued that if you went for mandatory reselection it would encourage factions such as the anti-abortion lobby, and it would work against the unions in that those who got seats would be slick media people.

I said I had been a Member for thirty years and, if my local Party wanted to get rid of me, they could just nominate somebody else and choose them. 'I don't believe for a moment that the trade unions will be disadvantaged. Indeed, I think they would benefit, because it is the media men that they want to get rid of and replace with good, solid local people. It will affect very few people, but it will mean that MPs listen to their GMCs.' Jim Callaghan got angry at this.

Moss Evans said, 'The Transport and General Workers' Union is firmly committed to mandatory reselection and so am I, but I am not mandated here. Therefore, I favour what Clive says, that if 40 per cent of a Party wanted it there would be mandatory reselection.'

Moss continued, 'Jim has shown that the evidence in favour of mandatory reselection is not strong and therefore I would like to build a bridge by laying down criteria that *60 per cent* of a Party would positively have to want a reselection conference before it was agreed.'

Clive said, 'No, there should be an obligation on all constituency Parties to hold reselections unless 60 per cent *don't* want it.'

It became a great muddle, and Bill Keys suggested we adjourn for five minutes. When we returned, David put the main question, ie that we supported last year's Conference resolution, and that was carried by 7 votes to 6.

So David Basnett said, 'Well, we've disposed of that', but Jim added, 'Ah no, we've got the question of *who* is going to reselect – a lot of people think it should be done by *all* the members of a local Party, not just the GMC.'

He went on, 'I can only tell you you have got a fight on your hands. The PLP will never accept this. I can't recommend this to the PLP.' And he picked up his papers and walked out; it was a tense moment, the Leader of the Party and a former Prime Minister picking up his bag and leaving a committee.

David Basnett said, 'We'll adjourn until tomorrow.'

Eric Heffer said, 'I am not accepting an adjournment.'

People began moving about, David Basnett picked up his stuff, and gradually the Left were the only ones who remained; it was very dramatic and people thought Jim would go back to London. We began discussing among ourselves what we would do and it was clear that there can't be any reversal of the vote. But we will vote for the GMCs to reselect because it's the only way it can be done.

I went down to have a drink and it was more dispiriting. Clive was sitting there absolutely depressed, and he said, 'You've wrecked it now', which Bill Keys repeated: 'You've wrecked it.'

'What have we wrecked?' I asked.

'You've wrecked the arrangment we had that the electoral college and the manifesto would be part of a compromise on reselection.'

I said, 'Well, look, if you intended that this was going to be a deal, you might have mentioned it to us so that we could have thought about it. I could have given you a better arrangement.'

They were really angry, and the truth is that the trade union leaders and Jim had tried to get this one through and Moss had let them down, because he wouldn't be able to face his Executive Council if he voted against mandatory reselection. I did wonder whether Jim had stormed out because he couldn't face the PLP.

Sunday 15 June

The Commission met at 9 with Eric Heffer in the chair. He said, 'As far as reselection is concerned, the question of the participation of all members of the Party in the process doesn't arise because we agreed we would adopt the reselection policy voted on at last year's Conference, which was that the GMCs would decide.' So that was that. 'Now we come to the Leader.'

To cut a long story short, when Eric Heffer put the final proposals to the vote, ours was lost 6–7, and Moss's was carried 7–6, and at least we established the principle that the electoral college would choose the leadership.

I had a word with Moss and Clive and tried to be friendly.

Drove home and slowly unpacked.

Looking back on the weekend, Eric, Jo, Norman, Frank, Joan and I stuck together. Clive Jenkins and Bill Keys are just fixers. Moss Evans is absolutely unaffected by the mandate of his trade union. David Basnett is devious and cynical but hasn't got real strength; you can beat Basnett. Duffy is much tougher and honest and straightforward. Jim is angry and cross, on his way out. Michael Foot is hopeless. Anyone who reads this will think what an awful man to say those things about his colleagues but I'm getting it off my chest.

Whitehall College itself is like an executive mansion for the chiefs of multinational companies to relax in. Eric Heffer said on the phone how corrupt it was, and this is the form the corruption takes. The saunas, the swimming baths and champagne, everything laid on, is corrupting and you can't produce reform unless you withdraw from that, challenge it. But when you do, and are serious, you are up against bitter opposition.

Saturday 28 June

Caroline went to the Socialist Educational Association Conference; I went with Dawn Primarolo to the Bristol City Farm, which is apparently the biggest and best in the country. It was lovely. There are geese, goats, rabbits, ponies, a barn, a workshop for mothers and children, and it is run by a heavily tattooed man of about twenty-five who had six ribs shot away and his liver damaged while serving in the army in Belfast.

Tuesday 15 July
I left for Birkbeck College for the debate with Eric Hobsbawm, the famous Marxist theoretician, which *Marxism Today* is going to publish in its September issue. He had sent me his line of questioning but I didn't prepare myself in any great detail for it, as I thought it would be better to be more informal. Eric Hobsbawm is Professor of Economic and Social History at Birkbeck, a very charming man of about sixty-three, a real intellectual with a pinched face and flowing hair. He looked like a thinner version of Jimmy Maxton. Bernard Crick, Professor of Politics at Birkbeck, and his wife were present. The meeting was packed out with research students and other people. I was then subjected to this most penetrating cross-examination. He was fair but pressing, and I'm not sure my answers were all that good. There were questions and answers from the floor which I enjoyed.

Tuesday 22 July
Went to the Commons and heard the unemployment figures – nearly 1,900,000, a jump of 250,000, I think, in a month. James Prior was not convincing and when Mrs Thatcher got up people shouted 'Resign' and 'Out'. Jim said there would be a motion of censure.

Tuesday 29 July
Went into the House to hear Prime Minister's Questions and the censure debate.

Jim Callaghan was heavy, concerned, sincere, and said it was wrong to spend money on the Trident missiles when the public services were being starved (even thought it is widely alleged that he spent £1,000 million on Chevaline without consulting the Cabinet; also, it is alleged in American reports that he was strongly in favour of the Trident). Next he called for import controls in a way that sent my mind back to the 1976 IMF discussions. But otherwise his remedies were trifling. They were just intended to edge the present Government back to the policy he had pursued – which hadn't been all that successful.

Thatcher got up and she just romped home. She quoted what Healey and Callaghan had both said in office. She demonstrated that there was no difference in analysis between herself and them but that, whereas they were weak, she wasn't. The Government were determined, they wouldn't do a U turn, the public supported her, and so on. It was a parliamentary triumph really.

Monday 22 September
To the new Labour Party headquarters, Walworth Road, at 10.20, and

there was Denis Healey standing outside. I said, 'I really liked your book of photographs. I had no idea what a good photographer you were.'

'Ah, you see, I'm not as daft as I look,' he replied.

'I always thought you were much *more* cunning than you appeared, but anyway they were really good pictures.'

So then he said, 'I enjoyed listening to your mother on the radio.' It was all very matey.

Tuesday 23 September
I have a terrible cough and cold, I haven't been smoking for a week. The cough and cold and sore tongue really frightened me, and I have a pain in my leg which makes me think I have got circulation trouble.

Friday 26 September – Labour Party Conference, Blackpool
The Imperial Hotel was more run down than ever. They have redecorated downstairs, but the rooms upstairs are really crummy.

There was a thundering disco going on all evening and the whole hotel vibrated with the noise until 2 am.

In yesterday's *Listener*, Barbara Castle's diaries were reviewed by Michael Foot, who was violent against diarists. Enoch Powell in *Now!* magazine was also strongly against them. It is interesting because Powell and Foot, who were thought of as tribunes of the people, want to keep the mystique of the state in order to make it easier to govern the people.

Watched *Newsnight*, which included a profile of me that Adam Raphael had put together. It lasted about sixteen minutes; I thought it really was an assassination job, done with considerable skill. Barbara Castle was quoted to my disadvantage and then David Owen, who said I was phoney and bogus for being 'ashamed of my middle-class background' and that the PLP didn't like phoney, bogus people. Sir Antony Part, my former Permanent Secretary at Industry, thought my problem was that I was a radical Minister in a non-radical government (which was quite fair). Then an awful interview with Joe Ashton, who said, 'The trouble with Tony is that he idealises the working class and there are as many shits in the working class as there are in the middle class – I know because I am in the working class.' There was no reference to the fact that my father had been a Labour MP.

Saturday 27 September
This evening I went to Jo Richardson's hotel room with Joan Maynard, Judith Hart, Neil Kinnock, Tony Saunois, Joan Lestor, Eric Heffer and Dennis Skinner, and we planned how we would handle the leadership question.

Sunday 28 September
Shirley Williams on Weekend World said she would leave the Party if the Conference voted to come out of the Common Market.

Monday 29 September
Michael Foot opened the economy debate with a speech entirely without content, just rhetoric.

On behalf of the NEC, I made a competent, 'prime ministerial'-type speech, putting forward the possibility of a Labour government creating a thousand peers to abolish the Lords and hence their power to delay our legislation on public ownership and industrial democracy.

Caroline attended the education debate as she has contributed to Party policy. Apparently Neil Kinnock got a standing ovation – for the second year – and he got it partly for saying that government cuts would have to be more than restored. Actually he had been saying elsewhere that he couldn't guarantee to restore them at all.

Wedneday 1 October
The Common Market motion was moved brilliantly by Clive Jenkins, talking about food mountains. He said, 'We have had a marvellous barley harvest. Next year we're having harvest festival in a hangar at Heathrow.' It was hilarious.

I went up to Ron Hayward and asked when Peter Shore was going to be called, and he said, 'I don't know whether Lena Jeger will call him.' I argued that he should; after all, he was the parliamentary spokesman. As a result the whole debate was given another ten minutes and Peter got in with a Churchillian-type speech. By 5 million to 2 million, we voted to withdraw from the Common Market. That is sensational, a fantastic victory.

In the afternoon we had three great debates on the constitutional changes.

The first was on mandatory reselection of Labour MPs. Joe Ashton made a notable speech against it. Joe is an old friend – he was my PPS – but he said something disgraceful.

'When you were sacked, Tony, from your seat by the House of Lords in a very unfair way, you fought and fought again, and you have never stopped fighting the House of Lords since . . . MPs who think they have been unfairly sacked will tend to react in the same way. Because if an MP gets the sack and walks away into the sunset, and says nothing, he does not get a penny redundancy. [But] if he stands and fights he can pick up nearly 13,000 quid.' This was a reference to MPs who, if they are defeated in an Election, get a lump-sum payment. He said it was letting a Trojan horse into the Party. 'If Roy Jenkins wanted to form a party of twenty-five sacked MPs now in this Parliament, they would be in business in six months', because, historically, sacked MPs won their seats when they stood as independents.

His speech did the PLP no good at all.

At the end Sam McCluskie delivered the most devastating argument in favour of mandatory reselection and it was carried: the Conference nearly went berserk.

Next was the manifesto. The NEC amendment was moved formally, and its effect would be to remove the Shadow Cabinet's joint control over the manifesto and to provide only *consultation with* the Leader. Very little was said during the debate. David Warburton of the GMWU, one of these well-dressed, right-wing, clever young trade union leaders, who are very pro-EEC, attacked the National Executive.

I was called to reply, and I described what had happened, why the manifesto was important, why in the past it was secretly killed, and then I dealt with Warburton and said all the measures Trade Unionists for a Labour Victory had wanted had been ruled out in the manifesto last year. I must say it was the best speech I have ever made at Conference, probably the best speech I have ever made in my life at a public meeting. It was followed by tumultuous applause from the CLPs and a standing ovation, while the trade union delegations sat looking very uncomfortable. By a narrow majority – 100,000 or so – the NEC motion was defeated, but I had heard that they had expected it to be lost by more.

Then we went on to the manner of election of the leadership, which Eric Heffer introduced in a halting way. He outlined the procedure the Conference had to follow, which was extremely complicated, and there was an absolute uproar when the Conference voted by a pretty narrow majority – 98,000 – to support the principle of an electoral college for electing the Leader and Deputy Leader. This was not what had been expected. Indeed, the *Express* said this morning that the Left would be defeated on all three issues.

It was a most thrilling day.

Caroline and I went to the *Tribune* meeting and 1,900 people were in the Pavilion Theatre. Neil Kinnock was extremely amusing during the annual collection – exceptionally talented and funny. After I spoke, the general consensus was that I went on too long.

Then Michael Foot, now the old lion, wound up and got a cheer although he hasn't been a figure of the Left for a decade. His usual line is to warn that we face the greatest crisis since Hannibal's march on Rome and that we must do nothing whatever that might interfere with total mental inactivity and 100 per cent loyalty to the Leader, whoever he may be – but particularly Callaghan, followed by Healey, followed, if all goes wrong, by Roy Mason and Eric Varley in about that order!

At 11pm Vladimir Derer, Tony Saunois, Joan Maynard, Margaret Beckett and others met in Jo Richardson's room. The general feeling was that at tomorrow morning's NEC we should propose a new constitutional amendment based on a division of 40 per cent to the PLP and 30 per cent each to the unions and constituencies, because that was thought the one most likely to get through. Tony Saunois, the YS representative on the NEC, emerged in the discussions as the most formidable, principled and serious politician, at the age of twenty-five.

However, just as I was going to bed, the phone rang and it was Frances Morrell, and a few minutes later, with Caroline and Melissa in bed, she plonked herself down in the same room and said this had been a terrible sellout. The Left never knew when it had won, we should not give the MPs 40 per cent but should insist on the unions getting 40 per cent because *anything* we put forward would be accepted tomorrow. Pressed and somewhat overpowered by Frances, who was in her full battlegear while I was in my underpants, I conceded that this seemed logical at 1.45 am and so she retired.

Thursday 2 October
When I went downstairs I found Stephen sitting in the hotel lobby with a typewriter, having worked all night on an emergency resolution about Chile.

'Benn's a Liar', 'Labour in Chaos', 'Anarchy Here', 'Callaghan Denounces Benn', and so on, the papers all said. I heard that Callaghan had denounced me at the miners' dinner, which did cause great offence to the miners because I had been a good Energy Minister.

The National Executive met at 8, and it was clear that Frances, Vladimir, Jon Lansman, Peter Willsman, Victor Schonfield and Francis Prideaux had bullied members of the Executive into agreeing to the new CLPD alternative – 40 per cent for the unions and 30 per cent each for the MPs and constituencies. We kicked this around for a bit, and eventually it was carried by 13 votes to 7, which was excellent.

Out of the blue, Jim announced that if this was implemented he would withdraw what he had said about Labour unity, he would open up a campaign and he would recommend to the PLP that they elect their own leader. Neil Kinnock said this was all rather regrettable.

I said, 'Jim has made a very important statement and I think we should consider it. If he tries to get the PLP to vote for a leader in this way, for which there is no provision in the constitution, either he would fail (and I think he will because most Labour MPs are good loyal members of the Party), or he will succeed and set up a centre party. Either way it would be very bad for us. All these threats do no good.'

So Jim announced, 'Well, I tell you that the Parliamentary Party will never accept a leader foisted upon them', and added, 'I'll tell you something else, they will never have Tony Benn foisted upon them.'

I said, 'Jim, you speak for yourself and nobody else.'

So, on that happy note, we went into the Conference. The morning debate was on defence, and passed two unilateralist resolutions overwhelmingly.

Then to the NEC statement agreed this morning on the election of the Leader, and Eric introduced the debate. To cut a long story short, there was a bitter debate, with Tom Jackson of the Post Office Workers accusing the Executive of being a conjuror producing white rabbits out of a top-hat, Andrew Faulds attacking 'the Right Honourable Anthony Wedgwood Benn' (inaudibly, since the mike was switched off), and Martin Flannery saying what he thought of Terry Duffy. In the end all the options for the electoral college were defeated, leaving only the principle agreed. Then David Basnett, who had spoken against the NEC constitutional amendment, moved an emergency resolution that we hold a Special Conference in January to resolve the method of electing the Leader of the Party, and that was agreed. So we are back where we started.

Friday 3 October
It has been a watershed of a Conference, of that there is no doubt, and, unlike any other Conference, it will continue to cast its influence over the PLP, over the leadership and over the future of British politics.

Sunday 5 October
The *Telegraph*, the *Sunday Times* and the *Observer* all presented the week entirely from a right-wing point of view – 'Representative Democracy Threatened', 'The Left Tyrannicals', and so on.

That it was the culmination of years of work to get a democratic Party in which the leadership was more responsive to the rank and file never surfaced at all. The *Sunday Express* raised the question whether the Queen could ask someone who had been made Leader by the Party outside Parliament to form a government.

Caroline has a bad cold. Got on with a bit of work but, having stopped smoking, I am putting on weight.

Sunday 12 October
We had guests at 8 – Norman Atkinson, Geoff Bish, Chris Mullin, Frances Morrell, Vladimir Derer, Tony Banks, Audrey Wise, Martin Flannery, Jo Richardson, Reg Race, Ken Coates, Stuart Holland and Julie Clements. There was some discussion as to whether we might have witnessed a real split in the Party. Sixty MPs have demanded that the PLP maintain the right to elect its own leader, and it looked as if they were calling for Callaghan to go.

Jo Richardson then proposed that if Michael Foot stood no one else should. Stuart Holland agreed.

Chris Mullin turned to me and asked, 'Tony, are you going to stand? You shouldn't. You have nothing to gain from standing, and everything to gain by abstaining.'

At some stage I was asked to speak. I said, 'First of all, this is a political and not a personal question. I have consulted my GMC and have made no commitment. Leaving aside the split question, we must see this in the wider context.' I thought the correct strategy was for us to challenge the leadership, the deputy leadership and the Shadow Cabinet appointments. I went on, 'The Party needs a strong leader now, and if the Left abstains there will be continued personal conflict with the left leader-in-waiting, and the incumbent will win in the electoral college. I don't think I could fight and win the college if I abstained now.'

But the unanimous view was that I shouldn't stand yet. After the discussion, I drafted a couple of resolutions, one for the NEC and one for the PLP.

Just to sum up the evening. First of all, it was a meeting of the Left in strength, and very formidable they are, but they were unanimous that I shouldn't stand and I am bound to take that seriously. I am in no hurry, and I have lots of meetings in which I can talk about the issues. But they were strong and firm, and clearly the view that Frances Morrell, Victor Schonfield, Dennis Skinner and others put forward earlier was right, so I simply bowed to the will of the majority.

Wednesday 15 October

To Coventry for a union meeting, and at the station I heard the news that Jim Callaghan had resigned. The media had all got in their taxis and cars and arrived at the station. Caroline had advised me simply to say, 'Although I have had many personal differences with Jim Callaghan, I feel that in the hearts of many people will be a desire to say thank you for his personal contribution; as to the future, nothing must be done that divides the Parliamentary Party from the Party in the country.' I said that several times.

Got home at 6, and on the news it was announced that Michael Foot had decided not to stand. I had a word with Eric Heffer, who said, 'Now look, I have consulted Doris' (very important, because Eric takes a lot of notice of his wife, quite properly) 'and if Michael Foot is not going to stand, and if there are no candidates other than Silkin and Healey, you and I should stand for the leadership and deputy leadership.'

Monday 20 October

At 5 Michael Foot declared. Then a couple of hours later we heard that Peter Shore was going to stand, so we have now got Healey, Foot, Shore and Silkin. Silkin will do badly. Michael gave the extraordinary reason that he had decided to stand because of the pressure of advice and because his wife would divorce him if he didn't. I think Foot has a good chance of beating Healey. So the whole thing looks shabby and calculating.

Sunday 26 October

The clocks went back so we had an extra hour in bed.

Caroline, Hilary and I went to Hyde Park for the CND march and rally. It was a fantastic day. I am not a descriptive writer but everything about it was thrilling. There were fourteen columns – the national column first, then Scotland and Wales, then East Anglia, and so on, right the way through. There was a huge balloon in the sky shaped like a hydrogen bomb with a mushroom cloud, and there was a children's puppet theatre. It had this element of gaiety and festivity about it, and there were tens of thousands of young people. I would think there were 100.000 in total.

Fenner Brockway, another old peace campaigner, spoke with amazing strength – he's ninety-three. I gave him a hug, I was so proud of him. The speakers were introduced by Lord Jenkins, Bruce Kent and Neil Kinnock. Sister Mary Byrne, the nun, upset the crowd by mentioning abortion.

Thursday 30 October
I voted last night for Michael Foot as Leader of the Party.

Friday 31 October
To Bristol to the Wills tobacco factory to meet the shop stewards. The President of the Tobacco Workers' Union was also present. Their joint complaint was that I had approved a resolution calling for the banning of cigarette advertising and they were angry with me, but it was really that they were terrified that the cigarette industry was running down, that Imperial Tobacco might be pulling out of Bristol. We calculated that there were about 35,000 people in Bristol who individually or in families derive their income from cigarette manufacture.

Monday 10 November
To a TULV dinner at St Ermine's Hotel. When Michael Foot came in, everybody rose and cheered, and he said, 'I want a double whisky and another double whisky. What I want to say is that I have got to go and record a programme, so do forgive me. But we will beat the Tories, we'll fight them on jobs and on nuclear weapons.'

He looked cheerful, and anyone who becomes Labour Leader becomes a little bit different. They step outside the mainstream, and now Jim Callaghan has dropped back into normality, as Harold Wilson has. Of course, an ex-leader still has a certain something, but they lose that magic power. With a new suit and a haircut, Michael already looked a bit different.

Tuesday 11 November
I heard tonight that the new electoral boundaries in Bristol will produce only four constituencies – North, East, South and West – and that means I will have to fight either Mike Cocks for the Bristol South nomination or Arthur Palmer, who will probably go for Bristol East. I must confess I am very uncertain about it, but clearly one seat will be winnable; I think probably

East and South will be Labour, and North and West, Tory. I'll have to mend some fences with the Bristol Labour leaders, otherwise there will be pressure to see I don't get in. I just won't worry about it.

Saturday 22 November
Caught the train to Newcastle for a book-signing of the Penguin paperback of *Arguments for Socialism*. A man came up at the station, produced a little plastic ID card and told me he was a police inspector. He said they had had a threat that I was going to be killed today when I visited a particular bookshop so wherever I went I would find plainclothes policemen and policewomen.

Thursday 4 December – Trip to United States
Up earlyish and caught the tube to Heathrow for the conference in Washington on 'Eurosocialism and America' arranged by the Democratic Socialist Organising Committee.

I was met at Dulles airport by the Ambassador and driven to the Capitol Hilton Hotel. As soon as I got in, I rang the Whips' Office and heard the result of the Shadow Cabinet elections.

Denis Healey's place was filled by Neil Kinnock and David Owen's by Gerald Kaufman. Neil Kinnock was lowest with 90 votes and I was the runner-up with 88, so I didn't get on. In a way, I am quite pleased because I think it would be wrong to be on at this moment. I certainly shan't accept a Front Bench job from Michael Foot because, if the PLP prefer Bill Rodgers and Roy Hattersley and Eric Varley to me, that's for them.

I rang Caroline. Then the phone in my hotel room went continuously – the *Daily Mirror*, the *Western Daily Press*, the *Daily Mail*, the *Daily Telegraph*. I simply said, 'No comment.'

Sunday 7 December
Woke at 6 and turned on the television and for one hour I listened to a man called Pat Robertson, who runs a right-wing born-again Christian evangelical movement. It was such a hair-raising programme that it undid all the optimism that I had begun to feel when I came to this conference. This guy Pat Robertson, who looked like a business executive of about forty-five with one of those slow, charming American smiles, was standing there with a big tall black man beside him, his sidekick, and he talked continuously about the Reagan administration, about the defeat of the liberals, about Reagan's commitment to the evangelical movement. He had a blackboard showing what in the nineteenth century 'liberal' meant. He then wiped that from the blackboard and said that today the liberals are Marxists, Fascists, leftists and socialists.

Then he showed an extract of Reagan saying, 'We want to keep big government out of our homes, and out of our schools, and out of our family life.' He went on and on for an hour like this. At the end, he said, 'Let us pray', and, his face contorted with fake piety, pleaded with Jesus to protect America, 'our country'.

I couldn't switch it off. It was so frightening, the feeling that we are now entering a holy war between that type of reactionary Christianity and Communism. It is a thoroughly wicked and evil interpretation of Christianity.

I checked out from the hotel and went into the conference to hear François Mitterrand give the keynote speech. I have heard him on a number of occasions and I find him rather boring and platitudinous, but today he was excellent. He made a most sensitive speech about the development of socialism, beginning in a very human way by showing a picture of the fist holding the rose and describing how it had developed. He went on to talk about economic and political democracy and traced the ideas of democracy through to the rights of man, together with the principles of the French Revolution, liberty, equality and fraternity. It went down extremely well.

After lunch Willy Brandt gave the closing speech and talked about the three challenges: new technology, the Cold War and the North–South divide. He went through it in his thoughtful way, as he always does, and he got a warm reception. I must say, my feelings did change a little. I felt more warmly disposed to them because they may sound pretty conservative in Europe, but when you hear them in America they are beacons of light in a dark continent.

Looking back on the conference, it was a significant event, although the media didn't cover it at all in America as far as I can make out.

Afterwards I went to the Aeronautical Space Agency museum with Edith Cresson, a French socialist deputy in the European Parliament, who is here with Mitterrand, and together we touched the piece of moonstone that was there – it was exciting to see and feel it.

Friday 12 December
The Prime Minister yesterday was in South Wales, where there was a big demonstration, with 1,200 police on duty and fifty-five arrests. And an egg hit her car. Then there were pictures on television of her speaking at a CBI dinner in Cardiff saying demonstrations don't help to get jobs – that it gives Wales a bad name for investors, and all the rest of it. Here is a woman entirely without any human sympathy whatever, applying rigidly capitalist criteria at a time of great hardship and deliberately widening the gap between rich and poor. The country is ready now for major unrest.

Monday 22 December
To the Friends of the Earth Christmas Party. What became clear from chatting to people there was that they were mostly pre-socialist in their thinking. One felt that all this concern was the middle class expressing its

dislike of the horrors of industrialisation – keeping Hampstead free from the whiff of diesel smoke, sort of thing. It was also a bit of a warning that local Labour Parties could become full of people like this, like the Liberal Party with no solid working-class and trade union experience behind it.

Friday 26 December

Late lie-in. Collected Melissa and she and I walked across the park. It was a fantastic year for press hysteria and violence; a few days free of that at the moment is welcome.

In 1981 there will be the Special Conference and I think some form of electoral college will be established. Michael Foot will certainly be re-elected unopposed. My intention at the moment is to stand against Denis Healey for the deputy leadership in order to pinpoint the real issues for the Party, but I don't expect to succeed.

I think the possibility is that there might be some minor breakaway from the Labour Party encouraged by Roy Jenkins and supported by Shirley Williams; if Mrs Thatcher gets into serious trouble, they may try to bring together a sort of national-reconstruction government with a federal European shift, a statutory pay policy and proportional representation. I have a feeling that the political fight that lies ahead will be a bitter one.

Monday 26 January 1981

Roy Jenkins, Shirley Williams, David Owen and Bill Rodgers were splashed all over the front pages with their 'Limehouse Declaration', so called because it was made from David Owen's home there in East London. It is a turning point in a way because from now on the Labour Party is going to be treated as if it is illegitimate, and resentment is growing strongly in the Party about this.

The big news tonight is that thirteen MPs are supporting the Council for Social Democracy, and the media are giving it massive coverage. If there is going to be a new political party, which the Gang of Four claim, that is important news. But the Left are holding their hand and I think that is right. I don't think it's sensible for us to attack the Social Democrats at the moment; let them come out with their own policies and then we shall raise the question whether Tom Bradley and Shirley Williams on the NEC, and Bill Rodgers in the Shadow Cabinet, can be allowed to plan a new political party while remaining in the Party. It is absolutely wrong.

Tuesday 27 January

Beause Bill Rogers has resigned from the Shadow Cabinet, I take his place. At 9.30 I went to see Michael Foot, and it turned into the most sensational interview.

He mentioned the NEC tomorrow, and said, 'I don't see why we should pass this resolution of Party loyalty. Why do we need it?'

I explained, 'Because the Social Democrats are saying they are going to leave.'

He said, 'It's quite unnecessary.'

So I replied, 'Well, it's quite straightforward: if you don't like it, vote against it.'

He was angry and red-faced.

I said something like, 'You're certainly very soft on the Right, buttering up Bill Rodgers all the time, but I notice you chose this morning to attack me violently in the PLP meeting. You have really been all over the shop to try and keep the Right in the Party, and you don't feel quite the same about the Left. Why didn't you attack Bill Rodgers for the "myths" *he* is spreading?'

He was angry about that. So then I said, 'I have come from the left group on the NEC who asked me to request a meeting with you.'

He snapped, 'Oh, so you meet before the NECs, do you?'

I said, 'Yes, we do.'

He said, 'Well, that's very disruptive of committees if people meet and discuss them in advance.'

'I don't know about that,' I remarked. 'You went round and saw people to try to get 50 per cent for the PLP at the Wembley conference.'

'I did not,' he said.

'I heard you had, but if I'm wrong . . .'

He repeated, 'It's very disruptive, a caucus of that kind.'

Well, since the husbands' and wives' weekly dinners met at his house throughout the whole of the Labour Government, to do exactly the same, I couldn't understand his anger.

Then he asked, 'You try to fix votes in advance, don't you?'

I said, 'No, I try to reach a sort of general agreement about things.'

'You're a bloody liar,' he said.

So I just walked out, and that was my first meeting with my leader as a member of his Shadow Cabinet. I am not being called a liar by anybody. I was pretty steamed up. So I went back to the left group of Eric Heffer, Tony Saunois, Eric Clarke, Norman Atkinson, Frank Allaun, Joan Maynard and Jo Richardson, and I told them what had happened. They said, 'Keep cool.' I said, 'I'm as cool as a cucumber.'

Later, while I was sitting in the Division Lobby waiting to vote, I talked to Peter Shore and told him that, in some ways, I admired David Owen because he was saying what he believed. I didn't agree with him, but at least he was arguing his case.

Peter said, 'If you admire that, you'll have a lot of admiring to do in the next year.'

'What do you mean?' I asked.

He said, 'Well, there's a lot of fighting going on and I shall be in on it.'

We went through the Lobby together and as we walked along the corridor I sensed an absolute reservoir of anger against me. Peter said I was obstructive; I think my relations with him are temporarily ruptured. As he is a very old friend, I am extremely sorry about that.

Monday 2 February
Went into the House and saw Michael Foot at 2.30. I said, 'Let's just forget last week completely. We were all under strain and I know you have got a great problem on your plate.' So that made things seem all right. I asked if the Gang of Four would go.

'It looks as if they will. I am seeing them this afternoon.'

I said, 'I don't want them to go, but at the same time I don't think we ought to offer them anything to keep them in.'

He replied, 'Well, I won't. On the question of a job, I can't really do a reshuffle of the Shadow Cabinet at the moment.'

I said, 'I understand that. Do whatever you need, but I would like Regional Affairs.'

I went to the Library and wrote out a brief which I dropped in for him to look at.

Thursday 5 February
Today a list of 100 Council for Social Democracy supporters was published. It included ex-Labour Ministers like George Brown and Jack Diamond, and Lord Donaldson, Michael Zander, Brian Flowers and the actress Janet Suzman. It was the middle class coming out in support of a break from the Labour Party. The BBC gave it tremendous coverage – the BBC is now the voice of Shirley Williams and Roy Jenkins.

I had an interesting phone call from Tony Saunois, saying that every member of the NUR executive except one had signed a letter condemning their General Secretary Sid Weighell for his recent statement that he would 'spit in Tony Benn's eye'.

Saturday 7 February
On the train back from Bristol I went to the front as we drew into Paddington, and a short, thin man of about sixty peered across and said in a Scottish accent, 'Are you Mr Benn?' I said, 'Yes.' He told me, 'Well, I was a fitter with your brother Michael in North Africa in 1943.' It gave me such pleasure to talk to someone who had known Michael, and he said, 'He was a nice man. Did he survive the war?' I told him he had been killed in 1944 at RAF Tangmere. At that point a big man with a trilby hat and moustache who was standing next to us said, 'RAF Tangmere? I was the station commander there. I was a wing commander in 1943.'

So at that moment, quite unexpectedly, on a Saturday night on a train from the West Country to Paddington, I tumbled back nearly forty years, and it gave me enormous pleasure.

Monday 9 February
I heard a rumour from a journalist that Shirley Williams had resigned from
the NEC. It was later confirmed, and Ron Hayward let me read her letter, in
which she said that the Party she had joined no longer existed. Such an
arrogant statement, and designed to do damage to us.

Thursday 12 February
Went into the Tea Room at 6.30 and I stayed there until the vote at 10,
talking to MPs, including Dale Campbell-Savours, who turned on me on the
question of reselection.

'Take John Sever, for example,' he said (the MP for Brian Walden's old
seat, Birmingham Ladywood). 'He's a good man, votes on the left, a decent
guy, and he's in danger of being deselected.'

Alex Lyon, who was sitting with us, said, 'Half a minute. When Brian
Walden sat in that seat he wouldn't let people join the Party. The selection
conference which selected John Sever was made up of twelve people: seven
were old ladies and five were from the Asian community and it was a rotten
Party; indeed, the agent there was a former member of the National Front.'

The discussion got wider and hotter. Alex said he had been a good right-
wing Jenkinsite until he went to the Home Office and realised that Roy
Jenkins wasn't remotely interested in socialism but only in himself.

Chris Price, the Member for Lewisham West, came and joined us. 'Look,
what really happened to the Party was that when Gaitskell became Leader
in 1955 there was a plot to put in an élite of Oxbridge right-wingers to take
the Party over. They were pro-American, pro-European and anti-Communist, and they got all the jobs in later governments. I never had a chance.' He
was bitter, absolutely right, and he threw a new perspective on the Party.

Friday 13 February
Went to Bristol for my surgery, an absolute mass of tragedies. Dawn picked
me up and took me to the constituency's Annual General Meeting. She had
written a marvellous report on the Bristol South East Party. At the end, we
had a discussion on my reselection and Cyril Langham said, 'Why bother
with a selection conference?' I said, 'That's the point; we must do it
properly.'

Then there was a series of speeches on the deputy leadership and the
meeting was unanimous, with one abstention, that I should stand, so in reply
I said, 'I think if we are going to use the reselection procedure for choosing
the MP here, we must use the electoral college to fight the deputy leadership.
This is not a personal but a political fight and defeat doesn't matter; if we let
the media pick the Leader, they'll soon pick the policy.'

Tuesday 17 February
Today, Duncan Campbell, a writer on the *New Statesman*, rang to tell me that

two years ago he had heard from an intelligence agent that Airey Neave had planned to have me assassinated if a Labour government was elected, Jim Callaghan resigned and there was any risk that I might become Leader. Then Neave was murdered, and now this agent was ready to give his name and the *New Statesman* was going to carry the story. He asked what I thought.

I said, 'I've never heard it before. I can't comment anyway; it would sound paranoid if I did. I get threatening letters of a similar kind.'

It doesn't ring true in a way; it sounds like the dirty-tricks department trying to frighten me by implying that a serious assassination attempt was being planned. No one will believe for a moment that Airey Neave would have done such a thing.

Stephen came over and we went for a meal at the House, and Mrs Thatcher came in to the dining room with Denis Thatcher and Ian Gow, her PPS. Last Sunday Mrs Thatcher had said that the only difference between Shirley Williams and me was that she was the slow-acting poison and I was the instant one. So later, as I left, I said to Ian, 'I hope the Prime Minister is taking the quick-acting poison. I wouldn't want anything to go wrong.' He laughed.

Voted at 11 and came home.

Wednesday 18 February
Talked to Caroline about the Duncan Campbell story, and her view was that this was the dirty-tricks department at work.

I rang Duncan Campbell and put this to him. But he said, 'This man is a cynical, right-wing intelligence man who has given me accurate information in the past; he gave me this story two years ago, when I discussed it with Bruce Page, but we sat on it.'

I said, 'It's probably come back because, whereas two years ago the likelihood that Labour would make me Leader was very remote, today, now that Callaghan has gone and we have got an electoral college, the possibility that I will be elected Leader when Michael Foot goes is obviously more real. Therefore this is more relevant now.'

Of course Bruce Page would be delighted at the publicity that would attach to the *New Statesman* though it would involve sinking to the *News of the World*'s level of coverage. Then if I was polished off, the *New Statesman* could say, 'Ah well, our man predicted it.'

Spoke to Frances Morrell, and she said I should write to the *New Statesman*, which I did, and later in the day they confirmed that they were going to publish my letter.

Friday 20 February
Melissa's twenty-fourth birthday.

Bought all the papers, and there was not one word about the *New Statesman* story – which was amazing, because if it is true it is the most sensational story for years.

To Bristol, and who should I see but Keith Joseph, the Secretary of State for Industry, so we got into an empty first-class compartment and talked all the way back to London. It was great fun.

I said, 'At least we agree on this, Keith, that the last thirty-five years have been a disaster!'

We talked about the centre party, and he asked what I made of it.

'Well, I have no time for them at all. Roy Jenkins is not very interested; Shirley is pessimistic; Bill Rodgers is an organiser; David Owen was jumped up as Foreign Secretary above his ability, and they all agree with David Steel and Ted Heath. I think now we have got to reorganise politics on the basis of three parties representing monetarism, corporatism and democratic social-ism.'

Keith didn't disagree with the analysis. He talked about crippled capitalism, and I talked about the log-jam in a market economy – we got on famously!

I told him, 'I respect Mrs Thatcher, but I think your way will lead to a breakdown of the social fabric and that actually in ten years' time our view will prevail. But we will see.'

He was saying the usual things about trade unions not representing their members properly, that they shouldn't be political, and talked about overmanning. I told him, 'You sound like Denis Healey.' He said I was a romantic about the shop stewards, and I said he was a romantic about market forces.

Keith talked about the possibility of the 'embourgeoisement' of the working class, and I answered, 'Capitalism can't afford to embourgeois people any more; it's got to return to unemployment. When will we get back to full employment?'

He said, 'I don't know.' He didn't care about lack of investment because he thought there was overmanning, and he didn't care about unemploy-ment because he thought it was the way to reduce overmanning.

I didn't ask him anything embarrasing about the miners or anything else; but he was interested in industrial democracy, who would take the decisions in co-operatives and so on.

It was great fun. I haven't had a discussion like that with him for ages. We talked about Russia and about defence and he said, 'Do you think the Russians would invade?'

'I doubt it. They are just a big power who want a cordon sanitaire.' I mentioned Switzerland and said that I would rather be neutral like the Swiss – better than wasting so much money on defence. Then I asked, 'Why don't you make *everything* commercial – commercial defence, commercial univer-sities and the coronation financed by Benson & Hedges?'

He laughed actually; I think the idea of further inroads into society by market forces appeals to him.

Then he said, 'You know, Enoch was right in the sense that we shouldn't have had immigration without consulting the people.'

I said, 'If you are a believer in the free movement of capital, why not the free movement of labour?' I repeated what Amir Hoveyda, the executed Prime Minister of Iran, had said to me in 1976: 'Money, like people, should have a passport to move about.'

He hadn't thought of that. 'The free movement of labour interferes with the whole cohesion of a society,' he argued.

So I asked, 'Well, what do you think the international movement of capital does? If firms or investors can move their money out of Britain and destroy the economy of this country, that's just as important and serious as bringing in a lot of people.'

'Why do you think you frighten people so much with your speeches?' he asked.

I said, 'Well, I don't. When I make speeches people ask me why I don't make more and I tell them I do.'

'Well, your language in the House of Commons is a bit extreme. It frightens people.'

'I don't believe I frighten people, but I do speak strongly in the House because I think there is a dangerous gap now between the feeling in the country and what is said in the House, and it is important that clear things are said in the House. So I rather deliberately pitch it hard there.'

Then he reverted to Russia, and I said, 'It just doesn't attract anybody any more. Soviet Communism is most unattractive.'

What satisfied me, apart from there being a friendly and non-provocative talk between us – and I have known Keith Joseph for thirty-five years – was that I was able to give the impression of confidence and show him how much I enjoyed life.

When we arrived at Paddington, blow me down, he said, 'I'll take you home.' He told me his government driver was waiting for him and he could drop me at Notting Hill Gate. As we walked off the train together, the engine driver leaned across and called out, 'I wish I could get a picture of you two buggers for the newspapers!'

On the midnight news were details of the first resignations of MPs from the Party: Ian Wrigglesworth, Member for Teeside Thornaby, Tom Ellis, the Member for Wrexham, and Richard Crawshaw, Member for Liverpool Toxteth.

Wednesday 25 February
Shadow Cabinet at 5, and predictably there was the usual unpleasant exchange. Michael Foot began by mentioning the fact that leaks from the

previous meeting had occurred. So Eric Varley said, 'I would like to say that it is very inhibiting having Tony Benn writing down everything we say.'

Michael replied, 'Well, people keep diaries. I'm not much in favour of them, but people do and can keep them.'

'I notice that in a letter to the *Guardian* recently Tony said that he had kept a note of a Cabinet discussion in 1974 – about who had spoken and so on,' remarked Eric.

I kept my mouth shut while this was going on. I thought: why be drawn into a row with Eric Varley?

Denis Healey suggested, 'Let's ban all diaries.'

Michael tried to defuse it. 'Well, people have funny habits.'

I let it go by, but it was just nasty.

Friday 27 February
Had a long telephone conversation with Frances Morrell, who is extremely depressed because the Left is in a state of disarray at the moment. Also she wonders whether she is going to get into Parliament, and I can understand the anxiety.

In the evening I went to a reception organised by the TGWU from the area round Bridgewater, Taunton and Wiveliscombe. A woman had been paid to sing and dance and I felt sorry for her because Somerset people are very taciturn and they didn't exactly enter into the spirit of it, but she managed to get four men to put funny hats on and play tambourines.

Saturday 28 February
Travelled to Bristol and was met by Dawn, who told me I wasn't doing enough in the constituency; I tended to appear like Lord Bountiful, and I should pop into ward meetings for a bit and listen to what members were saying. I wasn't appearing at local events, wasn't involved in the Labour Group, and so on. She was nice about it, but it was a serious criticism and I have sensed in a way that, with all the meetings I do around the country, I don't do enough in Bristol.

Tuesday 3 March
I have a great sense of relief at the resignation of the twelve Labour MPs and, I think, nine Labour peers – among them, Alf Robens, Hartley Shawcross, Dick Marsh, George Brown, Ray Gunter, Roy Jenkins, Herbert Bowden, David Owen, Shirley Williams, Bill Rodgers, Edmund Dell and Jack Diamond.

Melissa and I watched the news and it was fascinating. Mrs Thatcher was giving a speech in a church about Christian values and monetarism, and some young people got up and shouted, 'Jobs not bombs!' They were Young Communists, and of course that was all she needed. She said in her most pious way, 'Now you know what I am fighting against.' It will have given the

Communist Party a tremendous boost. They were very courageous, well-scrubbed, decent kids.

Then President Reagan was interviewed. He said Mrs Thatcher had admitted to him that she should have made more cuts sooner, but of course she had terrible problems because the Labour Party was split and the left wing was now dominant. As if that had in any way affected her position!

Sunday 8 March
Went to bed at 12.40 with a pain in my leg, which had gone very cold. I began to think I had overdone it.

Friday 13 March
Caught the train to Bristol for the NALGO meeting – a one-day strike of social workers against the cuts in social work in Avon has been called. I think they are sacking 210 people.

Then to a meeting with unemployed workers who are on job experience schemes under the Manpower Services Commission. It was one of the most depressing meetings I have ever been to. When I looked round, there were these kids of sixteen and seventeen, utterly hopeless and demoralised – punk rockers, a black boy with purple hair, guys in sort of Hell's Angels outfits with holes in their trousers.

One young guy with hair all over the place interrupted me all the time. The first thing he said was, 'What is the difference between nuclear weapons and machine-guns? You're still killing people.' He went on about that. He might have been an anarchist or nihilist.

They asked all sorts of questions – 'You're a millionaire anyway, aren't you?' 'There are millionaires in council houses, aren't there?' 'I've heard of one in Radstock.' 'Of course, you've got a bombproof shelter to go to, haven't you?' Then they expressed their hatred for the royal family – not the Queen, but all the hangers-on. 'Why should we pay for Prince Charles's wedding?' and all that. Then they said there was nothing they could do. 'You just come in here for our vote.' 'How much do you earn?'

It was a combination of the hopelessness, defeatism and bitterness bred in our education system and encouraged by unemployment. But at the same time a really bitter critique, and at least they were arguing, which showed some confidence. But, by God, I could see them joining the National Front, and I thought the only people who might possibly make something of this crowd would be the Militant Tendency with their philosophy and their analysis and their socialist explanations. I felt for the first time the collective guilt of anyone who has held Cabinet office over the last fifteen years and who has allowed unemployment to rise, and allowed education to remain as it was, and allow these people to be thrown into despair and apathy and hatred and confusion.

Tuesday 24 March

Went in to see Michael, who said, 'I asked you to come and see me about the deputy leadership, to find out if you are going to stand, because I think it would lacerate the Party if you did, would be deeply divisive, would ruin the annual Conference and would make it much harder for us to be elected in the next Election.'

I replied, 'Thanks for asking me. I have thought about it, and a number of people have pressed me to stand. I haven't finally made up my mind, but I think there is some support for a contest, and I will certainly take account of what you say. But, Michael, you fought Denis Healey only three months ago. I don't know why it should be right for you to do it and not for me.'

He said, 'That was quite different.'

'Well, I don't know that it was. I didn't think there should be an election at all, I thought you should have succeeded, as Deputy Leader, but given the fact that you were elected I think you have got a lot of support. You can tell that from the Party meetings.'

He got himself into a typical Michael Foot state where everything you want to do will always lose us the next Election. Well, as we followed his advice rigorously for the last five years of the last Labour Government and we did lose the Election in May 1979, I can't say I found it very credible.

But it must have been clear that I did intend to stand, and I said, 'If I do, I promise I'll let you know in advance. The real problem is that the people who have left the Party to attack it are now being matched by those *within* the Party who attack it, and somebody has got to get up and say we agree with Party policy and the electoral college decision at Wembley.'

'Well, I think we may change the decision to get one-third, one-third, one-third at the Conference this year,' he said.

'You may or may not; I am not particularly hyped on percentages. But that's not the point. The point is that the election will take place on the electoral college.'

Michael said, 'Well, it will be very much to your credit if you decide not to stand.'

'I am sure I will be clobbered if I stand, but I don't think that is really the issue. Denis wasn't elected by anybody, he was just allowed in unopposed, and so there is a genuine vacancy for the deputy leadership.'

That was how we more or less left it, but he was white and angry, as he always is.

Friday 27 March

Did a lot of phoning round and inviting people on Sunday to plan the deputy leadership campaign.

Saturday 28 March

A perfect spring day. The horrible winter seems to be behind us and the spring is coming; by God we need it.

The launch of the Social Democratic Party took place last Thursday and it was exactly as everybody predicted – a major media festival. It is unreal and potentially dangerous. It reminds me of what Tawney said. The attack on the two-party system, the attack on the democratic process, the attack on choice, the attack on debate, the attack on policy – all these have within them the ingredients of Fascism. Of course, as British politics returns to the nineteenth century, it is appropriate that there should be two bourgeois parties – the Conservatives and the Social Democrats. In my heart, I don't believe it can capture support, though it is going to be a huge long struggle to get through to the British people and to create conditions under which they can really govern themselves.

Sunday 29 March

The group arrived – Tony Banks, Ken Coates, Vladimir Derer, Jenny and Stuart Holland, Frances Morrell, Stephen, Chris Mullin, Reg Race, Victor Schonfield, Audrey Wise and Valerie Wise. We had three hours' intense discussion. First of all there was absolutely no doubt that I should stand as a candidate: it was unanimous. It was agreed that I should issue a statement announcing why I was accepting the candidature, and it was agreed that the issue should not be raised at the Tribune Group on the grounds that it had nothing to do with them.

It was also agreed that an attempt would be made to get people to sign a simple statement saying, 'I support the candidature of Tony Benn for the deputy leadership of the Labour Party', and these signatures would come to me by Wednesday. I would put out on 2 April a statement giving my reasons, a draft of which we went through very carefully. A lot of amendments were made.

Chris Mullin stayed, and we went through four chapters of the new book, *Arguments for Democracy*. I drove him home and then went to see Mother, who is a bit better, but I'll have to keep an eye on her, what with her arthritis, her heart trouble, her hernia, her eyesight, her migraine, her new knee and her bad hip. She needs watching, but her mind is as clear as a bell.

A very useful day and a historic decision taken collectively.

Thursday 2 April

The media reaction has been exactly as I expected; tomorrow it will be completely hysterical, just as at the time of the Common Market Referendum – but this time it is a six-month campaign which will blow itself out. What it has done, of course, is to force people to make choices. That's what's called polarisation, divisiveness and all the rest, but it's true. You can't go on for ever and ever pretending you're a socialist party when you're not, pretending you'll do something when you won't, confining yourself to attacks on the Tories when that's not enough. People want to know what the Labour Party will do and I think this process is long overdue; the Labour Party are having a Turkish bath, and the sweat and the heat and the discomfort are very unpleasant. I am sure Denis will win – I will put that on the record now – because the Party never sacks anybody, and why should it sack its deputy leader, particularly when many people think he should have been the Leader? But I think there will be a sizeable body of opinion which can't be entirely ignored or neglected.

Monday 13 April
Had lunch with Clive Jenkins, and we had a fancy meal – he really is a big-business executive.

In the course of the meal he said something like, 'You're not serious about it, are you?'

I replied, 'Of course I am serious about it.' And I realised immediately that the purpose of the lunch was to persuade me not to stand for the deputy leadership. I said, 'Clive, the policies may have been agreed at the Conference, but the argument has not been accepted by the Shadow Cabinet or by the TUC General Council.'

At the end of the lunch he asked if I would like a cup of tea, and on a tray in came the most beautiful loving-cup – a large china cup with two handles and a gold rim – and inscribed on the front in black letters was:

Elections can be poisoned chalices, Tony

and on the back:

Don't do it, Tony

I suppose he had thought this would be a consolation if I had agreed not to stand. Later today, I wrote and thanked him for lunch and added, 'I might need the cup again next year.'

Wednesday 29 April
Canvassing for Stephen in the GLC elections, I went to a block of flats, and people were terrified of coming to the door. They just called through the letterbox, 'What do you want?' The state of the stairways was awful. One of the people I called on was Christine Keeler, and she looked at me in a funny way, as if she recognised me – not that I've ever met her before, I might add.

Tuesday 5 May
I wasn't feeling very well today. I have had this tingling in my legs and now my hands, and my face has been very hot and my skin has been rough, and I did wonder whether I was getting high blood pressure. In the Lobby at

about 8, I asked Maurice Miller, who is MP for East Kilbride and a doctor, if I could consult him professionally. I went into the first-aid room with him and he took my blood pressure, examined my heart and looked at my eyes. He said my blood pressure was on the high side of normal, but he didn't see anything wrong and said it might be stress and I should take things easier. So, once he had told me there was nothing wrong, I felt much better.

Thursday 14 May
I got up early and went to see Dr Stein. I only see him about every five years, and after an hour's talk with him I feel much better. But I reported the fact that I have got this tingling in my legs. At the moment, walking is like having on wellington boots full of water with a sponge in the feet. I don't have any feeling in my feet and my hands tingle. I just don't feel well at all. He examined me, and there's nothing wrong with my blood pressure or my heart, so he thinks it might be some nerve condition.

Sunday 17 May
Hilary rang at 2 to say 'ASTMS have backed you!' And so they had, by a very narrow majority of about 650, in a vote of 28,000. So that gave me a huge boost, it is a real kick in the teeth for Clive Jenkins, with his 'poisoned chalice'.

Monday 1 June
Went to see Dr Stein again and he is sending me to see a neurologist at Charing Cross Hospital. I do take it seriously because it is really incapacitating me.

Joshua took me to County Hall, where there were about 1,000 people from the People's March for Jobs, sitting in the bright sunshine. I spoke and paid a warm tribute to the *Morning Star* for their support.

From 3.30 to 4 I stood outside St Stephen's entrance to the House, meeting the marchers. Some of them are worried because when the march is over they will be just unemployed people again.

Wednesday 3 June
Shadow Cabinet at 5, which was sensational. I didn't make very full notes but I have got a rough idea of what happened. By 5.20 we had come to 'any other business' and Michael said, 'I want to refer to the fact that, despite the Shadow Cabinet decision to abstain on the defence debate, a Tribune amendment was tabled. Tony Benn signed it, and voted against the Government. I take this as a criticism of me, and it makes a shambles, and I would like to ask him if he has anything to say.'

I answered, 'I think it would be more sensible to recognise that there really is here a very big constitutional issue, a conflict between two concepts of collective responsibility: one is the idea that the Shadow Cabinet can have collective responsibility; the other is that the collective responsibility is to the Party and Party policy and Conference policy, and I think that that is the way it should be looked at. As far as collective responsibility itself is concerned, in the House of Commons on 16 June 1977 Mrs Thatcher asked Jim Callaghan a question about collective responsibility and he replied, "Yes, I certainly think that the doctrine should apply except in cases where I announce that it does not." That is really what it is about. It is entirely arbitrary. It is seen as the power of the Prime Minister or the Leader of the Party. It has got no constitutional foundation. It isn't any good saying that this can be left to the Shadow Cabinet to decide whether or not they will do it.'

Michael said, 'Well, I now wish to read a statement that I am going to have published. There has been a great deal of suspicion and it is Tony's fault. There have also been a lot of leaks.'

I interrupted. 'May I make one thing absolutely clear. I know people in the Shadow Cabinet don't like me writing notes but I have never described what has happened in the Shadow Cabinet; and I know that other members of the Shadow Cabinet do. I want it to be absolutely established, whether people believe it or not, that I have never given a briefing on the Shadow Cabinet.'

Well, Michael then read this 25-page statement which showed he was in an absolute panic. 'In view of what he has said and done over recent weeks . . . I have told Tony Benn that, in my judgement, his only course now is to stand against me . . .'

He read it right through, and I won't repeat it here in full, but it was about how I was questioning his allegiance to Party policy, how the guidelines on collective responsibility were clear – he went through it all. It had obviously been drafted by Denis Healey, Peter Shore, John Silkin and Neil Kinnock. The main emphasis was that I must stand against him as Leader and let the Movement decide.

When he had finished, I asked, 'May I comment briefly?'

He said I could.

'I certainly welcome the suggestion that we have a discussion with the PLP. I welcome many of the policy points that are included in the statement, but I hope you won't publish it. First of all, it was written before you heard me today, and, secondly, it is very personal and it will confuse people. Two months ago you said I shouldn't stand against Denis, and now you say I *should* stand against *you*. But of course *you* stood against Denis. I really think it would be inadvisable to publish it.'

Michael said, 'On the deputy leadership, I warned you, and I shall make proposals for collective responsibility in the future. It is a question of trust and I have been humiliated.'

There was a lot of banging on the table by Shadow Cabinet people, and

John Silkin looked at me like a cat about to spring on a mouse; the hatred there was unbelievable.

Went to the Tea Room and showed Dennis Skinner the statement. He said as a joke, 'Perhaps you *should* stand against Michael, and John Silkin would beat Denis Healey.'

I staggered back to listen to the 9 o'clock news. I could hardly walk; I was pulling myself along by both arms in the corridor. It was banner headlines on the news. I rang Frances Morrell, who said, 'Don't get into a great argument with Michael, but you must let it be known you are not going to take up his offer.' So I asked her to ring the Press Association, which she did, and later I confirmed that it was authentic. Then I listened to the 10 o'clock news, which was all about it, but as a matter of fact I had established my position so clearly that I didn't really have to reply to Michael's arguments. The only thing was, I did have to say what I would be doing.

Caroline and I went and had a meal, and I drafted a statement on the following lines. 'I voted for Michael Foot when he stood for the leadership of the Party against Denis Healey last November. I continue to support him in that role, and there is no question of my standing against him for the leadership. I shall also continue to campaign for the deputy leadership in support of the policies of the Party as agreed at successive Conferences and without any references to personalities. I appeal to the whole Movement to back up those policies.'

Michael was on 'The World Tonight' interviewed by Anthony Howard for twenty-two minutes and it was the most muddled interview. 'Tony is in a difficulty', and 'Lenin said this' and 'Trotsky said that'. He sounded like Ramsay MacDonald in his rambling days.

I gave Chris Moncrieff of the PA my statement, having checked it with one or two people. Mik thought I should say, 'Unlike most other members of the Shadow Cabinet, I voted for Michael Foot.' But I thought that was silly.

When we got home, Hilary and Joshua turned up, and the family are rallying round like anything.

Thursday 4 June

I got up at about 4 am. I couldn't sleep, my legs were hurting, and so I worked for a couple of hours in case they keep me in hospital. Caroline has been looking in the medical dictionary and has found an illness that corresponds to all my symptoms.

Took Caroline breakfast just as a sort of final gesture, and outside the front door were a couple of camera and radio units and a lot of photographers. Hilary turned up early, went and bought all the papers, and there was a hysterical headline on every one, such as 'Fight Me Dares Foot'. Hilary put my bags in the car and then drove it round to the front door.

Hilary drove me to the Charing Cross Hospital and I was taken to see Dr Clifford Rose, who examined me. I hadn't got reflexes in my legs or arms.

He told me, 'I think I know what this is. If this was only a medical consideration, I would recommend you came into hospital at once.'

I said, 'Well, I'm perfectly happy to do that because I am simply incapacitated.'

So I was taken to the tenth floor and put in a single side-room. Hilary and I drafted a statement, which I checked with Dr Clifford Rose, saying that I had been admitted to hospital for tests for a suspected viral infection. The media then descended *en masse* on the hospital. The security people came and asked what they should do, so I said I wasn't going to see them.

I had my little television and I watched the various programmes and the discussion arising out of the Foot proposal, which was the big news story. What I need is a rest. I am not saying that it caused the viral infection, but I have been grossly overdoing it for ages, and a rest now comes at a convenient time because I am not really needed for the campaign. The issues have got across, and if I take a couple of weeks off I can come back whenever I like, provided I'm not thought to be unfit in a major way.

A Mars Bar from the Tony Benn fan club was delivered by two punks, and flowers and telegrams and letters poured in – including a letter from the Joint Shop Stewards Committee at the hospital asking if I would like to address their meeting on Wednesday, which I will do if I am still here.

Friday 5 June
I had all sorts of neurological tests today, and it may be necessary to have a lumbar puncture. Dr Rose was in yesterday morning, then Dr Kapidoo, who is the senior registrar, then Dr Clive Handler, who is the neurologist. Dr Lawrence comes and spends a lot of time getting my medical history and testing my reflexes. The nurses are extremely nice, and all the cleaners are members of NUPE. I received lots of flowers, so I put some in the day room, some in the cleaners' room, and gave some to the nurses.

Tony Benn's illness was eventually diagnosed as Guillain-Barré Syndrome, an attack on the nervous system starting from the feet, which can be fatal. He stayed in hospital from 6–17 June making retrospective notes on 20 June. While he was in Charing Cross hospital, the Sun *amongst others attempted by various unscrupulous means to get into his room.*

Saturday 20 June
On 17 June, our thirty-second wedding anniversary, I was discharged, and Hilary and Caroline arrived; we left to an onslaught of press, television and radio. We came out with Sister Ross and I gave an interview.

It was so lovely to be home, and Caroline had organised things so that the front room next to the bedroom will be my temporary office, where I can sit and work. When I got back I found Julie with Jon Lansman and Nigel Williamson, who are helping with the campaign. I brought home five sacks of unanswered mail.

Wednesday 24 June

I can start working at about 11 in the morning, though I have to rest in the afternoon, and it's still painful to walk. I'm reading *Red Shelley* by Paul Foot and am enjoying it very much indeed. The only book I have read about Shelley is *Ariel* by André Maurois, and that was when I was a student. What Paul Foot has shown beyond doubt is that Shelley was a genuine romantic revolutionary who was a republican, an atheist, a leveller and a feminist, and that he was the great inspiration of the Chartists and the working-class movement until all that was forgotten by poets who managed to suppress the political Shelley and emphasise his more precious poetry. It is a brilliant book, scholarly and very readable, and Paul Foot, whom I have met only once, added a note when he sent it to me: 'Just to show that not everybody from the *Daily Mirror* or the Foot family is hostile.' Very nice of him, and I wrote and thanked him.

Wednesday 29 July

Sat and watched the royal wedding on TV. There were perhaps two million people out in London, and this tremendous ceremonial display was watched throughout the world by 750 million people – without any doubt the biggest television audience that had ever seen anything. The image presented to the rest of the world was of a Britain about as socially advanced as France before the French Revolution! We are slipping back to eighteenth-century politics. We've got to fight like anything to recover the position that we had even in 1945. I had that feeling most strongly. It was feudal propaganda, turning citizens into subjects.

As an utterly convinced republican, I believe that a monarchical system of government is fundamentally undemocratic, and that the powers of the monarchy have got to be taken away. But republicanism frequently ignores the legal and constitutional powers of the monarchy and concentrates on attacking the royal family itself. Anyway, I've got my first reference to the monarchy in my book *Arguments for Democracy*.

Today the press were outside my door all day. They knocked on it once an hour from 9.30 to 4.30. I presume it was the *Sun* or the *Daily Mail*, a marvellous example of harassment.

Friday 25 September

The Times had a profile of the candidates in the deputy leader contest, and under me the caption included some absurd claims about my owning a farm in Essex and having a trust in the 'tax haven' of Bermuda.

Well, Julian Haviland rang me a couple of days ago and asked me about my financial position, and I told him I had inherited shares in Benn Brothers, the publishers, had bought a house in London which cost me £4,600 and had a house in Stansgate, Essex, bought by my father for £1,500 before the war. I also told him that I had never bought or sold a share in my life and I had some earnings from freelance work. He said, 'Well, we're doing a bit of financial background on each candidate.' *The Times* never mentioned that Healey had earnings from the *Daily Express* or that John Silkin had declared that his average private income over the last ten years had been £15,900 per year.

I decided to write to *The Times*, drawing attention to the lie they had printed in August 1977 about my children receiving private medical treatment. I rang them later and was told my letter had been set up in type and was before the Editor, Harold Evans, for approval.

Saturday 26 September – Labour Party Conference, Brighton

Got up about 6.30, very tired. *The Times* printed my letter and apologised, so I've caught *The Times* out on two lies now, the 1977 story and now this.

Packed up for the Brighton Conference. What an incredible time! It is pouring with rain but I am really looking forward to it and enjoying it.

We packed up all our stuff in tons of bags – video recorder, Joshua's VDU, etc – and we got to Brighton at 11.45 and found one of the London MEPs, Richard Balfe, and his wife Vivien and others had set up a marvellous office in the Grand Hotel with an electric typewriter, photocopier, radio, the lot!

Joshua was working on his computer and if the T&G and NUPE vote for me, then I'm home comfortably, even with forty abstentions and only 480 constituencies. If NUPE vote for Healey but the T&G vote for me, I could just win if I could scrabble together a few more MPs and a few more constituencies. If NUPE abstain, I could probably still win on forty abstentions and 480 constituencies, or it could be neck and neck. So there is clearly a sense of confidence about it which I have never had before.

Agreed to meet the campaign committee at 8.30 tomorrow morning. The word is going round now that we are going to win; I think confidence is the major factor, particularly with MPs, and that is what is going to decide the issue now. NUPE is in the balance. I don't know.

Sunday 27 September

The day of the election for the Deputy Leader. I didn't have time to read the papers. There was no word from Michael Foot, though I had expected there would be. The campaign committee had a meeting at 8.30 and we agreed on a last-minute leaflet.

There were photographers everywhere.

We went to the CLPD meeting in the Metropole Hotel at which Dennis Skinner made a brilliant speech. When we went in we heard that NUPE had decided to vote for Denis Healey – which most people thought was the finish of us, but we knew it wasn't.

Caroline drafted with me a statement for release after the result.

We went over to the conference hall at 5 pm. The press were hysterical, people were cheering and shouting, and, as I got my papers for the first ballot, we heard a rumour that the T&G, who were voting for Silkin in the first ballot, had in fact decided to abstain in the second. Well, that was a body blow! Joshua immediately worked out some computer predictions on the basis of an abstention from the TGWU on the second.

Anyway, we went in, and I was prepared for a massive defeat and was feeling pretty gloomy, but I tried to look as cheerful as I could on the platform. The Conference began with the usual address by the Mayor, the Chairman's address, the Conference Arrangements Committee report – during which some women made a terrific protest to get positive discrimination for women debated. Then the Chairman, Alex Kitson, took a show of hands on smoking, and that was banned from the conference hall.

At the end of that, the first ballot result was announced, and it showed precisely what Joshua had predicted – Healey 44.536 per cent (Joshua's figure, 45), me 36.639 per cent (Joshua's, 37.5), Silkin, with the T&G, 18 per cent. Rumours then began circulating on the platform that the T&G *had* decided to vote for me on the second ballot – which they did – and Joshua's prediction then was that Healey would get 51.3 and I would get 48.7 per cent.

The second ballot was called immediately, and while it was being counted there was a debate on South Africa. I got three separate messages that I had won, and finally, after the address by the Secretary of the Socialist International, the result was announced: Denis Healey got 50.426 and I got 49.547 per cent, which was an absolute whisker's difference.

I came off the platform, and all the press were there and I had a job saying anything. Then I picked up Caroline and we walked with a barrage of press and masses of cheering and pushing back to the hotel, where people cheered in the lobby and all the way up the stairs.

We had sandwiches and then decided to go out to the *London Labour Briefing* meeting at the Queen's Hotel, and it was packed out. I spoke briefly. Came out, and I declined to comment any further. Then Caroline and I walked to the fish and chip shop and the media followed us in there. We came back to the hotel and slowly we briefed ourselves on what had actually happened.

It has been a staggering result with all the media against us, the most violent attacks by the Shadow Cabinet, the full intervention of Michael, the abstention of a group of Tribune Group MPs who, in the end, turned out to be the people who carried the day – Stan Orme, Martin O'Neill, Neil Kinnock, Jeff Rooker, Joe Ashton, Tom Pendry. We got within 0.8 per cent of victory, and it was the best possible result, because if I had won by 0.8 per cent people would have shouted 'cheat'. It only requires four or six Labour MPs to join the SDP for Healey's majority to disappear, and then he will hold the post but not have the authority.

So sitting on the bathroom floor of the hotel, so as not to disturb Caroline, I bring to an end the report on the first electoral college ever held to allow the members of the Party to vote for the Deputy Leader of the Labour Party, and it has been far more successful than I could possibly have dreamed at the beginning.

Wednesday 7 October
Sally went in to University College Hospital and at 3.42 gave birth to a boy, Michael Graham Clark Benn – my first grandson. Hilary was there, and Caroline visited the baby in the afternoon.

Went to see Mother, who is now a great-grandmother. Came home and there was Hilary and 'Uncle' Joshua, and we were all very excited.

11

1981–83

Sunday 11 October

I read the typescript of Chris Mullin's new novel, *A Very British Coup*, the story of how a Labour government elected in 1989 is brought down by the security services.

Harry Perkins, the Prime Minister, is a steelworker who drinks tea from a mug with a tea bag and was a former Secretary of State for Energy who had rows with his civil servants about nuclear reactors. To cut a long story short, he is brought down by a scandal. It's very well done. I gave Chris a couple of hints and he's going to change a few details.

Caroline and I went for a walk.

Thursday 15 October
I went to the hospital to see Dr Clifford Rose, who told me that the electrical tests in July did show that there had been serious damage to my sensory nerves and it would be up to two years before they would know the extent of the recovery. I am beginning to realise that I may be handicapped for life. I would like to be able to run and jump about before I die but I've got to face the possibility that I never will. It was a bit of a shock, though I had guessed it.

In the evening Caroline and I went to Hilary's to visit little Michael. Hilary put him in my arms and I just looked at him for about half an hour. I am so thrilled with him.

Tuesday 3 November
Went to the Shadow Cabinet in the evening, and I must say I do find it an absolute nightmare. Sixty members of the Manifesto Group, the group of right-wing Labour MPs, have said that unless the Militant Tendency are expelled they will leave the Party. Well, candidly, if I had to trade the YS for some of them, I wouldn't be sorry to see them go.

Saturday 7 November
To Birmingham for a meeting and came back in the train with Fenner Brockway and Joan Lestor, who were also speaking there.

'As I get older I get philosophical,' Fenner said. 'There only ever was a tiny percentage of the Parliamentary Party who were socialists – thirty before the First World War, fifty in the days of the ILP and now probably fifty in the PLP. So we have to see ourselves as being a permanent minority in the sense that you never get a majority of people who convert to socialism. But the minority can offer leadership to the rest because the characteristic of the Right is that they are bankrupt. Their main concern is to fight off socialism, but the middle ground will swing with the victors. So if we did get a proper left leadership, which is not inconceivable with the electoral college, then we would go from being a quarter of the PLP to more than 50 per cent.'

I found that comforting. Fenner is a shrewd old man and I can't overemphasise my affection for him.

Monday 9 November
To the Organisation Committee, and we had a long discussion on the Croydon by-election defeat.

John Golding said that, wherever he went, the reason for the defeat was given as Benn and Livingstone.

Ron Hayward remarked, 'PLP morale is at a low level and the bitter attacks make it worse. The SDP are traitors, but, on the other side, when I went to a Cardiff rally and read a three-sentence message from Tony Benn who was lying ill in hospital, everyone on the platform cut me dead for doing so.'

Denis Healey said, 'Morale is very bad, the NEC has caused it, and *London Labour Briefing* calls for "no pity" on reselection.'

Neil Kinnock complained, 'Labour's internal war blanks out our policy. The next Election is lost and I will have wasted all my time on education. We are in big trouble. Unity is the only basis. Some people want us to lose the next Election, but fifty years of Callaghan is better than one year of Thatcher.' (That is really an indication that Neil Kinnock, in certain circumstances, would favour an alliance with the SDP rather than have a Thatcher government next time round.) He said, 'I am a unilateralist. We have got alternatives but people are deaf to them because of what has happened. I abstained in the deputy leadership election to give me a platform from which to say what I want.'

Tuesday 10 November
Went into the debate on North Sea oil at 3.30, and Merlyn Rees opened. I was in the debate most of the time, and Mother and Stephen came to listen. Towards the end, at 9, I wound up. I had determined that I would clearly get into Hansard the full range of Party policy: that we would renationalise without compensation; that we would take BP into 100 per cent ownership; that we would move towards 100 per cent ownership of oil; that we would use the revenues and other money for the alternative economic strategy, industry and the public services; that we would have planned trade and public ownership; that we would withdraw from the Common Market, and so on. When I made my speech the House was packed, and it went down like a bomb. When I came to renationalisation without compensation Lawson got up and asked me to clarify it, which I did. But when I sat down Michael Foot was absolutely fuming and Peter Shore was boiling like a kettle. I said, 'Well, it's all Party policy.' Actually my side gave me quite a cheer when I sat down, but that is clearly going to be a big issue.

Wednesday 11 November
Shadow Cabinet at 5 was a long and painful meeting. Michael Foot said he wished to make a statement and he had it all typed out, exactly as on 3 June this year. He said he wanted to make further reference to the question of unity. He then read out from the statement that dissent had distracted the Party from its real work and that the Social Democratic Party was 'our own creation'. He went on, 'After Brighton, I made an appeal that Denis Healey and Tony would serve in the Shadow Cabinet. I supported Tony on the NEC chairmanships. Tony was a party to the document agreed by the Shadow Cabinet on the renationalisation of North Sea oil and gas. The NEC on 28 October used the same wording, so there is unanimity in the light of Conference decisions. This is a clear illustration of the need for

collective Shadow Cabinet responsibility which is not a fuddy-duddy old rule but necessary to guard against conflict. With his speech yesterday Tony has brilliantly succeeded in throwing the Party into a fresh internal crisis and the whole responsibility rests with him. If Tony goes on in this way, his presence in this Shadow Cabinet will make it unworkable and our conduct will be a shambles. I would not and could not vote for him for Shadow Cabinet in these circumstances though I still hope he will stand on the terms I have set out. But I must make it clear that the main responsibility rests on Tony.'

I replied to Michael that there was no reason why I shouldn't have quoted in Parliament a Conference resolution and, as to the Shadow Cabinet elections, I intended to stand and the only way we could get unity was round Party policy.

Michael then said, 'On the oil compensation issue, there has been a change of attitude now. Why didn't you support Merlyn Rees in the debate? The Tory press had a field day. Common sense and comradeship would have pointed to the need not to do what you did. The Shadow Cabinet can't be run on a system of having debates in Parliament about what the policy of the PLP should be.'

Merlyn Rees spoke next. 'All right, the policy on compensation was decided at Conference, but Sam McCluskie changed it last year. The Shadow Cabinet will have to take collective decisions. At the Shadow Cabinet, Tony said nothing against a statement we issued on oil. I did not know what Tory was going to say in the debate but he made me look very foolish. The morale of the PLP and the constituencies is very low.'

Stan Orme commented, 'I heard both Merlyn and Tony yesterday and Tony was excellent until the last five minutes of his speech. The Shadow Cabinet must stick together. Labour MPs are shattered, and it shows the danger we are in.'

Neil Kinnock said he was a unilateralist, so he had been in the minority for years. He then delivered a lecture on Party unity and said, 'Our electoral standing is not due to ourselves. Tony, you are essential', and something like 'I address your conscience. You are being used by others. You are the most important single member of the Party.'

It was agreed we would come back to it next week.

The mood of the meeting was horrible, the atmosphere icy, and Michael was angry. I am used to it now. The things they said were extreme, but of course they are frantic. After that, it was quite clear that that was the end of me.

Wednesday 23 November
At 2 I went to Room W4, off Westminster Hall, for the first meeting of the Campaign Group, which has been constituted from the old deputy leadership campaign committee. Last night I had drafted a note saying:

'The Campaign Group, open to any member of the PLP, meets on Monday, Tuesday and Wednesday at 2 pm, and at 5 pm on Thursday with the following agenda each day: (1) Today's news; (2) Today's Commons business; (3) Liaison with the Labour Movement; (4) Business for the PLP; (5) Future work; (6) Media.'

We are in fact a different type of group from the Tribune Group, which is strictly parliamentary and doesn't have links outside, is closed to anyone who isn't a Member and only meets once a week.

Friday 4 December

Papers full of Foot's attack on Peter Tatchell, the Labour candidate for Bermondsey, and 'extremism' in the Party. The whole machinery of vilification is being set in motion again. Michael has made a tragic mistake and constituency Parties just won't go along with it. He now has to lie on the bed that he has made. I know he's trying to clean up the Party so that the SDP will rejoin, and that is the strategy of disaster. We'll have to go through a difficult time but at the end we shall come out much stronger.

At 6 I watched the news, and Peter Tatchell was interviewed. The reporter was completely unable to fault his arguments. He wouldn't criticise Michael Foot and he said he looked forward to meeting him.

Sunday 6 December

Caroline has persuaded me that not only should Party unity take precedence at the moment but that I am so damaged by my singlehanded combat against Denis Healey and Michael Foot that I'm a bit of an embarrassment to the Left. So I shall pull out a bit and see how things develop.

Monday 7 December

I went to the Organisation Committee of the NEC at 2.30 and the room was absolutely packed to discuss Peter Tatchell, the candidate in Bermondsey, who has condoned 'extra-parliamentary activity'.

Neil Kinnock said it was all a matter of political judgement. 'We were all extra-parliamentary – Michael was too – but the question is: are we talking of extra-parliamentary or anti-parliamentary behaviour?' It was so pompous, and I completely lost track of his argument. He went on interminably, as he always does, and got warmly cheered by Russell Tuck and Shirley Summerskill. You can't say more than that.

Eric agreed to amend his motion from 'investigate the Bermondsey Party' to 'report on the situation' and to shift it to the NEC. That suited me fine.

Kinnock droned on. He said we were really deciding the direction of the Labour Party, and we had to draw a line when candidates weakened the Party – Tatchell did weaken the Party and he did not have the welfare of the Party at heart. Russell agreed with Neil. We should endorse Michael, not

Peter Tatchell. Then someone added that the fact that Tatchell was a homosexual made him less inclined to support him.

Denis Healey thought the constitutional priority was that we had a right and a duty to judge whether candidates were suitable. However, no investigation was needed.

Michael Foot spoke, and more or less reiterated what he had said earlier. We must give him some leverage because the SDP would use it nationally. 'Many people within the Party on the left, right and centre were saying, "If you don't speak out we will", and, if I hadn't, people would have said I was a coward. Tatchell will not withdraw, and therefore I shall take the matter to the NEC.'

He gave the game away when he said he was pressed by MPs – no doubt he felt that if he hadn't acted they would have joined the SDP.

In the end, the substantive motion that we didn't endorse Tatchell was carried by 12 to 7, and will go forward to NEC.

Thursday 10 December
Jim Callaghan has a centre-page spread in the *Mirror* arguing that Labour must expel Militant, prepare for a coalition with the SDP after the Election and consider proportional representation. So that's Roy Jenkins, Jim and Ted Heath all contemplating a coalition; this is the beginning of the National Government which was a disaster in 1931 and will be this time. At least it's out in the open now, contrary to what Foot and Healey say. I know that Healey's research assistant told someone that you couldn't attack the SDP because we will be in with them after the Election.

Friday 25 December
Christmas Day. Caroline had bronchitis and was very poorly. Josh got up, and we began with a row, because I went down to my basement and found the washing-machine was leaking and the floor was awash with water, with my papers on the floor.

Later Val rang to say that Mark Arnold-Foster had died at lunchtime.

Monday 28 December
Caroline a bit better and eating. She slept a bit. We are both very physically and mentally exhausted.

Thursday 31 December
Lovely sunny day. In the evening we set off for Stansgate, arrived just before midnight, and sat and talked as the year came to a close.

Politically it has been the most dramatic year of my life – the deputy leadership campaign. Was it right? It's still arguable, but I think it was. It was also a year in which the Party became more politically educated than ever before, and a year in which the policies were agreed.

I became very ill with the Guillain-Barré syndrome, and it still affects me in that my legs are a bit wobbly and my fingers are not perfect. It will be two years before I am completely recovered.

Both of us were active politically. Caroline continued to work with the SEA and produced the Voluntary Schools Report, was involved with the TUC Education Alliance, with UNESCO, to which she was reappointed. She edited *Socialism and Education* and *Comprehensive Education*.

I think now – and my friends agree – that we should fight the General Election on a status quo agreement, whereby the policy is agreed, the constitutional changes are accepted, the Left holds off on further constitutional change, the purges are dropped, and the leadership is not challenged.

In early January 1982 a joint meeting of the National Executive and the PLP, and Trade Unionists for a Labour Victory (TULV) was held at the ASTMS country club at Bishops Stortford. Tony Benn circulated a paper 'Working for Unity', to the members of the NEC and to the trade union general secretaries, outlining the basis for a 'truce' within the Party. There was reached a tacit understanding that the next General Election could be fought under the existing leadership (ie Michael Foot and Denis Healey), with a manifesto based upon the 1981 Conference decisions, a moratorium on constitutional changes, and a halt to any purge of left individuals or groups.

As a result of the discussions over the two days, David Basnett was able to announce that 'peace had broken out' in the Labour Party, which was much trumpeted by the political commentators.

Sunday 10 January 1982
I had the first of my home meetings for some time with Norman Atkinson, Tony Banks, Vladi Derer, Jon Lansman, Ken Livingstone, Michael Meacher, Frances Morrell, Chris Mullin, Reg Race, Nigel Williamson, Audrey Wise and Valerie Wise.

There was a very good paper by Chris Mullin called 'The Basis for a Truce'. We had a long discussion that went on till about 10.45.

Williamson said there was a fear on the left that there had been a sellout, and Frances agreed it was a big change.

Jon Lansman said the Left was at a low ebb now and therefore we wouldn't lose by a truce – it was the best way to protect our gains.

Audrey Wise resented the idea of a deal or a truce and said we couldn't be private in any sense; we had to activate the rank and file to defend its rights.

Monday 11 January
Bitterly cold. The country is under the worst conditions within living memory.

Monday 18 January
Travelled back from Bristol, and a message came from the drivers asking if

I'd like to travel on the footplate. So I went along to their cabin and sat in a very comfortable chair and flew to Bath at about 90 miles an hour in this new 125, through the Brunel tunnel. I got out at Chippenham, went back to my compartment and worked on some papers.

Tuesday 2 February

I went to a press conference at the Commons to launch the report published today on the real cost of nuclear power. The conference was organised by the Committee for the Study of the Economics of Nuclear Electricity. It was packed with authors and scientists of nuclear power, like Colin Sweet, Professor J. Jeffrey, Edward Goldsmith and Sir Kelvin Spencer; David Penhaligon was in the chair. I sat at the back, but Kelvin Spencer kept insisting on bringing me in; I must say the old boy was marvellous. He said he had read all my books and asked me what was happening in the Labour Party now.

The meeting raised all the fundamental democratic questions about open government and information, chairmen of nationalised industries and the accountability problems of controlling technology.

Thursday 18 February

Home from an exhausting three-day trip to the United States. It was worthwhile – it is good to go to the US on occasions.

Reagan has made a tremendous impact on American politics. He is not quite like Mrs Thatcher, because he presides like a monarch over American society, whereas she is a leader and a teacher of a much more formidable kind. They have both won the battle of ideas, because the old New Dealers capitulated as the Old Left did in Britain, but in the course of fighting against that old decaying corporatist, liberal, capitalist structure a great generation of really tough people was bred, and they are now taking over and carrying through a counter-revolution. They are serious people to fight. We have to breed, by discussion and struggle, a group who are equally capable of doing what we want to do; the present leadership of the Democratic Party is no use at all. Edward Kennedy is a completely empty vessel who thinks of politics as a management job without any ideology.

America is very conscious of its fall in world power, and that is what makes it so very dangerous.

Tuesday 2 March

Norman Atkinson told me that Rupert Murdoch had had lunch with Mrs Thatcher no less than three times last week. He had heard that from Ian Gow, Mrs Thatcher's PPS, and he had the impression that the Tories were panic-striken that *The Times* might come out for the SDP. So they were offering Murdoch all possible help in return for support for the Tory Party.

Monday 22 March

To London Airport to get the flight to Glasgow, and who should I see at the airport but David and Debbie Owen going to Hillhead to campaign in the by-election for Roy Jenkins, who is standing as the SDP–Liberal Alliance candidate. Then George Brown came in and headed for the bar. So sitting in the airport were three people who had been Cabinet Ministers together at different times, and two of them had defected and were going to speak for Roy Jenkins. Brown and Jenkins – two former Deputy Leaders of the Labour Party.

I was met at Glasgow and taken to the Hillhead Labour Party committee rooms, where I had a cup of tea and a bun. Then I was taken into a little room in an old Co-op funeral parlour where the candidate, David Wiseman, and others were gathered – a panelled room where no doubt grieving Glaswegians were handed the bill for burying their relatives. Helen Liddell, the Secretary of the Scottish Council of the Labour Party, said they were frightened about my coming – Helen is very right-wing. They kept bringing up 'extremism' in the Party and said, 'Your Marx Memorial Lecture didn't help.'

I went to the meeting attended by 1,500–2,000 people. The SDP had put out a little red-baiting, McCarthyite-type leaflet referring to my lecture.

Thursday 25 March

Was picked up at 10.45 pm to go to the ITN studios to comment on Roy Jenkins's victory in the by-election.

Thursday 1 April

Met Graham Allen, Bob Cryer and Willy McKelvey, and for forty minutes we cried in each other's beer, because after Hillhead we are very depressed. The Party isn't doing well, the Left has lost the impetus, and the Right hasn't grasped it because they haven't anything to offer, but they are benefiting from the defeat of the Labour Party.

Friday 2 April

Today the Argentinian Navy were sent to the Falkland Islands, thousands of troops appear to have landed and overwhelmed the British garrison of seventy marines and a population of 1,800. The Government's defence policy has been completely shown up – not that I would favour sending the British forces in, because it's a colony we grabbed years ago from somebody and we have no right to it; neither has Argentina, though it is closer to South America. Some 1,800 British settlers do not constitute a domestic population whose views can be taken seriously, or rather whose views can be allowed to lead us into war. But of course the real interest there is the oil. There is oil around the islands, and Caroline pointed out that we should have done a deal years ago. Take the oil, divide it into two – say Argentina can have half the oil and overall theoretical sovereignty, while we would retain the administration and the population would be given shares in our oil. But that isn't the way these things actually work.

We have the Polaris submarine and nuclear hardware but absolutely no capacity to fight a war at that range.

Saturday 3 April
My fifty-seventh birthday.

The Falkland Islands is the big news.

The House was in the grip of jingoism. John Silkin and John Nott made very poor speeches, Nott trying to turn it into a party attack, which didn't go down very well. I came away full of gloom because it is obvious that a huge fleet of forty or so warships will set sail for the Falklands, arrive three weeks later, probably be attacked by the Argentinians, and then there will be a major battle. The Falklanders are in effect hostages, and I don't think the US will support us, since the last thing they want is a big British fleet in the South Atlantic overturning the Argentinian dictatorship. And that's what will happen, because General Galtieri, the Argentinian President who attacked the islands to divert attention from the fall in living standards in Argentina, could himself be deposed. The Americans don't want that, since the whole of Latin America would be set ablaze. Very difficult.

Monday 5 April
To the Tribune Group to discuss the Falklands. Stuart Holland said the real interest was the £5 billion investment in Argentina, and Lord Carrington and other Ministers had resigned because they disagreed with Thatcher's policy. He said there was high drama in the Tory Party about it.

Robin Cook pointed out that the Argentine Navy possessed British missiles and ships, and that nuclear weapons were useless. The Government had blundered, the position couldn't be reversed, and the Falklanders wouldn't want us back.

Mik said there was a danger of our being carried away. In the long term, was a Labour government committed to the return of the Falklands? A show of force was no use because we wouldn't be able to hold it afterwards. We could sink the Argentine Navy, raze Buenos Aires, sign a death warrant for the Falklanders and alienate the world, or we could evacuate the islands, compensate the islanders and have the fleet on standby.

I believed that it was a complex question about the remnants of empire, that we had to be realistic and recognise that the islands were indefensible. As with Suez, we would find that the Americans didn't support us in the end because they had great interests in Latin America. From their point of view the Anglo–American alliance was less important than their control over the whole of Latin America, and jingoism couldn't help us. We should take a clear and united stand condemning the Argentine Government for their invasion, holding Her Majesty's Government responsible for their failure to provide minimum military protection, believing that the prime concern of the Government should now be to secure the future of the Falklands under an administration that would safeguard their interests. We should decline to support the Government in its preparations for war against Argentina, a war which would cost many lives and threaten the life, safety and security of the Falklanders. We should urge the UN to take responsibility for seeking a settlement that would meet their needs, secured if necessary by the presence of a UN peacekeeping force while international negotiations took place.

Stan Orme agreed, arguing that we must fight Fascism and help the Argentine working class. A British presence may help to destabilise Argentina.

Afterwards I saw Norman St John Stevas in the corridor, and I asked him why Peter Carrington had resigned as Foreign Secretary today, together with all the Foreign Office Ministers. Did he think it was because Carrington didn't agree with Mrs Thatcher's policy? He said there could be a number of factors involved, but perhaps one of them was that he couldn't stand 'that woman' a moment longer!

Thursday 8 April
Chris Mullin came for a talk from 11.30 till 3.30. He's just been appointed Editor of *Tribune* to replace Dick Clements. *Tribune* has now admitted that circulation is down to 7,800; there are two months' unpaid print bills, and the whole paper has just been killed by a completely weak political line. I think now we are going to see some big changes. We discussed various ideas and plans. The paper will have a cutting edge, and that's important.

Monday 12 April
Easter Monday. The family watched Michael's bathtime; he was lying kicking and smiling.

I had a temperature of 102 and went to bed later. Falklands still dominant but no shooting yet.

Thursday 15 April
Chris Mullin rang to tell me the *Daily Star* had a heading 'Whose Side Are They On?' with pictures of the ten of us opposed to the Task Force, implying our treachery. It is bound to happen; you couldn't expect otherwise at this early stage of jingoistic fervour.

Friday 16 April
A very painful cough. My temperature was down to 94 degrees. Lay in bed all day – Falklands again dominating the news. Didn't feel at all well.

Saturday 17 April
This morning Caroline took me to the doctor, who diagnosed viral

pneumonia and put me on antibiotics and cough linctus. I felt very tired, and it was horrible to be stuck in my room on such a beautiful day.

Tuesday 20 April
The press covered my visit to the hospital, saying I was seriously ill. I feel a bit lonely at the moment.

Friday 23 April
Masses of letters pouring in about Argentina; the overwhelming majority in support of my position. There are a handful of really vulgar and abusive ones. I'm certain that a majority of the British people are against the war with Argentina but the media are preventing that view becoming apparent.

To Croydon for the funeral of Terry Parry, General Secretary of the Fire Brigades' Union, a very popular man. A fireman picked me up and took me to the entrance of the crematorium, and the fire brigade was out in force – hundreds of them – as Terry's body was carried on a fire engine covered with flowers and a Union Jack. Bill Jones, Walt Greendale, Moss Evans, Clive Jenkins, Len Murray, Jack Jones, Hugh Scanlon, Gordon McLennan, Mick McGahey, Jimmy Milne, Enoch Humphreys, Ken Cameron, Jim Mortimer – the Labour Movement's leaders were there in force.

The service, which was conducted by Bruce Kent, was really moving. Bruce said he had never known Terry Parry, but Terry had requested that he conduct the service. Jack Jones made an excellent speech, Len Murray not such a good one. A friend sang 'The Impossible Dream', and I'm afraid I sat there with tears rolling down my cheeks.

Afterwards I talked to fire officers from all over the country. I was invited to go in their coach to Crystal Palace Football Club for a little party.

Wednesday 28 April
An exhausting day. I got another 400 letters today, making 2,500 this week. Overwhelmingly supportive – I suppose coming primarily from middle-class people. Some white feathers and vulgar abuse. The mail is the biggest I've ever had.

Tuesday 4 May
To the House and heard Thatcher at Prime Minster's Questions. Tam Dalyell scored a direct hit by asking, 'Did the Prime Minister herself, personally and explicitly, authorise the firing of the torpedoes on the *General Belgrano*?' Thatcher said yes, in effect, she had the Task Force under political control.

Pym made a statement about his visit to the UN and looked uncomfortable, like Thatcher. I think they're beginning to worry in the Cabinet because of public disgust at the loss of life on the *Belgrano*.

I was called by the Speaker at the very end of Pym's interrogation, and I got in a pretty good point: 'Had the Foreign Secretary's attention been drawn to the fact that in the *Sunday Times* a public-opinion poll showed that 6 out of 10 people in Britain were not prepared to see one serviceman's life, or a Falkland Islander's life, put at risk, and that such a majority in Britain will not be rejoicing with the Prime Minister at the loss of life when the ship was torpedoed without a declaration of war well outside the Exclusion Zone? Will the Foreign Secretary take account of the desire for peace in Britain by agreeing to a ceasefire and to the transfer at once to the United Nations of sovereignty of the Falkland Islands and its administration pending a settlement under UN auspices?'

The House exploded at my comment 'not be *rejoicing* with the Prime Minister' – the Tories were furious because it echoed Mrs Thatcher's own use of the word on reacting to the *Belgrano* sinking. I simply repeated the point after the noise had died down. The public really are shocked by what's happened, and it had to be reflected in some way. The Labour benches weren't enormously warm in their response to me but they are uneasy. They are pleased with Michael's refusal to go into the secret talks between Mrs Thatcher, David Steel and David Owen this morning, and now of course the SDP and the Liberals are absolutely part of the government coalition and can't ask questions: David Steel didn't ask any while I was there.

Monday 10 May

One thing I record with regret and sadness. A woman from Portsmouth rang me up in great distress and started to abuse me. It transpired that her husband had gone down in HMS *Sheffield*, and she felt, as she was bound to, that his death had been in a good cause, and therefore she hated me for having opposed the war. I tried to tell her how sorry I was, but she rang off.

I wrote an article for *Tribune*, and sent a letter to the PM asking if the *Sheffield* had been armed with nuclear weapons when she was attacked.

Three nasty telegrams were waiting at the House. I'm sure things will get more unpleasant.

Thursday 20 May

About twenty-five MPs who oppose the war met at the House, under the chairmanship of Tam Dalyell – Andrew Faulds, Ray Powell, Bob Cryer, John Tilley, Mik, Judith Hart, Frank Allaun, Dafydd Ellis Thomas (Plaid Cymru MP) and so on.

A short press statement was drawn up saying that those who intended to vote against the Government tonight after the debate on the war were pressing for an immediate ceasefire, and they would vote against for the following reasons: (1) they wished to avoid the loss of life involved in a British landing, (2) they wished to continue negotiations in response to the latest appeal of the UN Secretary-General.

In the debate, Tam made a very good speech, and Denis Healey made an awful speech supporting the Government up to the hilt. When it came to the vote, Tam moved the closure at one minute to ten, and 33 Labour members went into the No Lobby; 296 voted for the Government – less than half the Commons. It wasn't a bad vote.

Tuesday 25 May
Heard on the 10 o'clock news this evening that another warship had been sunk. Absolutely tragic loss of life. People are going to ask how long this madness will last – 26,500 men out there and a hundred ships, of which we have already lost four, for 1,800 Falkland Islanders who could all be brought safely to Britain if they would only come. Absolutely crazy.

Monday 7 June
I rang Charles Douglas-Home, the Editor of *The Times*, and declined the column he had offered me, explaining that I wasn't principally a journalist, but if he was interested in publishing an article by me at any time, maybe a speech, I would be happy to contribute.

The NEC met at 5.30 – a very unpleasant meeting.

Healey attacked me for putting forward an emergency resolution on the Falklands, and attacked Judith, in the chair, for accepting it. Golding said it was dishonest and sharp practice to accept a resolution when we were there to discuss other things. Gwyneth Dunwoody appealed for us not to discuss it and also violently attacked Judith's 'egotism'. The idea that we should even discuss the resolution was defeated by 11 votes to 10.

President Reagan arrives in Britain today, and we considered a letter drafted by Denis Healey to Reagan from the Party. We deleted a reference to the fact that our post-war relationship with America revolved around NATO. I moved that we should make clear that our ultimate aim was the dissolution of NATO and the Warsaw Pact, and that was carried by 10 votes to 9. I got another change – that a Labour government would not permit the stationing of Cruise missiles, carried by 17 votes to 0. Finally I got this passage from the end of the letter removed: 'Throughout its history the people of the US have always shown themselves willing to sacrifice themselves for great causes, ignoring commercial and material advantage.' I said that wasn't true and we'd look stupid if we said it. So it was taken out.

Tuesday 8 June
The streets were packed with police for Reagan's visit. He began the day riding around Windsor Great Park in a coach and four with Nancy and the Queen and the Duke of Edinburgh, followed by 350 TV cameras.

Later he flew into London by helicopter and addressed both Houses of Parliament, in the Royal Gallery – an event I did not attend – and made a violent attack on the Soviet Union. He had lunch with Mrs Thatcher and another exchange of speeches. Back to Windsor Castle in the evening for a banquet at Queen Victoria's dining table, which seats 144. Michael Foot was there, I think, and Reagan made a speech about the Falklands, as did the Queen.

It was quite unlike the Pope's visit, which was much more human. Reagan is just a movie star acting the part of a king, and the Queen is like a movie star in a film about Britain. Mrs Thatcher is an absolutely Victorian jingoist. I find it embarrassing to live in Britain at the moment.

Monday 14 June
Caught the train to York, and talked to the first senior woman steward on BR. She got into an argument with a seaman from South Shields who is off tomorrow to join the Task Force in the South Atlantic.

While I was on the train, it was announced over the loudspeaker that there was a ceasefire in the Falklands, and it's obvious that the war is now over.

Tuesday 15 June
There has been an Argentinian surrender, and the reaction now is one of tremendous enthusiasm and support for Mrs Thatcher. However, this is not the moment to unbend but the time to reaffirm everything that we've said. It won't be popular, but if you take a principled position you don't withdraw from it.

I went to the House to hear the Prime Minister's statement announcing the surrender. Michael Foot congratulated her and her forces; somehow it was odious and excessive. I was called, and I asked if the PM would publish all the documents and the cost in terms of life, equipment and money of a tragic and unnecessary war. The Tories erupted in anger because this was Jingo Day. I said the world knew very well that the war would not solve the problem of the future of the Falkland Islands. 'Does she agree that in the end there must be negotiations, and will she say with whom and when she will be ready to enter into such negotiations?' She said she couldn't publish the documents, she saw no reason to negotiate with Argentina, she thought the war was tragic but not unnecessary, because the freedom of speech which the Right Honourable Gentleman made such excellent use of had been won for him by people fighting for it. Rubbish, but the Tories loved it.

Saturday 26 June
Tony and Sally Banks picked me up and we drove to the South Bank, where, built into one of the arches forming Waterloo Bridge, the famous Polish artist Feliks Topolski has his studio.

Topolski is seventy-five, came to England between the wars, knew Bernard Shaw and is vaguely left-wing. He has painted some portraits and sketches – Nye Bevan, for example – and he wants to paint me. His study was absolutely crammed with his work. His daughter Theresa was there, and she sat and talked to me while he was painting. I did feel inhibited. He autographed the bottom of a mug for me!

He seemed to get beneath the surface and capture my character, and I think if he didn't like someone the painting would not work. I think he was a bit uncomfortable too. Still, the oil painting was interesting – he gave me a long neck and a pipe.

Tony, Sally and I had a meal at an Italian restaurant.

Monday 12 July
The Organisation Committee met – an important meeting to consider Bermondsey and Peter Tatchell. I had tabled a resolution that Tatchell be endorsed on the spot, and Eric Heffer, who had visited Bermondsey, suggested they run another selection conference including Tatchell.

Michael Foot said Eric had done a good job in Bermondsey. Our position was based on the consequences to the Party of Tatchell's being the candidate, and he feared a disastrous by-election. But he had told Bob Mellish that he disapproved of what he did, and therefore he supported Eric's proposal that they hold a fresh selection conference with no bar on Tatchell. A total victory!

Friday 16 July
Today Hilary married Sally.

The family left for Acton Town Hall and arrived at 2.30, two weddings ahead of time. There was an Indian wedding in progress, with the women in the most beautiful colourful saris. Then another family and then us: the Benns, and Sally's parents, Aileen and Graham Clark (both architects), and their grown-up children.

At one point the registrar said, 'Now, Hilary and Salary . . .', which made us laugh. (We discovered that he had been engaged in wage negotiations that morning!)

We took photographs and all left for Ealing Abbey, the chic Catholic church in West London, where the priest greeted us. Mother read the lesson most beautifully and it was such a sight to see that old lady climbing up to the pulpit and reading the lesson, just as she had at Hilary's first wife Rosalind's funeral three years ago.

When I think of the tragedy of Rosalind's death and the tremendous suffering and unhappiness that Hilary has had, and indeed that Sally's older sister Caroline was killed about three years ago in a car smash, it was nice to think of this happiness coming to the family at this time.

Stephen referred in his speech at the reception to the fact that Rosalind and Caroline were in everybody's mind today.

Monday 26 July
I fell flat on my face today. If it hadn't been for my big black bag my face

would have hit the concrete. As it was my glasses frames were smashed and I grazed my knees, hurt my ankle and a finger – and I was badly shaken. Not as young as I used to be, and when you have a fall at nearly sixty it's more serious. A taxi driver was awfully kind – helped me pick up my wallet and things – and as I dragged myself up I thought I was going to have to go to hospital but after wiggling a few bones I was taken to the station and managed to walk to the train. The accident was a combination of not looking where I was going and the Guillain-Barré Syndrome, which meant my brain didn't tell my feet to avoid the kerb.

Friday 30 July
I feel somehow that we are at a real turning point in politics. I can't quite describe it. The military victory in the Falklands War, Thatcher's strength, the counter-attack of the Right of the Labour Party on the Left, the fact that unemployment has weakened the unions, and so on, make me feel more than ever before that I need to pause and think and work out a new strategy. Caroline has persuaded me that the press assassination of me was successful and that I've lived in a dream world believing it wasn't really happening. The NEC is in a bitter state, set on expulsions, ASLEF was sold down the river by the TUC, and even if they hadn't been I'm not sure how long they could have survived the Chairman of BR, Sir Peter Parker. The media are now in an absolutely hysterical state. I feel we have just come to the end of an era.

Saturday 25 September – Labour Party Conference, Blackpool
Compared to last year, when the Left was riding high with successes everywhere, this year the Left is very much tail-between-legs. We did unleash a violent backlash from the Right supported by the media and the general secretaries, and although the Party is pretty solid on policy it doesn't want divisions, so we are caught by the constraint of unity – whereas they, being on the warpath, are not, and are demanding the expulsion of the Left. It's very unpleasant but I shall just let it ride over me; at this stage we have to accept that the Right have won and there isn't much we can do about it.

Wednesday 27 October
The papers all week had been predicting the massacre of the Left at today's meeting of the newly elected NEC, which was due to decide on the composition of all its committees.

I decided to sit in a different place, opposite the Chairman, in recognition of the changes that were coming, and I had Dennis Skinner and Audrey Wise on either side of me to sustain me.

Shirley Summerskill moved that we ban smoking from the meeting – carried by 18 to 13.

After a bit of business, we came to the major question of the committees. John Golding was the prime mover in all the votes. Eric Heffer blew up. 'You buggers are trying to break the Party. For a year I haven't been on television but you say what you like on TV; when the Left had control we had the decency to vote right-wingers on.' He banged the table. But you can't shout and scream when you've lost. No one took the slightest notice.

In a nutshell, there was a clean sweep of the Left on all the committees. Foot appealed to us not to reveal what had happened, that we should leave it to the General Secretary. So when the Left had a majority, and Golding gave a press conference three times a day outside every committee, that was OK, but now that the Right are in power we are gagged.

As I went out I was pursued down the road by the media.

I feel quite liberated, frankly.

Had a call this evening to say that Tony Banks had beaten Arthur Lewis, Ted Knight, Dave Wetzel and Mandy Moore for the Newham North West candidacy. He had an overwhelming majority, and so he is in for life in a very, very safe seat – marvellous. I rang Sally. It shows that just when you think everything's gone wrong things begin to pick up.

Thursday 28 October

Bought all the papers, which were full of headlines such as 'Benn Gets Boot' and 'Benn Routed'. I've seen these headlines so many times, especially in 1975 after the Referendum. I'm tempted to look up the press cuttings, because I am sure they all said the same.

Friday 5 November

Taxi to the BBC for 2.30. From there I was driven to Marlborough to do 'Any Questions', picking up David Jacobs from Knightsbridge on the way.

On the panel were a go-ahead young businessman, Norman St John Stevas and Bea Campbell. Bea is a member of the Communist Party. She used to work for the *Morning Star*; now she is working for *City Limits*.

Back in the car with Norman St John Stevas in the front and Bea Campbell and me in the back. I asked Norman how things were, and he said the wets were totally in retreat. He told me he had seen Lord Home this morning, what a charming man he was, and how ignorant was that woman Thatcher. He thinks she hates his guts.

Norman told me about the moment when he realised he was going to be sacked; at the time he was Chancellor of the Duchy of Lancaster. Geoffrey Howe was late for the Cabinet. Norman said that 'the old hen' had come in, looked round the table and asked where the Chancellor was. Norman had said, 'I'm the Chancellor', and she had given him such a dirty look that all the other Ministers, who had been laughing at the joke, froze immediately. He realised then how much she hated him and that he would go.

Saturday 13 November
Last year Caroline felt it was unwise of me to stand for the deputy leadership.
When I look back, her advice has always been right. I think in future I will
actually take her advice. So on Thursday, if, as I expect, I am not elected to
the Shadow Cabinet, and if I decide not to stand for any seat in Bristol, I
shall be a senior Labour figure without a seat. There will then be an election
for the Leader while I am out of Parliament, someone else will be elected,
and I will then pass on to another phase. I just have to put all situations
involving personal advancement completely out of my mind. If you don't
want anything for yourself, you are less vulnerable to attack by the media. In
any case, since I failed against Healey in 1981, such damage was done that I
probably wouldn't succeed anyway.

Depressed at the moment – the reverses that have occurred in the last
twelve months have taken a long time to penetrate into my mind and at the
moment I'm feeling a bit like a burnt-out meteor. Still, it won't last for ever.

Monday 15 November
Drove to Newbury magistrates' court for the trial of eleven women from
Greenham Common, who were charged with action likely to cause a breach
of the peace for standing in a sentry hut a few yards inside the perimeter
fence on 27 August. They've been camping outside now for a year, first in
huts, which were destroyed, and then in tents and sleeping bags. Bruce Kent
was in court, and BBC, ITN and Channel 4 were present.

The court was packed, and there was applause as the women came in.
Two women barristers represented them. One of the magistrates was a
tough-looking man with greased hair and moustache.

The barristers asked for the proceedings to be recorded, and one tape
recorder was allowed, provided that any transcript was submitted for
authentication. The magistrates warned that they would remove people if
there were any disturbances. Then the defendants rose and were named,
and the prosecution began.

The prosecuting lawyer said, 'Eleven ladies have been brought before the
court, having occupied a hut, which caused inconvenience and was likely to
cause a breach of the peace.' The prosecution had been brought under the
1361 Justices of the Peace Act. He described the events of 27 August. He
admitted that the demo had been non-violent, but said that whether they
intended violence or not was irrelevant. The prosecution was not a criticism
of the ladies' demonstration against nuclear weapons but that their action
violated the rights of others over private property and the rights to privacy.
This campaign would not stop; it would get worse.

He went on to say that the 1361 Act as reported in the laws of England
was required 'for good behaviour towards the king and his people'. Then he
referred to Lord Justice Templeman, who had ruled that powers must exist
to deal with passive resistance and minimum force. He quoted Gandhi, who

had said that 'passive defence is only possible if it is successful'. All those who interfere with the lawful rights of others are guilty of a breach of the peace, the prosecuting counsel stated.

We had to leave at that stage. Caroline went back to London and I flew up to Scotland.

Thursday 20 January 1983

At the PLP meeting, Tam Dalyell began with a prepared speech, the gist of which was that the Prime Minister had lied to the House because she had known the invasion of the Falklands was coming and did have time to prevent it. He went on for so long that the Chairman, Jack Dormand, said, 'Look, Tam, we all appreciate the work you have done, but do you really want to say it all now rather than in front of the House during the debate?' So Tam curtailed it.

Jim Callaghan said there was a devastating case to be made against the Government, but added, 'I appeal to Tam not to pursue the case that Mrs Thatcher knew about the impending invasion and lied to the House, because there is no proof of that, while there are things in the report which we can take up. It was a slipshod government, we drifted into war, and Tam will get the headlines but will it help us politically? There is a jingoistic spirit now, in contrast to 1947, when we rationed food in order to send grain ships to India.'

Thursday 24 February

To Bristol, and stayed up to watch the end of the Bermondsey by-election, which was terrible. The 11,000 majority that Bob Mellish had received in the last Election was converted to a 10,000 majority for Simon Hughes, the Liberal candidate. Poor old Peter Tatchell, who had been massacred by the press, only got 7,600 votes, but he came out of it with considerable courage and dignity.

I resolved there and then in that hotel room not to desert Bristol, where boundary changes have affected my seat, and that, when I go to Scotland on Saturday for a meeting I will make a statement saying I couldn't accept nomination for Livingston.

Thursday 3 March

Went to the Commons in the afternoon, and Gordon McLennan, the General Secretary of the Communist Party, came to see me. We sat alone. He asked if Eric Hobsbawm had spoken to me, as he had suggested he should. Gordon thought there should be more talks between the Communist Party and the Labour Party, that the 'Eurocommunist' position (though he didn't like the term) was pluralistic, and he believed everyone should choose their own road to socialism. He said that *Marxism Today* had done some interesting analytical work on Thatcherism, on the Labour Movement of the future, on the trade unions and on the SDP–Liberal Alliance, which they took very seriously. He emphasised the importance of internationalism.

Gordon was pretty cold, actually. He said that the composition of the working class had altered, that the change in the make-up of the TUC General Council was a great threat, and that the CP now believe there should be a progressive alliance with autonomous developments under working-class leadership but not under a solely Labour Party umbrella. He thought Militant was a real danger, and disagreed with the view of one trade union leader that, 'without Tony Benn, Militant would never have been heard of'. On proportional representation, he believed it to be a basic democratic principle that must be upheld.

Sunday 1 May
In Liverpool for a public meeting with Eddie Loyden, the ex-MP for Garston, who has been selected to fight it again. I stayed overnight in the Liverpool Atlantic Tower Hotel.

At 1.30 in the morning I woke up coughing and choking. I was desperately trying to breathe in, and it was absolutely terrifying. I went into the bathroom and began turning blue, gasping for breath and coughing. I really thought I was going to die on May Day 1983. I won't say my whole life raced through my mind, but I did go through the likely sequence of my death – the final choking, the weakening, the extinction. But after a while the coughing began to ease and, although my throat was very sore and I was frightened, I managed to calm myself and finally went back to sleep.

Two hours later, I was woken up by the most appalling wailing noise as if a police car was in the bedroom. I leapt out of bed again, thinking it was the hotel alarm clock, which had a note on saying it did sometimes go haywire. I looked out of the window to see if it was a police car but it wasn't. So I went into the bathroom, where the noise was even louder. I tried to get out of the room to look along the corridor but I had locked the door, so I had to search for the key. By this time the noise was driving me crazy and I thought it must be some sort of fire alarm. Just as I got the door open, I saw the porter and the manager banging on all the doors, shouting, 'Evacuate the building at once.'

I was in my shirt and my underpants, but I thought I could put on my clothes, and I didn't want to lose my papers and wallet and tape recorder, so I got everything together. The manager said, 'Go down the stairs.' Well, it was *twelve* flights down! When I finally stumbled out at the bottom, somebody in the hall ushered me outside, where there were three fire engines but no sign of a fire. I had a little folding seat which I had put in my bag for the May Day march, so I sat there with my bags, just gazing out at Liverpool at 3.30 in the morning.

Eventually they said we could go back in. I was so exhausted by this time, I fell asleep on the bed fully clothed, and woke up three hours later when they brought me breakfast.

Saturday 7 May
To Bristol for a very important decision-making meeting with the officers of my party, before this afternoon's selection conference for the new Bristol South seat. I had worked out a timetable of decisions, and, to cut a long story short, I had drafted the case for staying and the case for running. Clearly Bristol East is not safe and will be less so as a result of the bitter press coverage, which, Ken Coates warned me, would be a 'lynching party'. I put the case for cutting and running from Bristol.

The case for staying was, however, much stronger. First, I had said I *would* stay and it was a question of integrity. Secondly, by going I would be condemning Bristol East and Kingswood to defeat by assuming that they would be lost. Thirdly, by assuming they would be lost, I would also be saying that the Labour Party would lose the Election because if they were lost we couldn't win the Election. Fourth, I did have a requirement to show leadership when things were going badly, and that carried the day. Meg Crack, Dawn Primarolo and George Micklewright, my election agent, agreed; Paul Chamberlain thought I should announce this afternoon that I was leaving Bristol.

I was driven to the Labour Club, where Bristol South delegates had gathered. Then I was shown into a room no bigger than a lavatory. Mike Cocks was there looking extremely worried.

I drew the straw first and went into a huge room where they were all sitting. I could see a few friends, but there was a sea of trade unionists who had been brought in under the Golding aegis, and women in their early sixties from the Co-op Women's Guild. I swear many of them had never been to a political meeting before in their lives. I knew I was going to lose, so I was relaxed, made a speech, answered a few questions and left. Then Mike Cocks went in.

I left the room, wandered round and had a word with a few journalists. When Mike Cocks came out I said, 'If you address the press, tell them I'll see them later if they want me to.'

He said, 'You're assuming I'm going to get the selection.'

'It's obvious you are.'

Anyway, Vic Jackson, the Chairman, came out and announced, 'The selection is for Michael Cocks.'

He and I went in and I looked at them all – it did change my attitude, being the defeated candidate. I remember thinking how awful it must have been in 1950 for Arthur Creech-Jones, a former Cabinet Minister, when I beat him. Anyway, Mike Cocks thanked them and said a word of thanks to me. I congratulated him and said that on my way here I had passed the Fighting Cocks pub and as it turned out he was.

I am glad I went. To be defeated does no harm unless you allow it to. He had worked like anything to fix the selection conference. Many of his supporters had never been before and will never attend again. But the Left will come back to haunt him.

During my press conference, Caroline arrived; it was lovely to see her. We had a cup of tea with Meg Crack and went over it all.

That was the end of a memorable day and possibly a turning point in my life, because, having been defeated for Bristol South, and facing the possibility of being defeated in the General Election at Bristol East, I would therefore be ineligible for the leadership of the Labour Party after the Election (if we lose it).

Sunday 8 May
Caroline and I had breakfast in our hotel room and read the papers. At 10 we went to the Bristol East selection conference in Ruskin Hall, Wick Road, the place where I had been carried shoulder-high by three lads after the count on 30 November 1950, and it looked exactly as it did then. Ron Thomas was there contesting the selection with me, and he is such a friend. There was quite a busy crèche with ten or twelve children being looked after by two men.

Ron knew I would beat him. It was a much smaller conference, and I made more or less the same speech. The vote was 46 to 3. Afterwards I paid tribute to Ron, who was very generous in defeat.

Monday 9 May
Someone from 'Channel 4 News' rang up to tell me that the Election would definitely be on 9 June. Shortly afterwards a phone call came cancelling the next NEC Organisation and Home Policy Committees.

Thursday 12 May
I went to my room in the House and cleared all the pictures, the NUM banner from Arthur Scargill, the typewriter, and so on, and put them in the car. As I left, I did wonder whether I would ever be a Member of Parliament again. I am relaxed about it, because I think the situation is so serious that socialists or representatives of socialism and of working people are being driven out of Parliament. I may have to help the Labour Movement and socialism without necessarily being in Parliament.

Tuesday 17 May
I've made hardly any reference to the Election campaign generally – which I suppose I should do.

The *Daily Star* came up with a MORI poll today suggesting that the Tory lead had been cut to 7 per cent. I watched the Tories' party political broadcast, which was just like a presentation to a group of businessmen, with pictures of the so-called Winter of Discontent, showing the Tories reducing inflation and so on, and finishing up with pictures of Mrs Thatcher. I found it informative, skilful and practical. Michael was on television pounding the table in Lancashire somewhere, and really looking quite good. I felt the atmosphere beginning to shift towards us a bit.

Thursday 26 May
Caught the train to Liverpool, where I was driven to the NUR club for a public meeting. On the platform were Terry Fields, the Labour candidate for Broadgreen, myself, Pat Phoenix (of 'Coronation Street') and the actor Tony Booth, the man she lives with. Derek Hatton of Liverpool Council was in the chair. There is tremendous excitement in Liverpool because of Labour's landslide victory in the district council elections, and it recharged my batteries.

Pat Phoenix and Tony Booth drove me to Manchester for 'Question Time' with Sir Geoffrey Howe and David Penhaligon, the Liberal MP for Truro. Back to Bristol in a BBC car and got to bed at about 1.15.

Monday 6 June
To the boot and shoe factory in Kingswood, where men and women were sitting in front of sewing machines which must have been sixty years old. When the hooter blows in the morning, they have a ten-minute break for tea, then at 12.30 they have an hour's lunch, after which they work straight through to 4.45. It was sheer wage slavery. HTV and BBC were there to take a picture of me, and I was presented with a beautiful set of boots and shoes.

Tuesday 7 June
Clive Jenkins arrived in Bristol, all bouncing, to campaign for me. We went round some shopping centres. Clive hogged the mike and went along like an emperor. You would have thought he was the candidate!

Wednesday 8 June
We drove to the Brislington shopping precinct and I spoke for a moment. Caroline went to a Community Enterprise Programme, where there were a lot of young blacks who said they weren't going to vote; she converted about seventeen of them with a few sharp words.

At Asda supermarket, the security man told me, 'The manager has asked you to leave the premises.'

So I replied, 'Perhaps you'd let me have that in writing.'

Nothing happened, so we carried on, and the manager came up with a heavy-looking guy and said, 'I must ask you to leave.'

I asked, 'Why?', and was told, 'Because our customers object to canvassing here.'

So I said, 'Well, I'm walking through your shop, and if you want me to leave you'll have to put it in writing. I'm a candidate.'

He said, 'Well, I hope we don't have a silly confrontation.'

'Well, I hope we don't either,' I replied.

I went on walking through the shop and then left.

Bill Owen, who plays Compo in a very popular television series called 'Last of the Summer Wine', arrived with my old friend, Ian Flintoff, to canvass for me.

To three eve-of-poll meetings. I resolved that tonight, as the Election is nearing the end, I would rehearse suitable farewell speeches to get on the record. Saw June Gibbs, with whom we had gone round in 1979 and with a spray gun had changed 'Benn must go' slogans to 'Benn must go on'.

Thursday 9 June – General Election

Caroline and I arrived at Transport House at about 9, and Paul Chamberlain and Alan Beynon, who have been solid friends and helpers throughout the whole of the campaign, had planned a route round the constituency. From 9 until about 4, we drove round to each of the polling stations and committee rooms. The weather was quite good and the turnout high for the early part of the day, which usually means that the Tories are voting and everything then depends on whether the Labour turnout is good at the end of the day – which, in the event, it was not. Caroline had been more cautious about the result; she thought we might *just* win by 500 but that the most likely result would be that the Tories would win by nearly 2,000. Of course, all the polls in the morning predicted an enormous Tory landslide, and also predicted that the Alliance might do better than Labour.

People were extremely friendly and there was more activity than I had seen before. All the committee rooms were fully manned and the canvassing was efficient.

I didn't go into the count itself; I just sat in Brislington school and watched on TV the defeat of our best MPs, with the obvious certainty that Labour would be badly beaten. Caroline came in at one stage and told me that, from the count so far, it looked as if we might be just marginally ahead, so I had a feeling that I might have scraped home. The enormity of what was to happen was not apparent. I had prepared what to say in advance and had kept it in the back of my mind – not that it would be much different whether it was a victory or a defeat for me, because clearly it was going to be a bad day for the Labour Party as a whole. A few people gathered in the room with us. Finally Caroline came to me at about 1.30 and said, 'They are almost ready. You have lost.' She had seen the votes piling up on the table.

So we walked out of the room, and all our Party workers gave me a dazed look, and I don't think they fully appreciated what had happened either. We walked arm-in-arm into the assembly hall, and when we got there we saw Sayeed and his wife and the Liberal candidate, Peter Tyrer, and the Ecology and the National Front candidates. The whole thing seemed like a dream. The returning officer read out the result, and I had lost by about 1,790 votes.

A great cheer went up among the Tories when they discovered they had won. Sayeed spoke and paid tribute to me, saying I could have fled Bristol and gone to one of the left-wing strongholds but I had stayed to fight. He said he would do his best for a better Bristol and a better Britain, or something.

I came forward, and there were film units trying to film me, and photographers and journalists jostling. I had resolved what I would say, and I paid a tribute to the Chartists and the suffragettes. I then thanked the people in Bristol for what they had done and said I didn't regret for one moment staying there to fight. The Labour Party still had things to do – to protect people, to build a mass party, or something or another. Finally, I said, 'If I may be allowed a personal word, I shall carry on with my commitment outside Parliament.' Then we all went outside the school and I had to say it all over again for the television and press waiting there. But this time I added, 'I hope nobody will shed any tears for me, because I am going to carry on my work.'

It was a warm evening, and we drove back to Transport House in Bristol. For the first time since 1950, I had been defeated. It was no longer an area which I represented but an area where I was a visitor. When we arrived, the media were all outside and one photographer from the *Observer* managed to get in, so we chased him out. I made a speech again, and the only person who marred it was a tall man who was drunk and kept leaning forward and interrupting. It is out of events like this that history is made; it was a rather moving occasion, all the Party people crying their eyes out, and here was this drunk saying, 'Why did you do it, Tony? Why didn't you leave Bristol?' But I managed to silence him, and then I went round and gave everybody a hug and thanked them.

I can't say I was surprised, but the campaign did buoy me up to the point where I thought I might have won.

12

1983–87

Saturday 11 June

The full scale of the Labour losses is enormous: Albert Booth, Neil Carmichael, Arthur Davidson, Joe Dean, David Ennals, John Garrett, Ted Graham, Frank Hooley, Alex Lyon (a great loss), Jim Marshall, Stan Newens, Ossie O'Brien, Gwilym Roberts, Chris Price, David Stoddart, Ann Taylor, Frank White, Philip Whitehead, Roland Moyle and many others. But there are a lot of good new Members now in – Tony Banks, Richard Caborn, Bob Clay, Frank Cook, Jeremy Corbyn, Terry Fields, Bill Michie, Dave Nellist, Bob Wareing.

Sunday 12 June

Chris Mullin had a post-mortem at his flat in Brixton. Most of our friends were there – Tom Sawyer, Jeremy Corbyn, Audrey Wise, Ann Pettifor, Francis Prideaux, Les Huckfield, Michael Meacher, Tony Banks, Mandy Moore, Frances Morrell, Reg Race, Jon Lansman, Jo Richardson, Stuart Holland, Alan Meale, Ken Livingstone. We sat in the garden at the back of Chris's flat.

I arrived early for a talk with Chris and Tony Banks. Michael Foot let it be known today, or rather it was known as a result of his refusing nomination for the Party leadership, that there would be a leadership contest, and Tony Banks, who has just been newly elected for Newham North West, offered to stand down so that I could have his seat and be eligible to contest the leadership. I wouldn't hear of it. It would be manipulative and I wouldn't contemplate such a thing. But I have *never* known anyone make such a generous offer before. Neil Kinnock, Roy Hattersley and Peter Shore have indicated that they will stand as leader.

Looking back on it, I suppose I should have played my cards differently. If I had not stood down from the Shadow Cabinet after 1979, had played a less active part in the campaign to change the policy and to bring about the democratic changes, and had not stood for the deputy leadership, and if I'd gone to find a safe seat this year, I would have been in the running now. I may even have won. But history didn't work out that way, and the price paid for playing it differently has been enormous in personal terms. I have lost successively my seat in the Shadow Cabinet, the deputy leadership of the Labour Party, the chairmanship of the Home Policy Committee last October after Conference and, this year, my seat in Parliament. Four major setbacks. But the reward is that the Party has, I think, been irreversibly shifted back towards socialism and is more democratic, and that is the most important thing of all.

We put Reg Race in the chair. Chris Mullin took some photographs and then we had a brief discussion on the campaign. I said I thought there should be no personal recriminations and we should look at the long-term developments we would need to bring about if we were going to secure a Labour victory next time on socialist policies.

Stuart Holland said, 'We must try and get a by-election for Tony, by getting somebody to stand down.'

'I don't want to stop you, but I couldn't possibly contemplate that,' I replied.

Les Huckfield said, 'Kinnock is the cause of our problems.'

Mandy Moore didn't like the idea of Heffer. 'He is in the old mould and is an abysmal choice for women. As for Kinnock, he seems ready to say anything to win. It will be tragic if we don't put up a candidate.'

Reg Race declared, 'I couldn't vote for Kinnock; under him, we'll have a witch-hunt, and he'll try to reverse the democratic changes in the Party. He would appease the Right. We would lose if we supported him, and anyway he does not believe in the policy commitments. We can't have him as Leader. Therefore we should run Eric Heffer, Jo Richardson or Michael Meacher. Really, Jo must do it.'

In effect, we decided that we hoped to persuade Michael Meacher to stand for the leadership or deputy leadership and that, if he stood for the leadership, Jo should stand for the deputy leadership.

Having sat and listened to all this, it seems to me inappropriate that I should be involved in this sort of discussion, particularly because it may be thought that I am trying to mastermind things outside Parliament. So I will keep up a good bilateral discussion with my friends, but I don't want to be involved in the plotting and planning.

The effects of the Election come over me in waves. Many people will suffer terribly under the Tories and it is immensely distressing. It's easy for us to sit round talking about what we should do, and overlook the fact that the inward-looking nature of the Party has done us down.

Monday 13 June

I ordered some stationery because I have been using House of Commons letter-heading for thirty-three years and I haven't even got any with my name and address. The cost of stamps is astronomical; at this present rate, assuming I get 1,000 letters a week, it would cost £120 on stamps alone. I did enquire about my redundancy pay, and I think I get £14,000 tax-free, and a couple of months' winding-up allowance. I'm keeping Julie on. I had a letter from Richard Gott of the *Guardian* inviting me to write a column every week, which will mean £175 a week coming in.

Wednesday 22 June

Went to the House for the first time since the Election feeling absolutely miserable. I never want to go near the place again but there are meetings to attend. I wasn't sure that I could go in through the private entrance by Westminster Underground station, but the policeman gave me a wink and said it was OK. I saw a couple of journalists, and found it pretty painful. I was allowed into Room 8 for the Campaign Group, even though non-MPs usually have to wait for the MPs to arrive. I shouldn't really feel embarrassed; after all, I fought a battle and was outvoted, and I don't feel defeated. Probably the feeling today was rather like that of a man thrown from a horse deciding to get on the horse again immediately.

The new Campaign Group was well attended – Bob Clay, Martin Flannery, Dennis Skinner, Brian Sedgemore, Frank Cook, Dave Nellist, Mark Fisher (the son of ex-Tory MP Sir Nigel Fisher), Willy McKelvey, Stuart Holland, Joan Maynard, Jo Richardson, Kevin Barron (the miner from Rother Valley), Ron Brown from Leith, Jeremy Corbyn, Harry Cohen, Michael Meacher and so on.

Again, the discussion revolved around the leadership. When Kinnock's name came up, Jeremy Corbyn said, 'Well, Kinnock lost the deputy leadership for Tony in 1981 deliberately and specifically, and he was busy preparing himself for the leadership campaign during the General Election. There must be a left candidate. Heffer is a candidate, he is against the witch-hunt, and I think we should consider him.'

Monday 27 June

Had a talk with Caroline in the evening. We are both sort of decoupling from the old style of political work. I am disenchanted with the Labour Party, and she feels she's getting nowhere with it.

Friday 1 July

Visited Bristol for a meeting at Baptist Central Hall; it gave me a very funny feeling. As I walked down the station approach, a man stopped me and said, 'Aren't you Mr Benn? I am so sorry . . .' Then at the corner of Old Market and Temple Way a disabled newspaper seller came out of his kiosk saying, 'I've followed you all through your career. I am sorry.'

I went into the Hall, a bit early, and sat down. A cleaner came in and asked, 'Don't I know you?' I said, 'You may have seen me.' She asked, 'Have you got a friend in Stoke Bishop?' I said, 'No.' She said, 'Well, who are you then?' I replied, 'I'm Tony Benn.' She said, 'Are you sure you haven't got a friend in Stoke Bishop?' So it was a good corrective for any superstar delusions I might have!

Sunday 24 July

The Kinnock–Hattersley leadership race has become more interesting. There was a violent exchange between Hattersley and Foot at the PLP meeting on Thursday night; apparently the Right had tried to get the Shadow Cabinet to recommend to the PLP 'one member one vote' in reselection procedures. So, when it came up at the PLP, the Kinnockites had packed the meeting to secure its defeat, and Max Madden (the MP for Bradford South) had moved that it not be discussed. Michael Foot had abstained. Hattersley had been furious, shouting, 'Where's the bloody leadership now?', and Michael Foot had allegedly replied, 'Don't ever speak to me again like that – I'll skin you alive.'

Saturday 30 July

At 4.20 Caroline and I went to Bristol for the farewell social at Bristol Transport House, where 750 people turned up, including the BBC and HTV with lights and cameras which upset people, particularly Caroline. Herbert Rogers and Dawn spoke, and Caroline was given a leather bag made by Arnold Smith. Pam Tatlow presented me with a beautiful illuminated address, drawn by Hazel Gower, which was decorated with pictures of Mars Bars, cups of tea and Concorde – everything that reminded the members of me; and also the text of a miners' hymn from the old days of the Bristol mines. We sang 'We'll eat pie in the sky by and by' and then the 'Internationale'. They played 'The Red Flag' as we walked out, and it was extremely moving. It's hard to believe that thirty-three years are over, but I'm glad the party was left sufficiently late for people to have recovered from the immediate shock of the defeat.

Driving back to London after what was a moving and tender and lovely evening, I did feel that the work had to begin again. At a personal level, I'll have no difficulty earning a living from media work, but talking about politics is not the same as being an active political figure; being engaged in the business of preparing to hold power is what provides you with a platform and gives greater meaning to what you're saying.

Sunday 31 July – Trip to Japan

I caught the Japan Airlines flight at 2.30 and the plane flew to Tokyo over the North Pole. I read the various briefs I had had prepared for the World Conference against Atomic and Hydrogen Bombs, including one on the General Council of Trade Unions (Sohyo), which is a sort of progressive, democratic and vaguely socialist federation, the largest in Japan, supported by the Japanese Socialist Party. I also read about Gensuikyo, the Japan Council against Atomic and Hydrogen Bombs.

Monday 1 August

To the reception, where a lot of journalists wanted to interview me, and I did speak to many people, but my deafness is a real barrier at the moment and the Japanese accent is very hard to get used to.

In a way, Japan is rather like Britain – they are both islands, self-contained, inward-looking, conservative and hierarchical, facing the same economic pressures which are driving politics to the right.

Tuesday 2 August

I had a fascinating talk with Robert Alvarez, an American from the Environmental Policy Institute in Washington, who is in Japan. I asked him about the sale of British plutonium to the United States. He told me that it started in 1959 and went on until 1979, when it was probably terminated by President Carter. It was a barter agreement under which the United States supplied us with tritium and high-enriched uranium for nuclear-powered Polaris submarines in exchange for plutonium from our Magnox civil nuclear power stations for use in American nuclear weapons.

Alvarez said the Americans wanted the Magnox plutonium because it was purer than that from the PWR. He told me that in 1980 the supply resumed, partly to fend off criticisms of Carter by Reagan on the eve of the presidential election.

From 1966 to 1970 and from 1975 to 1979 I was the Minister responsible for atomic energy, and I had absolutely no knowledge of this. Encouraged by my officials, I used to give talks on the uses of civil nuclear power, while all that time our civil power stations were supplying plutonium for American nuclear weapons. Recently Ross Hesketh of the CEGB made a statement in Britain in which he revealed this story, and he was promptly sacked by Sir Walter Marshall, Chairman of the CEGB – which has led to some argument in Britain.

Thursday 4 August
I was driven to see the Governor of Kanagawa, through these enormous industrial areas. It must be the greatest accumulation of industrialisation to be found almost anywhere in the world. It makes my heart bleed to think of all the previously productive areas in Britain which are now just decaying and declining.

Later I caught the flight to Hiroshima.

There I went to the meeting with the 'Hibakusha', as the victims of the actual bomb raids are called. An old lady, who said she was thirty-five in 1945, now seventy-three, was terribly badly injured and couldn't stand upright. She was working near Hiroshima in August 1945, for the military, and had been 1.1 kilometres from the epicentre of the explosion. She had seen the flash. She had been trapped in wreckage, was unconscious for two days and had suffered blindness, loss of hair, bleeding gums, fever and diarrhoea, and loss of power in her fingers and toes. All her organs were affected. She said, 'I try to lead a normal life. My father died of acute leukaemia in October 1945. I had breast and kidney cancer and operations for cataracts. My fingers and limbs still tremble. I can barely walk. And,' she said very quietly, 'I so much resent the production of nuclear weapons. Atomic bombs have made no positive contribution to the world. I am very old now, but I am still learning what we can do to help the world and I feel keenly that I must work for peace. I want to be of service and I hope to live to see peace established.' It was very moving.

There are 370,000 Hibakusha left but there is a rapid death rate among them, particularly recently through cancer. Two-thirds of them die of cancer. In Japan the doctors don't really reveal the cause of death. One man told me, 'It is most important to record our experiences before we die. There are no social security payments for the survivors, and most are suffering from a disease known as "atomic bomb bura-bura". The Government doesn't recognise it. Of course, the American Government is really responsible, but the Japanese Government is too.'

A Russian delegate told the meeting that he had lost his family among the twenty million Russians killed in the war. The bomb, he said, was dropped by American imperialists. Fixing the responsibility for dropping the bomb is very important. I had always accepted the general explanation that it was done to hasten the end of the war, but actually the then US Secretary of

Defense revealed that it was done to establish a strong position *vis-à-vis* the Soviet Union before the war ended.

I got back to the hotel at about 11.30 and dictated from my notes.

Friday 5 August

To the Peace Museum which was absolutely packed, and the exhibition moved me to tears. Children were handing out labels to the visitors saying 'No more war'.

There was a huge model of Hiroshima just after the bomb was dropped showing absolute devastation except for a few buildings that survived. From the ceiling hung a black rod at the bottom of which was a red blob showing where the epicentre was. Next was a vivid scene of a life-size model of a woman with her hair standing on end, bleeding, with the skin burned off her and another woman with a burned child. Behind them was a massive backdrop of Hiroshima burning. There were samples of the girders which had melted and children's little luncheon boxes containing food scorched by the bomb. There were some granite steps which had been outside a bank, with the permanent imprint of someone who had been sitting there when the bomb fell. It was terrifying. I wrote in the visitors' book, 'Every child in the world should see this museum.'

I had to go out to recover myself. No sane human being could possibly assent to the use of bombs 1,000 times as great as that. It cannot be right. There are some views you come to in life from which you can never be shaken, and nothing will ever shake me in the view that such a weapon cannot be used and therefore should not be built and must not be threatened. If it ever happens again, it will be the greatest crime in the whole of human history, because far more people will be killed.

Outside, in front of the car park, there was a disturbance involving some Fascists in blue overalls who were standing beside four vehicles displaying the old imperial Japanese flag. I took a few pictures. They were addressing us through loudspeakers, apparently saying that the future of Japan lies in nuclear energy, Japan must have nuclear weapons and Communism must be contained.

We went off to the atom bomb victims' hospital where the Vice-Director ran through a description of the various injuries they deal with – burns, blast, radiation, cancer, leukaemia, kidney trouble, cataracts, cheloids, purple spots, lassitude. I asked about genetic effects, but he had no information on that. The hospital is run by the Red Cross and gets no government money.

Monday 8 August

Had breakfast with the Venerable Sato. Sato was pleased with the conference and said the media coverage had been excellent. I thanked him very much indeed for making it possible for me to visit Japan.

Looking back on the week, it certainly was an interesting experience. The peace movement has a life and vitality of its own and its leading figures know each other well through having met at previous conferences. During the years that they were working on peace problems, I was a Minister in a government that was building nuclear weapons and following international policies which the peace movement itself found anathema.

Viewed from such a distance, Britain appears as a primitive, aggressive, feudalistic colony of the United States, gradually being taken over by the EEC, the multinationals and the IMF.

Tuesday 6 September
Sally went into the West London Hospital and our second grandson, James, was born to her and Hilary early on Wednesday morning.

Sunday 25 September
The *Mail on Sunday* carried an interview with Neil Kinnock by Jilly Cooper, and it was worse than I had been warned to expect. He was asked about various colleagues and came out with some astonishing remarks. He said Meacher was regarded as my vicar on earth – 'He's kind, scholarly and weak as hell'. He called me a spent force who 'couldn't knock the skin off a rice pudding', and denied he had once said I was a blindworm trying to be an adder. This clever-clever Kinnock, who has been getting away with funny remarks which endear him to the media, will find, as he approaches the leadership of the Party, that they give enormous offence. Apparently he rang Michael Meacher to apologise and said he had been misquoted. But he didn't ring me! That type of approach to personal relations, combined with his general inadequacy, is not going to be good for him.

I am feeling a bit depressed at the moment. I think the real effect of losing my seat is apparent, and no doubt being out of the leadership election has caught up with me. It is a fact that I have lost a platform and an income, and have no absolute certainty that I will get back. Indeed, if I do get back, I fear it may be on the basis of a tremendous battle with Shirley Williams or someone put up to fight me. I do understand how unemployed people lose their sense of self-worth.

Wednesday 28 September
At the NEC I passed a handwritten letter to Neil Kinnock.

Dear Neil,
　　I understand that you were misquoted in the interview with you that appeared in the *Mail on Sunday*. May I take it that these misquotations also covered the comments you were reported to have made about me?

I attached a photocopy of the article, in which Jilly Cooper had asked if it was true that he had once described me as a blindworm trying to be an adder. The relevant paragraph read: 'For a second Mr Kinnock flickered between discretion and the desire to be accredited with a wisecrack, then opted for the former, saying: "Attribute that to me and I'll kill you." '

I got a response later, as follows:

Dear Tony,

Many thanks. Yes, I was most certainly misquoted – misrepresented rather. In a statement I put out on Sunday, I said that my reference to you was in the context of the charges of extremism malevolently levelled at Tony Benn. My reference was entirely intended to dismiss those daft allegations and the quote should be in that context and should have said 'wouldn't', not 'couldn't' (knock the skin off a rice pudding).

. . . I am, incidentally, following your lead in getting a tape recorder.

Yours, Neil.

Well, that settles the matter as far as I am concerned.

Sunday 2 October – Labour Party Conference, Brighton

I confess that I am dictating this on 14 October from very accurate notes.

At the meeting of the NEC, there was an attempt to remit the T&G resolution committing the next Labour Government to scrapping all nuclear weapons systems unilaterally, but by 14 to 11 we accepted it. Kinnock abstained, made a big thing about abstaining and then tried to get the issue reopened, but Sam McCluskie wouldn't have it. I was confirmed to speak on the unemployment debate, and I reported that I would be moving the Irish resolution from the floor on behalf of Kensington GMC.

Neil Kinnock overwhelmingly won the leadership on the first ballot, and Roy Hattersley the deputy leadership on the first ballot. The TGWU went against the recommendations of their executive and voted for Hattersley instead of Michael Meacher, which was a scandal, but nobody referred to it because everybody wanted the 'dream ticket'. Meacher himself voted for Kinnock and not for Heffer, which was a disgrace, really.

Tuesday 4 October

I was elected top of the NEC constituency section again with the highest vote I have had for twenty years, the tenth year in a row I have received the most votes.

Michael Foot made his farewell speech and got tremendous applause. Caroline went back to London to take her evening class; she doesn't like Conference.

Thursday 6 October

In the afternoon Kinnock made his first speech as Leader. It was pretty vacuous, I thought, but he got a huge ovation.

Friday 11 November

I went to Bristol to attend a memorial meeting for Alan Mason, the South West Regional Organiser, who died recently. While I was there Mike Cocks told me privately that Eric Varley is meeting his Party's executive committee in Chesterfield tonight and intends to announce that he is resigning from Parliament to become Chief Executive of Coalite. I must admit it took some time for this to sink in, but it became quite clear that this would mean a by-election in a seat with a 7,000 Labour majority.

When I got home (on the last train) I spoke on the phone to Arthur Scargill, who had a word with Peter Heathfield, General Secretary of the Derbyshire Miners, who is also a member of the GMC of the Chesterfield Party, and Arthur rang me back and said, 'You must move quickly. We will get statements put out in the constituency to the effect that they would like you, and you must be ready to say you would be pleased to respond.'

My prospects may possibly have changed a bit.

Saturday 19 November

I have been in touch with Tom and Margaret Vallins, who are both on the Chesterfield executive committee. Apparently the NUM are allowed only five delegates at the selection conference out of a total of 132 votes, so the miners haven't actually got a dominating role. They have decided to nominate a miner, and vote for me on the second ballot – which is better than nothing. The YS have nominated me, but whether that's a good start or not I don't know. The AUEW are pretty strong. Alan Tuffin of the Union of Communication Workers sent instructions to the UCW there to nominate Charles Morris, who lost his Manchester seat in the boundaries redistribution. That caused some resentment among the UCW people in Chesterfield. ASLEF have got a strong branch there. Tom Sawyer is getting on to NUPE and there are two or three wards that could nominate me, so I might end up with a few nominations. The first hurdle is to get shortlisted, the second hurdle is to get into the final ballot, and if that happened I think I would have a reasonable chance.

David Blunkett told me that when he was in Chesterfield he found that a lot of people had been influenced by the hostile press campaign. The local papers and the *Daily Mail* have been using polls to influence the selection process.

Doesn't look too good, but it's not entirely impossible.

Sunday 11 December

Caught the train to Chesterfield to meet Party members. The train didn't actually stop in Chesterfield station but went straight through, then halted, and I thought the driver had forgotten to stop in Chesterfield, so I opened the carriage door and jumped on to the line and walked back about half a mile. In fact they were having to back the train into the platform. It was a risky thing to do, but I couldn't afford to be late.

Ken Coates and Tom Vallins took me over to the old Market Hall for a pre-selection meeting between the candidates and members of all the wards. The other candidates were John Lenthall, the treasurer of the Chesterfield Party, Cliff Fox, the NUM candidate, Bill Flanagan, leader of the council Labour Group, Phillip Whitehead and Paul Vaughan, President of the Party. I had prepared my speech too much, and it was a bit offputting because it was so rigidly controlled. I was asked three questions. One was about the media attacks, another about my age and health and one, from the YS, asking if I was in favour of MPs taking the average workers' wage. I felt very discouraged.

Wednesday 14 December

To Chesterfield for the St Helen's Ward nomination meeting. I was absolutely certain that Paul Vaughan, who is Chairman of the ward Party, would get it.

When I got home, I rang Tom Vallins for the result and heard I had won the ward by 11 to 8. Then I heard that in Moor Ward, where they nominated without hearing the candidates, there was a tie between me and Paul Vaughan, and the Chairman gave his casting vote in support of Paul.

Wednesday 21 December

Bea Campbell came to do an interview for *City Limits*. She pursued me on a number of points but she is obsessed with my class. She was trying to suggest that on a particular day in 1966 I met a worker at the Upper Clyde Shipbuilders and this was when the scales fell from my eyes. It isn't quite as simple as that, but it was a useful discussion, and she wants to come back and pursue Hobsbawm's argument for a popular front, she being a member of the Eurocommunist wing of the CP.

Wednesday 4 January 1984

Arkady Maslennikov, the London correspondent of *Pravda*, came to interview me. He had said he would very much like to see how my computer worked, so, before he arrived, I prepared 'a message from the Central Committee of the CP in Moscow to the London *Pravda* correspondent'. The message stated that it was amazing that he was still using a typewriter, which was a tsarist invention, that he might even be using a medieval instrument known as a pen, that all correspondents had to equip themselves with computers in order to demonstrate the Soviet lead in technology, and 'would he please confirm the receipt of this message by sending a carrier pigeon at once to Moscow'. Maslennikov laughed heartily when I called up the message on the screen. Then I showed him how it could be printed in various typefaces, and he took four copies away with him.

Sunday 15 January
We left for Chesterfield at 8 am for the selection conference of the GMC, and arrived in snow and blizzards. Caroline dropped me off at the NUM offices in Saltergate, where there was an enormous crowd of media people standing about as the snowflakes fluttered down. There was the usual checking of Party membership cards and trade union membership as delegates arrived. I drew number six in the speaking order.

The final list was Cllr Dave Wilcox of USDAW, Phillip Whitehead, Bill Flanagan, Cliff Fox, John Lenthall and me.

I finally went in just after 6pm. I had only been speaking for two minutes when a miner in the front row had an epileptic fit and had to be carted out. He was a very heavy man and had been sick, but they managed to move him and left him at the back so officially he could hear the speeches. I had to recover after that incident. I was asked the obvious questions – 'Didn't we lose the General Election because you fought against Healey?', 'How would you deal with the media?', and so on.

There were three ballots, and, to cut a long story short, I was selected. I shook hands with the others and said I hoped to see them all in Parliament in other seats after the next General Election. Phillip Whitehead and Bill Flanagan made little speeches of congratulations, then all hell broke loose. As I went out the front door, there were the media surging about with cameras. We moved slowly across their ranks to the Labour Club, where I gave a press conference. Afterwards I had a word with all my supporters and then Caroline and I drove home.

Caroline was marvellous all day. I have overcome the biggest hurdle, despite the huge press campaign designed to prevent my being selected. I did actually win with more votes than the next two candidates combined, so that was something.

Tuesday 7 February
Visited the Arkwright colliery, where the manager had told the media they were not allowed to come inside. I went down the pit for the first time since my illness in 1981, and I did wonder whether I would stand up to it because my legs are still a bit shaky. Fortunately it was a drift mine, and they took me down in the man-rider. I still had to walk three and a half miles underground on a 1:4 gradient. John Burrows, the treasurer of the Derbyshire NUM, and Cliff Fox came with me. I went and talked to the media in my pit clothes before I had a bath.

Sunday 12 February
Laurie Flynn, who is a friend of Maxine Baker on 'World in Action', came to discuss a programme they want to do on the media coverage of the by-election. I was a bit suspicious, truthfully.

Today Meg Crack, Chris Mullin, Ian Flintoff and Jon Lansman arrived;

my team is beginning to assemble. I visited a Labour club, where, I think, Vincent Hanna had interviewed people and, seemingly, only two out of 150 supported me. They began the bingo, and when number 10 was drawn they called out, 'Number Ten, Wedgie's Den.' Everybody laughed; it was a sort of sign of acceptance, and Dennis Skinner, who organised it, was absolutely thrilled.

It's bitterly cold at the moment, and I have to wear two pairs of socks and two woolly jumpers.

Sunday 19 February
Seventeen candidates have been nominated – a record. I should mention a couple of the other candidates. Screaming Lord Sutch, David Sutch, of the Monster Raving Loony Party Last Stand, turned up at some of my meetings. He has become something of a friend. He's a decent guy, he is actually quite serious and liked the things we were saying, and my view of him altered completely. He appears to be making fun of the Election but he's shrewd: he's a court jester in the medieval sense.

Neil Kinnock came up today. I met him at lunchtime at the Labour Club and there was a photo-call. For the purpose of the battle, you have to be seen side by side, and he played it very well. We went on a walkabout in the market and were mobbed by the media; there must have been sixty of them walking backwards in front of us. I wonder whether it was worth doing, because hardly anyone in the market could get near us. Even when we went for a cup of tea they surrounded us.

Kinnock performed his part excellently. At the public meeting, we held up our hands together and I called it 'The Return Ticket', a comment on the so-called 'Dream Ticket'.

I did have a chance to talk to Neil about his visit to America. He had seen Reagan, who had said to him, 'Do you think the United States would ever have used nuclear weapons on Japan if Japan had had the bomb?' So Kinnock replied, 'Well, that would be Qadhafi's case for having the bomb!' Reagan couldn't think of an answer to that one.

Kinnock was quite friendly throughout, but it was a formal occasion. That part of the campaign is over, and Kinnock must want it to succeed.

Friday 24 February
I went to the Chesterfield Royal Hospital. Patricia Moberly and Jenny Holland from Vauxhall were here canvassing. Hilary, Sally, Michael and James turned up, and it was lovely to hear Michael cry out, 'Dandan!', which is what he calls me.

At the NHS rally in the evening with 500 people, I did a very silly thing. To show how fit I was (I suppose), I tried to leap on to the platform, which was only about 18 inches off the ground, but I missed and fell and broke my specs. It hurt like anything, but I was determined not to show it.

Sunday 26 February
The last Sunday before polling day. Pat Phoenix, Tony Booth, Dennis Skinner, Caroline and I went out for four hours in the morning and four hours in the afternoon. It was cold and wet and exhausting, but I must say Pat Phoenix was marvellous. There were over 1,000 helpers from all over the country – a great response.

Monday 27 February
Jim Mortimer, Eric Heffer and Denis Healey arrived for a public meeting. I must say Denis played it like an old trouper. He spoke before me, and just as he said, 'Tony and I are inseparable, like Torvill and Dean', the Party banner behind us fell off the wall; it was hilarious, and it was impossible not to laugh uproariously. He made a great speech and got a good reception. Then we went to the Hopflower pub, where he played the piano and we sang together, 'Here we are again, happy as can be, all good pals and jolly good company!' He was extremely good, and even the press were laughing.

Wednesday 29 February
Eve of poll. Went canvassing with Colin Welland, who wrote *Chariots of Fire*, which was such a success, and Stephen Lewis, who plays an inspector in 'On the Buses'; he is a committed socialist and extremely amusing, very direct and couldn't have been better. At a canteen meeting and later at the Brimington Ward eve-of-poll meetings I spoke about restoring our self-respect and getting rid of the Tories.

A series of eve-of-poll meetings with Jo Richardson, Ken Coates, Peter Heathfield and Stuart Holland. Bed at 12.

Thursday 1 March – Chesterfield by-election
Joshua worked all day feeding canvassing information into the computer system set up at the Westdale Hotel. I went round the constituency all day.

The *Sun* had an article, 'Benn on the Couch – a top psychiatrist's view of Britain's leading leftie', in which they said they had fed my personal and political details to a psychiatrist in America who had concluded that I was power-hungry, would do anything to satisfy my hunger, was prone to periods of fantasy and so on.

Dozed, had a bath at the Westdale, then watched TV.

Just after midnight, we walked over to the Goldwell Rooms in the snow and the rain for the count. When we arrived, there was a huge crowd outside being held back by police. I did a few interviews, and the result was declared – Labour 24,633, Liberal 18,369, Tory 8,028. So the majority was 6,264, which was 663 higher than Varley's. There were rowdy scenes as we got on the platform, and all the young Labour people came in chanting, 'Tony Benn, Tony Benn!' I made my victory speech. Payne, the Liberal, made an angry one which was greeted with so much noise that I had to quieten people down in order to allow him to be heard. Bourne, the Tory, spoke briefly.

We withdrew like boxers after a big match and went back to the Labour Club with the media around in huge numbers, the police having a job to hold them back. Outside the Labour Club I spoke to the crowd again. Then I went inside and stood on a table and addressed the members.

Got to bed at 5 exhausted, but what an extraordinarily good result it was, though 'Newsnight' were able to describe it as a very poor result for Labour. I must confess it was a triumph for the Left and showed that socialist policies are not a deterrent.

Thursday 15 March

The miners' strike has been triggered off by the Government's decision to accelerate pit closures, and there has been a ballot in the various areas. Derbyshire voted by only 16 votes against striking, and Nottingham by 3 to 1. It has precipitated a great new crisis in the mining industry and a big political crisis in Britain. I attacked the Home Secretary, Leon Brittan, in the House when he made his statement on picketing, saying that a 'major co-ordinated police response, involving police officers throughout the country, has been deployed to ensure that any miner who wishes to work . . . may do so.'

Friday 16 March

I drove to Chesterfield for a surgery. Margaret and Tom Vallins have got it all organised, and Margaret has agreed to be my constituency secretary, part-time.

Monday 19 March

Thousands of police are being used to stop the miners from picketing; in Kent, miners were stopped from travelling through the Dartford Tunnel. I heard that Michael Foot, Merlyn Rees, Eric Heffer and Tony Banks had protested to the Press Council about the *Sun* story, 'Benn on the couch'.

Tuesday 20 March

Went to the Commons for Prime Minister's Questions, and got in one about the use of the police in the strike. The whole mining industry is now up in arms because of flying policemen coming from all over the country to try to stop picketing in Nottinghamshire.

Thursday 22 March

Caught the train to Chesterfield. Tom and Margaret met me and we went straight to the Duckmanton miners' wives meeting which had been organised by Margaret Vallins and Betty Heathfield. One woman, whose five-week-old baby had died in a cot death in January, had received a bill for

£206 for a headstone, to be paid by the end of March. She was getting no strike pay from her husband.

Friday 4 May

Apparently some of the men still working in the pits are waving their £50 bonuses in the faces of the pickets. In Nottinghamshire, 10,000 tons of coal a day is being produced instead of 28,000 tons, and that means the subsidy on it would be £70–80 a ton.

Saturday 5 May

It looks as though the miners cannot beat the Government. However, with 85 per cent of the pits out, coal stocks must be shrinking like anything, and the steel industry is beginning to be affected. The miners won't budge, and it is a very long strike, already longer than the 1926 strike. The TUC has got to back them, because, to put it bluntly, if the miners are beaten, the Government will ride all over everybody and workers couldn't stand up to it again, so the miners *mustn't* be beaten.

The success or failure of the Government doesn't depend on their capacity to bring in police to beat a particular group of workers, it depends on whether they carry the public with them, and they have gone so far over the top on democracy, trade union rights and brutality against the poor that the public are beginning to see it; but what a battle it is.

Tuesday 15 May

Roy Hattersley sat down next to me at tea and I had a chat with him. He told me he thought the miners would lose, and I said I thought we ought to take a stronger line because there were votes to be gained from strength and there was a sense of weakness prevailing at the moment. He agreed with that. He said he had had to protect Kinnock from getting the wrong line on Liverpool, and there was a twinkle in his eye.

I followed this up by saying, 'I suppose Neil will be the first Prime Minister at Number 10 who has never held any ministerial office.'

He said, 'No, there was Ramsay MacDonald!'

It was quite a friendly talk and I think the truth is that Roy Hattersley would like to build up alliances on the Left a bit. In that situation, Hattersley would be easier to deal with than Kinnock, just as Healey would have been easier to deal with than Foot.

Wednesday 16 May

I went to the House for a meeting of the PLP.

There were a number of motions asking for a censure debate on the miners' dispute and for a £5 levy on MPs towards the miners' strike. Max Madden, MP for Bradford West, made a brilliant speech, describing how miners and nurses had stood together on the hospital picket lines to try to prevent the closure of Thornton View Hospital, which was in his constituency. He said that in Chesterfield he had met a miner who said, 'For the first time we are beggars, and we never thought we would be.' He told us that huge sacrifices were being made, and at the moment a miner's wife had only £13.85 a week to live on. At his GMC, £80 had been raised, and tinned food was being collected outside supermarkets. He moved a motion for a £5 levy from all Labour MPs. He said he was disappointed at the amendment which had been put against the £5 levy and he hoped those responsible would withdraw it. He stressed, 'Money is vital, because this will be a long dispute.'

Willie Hamilton, the MP for Fife, who is a hardline right-winger, gave his credentials: he was the longest-serving member of the PLP and he had always supported miners (the sort of statement that warns you that betrayal is coming). He said there had never been a motion for a levy of Labour MPs before, it was a dangerous precedent, and what would happen if a similar motion was put forward for the nurses, the engineers or the civil servants? The PLP would become a supplementary benefit organisation. 'This is not the way to help the miners. The Government has got its responsibility, and the Notts miners are good, sound working people. The strike is harming the Party and Thatcher is trying to say that we are responsible.'

Kinnock declared, 'I want the miners to win. I agree with Max Madden that there are massive sacrifices being made in the coalfields and the Movement is trying to help. My own constituency has given £500. I accept also that £5 is not a sacrifice for MPs. The amendment has nothing to do with any objection to the money, but if we levy now we must continue to levy, and we, the Shadow Cabinet, are against it. A levy gives the impression that there is a reluctance to contribute, and if the levy fell below its official sum, there would be a propaganda point for our enemies.'

Joe Ashton was excellent. He said, 'We are now attempting to substitute a discussion about payments for a debate on policy. The Shadow Cabinet have been sitting on the fence for ten weeks and have now come up with this amendment against the miners. We have had no policy for ten weeks, and 2,300 miners have been arrested. The police are now in charge of industrial relations. The Labour Party's gains in the opinion polls have levelled off because we are dithering. What are we scared of? We are just keeping our heads down, and we need leadership from the PLP. We should take the initiative. The strike is about despair. We should support the miners or we will lose.'

In the end, the motion was carried unanimously. This is the second time within a week that I have witnessed Kinnock withdraw. He did so in the Liverpool case by accepting a meaningless amendment, and he did so in this case by accepting a meaningless concession. It does confirm my view that, if you keep the pressure up, the man will always give way.

Friday 18 May
Up at 6.30 for the soup run at 7.30. It was cold and a bit miserable, and I detected a different atmosphere. The miners were unshaven, looked unwell, were probably unfed, and the police were more aggressive. I was told that at one place the police had stood right up against the miners, staring at them and rhythmically beating their truncheons on their gloved hands. It is just very frightening and intimidating.

I talked to Betty Heathfield about the attempt by the Electricity Board to cut off domestic supplies to the miners, and I wrote some letters to try to prevent it. She told me that the villages of Welbeck and Church Warsop had been virtually occupied by the police. They had put foot patrols on every corner, gone into the houses of striking miners, interrogated the families to find out if they were billeting pickets from Yorkshire, and were evicting those Yorkshire miners, though they had absolutely no right to do so. They were alleged to be 'investigating intimidation' by striking miners against working miners. Betty thought the police were trying to break up the Women's Action Group, because the Barnsley group had been arrested and the police were attacking women pickets.

Sunday 20 May
Heard Neil Kinnock on the one o'clock news. His interviews are like processed cheese coming out of a mincing machine – nothing meaty, just one mass of meaningless rhetoric that defuses and anaesthetises the listener. The last thing we want is a row with him because he is still on his honeymoon, but the fact is that the Labour leadership has totally failed to support the working class when in struggle.

Wednesday 23 May
NEC, which was nasty at times. At one stage, Dennis Skinner described it as a 'right-wing mediation committee'.

Neil Kinnock snarled, 'You're mad, you're mad!'

I've never seen Neil Kinnock lose his cool like that.

Eric Heffer said, 'Right, we'll suspend the meeting for five minutes.'

Dennis argued, 'We've been voting all night, and the Front Bench sloped off after a deal and left us to hold the fort . . .' and so on.

Neil Kinnock shouted, 'The time's coming when you'll have to put up or shut up!'

I had a reply today from Mrs Thatcher to the fax I had sent her about the use of troops in the miners' dispute, and the wording she uses, such as 'no authorisation has been given', is very different from saying that it isn't happening – a highly unsatisfactory response. So I think I might possibly keep that alive a bit.

Friday 25 May
I had resolved that while Caroline was in America I would do some repairs

around the house. I started work at 4 pm and it was an absolute disaster. The first job I attempted was to replace the old lavatory seat, but I couldn't get the old fittings off, so I banged with the hammer and bust the lavatory bowl, and now the water comes out the back when you flush. The cost of that intervention will be £70 or £80. Then I tried to repair a faulty switch outside the bedroom, but I wasn't sure what to connect to what, so ended up putting the old broken switch back on. Then I replaced bulbs round the house.

This morning, Hilary had the whole centre page in *Tribune* on the Common Market; he is a great authority on Europe.

Thursday 31 May
Over the last few days there have been terrible scenes outside the Orgreave Coke Depot, where 7,000 pickets have been attacked by mounted and foot police with riot shields and helmets. It looks like a civil war. You see the police charging with big staves and police dogs chasing miners across fields, then miners respond by throwing stones and trying to drag a telegraph pole across a road; there are burning buildings and roadblocks. It is like looking at scenes from Northern Ireland or Central Europe. Yesterday Arthur Scargill was arrested.

I was asked to go on 'The World at One' to comment on the fact that the Police Federation had suggested that the Coal Board take legal action under the Employment Acts to deal with the miners' opposition to the pit closures. I agreed to go on, but I said, 'You will have to give me a couple of minutes to say what *I* think is happening.'

They replied, 'We can't do that.'

I told them, 'If you want me on, I want the opportunity to say what I think is happening in the dispute.'

They said, 'Well, you'll be interviewed.'

So I had a flaming row with the editor, who said, 'We can't make special rules for you.'

'I'm not going to be interviewed and treated as if I was on trial for my life and be prevented from saying what I want to say.' I left it at that.

Saturday 2 June
With Tom Vallins to a rally in the village of Ollerton in the North Nottinghamshire coalfield. When we arrived, there were police about every hundred yards walking in pairs up and down the village street. Some 5–6,000 people marched round the town singing 'I'd rather be a picket than a scab' to the tune of the Simon and Garfunkel song 'I'd rather be a hammer than a nail', and pointing to the houses of miners who were working. It's such a small community, everybody knows what everybody else is doing.

We marched to a field outside the Miners' Welfare Club. Tommy

Thompson, Vice-President of the Yorkshire miners, who was extremely clear and direct, described how he had been invited by Stan Thorne, the MP for Preston, to speak at an unemployment meeting alongside Neil Kinnock, but then Stan Thorne had taken Tommy aside and asked him not to speak: 'You will appreciate, it would be a real embarrassment to Neil Kinnock if you, as a Yorkshire miner, were to speak on the same platform as him.' Tommy said, 'My family have done more for the Labour Movement than Neil Kinnock will do until the day he dies.'

I was presented with a stick carved with a miner's head, and a miner's lamp. I was also given a thick plastic file full of statements by Nottinghamshire miners about police arrests and brutality.

Two women who spoke – miners' wives – were brilliant, and they told me afterwards that it was the first time they had ever spoken from a platform.

Thursday 7 June

Miners had come from all over the country for a mass demonstration in London; a very exciting occasion. It was headed by Arthur Scargill, Mick McGahey, Eric Clarke, Eric Heffer and Jim Mortimer. People were waving and cheering out of the windows as we walked along Farringdon Road. It was a beautiful day, and there must have been 10–20,000 people.

Outside the *Sunday Times* offices the SOGAT chapel had their banner on the pavement and were cheering and waving; that was really something for the *Sunday Times*. We turned down Fleet Street and passed the *Daily Express* building and the miners shouted out, 'Lies, lies, lies, lies!' – that was exciting and long overdue. The miners were in a jolly mood, and some of them were drinking cans of beer and had stripped off to the waist, showing off their tattooed bodies. There were some hostile looks, as you would expect, and large numbers of police. At one stage, when the miners saw the mounted police, they shouted, 'Sieg Heil, Sieg Heil, Sieg Heil!' Relations between the miners and police are at rock bottom.

Just as I was going through the Lobby at 10.15, Dennis Skinner said, 'Sixty-seven miners are being held in Rochester Row police station as a result of scuffles in Parliament Square. Will you go and see them?'

So Brian Sedgemore, Tam Dalyell and I drove to the police station, where a group of miners were waiting anxiously outside. We went in and spoke to a man with two pips on his shoulder, a young officer type in his late twenties who was very courteous. He asked us to wait, and while we were waiting, we met a lawyer brought over by the NUM, a woman in her late twenties. She was a most determined woman. She said, 'These people are being held five to a cell intended for one, they have had no food, have been here six or seven hours, and the situation is really awful.' We were told that one man of sixty-seven who had a heart condition had been released from the cells because he was suffocating, and another man with migraine had

had to be released. Somebody had been struck on the eye by a policeman, and a doctor had said it should be stitched, but nothing had been done.

The commander of A Division, which covers the whole area, came to see us. He was a rather decayed-looking man in his late forties or early fifties, wearing a peaked cap with a lot of encrusted silver on it.

We were all taken up to what was obviously the officers' dining room and the commander sat there with the other officer. I kept my tape recorder running in my bag. I did wonder whether it was entirely proper, but I thought: When you're dealing with the enemy, why not?

In the course of the discussion I said to the senior officer, 'I cannot understand, Commander, how it is you allow the police to be used in this way. You are provoking people and you are being used by the Government for political purposes.'

He said, 'I can't comment on that.'

'Well, maybe you can't, but can you explain why it is that Metropolitan police constables in Derbyshire are waving their £600-a-week pay slips at miners who have got nothing to live on?'

'Well, obviously you can't justify that,' he replied.

Brian Sedgemore, who is a big, tall man, a barrister, made the point that there was no justification whatever for keeping the arrested men for hours without food, for treating them like this, when they were only charged with obstructing the highway, threatening behaviour or obstructing the police, which are pretty minor offences. We heard later that the ventilation in the cells had broken down, and the heat was intolerable.

Anyway, at about 11.45 we were told they had all been released. We never saw them in the cells, as we had asked, but we did insist upon seeing the cells afterwards. Each cell measured only 7 feet by 6 feet and had a recess across which was a wooden board with a mattress covered in plastic. Even with the door open, you could hardly breathe, and all the ventilation came in through a small plate, just about big enough to provide air for one person, but with a high summer temperature and a broken ventilator it was impossible to breathe. To have been shut up in there with no ventilation must have been a nightmare.

As we left, the commander said, 'Goodnight.' I couldn't shake him by the hand, and I told him, 'I shall never forget tonight.' We went out and talked to the miners outside.

Having taken all the details and listened to everything that had happened, I went home. I was so upset and angry to think that this is happening in Britain. The police are accountable to nobody. As Tam, Brian and I parted, we agreed to write a letter to the Home Secretary over the weekend, and we will probably release it to the press.

Saturday 7 July
To Chesterfield. Went over to the club and there was Peter Heathfield, so I

asked him about the talks being held between the Coal Board and the NUM, I must say Peter is marvellous; he's got a tremendous sense of humour, and he looked tanned and cheerful. He said the talks had gone well from the point of view of the NUM. Ian MacGregor, the Chairman, was trying to be friendly, but after nine hours he had begun to get a bit knackered. He said Jim Cowan, the Deputy Chairman of the Coal Board, was taking a hard line, although that may have been their strategy. Ned Smith, the industrial relations director, was probably less rigid. The three of them – Peter Heathfield, Arthur and Mick McGahey – are working extremely well together. Arthur is totally unyielding and is a field commander; Peter is a negotiator, a diplomat; and Mick McGahey is a straightforward old statesman. They are a fantastic team and totally united. The Coal Board and the NUM have agreed that there's no problem with closures of pits on the grounds of exhaustion or geological faults, but they are trying to find a new definition of 'uneconomic pits', a term which the NUM are not prepared to accept.

I said, 'What about suggesting to them that the finance for "uneconomic pits" should come from nuclear power?'

Peter said, 'MacGregor might agree, but that's a different matter.'

'Well, bring in the Government.'

'We don't want to involve the Government,' said Peter.

'Couldn't you suggest that the "uneconomic" coal be given to pensioners?' I asked.

'MacGregor would say that had nothing to do with it.'

It became absolutely clear – and this is what I wanted to hear – that the NUM are not going to give MacGregor an agreement. They are not going to let him come out of it with any credit.

Peter said MacGregor was trying to be very friendly and saying, in his Canadian accent, 'Come on, Arthur' and 'Peter, you must come fishing with me in Scotland' and 'What about a game of golf, Mick?' McGahey, in his Scottish brogue, had replied, 'I've never played golf in my life; it's a total waste of time!' It would be fascinating to be a fly on the wall. MacGregor had said to Arthur, 'Now, Arthur, I've got my audience to consider and you've got your audience to consider, but the important one is the third audience, the people not directly involved.' The fact is that the miners now think they are winning.

Peter was prepared to say a great deal in confidence. The morale of the miners is fantastic, the money is coming in and they can manage. He thought the strike wouldn't finish until the end of August or the beginning of September, another eight weeks.

Sunday 15 July
Alan Meale rang to tell me about the Durham Miners' Gala yesterday. Apparently 100,000 people were there; Dennis Skinner made a brilliant

speech which got a standing ovation, but, when Neil Kinnock got up to speak, three bands started playing and moving off the field, and about 85,000 people with twelve banners just began moving away. All Neil did was to attack the Tories – he didn't give support for the miners.

Thursday 2 August

Lawson's comment that the miners' strike was a worthwhile investment was followed by the statement that if he had wanted a strike in 1981 he could have had one – which proves that he wasn't ready then and is ready now. The Prime Minister was on radio and television today saying that she thought the strike had gone on too long; I think they are worried.

Thirty-six years ago today I met Caroline. She put on the very same dress she wore that day and it fitted her perfectly. She looked lovely in it, and it is fantastic that we should have had thirty-six years together. We went out for a meal.

Tuesday 14 August

I do get the feeling that the strike is building up to a real crisis, particularly when you get accounts of incidents like a policeman threatening to stick a man's darts up his nose, stories of the police being drunk and breaking cars. They are completely out of control. Went on to Warsop, where I heard that at 3 am the police had got out of their vans with their riot shields and walked in front of cottages, banging their batons rhythmically, frightening people.

Friday 24 August

This evening Kathy Ludbrook looked in to discuss the possibility of becoming my secretary to replace Julie. She has exceptional political knowledge and experience. She said one thing to me: 'I am afraid I am very sensitive to smoking. Do you smoke a lot?' That really worried me, but we'll try it out.

Thursday 13 September

The Acting Chief Constable of Derbyshire, Mr Leonard, had written to me saying he would like to see me, and he arrived at the Labour Club accompanied by another officer. I had with me Gordon Butler and Johnny Burrows.

Leonard said at the beginning, 'I thought it would be a good idea to have a talk, because from some of the things you have been saying about police action you misunderstand that *I* have complete operational control. I have only got 1,800 policemen in the whole of Derbyshire.'

I listened carefully, and said, 'Thank you very much, but remember I have a certain amount of Whitehall experience as a Minister. I was in the Cabinet during the Winter of Discontent, and I know perfectly well that the Home Secretary chairs a meeting with the police, the army and Ministers and that all the instructions are given by the Home Secretary. So please don't ask me to believe that you are in charge. I don't honestly believe you are.'

Then he made a great point about how in Derbyshire they had not closed the motorways, that the Metropolitan police officers who had been brought in were under his control and they weren't as bad as we thought. He said he briefed the police every Sunday night about the history and traditions of the Derbyshire miners. He then remarked, 'You may think me cynical and think I am scapegoating, but it suits our books to see the Met criticised because, when the strike is over, the Derbyshire Constabulary will be able to resume normal relations with the local people and say it was the Mets who caused trouble.'

I thought he was taking a bit of a risk saying that. He's an intelligent person and, personally, quite a nice guy. He certainly will be a Chief Constable; he is standing in for the Chief Constable.

Then I gave him some examples of people's fear of the police breaking into their homes in the middle of the night. Generally speaking, I indicated that the situation was explosive and there was no point in pretending otherwise. 'If I may say this to you, Chief Constable, I believe that you, as individuals, should make it clear to the Home Office that you resent the police being used for what are, in effect, political purposes, and that you are being used to cover up for a failure of government policy.'

He said, 'Police dislike the idea of being described as "under the control of left-wing extremists in the local authorities". Well, I am equally against right-wing extremists in the Cabinet controlling us' (a hostage to fortune). 'I am quite independent. I am here to keep the peace and enforce the law, and, if there is a conflict between the two, I have, probably, to keep the peace.'

He was looking forward to the time when it would all be over, and I said, 'I think your problems will begin then.'

Tuesday 2 October – Labour Party Conference, Blackpool
Neil Kinnock made his Conference speech, which lasted forty-five minutes. I was sitting next but one to him, so I had to listen. He got a standing ovation of a most forced kind. People rose to their feet and clapped in order to prolong it. Glenys was brought on and they held up their hands. Then he himself stopped it because it was getting to the point where people were standing like a sullen crowd clapping to try to get the pub doors open! Arthur Scargill had got a spontaneous and passionate ovation, and Neil didn't want comparisons drawn with Arthur.

Friday 12 October
At 3 o'clock this morning a bomb exploded in the Grand Hotel in Brighton, and four people were killed. Norman Tebbit and his wife were injured, and it just missed Mrs Thatcher, who emerged unscathed. The IRA have

claimed responsibility. It is a big event, like the Gunpowder Plot or the Cato Street Conspiracy. The IRA issued a statement, which the press never printed, saying that they had planted the bomb because prisoners in Northern Ireland were being tortured.

Saturday 13 October

Caught the 7.45 to Chesterfield. There were a couple of young striking miners from South Derbyshire on the train. They had no money at all and I bought them a cup of tea. We had two problems: first, how to get them to Derby without a ticket, then how to get them past the ticket collector in Derby. I spoke to the ticket collector on the train, who initially got very tough and said, 'I'll have to take their names and addresses.' Then he whispered to me, 'The man behind me is one of my gaffers from BR, a retired inspector.' So he took their details but won't act on it. I wrote a note to the ticket collector at Derby, explaining their situation and saying that, as the NUR was showing solidarity with the miners, I would be grateful if they could be allowed through and, if there was a problem, they should send the bill to me. I think everything was all right in the end. It gave me great pleasure that there was this sort of network of help.

Monday 19 November

In the House of Commons a statement was made about the Animal Liberation Front, who claimed to have poisoned Mars Bars with rat poison, as a result of which the Mars Corporation had taken their chocolate out of the shops. The ALF said Mars were funding experiments on animals. Well, there was shock-horror-disgust from all sides of the House. The only person who spoke up and said the Government had been slow to deal with animal welfare was Dale Campbell-Savours of all people. Everyone else just poured contempt on the ALF and said how the RSPCA was being undermined by this sort of irresponsible behaviour.

Wednesday 21 November

I went into the House at 10 pm. After a division, Mick Welsh, Labour MP for Doncaster North, a Yorkshire miner, got up, and he was so incensed at the cut of a further £1 a week from the benefit paid to the families of miners on strike that he stood shaking his finger. Quite spontaneously, Eric Heffer, Dennis Skinner, Dave Nellist and Terry Fields went and stood in front of the mace; a number of people joined them, including myself. I remember the same thing happening over the Industrial Relations Act. On this occasion the Speaker suspended the sitting for ten minutes. There was uproar in the House, and I believe Dave Nellist tore up the statement that the Social Services Secretary, Norman Fowler, was making. The Speaker came back, saw people still standing and adjourned the House. It was a tremendous row, and gave publicity to the miners' strike and the demand for a debate.

Things happen when you make a row, and if you don't make a row people don't give a damn.

Thursday 22 November
To Brussels for a meeting with the British Labour Group in the European Parliament, and we collected £400 for the miners.

Friday 14 December
At 10.35 pm, Joshua rang to say that William Graydon Feeney Benn had been born – our third grandchild. He is six weeks early, but seems to be all right.

Tuesday 8 January 1985
Bought four rather clever attachments to put on my shoes so that I wouldn't slip on the ice. I've been afraid of falling and breaking my hip or something. With the remains of the Guillain-Barré Syndrome I'm still not getting a perfect set of messages from my feet.

Thursday 31 January
Peter Heathfield said there were pickets who simply couldn't go on any more because their shoes had worn out, they hadn't got any warm clothes, they had been evicted from their homes, and their gas and electricity had been cut off. The union hadn't any money; they needed £150,000 a week to keep the strike going.

Sunday 10 February
The judge in the Ponting case apparently said that the interests of the state were the interests of the Government of the day, implying that criticism of the Government was unacceptable.

Monday 11 February
We heard on the news that Clive Ponting had been acquitted – a tremendously significant victory, particularly after the judge had given a violently anti-Labour summing-up. He almost directed the jury to convict.

Wednesday 13 February
A man in Wales has left me in his will many personal papers, including letters from Keir Hardie to Emrys Hughes's sister (while Emrys was in prison as a conscientious objector during the First World War), and a lovely ebony stick which Mahatma Gandhi gave to Hardie, and a small armchair.

Tuesday 19 February
The press generally presented yesterday's debate on the *Belgrano* as a great government triumph, with Heseltine having completely destroyed the

reputation of Clive Ponting. The Labour attack hasn't really registered, and that is the problem that we are facing as a party.

Sunday 3 March

Today the delayed miners' delegate conference took place at TUC headquarters. The NUM executive had been split 11:11 on the continuation of the strike, and Arthur had refused to use his casting vote. The delegate conference itself ultimately voted by 98 to 91 for an organised return to work.

I felt like weeping when I heard it on the news, after this great struggle – at the fact that the people who had been victimised were not being negotiated back, and at the Coal Board's and the Government's arrogance.

The strike has been a monumental and titanic struggle. The overwhelming majority of the miners and their families have supported it to the last, and the crude use by the Government of the apparatus of the state to crush the miners has been on an unprecedented scale. The lessons to be learned from that are enormous. The Coal Board as a nationalised industry has completely abandoned any legitimate loyalty from the miners – they are just state coal-owners.

The other unions who have supported them – the NUR, the NUS, and so on – have been marvellous. The TUC has been pathetic. The Labour hierarchy has been shown to be quite inadequate. But at grassroots level there has been a formidable development of support groups and so on. I think that is where we will see the moves coming now.

Tuesday 5 March

Chesterfield. Still have a filthy cough. I got up at 4, and at 4.50 we gathered in the pitch dark outside the Labour Club. We decided to go with Johnny Burrows to Markham colliery, and as the sun began to rise people gathered round.

All the miners and their wives, carrying banners, marched down the hill under the railway bridge towards Markham. It was an extraordinary day. Betty Heathfield was on the brink of tears and I hugged her. I felt drained by the end of it because every emotion swept through me like a gale – tragedy, wanting to weep at seeing these people who had sacrificed so much having to go back without having won; then tremendous pride that they could go back with their banners high and not give any sort of impression that they were beaten; then feelings of intense hate as a scab came forward dressed in his pit clothes and photographed them. They began shouting 'Scabby bastard!', and the level of hatred is frightening. Then I had feelings of hope and dignity as we stood there and applauded as they all marched into the colliery.

Later, on TV, we saw pictures from other collieries. At Maerdy, the last pit in the Rhondda, where not a single man had scabbed, they marched round the whole village and went in together. In Yorkshire Arthur Scargill led them back and was stopped by three Kent miners, who had come up all the way to picket that particular colliery because the Kent men are still out. So they all turned back and didn't go into work that day. The media will try to dance on the grave of the NUM, but they will make a terrible mistake.

Thursday 28 March

Brought my diary up to date. It would be so lovely if I had my own room at the Commons. I'm a nomad with a desk, and I can't even make private phone calls – every word can be overheard.

I have a huge burden of work at the moment but it is enjoyable, and now that I've been squeezed out of the top of Labour politics I'm determined to do a really good job as MP for Chesterfield.

Monday 1 April

I have had five invitations to go on chat shows, because it's my sixtieth birthday on Wednesday. I suppose when you reach sixty the journalists think they can rehabilitate you as an eccentric, lovable old character. These shows would be entirely personal, nothing to do with politics, and I would be presented as an attractive person if I was prepared to go along with it on their terms. But people at home who know me as a fighter would say, 'God, he's sold out.'

Tuesday 23 April

Today was the christening of Joshua's son, William, in the Commons Crypt. Michael and little James ran around and took no notice of the service at all. When the vicar asked us to stand for a prayer, Michael could be heard saying, 'We've got to stand again.' But it went beautifully, and William didn't cry at all. Afterwards we all went up to the Members' Dining Room and had tea.

Wednesday 24 April

Bought the *New Socialist*, and there was the article by Patrick Seyd called 'Bennism without Benn' of which I had been warned. To find a socialist journal carrying an article as personal as this is revolting. Stuart Weir, the Editor, is of the Hobsbawm school, and what the article says in effect is that Ken Coates, Michael Meacher, Tom Sawyer, Stuart Holland and Frances Morrell have all completely deserted me and joined the Kinnock camp and that I am now alone with 'Dennis Skinner and the headbangers'.

Thursday 25 April

New Left Review carried an article by Ralph Miliband in which he patiently took to pieces the arguments of the new revisionists – everyone from the Eurocommunists to the soft Left of the Labour Party. He described how people had detached themselves from the Left and were being drawn towards Kinnock with a view to 'saving Kinnock from the Right', the old argument that I heard Crossman and Castle use in relation to Wilson time and again.

I had a letter from Stuart Weir, offering me the right of reply in *New Socialist* and saying the Seyd article did not represent the paper's view.

Sunday 5 May

In the evening I had a useful meeting with the *New Left Review* people, organised by Ralph Miliband: John Palmer, Perry Anderson (Editor of the *NLR*), Tariq Ali, Hilary Wainwright and Robin Blackburn. Caroline sat in – which was a great tribute to them.

Ralph outlined the three elements of the Left: the ultra-Left (eg the Workers' Revolutionary Party and Militant) and some radical feminists, who were intransigent; the Hattersley to Hobsbawm Left (including Frances Morrell and possibly Ken Livingstone), who lean towards the leadership; and the independent socialist Left, the Bennites inside and outside the Labour Party, who wanted socialism without rocking the boat. Ralph wanted to see this last element strengthened.

He said Bennism could be summarised as 'the need for a democratic revolution' in Britain to tackle corporate power and the class structure. But how?

John Palmer was reminded of 1962–64 when Wilson had been able to co-opt the old Left because it had not prepared its position. Kinnock was attempting to do the same thing. John's fears for the next Election were that a Labour or Labour/SDP government might come to power and then fail, and that would produce a strong backlash of the Right, currently held in check by Thatcherism itself. He didn't agree entirely with me on the EEC but did agree on the question of NATO.

He continued, 'We must arm the Left with all sorts of weapons, weapons which may have to be used even against a Labour government. The defeat of the miners' strike was a blow to the Left, and helps to explain the shift towards Kinnock. The Left has to utilise its resources to mount a massive and serious anti-Thatcher campaign, because there is no attack on capitalism by Labour at the moment.' He said there would be a hard fight inside Parliament of fifty to sixty new Labour MPs who must tell the next Labour Government, 'We will not support what you propose – neither the acceptance of Cruise nor any attacks on the working class.'

Robin Blackburn believed we must attack British capitalism and not Thatcherism, which was the worst form of capitalism we'd ever had but had meant great success for the City. We must examine the empowerment of workers and the democratisation of British capitalism.

We discussed the accusation of 'boat-rocking'. John Palmer said that rocking the boat couldn't be avoided; there shouldn't be a leadership contest but there was a need for a clear challenge to Kinnock's position.

So from that beginning we decided to call ourselves the Independent Left Corresponding Society (ILCS) and meet monthly. It is what Ralph had in mind as a 'think tank', and I think we all enjoyed it. There has been a major political shift and we have to accept it without bitterness. The 'new realists' have been propelled towards Kinnock partly by the defeat of the miners and the local authorities, partly by the fact that if Kinnock becomes PM he will have a lot of patronage to offer and their own careers will be promoted. The media have been making it tough for the Left. The so-called Bennites are trying to find a new base from which to advance, rooted in the trade union movement and the constituency Parties.

Friday 19 July
Train to Chesterfield. As I went to get some tea a woman asked me if I was Tony Benn. She said, 'I'm Gareth Peirce.' Well, Gareth is one of the solicitors who has been defending the miners on trial for rioting at Orgreave, and we talked and talked. She told me the trial was of tremendous historical importance. At the beginning, the prosecution had said it was one of the gravest cases of riot in Britain, but the defence counsel had so successfully cross-examined the prosecution witnesses that it had gradually emerged, from the clear evidence of video recordings and photographs, that the police account was flawed.

She said that from reading the *Public Order Tactical Operations Manual* – the police training manual – detailing the use by the police of short and long shields, of mounted police and truncheons, it was clear that unarmed civilians were being exposed to paramilitary tactics unauthorised by common law. I am going to raise it in the House on Monday. It was a military operation without doubt – nothing to do with protecting law and order. She is going to get me extracts of the manual used at the trial.

Tuesday 1 October – Labour Party Conference, Bournemouth
I dropped from first to third place in the NEC elections, which is almost inevitable. Blunkett came first. The only people whose vote went up were Dennis Skinner and Jo Richardson. No one took much interest really, and nor did I, because as the day progressed it became more and more apparent what a misery it is to be in the Labour Party.

We had the health service debate, and Margaret Vallins spoke. She stood for the women's section of the NEC and got 59,000 votes – about 10 per cent of the whole – which was amazing.

Kinnock's Conference speech, and I sat through an hour and a quarter of it. The first part was very clever – hard, harsh Kinnock mocking the Government, stressing the importance of winning. But he ended with a violent attack upon Militant in Liverpool saying, 'Implausible promises don't win victories . . . you end in the grotesque chaos of a Labour council hiring taxis to scuttle around a city handing out redundancy notices to its own workers. You can't play politics with people's jobs . . . or their homes.' He spoke as if the Liverpool councillors wanted to fire people, when actually they are themselves victims of government policy. It was all part of his strategy, going back to 1983, to kill off any left-wing challenge by appealing for unity and on that basis to get a right-wing NEC and accuse the Left of being divisive. As a result of this strategy, power over policy-making has been passed to the Shadow Cabinet, a lot of charters (which have no policy status) have been issued, and the policy and the work of the International Department have been wound up.

Kinnock's speech led to a walkout by Eric Heffer and shouting from Derek Hatton and Tony Mulhearn. Kinnock has released the hatred of the Tory press against his own people in the middle of a struggle, in the hope that he can pick up the ex-Labour voters who supported Owen, knowing that real socialists and the rump of the working class have no alternative but to vote for him. He is pioneering a presidential style of government which is quite foreign to our own traditions.

I left because I couldn't bring myself to stay after that. I saw a woman delegate crying, and I put my hand on her shoulder and she said, 'I can't understand what they've done to our Party.' I told her not to worry, and I began to cry – not at what was happening, which I've seen before, but at this woman's distress. It absolutely shattered her.

It has been a historic day in the Party. What Gaitskell attempted in 1960 has been done again – an attempt to destroy the Left, the Conference and the unions. Some people will want a candidature against Kinnock next year, but he would smash his critics and crush the Left, probably even expel it. On the other hand, we don't have any obligation any more to go along with what is said, and I think it is perhaps the restoration of the freedom to speak out that is more important.

Wednesday 2 October
Debate on the miners' amnesty resolution. Arthur Scargill made an exceptionally good speech to the Conference.

Alan Hadden, who was chairing the Conference, managed to dredge up two delegates who were against the miners, and he also called Basnett, Gavin Laird and Eric Hammond against. He didn't call a single pro-NUM union leader such as Ray Buckton, Jimmy Knapp or Ron Todd.

It was an extraordinary debate – memorable for the fact that Eric Hammond described the striking miners as 'lions led by donkeys'. It caused an uproar in the hall, and just before Kinnock was due to wind up the debate, delegates were so angry that they stood up and just pointed at Ron Todd – like iron filings aligning themselves around a magnet – shouting. 'Todd! Ron Todd! Todd! Ron Todd!' so Hadden had to call him.

Ron made a very powerful speech. He was extremely angry. In response to Hammond he said, 'I am an animal lover. I prefer donkeys to jackals.' A good response, but it might have been better to have left it without reciprocal abuse.

Kinnock ended the debate. He spoke much more softly than yesterday, but his speech was really a denunciation of the whole strike, not just the resolution. He attacked the miners' leaders for the whole way in which they had conducted the campaign. A horrible speech.

I was told later that miners in the gallery were crying. However, the resolution was carried by 3,542,000 to 2,930,000, but it did not get a two-thirds majority, and that is the comfort Kinnock will cling on to.

We came later to the local-government debate, and David Blunkett was to move the NEC statement calling for reimbursement of councillors who had suffered financially through rate-capping legislation. There he was, this Christ-like bearded blind man, standing on the rostrum appealing to Derek Hatton to withdraw his Liverpool resolution asking for industrial action in support of councillors 'not prepared to carry out Tory cuts'.

'Will you do that? Will you do that, Derek?' He stood there waving his hands into the darkness.

So Hatton, who is a bit of a smart alec, ran towards the rostrum in his neat suit, got up on to the rostrum and said, 'Yes, in the interests of unity, Liverpool will withdraw its resolution.'

There was an explosion of applause. I believe the right wing were angry with Blunkett for having done that.

Thursday 9 January 1986

Michael Heseltine resigned from the Cabinet today over the Westland affair, giving as his reasons that the Prime Minister had refused to allow the matter to be discussed and had told Ministers to clear any statements with the Cabinet Secretary, Robert Armstrong. No doubt Armstrong himself suggested that in order to protect the PM from this continuing public row.

I remember that in 1974 I wanted to bring Westland Helicopters into British Aerospace, but Westland were making a lot of profits and didn't want to have anything to do with it. Then when Westland got into difficulties the Government wouldn't help them, and they were forced to look to the Sikorsky company in America, with whom they had links, and who put in a rescue package. This frightened the Europeans, and Heseltine, who is very pro-Common Market, supported the Europeans.

That disturbed Mrs Thatcher, who is pro-American, so she said that it should be left to the shareholders to decide, but it seemed she and Leon Brittan, the Trade and Industry Secretary, were indicating to Westland that it would be against the national interest for them to accept the European bid.

It has come at an interesting time, because there is this intense US domination of Britain, intense European hostility to America and a growing feeling that Mrs Thatcher is too overbearing. Heseltine, with his he-man image, has also spoken up for men against a woman's dictatorship in Cabinet.

Tuesday 14 January
Went into Prime Minister's Questions to see how she did on the Westland affair, and she was in complete control. Kinnock was quite ineffective.

Friday 17 January
The Westland shareholders are meeting at the Albert Hall – rich and powerful people deciding the future of the whole company and its workers. It is disgraceful.

Monday 27 January
The Westland debate, and it was one of those 'great parliamentary occasions'. It was opened by Kinnock, who waffled, talked for too long and didn't put the crucial questions. Thatcher brazened it out and didn't look at all worried. The only people whose faces were like thunder were the two law officers – Sir Patrick Mayhew, the Solicitor-General, and Sir Michael Havers, the Attorney-General – who appear to have been used by Thatcher to try to destroy Heseltine. When Heseltine spoke he attempted to recover his role as a Tory leader. Leon Brittan, who had resigned last week, made a cringing little speech. Michael Foot made a good one.

My speech was listened to in silence by the Labour Members. The Tories didn't like it and there were a lot of interruptions. I said that Mrs Thatcher had asked, 'Who will rid me of this turbulent priest?', and that her civil servants had done the rest and got Heseltine out. I also attacked the lobby briefing system.

Sunday 9 February
Watched Neil Kinnock on the Brian Walden interview on television. He is now advocating a Franklin D. Roosevelt approach. He declared that individual freedom must come above equality, that production must come above redistribution, and that taxes would not be raised except on the very rich, ie the top 3 or 4 per cent of earners. These statements, combined with his praise of the Japanese industrial system, put Kinnock and Hattersley squarely in the SDP camp.

I thought once again we must put up a candidate against Kinnock to challenge this consensus, but, as Caroline said, 'Nobody would understand what it would be about if you did it. You sacrificed yourself in 1981, when I advised you not to do it. You used up your goodwill at that moment and it isn't available to you now.'

Friday 14 February
The Turkish authorities have banned my proposed trip to Istanbul. Turgut Ozal, the Prime Minister, is coming to Britain on Monday.

Sunday 23 February
There was a small piece in the *Guardian* yesterday saying that Peter Mandelson had rung up the BBC to try to get me taken off the panel for 'Question Time', which I am doing on Thursday. This is a reaction to the fact that yesterday the NEC voted to start proceedings against Militant supporters in Liverpool District Labour Party. So I decided to write to Larry Whitty. To be banned from Turkey and 'Question Time' is quite something!

Saturday 22 March
I decided to go to Wapping for the printworkers' march on Murdoch's empire. The police are behaving in an appalling way.

Last Sunday the pickets did succeed in delaying the distribution of the papers by five hours, and late newspapers are just waste paper, so it's worth going.

It was an incredible night. A few years ago you would never have believed it could happen in the middle of London. Passing the Tower of London, grey-stoned and illuminated, you just felt as if you were back in the Middle Ages and it was only one step between the police charging you and hauling you away for execution in the Tower. We saw one of the huge lorries loaded with papers, coming out of the plant. But the spirit was good, just as good as during the miners' strike. I haven't as yet had to face a police horse or been struck by a truncheon, but tonight was a night to remember.

Monday 24 March
At 5 I went to the Party's Campaign Strategy Committee, where four men and a woman from something called the Shadow Agency made a presentation entitled 'Society and Self'. They said it was a qualitative survey in which thirty groups of eight people, 240 people in all, had been interviewed for an hour and a half. We were told that the purpose was to understand the nature of the target vote. Primarily, they were non-committed Labour voters.

They flashed up on to a screen quotes which were supposed to be typical of Labour voters, for example: 'IT'S NICE TO HAVE A SOCIAL CONSCIENCE BUT IT'S YOUR FAMILY THAT COUNTS.'

What we were being told, quite frankly, was what you can read every day in the *Sun*, the *Mail*, the *Daily Express*, the *Telegraph*, and so on. It was an absolute waste of money.

They went on to talk about images and how the Party image was made up of current issues, leadership and historical ideas. They said the public were more interested in people than ideas, and figures like Livingstone and Hatton did us great damage.

Why should we pay them to tell us that our own people are damaging?

Labour was associated with the poor, the unemployed, the old, the sick, the disabled, pacifists, immigrants, minorities and the unions, and this was deeply worrying. The Tories were seen to have the interests of everyone at heart including the rich. Labour was seen as yesterday's party. The SDP gave hope but had no ideology or history.

The Labour Party was seen as disunited, squabbling, with Militants or infiltrators, and lacking in government experience. 'The party of my father' was one of the quotes; 'If I had a brick, I would throw it into Arthur Scargill's face' was another.

What was required in the Party leadership was decisiveness, toughness and direction: people wanted a tough person at the helm. Leadership was what it was about. Who was the Leader and what did he look like?

It was a Thatcherite argument presented to us: 'You had better be more like Thatcher if you want to win.'

I came out feeling physically sick; I'm not kidding, I really felt unwell, because if this is what the Labour Party is about I've got nothing whatever in common with it.

Sunday 4 May

To Chesterfield. Went over to the Labour Club, and there were six women who had been at Wapping, and all had the same horrific accounts of the night.

Monday 19 May

Went over to the House of Commons for the Campaign Strategy Committee in Neil Kinnock's office. This is the holy of holies.

For the second half of the meeting we had another presentation from this Shadow Agency, which is made up of people from different advertising agencies who have offered to help the Party prepare for the Election.

It was a real management presentation with words and phrases being flashed up on a screen, like 'qualitative research', 'hypothetical solution', 'targeted'. This went on for ages, and Blunkett asked, 'What about democracy?'

'We haven't got round to that.' They continued, 'We must be credible, our promises must be backed by machinery. We must have sympathetic values. We must be able to answer the question "Where will we get the money from?" '

After the presentation was over, Robin Cook reflected my view. He said it didn't excite him because it wasn't rooted in experience.

Thursday 22 May

The NEC met all morning to consider the Militant Tendency members.

At 4.30 in the afternoon, Councillor Harry Smith from Liverpool Council was brought in – a short, round-faced man with curly hair and twinkling eyes – and with him was a sallow-faced man with dark hair who kept whispering in his ear.

Smith said, 'I should introduce the man I have brought with me. His name is George Nibbs – of course, that's only his pen-name.' Everybody burst out laughing, he was a very amusing man, though deadly earnest in what he said. He was only being charged with membership of the Militant Tendency, not with malpractice.

They asked for a deferment and withdrew, and Kinnock moved that we did not let him consult with his solicitor. Blunkett said he thought we should wait. Hattersley moved that we proceed, and that was carried 12 to 7. When they came back in, Harry Smith protested. 'What would happen if I walked out? I am very nervous. Ian Lowes has been done in and I'm afraid you are going to do me in too. It's like two murderers before a court. The judge says, "We've hanged one now, we'd better hang the other." I'm going.'

So he left, but at 5.30 he returned and said, 'I want to make a political statement. You don't know who I am, and I want to tell you who I am.' Then he gave the most riveting account of his life.

'My mum and dad were married, and I was born six months later, so it doesn't take a very clever man to realise what they were up to. They were High Church. I was racist as a young man, and I lived in the Edge Hill constituency. At fifteen I joined the electricians' union, which was when my political education started. My family are still Tories, and I come from a reactionary, working-class Protestant family. I worked all my life on building sites and in maintenance jobs, and I got married at eighteen. My son was born when we had been married six months, so you can see at least my son has got something in common with me.' Everybody laughed.

He continued, 'I joined the Labour Party in Wavertree Ward, which only had one or two working-class members. I helped in the ward, canvassed for new members and converted it into a political ward. I got appointed eleven months later as the election agent. I later became treasurer for Wavertree, and I ran the tote—'

Syd Tierney interrupted, 'I am not trying to stop you, but can you please come to the point?'

I said, 'Half a minute. This man is giving the reasons why he holds the views he does, and I want to know at what stage he may have heard about the ideas of Militant.'

Harry Smith went on, 'I stood as a council candidate, and gave an undertaking that I would carry out the policies. I was very nervous about speaking, but I wanted better services in the city. I had never been in any other political organisation – only the Church, boy scouts and youth clubs. I have never joined any other political organisation, I have never been a member of Militant. I read the paper. I've been thrown into a high prominence by my activity for a minimum wage and a 35-hour week, but I can't say I won't do it again because I haven't "done it" in the first place.'

I just note that at this stage it was clear that Sam McCluskie and Alex Kitson were going to vote in support of Harry Smith because he was creating such a good impression.

Smith carried on, 'All I can really do is speak. I did get invited to two meetings in Coventry and Llandudno' (which Hattersley had raised) 'but they were given to me to represent the Party.'

Frances Curran asked, 'Who booked you for these meetings? Wasn't it the City Council?'

'Yes, and all the speeches I did were through the Campaign Unit. I have never spoken other than for the council or for the Education Committee, or on the 35-hour week or the minimum wage.'

Kinnock asked him, 'When you discovered that Militant had taken you for granted, were you angry?'

'I'm easygoing. My wife says people take advantage of me, and perhaps they do. My school report says that if I had given more attention to my work I might have been a brain surgeon.' He was hilarious.

At 6.42, by which time he had completely charmed the meeting, we had the final statement. He said, 'I apologise for leaving when I did. It has been a comradely meeting. I hope you believe me. I hope I have satisfied you, and I would like to thank you for the comradely treatment I have received.'

It was quite clear that, with McCluskie, Kitson, Blunkett and Meacher voting in favour, Kinnock would lose. So Kinnock said, 'We've heard the explanation, a very candid reply. Not being disingenuous, I think we should withdraw the charges to prove that we listened carefully.' This was the point – he was anxious to let one person off so he could argue that he had been fair. He knew he would lose, and I think he was quite happy to let Smith off to ensure there was no vote.

By 9.30 pm we had expelled two more members, and acquitted Harry Smith.

Monday 16 June
Went with Tom to Chesterfield Crematorium for Frank Cousins's funeral. Many figures from the Labour Movement were there – Arthur Scargill, Peter Heathfield, Henry Richardson from the Nottinghamshire area NUM, Michael Foot, Geoffrey Goodman and his wife, Bill Howden from the GMB, Dennis Skinner, and Malcolm Gee from the AUEW.

But the chapel wasn't full, and the vicar, who knew nothing about Frank Cousins, gave a totally inadequate tribute, another of these sausage-machine funerals that I have attended for so many members of the Labour Movement. Caroline has always wanted a book of socialist writings from which you could quote – Keir Hardie, Tom Paine, and so on – and then you could sing socialist anthems and hymns.

Nance Cousins was absolutely magnificent.

Monday 7 July – Visit to Poland

At Warsaw I was met by two officials from the Scientific Secretariat of the Institute of International Affairs and an interpreter. They took me to a government hotel, in a batch of buildings where there are a lot of embassies.

Unpacked, and went down to dinner with members of the institute, a charming crowd. I asked what they thought the prospects of a Soviet invasion had been, and they said it was inconceivable that after the experience of Hungary and Czechoslovakia the Soviet Union would have invaded Poland – unless Poland had actually changed sides in the Cold War.

They were keen to stress that democracy was the key question everybody was discussing. They have tribunals to identify 'failures of socialist legitimacy' and so on. I said I thought tribunals were all right but actually democracy was a way of life; it was controversial and it took power away from people at the top, who didn't like it.

My impression is that Poland is much more open now (but probably the economic problems are making them cautious and conservative and managerial), that Communism in Eastern Europe is moving towards social democracy and there is a sort of convergence – although at the same time, alas, social democracy is moving towards monetarism.

Wednesday 9 July

I had a message to say that Cardinal Glemp would see me this afternoon. He was due to be away on holiday but had agreed to stay in Warsaw to see me. I was told that priests in Poland were the social aristocrats, with a powerful position in the villages (whereas in Italy, for example, they are poor).

I put on a white shirt and a smart suit to see Cardinal Glemp. We arrived at the Primate's Palace and walked through a long garden. The door was opened by an immensely tall and handsome young priest who was obviously the Primate's chaplain. He looked at Bozena, my interpreter, held out his hand and pointed with his finger at his watch – because we were one minute and a few seconds late, and I suppose you don't keep cardinals waiting, but he did it in a jovial sort of 'naughty-naughty' way.

We were shown into a room which had a throne at one end and oil paintings of all the previous primates of Poland hanging on the walls. Through another door came Cardinal Josef Glemp, a short man of about fifty-five, not a grey hair on his head, wearing a red cardinal's cap and a black cassock with a pectoral cross over it; he was rather expressionless. He beckoned us to sit at the table, and then sat at the other end, facing the throne. He had big ears that stuck out and a rather cunning expression. I got to like him more as the discussions progressed, but to begin with I was apprehensive of him because the Primate of Poland is a powerful man, and to establish a relationship of equality for the purpose of discussion was going to be difficult.

I thanked him very much indeed for seeing me. Then I said that Basil Hume was very popular in Britain, a modest man who had great influence. I mentioned the Pope's visit to Britain and his meeting with Archbishop Runcie at Canterbury Cathedral.

Glemp said, 'Basil Hume is a good man. I have asked Archbishop Runcie to come to Poland, but he can't come, so he is sending one of his senior officials or bishops.'

I told him I would be grateful if he could give me his assessment of the situation in Poland.

'Well,' said Glemp, with a slight glint in his eye, 'of course, I can only comment on Church matters, but there is a very serious conflict between Christianity and Communism. The Church is concerned with morality, and a serious demoralisation has occurred in Poland. When the Communists took over private property and made it collective, it was simply a utilitarian policy, and I am afraid there is no feeling of conscience by the public about common property. The Church must be able to help the community decide what is good and what is evil.'

That was what Lopatka had said about policies designed for angels.

'I am afraid there are deep-rooted evils in Polish society caused in part by partition, in part by the occupation, and the most serious evil is alcoholism. The alcohol industry produces the greatest profits, and this is one reason why it continues to exist. We need to produce less alcohol in Poland.

'Then we come to the question of family morality. The Communist philosophy and Western values are undermining young people. Women are working as men do, but at lower wages. The divorce rate is rising and there is lower morality in Poland. Those are the Church's concerns in the area of public affairs.'

I mentioned that, as he would be well aware, the standard of morality in the West was pretty low; there was drunkenness and drugs and pornography and vice and competitiveness.

'That is true,' he said, 'but the Communist Party defends collective values, and we also have to have regard for individual rights. Actually, the Communist Party is only against drugs because it wants people to be subservient, and if people are on drugs they can't be made subservient.'

So I told him I thought that because drugs removed people from situations of conflict, and neutralised them, some regimes actually encouraged drugs because they produced a quiescent population.

He said, 'I think the Communist Party is afraid that drugs will mean that young people won't listen to what the Ministers say.'

I turned the subject to liberation theology. In Latin America, for example, it appeared that there was a unity between socialists and Christians on the basis of social justice. What did he think about that?

'Of course, we have liberation theology in Poland too but it is different. In Latin America, the basis of it is social injustice, and the Communist Party wants to take advantage of social injustice to manipulate it for its own ends. This is designed to separate the faithful from the bishops. The theology of liberation in Poland is quite different because the Church does not want the priests to be active in Solidarity.'

I asked, 'Have you possibly been using Solidarity to undermine the faith of the people of Poland in their government, in the same way as you say the guerrilla leaders in Latin America have used liberation theology to undermine the faith of the people in their bishops?'

He misunderstood me, and said, 'Oh no, nothing could undermine the faith of the Polish people in their bishops.'

I said, 'No, no, have you used Solidarity to undermine the people's faith in their *government?*'

He said, 'Oh no, there is no intention of using Solidarity to undermine confidence in the Government. We have only supported it as a trade union. That is the only circumstance under which the Church would support Solidarity. We never supported it as a political party, and we have not used it to defeat the Government. But I must admit that the impact of Solidarity has brought some changes and some better prospects which the Party appreciates and which have led it to change many of its policies and personalities. The ideas of Solidarity have won support from the people, but Solidarity itself is political and anti-Communist.'

This is exactly what people have been saying to me over the last few days.

I asked him, 'How many political prisoners are there now?'

He replied, 'About 220, and the Church cares for them. Many of them have not been involved in anything really. They might distribute a leaflet and find themselves in prison.'

I said, 'Can I now turn the subject to the bomb, because there are formidable moral questions in the use of nuclear weapons, and I would like to ask you whether you think Gorbachev is sincere, what future for Europe you see, and what the Church's role is in dealing with the threat of nuclear war.'

He answered, 'Rearmament is a political game. It is a crime against humanity to build nuclear weapons. I think Gorbachev is perfectly sincere in wanting peace, because the Soviet Union needs to divert resources from weapons of war, which are very expensive, and use skilled labour. But what can the Church do? I know the French and the German bishops have issued a statement, and the bishops have presented papers, but I don't think we know what to do.'

So I commented, 'I suppose, Your Eminence, you could say publicly what you have said to me, which I think is very important, particularly in your assessment of Gorbachev.'

Then he made the most important remark of the whole interview. 'If I did this, it would create difficulties for the Church, because Radio Free Europe and Voice of America and the BBC are violently anti-Soviet, and the Polish people listen to these broadcasts. They shape Polish opinion, and if I were to say publicly what I have said to you it would create tension in Poland. Poles would say to me, "You are pro-Communist", and so, perhaps, would Radio Free Europe, the BBC and the Voice of America. I am accused of being pro-Communist anyway.'

'Well, that indicates the power of the media.'

He sort of nodded rather wryly and it was amazing that the Catholic Church recognises that the media are more powerful than it is in getting the message across.

'At least you could argue that through martial law Jaruzelski had preserved Polish independence from the Russians, because I presume that if things had gone wrong the Russians might have intervened.'

'Ah,' said Glemp, 'on 13 December 1981 the Church remained absolutely quiet on the question of martial law, and if I had spoken, and had called the people out against it, the Soviet troops, who were on the border, would have come in.'

Then I asked him, 'Can I explore with you the question of your dialogue with the Government?'

He said, 'Communist governments treat the Church differently in each country – Hungary, Czechoslovkia and Yugoslavia. I have no illusions: Communism wants the Church to become subservient.'

I said, 'Are you saying that there is a permanent holy war between Catholicism and Communism?'

'Well, there is a conflict between the idea of collectivism and individualism, and we may find some form of reconciliation.'

I put it to him that, just as Marx was entirely innocent of what happened under Stalin, you could not blame Jesus for what happened at the time of the Spanish Inquisition. You could also argue that socialism was a faith but that Communist parties were institutions, like the Church, in relation to belief. 'These are factors that you might take into account.'

He agreed with me on a number of things but not on this one. 'Is socialism a religion? No, it isn't because the Soviet bloc leaders do not actually believe in socialism, they just use ideology as a way to achieve personal power.'

Of course, that is an argument that Marxists have used against the Churches for years! They have said the Church leaders don't believe in God but they use their faith and the faith of the faithful to get themselves power.

I said, 'There have been occasions, I suppose, in the long history of the Church, over the past 2,000 years, when the Church has been concerned with power. I suppose you could compare Martin Luther with Solidarity –

Martin Luther identified certain weaknesses in the Church and challenged it, and as a result, the Church modified its position.'

He thought it was an interesting argument.

I had been there for about an hour and a half, so I thought it was my duty to bring the discussion to a conclusion. I thanked him very much, and said, 'I must tell you that the people I have met in Poland, the Ministers and the officials, seem to me to be good people. You may disagree with what they are trying to do, but they seem to me to be sincere people who are trying to do their best.'

He gave me rather a warm smile.

Thursday 10 July
At 7 in the evening there was a farewell dinner in a private room of the hotel, with the Deputy Speaker, the Director of the Polish Institute and a couple of other Poles. It was an extremely jolly evening, with some political discussion but mainly endless jokes.

They told one funny story about a German dog that came over the border to Poland one night, and said, 'Oh, the bones in Germany are delicious. They are the best dog bones in the world!' The dog came back the next night and said to the Polish dogs, 'You sleep in the garden, but in Germany we have blankets – luxury!' The dog came night after night, so eventually the Polish dogs asked him, 'Why don't you stay in Germany?' 'Ah,' he replied, 'you are not allowed to bark in Germany.' They did make fun of the Germans.

Friday 11 July
Up at 5 and left for the airport.

Tuesday 30 September – Labour Party Conference, Blackpool
After lunch I went back in for Neil Kinnock's speech, which lasted interminably, and I had my usual annual agonies on whether to join in the standing ovation at the end. But I came to the conclusion that it was part of the eve-of-Election game you had to play. The high point was when he said, 'I would be prepared to die for my country but I don't want my country to die for me' – the most crude demagoguery, which will satisfy people that he is in favour of defence, but I thought it poor stuff. The standing ovation lasted for six minutes; Glenys was brought down from the balcony and he kissed her and waved, and then she went back. The whole thing was like a Nuremberg rally, phoney to a degree.

Friday 3 October
The finale of Conference is always a bit of an anticlimax. Eric had heard from the organist that she had been told the Conference was not singing 'The Red Flag', but there had been such a row about it that it was agreed

that she would play it after all. As the pale pink rose is now the symbol of the
Labour Party, I wrote an alternative version of 'The Red Flag' to take
account of it:

> *The people's rose in shades of pinks*
> *Gets up my nostrils and it stinks,*
> *But 'ere our limbs grow stiff and cold*
> *Our old Red Flag we shall unfold.*
> *With heads uncovered swear we all*
> *To let rose petals fade and fall.*
> *Though moderates flinch and media sneer*
> *We'll keep the Red Flag flying here.*

At the end, believe it or not, Neil and Glenys threw a whole mass of red roses
at the delegates from the platform. It was a disgusting spectacle, and I simply
couldn't stand it, so I rushed out before the crowd left and caught the train to
London.

Tuesday 4 November
Caught the train to Chesterfield, and a ticket collector came up, a man of
about thirty-four, and asked if I was Tony Benn. When I said yes, he asked if
I had been involved in the miners' strike.

I said I used to go on the picket line, and he said, 'Did you know the army
was used, dressed in police uniform?'

I told him we suspected it but were never able to prove it.

He said, 'I know, because I was in the army until last year, and during the
miners' strike I was at Catterick Camp and we were regularly put into police
uniforms and sent on the picket lines. We didn't like it particularly.'

I asked him how many men.

He replied, 'At Nottingham, of the sixty-four policemen in our group,
sixty-one were soldiers and only three were regular policemen – an
inspector, a sergeant and one bobby. We didn't wear any numbers, didn't
get paid overtime as the police did, and were told not to make any arrests
because the police would do all that.' He said the soldiers used were from the
Military Police, the SAS and the Green Jackets. He himself had been a
military policeman. 'I shouldn't really be saying all this because of the
Official Secrets Act.'

Then he added, 'Surely you could tell us because of the way we marched,
and we had short hair. We were obviously the army. The police knew we
were soldiers. Of course, you realise the army are now being used for civil
defence.'

I told him he should write it all down before he forgot it.

He said, 'There's the Official Secrets Act, and I would deny I ever said it if
you told anyone. But we must get rid of Thatcher.'

Wednesday 19 November
In the *Financial Times* this morning Mrs Thatcher was reported as saying that
two more terms of office would exterminate socialism. I saw Clare Short,
who asked if I had seen it, and I replied, 'Yes, but I think she'll have a job to
outdo Kinnock.'
   'Don't be so depressed,' she said.
   'I'm not, I'm just being realistic.'

Thursday 27 November
Sat through Prime Minister's Questions, listening to the Prime Minister
trying to cope with the rising crisis in Australia; Sir Robert Armstrong has
been sent there to stop the publication of *Spycatcher* but he will fail.
   Went to the PLP meeting, and next week's business was announced; it
included Wednesday's debate on the security services, called by the SDP. I
chipped in to say I thought it was all very well making Thatcher look a fool,
and having a lot of fun over Lord Rothschild and the 'fifth man', but the
really important issue was that the security services were out of control.
People thought Harold Wilson was paranoid when he claimed he was
bugged, but he *was* bugged, and burgled; of course, Wilson himself had
tapped trade unionists' phones during the National Union of Seamen's
strike in 1966. I said we really did have to establish some principle of
accountability through Parliament, a proper statute governing the security
services' conduct. It was the first time I've spoken at a PLP meeting for some
time.

Wednesday 31 December
Looking back over 1986, I think the most important event on the world
scene was probably the Reykjavik summit. Gorbachev offered total nuclear
disarmament and Reagan accepted but insisted on Star Wars, which
wrecked the summit but left on the table something that could officially be
picked up if Star Wars were dropped – the total nuclear disarmament of
Europe. This caused flutters of alarm through the European NATO
members including Thatcher, Kohl and Mitterrand. What it did was to
confirm the seriousness and purpose of the Russians, the Americans' lack of
seriousness and purpose and the Europeans' utter commitment to nuclear
weapons.
   In Britain, Mrs Thatcher got into trouble over the Westland affair and
lost Michael Heseltine, the Defence Secretary, and Leon Brittan, the Home
Secretary, early in the year. She was in further difficulties about Leyland,
and was unpopular also for authorising the use of British bases for the
American raid on Libya. Later in the year, *Spycatcher* led Sir Robert
Armstrong to face an arrogant, young, up-and-coming Australian barrister
called Malcolm Turnbull; the humiliation should have put the Government

into an appalling position; but there was no credible opposition on the part of the Labour Party.

The Labour Party is a story of continuing tragedy. At the end of the year, despite everything that was done to boost Kinnock against the Left, the Tories had a lead of 8 per cent – which is quite unheard of on the eve of an Election after a party has been in government for seven years. It is a tragedy for the Party, but it is no exaggeration to say that 90 per cent of NEC time this year has been spent in trying and expelling people in Liverpool and hounding Militant in a general witch-hunt. It has led to great bitterness, though nobody speaks up for fear of 'rocking the boat'.

A National Constitutional Committee is being elected; it was established after the Party Conference, in order to take some of the load of expulsions and discipline off the shoulders of the NEC.

The policy of the Party is now vaguer and more muddled than ever before. The 'Jobs and Industry' campaign was followed by the 'Freedom and Fairness' campaign; and now 'A Modern Britain in a Modern World' has been launched to put forward our defence arguments. But actually it is the biggest fallback from our position there could be, because although we are going to decommission the Polaris it doesn't say when; the Americans will be asked to leave their nuclear bases in Britain by agreement; and the money spent on nuclear weapons is to go into conventional defence. So I don't think that will help us much.

I do find the House of Commons an extremely unpleasant place at the moment. Talking in the Chamber itself is like being in a zoo where the animals bray at you. The PLP is like an icebox; they are terrified anything you say might lose them their seats. Being on the NEC is like being a member of the Inquisition.

I should think David Owen will try to merge the SDP with the Tory Party and leave the Liberals in the lurch, having used them as a launching pad in the interim – because that man is not going to be content to go through life as just a sort of independent media commentator.

Nevertheless, I look forward immensely to 1987. There will almost certainly be a General Election, and my guess is that, with a completely gutless and right-wing Labour leadership, the Tories could win outright.

Saturday 7 February 1987
Today we heard that now the NGA has pulled out of supporting the strike against Rupert Murdoch. The printers, like the miners, are strong, and that is why the Government has gone for them. Until there is a really big change of attitude by the trade unions, the Labour Movement will continue to be entirely subservient to Thatcher.

Sunday 8 February
We went to see Sally and Hilary's new baby, who hasn't got a name yet. He

has webs about a third of the length of his toes, and when I looked at mine I found I have the same!

Monday 16 February
Today we had a meeting of the NEC and the Shadow Cabinet – the first, I think, since Neil Kinnock became Leader.

Kinnock introduced the meeting and spoke for about twenty minutes on how we were geared for Election victory. My general impression was of a very insecure chairman of a company addressing shareholders, or rather sales representatives in the field – we were told what to do, and there was no sense of being genuinely consulted at all.

We went on to the polling presentation, and Peter Mandelson said a few words. I find Mandelson a threatening figure for the future of the Party. He came in from the media eighteen months ago and has taken over, and he and Kinnock now work closely together. Whitty is just a figurehead, and Geoff Bish has been pushed into the background.

Then the Shadow Agency, or Shadow Communications Agency as it is called, analysed their findings. They said that there had been a shift from the collective to the individual, and that people were afraid of the loony Left, afraid of the future, afraid of inexperience. It was totally defensive; but on the positive side we had 'a leader in control' and so on.

There was a discussion, in which Denis Healey said, 'Not for the first time, I agree with 95 per cent of what Tony Benn has said. The psychosis of the Cold War has had to be revived to justify the Trident. There are important changes in the Soviet Union, and it would be a historic crime to miss the opportunity that Gorbachev is opening up. The Trident depends on American targeting. Britain is not in the first division any more, it is in decline, and because of the Falklands War and our attitude to South Africa we are not taken seriously in the UN Security Council.' We had another twenty-five minutes of Neil Kinnock summing up.

Tuesday 17 March
My first visitors at 9 am were Alan Plater, the playwright, Mick Jackson and Sally Hibbin, who are turning Chris Mullin's book *A Very British Coup* into a three-part television series. They wanted to ask me what situation would face an incoming radical Prime Minister, what his relations would be with the security services, the Americans, the Governor of the Bank of England, and so on.

In a way, Chris's book has been a bit overtaken by events in a number of respects. First of all, the likelihood of a left-wing Labour leader is absolutely minimal. Secondly, there won't be a Labour government. Thirdly, when Chris wrote about 'dirty tricks' in 1982 they were considered a bit way out but are now sort of taken for granted. However, the general idea is interesting, and I thoroughly enjoyed meeting them.

Saturday 28 March

Kinnock and Healey returned from America today, Reagan having given them less than half an hour. It was a disaster, whereas Thatcher's visit to Moscow has been trumpeted everywhere. It's sad for the Party, because all Kinnock did was to reassure Reagan that Britain would remain in NATO and never put Labour policy forward at all, as far as I can make out. Healey is angry about it.

Sunday 26 April

A beautiful day, the blossom is out, and London looks lovely.

It is clear the Election will be in June, and the Tories have an 11 per cent lead.

Wednesday 29 April

I was driven early to the BBC for a television interview about *Spycatcher* and MI5. Just before I went on the air, the producer leaned over to my seat and said, 'You cannot mention any of the allegations in the Wright book.' Since I was there to *discuss* the allegations in the Wright book, it seemed to me incredible, so I asked why, and she said, 'Our lawyers have advised us.' I was expected to sit there and discuss *Spycatcher* without saying what it was about. I said, 'I'm very sorry, but I'm not prepared to do that.'

So when we came to the broadcast I not only spelled out the allegations with absolute clarity but mentioned the attempted assassination of Nasser. I also stated that I had been approached just before we went on air not to talk about the allegations.

Monday 11 May

Spent most of the morning waiting for news of the Election date, and it was announced at about 2.15 – 11 June, as we'd expected.

Tuesday 12 May

Went into the Commons, then to the Clause 5 meeting which was being held in Transport House to discuss the manifesto. There was a huge crowd outside with red balloons, and television cameras filming it. Neil was standing on the steps waving – it had all been stage-managed. The members of the Shadow Cabinet and the NEC filed in.

Not having seen the manifesto in advance, I didn't know what would be in it, but I had typed out a whole range of 'amendments', which I called a checklist, and gave copies to Larry Whitty, Audrey Wise, Geoff Bish, Jo Richardson, Joan Maynard, Dennis Skinner, and Linda Douglas, the NEC Young Socialist. Looking round the meeting, I was reminded of Brezhnev's Central Committee; the same thing which brought the Stalin era to an end in Russia will bring the Labour Party domination of British politics to an end – an authoritarian, right-wing, passionately anti-democratic streak.

At the end, Kinnock said, 'We've discussed this for two hours, and the meeting has been held in goodwill; nobody should go away with animosity. It is not only policy we're talking about but our presentation.' He stressed our unity.

By 30 to 6, which is a ratio of 5 to 1, that meeting overturned Conference policy which itself had been carried by 5 to 1. I couldn't find anyone sympathetic except our little gang.

Wednesday 13 May

The press today had all the headlines Kinnock would have wanted – 'Kinnock Beats the Left' and so on. He wants to begin the Election with a victory over the Left to show he is in charge. The *Evening Standard* said that, if he wins, he'll be able to disregard the Left and the Conference. But, if he loses, nobody will be able to say that the Left lost him the Election, because it will be his personal victory or his personal defeat.

Typed my Election address, including a warm tribute to myself, and left it on the photocopier at the Commons. When I returned to retrieve it, Ivan Lawrence and another Tory MP were sitting there with it.

Ivan said, 'Not bad. If I were a Labour man in Chesterfield, I think I'd vote for you. I've never thought of describing myself in such glowing terms; I've always left that to my admirers.'

'I suppose, if you wrote it yourself, you could say it was written by an admirer!'

They laughed.

Friday 15 May

A poll published today gives the Tories an 18 per cent lead. Mrs Thatcher was so confident and clear on the television news, and Kinnock was so boastful and wordy and weak. His popularity is falling rapidly.

Thursday 21 May

I watched the party political broadcast, which opened with the title 'Kinnock'. It began with a bomber flying, then a bird flying, then Neil and Glenys on a mountain top, then Kinnock talking straight to camera about his inspiration, a woman from Wales saying, 'We always knew he would make it'; he talked about his parents and Glenys was brought in again. They showed speeches by Kinnock, with tremendous applause. The centre point was his attack on Militant at the Bournemouth Conference, and the camera flashed to Derek Hatton. The high peak of his strength is that he attacked the Militant Tendency. It made my blood run cold.

Friday 22 May

Spent most of the day in Duckmanton and Poolsbrook, mining villages on the outskirts of Chesterfield. Visited a few old people's homes. Quite a few people said they thought the Kinnock broadcast was brilliant and would have a tremendous impact.

Wednesday 27 May

Got the papers, and the slanging match between the leaders goes on.

Reagan has said how much he admires Mrs Thatcher and how he thinks he would be able to live with a Labour government. His intervention must make people hopping mad, I would imagine.

David Steel has produced a list of '101 hard-left' MPs, and of course I was on it. So was Tam Dalyell! It was astonishing. Even Harry Barnes in Derbyshire North East is listed as a dangerous red!

Thursday 4 June

I went to the market and made two little speeches, and people did listen carefully. There was a round of applause at the second meeting – like a village cricket match when somebody scores a run.

Returned to the NUM offices in the afternoon, and Jack Dash, the old dockers' leader, had arrived for an Election meeting. He is nearly eighty-one, led many of the dock strikes, is a long-term member of the CP, and a man whom I deeply respect. He had written such a nice letter saying he would like to help, so Johnny Burrows paid his fare up from London and Bas Barker, a Chesterfield trade unionist and CP member, had organised a meeting of about thirty or forty pensioners. He made a marvellous, reflective speech.

Saturday 6 June

Went to the Market Square for the hustings with the other two candidates. There were 4–500 people listening, and it was enormously worth while. There was some friendly heckling. Several old characters turned up – Tommy Tatters with his cap and his placard saying 'Mrs Thatcher's worse than Attila the Hun', and Gloria Havenhand, who used to be leader of the Tory Group on the council, all dolled up. She kept shouting, 'That! From a man who went to a public school!' – at which Johnny Burrows replied, 'That! From a woman with no education!' Then there was a weird local doctor who asked whether the Americans would press the nuclear button if Labour was elected.

Thursday 11 June

In the car to all the committee rooms and to some polling stations. It appeared from the first results that it was going to be a Tory landslide. Caroline and I walked over to the Winding Wheel centre where the count was, and I did actually worry about my own position.

The media were already beginning their usual chorus about why we had done badly – the hard Left, the loony Left, and so on, although the results weren't suggesting that at all. Eric Heffer, for example, had a huge increase in his majority from 15,000 to 23,000. Terry Fields and Dave Nellist doubled their majorities in Liverpool Broadgreen and Coventry South East. Chris Mullin won in Sunderland South, increasing the Labour vote, and my majority over the Liberal Alliance candidate was 8,500. It was in the south of England that things went badly for Labour.

13

1987–90

Wednesday 17 June
Our thirty-eighth wedding anniversary.

Went to the Commons for the first PLP meeting, and my instinct was to sit and listen and get the feel of it.

At 12.10 Neil Kinnock spoke. He said, 'This is the most successful campaign in the history of the Party. It has been recognised as such by our opponents and the pundits. It was well organised, the performances were good, and, comparing speech for speech, interview for interview and press conference for press conference, we beat them all along the line. We fought as a team together and we have achieved a great deal. We made gains – for the first time the number of Labour women MPs is up to twenty-one, and for the first time we are a multiracial party, which I hope will affect the self-image of black voters.' He congratulated the four black and Asian Members, Diane Abbott, Paul Boateng, Bernie Grant and Keith Vaz, (the new MPs for Hackney North and Stoke Newington, Brent South, Tottenham, and Leicester East).

Kinnock went on, 'I must mention some failures. One is that we failed to win the Election, and there is no consolation for defeat in any form. Millions will suffer, the young will be isolated, the old will be frightened, the sick and the unemployed will have no prizes; but the result provides a better basis for building up.'

Then, with a lot of rhetorical flourishes, he said, 'We must show we are in charge of events. We must emphasise freedom. We must seek a refreshment of the values which we inspire. There must be a strategy for dealing with change or we will lose again. There is a great deal to play for.' He continued in this vein, and became hectoring. 'With every word, every action and every deed we must support the idea of victory. We must convince people. There is a demand for unity from the Movement to disappoint the commentators, to deny them the splits. The SDP and the Liberals are divided but they are treated with kid gloves. There must be energy and commitment, the characteristic of the future. We must ensure that none of us has to dismiss this group or that group in any interview or be distracted or diverted. We must accept the light burden of self-discipline.'

Dave Nellist observed, 'We couldn't win the Election in three and a half weeks. Sixty per cent decided how to vote before the campaign, and there was a lot of time wasted on expulsions. The best swings to Labour were in Liverpool.' He said he hoped the PLP would fight outside Parliament.

There was a lot of shouting at this.

Clive Soley said, 'We want to avoid internecine war. The London situation is not the responsibility of the Party or of individuals but of the inherent situation in London.' That was quite a sensible point.

At 9 Lev Parshin from the Soviet Embassy came to see me at home. I'm sure the security services think it is some deep plot, but all he wanted was a briefing on the Election, what I thought of Kinnock's and Thatcher's positions, and so on.

Parshin said he would like the television programme 'Spitting Image' to be available in the Soviet Union, because it makes fun of Soviet leaders. Altogether, the whole thing was so relaxed. When I look at my diary for the mid-Sixties, I realise the Soviet people I met then were not all that different but they wouldn't accept criticism.

Sunday 12 July
Chunks of Peter Wright's book were published in the *Sunday Times*. I must say, reading his words did make my blood run cold. Here was the American CIA trying to destroy an elected Prime Minister, and Peter Wright himself said that half the MI5 officers were trying to get rid of the Labour

Government and that they 'bugged and burgled' their way across London. He also referred to the assassination attempt on President Nasser.

Sunday 2 August
Turned up in Hyde Park at Speakers' Corner early and met someone from the Campaign for Press and Broadcasting Freedom; they had asked me to read from *Spycatcher* in defiance of the ban.

I had prepared my speech with enormous care. I read it out and included long passages from *Spycatcher*. There was a bit of heckling from a man wearing a T-shirt with the words 'Colonel North for President' and 'Help the Russians Join CND', and shouting silly slogans.

Thursday 13 August
Stansgate. Lovely day with a little rain. Caroline is working on the Keir Hardie correspondence left to me in the will of Hedley Dennis. Hardie was obviously a difficult man, a loner who quarrelled with everybody. Various biographies have been written to suggest that he wasn't a socialist but just an old Christian radical. Every generation of historians rewrites history to bring it into line with the current philosophy.

Joshua phoned from the United States to say the Hyde Park reading of *Spycatcher* was front-page news there.

The House of Lords announced their judgment on *Spycatcher*, and by 3 to 2 they voted to uphold the injunction. The lessons of *Spycatcher* are getting broader and broader – not only that there is secret material that Mrs Thatcher doesn't want publicised but that the judges are tools of the Government. The BBC World Service can't broadcast material that is broadcast by every other world broadcasting organisation.

Friday 14 August
Worked on letters. Listened to Danish radio, which had a programme, in Danish, on *Spycatcher* in which the extracts from it were in English, mostly the ones I had read in Hyde Park. I felt rather like someone in the French Resistance sitting in an attic with a radio.

Saturday 29 August
Chris Mullin's wife Ngoc, whom he met two years ago in Vietnam, arrived from Saigon a few days ago, so I drove to his flat in Brixton Road to meet her. There had been television cameras at the airport when she arrived.

Thursday 17 September
The Liberal Assembly in Harrogate voted overwhelmingly to merge with that part of the SDP that wants to, and set up a new party. It is a historic moment, because the Liberal Party has been in existence for about 150 years, had a fine tradition of its own and is now throwing in its lot with

people who don't share its principles, approach or anything else. It is bound to fail. David Owen's achievement is amazing. First of all, he tries to split the Labour Party and fails, then he splits the SDP, and now he has split the Liberal Party and persuaded them to go out of existence.

Friday 2 October – Labour Party Conference, Brighton
Heard Dennis Skinner deliver a brilliant speech on legal reform which brought everybody to their feet as always. He is an inspired man, extremely funny, very serious and absolutely to the point.

Michael Meacher and I were asked to do a recorded interview for 'Newsnight', presented by Peter Snow who is the media leader of the SDP. For years 'Newsnight' has done nothing but show the Labour Party as unelectable, boost the Alliance and give David Owen lots of time. They had set up in one of the lobbies of the conference centre, and it turned out they had got together a film in which Martin Jacques, the Editor of *Marxism Today*, appeared. The last sentence in the little film was Martin saying that I personally was a spent force.

So Peter Snow turned to me and asked, 'Are you a spent force, as Martin Jacques says?'

I said, 'Martin Jacques is a Eurocommunist who believes in an alliance with the SDP.'

'Will you answer the question?' he demanded.

I turned on him. I used some of the arguments I've just listed, and added, 'If democracy ever dies in Britain, it will be because of you.'

Around the studio set, with Michael Meacher sitting behind me, was a crowd of about fifty people – delegates, officials, security people and so on – and my attack on the BBC led to a great round of applause.

So then Peter Snow turned to Michael Meacher, who said the Left was actually in charge of the Party (which was a load of old rubbish) and the policy reviews would be undertaken with balanced views, and so on.

Then Snow came back to me. 'Now, Mr Kinnock says that he is not going to let the tail wag the dog.'

I said, 'I'm not going to discuss Mr Kinnock. His own position is clear.'

Then he asked, 'What new ideas have come from the Left?'

I replied, 'All the ideas about non-alignment; that the Russian military threat is not true, that the Americans don't speak for freedom and democracy, that Chernobyl shows that nuclear weapons don't make you safe.'

This threw him completely, and he went back to Michael Meacher. At one point I said to him, 'Don't act the part of God', and everybody round burst into cheers. He had never had to do his interview in a public meeting before. It has always been in the safety of his own constituency, which is Lime Grove North!

It was a marvellous little incident. Needless to say, they didn't use the interview at all.

Went back to the Conference and stood between Joan Maynard and Audrey Wise, both of whom had lost their seats on the NEC and were in tears. Audrey is an MP, so she is all right, but Joan has retired from Parliament and she is such a strong woman that it was very sad to see her upset.

My thoughts on leaving the Conference are that the whole thing was a media show. Socialism was mentioned in every sentence, and then by nudges and winks from the platform the media were told, 'Don't worry, we don't mean what we appear to mean.' They were using that to imply that the Left were a ridiculous tiny minority against a socialist majority led by Kinnock.

I don't think we should contest the leadership, but John Prescott may put up against Hattersley and Michael Meacher may then throw his hat into the ring. I'm not getting mixed up in that.

Friday 9 October
The Tory Party Conference ended with an eleven-minute standing ovation for Mrs Thatcher, the singing of 'Rule Britannia', waving of flags and so on; yet, although they sound on the up and up, I think the base is not very secure, what with the poll tax, the attacks on the NHS and local government, and nuclear rearmament.

Friday 16 October
In the middle of the night we had the worst storm since 1703, with the wind speed in London reaching 94 mph. Trees were torn up all over the place. In Kew Gardens it will take 200 years for the trees that were lost to be replaced to maturity. The weather men never predicted it, though it was actually a hurricane. There are trees lying all over the streets. Caroline has been staying at Stansgate, where there was a power cut. Enormous damage has been done. The whole thing was unreal; it was like a day that didn't exist, one of those days that has a special character of its own.

Saturday 21 November
Began packing for Russia. When you go to America you just take a toothbrush and know you can get anything you need there, but when you go to the Soviet Union you have to be self-contained. So I packed a kettle, batteries, cassettes, medicines and so on. The bag was so heavy that I couldn't carry it, so I'll have to unpack some of it.

Monday 23 November – Trip to USSR
Caught the 9.50 am flight to Moscow, where the temperature was −18°C.
I waited two and a half hours for my bag, amidst people coming and going

in fur hats. I could see a thin layer of snow outside, and as the snow fell it was quite romantic really, reminding me of some of the scenes from the film *Reds*. We discovered that my bag had been mistaken for that of the Kampuchean Ambassador, so we drove to the Kampuchean Embassy, where there were two officers standing in the courtyard. The officers accompanied us to the door, and one of them, wearing a blue overcoat and fur cap and belt and pistol, banged on the front door, which finally opened, and there inside was my bag. By this time it was four hours since I had landed.

I was taken to the hotel and waited for one hour to register! There were twenty people waiting and only one woman, absolutely at her wits' end, authorised to check people in. There were people arguing and shouting at her. It was clear they didn't have enough rooms and they were offering middle-aged businessmen rooms to share, which they didn't want. There was one plump blonde woman with a Swiss passport who spoke fluent Russian, and two men laughing because she was saying she didn't want to share a room with them and two Germans. I tried to persuade the receptionist to take an interest in me by leaning over to point at my name on the computer printout, and she sort of smacked my hand! At nearly 9 o'clock I was given a bit of paper which I had to take to another desk to get the key for my room, which turned out to be a beautiful one overlooking the city.

Had dinner downstairs in a fancy restaurant with several people from the Institute of International Relations and World Economy. What is so nice is that one can now talk absolutely openly to the Russians about anything – Stalin, Trotsky, the Cold War, the Labour Party – and there is no restraint. They couldn't have been more friendly, though the Russian intellectuals are a bit heavy.

Tuesday 24 November
Went to the Institute and gave my lecture. I had a lot of questions, such as what changes have occurred in the nature of the working class, and how do you deal with the problems of technological unemployment? If Mrs Thatcher claims to have helped capitalism, why has industrial production declined to the point at which Britain has now dropped below Italy from fifth to sixth place in the world production table? How would you define the difference between left and right? Even, what was the reaction to the Chesterfield Conference?

At the end Professor Bolodyn, who is a great expert on perestroika and the economic situation, said, 'Contrary to what you have suggested in your lecture, there is no danger of any breakdown of central planning. The danger is that Gosplan is trying to hold on to its real power. It still has powers to develop the five-year plan and decide economic rates of growth, and factories simply have to comply. Next year 60 per cent of the profits will come back in taxation.' He added, 'Socialist ownership will not be changed, of that I assure you.'

After that, I talked to Igor Guriev, a deputy director of the Institute, and Professor Efim Khesin. Guriev said they were in a revolutionary situation in the Soviet Union. 'If we do not succeed in changing our society soon, there will be a real and characteristically vigorous Russian response and opposition to the Government.'

I asked if it would be violent, and he said, 'I don't know, but we are stagnating.'

I put the point that bourgeois democracy allows you to change your management by elections without changing your system, and that could be applied to Communism.

He said, 'We are attempting that by allowing rival candidates to stand for office, but our situation is really urgent. Perestroika has produced nothing yet; we have only talked about it.'

Listening to him, I thought the Soviet Communist Party seemed really frightened at the enormity of the crisis, with stagnation, shortages and poor quality leading to public anger and inertia. They are determined not to move towards capitalism, but they recognise that bureaucratic command Communism has not worked either. I think probably for them this is more important than disarmament. They want to reduce the burden of defence, but that is nothing like as important as getting their own economy going.

When I asked if the changes in the Soviet Union would be like those in Poland, they thought probably not, because the opposition to the Government in Poland was highly organised. In the USSR it would be sporadic and unorganised. The nature of the USSR's problems were to do with inefficiency and lack of democracy. They emphasised that there is no repression now and criticism is tolerated.

Wednesday 25 November
Went shopping, and I saw some cassettes of Russian music displayed in a shop. So I went in and asked for one, and was told they did sell them but they didn't have any. Went to buy some food, and the shop had no bread or butter.

Met Sacha to go back to the Institute to meet Alexander Kislov, a deputy director. The taxi we had ordered didn't turn up, so we rang the Municipal Transport Service, which runs the transport for Moscow, and they said the taxi was there, but it wasn't. So we caught an ordinary taxi, which broke down, and we hailed another one, which also broke down. I didn't get a very favourable impression of Moscow transport.

I was terribly depressed, and I thought to myself: How on earth can the Soviet Union get itself out of this mess? It is like an elephant with multiple sclerosis, huge but it can't move. The Russians are a patient people, though slightly sad and resigned, and some of the young ones are cynical.

I wondered whether there was any possibility of rival political groups being set up within the socialist system, but it was pointed out to me that there was no experience of bourgeois democracy before the revolution. There would be resistance from the Communist Party itself because the bureaucrats do not like being challenged. Then there is a danger of foreign interference; political groups would inevitably be financed and supported from outside with a view to destabilisation. Lastly, there might be nationalist pressure from the republics against the Soviet Union itself. They are absolutely right to talk about it openly, and Gorbachev's speeches about perestroika and glasnost have encouraged discussion. But the remedy is really political rather than economic.

When we arrived at the Institute I was taken to see Alexander Kislov whom I met at the Japan Peace Conference in 1983, and I had a long talk with him and two doctors. I came straight to the point. 'I have some proposals. The first is a treaty of friendship.'

Kislov said, 'That is not realistic with the Thatcher Government.'

I replied, 'I know that very well. I don't want to promote it if it wouldn't be acceptable to the Soviet Government. I don't want to be repudiated in Moscow.'

I asked about the speech by Boris Yeltsin which had led to his removal as Secretary of the Moscow Communist Party just before I arrived there, and they said it had not been published, but he had undoubtedly offended the bureaucracy.

Later in the day I talked to Martin Walker, the *Guardian* correspondent, who told me that people he knew believed that Boris Yeltsin had not criticized Raisa Gorbachev (as some had said), but he had made a reference to the personality cult and had gone right over the top, accusing Ministries of inflated size. So he had been removed by the Moscow District Committee. Martin Walker said the hearings against him sounded like a witch-hunt or a denunciation.

Thursday 26 November
At 3.15 I went to the Institute of Economics of the Academy of Sciences and was greeted by a man of about fifty, Leonid S. Yagodovsky. We were joined later by a specialist on East Germany.

Yagodovsky repeated what I had heard elsewhere, that they must make greater use of the credit system. He said they have got to reduce state financing, and the state must earn its keep and use credit. 'We need a flexible system of prices and incentives for workers. There will inevitably be greater inequality of incomes, and we need some form of market mechanism.'

He went on, 'Planning, decentralisation and self-management are the key to the new laws of state enterprise and industrial democracy which will come into force on 1 January 1988. There will be an Enterprise Council with the workers, the managers, the Party, the trade unions and the youth movements and *they* will adopt a plan of enterprise, not the Ministry.'

I commented, 'I find what you say about self-management very exciting, but when I say this in Britain they call me a Trotskyite.'

'Oh,' said Yagadovsky, 'Trotsky's concept was quite different. He believed the trade unions should be an instrument of state power, and actually Trotsky's view was implemented by Stalin. Stalin was Trotsky in practice.'

So I said, 'You had better send us a lecturer on Trotsky to argue with Trotskyite parties!'

He told me, 'Trotsky claimed he was expelled because his ideas were rejected, but actually his ideas were implemented. But Trotsky said that the USSR could not build socialism in one country, wheras Stalin thought it could, and it was.'

Friday 27 November

Spent twelve hours in bed tossing and turning, and obviously had a fever. I woke feeling very unwell.

Went out with a guide for sightseeing, but I had already seen Red Square and the various cathedrals. It was terribly cold, and I could feel this freezing air going into my chest. Walked to the cemetery, and it was so icy that it was like walking on glass: I was terrified I was going to fall, so altogether I wasn't in the happiest of moods. In the graveyard were statues of Pushkin and Khrushchev. Between coughing and walking and slipping on the ice, I managed to get a glimpse of them and other interesting ones.

But the greatest point of interest was my conversation with my guide, Yuri, who said he wasn't a member of the Party and didn't have any interest in being a member of the Party: he was really a budding Russian entrepreneur.

I asked about Boris Yeltsin, and he said there was certainly no glasnost about his dismissal. 'It was the old-style removal of somebody who threatened the bureaucracy. In fact, Yeltsin and Gorbachev were old friends, and Yeltsin was very go-ahead, but he had been frustrated and had previously offered to resign his job because he couldn't make any progress. He did not attack Gorbachev or his wife, but he did make some reference to avoiding the cult of personality. Actually, the bureaucracy removed Yeltsin, but the public outcry at his removal was so great because he was a popular figure that he was reinstated as Deputy Construction Minister with the rank of Minister.'

Had a farewell dinner with Alexander Kislov, Igor Guriev, Sacha, Professor Khesin and Sergei Peregudov, who is studying the Labour Left and asked me to send him some material.

I asked them lots of questions, including the one often put to me: 'Do the people of Russia really want perestroika?'

Kislov replied, 'I remember talking to a Saudi Arabian slave who had been liberated, and he said he was happier when he was a slave because people looked after him, and now he was on his own.'

I drew a comparison between the Vatican and the Kremlin and said I thought they were similar in their structure.

Guriev laughed. 'You said it; I didn't.'

I asked about Khrushchev, and they said he lost a lot of support from the people and from the bureaucracy because he attacked Stalin, and the bureaucracy had worked with Stalin.

I was told the other day that on the occasion in 1960 when Khrushchev hammered the UN rostrum with a shoe, somebody took a photograph of him and he was wearing both his shoes, so he had obviously brought a spare one in his bag.

They told me that in 1985 Gorbachev had been elected as General Secretary of the party by only a one-vote majority, and one of the anti-Gorbachev members of the Politburo had been detained in America because of a problem with the plane; if he had got back in time, Gorbachev would not have won.

They asked who the people were to watch on the Labour Left, apart from myself, Ken Livingstone and Joan Ruddock. I said, 'Jeremy Corbyn, Dennis Skinner, Brian Sedgemore, Dawn Primarolo, Tony Banks, Harry Cohen and Bob Cryer.'

They were very critical of the *Morning Star*, and thought it was simplistic. I defended it by saying, 'When you're on the defensive, which we are, you repeat old slogans – that may be what your criticism is.'

Saturday 28 November
Up at 5 and packed. Sacha arrived with some gifts – a beautiful book of Russian still-life pictures and a guide to Kiev. We went to the airport together and I watched my bag like a hawk!

Friday 8 January 1988
To Chesterfield for a seven-hour surgery. There was a delegation of twenty-five people from Donkin's, the engineering factory, who had been sacked with twenty minutes' notice just before Christmas. They had been called in and told, 'You're redundant', and that they had to be off the plant within twenty minutes. Some of the workers had been there for twenty-two years.

Monday 11 January
This afternoon John Hughes, Labour MP for Coventry North East, a very devout Catholic and a member of the Campaign Group, was so incensed at the death of a constituent's child, denied a heart operation because of the NHS cuts, that he interrupted prayers and made a protest. It will not be included in Hansard because Hansard does not record prayers. It was a highly principled thing to do. He was subsequently suspended, and twenty-

one Labour MPs including Kinnock and Hattersley voted for his suspension.

Monday 14 March

I had a talk with Mark Schreiber of the *Economist*. He told me that there was a serious possibility of Mrs Thatcher being opposed by a Tory MP in the new session. If they did put someone up as a 'stalking horse', as he called it, they would be able to get some indication of Mrs Thatcher's popularity and they could then repeat the process next year to pave the way for her removal. I can imagine quite a lot of Tory MPs saying to themselves, 'Thatcher's safe but there's no harm in giving her a bit of a shock.'

Tuesday 15 March

Took a party of business studies students from Chesterfield College of Technology and Arts around the House. Their lecturer told me with some embarrassment that politics and economics had now been transformed into business studies. He said they had businessmen in to talk about businesses.

I asked, 'What about the trade unions?'

'We have to tell the students that trade unions are about human resources, and their relationship with employers is discussed in that context.'

I asked about socialism, and he said, 'We never mention that.'

Nine years after Thatcher came to power, we have a new wave of people coming through the system for whom capitalism is not only absolutely normal but the only thing they are taught about.

Sunday 20 March

Went to the AGM of the Chesterfield Party's general committee; it had been agreed last week that we would decide whether I should put up as a candidate in the leadership election.

At the end Johnny Burrows summed up. 'I think the balance of opinion expressed today has been pretty fair. John Prescott's attempt to be considered for the deputy leadership was described by Kinnock as an "unforgivable diversion". I wonder if in the next Election Mrs Thatcher will say an Election is an "unforgivable diversion". I will not accept that we should shut up for anyone. We have a right to a General Election every five years, and it is right to contest the leadership and deputy leadership of the Party.'

Then Peter Heathfield said, 'I nominate Tony Benn for the leadership if he is chosen by the Campaign Group.'

Of the ninety-six delegates there, eight voted against. I think probably about eighty people voted. Peter Coleman said he thought it was about three-quarters for and a quarter against and some hadn't voted. There was a slightly nasty flavour, but you can't expect constituency Parties to be unanimous on these things, and the old right wing of the Party would be opposed to it.

Wednesday 23 March

I had a message to ring Jim Mortimer, who has always been cautious and thought it would be inadvisable of me to stand, but today he said, 'I've been thinking about it and I think you should stand.'

That played a big part in my mind, so at 5.30 I went to the Campaign Group much more evenly balanced, I addressed the group, while Jeremy Corbyn took the chair.

Then I withdrew and went up to my room and had a cup of tea. I had a call saying they'd decided to nominate me and Eric for Leader and Deputy Leader. So I went downstairs, fighting my way through a huge mass of journalists who had got wind of the fact that a decision was being taken. Margaret Beckett, Dawn Primarolo, Gavin Strang, Audrey Wise, Chris Mullin, Joan Walley were against a contest. Gerry Bermingham abstained. That was 21 in favour.

The vote for Eric as Deputy Leader was carried by 25 and only 4 against – Diane Abbott, Margaret Beckett, Gavin Strang and Chris Mullin.

I gather a great deal of pressure was put on Audrey Wise to stand for the deputy leadership but she just wouldn't do it.

Having been doubtful, I felt more peaceful in my own mind about it. It was a collective decision. I had given the best advice I could, I had reflected the arguments for and against, and there is an excitement about doing it.

Thursday 24 March

The press was packed with reports of the decision, all beginning with 'Labour was launched last night into another bitter row . . .' and so on. The phones rang continuously.

Tuesday 29 March

This evening at the Campaign Group we heard that Clare Short, Margaret Beckett, Joan Ruddock and Jo Richardson had withdrawn from the group. I got angry and I said to Audrey, 'If only you had agreed to stand, they wouldn't have gone.' She got quite upset; she is under considerable pressure, and of course some of the women think this is just a macho male contest and don't like doing it this way. On the other hand, having demanded a proper say in the affairs of the Party, why shouldn't they play their part? That's the way I see it. The people who have withdrawn all have Front Bench responsibilities – apart from Joan Ruddock, and she's a close friend of Neil's, so it would be difficult for her.

Wednesday 25 May
NEC to consider the seven policy statements by the Policy Review Groups, and a historic meeting it was.

The first of the statements, 'The Productive and Competitive Economy', was presented by Bryan Gould. It was weak in analysis and vague in prescription, very backward-looking.

I said, if you worked in a profit-based society you couldn't do much about the centralisation of power. Intervening in markets wasn't any good, and I had spent a lot of my time in government trying to bribe and bully businessmen, entirely without success.

Livingstone remarked that it was 'pure Wilson'.

Skinner said it was fudge and mudge and that unemployment would rise, particularly after the American elections. We as a party were moving towards Thatcherism.

John Smith presented the next paper, 'Economic Equality'.

I said the trouble about this paper was that it did not recognise that there was a conflict of interest between those who created the wealth and those who controlled it. The paper declined to write off the debt that is owed by the poor to the Social Fund and pledged not to increase the highest levels of taxation above the level in Europe.

Skinner said, 'I could be taxed higher. The papers must be clear on higher taxation.'

Blunkett argued, 'We have got to re-establish the idea of the social wage.'

Eric Clarke agreed with Dennis Skinner.

Smith said he also agreed with Skinner. 'But we must persuade the rich of the need for fairness, and we are going to hit the rich on the capital side.'

That paper was carried by 20 to 3, with Livingstone abstaining.

Eddie Haigh then presented 'People at Work'.

Skinner didn't like it because it accepted the regulation of the trade unions.

I said that Thatcher had actually identified the obstacles to her policy, which were trade unions, local government and the public sector, and she had set out to destroy them. 'Are we going to repeal her Acts? What about using democracy, the votes of workers, to remove the boards of companies? This is a great missed opportunity.'

Kinnock said, 'As far as Tony is concerned, Thatcher didn't disclose her policy in advance, so why should we? The public don't perceive themselves as being dominated by employers, and anyway industrial democracy was an anarchist idea used in the Spanish Civil War.'

The paper was carried by 11 to 4.

Next was 'The Physical and Social Environment', which John Cunning-ham described as radical, interventionist, evolutionary and international.

I criticised it because it left out the issue of nuclear power, which was central to the environment. Secondly, it didn't mention the ownership of land, which was crucial.

The paper was carried by 20 votes to 1 (Dennis Skinner). I abstained.

Kaufman presented 'Britain and the World', saying, 'It accepts the Common Market and leaves disarmament open.'

Livingstone wanted the repeal of Section 2 of the European Communities Act, which would have the effect of restoring sovereignty over legislation and statute and he moved it be included.

'Repeal of Section 2 equals withdrawal,' Kinnock argued. 'The electorate rejected that in the 1983 Election, and it would wreck the economy if we withdrew.' So he has come out as a full Marketeer.

On defence, Ken Livingstone moved an amendment that we should agree to the mutual dissolution of the NATO and Warsaw pacts.

On withdrawal from the EEC, 8 were for and 13 against, with Gould abstaining.

On repeal of Section 2 of the European Communities Act, Livingstone moved the amendment, and I added: 'and to restore full powers to the British Parliament'. That was defeated by 16 to 7. Ken's amendment on mutual dissolution of the two pacts was carried by 19 to 2, with Kinnock abstaining. A motion to reduce defence expenditure to the level of that of European members of NATO was defeated by 13 to 7. The question of debt was not discussed. The whole document 'Britain and the World' was carried by 17 to 4.

The consumer document was carried without much discussion. Hattersley then moved 'Democracy and the Individual'.

I said, 'In order to be constructive, I will move two amendments: that the House of Lords be abolished; and that the security services be subjected to the same ministerial and parliamentary control as the defence forces.'

Hattersley agreed.

On a vote, my amendment on security accountability and control was defeated by 12 to 8, with Kinnock against: my amendment on abolition of the House of Lords was defeated by 18 to 4.

To cut a long story short, this is the Thatcherism of the Labour Party. We have moved now into the penumbra of her policy area, and our main argument is that we will administer it better than she will. Kinnock has won because the trade union leaders don't like the Left, but also because they haven't any idea of what to do, they have lost confidence in themselves and think this is the best way of winning an Election. So they went along with it. But I think the arguments we put forward were strong.

Saturday 4 June

I woke up this morning, and out of the corner of my eye I saw a flash. There was a sheet of flame about 2 feet high stretching across the end of the bed – the electric blanket had caught fire. I leapt out and poured a cup of water over the mattress, which was beginning to burn, and threw the electric blanket out into the garden. Half an hour later it was still burning.

Tuesday 21 June

There was an astonishing report in the *Independent* this morning. Neil Kinnock had had lunch with its editorial board yesterday and had said, 'Turn the tape recorder on, it's all on the record', and what he said was so muddled that, in effect, he said that his recent television broadcast attacking unilateralism as 'something for nothing' had not been a repudiation of unilateralist policy. Peter Shore described it as 'the Grand Old Duke of York, who marched his men to the top of the hill and marched them down again'.

Wednesday 22 June

The papers today are full of adverse comment on Kinnock's volte-face. Nobody knows where he stands at all now.

The Executive was awful as usual. We were told about phase 2 of the Policy Review, and how they would handle the reviews at this year's Conference. Neil said there was going to be a positive policy of consulting the constituencies and the unions, having 'open hearing' days, one-day regional policy conferences, and so on.

Wednesday 13 July

Drafted a notice to put in the broom cupboard in the Crypt of the Commons about the suffragette who hid there on the night of the census of 1911.

When I got to the Crypt I was told it was locked until after the Glorious Revolution celebrations, and I couldn't get the key, so I went to see Miss Frampton in the Serjeant at Arms' office. Miss Frampton is a most terrifying creature, a woman in her fifties, plump, determined, like the headmistress of a girls' school. So I said, 'Miss Frampton, I want your help.'

'What?' she said, with a frosty look.

I showed her my little notice, and to my amazement she was tickled pink. She laughed, and said, 'I'll take you down to the Crypt.'

We went down a secret staircase I didn't know existed and we arrived in the Crypt chapel. I showed her the broom cupboard, and we closed the door, stood there surrounded by mops and brushes and hoovers and wires. I had brought six strong brass thumb-tacks and a hammer, and we hammered this notice to the back of the door. It was like a sort of midnight feast with the headmistress, and as we left I gave her a wink and said, 'We mustn't go on having assignations like this.' She giggled. Anything Miss Frampton approves is OK.

I knew she was a descendant of Squire Frampton from Dorchester, and I told her that the secretary of my local Party when I was first elected to Bristol in 1950 was Edna Loveless, who was a descendant of George Loveless, one of the Tolpuddle Martyrs whom her great-great-great-grandfather had sent to Australia. She said she knew there were Lovelesses still in Dorchester. I also told her about the Reverend William Benn, who had been ejected in 1662 from his Dorchester parish.

Monday 25 July
Our grandsons Michael, James and William, who had been out for the day with Caroline, came back for tea, and we set up three committees. The 'London Wildlife Committee' was chaired by Michael; James and William were deputy chairmen. We voted by 4 to 0 for more parks and by 4 to 0 for more nesting boxes for birds, and I pretended to ring Mrs Thatcher to give her their news. We had a 'Bus Committee', voting for more buses by 2 to 2, and for cheaper buses by 4 to 0. Michael put up a big poster and called himself 'the Socialist Wildlife candidate'.

Sunday 4 September
I must confess I am a bit low at the moment. The coverage of the leadership campaign is poor and, despite enormous effort, no progress seems to have been made.

Saturday 17 September
Came back to London and went with Caroline to see Hilary and Sally's new baby, Caroline Rosalind Clark Benn, our first granddaughter. Then we went for a meal in a little Chinese restaurant in Westbourne Grove.

Friday 30 September – Labour Party Conference, Blackpool
Caroline and I caught the train to Blackpool and unpacked at the Florida Apartments, a nice place between the Imperial Hotel and the Winter Gardens.

I set up the fax machine, the answering machine, the video, the typewriter, and so on.

Sunday 2 October
We walked over to the Conference, and Caroline advised me on what I should say after the result was announced. When the result came, it was appalling. My total of the electoral college came to 11 per cent. I did my best to look impassive and cheerful on the platform. I just touched Neil Kinnock on the shoulder and smiled.

Caroline and I went to the T&G party because I thought it wouldn't be a bad idea to show ourselves. There were a few embarrassed faces on the so-called Left on the T&G executive who had urged me to stand and then voted for Kinnock and Hattersley. The T&G had decided not to ballot its members. I went right up to Ron Todd's table, shook his hand, and thanked him for inviting us to the party.

Wednesday 5 October
I had been asked to reply for the NEC to the debate on safety in the North

Sea oil industry. I had worked extremely carefully on my speech and decided to make it an occasion for criticising market forces, the market economy and the multinationals, and to use the industry and its safety record as an argument for socialism and trade unionism. I got a tremendous response from the delegates. Dennis Skinner, who is slow to comment on these things, thought it was the best Conference speech I had made for many years. He was in the chair for the afternoon.

Got back to the flat utterly exhausted.

Thursday 6 October

Ron Todd in the news as the man who is challenging Kinnock's modernisation. He's the bogeyman this year. There is a lot of resentment within the T&G, and the Party doesn't work unless the T&G supports the leadership, so in that sense it's a bit like 1960, when Frank Cousins opposed Gaitskell.

Saturday 8 October

The wedding of Stephen to Nita Clarke. The family arrived and we all went to the Chelsea Register Office. Stephen was dressed up in a frock-coat, and Nita was in a cream wedding dress with a train.

Then we went to the House of Commons, where a few more people had gathered. Richard Moberly, the industrial chaplain at the *Daily Mirror*, conducted the service in the Crypt. It was a beautiful occasion. Pratima Bowes, Nita's mother, read something in Hindi from Rabindranath Tagore. Mother, who had come in on crutches and was slumped behind the reading desk causing great concern to Richard Moberly, stood up at the appropriate moment and delivered a marvellous sermon about the Corinthians. She was splendid.

At the reception held in the Strangers' Dining Room over 600 people turned up. Caroline and I stood in the receiving line as these people piled in. I had been nervous and thought it might be over the top, to be candid, but it was very successful, Caroline pointed out that the Labour Right had also come, and they obviously had a whale of a time.

Thursday 13 October

The injunctions against the *Guardian* and the *Sunday Times* on *Spycatcher* were lifted. The Government must have spent millions pursuing Peter Wright around the world. It is incredible that a man can confess to crimes against an elected government, yet all the British Government want to do is prevent him publishing it rather than investigate the charges.

The Law Lords compared Wright to Philby and stated that he owed 'a lifelong obligation of confidentiality to the Crown', a most extraordinary judgment. I think this ought to be the subject of some parliamentary action.

The Thatcher years are coming to an end, and it wouldn't surprise me if this time next year she was on her way out and some Baldwin-like figure was brought in (John Biffen or Sir Geoffrey Howe) to lower the temperature of debate.

Thursday 8 December
Following the horrific news of the earthquake in Armenia, the response of sympathy and understanding is amazing, with the Soviet Embassy open for gifts and messages.

Gorbachev's unilateral announcement of cuts of half a million troops has put Russian diplomacy right at the top, has ended the Cold War at a stroke and may bring hope to millions. What is so absurd is that the British defence policy is based on building bombs which would create a tragedy ten times as great as the earthquake and we are pouring money in to help Armenia. It is totally contradictory. The Labour Party has absolutely failed to think anything out.

Caroline said disarmament will lead capitalism to collapse and could lead socialism to prosper, and I think she's right.

Thursday 22 December
There has been an awful air crash. A Pan-Am jumbo aircraft crashed at Lockerbie, near Dumfries in Scotland, killing everybody on board and about twenty-seven people on the ground. The plane came down on a petrol station and burst into flames. A most terrible tragedy, and of course people are worried about whether it was caused by a bomb.

Friday 6 January 1989
Today the UN Security Council discussed the US bombing of Libya over the Lockerbie disaster. The Americans were on the defensive because the Third World has joined almost unanimously in supporting President Qadhafi of Libya. The Americans now behave like cowboys fighting Indians: if you're a Third World country, the Americans can just do what they like – they can invade you, shoot you, bomb you.

Sunday 29 January
In the evening Caroline and I went to a Socialist Conference fund-raising party in Highgate. About 150 people turned up, including Salman Rushdie, who made a little speech about the burning by Muslims of his new book, *Satanic Verses*, which he autographed and auctioned at the party.

Wednesday 15 February
At the Campaign Group we discussed Salman Rushdie and his *Satanic Verses*. Earlier this week Ayatollah Khomeini called for his execution and

another mullah put a million pounds on his head. This has sent shockwaves through the British Muslim community.

Bernie Grant put forward a motion with Max Madden which proposed extending the blasphemy laws and called for a meeting with the Islamic Council. Bernie said that Rushdie knew what he was doing and that they'd cut off people's hands for years in the Muslim world. He appeared to be criticising Rushdie.

Diane Abbott said this was a matter of principle. The Muslims were being misled, and she was opposed to censorship because minorities would suffer.

Alice Mahon said the zealots of Islam had persecuted women, and they went as far as stoning women who'd been raped. She had no sympathy for their case.

Audrey Wise said she hadn't read the book but Rushdie was simply looking at the world with questioning eyes. Khomeini's death threat encouraged racism. She had 6,000 Muslims in the constituency in Preston, and many had written to her asking for the book to be banned, but she had refused, and she had had no criticism of her response.

Mildred Gordon said all fundamentalists and all established Churches were enemies of the workers and the people. All religions were reactionary forces keeping the people down and denying the aspirations of working people. She opposed all blasphemy laws.

Bernie Grant kept interrupting, saying that the whites wanted to impose their values on the world. The House of Commons should not attack other cultures. He didn't agree with the Muslims in Iran, but he supported their right to live their own lives. Burning books was not a big issue for blacks, he maintained.

Pat Wall said his constituency, Bradford North, had the second largest Muslim population but he couldn't sign Max Madden's motion. He read us a letter he was sending out, refusing to support the banning of the book. The real question was the power of the imams and the mullahs and the fundamentalists, and no socialist could support Khomeini. Class was the issue.

Bernie Grant asked why the Muslims should be insulted. They had nothing to live for but their faith, he said.

Eric Heffer thought the history of our own country and the banning of books should be warning enough. Tom Paine's *Rights of Man* had been banned. Many Muslims hadn't even read the book. He couldn't agree to the burning of books, because that led to the burning of people.

We left it there, and it raised all sorts of questions.

Saturday 25 February
To an anti-poll tax public meeting in Sheffield, the first meeting at which I had spoken specifically on the poll tax, and it was clear that mobilisation against it had begun. There was a great deal of anger there, and the ultra-

Left attacked people who said they would pay the poll tax and asked me if I intended to pay. I said it was easier for me because my poll tax was much less than my rates, but I wasn't going to tell anyone else to pay the poll tax, since I thought that would just divide us.

Friday 7 April
Gorbachev had lunch today with the Queen at Windsor Castle, where she gave him some jewellery and an oil painting of a tsar. Gorbachev is going flat out to endear himself to the establishment in the West, and I suppose he's gaining a worldwide reputation which he can use for domestic purposes in the Soviet Union. Meanwhile Boris Yeltsin is quoted as saying he is a tremendous fan of Mrs Thatcher; the praise heaped on Yeltsin is obviously being given because he is thought to be the man who might dismantle socialism.

Monday 8 May
I worked this morning on an alternative paper to 'The Productive and Competitive Economy', which we are discussing today at the special NEC on the policy reviews, together with 'Economic Equality' and 'Consumers and the Community'.

The TV cameras were at Transport House, and I complained to Larry Whitty about Mandelson, who was telling them who and who not to film.

Ken Livingstone, Hannah Sell, the Young Socialist on the NEC, Dennis Skinner and I voted pretty well together.

Gould introduced 'The Productive and Competitive Economy'. When he finished, I said it reminded me of 1931, when Ramsay MacDonald had said that what he recommended went against everything the Party stood for but it was necessary. The trouble with the document was that it contained no analysis, no history, nothing about the power of capital or the impact of the EEC, nothing about the fact that technology gave you a choice, nothing about post-Fordism, nothing about public assets, nothing about the problems that would face an incoming Labour government. I submitted my alternative draft.

Ken Livingstone agreed about the weakness of analysis. He talked about the balance of payments and moved two amendments, one to cut the defence burden and the second to control the export of capital.

Kinnock said there was no need for a historical analysis; it would daunt us. We lived in a capitalist world and we must accept the limitations of capitalism and control technology; unless we could win we couldn't tackle these problems. He said that my proposals were a detachment from reality because there was no easy way. The British public did believe in the market and we had to face that fact.

On cost, he said Ken had helped our enemies by drawing attention to the fact that we couldn't afford our policies. We must build the basis for sustainable growth and we must not promise to spend what we hadn't got. We must create growth and distribute it more fairly – shopping-list socialism was dreaming, and we should leave dreams to others.

Then 'Economic Equality' was introduced by John Smith and Diana Jeuda. I moved that we remove the 50 per cent upper-limit tax pledge. That was defeated.

We adjourned and had a quick meal, then came back to the NEC at 7 for 'Consumers and the Community'. I suggested we change it to '*Citizens* and the Community' – that wasn't accepted.

The atmosphere at the meeting was quite friendly. Four of us, Ken, Dennis, Hannah Sell and I, stuck firm. It is a major change, and by far the most right-wing policy during my time in the Party. Kinnock is openly arguing for capitalism, and the rest are accepting that Thatcher has won the argument but her government might be replaced. I was as cheerful as I could be, and there was no hostility because the majority against was so enormous. As Peter Jenkins said on the news, Kinnock needs a fight to show there has been a change.

Looking back on it, I must recognise that the Labour Party has never been a socialist party, it has never wanted social transformation, it has always had a right-wing leader, it has always wanted to pursue these policies, and it is only when circumstances require a change that the pressure comes from underneath for a transformation. When we win the Election, there will be high expectations and enormous pressure on us, and it is an inadequate economic policy for that situation.

Tuesday 9 May
To Transport House early in order to be able to give a long press interview before I went into the Executive for the second day on policy reviews.

At 10.07 we began work on 'Democracy, the Individual and the Community'. I had put in an alternative paper, and I moved the two amendments at the beginning of my paper – that we remove US bases and take back control from the EEC. They were both defeated by 19 to 3.

We came to the paper called 'Britain in the World' – a defence policy for Britain, presented by Gerald Kaufman. I argued that this really was reiterating Gaitskell's speech in 1960 – fight, fight and fight again. After Chernobyl it was clear that nuclear weapons were unusable. But the PLP had never put forward Conference policy on unilateralism, and, if you looked at the history, Labour governments had in fact been associated with unilateral nuclear *re*armament. Attlee built the bomb, Chevaline was endorsed by Callaghan, and now we were coming along with Trident, which would multiply our nuclear capacity ninefold.

Kinnock said we were not interested in the history of Attlee, Bevin or Gaitskell. This document was put forward in the interests of the British people. He declared, 'I have been to the White House, I have been to the

Kremlin and to the Elysée arguing for unilateral disarmament. They couldn't comprehend the idea of giving up weapons with nothing in return – they couldn't understand "something for nothing". We cannot sustain the argument for unilateralism. Tony says the debate is unrealistic, but patriotism and common sense tell us that there is nothing incompatible between unilateralism and multilateralism. Realism is the greatest weapon in my argument. I have ambitions for a non-nuclear world, and we can get public support for Labour and win the Election; the choice is disarming under Labour or having a Tory government that rearms. We want partners in negotiation and we must get to power.'

The Right clapped him, and that was the first and only applause of the whole two days.

I suppose I ought to put my reflections down. It was a remarkable two days. The NEC *has* abandoned socialist aspirations and any idea of transforming society; it has accepted the main principles not only of capitalism but of Thatcherism, and it thinks that now the Party has a chance of winning office.

On peace, we have abandoned unilateralism and, however we dress it up, we are going to keep the bomb. That is catastrophic, because lots of people are just not going to support Labour – they'll vote Green or something. I think the Labour Party may be in a state of terminal decline.

That doesn't mean I want to join another party or set one up. I don't want the Labour Party to lose, but I want people to understand clearly what is really happening, otherwise they are going to waste their time, they'll be cynical, frustrated, and so on.

That's my work from now until the end of my life.

Wednesday 31 May

I went to Chesterfield Royal Hospital with Tom and Margaret, and we were taken round by the unit manager, who, of course, is a chartered accountant. It is a beautiful hospital. When we came to the premature baby unit, she dropped her voice and said, 'Mr Benn, this is the most expensive end of the business.' I thought, 'God! If premature babies are uneconomic units, where the hell are we?'

Tuesday 15 August

Went to St Thomas's Hospital, where Mother had been taken by ambulance after a fall. She was in a poor way. Her face was vacant, her skin was white and her wig was at an angle. I talked to Dr Norman Jones, the consultant, who said she had a touch of pneumonia, and it is a high-risk situation for the next four or five days.

Wednesday 16 August

I went off to the hospital at 11 and Mother was still looking very poorly. She cried and said, 'My time has come. What is there to live for? I've lived long enough. I am ninety-two. There is no point in going on. I have nothing to look forward to.' It made me cry too.

I decided I must try to cheer her up, so I said, 'You've got a new great-grandchild due next month, Stephen and Nita's baby. You've got your eye operation on 11 September and then you've got your book to finish.'

She slowly came round. We talked about the old days and about her parents, and how her father, D.T. Holmes, had been one of three survivors out of eight children. Then Joshua arrived, and she had lunch and began to perk up. She looked out of the window at Big Ben across the river.

Sunday 1 October – Labour Party Conference, Brighton
To the Conference NEC, where we spent about an hour organising our responses to the Conference resolutions.

What was clear to me was that Kinnock apparently did not want us to be committed to anything, even to the rundown of nuclear power within fifteen years. He was just convinced that we have got to get power first. Still, we've got a 10 per cent lead, and the press is giving him smashing support.

One of the most interesting discussions was on proportional representation, which is supported by Robin Cook, Ken Livingstone, John Evans and Clare Short. Hattersley, Kinnock, Gould, Beckett and I spoke against it. In the end there was a vote, with 23 to 4 against even having an NEC inquiry into it.

Wednesday 4 October
Stephen and Nita had their first baby – Emily, born by Caesarian section at 2.59 pm.

Friday 6 October
Geoffrey Parkhouse from the *Glasgow Herald* gave the traditional vote of thanks to Conference on behalf of the press, and referred to the fact that during the debate on labour relations Emily Benn had been born, and he looked forward to hearing her views on her grandfather in years to come. There was a lot of laughter at that.

At the end we sang 'The Red Flag', 'Auld Lang Syne' and this new song 'Meet the Challenge, Make the Change'. Neil and Glenys stood carrying a little baby, and members of the staff of Walworth Road threw roses at the audience. It was just like an American convention. The Conference has been disastrous for the Left.

Cleared up and drove to May Day Hospital, Croydon, where I saw Emily.

Thursday 26 October
It was announced on the 6 o'clock news that Nigel Lawson, the Chancellor

of the Exchequer, had resigned because he was not prepared to work with Thatcher's economic adviser, Professor Alan Walters. Well, earlier this afternoon the Prime Minister had announced that she had full confidence in Lawson, although it became clear that she knew of his decision to resign before she made that declaration. So when Geoffrey Howe, standing in for her, made a statement later I got in a question, saying that, in view of the fact that the Prime Minister knew that the Chancellor had resigned before she made her statement, she had misled the House. As she is first Lord of the Treasury, she ought to take responsibility for her actions.

For the first time for a long time, our people cheered at my question. It is an enormous political event, and everyone was gossiping in the lobbies. Then we heard that Professor Alan Walters had himself resigned – not that that makes much difference, because he can still feed his advice through to her privately. But it was seen as another massive blunder by Thatcher. She lost Heseltine and Brittan over Westland. I think the fact is that the economy is in a real mess, and Nigel Lawson is happy to get out in good time. Secondly, the British Establishment want to get Britain into the European Monetary System, and therefore they want to discredit the Prime Minister, who is opposed.

Friday 10 November
Out of the blue, and quite amazingly, the Berlin Wall is being removed. The Brandenburg Gate was opened yesterday, and today bulldozers and cranes went in and began hammering holes in the wall and thousands of East Germans are coming over into the West. But in reality it is causing enormous anxiety in NATO because the whole defence argument has changed, while the Labour Party continues to call for three Trident submarines as a first priority. So it is an extremely important event, and very moving.

Wednesday 15 November
I was picked up by car and taken to a studio for a programme called 'Head On', done 'down the line' from Glasgow. Richard Shepherd, the Tory MP for Aldridge-Brownhills, also took part at my suggestion. He is such a sensible person, and we were able to have a serious discussion.

After it was over, Richard and I fell to talking. He thinks there could well be a 'stalking horse' against Thatcher this winter. He said, 'It would be better to have a centre-right figure than a wet.' He thought a lot of people would abstain and, if there was a poor result, Norman Tebbit would go to Mrs Thatcher and tap her on the shoulder and say, 'Time to go.'

Tuesday 5 December
In the House, I heard that the Tory MP Sir Anthony Meyer, who decided to

stand against Mrs Thatcher for the Tory leadership, received 33 votes. It has obviously shaken the Prime Minister a bit more than she would like.

Sunday 31 December

A tumultuous decade and a dramatic year have ended.

World politics in 1989 were earth-shattering. In Poland, Lech Walesa came to power and emerged as a real right-wing, Thatcherite, Catholic nationalist for whom I have very little sympathy. He came to Britain saying he was going to offer cheap Polish labour to British investors, and told the CBI he wanted profit to play a larger part. Then there were demonstrations in Prague, which were put down by force and led to the total overthrow of the Czech regime and a new government. Hungary developed in a similar way. Then the Berlin Wall came down after tremendous outpourings of public feeling, the East and West German governments came together, and there was talk of German reunification. All this was accepted by Gorbachev, who is still desperately trying to make a go of his reforms in Russia, but there are problems in Armenia and the Baltic States, and the economic situation is terribly difficult. The Tories arued that this had all come about due to the fact that we had nuclear weapons, but people didn't really believe it any more.

Sunday 21 January 1990

I have been thinking a lot lately about the role of conscience. I realise that I have got built into me, through my upbringing or whatever, a tremendously strong inner voice saying what I should do at any one moment. It says: You should get up and get the breakfast. You should ring the children. You should not smoke. You should get on with your work. You should go to bed earlier. If I disregard it – as I regularly do over a whole range of issues – then it builds up an unhappiness in me which comes out in other forms. People say I'm a workaholic, but if an inner voice is telling you all the time to do something or another, you can't avoid it. It is the 'still small voice', though sometimes it becomes quite loud.

Sunday 11 February

Had a phone call telling me that Mandela would be released today and asking me to go to Trafalgar Square at 12.30. There were hundreds of people gathered there and the organisers were, of course, the City of London Anti-Apartheid Group, who had been picketing outside South Africa House in Trafalgar Square non-stop for 1,395 days. There was a tremendous sense of excitement. People were singing and waving their arms and kissing and hugging. Somebody had draped on Nelson's column a banner with the words 'Nelson Mandela's Column', and I was pushed on to a platform.

I'm afraid my speech wasn't very clear. I simply said, 'This is a great day.

Free Mandela. Free South Africa. Free Britain. Free working people from exploitation.' There was a cheer, but I don't think people could hear much, and I could hardly hear myself.

It was a marvellous event; people were dancing and shouting, and an ANC choir were singing. It was fantastic. I don't think there has been anything like it since 1945 when the war ended.

A really great day. On television live from Cape Town was Mandela, this tall, slim, distinguished man with a strong voice, walking out of prison and reaffirming the need for the armed struggle.

Tuesday 27 March

To County Hall for the last meeting of ILEA. It was really rather moving to think that there had been a London education authority for over 100 years, that my grandfather had been a founder member in 1889 and that my son, Stephen, was a member as it ended. Nita and little Emily were present, and Emily sat on my lap in the Council chamber and listened to her dad speaking.

Saturday 31 March

To the anti-poll tax demonstration, which started from Kennington Park and marched to Trafalgar Square.

We came up Whitehall and on into Trafalgar Square, which was absolutely crammed. There must have been 150,000 people. I was pleased to see George Galloway there. Jeremy Corbyn was there, but before he was due to speak the rally was stopped because of the trouble which occurred.

I got off the platform and began walking back down Whitehall, but found the police had thrown a barrier across the road, so that people couldn't get up or down, though they let me through. In the crowd I found myself being pressed from behind by riot police and mounted police. People were terribly frightened. I forced my way through until I came to the line of police, who didn't look like police at all. I wondered if they were soldiers in police uniform. I asked where the senior officer was and finally was introduced to a man with a crown on his shoulder.

I had a tape recorder running part of the time, and I asked, 'Why don't you let them go by?'

He said, 'They won't move.'

Well, that wasn't true. He claimed there had been a lot of violence. I think that what they had done was to break the march up, squeeze the people in the middle and frighten them, and then no doubt some bottles and things were thrown. It reminded me a bit of Wapping.

I said to the commander, 'Don't forget what the Northamptonshire police said about the behaviour of the police at Wapping.'

He got a bit angry and said, 'A few mistakes were made then.'

Sunday 1 April
The papers were full of the riots and looting in Trafalgar Square. A man rang me and left a message on my answerphone: 'You fucking cunt. Now you've lost the next Election for us.' That was the only unfriendly one.

Wednesday 11 April
Most of the letters are pretty supportive. Three Anglican bishops, a Catholic bishop and five free churchmen came out today in favour of non-violent protest against the poll tax.

Tuesday 8 May
Jeremy Corbyn and I had a bite to eat, and then went down to the Commons Crypt with a Black & Decker drill and my brass plaque commemorating Emily Wilding Davison. We screwed it on the door, in place of the temporary notice I had put up with Miss Frampton's help.

Monday 23 July
I saw Heseltine in the post office of the Commons today, and said to him, 'I noticed when you were interviewed not long ago on television that one of my books was on the shelf behind you. I presume it was there to impress people!'
    'I'll remove it at once,' he replied.

Wednesday 1 August
On holiday at Stansgate. Absolutely perfect weather, temperature in the nineties – higher than in Athens or North Africa. In the evenings the sunsets are beautiful, and we saw two swans with their cygnets on the river, just heavenly. Caroline is so happy working on her biography of Keir Hardie.

Friday 3 August
Serious news today of the Iraqi invasion of Kuwait. Alliances are being built up; the Americans and Russians issued a statement, Thatcher is going to America, Bush warned that Saudi Arabia mustn't be attacked because Baghdad can't be allowed to control two-thirds of the world's oil supplies. We could be hovering on the edge of a Third World War, and the only comforting thing you can say about it is that the Cold War is over and the superpowers are not fighting this war by proxy. King Hussain of Jordan, who is a great friend of Britain but is also a friend of the Baghdad Government, has been to Iraq.

When the Iraqi Army invaded Kuwait, the Iraq Government claimed a list of grievances against Kuwait – some of which originated in the historical settlement of the borders in the region by the victorious powers after the First World War.
    In 1922, the British High Commissioner, Sir Percy Cox, had delineated the borders of Iraq, Kuwait and Saudi Arabia, giving Kuwait a coastline of 310 miles, and Iraq one of

only 36 miles, at the top of the Gulf. The kingdom of Iraq had comprised the former provinces of Mosul, Baghdad and Basra (which had included Kuwait).

In 1990, therefore, Iraq tried to argue that it had old territorial claims to Kuwait. But the two countries had more recent differences, including the ownership of the Rumaila oilfield, lying under the Iraq–Kuwait border; Kuwait's refusal to lease two islands in the Gulf to Iraq to give her a deep-water port; and serious debt.

Sunday 5 August

Read the papers, and it was just like Suez, with the dire warnings of war, so I decided to send a message from Stansgate (where I had taken my little fax machine) to Neil Kinnock, asking him to consider the recall of Parliament. Certainly if British troops are to be deployed it should be done. I rang the *Guardian*, the Press Association and the *Independent* news desks about it.

Tuesday 7 August

I decided that I would formally request the recall of Parliament, so I typed a letter to the PM, with copies to the Speaker and Neil Kinnock, warning that we could be involved in decisions in which we had played no part. I also stated that a pre-emptive strike by the United States could have the opposite effect to that intended and destroy the unity that had been built up and which I welcomed in the resolution of the Security Council. I pointed out that in former years Parliament was recalled during the recess – in the case of the Suez crisis and the Soviet invasion of Czechoslovakia; MPs had the right to hear the Government's views and ask questions and express their own opinions.

The hostility to Saddam Hussein is so great, as he is being built up as a new Hitler, that any cautious voice even calling for discussion is going to be disregarded and silenced.

Kinnock is on holiday in Italy. Kaufman appears on the television every now and again demanding more urgent action. Israel says that if Iraqi troops enter Jordan it will be an act of war, even though Jordan might agree to have them there. It could be catastrophic.

Wednesday 8 August

Today Bush did a broadcast with tremendous hyping up – American wives weeping as sailors left in aircraft carriers and all that. The British are sending forces to help King Fahd of Saudi Arabia, apparently because he requested them. In the end, it's an Anglo-American force that is in the Gulf. Saddam Hussein soon afterwards announced that Kuwait was to be permanently annexed to Iraq.

In the afternoon I was quite desperate, and rang the BBC. I asked them, 'Why won't you broadcast the fact that a request has been made to recall Parliament?' But they won't do it.

Monday 13 August
The Prime Minister turned down my request for the recall of Parliament.

Wednesday 15 August
Began serious work on my Government of Britain Bill. It's extremely difficult writing a completely new constitution from scratch on your own. On the other hand, having a blank piece of paper and knowing how power works and is abused is helpful as a starting point.

The problem will be devising a constitution for Scotland and Wales. I think I shall make provision for national parliaments for Scotland and Wales, and they must decide on their own constitutions. So I am left with the English Assembly and how it should work. There is a difficulty about proportional representation and a second chamber. I've been talking about this for two years, and now everyone else is moving on it, and I shall be left behind if I don't make some progress soon.

Thursday 30 August
I rang Andreas Whittam Smith, Editor of the *Independent*, and said, 'Don't you think it would be a good idea if your readers had a chance of hearing what the peace case is?' He was terribly polite and asked me to write something, which I did immediately and faxed to him. They are going to print it tomorrow.

Later today I heard Parliament had been recalled for Thursday and Friday next week, and so there will be a Commons debate.

There is going to be a demonstration in Hyde Park or Trafalgar Square.

Thursday 6 September
To the Commons for what turned out to be a difficult meeting of the Campaign Group. I circulated a motion which had the broad agreement of the Stop the War campaign – that we condemn the aggression, support the sanctions, say there is a prospect of a peaceful settlement and then demand that the Government give an assurance that they won't authorise offensive British military action without a special resolution by the UN. We should decline to support the Government in the absence of such a declaration.

Perhaps not to my surprise, there was a lot of argument about my resolution.

Dave Nellist said he didn't believe in the UN at all. He insisted that there had to be an overthrow of the Iraqi regime from within – I don't disagree with that.

Dennis Skinner said we should raise the question of the oil companies and their exploitation, otherwise it looked a bit academic.

Diane Abbott was doubtful about signing it, because she thought the UN could be the instrument of oppression of the Third World by the rich white countries.

Jeremy Corbyn was doubtful because of the UN, and thought we should say simply, 'Get out of the Gulf.' I should have cleared it with Jeremy first, because we are both officers of the Campaign Group.

To cut a long story short, most of them signed it, but Terry Fields and Dave Nellist wouldn't.

The debate in the House was opened by Thatcher. I put a question to her about the use of force. Kinnock made a more militant speech than Thatcher, and he called for the destruction of the Iraqi war machine, which is nothing whatever to do with Kuwait.

Ted Heath and Denis Healey spoke urging caution. The debate went back and forth, and I was called by the Speaker shortly after 5.40 and spoke for twenty-two minutes. The Chamber filled up with Members, because it was known by then that I was going to divide the House. Looking back on it, I wasn't terribly pleased with the speech – I don't know why. I felt very flat afterwards. Sir John Stokes, who is a right-wing old Tory, said he thought I had been flippant. I don't think I quite got it right, although the argument was correct.

Friday 7 September
Second day of the debate, opened by Tom King, and we had a speech from Martin O'Neill, our defence spokesman, which was very militant.

Then we had a series of speeches of which infinitely the most moving was from Eric Heffer, who is very thin and white. Everybody knows he is dying, and he spoke against war with great passion. David Winnick got up to interrupt him, but Eric said, 'I am not giving way. This may be my last speech in the House.' When he sat down he was exhausted, his head fell forward on to his hands and he crossed himself. It was deeply, deeply moving.

Douglas Hurd spoke last, and added something about the possibility of a post-Cold War 'new world order', which is what everybody has been talking about. 'Opposition Members talk . . . in terms of great aspirations and the brotherhood of man. I see it in more traditional Tory terms as an increasingly effective concert of nations.'

This summed it up: a return to a pre-1914 situation in which the great powers – Washington, Moscow, and no doubt Tokyo and Berlin – will get together and run the world. With the disappearance of socialism from the international agenda, we are getting back to great-power politics, to nationalism, to racism, to imperialism, and to all sorts of other unattractive xenophobic characteristics.

The division was 437 to 35. But, taking the Labour backbenchers, 49 per cent voted for the Government, 25 per cent against and 26 per cent abstained. In others words, 51 per cent of Labour backbenchers didn't vote with the Government.

Monday 17 September
To Friends' Meeting House, Euston Road, for the Committee to Stop the War. The Left is marvellous! When I arrived I walked into a flaming row, because Mark Osborn of *Socialist Organiser* had issued a leaflet to which CND and the *Marxism Today* lot took exception. He asked on behalf of his committee to affiliate to Stop the War, but that was turned down, and he was requested to leave the meeting.

I said, 'I don't think we have any authority to do that. It's Stalinist.' So that upset the CND people.

The row went on and on, and Ann Pettifor said Mark Osborn should be told to leave. I nearly walked out myself!

Monday 24 September
I had asked to see Ted Heath, and at 5.45 I arrived at his house. I expected a police guard, but the door was open and his chauffeur was carrying in a box of apples, which he told me Mr Heath had picked from his garden in Salisbury. Out came a Spanish lady in her sixties, who said, 'Mr Benn, what a pleasure to see you in the flesh. Do come in. Mr Heath will be here in a few minutes.'

She took me up to his sitting room on the first floor of quite a small house, beautifully furnished, with pictures of yachting scenes, and his piano, and two couches facing each other. As I walked up the stairs I could see him working in his office in his pullover.

He came in and shook hands, and I thanked him for sparing the time. He offered me a drink, and I said I was a teetotaller – which he didn't know. I had a ginger ale.

I said I thought his broadcast a week before had been very wise and reflected a widely held opinion in Britain. I wondered whether he might consider joining with other senior political figures, many of whom, like himself, had been 'through the chair', to issue an appeal for peace along the lines of his broadcast. He sat there, impassive, looking at me.

His Private Secretary had told me that after his broadcast he had received eighty-five letters, most of them sympathetic.

I told him, 'I have had over a thousand now, from all over the world, and only thirty-one of them were critical.'

We discussed the UN's position, and I said, 'People don't want another Korean War.'

'I agree with that.'

It wasn't a cold meeting exactly, but it was formal, and I suppose he must be suspicious of me because I fought him very hard when he was Prime Minister, opposed him on the Common Market, and criticised him sharply on a number of occasions.

Just before I left, I said, 'My wife sends her kind regards. We have never forgotten the time we came to dinner at Number 10 when you were Prime

Minister and you were dining a West African president, I forget who it was. After the dinner we had some lovely music played by African musicians, sitting on the floor and playing their instruments.' All of a sudden he was transformed. His body began shaking with the old Ted Heath laugh, and he said, 'We always had music at Number 10 dinners.'

I got up and left. It was a memorable little event. Perhaps he will do something about it, but, if he doesn't, there you are.

Sunday 30 September – Labour Party Conference, Blackpool
Two well-dressed men came up to me at the Conference and said, 'Excuse me, sir, we are from the police. We have to advise you that somebody with a northern accent rang the *Daily Mirror* this morning saying that a contract had been put out to kill you and Ken Livingstone. Do you know where Mr Livingstone is?'

I said, 'I'll see him later, and I'll tell him. Thanks.'

I daresay we are back in the old routine of death threats, with the Gulf crisis.

The layout of the Conference is fantastic – lots of photographs and the slogan 'Looking to the Future'. The rostrum is quite separate from the platform, and everybody had been pushed up on to the second row, except for 'leading figures'. It is now all stage-managed for the telly. It is symbolic of the separation between the leadership and the membership.

Monday 1 October
I was disappointed that the Conference rejected by 3 million-odd to 2,788,000 a motion to phase out nuclear power over fifteen years.

Looking at the platform in the afternoon, I though that all these impressive Front Bench people – Tony Blair, Michael Meacher, Jack Straw, Frank Dobson, John Cunningham – made a much better team man for man, or woman for woman, than the Tories. I think people have had enough of the Thatcher philosophy, and they want a change.

Wednesday 3 October
Up at 6.45, and I practised and timed my speech on the emergency resolution on the Gulf, on which I intended to speak from the floor.

Ken Cameron moved the emergency resolution very well, seconded by somebody from Bolsover who sounded just like Dennis Skinner and was brilliantly funny. Then Denis Healey spoke, and John Edmonds made an outrageous speech in which he asked about the commanders of British troops in Saudi Arabia, 'Are they not to be allowed to make a pre-emptive strike?'

I got up after every speech, expecting to be called, and finally Jo Richardson, the Chair, said, 'That's where we must leave it. The Conference Arrangements Committee have allowed us five speeches from the floor.' So people on the floor shouted, 'Call Tony Benn!' Jo said, 'I've called two MPs, and nobody has a special right to speak.'

I didn't complain, but, as a result of all the fuss being made about my being excluded, the media gathered round, and in fact I did masses of interviews on what I would have said anyway. I was very sharp at Edmonds: 'For a general secretary sitting in his comfortable armchair to call for a pre-emptive strike against Baghdad when he is not going to be killed himself is disgraceful.'

Sunday 21 October

Ted Heath saw Saddam Hussein today and is hoping to come out with some of the British hostages. Bit by bit, one could see the whole of the Gulf War enterprise grinding to a halt, with the American President in deep trouble domestically over his budget.

Thursday 1 November

A bombshell today: Geoffrey Howe, the Deputy Prime Minister and Leader of the House, has resigned from the Government – the last surviving member of the original 1979 Cabinet. He is a very nice man; I like him personally.

Willy Brandt is going to Baghdad. I feel a certain pride in this because Ralph Miliband had suggested I approach Ted Heath, and then I suggested to Heath that Willy Brandt might be brought in. It may have come from that. Brandt is going to Baghdad with the goodwill of the UN Secretary-General, although Douglas Hurd has complained to the German Government about it.

Howe's resignation has put the Tories into a panic, and there may be a leadership election; if Heseltine became Leader, there's not much difference between him and Kinnock, except that he has had a lot more experience.

Tuesday 6 November

The Iraqi Embassy rang, saying the Ambassador would like to see me. I wasn't prepared to go to the Embassy, so they said the Ambassador would come to my home at 1.30. I informed the Foreign Office, so that it was all above board.

The Ambassador, Dr Shafiq al-Salihi, came with his Third Secretary, and Ruth Winstone, who is working on my diaries, greeted them in Arabic – which I think created a favourable impression.

He said straightaway, 'We have been following your statements on the Gulf crisis and I have been instructed by my government to invite you to visit Baghdad.' He then asked if I had any advice as to how the matter might be resolved.

I said, 'Yes, I have. I think you should release all the hostages, because they are not worth anything to you in terms of bargaining. They won't protect you from a war and, if they were all released, the whole thing would look quite different. After that, I think, you would have to be prepared to put Kuwait under the control of the UN and then sit down without preconditions to consider the implementation of all the resolutions.'

'I hadn't thought of the hostage point,' he said, and added, 'If the President's programme permits, he will see you in Baghdad.' He also told me that I 'wouldn't come back empty-handed', which implied that some hostages would return.

I told him, 'My prime interest would not be in the humanitarian appeal for some being allowed out but in the political case for *all* of them coming out.'

He looked very uncomfortable. Then he asked me to dinner, and I thanked him.

When they left I rang Ralph Miliband, who was responsible for the whole idea of my approaching Heath. I also rang Heath's Private Secretary, who told me that Heath had put that very point about the hostages and had also spoken to Bob McNamara in California.

I told the UN Secretary-General's office about the approach, and faxed them my account of the meeting.

Later in the day, I spoke to Heath (who got thirty-three hostages released) and said, 'I haven't seen you since you went to Iraq. Congratulations. I have had an invitation. Shall I go?

'Yes, of course,' he replied.

So everyone I have asked thinks I should go. I'll have to work out carefully what to say, and I will make it an explicitly political mission, not one about humanitarian issues. The air tickets will cost £825.

Friday 9 November
I made it clear to the Iraqis that if I went to Baghdad I would want to see Saddam Hussein, I would want some hostages released, and I wanted to see King Hussain in Jordan.

Yesterday in the Commons Douglas Hurd had urged me not to go to Baghdad. On the other hand, letters and telephone calls of support are pouring in. Two people offered to act as interpreter. Richard Branson's office rang to say he would be happy to send one of his Virgin Airline planes to Baghdad to bring any hostages back.

To Chesterfield. Johnny Burrows had been a bit upset that he hadn't been told I was going, and he felt I wasn't consulting the local Party. But after a talk he supported me 100 per cent.

Saturday 10 November
Looked in to see Melissa, and found Joshua and some of the grandchildren there. They were very concerned about my safety in Baghdad, so I rang an Irish PhD student, Paul Lalor, who is a brilliant Arabist and who had offered

his services as an interpreter, and said I might be able to take him. There is such a lot to do, and the hostages' relatives keep ringing the office with requests. Michael, my eldest grandchild, asked, 'Are you going to be killed in Baghdad, Dan-Dan?'

I said no, and he looked relieved and went on watching the telly.

Sunday 11 November
I spoke to Paul Lalor, the Arabic speaker, an Irishman of thirty-two who is at St Antony's College, Oxford. He has agreed to come if I pay his airfare and expenses.

Tuesday 13 November
Geoffrey Howe made his formal resignation speech, which was devastating; he savaged Mrs Thatcher, was amusing and committed. It was all about Europe and the maintenance of the free market and so on. It has certainly transformed everything. We have really come to the end of the Thatcher era, I think.

Friday 16 November
I rang a former Jordanian Ambassador, who was most courteous and friendly and advised me how to approach Saddam Hussein and King Hussain of Jordan.

Later in the day, the Leader of the Democratic Opposition in Kuwait rang me and described the atrocities in Kuwait – the torture and rape and looting – and said he thought war was inevitable. I said, 'I suppose you don't think I should go.' He said, 'No, I don't.'

Tuesday 20 November
To the House, and went to the Committee Corridor because I wanted to see what was happening in the first ballot for the Tory leadership – Michael Heseltine versus Margaret Thatcher.

It is quite a historic event. By secret ballot, Tory MPs have the power to remove as Leader of their party a Prime Minister who has been elected three times by the British people.

When I got there, the whole corridor was packed from the upper waiting hall right down to the far end, with hundreds of people. I had my radio with an earpiece and the aerial sticking up, and I must have looked like a man from outer space. I stood on a bench so that I could see everyone – Tory, Labour and Liberal MPs, clerks, secretaries, journalists – a sea of faces.

There was a bit of scuffling further up, and then all of a sudden, through the crowd, came a number of journalists, who ran by so quickly I could hardly recognise any of them. The crowd opened like the Red Sea. One of the journalists said to me, 'Second ballot. Can you comment?'

So I said, 'It is appropriate that it should have happened to her when she was in Versailles' – a point Caroline had made to me.

He said, 'Brilliant', and rushed off.

It wasn't for some time that I heard the results. Margaret Thatcher had got 204 and Heseltine 152. It was four short of an outright victory for her on the first ballot. Almost immediately I heard her on my radio from Paris, where she is attending the Conference on Security and Co-operation in Europe, announcing she was going to fight in the second ballot.

Heseltine said he had let his name go forward to the next ballot, so the crisis continues for another week.

The Labour Party is of course keen to keep Thatcher, and Kinnock has put down a motion of censure against her, for Thursday, to try to consolidate Tory support around her. It is a disgrace that in eight years this is the first motion of censure against the Government.

At 10, when a statement was made that there would be a motion of censure against the Government on Thursday, Jim Sillars made exactly that point.

Wednesday 21 November

Mrs Thatcher arrived back from France. The rumour going round at the moment is that the men in grey suits went to see her to say, 'Time to go.' Indeed, I think Willie Whitelaw went to see her. But according to rumours she just absolutely refused to have anything to do with that advice, so then the Cabinet was polled privately and, whatever they thought individually, they took a common line to support her. So Hurd has nominated her again, and Major has signed her nomination. Actually, if you look round, there isn't a dominant alternative figure. Hurd and Major aren't really up to it, but Heseltine is flamboyant and experienced and is getting marvellous press.

In terms of stamina and persistence, you have to admit Margaret Thatcher is an extraordinary woman. She came out of Number 10, saying, 'I fight on. I fight to win.' Then she went to the House and made a statement on the Paris CSCE talks. You would think she would be downcast after that setback, but not at all. When Paddy Ashdown got up and said that the Paris Treaty was one of the great moments of the twilight of her premiership, she replied, 'As for the twilight, people should remember that there is a 24-hour clock', which was a smashing answer.

Kinnock tried to be statesmanlike but couldn't manage it. I then went upstairs to see Douglas Hurd about my Iraq trip, and there were three officials in his room. It was the very same room in which George Brown had tried to summon Harold Wilson in 1968 on the night George resigned as Foreign Secretary, and I told the civil servants the story. They asked how I thought history would see Margaret Thatcher.

I said, 'Everyone drops into the darkest of all worlds between the headlines and the history books. Not many live long enough to come back again, but it is too soon to say.' I didn't want to be offensive. I asked, 'Who do you think will win?'

One of them said he thought Heseltine would.

Hurd came in. He is a weakling and hasn't got any stuffing.

After the pleasantries he said, 'What I am afraid of is that you might give Saddam Hussein the impression he wouldn't have to leave Kuwait.'

I replied, 'Quite the opposite. As a matter of fact, I am going to tell him that there is going to be a war.'

'Nobody wants a war,' he said.

'Well, in my opinion, that's what it is all building up to.'

Hurd was slightly thrown.

I told him, 'I am going to try and bring out some hostages, obviously, but my main argument is that he should release them all and explore the possibility for negotiations.'

He said, 'He gave Ted Heath a very rough time, talked about chemical warfare and made his flesh creep.'

'I'm too old for that! You are a diplomat and are experienced at diplomacy, and it must be frustrating that you can't do anything about it, using your diplomatic skill.'

I got the feeling he was uneasy. I think he is really a dove in this situation.

He said, 'It's very easy for him. He has only got to withdraw from Kuwait.'

'It's not quite like that. The Prime Minister talks about a war crimes tribunal, about destroying his military capacity and about compensation, and I am not sure that withdrawal from Kuwait would necessarily do the trick.'

At the end, I was given the latest list of hostages compiled by the FO. But I could feel the awful pressure from all these reasonable civil servants and Tory Ministers.

Thursday 22 November

I was in the middle of an interview about the war in the Gulf for 'Dispatches' on Channel 4 when my secretary Kathy burst in to say Margaret Thatcher had resigned. Absolutely dazzling news, and it was quite impossible to keep my mind on the interview after that. So people have been to her and told her that she can't win. She called the Cabinet together this morning and told them. But the motion of censure is still taking place this afternoon.

To the House, which was in turmoil. We had the censure debate, and Kinnock's speech was flamboyant and insubstantial. When he was cross-examined about the European currency he simply couldn't answer. Thatcher was brilliant. She always has her ideology to fall back on; she rolled off statistics, looked happy and joked.

Monday 26 November

We were met at Baghdad by three MPs from the International Relations

Committee of the Iraqi Parliament, and we sat in this beautiful, glamorous new airport which was absolutely deserted because there are no flights other than internal ones. Gave a press conference.

We were driven to the Al-Rasheed Hotel; in the car we were given the government line about how the Iraqis were prepared to make any sacrifices and die for their people, and so on. Who should be at the hotel but Svend Robinson MP, of the Canadian New Democratic Party, whom I met two years ago. He has been here for a week with an all-party Canadian delegation but has not yet succeeded in seeing Saddam.

We went down to dinner with the Iraqi MPs, who said Saddam would see me. I asked if they could give me an indication of how many hostages were likely to be released; they said the number would be on the same sort of scale as Willy Brandt was allowed.

Tuesday 27 November
At 7.45 am I was taken in pouring rain to the tented encampment in the garden of the British Embassy, which looked like a refugee camp. There are about fifty-seven people in the tents, and they eat in a place they call the Oasis Club, a sort of hut with some basic cooking facilities. They are all British, work for Bechtel, and have been living there since the beginning of the crisis. They are in engineering, construction, procurement and information technology, all working on contracts for the Iraqi Ministries. They are all being paid and buy food from the streets with company money. A doctor visits once a week and a nurse twice a week. One of them said that on the streets they had encountered growing public hostility to Saddam Hussein.

Heard on the news that John Major has won the leadership of the Tory Party with 185 votes against 56 for Hurd and 131 for Heseltine; as he was only two votes short of an overall majority, Hurd and Heseltine had immediately withdrawn. So he becomes the youngest Prime Minister this century; a competent person from a simple background, like the Archbishop of Canterbury, George Carey. He is a new type of Thatcherite really; not strident, probably slightly less ideological, more sympathetic to Europe, a hard man in terms of financial policy, but confident.

Wednesday 28 November
The *Spectator* has voted me Backbencher of the Year. Fat lot of good that does! Tony Banks is accepting on my behalf at the Savoy Hotel today.

Up at 6.30 and had breakfast with four members of the 'Committee of the British Community', and their description of British Embassy treatment was awful. They were not welcomed at the Embassy, had had absolutely no help from it, and had even been told they had to put stamps on their letters home. Because they are not British taxpayers, they were told they couldn't expect any concessions. One man's mother-in-law had died, somebody's sister was dying of cancer, and their anger at the British Embassy was great. But they have organised themselves well.

Went downstairs after breakfast with a view to meeting the Deputy Prime Minister, when I recognised the President's interpreter, Dr Sa'doon Zubaydi, and all of a sudden I realised that this was the big meeting. I said I would be taking Paul with me as my adviser, and they said, 'You can't; we haven't permission.' If I had put my foot down, I may have been able to insist, I don't know. However, not only did they refuse Paul, they took my bag off my shoulder and said I would have to leave that behind. So I put my hand in my bag to pull out some papers, and I thought that I had pulled out the full list of hostages which we had been advised should be handed in at the Presidential Office. But owing to the hurry – I wasn't even in my best suit, which I had brought for the meeting – I failed to take the list and also the box of medicines which I brought to give Saddam.

Anyway, we got into the car and had a candid talk. Dr Zubaydi asked if there were many matters I would like to discuss. So I took my opportunity and said, 'There is great anxiety in Britain about the Kurds. I know you have given them a lot of autonomy, but this is a problem. There is great anxiety about human rights.' He looked a bit uncomfortable, but at least I did raise these matters. I added, 'But I don't want to raise this now, because the central question is peace.'

We drove through Baghdad, on a circuitous route, and finally we came to a line of ordinary-looking little villas and drove into the front garden of one. This was where I was to meet the President. It reminded me of the villa at which I had met Rajiv Gandhi last year but without the three encampments and barbed wire.

There was a gathering of people in the waiting room – Tariq Aziz, the Foreign Minister; Dr Sa'doon Hammadi, whom I had met yesterday; Mr Latif Jassim, the Minister of Culture and Information; Hamid Yousif Hammadi, the President's Private Secretary, who apparently has Cabinet rank; Muhsin Khalil, the press secretary; Sa'doon Zubaydi, the chief interpreter; and two other aides.

The Foreign Minister asked about John Major and said, 'I met him a couple of years ago in Geneva and I found him a good listener. I knew Carrington before and I didn't find him very helpful' – which didn't surprise me. I thought that was an indication that they would like better relations with the British Government.

At about 10.15 we were ushered into a room furnished with blue curtains and seats, with flowers on the table, and two television cameras and photographers. There was Saddam Hussein dressed in uniform, and I said, 'Salaam Alaikum', and he said, 'Wa Alaikum a Salaam'; at least I remembered that. We sat down, and when the cameras were on us I didn't know whether we were supposed to start speaking, so it was a bit awkward for a moment. Anyway, I thanked him for inviting me.

I began by saying that I was very conscious that between the Tigris and the Euphrates was the cradle of world civilisation, so that I was coming to the source of my own civilisation.

Then I said, 'I bring you messages of peace', and I placed the papers I had brought with me on the table – telegrams I had received from Nelson Mandela, Willy Brandt, Ron Dellums, Papandreou, and so on. 'I have also brought some letters, Mr President, that were sent to me in London with the request to give them to you.' (These were personal pleas from relatives of hostages to Saddam.)

'May I say a personal word,' I continued. 'I come from a family that for a long time has supported the Arab nation. My father was a Secretary of State in 1945 and worked to bring about the evacuation of the British base in Tel El-Kebir. I opposed the Suez War and participated in big demonstrations, like now.

'My little grandson, James, who is six, asked me the other day, "Dan-Dan" (which is what he calls me), "are you in favour of war?" I said, "No, James, I am not." "Does Saddam Hussein want a war?" I said, "No, he does not." So James said, "I understand now why he invited you to Baghdad." '

They all smiled.

I went on, 'But you know my position. May I speak frankly?'

'Yes.'

'I think the time has come for a major new Iraqi peace initiative.

'I would like to turn to the case for restoring free movement to the foreign residents now in Iraq. The holding of these residents is no protection against war, and indeed the American and British governments are using the fact that you are holding them as arguments for their policy, which is one reason why the British Government have refused to give me help on my visit. There is a special problem of the foreign residents in Kuwait who do want to see Kuwait liberated and want to protect their Kuwaiti friends.

'What is needed is a historic statement by the Iraqi Government that all residents can come and go freely. They would all be ambassadors for peace – which would transform the political situation, reaffirm the traditional reputation of the Arabs for hospitality, and open the way to peace talks. And I hope I may take our people home with me.'

I should add that he had said he thought there was a complex conspiracy between the Americans, the Kuwaitis, the Israelis and the Saudis, and that actually the Americans had been paid money by the Saudis to come in and protect the Saudi royal family. He asked if I thought the Americans would be there if the costs weren't being paid by Kuwait and Saudi Arabia.

I said, 'We must get off the war machine and on to the peace process, and I think it would be very, very helpful if there was anything you could say, Mr

President, that indicated your long-term perspective for peace. Today is the crisis, tomorrow the war, but there is a day after.'

I then told the story (a dangerous story to tell because emotion overcomes me) about the old lady of seventy-seven from Arbroath who sent me £5 to wish me good luck in my mission for peace and wrote, 'My father was killed in Iraq in 1921, shot through the head while defending a British pipeline. I have sent the money in case you find his grave, put some flowers on it, take a photograph and send it to me.'

As I told this, my lip quivered, and it had a quite electric effect on the meeting and they all paused for a second. I said, 'It may seem rather an emotional point, but politics *is* about emotion and not just about statistics.'

Then we went on to the question of Palestine, and I said, 'I support you 100 per cent on Palestine and the right to a Palestinian state, but, if there is a war, think of the consequences. You can't have a Palestine without Palestinians, and they may all be killed.'

After three hours he said, 'I have detained you too long.' That was a clear sign, so we stood up and shook hands.

This was where I made my big mistake, because I had been so high-minded about not pleading for hostages and talking about politics that I had forgotten to do what Paul would have done if he had been allowed to come – that is, to ask how many hostages would be allowed out, when they could come out, and so on. I missed the boat, and, when I got back with Sa'doon Zubaydi, Paul was obviously extremely disappointed that I had failed to do the fundamental thing. I felt I had let him down most terribly.

But you must have faith, and I tried to keep it up during a pretty gloomy afternoon press conference, with the journalists all clamouring around and asking, 'How many have you got, Mr Benn?' as if it was a cricket match.

I described the meeting in a way that didn't betray Saddam Hussein's confidence, and the press were quite generous to me. I said, 'Well, I can't tell you. There are a lot of ends to be tied up. I was very bold and asked for the lot.'

By the evening, the full impact of my failure was beginning to dawn on me.

Sa'doon Zubaydi, incidentally, asked me to send him the particulars of the grave the Scottish woman had written to me about. Late in the day, a message came through that the Iraqi Government would provide me with a private jet to Amman, which means I might be able to see King Hussain on my way back.

Paul and I were in a state of gloom, but in fact a very amusing, kind Member of Parliament came to see us, and I told him I had forgotten to ask the critical question. He laughed, and he is going to try to talk to the Speaker. Later I heard that fifteen hostages had been identified to be released. It's not bad, but not as many as I had hoped.

Incidentally, I heard that, when Willy Brandt met Saddam Hussein, at one point he had looked down at his knees and said very quietly, 'Mr President, you won't like what I am going to tell you, but . . .' Then he had told him that he should withdraw from Kuwait. Afterwards Saddam had said he thought Willy Brandt was 'sweet'!

Just after midnight, Sa'doon rang to check the final list of fifteen names. He commented on some of the people who have been to see Saddam Hussein, and told me, 'Jesse Jackson is a complete fake.'

I asked, 'What do you mean?'

'He came over with a television crew; Saddam Hussein wanted to talk to him about the crisis, and he said, "I'm just here doing television programmes." He created a very poor impression.'

Thursday 29 November
We were taken to the old airport in Baghdad and took off in this comfortable little jet – just Paul, myself and the Iraqi Ambassador to Jordan, who had been for talks in Baghdad. We flew for an hour across nothing but desert except the Euphrates, and landed in Amman at about 10.

We landed at London Airport at about 4pm and came through quickly, and there was Caroline waiting for me. I felt totally at home again. There were forty journalists, and I felt as if I were in front of a firing squad. They asked some hostile questions.

Saturday 1 December
This week saw the removal of Mrs Thatcher from Number 10, and apparently, as she left the building, people detected a tear in her eye. But she turned up in the House the following day, sitting in the seat Geoffrey Howe had occupied when he had made his resignation speech, and she listened to John Major. According to the opinion poll, Labour is slipping and the Tories are rising, and I think the media have at last found a candidate they can openly and uncritically support.

Yesterday I actually had a handwritten letter from Kinnock in which he congratulated me on the success of my 'humanitarian efforts'. I thought I had better take it as a peace gesture, so I rang and thanked him, and arranged to go and give him a briefing.

Thursday 6 December
During the day we heard that Saddam Hussein had announced that he is granting 'freedom of movement' to all foreign residents i.e., releasing them – the very thing I asked him to do last week. I could hardly believe it.

At 8 Caroline and I went to a lovely dinner at the Commons that had been arranged to celebrate my fortieth year in Parliament. Ruth Winstone had decorated a cake with the Commons portcullis symbol on it. Tony and Sally Banks gave me a Gladstone plate from their own collection, which was extremely generous. Also invited were Chris Mullin, Ralph and Marion

Miliband and their friend John Saville, the historian, who was riveted by Caroline's work on Hardie, Richard and Patricia Moberly, Jeremy and Claudia Corbyn and Maxine Baker.

At one point, the lights went out in the Harcourt Room, which is where a lot of Tory MPs have dinner, and in came the cake, and the Tory MPs sang 'Happy Birthday', not knowing what was going on.

Principal Persons
Political and Official

Biographical notes describe individuals according to their status at the start of the book i.e.
Winston Churchill, not Sir Winston Churchill, etc

ACLAND, Sir Richard. Founder of Common Wealth Party 1942. Liberal
    MP (Barnstaple), 1933–45; Labour MP (Gravesend), 1951–5.

ALLAUN, Frank. Chairman of the Labour Party, 1978/9, and Labour MP
    for Salford East, 1955–83. Vice-President of CND and President of
    Labour Action for Peace.

ARMSTRONG, William (1915–80). Head of the Home Civil Service, and
    Permanent Secretary of the Civil Service Department, 1968–74. Joint
    Permanent Secretary of the Treasury, 1962–8. Created a life peer in 1975.

ASHTON, Joe. PPS to Tony Benn, 1975–6. Labour MP for Bassetlaw since
    1968.

ATTLEE Clement (1883–1967). Clement Attlee, Leader of the Labour
    Party, 1935–55; and Prime Minister, 1945–51. MP for Limehouse,
    subsequently West Walthamstow, 1922–55. Created an earl in 1955.

BALOGH, Thomas (1905–85). Oxford economist of Hungarian birth.
    Minister of State at the Department of Energy, 1974–5; and Deputy
    Chairman, British National Oil Company, 1976–8. Close adviser to
    Harold Wilson in the 1950s and early 1960s, and Economic Adviser to
    the Cabinet, 1964–8. Created a life peer in 1968.

BANKS, Tony. Assistant General Secretary, Association of Broadcasting
    and Allied Staffs, 1976–83; and Head of Research, Amalgamated Union
    of Engineering Workers, 1968–75. Last Chairman of Greater London
    Council, 1985–6. Labour MP for Newham North West since 1983.

BARNETT, Joel. Chief Secretary to the Treasury, 1974–9. Labour MP for
    Heywood and Royton, 1964–83. Created a life peer in 1983.

BASNETT, David (1924–89). General Secretary of General and Municipal
    Workers' Union 1973–86. Chairman, TUC General Council, 1977–8,

and of Trade Unionists for a Labour Victory, 1979–85. Created a life peer in 1987.

BEVAN, Aneurin (Nye) (1897–1960). Labour MP for Ebbw Vale. Minister of Health 1945–51; Minister of Labour and National Service, 1951. Married to Jennie Lee.

BEVIN, Ernest (Ernie) (1881–1951). General Secretary, TGWU, 1921–40. Labour MP for Central Wandsworth, subsequently for Woolwich East. Minister of Labour and National Service, 1940–5. Foreign Secretary, 1945–51.

BIFFEN, John. Chief Secretary to the Treasury, 1979–81; Secretary of State for Trade, 1981–2; and Lord President of the Council, 1982–3. Leader of the House of Commons, 1982–7. Conservative MP for Oswestry, subsequently Shropshire North, since 1961.

BLACKETT, Patrick (1897–1972). Chief Scientific Adviser at the Ministry of Technology. Pre-eminent nuclear scientist. President of the Royal Society, 1965–70. Created a life peer in 1969.

BONDI, Hermann. Chief Scientific Adviser to Ministry of Defence, 1971–7. Chief Scientist, Department of Energy, 1977–80.

BONHAM CARTER, Violet (1887–1969). Leading Liberal, President of the Liberal Party, 1945–7. Daughter of Liberal Prime Minister, Herbert Asquith; mother-in-law of Liberal Leader, Jo Grimond. Created a life peer in 1964, as Lady Asquith.

BOOTH, Albert. Minister of State, Department of Employment, 1974–6, and Secretary of State, 1976–9. From 1966 to 1983 he was Labour MP for Barrow-in-Furness.

BOOTHBY, Robert (Bob) (1900–86). Conservative MP for Aberdeenshire East. Broadcaster.

BOYLE, Sir Edward (1923–81). Friend from university days. MP for Birmingham Handsworth. Economic Secretary to Treasury, 1955–6.

BRETHERTON, James. Principal Private Secretary at the Department of Energy, 1976–8.

BROCKWAY, Fenner (1888–1988). Founder of the Movement for Colonial Freedom in the 1950s. Labour MP for East Leyton, 1929–31, and for Eton and Slough, 1950–64. Leading member of the Independent Labour Party between 1922 and 1946. Created a life peer in 1964.

BROOK, Norman (1902–67). Chairman of the Governors of the BBC, 1964–7; previously Joint Secretary of the Treasury. Secretary of the

Cabinet, 1947–62; Head of the Home Civil Service, 1956–62. Created a life peer, Lord Normanbrook, in 1963.

BROWN, George (1914–85). Deputy-Leader of the Labour Party, 1960–70, and in that capacity member of the National Executive and Chairman of the Home Policy Committee. Held office in the 1945–51 Government, finally as Minister of Works. First Secretary of State at the Department of Economic Affairs, 1964–6; and Foreign Secretary, 1966–8. Ardently pro-Common Market: tried to negotiate Britain's entry in 1967. Labour MP for Belper, 1945–70. Created a life peer, Lord George-Brown, in 1970. Resigned from the Labour Party in 1976 and later joined the SDP.

BUTLER, David. Political scientist and broadcaster, whose special subject is the study of elections; the first person to coin the term 'psephology'. Co-author of *British Political Facts 1900–83*. Lifelong friend.

CALLAGHAN, James (Jim). Prime Minister, 1976–9; and Leader of the Labour Party, 1976–80. Held junior posts in the 1945–51 Labour Government; was Chancellor of the Exchequer, 1964–7; and Home Secretary, 1967–70. Foreign Secretary, 1974–6. Chairman of the Labour Party, 1973/4; and Labour MP for South, South-East and again South Cardiff, 1945–87. Created a life peer in 1987. Married to Audrey Callaghan.

CASTLE, Barbara. Leader of the British Labour Group in the European Parliament, 1979–85. Secretary of State for Social Services, 1974–6; dismissed by James Callaghan when he formed his government in 1976. Minister of Overseas Development, 1964–5. Minister of Transport, 1965–8; Secretary of State for Employment and Productivity, 1968–70. Chairman of the Labour Party, 1958/9. Labour MP for Blackburn, 1945–79. Created a life peer in 1990.

CHAPPLE, Frank. General Secretary of the Electrical, Electronic, Tele-communications and Plumbing Trade Union, 1966–84. Created a life peer in 1985.

CHURCHILL, Winston (1874–1965). Prime Minister and Minister of Defence, 1940–5; Prime Minister, 1951–5; Home Secretary, 1910–11; First Lord of the Admiralty 1911–15; Secretary of State for War, Air and the Colonies 1919–22; Chancellor of the Exchequer 1924–9. Parliamentary career began in 1900 as Conservative MP for Oldham, and ended in 1964 as Conservative MP for Woodford, Churchill sitting as a Liberal MP, 1904–22. Out of Parliament for only two years, 1922–4.

CLARKE, Lucille. Personal Secretary to Tony Benn for many years from 1968.

CLARKE, Richard (Otto) (1910–75). Permanent Secretary at the Ministry of Technology. Formerly a senior Treasury official. Retired 1970.

CLEMENTS–ELLIOTT, Julie. Personal Secretary to Tony Benn, 1976–84.

COCKS, Michael. Opposition Chief Whip, 1979–85. Government Chief Whip, 1976–9. Labour MP for Bristol South, 1970–87. Created a life peer in 1987.

CORBYN, Jeremy. Official of National Union of Public Employees, 1975–83. Labour MP for Islington North since 1983.

COUSINS, Frank (1904–86). General Secretary of the Transport and General Workers' Union, brought into the Labour Cabinet as Minister of Technology in 1964. Resigned in 1966 over government policy and returned to the union until his retirement in 1969. Labour MP for Nuneaton, 1965–6.

CRAIGIE, Jill. Author and journalist, married to Michael Foot.

CRIPPS, Francis. Economic adviser to Tony Benn, 1974–9. Founder member of the Cambridge Economic Policy Group.

CROSLAND, Anthony (1918–77). Foreign Secretary from 1976 to his sudden death in February 1977. In the 1964–70 Government he was successively Minister of State for Economic Affairs, Secretary of State for Education and Science, President of the Board of Trade, finally Secretary of State for Local Government. Secretary of State for the Environment, 1974–6. Labour MP for South Gloucester, 1950–5, and Grimsby, 1959–77. Married journalist Susan Barnes in 1964. A personal friend from the war years.

CROSSMAN, Richard (1907–74). Labour MP for Coventry, 1945–74; and senior Cabinet Minister in the 1964–70 Wilson governments; his *Diaries of a Cabinet Minister* were published posthumously.

CUDLIPP, Hugh. Succeeded Cecil King as Chairman of Daily Mirror Newspapers, 1963–8. Deputy Chairman, then Chairman, of International Publishing Corporation (IPC), 1964–73. Created a life peer in 1974.

CUNNINGHAM, John (Jack). Labour MP for Whitehaven, 1970–83, Copeland since 1983. Parliamentary Under-Secretary of State, Department of Energy, 1976–9. PPS to Jim Callaghan, 1972–6.

DALY, Lawrence. General Secretary of the National Union of Mineworkers, 1968–84, previously General Secretary of Scottish NUM. Member of the TUC General Council, 1978–81.

DALTON, Hugh (1887–1962). Labour MP for Bishop Auckland. Chancellor of the Exchequer 1945–7. Forced to resign over inadvertent Budget leak in 1947.

DALYELL, Tam. Labour MP for West Lothian. 1962–83, and Linlithgow since 1983. PPS to Richard Crossman, 1964–70.

DAVIES, John (1916–79). Chancellor of the Duchy of Lancaster with responsibility for Europe, 1972–4. Director-General of the Confederation of British Industry, 1965–9. Minister of Technology from July to October 1970, when Mintech was abolished. Secretary of State for Industry, 1970–2. Conservative MP for Knutsford, 1970–8.

DE FREITAS, Geoffrey (1913–82) Labour MP for Central Nottingham and later Lincoln.

DELL, Edmund. Secretary of State for Trade, 1976–8. Minister of State at the Board of Trade, 1968–9. and at Employment and Productivity, 1969–70. Joined the SDP. Labour MP for Birkenhead, 1964–79.

DERER, Vladimir. Secretary, Campaign for Labour Party Democracy.

DIAMOND, Jack. Chief Secretary to the Treasury, 1964–70. Labour MP for Blackley, 1945–51; Gloucester, 1957–70. Chaired the Royal Commission on the Distribution of Income and Wealth, 1974–9. Created a life peer in 1970 and became leader of the SDP in the House of Lords.

DONOUGHUE, Bernard. Senior policy adviser to the Prime Minister and head of the Policy Unit at Number 10, 1974–9. Member of staff at the London School of Economics, 1963–74. Created a life peer in 1985.

DOUGLAS-HOME, Alec. Foreign Secretary, 1960–3, in the House of Lords. Before inheriting his peerage, the Earldom of Home, in 1951 he was Conservative/Unionist MP for Lanark, 1931–51, using his courtesy title of Viscount Dunglass. He succeeded Macmillan and renounced his title in 1963. Prime Minister from October 1963 until October 1964, and MP for Kinross and West Perthshire, 1963–74. In 1974 he was created a life peer and re-entered the Lords as Home of the Hirsel.

EDEN, Anthony (1897–1977). Conservative MP for Warwick and Leamington. Foreign Secretary, 1951–5. Prime Minister, 1955–7. Created an earl, Lord Avon, in 1961.

EMMETT, Bryan. Principal Private Secretary to Tony Benn at Department of Energy, 1975–6; subsequently Chief Executive of the Employment Division of the Manpower Services Commission, and Head of the Oil Division at Energy.

ENNALS, David (1922–95). Secretary of State for Social Services, 1976–9.

Secretary of the Labour Party's International Department, 1958–64. Labour MP for Dover, 1964–70, and Norwich North, 1974–83. Created a life peer in 1983.

EVANS, Ioan (1927–84). PPS to Tony Benn as Postmaster General. Government Whip, 1968–70. Labour MP for Yardley, 1964–70, Aberdare, 1974–83, and Cynon Valley, 1983–4.

EVANS, Moss. General Secretary of the Transport and General Workers' Union, 1978–85. National Officer of the TGWU, 1969–78.

FLOWERS, Brian. Chairman of the Royal Commission on Environmental Pollution, 1973–6, and the Standing Commission on Energy and the Environment, 1978–81. Nuclear physicist, Atomic Energy Research Establishment, 1946–58. Rector of Imperial College, 1973–85; Vice-Chancellor of London University since 1985. Created a life peer in 1979.

FOOT, Michael. Deputy Leader of the Labour Party, 1979–80, and Leader, 1980–3. Lord President of the Council and Leader of the House of Commons, 1976–9. Secretary of State for Employment, 1974–6. Labour MP for Devonport, 1945–55, Ebbw Vale, 1960–83, and Blaenau Gwent, 1983–92. Biographer of Aneurin Bevan. Married to Jill Craigie.

FREEMAN, John. Labour MP for Watford, 1945–55. Later British High Commissioner in India and Ambassador in Washington. Broadcaster.

GAITSKELL, Hugh (1906–63). Leader of the Labour Party, 1955–63. Held office, 1945–51, as Minister of Fuel and Power, Minister of State for Economic Affairs, and Chancellor of the Exchequer. Labour MP for South Leeds, 1945–63.

GARDINER, Gerald (1900–90). Lord Chancellor, 1964–70. Created a life peer in 1963. Former Chairman of the National Campaign for the Abolition of Capital Punishment and from 1973–8 Chancellor of the Open University.

GENTLEMAN, David. Designer of stamps for the GPO in the 1960s. Member of the Design Council, 1974–80.

GERMAN, Sir Ronald (1906–83). Director-General at the GPO from 1960 until his retirement in 1966. Formerly Postmaster-General for British East Africa, 1950–8.

GILL, Ken. General Secretary, Technical and Supervisory Section of Amalgamated Union of Engineering Workers, 1974–88.

GOODMAN, Arnold (1913–95). Prominent lawyer, adviser to Harold Wilson, 1964–70. Created a life peer in 1965.

GOODMAN, Geoffrey. Industrial editor of the *Daily Mirror*, 1969–86; and Head of the Counter-Inflation Publicity Unit, 1975–6. Biographer of Frank Cousins.

GORDON WALKER, Patrick (1907–80). Foreign Secretary, October 1964–January 1965. He was defeated in the 1964 Election as Labour MP for Smethwick, a seat he had held since 1945. Fought and lost Leyton, 1965, but elected Labour MP for Leyton, 1966–74. Returned to Cabinet as Secretary of State for Education and Science, 1967–8. Created a life peer in 1974.

GORMLEY, Joe (1917–93). President of the National Union of Mineworkers, 1971–82. Member of the National Executive, 1963–73. Created a life peer in 1982.

GREENE, Hugh (1910–87). Director-General of the BBC, 1960–9. *Daily Telegraph* correspondent in Germany in the 1930s; appointed Head of BBC German Service in 1940.

GREENWOOD, Anthony (1911–82). Colonial Secretary, 1964–5. Minister for Overseas Development, 1965–6. Minister of Housing and Local Government, 1966–70. Chairman of the Labour Party, 1963/4. Labour MP for Heywood and Radcliffe, subsequently Rossendale, 1946–70. Created a life peer in 1970.

GRIFFITHS, James (Jim) (1890–1975). Labour MP for Llanelli 1936–59. Deputy Leader of the Labour Party, 1955–9.

GRIGG, John. Journalist and author who inherited the title Baron Altrincham in 1955 and disclaimed it in 1963. Biographer of Lloyd George.

GRIMOND, Jo (1913–93). Leader of the Liberal Party, 1956–67. Liberal MP for Orkney and Shetland, 1950–83. Created a life peer in 1983. Son-in-law of Lady Violet Bonham Carter.

GUNTER, Ray (1909–77). Minister of Labour Party, 1964–8. Labour MP for Essex South East, 1945–50, Doncaster, 1950–1, Southwark 1959–72. Resigned from the Labour Party, 1972.

HAINES, Joe. From 1977–84 senior journalist on the *Daily Mirror*, political editor of the Mirror Group since 1984. Chief Press Secretary to Harold Wilson, 1969–76, previously political correspondent of the *Sun*.

HALL, Glenvil (1887–1962). Labour MP for Colne Valley, 1939–62. Financial Secretary to the Treasury, 1945–50. Chairman of the Parliamentary Labour Party, 1950/1.

HART, Judith (1924–91). Chairman of the Labour Party, 1981/2. Minister for Overseas Development, 1974–5; sacked by Harold Wilson after the Referendum, and reinstated 1977–9. In the 1964–70 Government she was Paymaster-General and Minister for Overseas Development.

Labour MP for Lanark, 1959–83, Clydesdale, 1983–7. Married to Tony Hart.

HATTERSLEY, Roy. Deputy Leader of the Labour Party, 1983–92. Secretary of State for Prices and Consumer Protection, 1976–9. Minister of State at the Foreign and Commonwealth Office, 1974–6. Labour MP for Birmingham Sparkbrook since 1964.

HAWKINS, Sir Arthur. Chairman of the Central Electricity Generating Board, 1972–7. Joined CEGB as planning engineer, 1957.

HAYWARD, Ron. General Secretary of the Labour Party, 1972–82.

HEALEY, Denis. Deputy Leader of the Labour Party, 1980–3. Chancellor of the Exchequer, 1974–9; Secretary of State for Defence, 1964–70. Labour MP for Leeds South East, 1952–5, and Leeds East, 1955–92. Created a life peer in 1992.

HEATH, Edward. Conservative MP for Bexley, subsequently Old Bexley and Sidcup since 1950. Leader of the Conservative Party, 1965–75. Prime Minister, 1970–4. Minister of Labour, 1959–60; Lord Privy Seal, 1960–3; Secretary of State for Industry and Trade and President of the Board of Trade, 1963–4.

HEATHFIELD, Peter. General Secretary of the National Union of Mineworkers since 1984. Previously Secretary of the Derbyshire Area, NUM.

HEFFER, Eric (1922–91). Labour MP for Walton, Liverpool, 1964–91. Minister of State at the Department of Industry, 1974–5; sacked by Harold Wilson over the Common Market. Chairman of the Labour Party, 1983/4. Married to Doris Heffer.

HESELTINE, Michael. Minister for Aerospace and Shipping at Department of Trade and Industry, 1972–4. Secretary of State for Environment, 1979–83, and for Defence until his resignation in 1986. Conservative MP for Tavistock, 1966–74, and Henley since 1974. Contested party leadership, 1990.

HILL, John. Chairman of the UK Atomic Energy Authority, 1967–81, and of British Nuclear Fuels, 1971–83. Member of the Advisory Council on Technology, 1968–70.

HOGG, Quintin. Conservative MP for St Marylebone, 1963–70. Disclaimed his peerages in 1963 during the contest for the Conservative Party leadership. Previously sat as MP for Oxford City, 1938 to 1950, when he succeeded his father as 2nd Viscount Hailsham. Held ministerial posts in the House of Lords during the 1951–64 Conservative governments, including Secretary of State for Education in 1964.

Returned to the Lords with a life peerage in 1970. Lord Chancellor, 1970–4 and 1979–87.

HOLLAND, Stuart. Labour MP for Vauxhall, 1979–89. Formerly Economic Assistant, Cabinet Office, 1966–7; and Personal Assistant to Prime Minister, 1967–8.

HOUGHTON, Douglas. Chairman of the PLP, 1967–74. Chancellor of the Duchy of Lancaster, 1964–6; Minister without Portfolio, 1966–7. Labour MP for Sowerby, 1949–74. Created a life peer in 1974.

HOWE, Geoffrey. Chancellor of the Exchequer, 1979–83. Foreign Secretary, 1983–9. Solicitor-General, 1970–2; and Minister for Trade and Consumer Affairs, 1972–4. Conservative MP for Reigate, 1970–4; Surrey East, 1974–92.

HUNT, John. Secretary of the Cabinet, 1973–9. Created a life peer, Lord Hunt of Tanworth, in 1980.

HURD, Douglas. Minister of State, in Foreign and Home Offices, 1979–84. Home Secretary, 1985–9; and Foreign Secretary, 1989–95. Conservative MP for Witney since 1983, for Mid-Oxon, 1974–83. Contested party leadership, 1990.

INGHAM, Bernard. Chief Press Secretary to the Prime Minister, 1979–90. Director of Information at the Department of Energy, 1974–8; Chief Information Officer at the Department of Employment and Productivity, 1968–73. Reporter on the *Yorkshire Post* and the *Guardian,* 1952–67.

JAY, Douglas. President of the Board of Trade, 1964–7. Labour MP for North Battersea, 1946–83. Created a life peer in 1987.

JENKINS, Clive. General Secretary of the Association of Scientific Technical and Managerial Staffs, 1970–88. Member of the General Council of the TUC, 1974–8.

JENKINS, Roy. President of the European Commission, 1977–81. Minister of Aviation, 1964–5; Home Secretary, 1965–7. Chancellor of the Exchequer, 1967–70. Home Secretary, 1974–6. Deputy Leader of the Labour Party, 1970–2. Labour MP for Central Southwark, 1948–50, for Stechford, 1950–76. Leader of the SDP, 1981–3; and SDP MP for Glasgow Hillhead, 1982–7. Created a life peer, Lord Jenkins of Hillhead, in 1987.

JONES, Elwyn (1909–89). Lord Chancellor, 1974–9. Attorney-General, 1964–70. Labour MP for Plaistow, 1945–50, for West Ham South, 1950–74, and for Newham South, February to May 1974, when he was created a life peer, Lord Elwyn-Jones.

JONES, Jack. Assistant General Secretary of the Transport and General

Workers' Union, 1963–9, General Secretary, 1969–78. Vice-President of Age Concern since 1978.

JOSEPH, Keith (1918–95). Secretary of State for Social Services, 1970–4, for Industry, 1979–81; and Education and Science, 1981–6. Junior Minister from 1959–64. Conservative MP for Leeds North East, 1956–87. Created a life peer in 1987.

KAUFMAN, Gerald. Minister of State, Department of Industry, 1975–9. Labour Party press officer, 1965–70. Previously journalist on *Daily Mirror* and *New Statesman*. Labour MP for Manchester Ardwick, 1970–83, and Manchester Gorton since 1983.

KEARTON, Frank. Chairman and Chief Executive of the British National Oil Corporation, 1975–9. Chairman of Courtaulds, 1964–75. First Chairman of the Industrial Reorganisation Corporation, 1966–8. Created a life peer in 1970.

KING, Cecil (1901–87). Chairman, International Publishing Corporation (IPC), 1963–8. A director of the Bank of England, 1965–8. Chairman of Daily Mirror Newspapers Limited, 1951–63.

KINNOCK, Neil. Leader of the Labour Party, 1983–92, Chair, 1987/8. Labour MP for Bedwelty, 1970–83, Islwyn, 1983–94.

KNIGHTON, William. Principal Private Secretary to Tony Benn at the Ministry of Technology, 1966–8.

LANSMAN, Jon. Coordinator of Benn's deputy leadership campaign, 1981.

LEE, Jennie (1904–88). Under-Secretary, then Minister at the Department of Education and Science, 1965–70, responsible for establishing the Open University. Chairman of the Labour Party, 1967/8. MP for North Lanark, 1929–31, and Cannock, 1945–70. Widow of Aneurin Bevan, Deputy Leader of the Labour Party. Created a life peer in 1970.

LESTOR, Joan. Under-Secretary at the Foreign and Commonwealth Office, 1974–5, and at the Department of Education and Science, 1975–6, resigning her post over public-expenditure cuts. UnderSecretary at the Department of Education and Science, 1969–70. Chairman of the Labour Party, 1977/8. Labour MP for Eton and Slough, 1966–83, and Eccles since 1987.

LEVER, Harold. Chancellor of the Duchy of Lancaster, 1974–9. Financial Secretary to the Treasury, 1967–9; Paymaster-General, 1969–70. Created a life peer, Lord Lever of Manchester, in 1979.

LIVINGSTONE, Ken. Leader of Greater London Council, 1981–6. Labour MP for Brent East since 1987.

MABON, Dickson (Dick). Minister of State at the Department of Energy, 1976–9. Chairman of the Labour Committee for Europe and the European Movement between 1974 and 1976. Labour MP for Greenock from 1955. Joined the SDP in 1981 and sat as SDP Member, 1981–3.

McELHONE, Frank (1929–82). Under-Secretary of State for Scotland, 1975–9. PPS to Tony Benn, 1974–5. Labour MP for Gorbals, 1969–74, Glasgow Queen's Park, 1974–82.

McGAHEY, Mick. Vice-President, National Union of Mineworkers, 1973–87. President, Scottish Area of the NUM, 1967–87. Chairman of the Communist Party of Great Britain, 1974–8.

MACLEOD, Iain (1913–70). Leader of the House of Commons, 1961–3, and Chairman of the Conservative Party during that period. Served in the 1951–64 Conservative governments as Minister of Health, Minister of Labour and Colonial Secretary. Chancellor of the Exchequer, June–July 1970. Conservative MP for Enfield, 1950–70.

MACMILLAN, Harold (1894–1986). Prime Minister from 1957 until his retirement in October 1963, previously Minister of Defence, 1954–5; Foreign Secretary, 1955; and Chancellor of the Exchequer, 1955–7. Created Earl of Stockton, 1984. Conservative MP for Stockton-on-Tees, 1924–9, 1931–45, and for Bromley, 1945–64.

MANLEY, Ivor. Principal Private Secretary to Tony Benn at the Ministry of Technology, 1968–70. Principal Establishment Officer, Department of Energy, 1974–8, and Deputy Secretary since 1981.

MARSH, Richard. Minister of Power, 1966–8. Minister of Transport, 1968–9. Labour MP for Greenwich, 1959–71. Resigned his seat and became Chairman of British Railways Board, 1971–6. Created a life peer in 1981, and left the Labour Party.

MARSHALL, Walter. Chief Scientist, Department of Energy, 1974–7; Deputy Chairman of the United Kingdom Atomic Energy Authority, 1975–81. Chairman of the UKAEA, 1981–2, and of the Central Electricity Generating Board since 1982. From 1968–75, Director of the Atomic Energy Research Establishment, Harwell. Created a life peer, Lord Marshall of Goring, in 1985.

MASON, Roy. Secretary of State for Northern Ireland, 1976–9. Minister of Defence, 1967–8, and of Power, 1968–9; and President of the Board of Trade, 1969–70. Secretary of State for Defence, 1974–6. Labour MP for Barnsley, 1953–87. Created a life peer in 1987.

MAXWELL, Robert (1923–91). Owner of Pergamon Press and Labour MP for Buckingham, 1964–70, Chairman of the Mirror Group of Newspapers.

MAYHEW, Christopher. Appointed Minister of Defence for the Royal Navy in 1964, resigned in 1966. Labour MP for South Norfolk, 1945–50; and for Woolwich East, 1951–July 1974, when he resigned from the Labour Party to join the Liberal Party. Sat as a Liberal MP for Woolwich East for three months. Created a life peer in 1981.

MAYNARD, Joan. Labour MP for Sheffield Brightside, October 1974–87. Vice-Chairman of the Labour Party, 1980/1.

MEACHER, Michael. Labour MP for Oldham West since 1970. Parliamentary Under-Secretary of State for Industry, 1974–5, Health and Social Security, 1975–6, and Trade, 1976–9.

MELLISH, Robert. Labour MP for Bermondsey from 1946 to 1982, when he resigned from the Labour Party and sat as an Independent. Deputy Chairman of the London Docklands Development Corporation from 1981. Government Chief Whip, 1969–70 and 1974–6. Opposition Chief Whip, 1970–4. Created a life peer in 1985.

MELVILLE, Ronald. Permanent Secretary in the Ministry of Aviation, subsequently Ministry of Technology, 1966–71.

MIKARDO, Ian (1908–83). Labour MP for Poplar, 1964–74, and for Bethnal Green and Bow, 1974–87. MP for Reading, and South Reading, 1945–59. Chairman of the Labour Party, 1970/1. A close associate of Aneurin Bevan and sometime chairman of the Tribune Group of Labour MPs.

MILIBAND, Ralph (1924–94). Professor of Politics, Leeds University, 1972–7, and visiting Professor of the Graduate School, City University of New York.

MONCKTON, Sir Walter. Conservative MP for Bristol West. Minister of Labour, Minister of Defence and Paymaster-General consecutively, 1950–7.

MORRELL, Frances. Leader of Inner London Education Authority, 1983–7. Political adviser to Tony Benn, 1974–9. Press officer for the National Union of Students and the Fabian Society, 1970–2. Previously a schoolteacher, 1960–9.

MORRISON, Herbert (1888–1965). Deputy Prime Minister, 1945–51; and Deputy Leader of the Labour Party, 1945–55. Foreign Secretary, 1951. Labour MP for South Hackney, East Lewisham and South Lewisham intermittently between 1923–59. Chairman of the Labour Party, 1928/9. Leader of the London County Council, 1934–40. Served in the wartime coalition Cabinet. Created a life peer in 1959.

MORTIMER, Jim. Chairman, Advisory, Conciliation and Arbitration

Service, 1974–81. General Secretary of the Labour Party, 1982–5.

MULLEY, Fred (1918–95). Secretary for Defence, 1976–9. Minister of Transport, 1969–70, and Secretary of State for Education and Science, 1975–6. Chairman of the Labour Party, 1974/5. Labour MP for Sheffield Park, 1950–83. Created a life peer in 1984.

MULLIN, Chris. Editor of *Arguments for Socialism* and *Arguments for Democracy* by Tony Benn; editor of *Tribune*, 1982–4. Author of *A Very British Coup*, and other political novels, and *Error of Judgement*. Labour MP for Sunderland South since 1987.

MURRAY, Len. General Secretary of the TUC, 1973–84. Member of the TUC staff from 1947. Created a life peer, 1985.

ORME, Stan. Labour MP for Salford West, 1964–83, and for Salford East since 1983. Minister of State for Social Security, 1976–7; and Minister for Social Security, 1977–9. Minister of State, Northern Ireland Office, 1974–6. Chairman of the PLP since 1987.

OWEN, David. Labour MP for Plymouth Sutton, 1966–74, and Plymouth Devonport, 1974–81. Founder member of the SDP, 1981; and sat as SDP Member, 1981–3; SDP MP for Devonport, 1983–92. Minister, Foreign and Commonwealth Office, 1976–7; then Foreign Secretary, following Tony Crosland's death, 1977–9. Parliamentary Under-Secretary of State, then Minister of State, at the Department of Health and Social Security, 1974–6. Created a life peer in 1992.

PAGET, Reginald (1908–90). Labour MP for Northampton, 1945–74. Created a life peer in 1974.

PANNELL, Charles (1902–80). Minister of Public Building and Works, 1964–6. Labour MP for Leeds West, 1949–74. Created a life peer in 1974.

PART, Antony (1916–90). Permanent Secretary at the Department of Trade and Industry, 1970–4, and the Department of Industry, 1974–6.

PEARSON, Denning (Jim). Chairman of Rolls Royce, 1969–70. Joined Rolls Royce in 1932. Member of the NEDC, 1964–70.

PEAY, Ken. Broadcasting officer, Labour Party headquarters.

PENNEY, William. Chairman of the Atomic Energy Authority, 1964–7. A wartime pioneer of nuclear weapons. Director of the Atomic Weapons Research Establishment, Aldermaston; and Rector of Imperial College, London, 1967–73. Created a life peer in 1967.

PLIATZKY, Leo. Under-Secretary at the Treasury, 1967–71, and Second

Permanent Secretary, 1971–6. Permanent Secretary at the Department of Trade, 1977–9.

POWELL, Enoch. Minister of Health, 1960–3. Conservative MP for Wolverhampton South West, 1950–74. Stood down as Conservative candidate in February 1974. United Ulster Unionist MP for Down South, October 1974–9, Official Unionist Party, 1979–87.

PRENTICE, Reg. Labour MP for East Ham North, 1951–74, Newham North East, 1974–9. Crossed the floor in 1977 and sat on the Conservative benches until 1979. In 1979 he was elected Conservative MP for Daventry and sat for Daventry until 1987; he was Minister for Social Security, 1979–81, in the Conservative Government.

PRESCOTT, John. Labour MP for Hull East since 1970. Member of European Parliament, 1975–9. Contested Party deputy leadership in 1988.

PRIMAROLO, Dawn. Secretary of Bristol South East Labour Party, 1979–83. Labour MP for Bristol South since 1987.

PRIOR, James (Jim). Secretary of State for Employment, 1979–81; Secretary of State for Northern Ireland, 1981–4. Lord President of the Council and Leader of the House of Commons, 1972–4. Conservative MP for Lowestoft, 1959–83, and Waveney, 1983–7. Created a life peer in 1987.

RAMPTON, Jack. Permanent Under-Secretary of State at the Department of Energy, 1974–80. Formerly a senior official at the Ministry of Technology and the Department of Trade and Industry, 1968–74.

REES, Merlyn. Home Secretary, 1976–9. Parliamentary Under-Secretary of State at the Ministry of Defence, 1965–8, and Home Office, 1968–70. Secretary of State for Northern Ireland, 1974–6. Labour MP for South Leeds, 1963–83, and for Morley and Leeds South, 1983–92. Created a life peer Lord Merlyn-Rees in 1992.

RICHARDSON, Jo (1923–94). Labour MP for Barking, February 1974–1994. Chair of Labour Party, 1989/90.

RIDLEY, Nicholas (1929–93). Parliamentary Secretary to Minister of Technology, 1970; and Under-Secretary of State at the Department of Trade and Industry, 1970–2. Minister of State at the Foreign and Commonwealth Office, 1979–81; Financial Secretary to the Treasury, 1981–3; Secretary of State for Transport, 1983–6, and for the Environment. Conservative MP for Cirencester and Tewkesbury, 1959–XX. Created a life peer in 1992.

RODGERS, William (Bill). Secretary of State for Transport, 1976–9. Labour MP for Stockton-on-Tees (Teesside, Stockton from 1974), 1962–81. Founder member of the SDP in 1981 and sat as SDP MP for same seat, 1981–3. Created a life peer in 1992.

ROGERS, Herbert. Election Agent for Tony Benn, 1951–70. Secretary of the East Bristol Independent Labour Party from 1912.

ROOSEVELT, Franklin D. (1882–1945). President USA, 1933–45.

ROSS, William (1911–88). Secretary of State for Scotland, 1964–70, and 1974–6. Labour MP for Kilmarnock, 1946–79. Created a life peer in 1979.

ROTHSCHILD, Lord (Victor Rothschild) (1910–90). Director-General of the Central Policy Review Staff ('Think Tank'), 1970–4. Scientist and Chairman of Shell Research Ltd, 1963–70. Member of the Central Advisory Committee for Science and Technology, 1969.

RYLAND, William (1913–88). Managing Director, Telecommunications, at the GPO, 1967–9. In the reorganised Post Office Corporation Ryland became Chairman, 1971–7.

SAWYER, Tom. National Union of Public Employees' member of National Executive since 1982. Chair of Labour Party, 1990/1.

SCANLON, Hugh. President of the Amalgamated Union of Engineering Workers, 1968–78. AEU organiser, 1947–63. Created a life peer in 1979.

SCARGILL, Arthur. President of the Yorkshire Area of the National Union of Mineworkers, 1973–81. President of the NUM since 1981.

SEDGEMORE, Brian. PPS to Tony Benn, 1977–8. Labour MP for Luton West, 1974–9, and for Hackney South and Shoreditch since 1983.

SHAWCROSS, Hartley. Labour MP for St Helens, 1945–58. Attorney-General, 1945–51. President of Board of Trade, 1951.

SHINWELL, Emmanuel (Manny) (1884–1986). Chairman of the Parliamentary Labour Party, 1964–7. Minister of Fuel and Power and Minister of Defence in the 1945–51 Labour Government. Labour MP for Linlithgow, 1922–4 and 1928–31, for Seaham, 1935–50, and for Easington, 1950–70. Chairman of the Labour Party, 1947/8. Created a life peer in 1970.

SHORE, Liz. Deputy Chief Medical Officer for the Department of Health and Social Security, 1977–85. Former Post-Graduate Medical Dean, North West Thames Region. Married to Peter Shore.

SHORE, Peter. Secretary of the State for the Environment, 1976–9. Head of Research Department of the Labour Party, 1959–64. PPS to Harold Wilson, 1965–6. Joint Parliamentary Secretary at the Ministry of Technology, 1966–7. Secretary of State for Economic Affairs, 1967–9. Minister without Portfolio, 1969–70. Secretary of State for Trade, 1974–6. Labour MP for Stepney, subsequently Stepney and Poplar, and then Bethnal Green and Stepney, since 1964. Married to Liz Shore.

SHORT, Clare. Civil Servant in the Home Office, 1970–5. Labour MP for Birmingham Ladywood since 1983.

SHORT, Edward. Deputy Leader of the Labour Party, 1972–6; and Lord President of the Council and Leader of the House of Commons 1974–6. Government Chief Whip, 1964–6. Postmaster-General, 1966–8. Secretary of State for Education and Science, 1968–70. Labour MP for Newcastle-on-Tyne Central, 1951–76. Created a life peer, Lord Glenamara, in 1976.

SILKIN, John (1923–87). Minister for Agriculture, Fisheries and Food, 1976–9. Chief Whip, 1966–9. Minister of Public Building and Works, 1969–70. Minister for Planning and Local Government, 1974–6. Labour MP for Deptford, 1963–87.

SILKIN, Sam (1918–88). Attorney-General, 1974–9. Leader of UK delegation to European Assembly, 1968–70. Labour MP for Dulwich, 1964–83. Brother of John Silkin (see above). Created a life peer in 1985.

SIMON, Brian. Professor of Education and subsequently Emeritus Professor at the University of Leicester. Has published a large number of books on education including *Half Way There: Report on the British Comprehensive School Reform* (1970) with Caroline Benn.

SKINNER, Dennis. Labour MP for Bolsover since 1970. Chairman of the Labour Party, 1988/9. President of the Derbyshire NUM, 1966–70.

SLATER, Joe (1904–77). Assistant Postmaster General, 1964–9. Previously PPS to Hugh Gaitskell and Harold Wilson. Labour MP for Sedgefield, 1950–70. Created a life peer in 1970.

SMITH, Charles Delacourt (1917–72). General Secretary of the Post Office Engineering Union, 1953–72. Formerly Labour MP for Colchester, 1945–50. Created a life peer in 1967, and was Minister of State at the Ministry of Technology, 1969–70.

SMITH, Ron. General Secretary of the Union of Post Office Workers, 1957–66.

STEEL, David. Leader of the Liberal Party, 1976–88; and the joint Leader of the Liberal and Social Democratic Alliance during 1987. Liberal MP for Roxburgh, Selkirk and Peebles, 1965–83, and Tweeddale, Ettrick and Lauderdale since 1983.

STEWART, Michael (1906–90). Secretary of State for Education and Science, 1964–5; Foreign Secretary, 1965–6; Secretary of State for Economic Affairs, 1966–7; Foreign and Commonwealth Secretary, 1968–70. Labour MP for Fulham East, subsequently Fulham and then Hammersmith and Fulham, 1945–79. Created a life peer in 1979.

STOKES, Donald. Managing Director and Deputy Chairman, subsequently Chairman, of Leyland Motor Corporation from 1963. Chairman and Managing Director of British Leyland in 1973, President in 1975. Created a life peer in 1969.

STONEHOUSE, John (1925–88). Minister of State at the Ministry of Technology, 1967–8. Postmaster-General in 1968, and Minister of Posts and Telecommunications, 1969. Labour Co-operative MP for Wednesbury, 1957–74, and Walsall North, 1974, until his resignation in 1976. Imprisoned for fraud, 1976.

STRACHEY, John (1901–63). Labour MP for Aston, 1929–31, for Dundee 1945–63. Minister of Food, 1946–50. Secretary of State for War, 1950–1.

TAVERNE, Dick. Labour MP for Lincoln from 1962 until resigning in 1972. Regained the seat in a by-election in 1973, as Democratic Labour candidate, lost it in the October 1974 Election. Financial Secretary to the Treasury, 1969–70.

THATCHER, Margaret. Leader of the Conservative Party, 1975–90. Prime Minister, 1979–90. Secretary of State for Education and Science, 1970–4; previously a junior Minister in the Ministry of Pensions and National Insurance, 1961–4. Conservative MP for Finchley, 1959–92. Created a life peer in 1992.

THOMAS, George. Speaker of the House of Commons, 1976–83 (Deputy Speaker 1974–6). Minister of State at the Welsh Office, 1966–7, and Commonwealth Office, 1967–8. Secretary of State for Wales, 1968–70. Labour MP for Cardiff Central, 1945–50, Cardiff West, 1950–83 (sat as Speaker from 1976). Created a hereditary peer, Viscount Tonypandy, in 1983.

THOMSON, George. Chairman of the Labour Committee for Europe, 1972–3; appointed an EEC Commissioner, 1973–7. Secretary of State for Commonwealth Affairs, 1967–8. Minister without Portfolio, 1968–9. Labour MP for Dundee East, 1952–72. Created a life peer in 1977.

THORNEYCROFT, Peter (1909–94). Conservative MP for Stafford, subsequently for Monmouth. Chancellor of the Exchequer, 1957–8.

THORPE, Jeremy. Leader of the Liberal Party, 1967–76. Liberal MP for North Devon, 1959–79.

TILLING, Henry. Private Secretary to Tony Benn as Postmaster General, 1964–5. Deputy Director of Finance at the GPO, 1965; and subsequently became Secretary of the Post Office, 1973–5.

TODD, Ron. National Organiser of the Transport and General Workers' Union, 1978–85. General Secretary, 1985–91.

TREND, Burke (1914–87). Secretary of the Cabinet, 1963–73. Created a life peer in 1974.

UNDERHILL, Reg. National Agent of the Labour Party, 1972–9. Labour Party official since 1933. Created a life peer in 1979.

VALLINS, Margaret. Member of Chesterfield Labour Party. District Councillor, 1987–91. Constituency Secretary to Tony Benn since 1984.

VALLINS, Tom. Member of Chesterfield Labour Party. Election agent to Tony Benn since 1987.

VARLEY, Eric. Labour MP for Chesterfield, 1964–84. Secretary of State for Energy, 1974–5, exchanging Cabinet jobs with Tony Benn to become Secretary of State for Industry, 1975–9; PPS to Harold Wilson, 1968–9. Retired in 1984 to become Chairman of Coalite Group. Created a life peer in 1990.

VAUGHAN, Ron. Official driver to Tony Benn at the Ministry of Technology, 1968–70, and at the Departments of Industry and Energy, 1974–90.

WALKER, Peter. Minister for Agriculture, Fisheries and Food, 1979–83, Secretary of State for Wales, 1987–90. Secretary of State for the Environment, 1970–2, and for Trade and Industry, 1972–4. Deputy Chairman of Slater, Walker Securities, 1964–70. Conservative MP for Worcester, 1961–92. Created a life peer in 1992.

WEATHERILL, Bernard (Jack). Conservative MP for Croydon North East, 1964–83. Speaker of the House of Commons and MP for Croydon North East, 1983–92. Created a life peer in 1992.

WEINSTOCK, Arnold. Industrialist. Managing Director of GEC since 1963, of Radio and Allied Industries, 1954–63. Created a life peer in 1980.

WHITELAW, William (Willie). Home Secretary, 1979–83. Secretary of

State for Employment, 1973–4; previously Leader of the House of Commons and Secretary of State for Northern Ireland, 1972–3. Chairman of the Conservative Party, 1974–5. Created a hereditary peer, Viscount Whitelaw, in 1983.

WHITTY, Larry. Official of the General and Municipal Workers' Union, 1973–85. General Secretary of the Labour Party, 1985–94.

WILLIAMS, Marcia. Personal and Political Secretary to Harold Wilson, 1956–95. Created a life peer, Lady Falkender, in 1976.

WILLIAMS, Roy. Principal Private Secretary to Tony Benn, 1974. Under-Secretary, subsequently Deputy Secretary, of the Department of Industry (later the Department of Trade and Industry).

WILLIAMS, Shirley. Founder member of the SDP in 1981, President in 1982; and SDP MP for Crosby, 1981–3. Secretary of State for Education and Science, and Paymaster-General, 1976–9. Minister of State, Education and Science, 1967–9, and the Home Office, 1969–70. Secretary of State for Prices and Consumer Protection, 1974–6. Labour MP for Hitchin, 1964–74, for Hertford and Stevenage, 1974–9. Created a life peer in 1993.

WILSON, Harold (1916–95). Leader of the Labour Party, 1963–76. Prime Minister, 1964–70, and 1974–6. Resigned in 1976 and did not hold office again. President of the Board of Trade, 1947–51, when he resigned with Aneurin Bevan. Chairman of the Labour Party, 1961/2. Labour MP for Ormskirk, 1945–50, and Huyton, 1950–83. Created a life peer, Lord Wilson of Rievaulx, in 1983. Married to Mary Wilson, poet and writer.

WISE, Audrey. Labour MP for Coventry South West, 1974–9, and for Preston since 1987.

WOODCOCK, George (1904–79). General Secretary of the TUC, 1960–9. Assistant General Secretary, 1947–60.

WRATTEN, Donald. Private Secretary to Tony Benn as Postmaster General, 1965–6; Head of Telecommunications Marketing Division, 1966–7.

WYATT, Woodrow. Journalist and Labour MP for Aston, 1945–55, subsequently for Bosworth, 1959–70.

ZANDER, Michael. Lecturer, subsequently Professor in Law at the London School of Economics. Assisted Tony Benn during the peerage campaign, 1960–1. Left the Labour Party to join the SDP.

ZUCKERMAN, Solly (1904–93). Zoologist. Longtime government adviser. Chief Scientific Adviser to Harold Wilson, 1964–70, and to the

Secretary of State for Defence, 1960–6. Chairman of the Central Advisory Committee for Science and Technology, 1965–70. Created a life peer in 1971.

Personal

ARNOLD-FORSTER, Mark (1920–81). Political commentator, worked on *Guardian, Observer,* and ITN, 1946–81. Married to Val Arnold-Forster, Journalist. Family friends.

BENN, Caroline. Born in the USA. Postgraduate degrees from the Universities of Cincinnati and London. Founder member of the comprehensive education campaign in Britain and editor of *Comprehensive Education* since 1967. Author of educational publications including *Half Way There* with Professor Brian Simon (1970) and *Challenging the MSC* with John Fairley (1986). Biographer of Keir Hardie (1992). President, Socialist Educational Association since 1970. Member, Inner London Education Authority, 1970–7. Member, Education Section, UNESCO Commission, 1976–83. Governor of several schools and colleges, including Imperial College, London University and Holland Park School, from 1967. Lecturer, adult education service, 1965–present. Married Tony Benn, 1949. Four children (see below).

BENN, David Wedgwood. Younger brother of Tony Benn; a barrister; worked for the Socialist International and later for the External Service of the BBC. Head of the BBC Yugoslav Section, 1974–84. A writer specialising in Soviet affairs.

BENN, Hilary. Son, born 1953. Educated at Holland Park School and Sussex University. Head of research, MSF. Deputy Leader of Ealing Council and Chair of the Education Committee, 1986–90. In 1973 married Rosalind Retey, who died of cancer in 1979. Married Sally Clark in 1982. Three sons, one daughter.

BENN, Joshua. Son, born 1958. Educated at Holland Park School. Founder of COMMUNITEC Computer Training Consultancy, 1984–8. Co-author of *Rock Hardware* (1981). Employed by the Housing Corporation since 1988. Married Elizabeth Feeney in 1984. One son.

BENN, June. Former lecturer; novelist writing under the name of June Barraclough. Married David Benn in 1959. Two children, Piers, born in 1962, and Frances, born 1964.

BENN, Melissa. Daughter, born 1957. Educated at Holland Park School and the London School of Economics. Socialist feminist writer and journalist. Author of *Public Lives* (1995). Contributor to several essay collections on feminism, the media, the police and crime; contributor to *Guardian, New Statesman, Marxism Today, Spare Rib, City Limits*. One daughter.

BENN, Stephen. Son, born 1951. Educated at Holland Park School and Keele University. PhD for 'The White House Staff' (1984). Former assistant to Senator Thomas F. Eagleton. Parliamentary Affairs Officer for Royal Society of Chemistry since 1988. Composer. Married Nita Clarke in 1988. One daughter, one son.

CARTER, Peter. Family friend. Architect.

CLARKE, Nita. Chief press officer, GLC, 1980–6. Married to Stephen Benn since 1988.

GIBSON, Ralph. Barrister and judge. Married to Anne. Close family friends.

RETLEY, Rosalind (1953–79). Married Hilary Benn in April 1973. Rosalind contracted cancer in 1978, and died at home in June 1979. A fund in her memory has been established at Holland Park, her former school, under the control of the students.

STANSGATE, Lady (1897–1991). Margaret Holmes. Daughter of Liberal MP, D.T. Holmes. Married William Wedgwood Benn in 1920. They had three children (the eldest son, Michael, was killed while serving as an RAF pilot during the Second World War). A longstanding member of the Movement for the Ordination of Women, the first President of the Congregational Federation, served on the Council of Christians and Jews, and the Friends of the Hebrew University. Fellow of the Hebrew University. Joint author of *Beckoning Horizon*, 1934.

STANSGATE, Lord (1877–1960). William Wedgwood Benn. Son of John Williams Benn, who was Liberal MP for Tower Hamlets and later for Devonport, and Chairman, 1904/5, of the London County Council of which he was a founder member. William Wedgwood Benn was himself elected Liberal MP for St George's, Tower Hamlets, in 1906. Became a Whip in the Liberal Government in 1910. Served in the First World War and was decorated with the DSO and DFC, returning in 1918 to be elected Liberal MP for Leith. Joined the Labour Party in 1926, resigned his seat the same day, and was subsequently elected Labour MP for North Aberdeen (1928–31) in a by-election. Secretary of State for India in the 1929–31 Labour Cabinet. Re-elected as Labour MP for Gorton in 1937. He rejoined the RAF in 1940 at the age of sixty-three, was made a peer, Viscount Stansgate, in 1941, and was Secretary of State for Air, 1945–6, in the postwar Labour Government. World President of the Inter-Parliamentary Union, 1947–57.

WINCH, Olive (Buddy). Miss Winch was with the family as a children's nurse from 1928 until 1940, when she left to undertake war work. A life-long friend.

INDEX